中国民政统计年鉴

（中国社会服务统计资料）

CHINA CIVIL AFFAIRS' STATISTICAL YEARBOOK

(Statistics of China Social Services)

2015

中华人民共和国民政部　编

Compiled By Ministry of Civil Affairs of the People's Republic of China

中国统计出版社
China Statistics Press

图书在版编目（CIP）数据

中国民政统计年鉴 ：中国社会服务统计资料．2015 ：汉英对照 ／ 中华人民共和国民政部编．
-- 北京 ：中国统计出版社, 2015.7
ISBN 978-7-5037-7461-4

I.①中… II.①中… III.①民政事务－统计资料－中国－2015－年鉴－汉、英 IV.①D632-66

中国版本图书馆CIP数据核字（2015）第139982号

中国民政统计年鉴－2015（中国社会服务统计资料）

作　　者／ 中华人民共和国民政部
责任编辑／ 郭　栋　　李　冲
封面设计／ 李雪燕
出版发行／ 中国统计出版社
通信地址／ 北京市丰台区西三环南路甲6号　　邮政编码／100073
电　　话／ 邮购 (010)63376909　　书店 (010)68783171
网　　址／ http://www.zgtjcbs.com/
印　　刷／ 河北天普润印刷厂
经　　销／ 新华书店
开　　本／ 880 × 1230mm　　1/16
字　　数／ 1300千字
印　　张／ 42.75
版　　别／ 2015年8月第1版
版　　次／ 2015年8月第1次印刷
定　　价／ 280.00元

本书附同版本CD-ROM一张，光盘内容以书面文字为准。
如有印装错误，本社发行部负责调换。

《中国民政统计年鉴-2015》

（中国社会服务统计资料）

编委会和编辑出版人员

编者说明

《中国民政统计年鉴－2015》(中国社会服务统计资料)是一部全面反映2014年中国社会服务发展的资料性年刊。2014年度社会服务统计资料是根据各省、自治区、直辖市以及计划单列市民政厅（局）报送的社会服务业统计年报及有关部门的报表编制而成。本书内容由六个部分组成：第一部分是专文，2014年社会服务发展统计公报；第二部分是社会服务主要数据图表；第三部分是社会服务综合统计资料；第四部分是社会服务历年统计资料；第五部分是社会服务当年分省统计资料；第六部分是附录，《中国民政统计年鉴－2014》勘误。本书对各级政府有关部门、从事社会服务研究和教学的人员，以及社会各界了解和研究社会服务发展状况、提高政府管理和决策水平，具有重要的参考价值。

书中涉及到的全国性统计数据均不包括香港特别行政区、澳门特别行政区和台湾省；表格中“——”符号表示数据不足本表最小计量单位；“空格”符号表示该项统计数据为零；“#”表示其中主要项。

本书凝聚了全国民政系统广大规划财务部门统计工作者和有关部门统计人员的辛勤汗水和工作成果。本书的编辑出版得到了各级领导和统计战线同仁们的热情支持和帮助。在此，向所有关心和支持该书出版发行的领导和同志表示衷心的谢意。

目　录

第一部分：专文

第二部分：社会服务主要数据图表

综合

社会工作

成员组织和其他社会服务

第三部分：社会服务综合统计资料

综合

社会工作

成员组织和其他社会服务

第四部分：社会服务历年统计资料

综合

社会工作

成员组织和其他社会服务

第五部分：社会服务当年分省统计资料

综合

行政区划和行政机关

社会服务业态总体情况

社会工作

提供住宿的社会服务活动

为老年人与残疾人提供住宿服务的机构

为智障与精神疾病人提供住宿服务的机构

为儿童提供住宿的社会服务机构

其他提供住宿的社会服务机构

不提供住宿的社会服务活动

为社区居民提供的服务

为老年人提供的服务

为残疾人提供的服务

为儿童提供的服务

为生活困难群众提供的服务

为受灾群众提供的服务

为弱势群体筹集资金的活动

为军队有关人员提供的服务

成员组织和其他社会服务

成员组织

其他社会服务

其他

第六部分：附录

CONTENTS

Part one: Feature Articles

Part two: Key Data Figures of Social Services

I. Synthesis

II. Social Work

III. Member Organizations and Other Social Services

Part Three: Comprehensive Statistics of Social Services

I. Synthesis

II. Social Work

III. Member Organizations and Other Social Services

Part Four: Historical Statistics of Social Services

I. Synthesis

II. Social Work

III. Member Organizations and Other Social Services

Part Five: Provincial Statistics of Social Services

I. Synthesis

Administrative Divisions and Administrative Organs

Situation of Social Service Industry

II. Social Work

Social Service Activities with Accommodation

Social Service Activities without Accommodation

III. Member Organizations and Other Social Services

Member Organizations

Non-governmental Organizations

Self–governing Organizations

Other Social Services

Marriage Service

Funeral and Interment Service

Other Institutions

Part Six: Appendix

专 文

01

中华人民共和国
2014年社会服务发展统计公报

中华人民共和国民政部
2015年6月8日

2014年，全国民政系统认真贯彻党中央、国务院决策部署，积极履行保障基本民生、创新社会管理、促进国防建设、强化社会服务等方面的职能，扎实推进各项重点工作，民政事业实现了新突破新发展，服务了党和国家工作大局，促进了社会生产力发展，增强了社会活力，使发展成果更多更公平惠及全体人民。

一、综合

截至2014年底，全国共有省级行政区划单位34个（其中直辖市4个、省23个、自治区5个、特别行政区2个），地级行政区划单位333个（其中地级市288个、地区12个，自治州30个、盟3个），县级行政区划单位2854个（其中市辖区897个、县级市361个、县1425个、自治县117个、旗49个、自治旗3个、特区1个、林区1个），乡级行政区划单位40381个（其中区公所2个、镇20401个、乡11111个、苏木151个、民族乡1019个、民族苏木1个、街道7696个）。

2014年，共联合检查省界14条，完成了总长度约为7874公里的联检省界任务。

图1 乡镇、街道变化情况

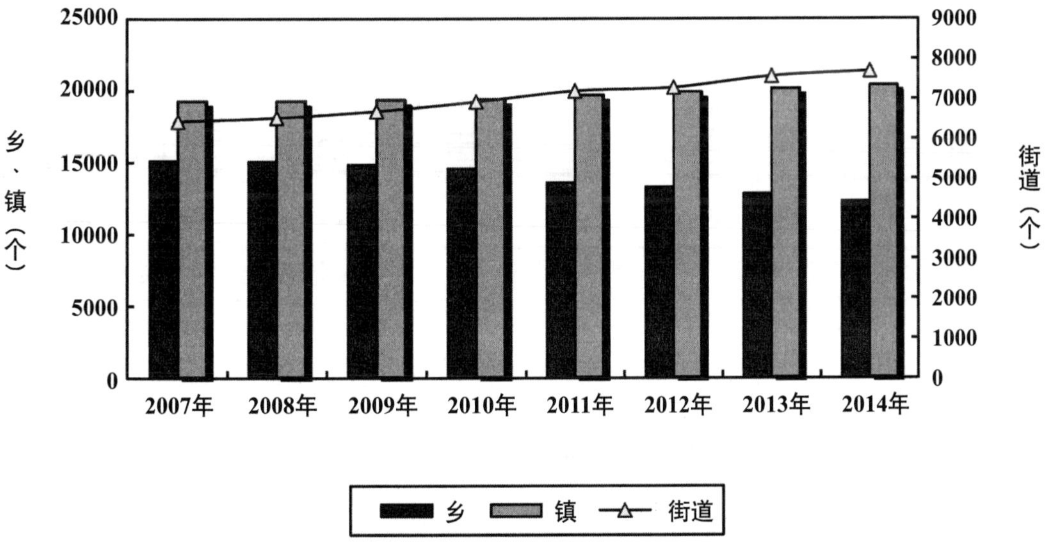

表 1 乡镇、街道变化情况

单位：个

指标	2007年	2008年	2009年	2010年	2011年	2012年	2013年	2014年
乡	15120	15067	14848	14571	13587	13281	12812	12282
镇	19249	19234	19322	19410	19683	19881	20117	20401
街道	6434	6524	6686	6923	7194	7282	7566	7696

截至2014年底，全国共有社会服务机构166.8万个，比上年增长6.8%，职工总数1251.0万人（全国持证社会工作者共计16.0万人,其中：社会工作师3.9万人，助理社会工作师12.0万人），固定资产总值为7213.0亿元，比上年增长5.9%，增加值为2515.2亿元，比上年增长11.7%，占第三产业的比重为0.8%。

截至2014年底，全国社会服务事业费支出4404.1亿元，比上年增长3.0%，占国家财政支出比重为2.9%。中央财政共向各地转移支付社会服务事业费2150.0亿元，与上年基本持平，占社会服务事业费比重为47.8%。社会服务事业基本建设施工项目14001个，全年完成投资总额282.2亿元。

图2 社会服务基本情况

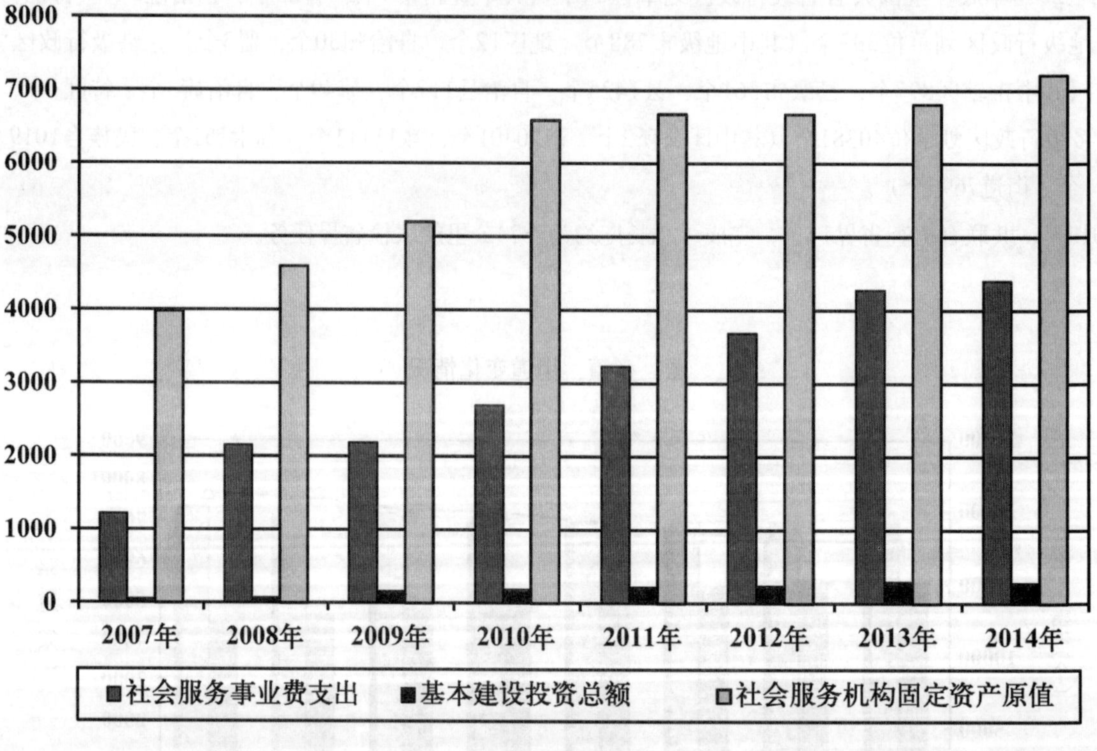

表2 社会服务基本情况

单位：亿元

指标	2007年	2008年	2009年	2010年	2011年	2012年	2013年	2014年
社会服务事业费支出	1215.5	2146.5	2181.9	2697.5	3229.1	3683.7	4276.5	4404.1
基本建设投资总额	47.7	66.6	157.0	183.0	218.5	235.0	292.8	282.2
社会服务机构固定资产原值	3973.0	4592.8	5198	6589.3	6676.7	6675.4	6810.2	7213.0

二、社会工作

（一）提供住宿的社会服务

截至2014年底，全国各类提供住宿的社会服务机构3.7万个（其中登记注册为事业单位机构1.6万个）；床位613.6万张，比上年增长16.5%；每千人口平均拥有社会服务机构床位4.5张，比上年增长15.4%；收留抚养334.9万人，比上年增长3.8%。

图3 社会服务机构床位

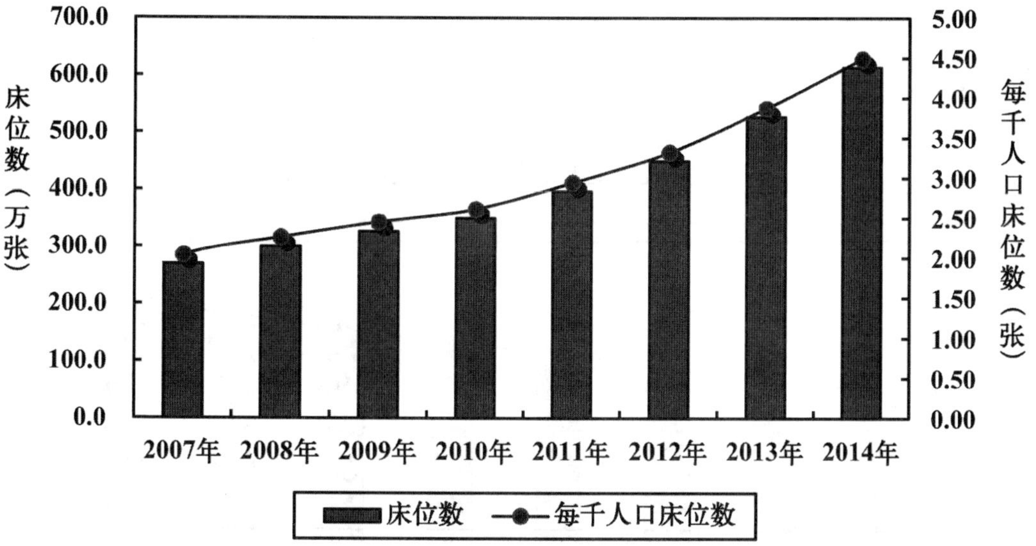

表3 社会服务机构床位

单位：万张、张

指标	2007年	2008年	2009年	2010年	2011年	2012年	2013年	2014年
床位数	269.6	300.3	326.5	349.6	396.4	449.3	526.7	613.5
每千人口床位数	2.04	2.26	2.45	2.61	2.94	3.32	3.87	4.49

1.提供住宿的养老服务。全国各类养老服务机构和设施94110个，其中：养老服务机构33043个，社区养老服务机构和设施18927个，互助型的养老设施40357个，军队离退休干部休养所1783个；各类养老床位577.8万张，比上年增长17.0%（每千名老年人拥有养老床位27.2张，比上年增长11.5%），其中社区留宿和日间照料床位187.5万张；年末收留抚养老年人318.4万人，比上年增长4.2%。

2.提供住宿的智障与精神病服务。全国民政部门管理的智障与精神疾病服务机构共有254个，拥有床位8.0万张，比上年增长8.1%。其中社会福利医院（精神病院）156个，床位数4.9万张，比上年增长8.9%，年末收留抚养各类人员4.0万人；复退军人精神病院98个，床位数3.1万张，比上年增长6.9%，年末收留抚养各类人员2.5万人。

3.提供住宿的儿童福利和儿童救助服务。全国共有儿童收留抚养救助服务机构890个，拥有床位10.8万张，年末收养各类人员5.9万人。其中儿童福利机构545个，床位9.6万张，比上年增长10.3%；未成年人救助保护中心345个，床位1.2万张，全年救助生活无着流浪未成年人17.0万人次。

4.其他提供住宿的社会服务。全国共有其他提供住宿的社会服务机构2622个，床位17.0万张。其中救助管理站1949个，床位9.9万张，全年救助生活无着流动人员351.7万人次，其中在站救助299.5万人次，不在站救助52.1万人次；安置农场13个；军供站327个，床位3.7万张；其他收留抚养机构333个，床位3.3万张，年末收留抚养各类人员1.6万人。

（二）不提供住宿的社会服务

1.为老年人提供的服务。截至2014年底，全国60岁及以上老年人口21242万人，占总人口的15.5%，其中65岁及以上人口13755万人，占总人口的10.1%。截至2014年底，全国共有老龄事业单位2558个，老年法律援助中心2.1万个，老年维权协调组织8.0万个，老年学校5.4万个、在校学习人员733.1万人，各类老年活动室34.9万个。

图4 60岁及以上老年人口占全国总人口比重

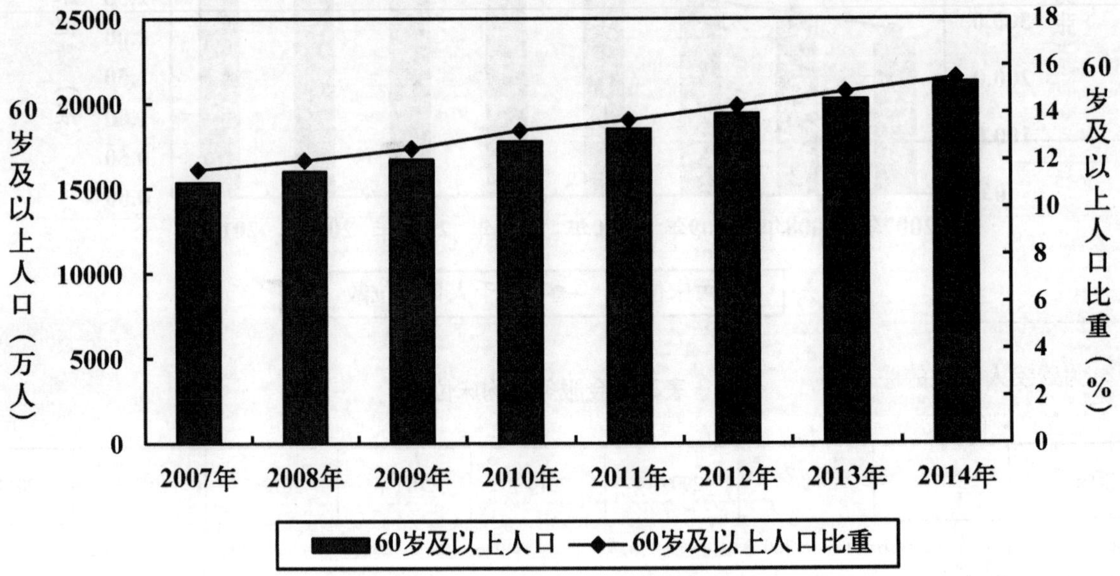

表4 60岁及以上老年人口占全国总人口比重

单位：万人、%

指标	2007年	2008年	2009年	2010年	2011年	2012年	2013年	2014年
60岁及以上人口	15340	15989	16714	17765	18499	19390	20243	21242
60岁及以上人口比重	11.6	12.0	12.5	13.26	13.7	14.3	14.9	15.5

2.为儿童提供的服务。截至2014年底，全国共有孤儿52.5万人，其中集中供养孤儿9.4万人，社会散居孤儿43.2万人。2014年全国办理收养登记22772件，其中：内地居民收养登记19694件，港澳台华侨收养登记191件，外国人收养登记2887件。

图5 家庭儿童收养

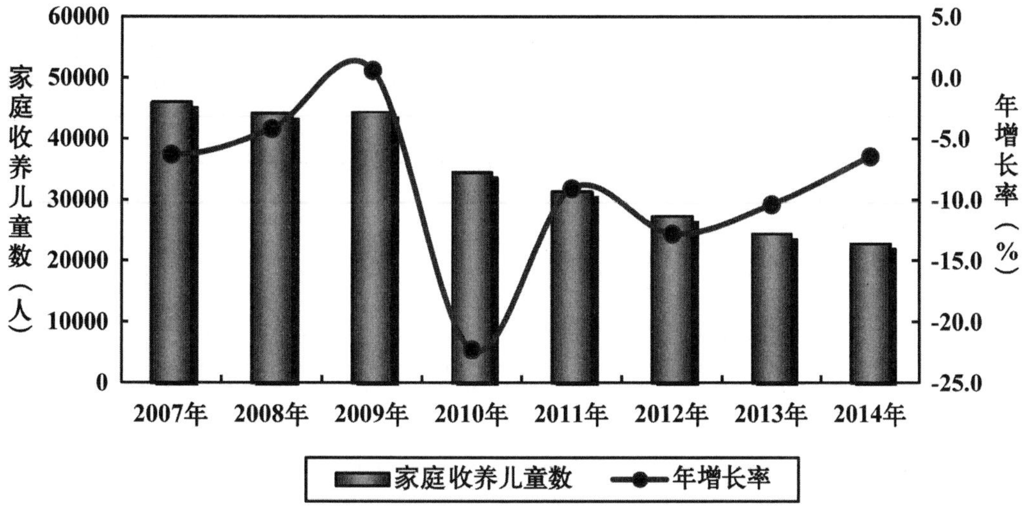

表5 家庭儿童收养

单位：人、%

指标	2007年	2008年	2009年	2010年	2011年	2012年	2013年	2014年
家庭收养儿童数	46047	44115	44359	34473	31329	27310	24460	22876
年增长率	−6.3	−4.2	0.6	−22.3	−9.1	−12.8	−10.4	−6.5

3.为残疾人提供的服务。截至2014年底，全国共有为残疾人提供服务的机构16389个；增加值为757.0亿元，占第三产业的比重0.25%；吸纳残疾职工47.9万人就业；实现利润95.2亿元；年末固定资产1789.5亿元。

图6 为残疾人提供服务机构中的残疾职工

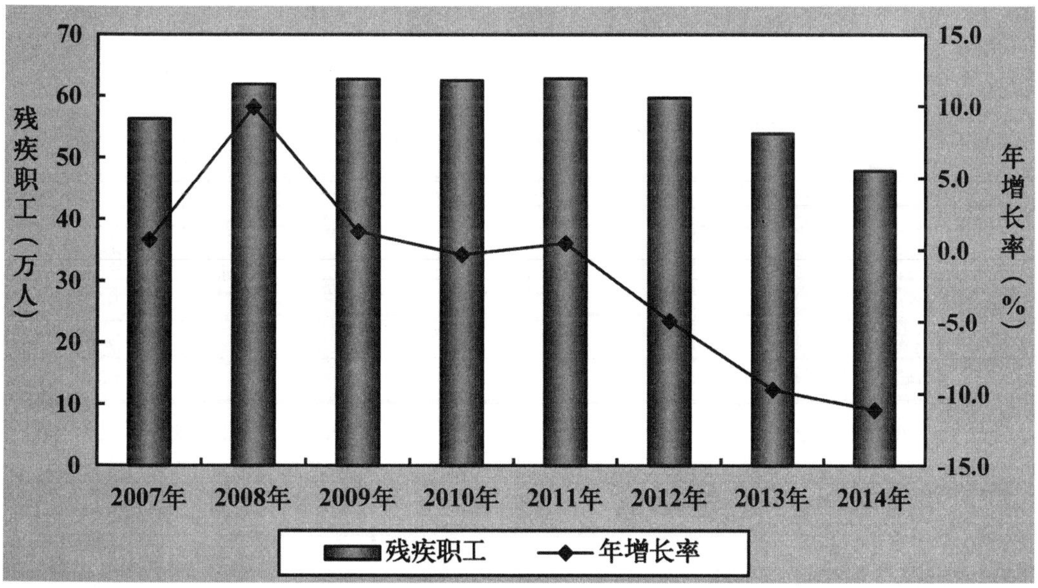

表6 为残疾人提供服务机构中的残疾职工

单位：万人、%

指标	2007年	2008年	2009年	2010年	2011年	2012年	2013年	2014年
残疾职工	56.3	61.9	62.7	62.5	62.8	59.7	53.9	47.9
年增长率	0.7	9.9	1.3	−0.3	0.5	−4.9	−9.7	−11.1

4.社会救助。

城市低保。截至2014年底，全国共有城市低保对象1026.1万户、1877.0万人。全年各级财政共支出城市低保资金721.7亿元，其中中央财政补助资金518.88亿元，占总支出的71.9%。2014年全国城市低保平均标准411元/人、月，比上年增长10.1%；全国城市低保月人均补助水平286元，比上年增长8.3%。

城市“三无”救济。2014年救济城市“三无”7.6万人。

农村低保。截至2014年底，全国有农村低保对象2943.6万户、5207.2万人。全年各级财政共支出农村低保资金870.3亿元，其中中央补助资金582.6亿元，占总支出的66.9%。2014年全国农村低保平均标准2777元/人、年，比上年提高343元，增长14.1%；全国农村低保月人均补助水平129元，比上年增长11.4%。

农村五保。截至2014年底，全国有农村五保供养对象529.1万人，比上年下降1.5%。全年各级财政共支出农村五保供养资金189.8亿元，比上年增长10.2%。其中：农村五保集中供养174.3万人，集中供养年平均标准为5371元/人，比上年增长14.6%；农村五保分散供养354.8万人，分散供养年平均标准为4006元/人，比上年增长14.5%。

图7 社会救助情况

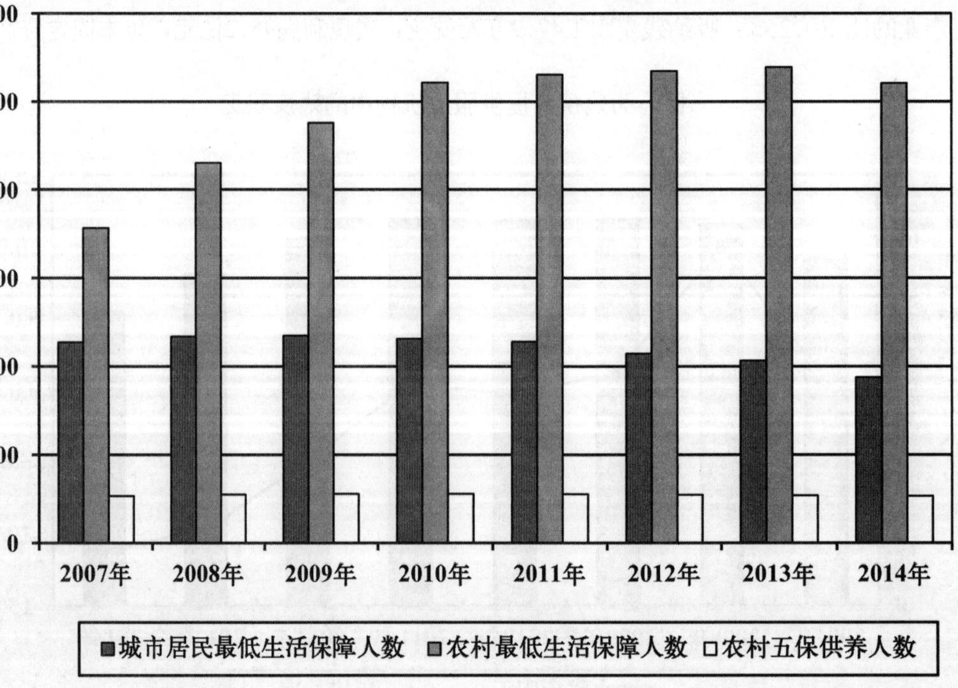

表7 社会救助情况

单位：万人

指标	2007年	2008年	2009年	2010年	2011年	2012年	2013年	2014年
城市居民最低生活保障人数	2272.1	2334.8	2345.6	2310.5	2276.8	2143.5	2064.2	1877
农村最低生活保障人数	3566.3	4305.5	4760.0	5214.0	5305.7	5344.5	5388.0	5207.2
农村五保供养人数	531.3	548.6	553.4	556.3	551.0	545.6	537.2	529.1

农村传统救济。2014年农村传统救济74.5万人。

医疗救助。2014年全国实施医疗救助9119万人次，其中住院救助1106.6万人次，门诊救助1288.7万人次，资助参保参合6723.7万人。支出医疗救助资金252.6亿元，其中住院救助180.2亿元，门诊救助24亿元，资助参保参合48.4亿元。住院救助、门诊救助、资助参保参合水平分别达到人次均1628元、186元、72元。

2014年全年累计医疗补助优抚对象474.6万人次，人均补助水平661.8元，各级财政共支出优抚医疗补助资金31.4亿元。

临时救助。2014年临时救助650.7万户次，其中，按户籍性质分类城市家庭333.5万户次，农村家庭317.2万户次；按属地分类当地常驻户口631.5万户次，非当地常驻户口19.2万户次；按救助类型分类支出型临时救助533.9万户次，应急型临时救助116.8万户次。全年支出临时救助资金57.6亿元。

5.防灾减灾。2014年全国各类自然灾害共造成2.4亿人次不同程度受灾，因灾死亡失踪1818人，紧急转移安置601.7万人次；农作物受灾面积2489.1万公顷，其中绝收面积309.0万公顷；倒塌房屋45万间，不同程度损坏254.2万间；因灾直接经济损失3373.8亿元。国家减灾委、民政部共启动3次预警响应和28次应急响应，协调派出22个救灾应急工作组赶赴灾区，财政部、民政部下拨中央救灾资金98.73亿元，民政部调拨帐篷11.4万顶、棉衣被16.4万件（床）、折叠床4.7万张等中央救灾储备物资，累计救助受灾群众7500万人次，受灾群众基本生活得到妥善保障。

图8 因灾死亡（含失踪）人口

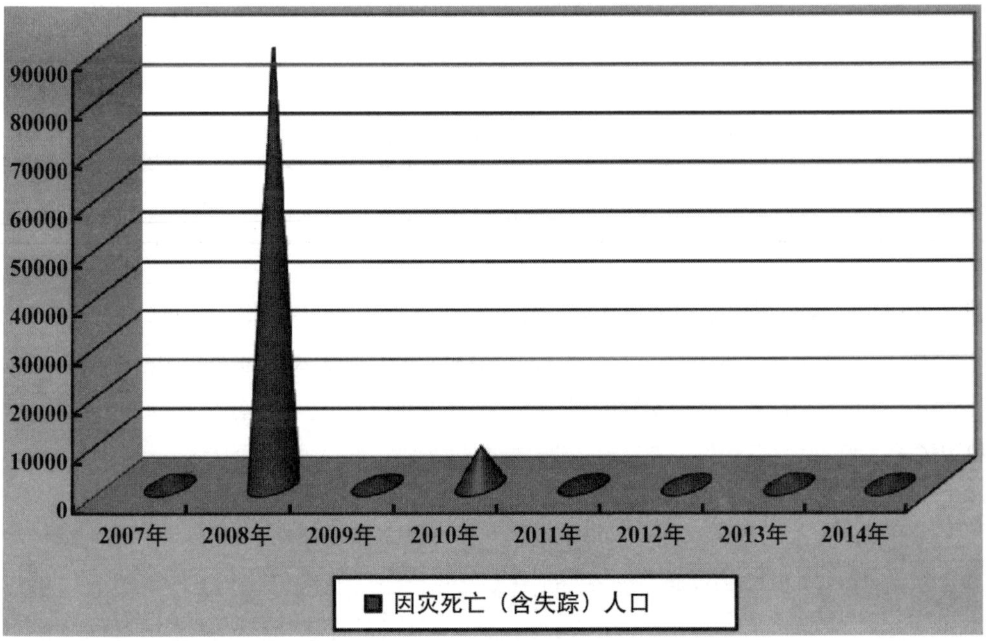

表8 因灾死亡（含失踪）人口

单位：人

指标	2007年	2008年	2009年	2010年	2011年	2012年	2013年	2014年
因灾死亡（含失踪）人口	2325	88928	1528	7844	1126	1530	2284	1818

6.慈善事业。

慈善捐赠。截至2014年底，全国共建立经常性社会捐助工作站、点和慈善超市3.2万个（其中：慈善超市10174个）。全年各地共接收社会捐赠款物604.4亿元，其中：民政部门直接接收社会各界捐款79.6亿元，各类社会组织接收捐款524.9亿元。全年各地接收捐赠衣被5244.5万件，捐赠物资价值折合人民币8.0亿元。间接接收其他部门转入的社会捐款2.2亿元，衣被105.6万件，捐赠物资折款39011.6万元。全年有1694.9万人次困难群众受益。全年有1095.9万人次在社会服务领域提供了2711.1万小时的志愿服务。

图9 接收社会捐款和衣被

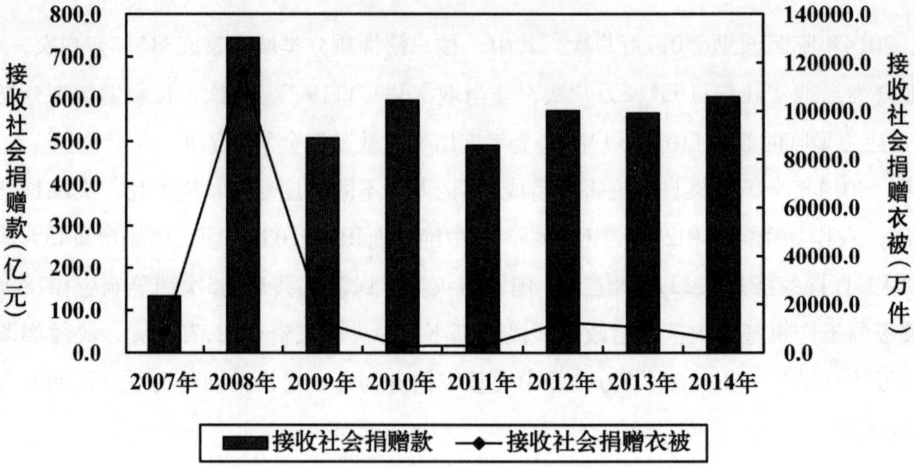

表9 接收社会捐款和衣被

单位：亿元、万件

指标	2007年	2008年	2009年	2010年	2011年	2012年	2013年	2014年
接收社会捐赠款	132.8	744.5	507.2	596.8	490.1	572.5	566.4	604.4
接收社会捐赠衣被	8756.8	115816.3	12476.6	2750.2	2918.5	12538.2	10405.0	5244.5

福利彩票。2014年中国福利彩票年销售2059.7亿元，比上年增加294.4亿元，同比增长16.7%。全年筹集福彩公益金585.7亿元，比上年增长14.7%。全年民政系统共支出彩票公益金231.3亿元，比上年增加35.8亿元；其中：资助用于抚恤5.9亿元、退役安置0.9亿元、社会福利143.6亿元、社会救助29.1亿元、自然灾害2.2亿元、其他49.7亿元。

图10 福利彩票

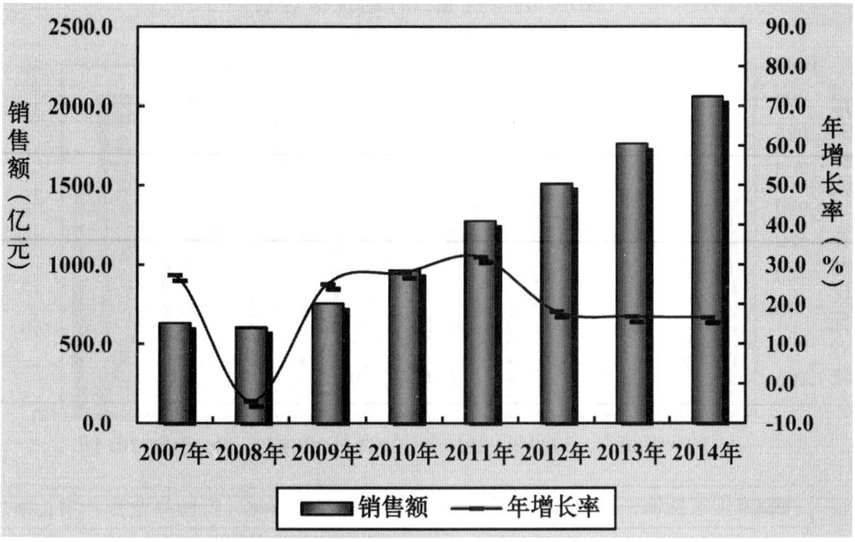

表10 福利彩票

单位：亿元、%

指标	2007年	2008年	2009年	2010年	2011年	2012年	2013年	2014年
销售额	631.6	604.0	756.0	968.0	1278.0	1510.3	1765.3	2059.7
年增长率	27.4	−4.4	25.2	28.0	32.0	18.2	16.9	16.7

7.**优抚安置**。截至2014年底，国家抚恤、补助各类重点优抚对象917.3万人。其中：伤残人员76.6万人，带病回乡退伍军人124.2万人，在乡复员军人99.3万人，60岁以上农村籍退伍军人374.8万人，在乡退伍红军老战士341人，在乡西路军红军老战士87人，红军失散人员11269人；烈士遗属19.8万人，因公牺牲、病故军人遗属11.3万人。

表11 国家抚恤、补助优抚对象

单位：万人、亿元、%

指标	2007年	2008年	2009年	2010年	2011年	2012年	2013年	2014年
国家抚恤、补助优抚对象	622.4	633.2	630.7	625	852.5	944.4	950.5	917.3
抚恤事业费	210.8	253.6	310.3	362.7	428.3	517	618.4	636.6
抚恤事业费年增长率	17.9	20.3	22.4	16.9	18.1	20.7	19.6	2.9

图11 国家抚恤、补助优抚对象

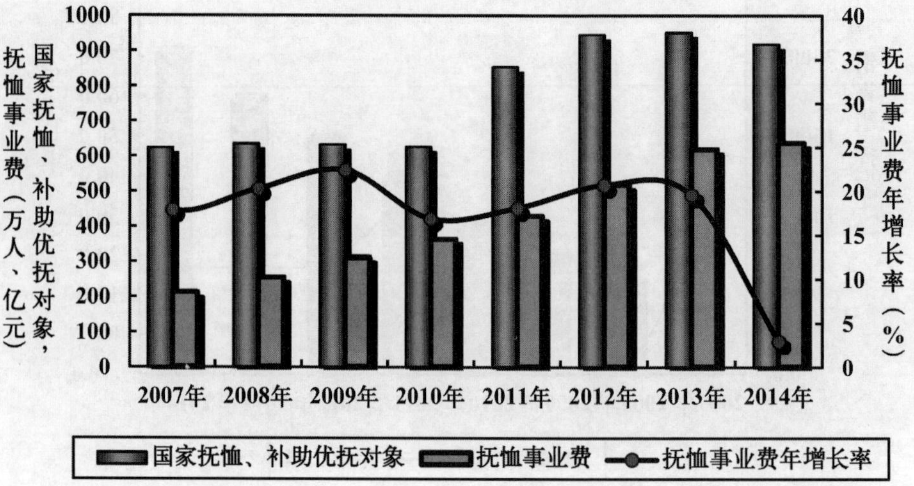

2014年新增领取烈士褒扬金人员267人。截至2014年底，全国共有烈士纪念设施管理机构1516个，占地面积4564公顷，机构内烈士纪念设施9289处；零散烈士纪念设施11365处。

2014年共接收军队离退休干部（含退休士官）、无军籍退休退职职工、复员干部2.8万人。军队离退休人员管理中心185个，年末职工0.2万人；军队离退休人员活动中心30个，年末职工0.1万人。

8.**社区服务**。截至2014年底，全国共有各类社区服务机构31.1万个，社区服务机构覆盖率45.5%；其中：社区服务指导中心918个，社区服务中心23088个，比上年增加4074个，社区服务站120188个，比上年增加11811个，社区养老服务机构和设施18927个，互助型的养老设施40357个，其他社区服务机构10.7万个。城镇便民、利民服务网点30.9万个。社区志愿服务组织10.9万个。

图12 社区服务机构

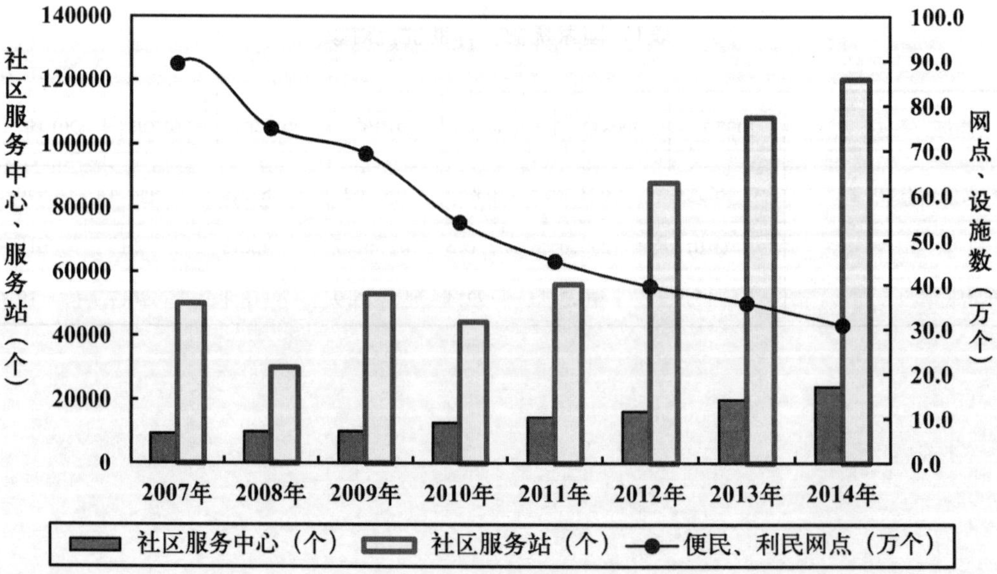

表12 社区服务机构

单位：万个、个

指标	2007年	2008年	2009年	2010年	2011年	2012年	2013年	2014年
社区服务机构	12.9	14.6	14.6	15.3	16.0	20.0	25.2	31.1
社区服务中心	9319	9873	10003	12720	14391	16306	19904	23088
社区服务站	50116	30021	53170	44237	56156	87931	108377	120188
便民、利民网点	89.3	74.9	69.3	53.9	45.3	39.7	35.9	30.9

三、成员组织和其他社会服务

（一）成员组织

1.社会组织。截至2014年底，全国共有社会组织60.6万个，比上年增长10.8%；吸纳社会各类人员就业682.3万人，比上年增加7.2%；形成固定资产1560.6亿元；社会组织增加值为638.6亿元，比上年增长11.8%，占第三产业增加值比重为0.21%；接收各类社会捐赠524.9亿元；全年共查处社会组织违法违规案件4246起，其中取缔非法社会组织46起，行政处罚4200起。

全国共有社会团体31.0万个，比上年增长7.2%。其中：工商服务业类34099个，科技研究类16923个，教育类11412个，卫生类10060个，社会服务类44630个，文化类30101个，体育类20848个，生态环境类6964个，法律类3270个，宗教类4898个，农业及农村发展类60202个，职业及从业组织类19867个，国际及其他涉外组织类516个，其他45946个。全年共查处社会团体违法违规案件2312起，其中取缔非法社会团体4起，行政处罚2308起。

全国共有基金会4117个，比上年增加568个，增长16.0%，其中：公募基金会1470个，非公募基金会2610个，涉外基金会9个，境外基金会代表机构28个。民政部登记的基金会（含涉外基金会）227个。公募基金会和非公募基金会共接收社会各界捐赠374.3亿元。全年对基金会作出行政处罚13起，取缔1起。

全国共有民办非企业单位29.2万个，比上年增长14.7%。其中：科技服务类15110个，生态环境类398个，教育类163681个，卫生类23404个，社会服务类42244个，文化类14148个，体育类11901个，商务服务类5915个，宗教类82个，国际及其他涉外组织类4个，其他15308个。全年共查处民办非企业单位违法违规案件1920起，其中取缔非法民办非企业单位41起，行政处罚1879起。

表13 社会组织

单位：万个、个

指标	2007年	2008年	2009年	2010年	2011年	2012年	2013年	2014年
社会团体	21.2	23	23.9	24.5	25.5	27.1	28.9	31.0
基金会	1340	1597	1843	2200	2614	3029	3549	4117
民办非企业单位	17.4	18.2	19	19.8	20.4	22.5	25.5	29.2

图13 社会组织

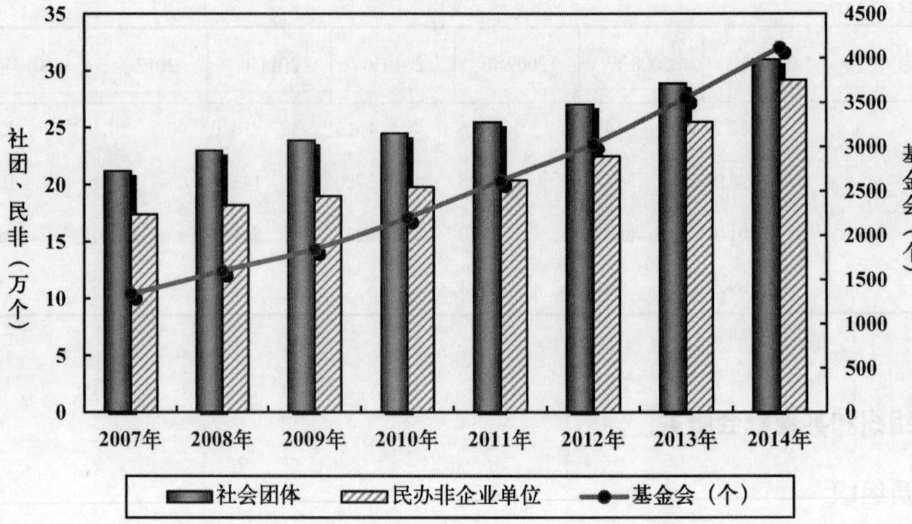

2. **自治组织**。截至2014年底，基层群众自治组织共计68.2万个，其中：村委会58.5万个，村民小组470.4万个，村委会成员230.5万人；居委会96693个，比上年增长2.2%，居民小组135.8万个，居委会成员49.7万人，比上年增长2.7%。全年共有33.0万个村（居）委会完成选举，参与选举的村（居）民登记数为4.3亿人，参与投票人数为3.4亿人。

图14 自治组织

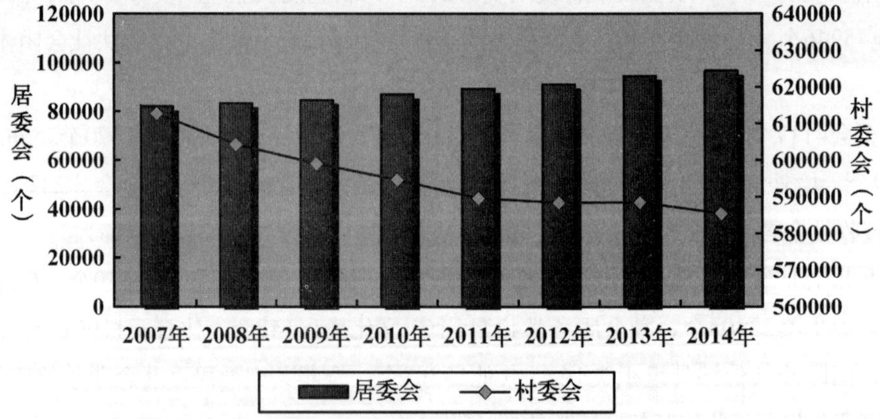

表14 自治组织

单位：个

指标	2007年	2008年	2009年	2010年	2011年	2012年	2013年	2014年
居委会	82006	83413	84689	87057	89480	91153	94620	96693
村委会	612709	604285	599078	594658	589653	588475	588547	585451

（二）其他社会服务

1.婚姻服务。2014年全国共有事业单位性质的婚姻登记机构2236个，办理婚姻登记的处数6797处。全国共依法办理结婚登记1306.7万对。其中：内地居民登记结婚1302.0万对，涉外及华侨、港澳台居民登记结婚4.7万对。结婚率为9.6‰。2014年25–29岁办理结婚登记占结婚总人口比重最多，占38.0%，比上年提高2.8个百分点。

2014年依法办理离婚363.7万对，比上年增长3.9%，离婚率为2.7‰，比上年增加0.1个千分点。其中：民政部门登记离婚295.7万对，法院办理离婚67.9万对。

图15 结婚率和离婚率

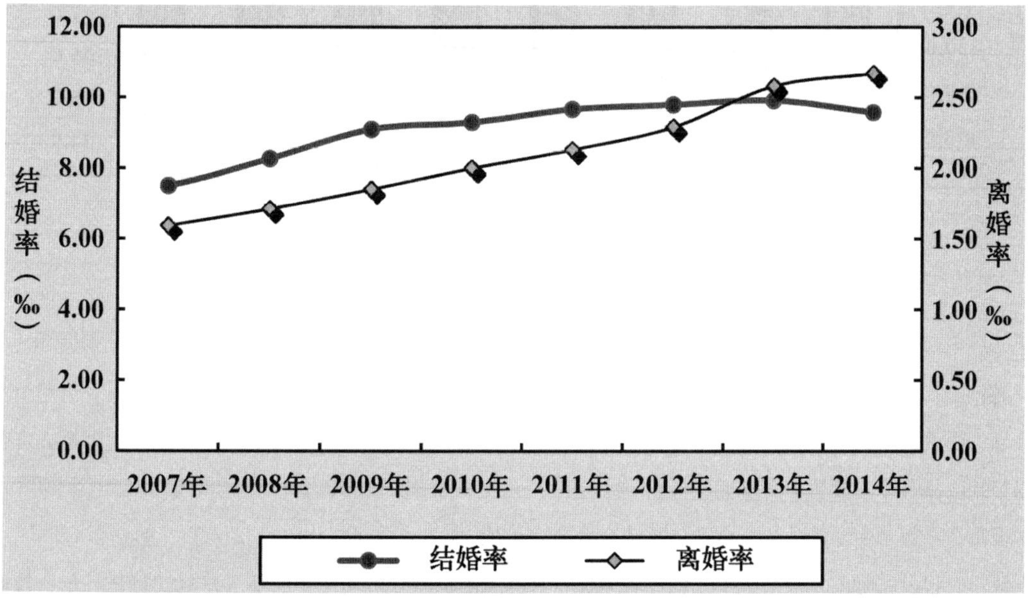

表15 结婚率和离婚率

单位：‰

指标	2007年	2008年	2009年	2010年	2011年	2012年	2013年	2014年
结婚率	7.50	8.27	9.10	9.30	9.67	9.80	9.92	9.58
离婚率	1.59	1.71	1.85	2.00	2.13	2.29	2.58	2.67

2．殡葬服务。截至2014年底，全国共有殡葬服务机构4559个，其中殡仪馆1801个，殡葬管理机构1141个，民政部门管理的公墓1598个。殡葬服务机构职工共有8.3万人，其中殡仪馆职工4.6万人。火化炉5908台，火化遗体459.3万具。火化率47.0%。

表16 火化遗体情况

单位：万具、%

指标	2007年	2008年	2009年	2010年	2011年	2012年	2013年	2014年
火化遗体数	442.1	453.4	454.2	474.1	468.1	477.7	468.9	459.3
火化率	48.4	48.5	48.2	49.0	48.8	49.5	48.2	47.0

图16 火化遗体情况

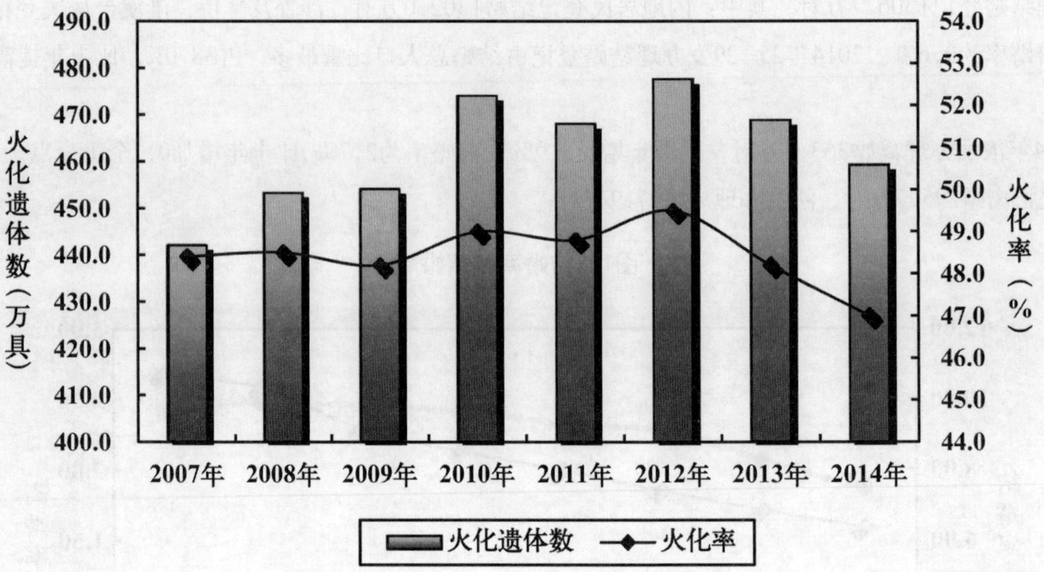

注释：

1. 图1和表1中“乡”包含“民族乡、苏木和民族苏木”。
2. 财政部、民政部下拨中央救灾资金不包含中央级救灾物资采购经费和中央拨付新疆生产建设兵团救灾资金。
3. 2014年社区服务中心数量中含社区服务指导中心。
4. 部本级基金会数量中含涉外基金会和境外基金会代表机构。
5. 由于每年公报发布时间，社会组织年检还未完成，社会组织捐赠款数均使用的是上年（2013年）年检数据。
6. 离婚登记服务中法院判决、调解离婚数据来源于最高人民法院。
7. 本资料中的民政对象人数和机构数均为当年实际发生数和注册登记后的法定机构数，与当年批准数、计划数和预算数不可比。
8. 本资料部分数据因四舍五入原因，存在分项数据与合计数据不等情况，由此产生的误差，均未作机械调整。
9. 各项统计数据均未包括香港特别行政区、澳门特别行政区和台湾省。

Statistical Report of the People's Republic of China on the Development of Social Services in 2014

Ministry of Civil Affairs of
the People's Republic of China
June 8th, 2015

In 2014, the system of national civil affairs earnestly implemented decisions and arrangements of the Party Central Committee and the State Council, actively safeguarded basic livelihood of people, innovated social management, improved national defense construction, and intensified social services. The performance of these functions improved the implementation of key points, made new development of civil affairs, served the overall work of the Party and the country, promoted the development of social productivity, intensified social vibrancy and made more development results benefit all people more fairly.

I. Synthesis

By the end of 2014, there were altogether 34 administrative areas at the provincial level in China (4 municipalities directly under the central government, 23 provinces, 5 autonomous regions and 2 special administrative regions), 333 administrative areas at the prefecture level (288 cities at the prefecture level, 12 prefectures, 30 autonomous prefectures and 3 leagues), 2,854 administrative areas at the county level (897 districts under the jurisdiction of cities, 361 cities at the county level, 1,425 counties, 117 autonomous counties, 49 banners, 3 autonomous banners, 1 special zone and 1 forestry district), 40,381 administrative areas at the township level (2 district public offices, 20,401 towns, 11,111 townships, 151 sumus, 1,019 ethnic townships, 1 ethnic sumu, 7,696 street communities).

In 2014, the joint inspections covered 14 provincial boundaries (7,874 kilometers).

Figure 1: Changes in Townships, Towns and Street Communities

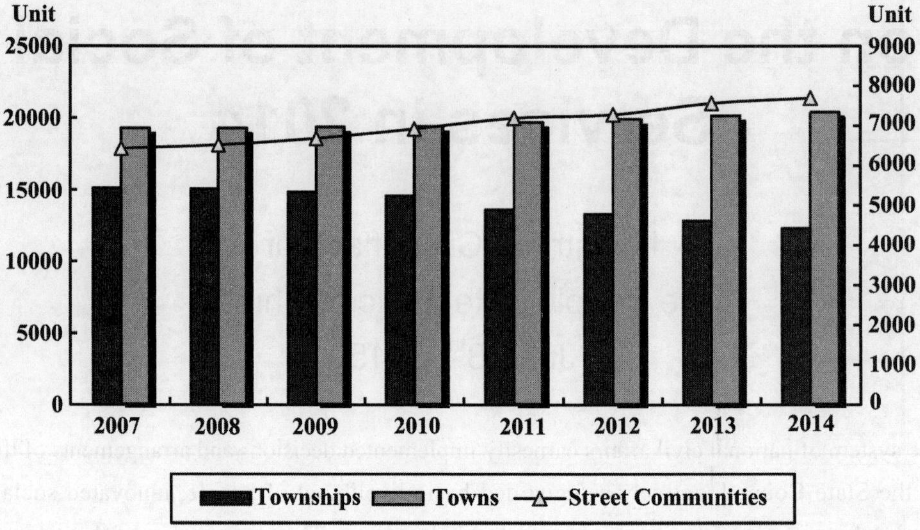

Table 1: Changes in Townships, Towns and Street Communities

Indicators	2007	2008	2009	2010	2011	2012	2013	2014
Townships (Unit)	15120	15067	14848	14571	13587	13281	12812	12282
Towns (Unit)	19249	19234	19322	19410	19683	19881	20117	20401
Street Communities (Unit)	6434	6524	6686	6923	7194	7282	7566	7696

By the end of 2014, there were 1.668 million various registered organizations on social services, a rise of by 6.8 percent over the previous year. The total number of staff was 12.51 million (The total number of National certified social workers is 160,000, 39,000 of them were social workers and 120,000 of them were assistant social workers.) The total fixed assets stood at 721.30 billion yuan, which rose 5.9 percent over the previous year. The added value reached 250.37 billion yuan, which rose 11.2 percent over the previous year. It occupied 0.8 percent of the proportion of tertiary industry.

By the end of 2014, the total expenditure on social service industry reached 440.41 billion yuan, a rise of 3.0 percent over the previous year. The proportion of total expenditure on social service industry in the share of national financial expenditure was 2.9 percent. The transferred payment of the central government to social service industry amounted to 215.00 billion yuan, basically the same as that in the previous year. It took up 47.8 percent of the total social service expenditure. There were 14,001 construction projects for social services. The total investment reached 28.22 billion yuan.

Figure 2: Basic Situation of Social Service Industry

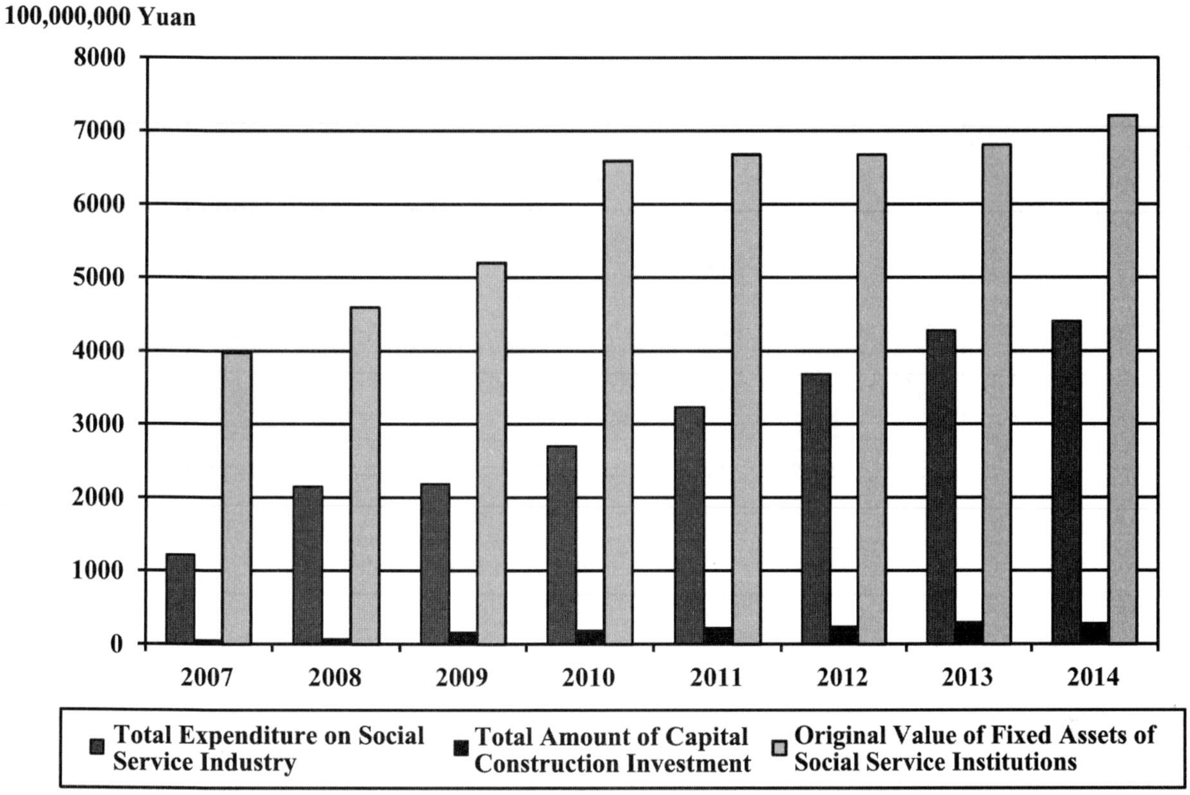

Table 2: Basic Situation of Social Service Industry

Indicators	2007	2008	2009	2010	2011	2012	2013	2014
Total Expenditure on Social Service Industry (100,000,000 Yuan)	1215.5	2146.5	2181.9	2697.5	3229.1	3683.7	4276.5	4404.1
Total Amount of Capital Construction Investment (100,000,000 Yuan)	47.7	66.6	157	183	218.5	235	292.8	282.2
Original Value of Fixed Assets of Social Service Institutions (100,000,000 Yuan)	3973.0	4592.8	5198	6589.3	6676.7	6675.4	6810.2	7213.0

II. Social Services

A. Social Services with Accommodation

By the end of 2014, there were 37 thousand social service institutions with accommodation (16 thousand of them were registered as public institutions). They offered 6.135 million beds, a rise of 16.5 percent over that of the previous year. The average number of beds in social service institutions was 4.5 per thousand people, a rise of 15.4 percent over the previous year. The number of adoptees in these institutions reached 3.349 million, a rise of 3.8 percent over the previous year.

Figure 3: Beds in Social Service Institutions

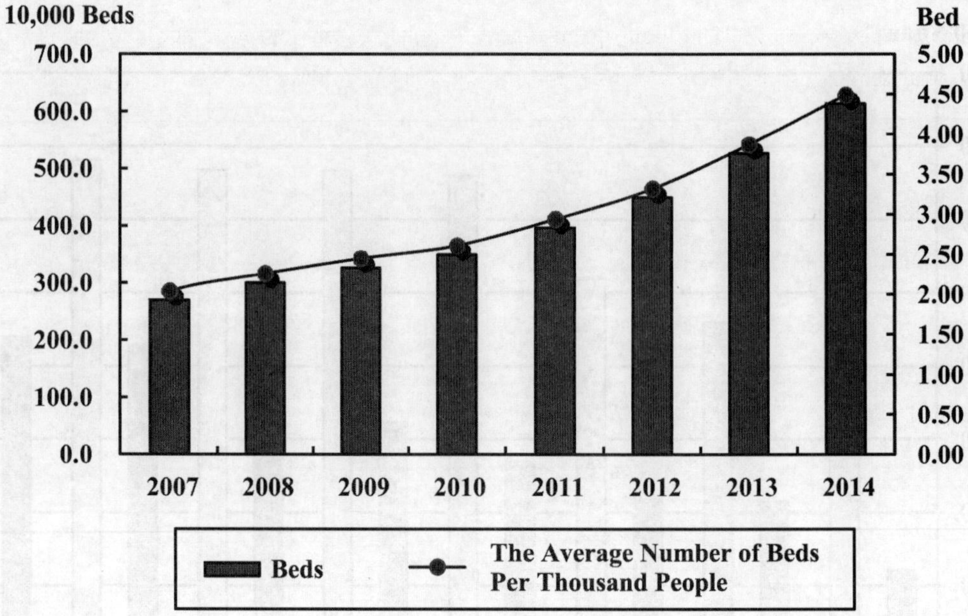

Table 3: Beds in Social Service Institutions

Indicators	2007	2008	2009	2010	2011	2012	2013	2014
Beds (10,000 Beds)	269.6	300.3	326.5	349.6	396.4	449.3	526.7	613.5
The Average Number of Beds Per Thousand People (Bed)	2.04	2.26	2.45	2.61	2.94	3.32	3.87	4.49

1. Social Services with Accommodation for the Aged

The number of welfare institutions and facilities for the aged was 94,110. Thereinto, there were 33,043 welfare institutions, 18,927 community welfare institutions and facilities, 40,357 mutual aid facilities, and 1,783 sanatoriums for retired military cadres. The number of all kinds of beds for aged people was 5.778 million, a rise of 17.0 percent over the previous year (the average number of beds per thousand seniors was 27.2, a rise of 11.5 percent in comparison with last year). Thereinto, 1,875 thousand were used for community accommodation and daytime care. At the end of 2014, 3.184 million aged people were adopted, a rise of 4.2 percent over the previous year.

2. Service Agencies with Accommodation for Mental Retardations and Psychiatric Disorders

There were 254 service agencies for mental retardations and psychiatric disorders under the management of the civil affairs departments with 80 thousand beds, an increase of 8.1 percent over the previous year. Thereinto, there were 156 social welfare homes (mental hospitals) with 49 thousand beds, an increase of 8.9 percent over the previous year. By the end of 2014, 40 thousand people were adopted. There were 98 mental hospitals with 31 thousand beds for ex-servicemen, a rise of 6.9 percent over the previous year, and 25 thousand people were adopted by the end of the year.

3. Welfare Homes and Salvation Institutions with Accommodation and for the Children

By the end of the year, there were 890 adoption and salvation institutions with 108 thousand beds for children, and 59 thousand children were adopted. Thereinto, there were 545 welfare homes for children. They offered 96 thousand beds, which rose by 10.3 percent in comparison with last year. There were 345 children relief and protection centers with 12 thousand beds. They received 170 thousand minor vagabonds (person-times) in the whole year.

4. Other Social Service Institutions with Accommodation Service

There were 2,622 other social service institutions with 170 thousand beds. Thereinto, there were 1,949 relief and management shelters with 99 thousand beds. In the whole year, they received 3.517 million street people (person-times) who had no means of support. 2.995 million of those got in-shelter reliefs and 521 thousand got out-shelter reliefs. There were 13 arrangement farms. There were 327 military depots for military supplies, which had 37 thousand beds. There were 333 adopt institutions of other kinds, and they offered 33 thousand beds and adopted 16 thousand people by the end of 2014.

B. Social Services without Accommodation

1. Aging Service

By the end of 2014, there were 212.42 million aged people at or above 60 years old, consisting of 15.5 percent of the total population. Among those aged people, 137.55 million were at or above 65 years old, consisting of 10.1 percent of the total population. By the end of 2014, there were 2,558 public institutions on aging, 21 thousand legal aid centers for the aged, 80 thousand rights safeguarding institutions for the aged, 54 thousand schools for the aged with 7.331 million students in these schools and 349 thousand activity rooms for the aged.

Figure 4: Percentage of Aged Population 60 Years Old or above in the Total National Population

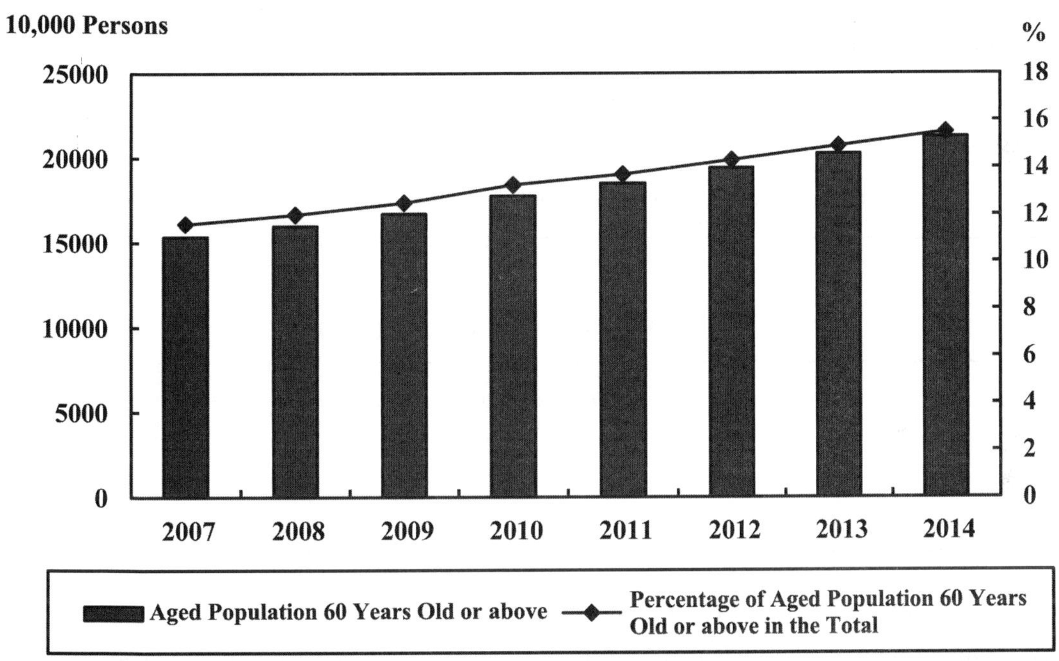

Table 4: Percentage of Aged Population 60 Years Old or above in the Total National Population

Indicators	2007	2008	2009	2010	2011	2012	2013	2014
Aged Population 60 Years Old or above (10,000 Persons)	15340	15989	16714	17765	18499	19390	20243	21242
Percentage of Aged Population 60 Years Old or above in the Total National Population (%)	11.6	12	12.5	13.26	13.7	14.3	14.9	15.5

2. Children Welfare

By the end of 2014, there were 525 thousand orphans in China, of which 94 thousand orphans were collectively adopted, 432 thousand orphans scattered. In 2014, registered family adoptions totaled 22,772 cases. Thereinto, 19,694 cases were completed by mainland citizens, 191 cases were completed by overseas Chinese and residents in Hong Kong, Macao and Taiwan, 2,887 cases were completed by foreigners.

Figure 5: Children Adopted by Families

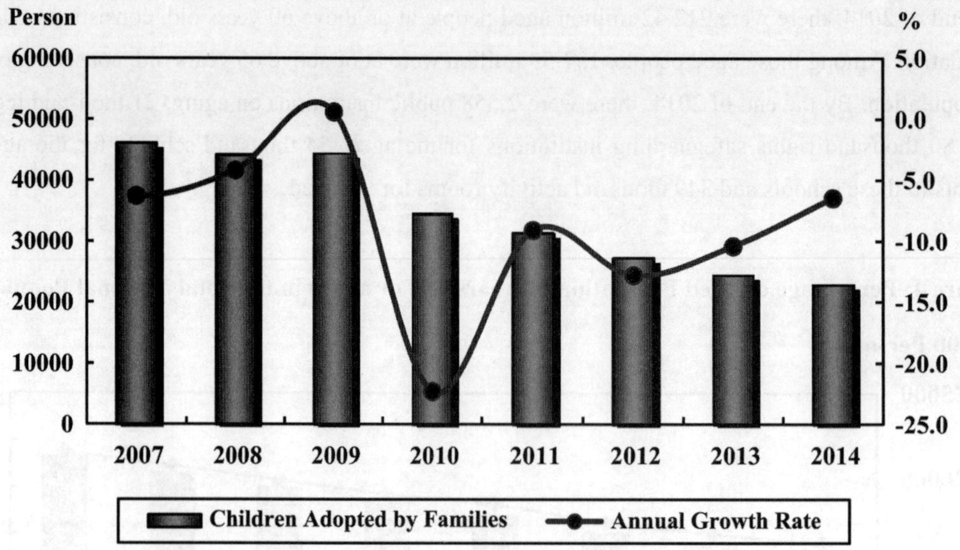

Table 5: Children Adopted by Families

Indicators	2007	2008	2009	2010	2011	2012	2013	2014
Children Adopted by Families (Person)	46047	44115	44359	34473	31329	27310	24460	22876
Annual Growth Rate (%)	−6.3	−4.2	0.6	−22.3	−9.1	−12.8	−10.4	−6.5

3. Agencies Providing Services for Disabled

By the end of 2014, there were 16,389 social welfare agencies providing services for disabled across the country. The added value was 75.70 billion yuan, which accounted for 0.25 percent of the tertiary industry. These agencies employed 479 thousand disabled people. The profits reached 9.52 billion yuan. By the end of 2014, the fixed assets valued 178.95 billion yuan.

Table 6: Disabled Employees in Social Welfare Enterprises

Indicators	2007	2008	2009	2010	2011	2012	2013	2014
Disabled Employees in Social Welfare Enterprises(10,000 Persons)	56.3	61.9	62.7	62.5	62.8	59.7	53.9	47.9
Annual Growth Rate(%)	0.7	9.9	1.3	−0.3	0.5	−4.9	−9.7	−11.1

Figure 6: Disabled Employees in Social Welfare Enterprises

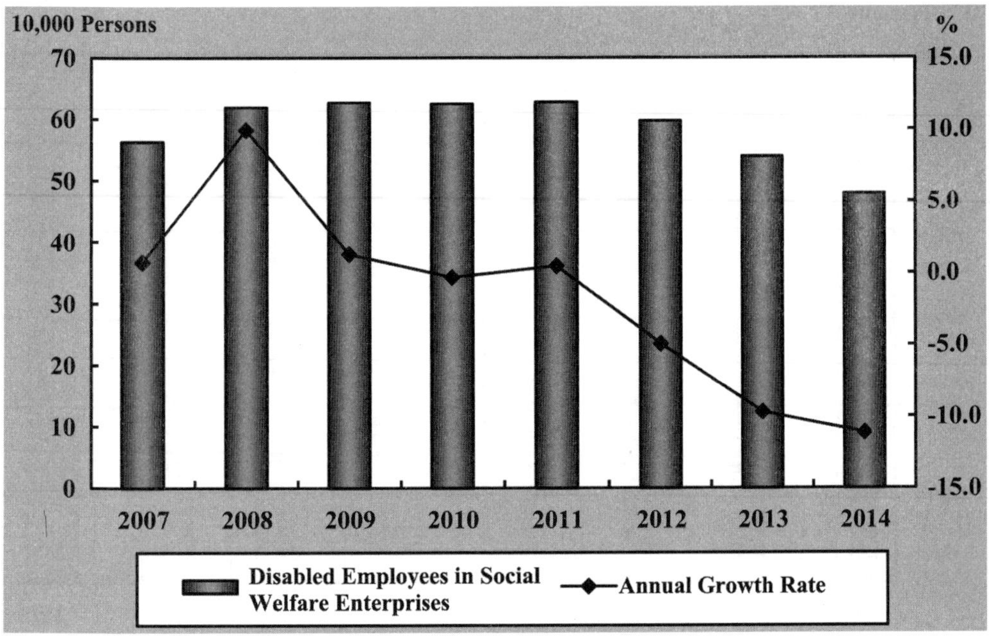

4. Social Relief

- Urban Minimum Life Guarantee

By the end of 2014, there were 10.261 million households or 18.77 million urban residents entitled to minimum living allowances. In 2014, the total fiscal expenditure on the urban minimum life guarantee reached 72.17 billion yuan. There were 51.888 billion yuan came from the central financial subsidy funds, accounted for 71.9 percent of the total expenditure. In 2014, the average expenditure standard of urban minimum life guarantee was 411 yuan per person every month, a rise of 10.1 percent over the previous year. The per capita urban minimum life guarantee was 286 yuan every month, a rise of 8.3 percent over the previous year.

- Relief of the Urban Three-Without People

In 2014, 76 thousand urban Three-Without people had been relieved.

- Rural Minimum Life Guarantee

By the end of 2014, there were 29.436 million households, 52.072 million people who were covered by the rural minimum life guarantee system. A total of 87.03 billion yuan was distributed by governments at all levels in the whole year. It contained the central government subsidy of 58.26 billion yuan, accounting for 66.9 percent of the total expenditure. In 2014, the average expenditure standard of rural minimum life guarantee of the country was 2,777 yuan per person per year, which was an increase of 343 yuan over that of the previous year, a rise of 14.1 percent. The per capita rural minimum life guarantee was 129 yuan every month, a rise of 11.4 percent over the previous year.

- Five Guarantees in Rural Areas

By the end of 2014, there were 5.291 million people who had received relief allowances from the five guarantees system in rural areas across the country, decreased 1.5 percent over the previous year. A total of 18.98 billion yuan for rural five guarantees was distributed by government at all levels in the whole year. It was an increase of 10.2 percent over the previous year. There were 1.743 million people who were cared collectively in welfare institutions, with an average expenditure standard of 5,371 yuan per person per year, a rise of 14.6 percent in comparison with last year. There were 3.548 million people who were cared separately in communities, with an average expenditure standard of 4,006 yuan per person every year, a rise of 14.5 percent in comparison with last year.

Figure 7: Situation of Social Relief

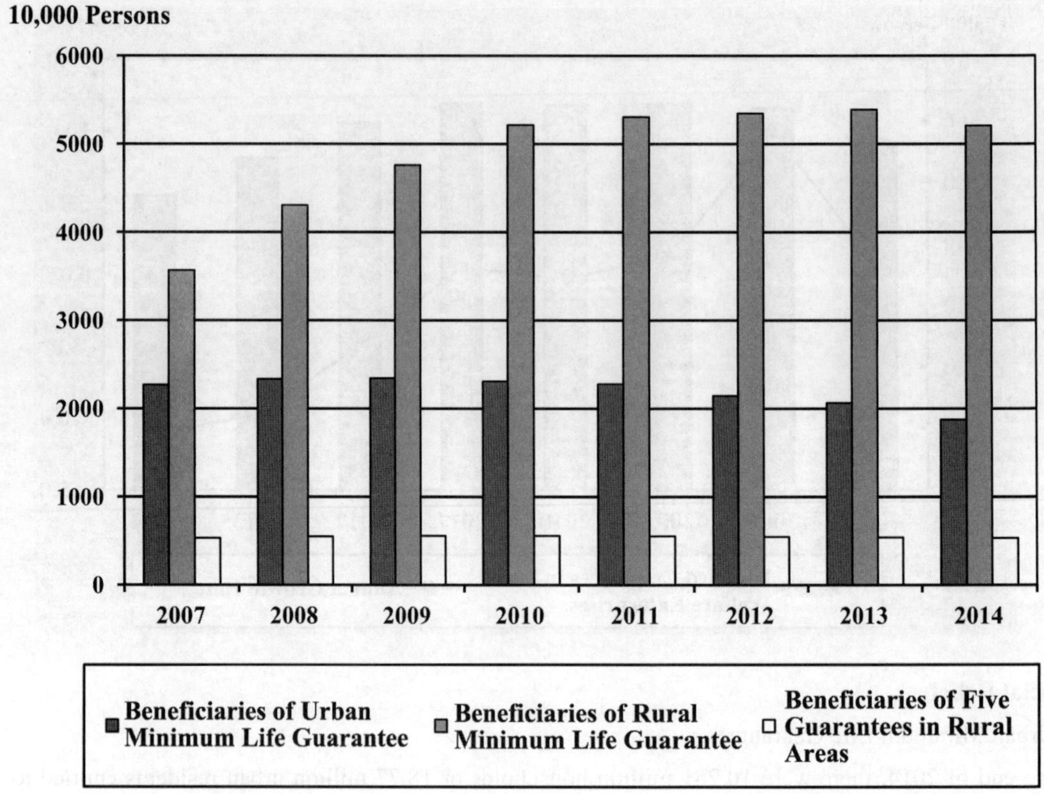

Table 7: Situation of Social Relief

Indicators	2007	2008	2009	2010	2011	2012	2013	2014
Beneficiaries of Urban Minimum Life Guarantee (10,000 Persons)	2272.1	2334.8	2345.6	2310.5	2276.8	2143.5	2064.2	1877
Beneficiaries of Rural Minimum Life Guarantee (10,000 Persons)	3566.3	4305.5	4760.0	5214.0	5305.7	5344.5	5388	5207.2
Five Guarantees in Rural Areas (10,000 Persons)	531.3	548.6	553.4	556.3	551	545.6	537.2	529.1

- Traditional Rural Relief

In 2014, there were 745 thousand residents who received the traditional rural relief.

- Medical Aid

In 2014, there were 91.19 million people (person-times) that received medical aid. 11.066 million of them were aided as inpatients and 12.887 million were aided as outpatients. 67.237 million people received subsidized aid for medical insurance. The total expenditure on medical aid was 25.26 billion yuan. It includes the fund for medical aid as inpatients of 18.02 billion yuan (1,628 yuan per persontime), the fund for medical aid as outpatients of 2.4 billion yuan (186 yuan per person-time) and the fund for subsidized aid for medical insurance of 4.84 billion yuan (72 yuan per person-time).

In 2014, the number of people who were covered by state pension and preferential treatment program and who received medical subsidy reached 4.746 million (person-times). The average expenditure was 661.8 yuan per person. The financial expenditure on medical subsidy at all levels totaled 3.14 billion yuan.

- The Provisional Relief

In 2014, there were 6.507 million households (times) that received provisional relief. According to the types of the household registrations, 3.335 million (times) were registered as urban households and 3.172 million (times) registered as rural ones. According to the classification of the households, 6.315 million households (times) belonged to local permanent residence and 192 thousand households (times) belonged to non-local permanent residence. According to the types of the provisional relief, 5.339 million households (times) received the provisional relief in expense pattern and 1.168 million households (times) received it in emergency pattern. The total annual expenditure on the provisional relief was 5.76 billion yuan.

5. Disaster Prevention and Relief

In 2014, 240 million people (person-times) were influenced by various natural disasters. There were 1,818 deaths and abscondences caused by disasters. There were 6.017 million people (person-times) who were transferred and resettled urgently. There were 24.891 million hectares of farm crops hit by disasters, thereinto, 3.09 million hectares of crops were demolished. Collapsed buildings reached 450 thousand and 2.542 million buildings were damaged. The direct economic loss which was caused by disasters stood at 337.38 billion yuan. The China National Commission for Disaster Reduction and the Ministry of Civil Affairs totally started mechanism of early warning for 3 times and emergency response for 28 times. Twenty two disaster assistance response teams rushed to disaster areas. The Ministry of Finance and the Ministry of Civil Affairs allocated 9.873 billion yuan as central relief funds, and the Ministry of Civil Affairs allocated 114 thousand tents, 164 thousand pieces of cotton-padded clothes and quilts and 47 thousand folding beds. 75 million people (person-times) received the disaster relief. The basic needs of people afflicted by natural disasters were guaranteed.

Figure 8 : Deaths (Abscondences) Caused by Disasters

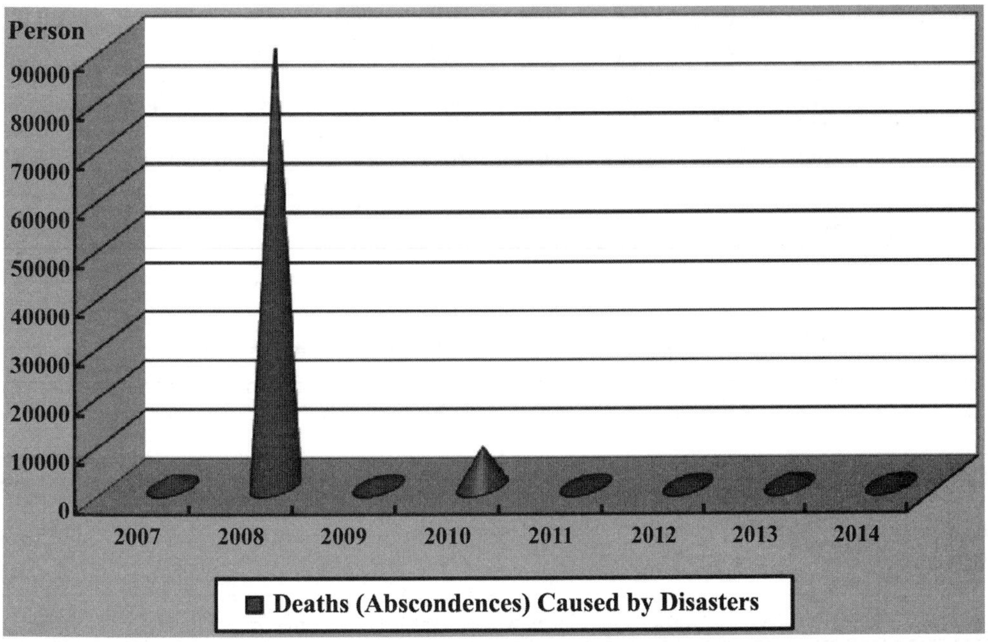

Table 8 : Deaths (Abscondences) Caused by Disasters

Indicators	2007	2008	2009	2010	2011	2012	2013	2014
Deaths (Abscondences) Caused by Disasters (Person)	2325	88928	1528	7844	1126	1530	2284	1818

6. Social Charity

- Charitable Donations

By the end of 2014, there were 32 thousand regular workstations of social donations and charity supermarkets (10,174 of which were charity supermarkets). The total social donations reached 60.44 billion yuan. Of this total, the civil affairs departments received direct donations of 7.96 billion yuan and social organizations received donations of 52.49 billion yuan. In 2014, the donated quilts and clothes reached 52.445 million pieces, valued at 800 million yuan. The indirect social donations which were transferred from other departments were 0.22 billion yuan, and there were also 1.056 million pieces of indirect-donated quilts and clothes. The donated materials were worth 390.116 million yuan. Over 16.949 million people (person-times) in difficulties benefited from the charitable donations. There were 10.959 million volunteers (person-times) who provided 27.111 million hours of social services in 2014.

Figure 9: Social Donations and Donated Quilts and Clothes

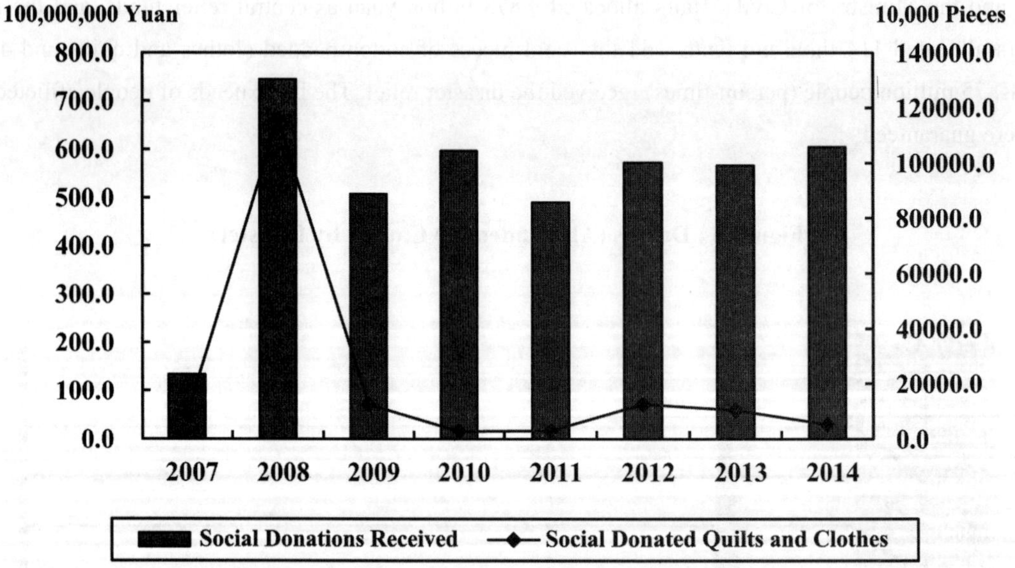

Table 9: Social Donations and Donated Quilts and Clothes

Indicators	2007	2008	2009	2010	2011	2012	2013	2014
Social Donations Received (100,000,000 Yuan)	132.8	744.5	507.2	596.8	490.1	572.5	566.4	604.4
Social Donated Quilts and Clothes (10,000 Pieces)	8756.8	115816.3	12476.6	2750.2	2918.5	12538.2	10405.0	5244.5

- Welfare Lottery

In 2014, the sales of welfare lottery reached 205.97 billion yuan, an increase of 29.44 billion yuan over the previous year, a rise of 16.7 percent over the previous year. The public lottery funds reached 58.57 billion yuan, a rise of 14.7 percent in comparison with last year. The expenditure of public lottery funds by the civil affairs departments totaled 23.13 billion yuan, an increase of 3.58 billion yuan over the previous year. It included 590 million yuan on state pension, 90 million yuan on the placement of retired servicemen, 14.36 billion yuan on social welfare, 2.91 billion yuan on social relief, 220 million yuan on disaster relief and 4.97 billion yuan on other expenses.

Figure 10: Welfare Lottery

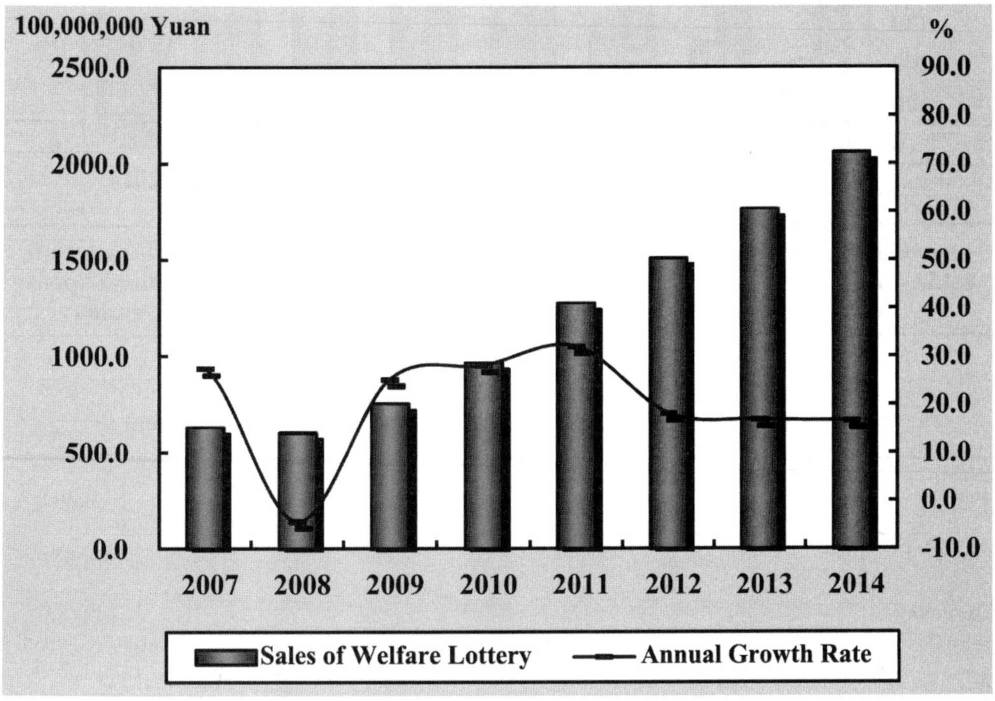

Table 10: Welfare Lottery

Indicators	2007	2008	2009	2010	2011	2012	2013	2014
Sales of Welfare Lottery (100,000,000 Yuan)	631.6	604.0	756.0	968.0	1278.0	1510.3	1765.3	2059.7
Annual Growth Rate (%)	27.4	-4.4	25.2	28.0	32.0	18.2	16.9	16.7

7. Preferential Treatment and Placement

By the end of 2014, there were 9.173 million people who were covered by state pension and preferential treatment program. Of this total, there were 766 thousand wounded servicemen, 1.242 million ailing ex-servicemen, 0.993 million rural retired servicemen, 3.748 million ex-servicemen above 60 years old with rural registration households, 341 veterans of the Red Army in rural areas, 87 veterans of the West-Road Red Army in the rural areas, 11,269 veterans who lost touch with the Red Army, 198 thousand family members of martyrs, 113 thousand family members of servicemen who died on duty or of illness.

Figure 11: Beneficiaries of State Pension and Preferential Treatment

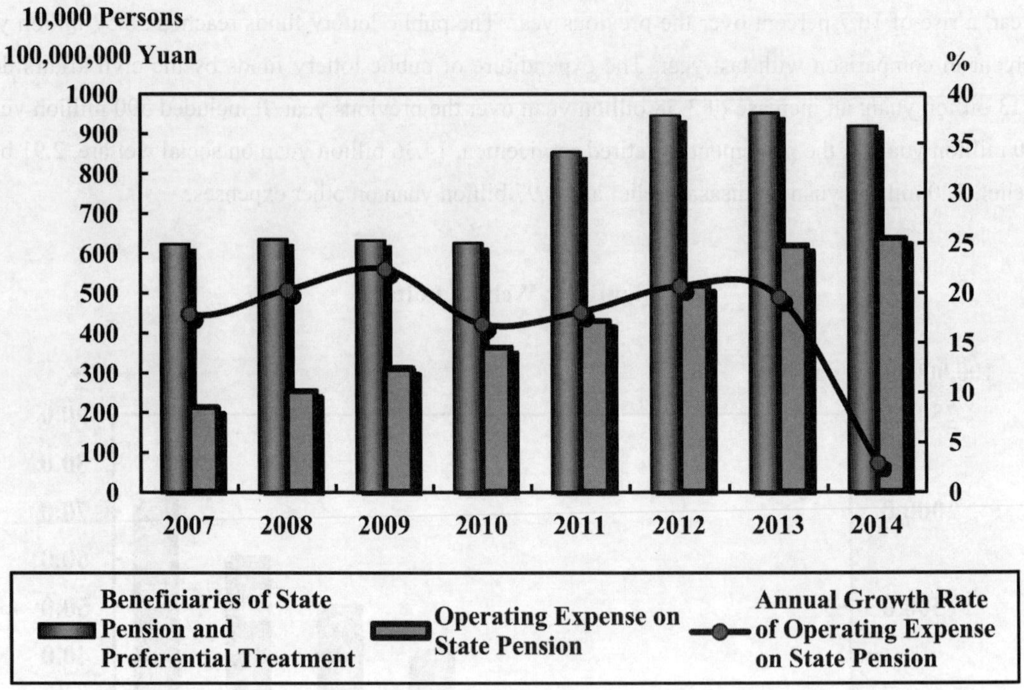

Figure 11: Beneficiaries of State Pension and Preferential Treatment

Indicators	2007	2008	2009	2010	2011	2012	2013	2014
Beneficiaries of State Pension and Preferential Treatment (10,000 Persons)	622.4	633.2	630.7	625	852.5	944.4	950.5	917.3
Operating Expense on State Pension (100,000,000 Yuan)	210.8	253.6	310.3	362.7	428.3	517	618.4	636.6
Annual Growth Rate of Operating Expense on State Pension (%)	17.9	20.3	22.4	16.9	18.1	20.7	19.6	2.9

In 2014, the government allocated prizes to newly increased 267 martyrs. By the end of 2014, there were 1,516 management organizations of martyrs' monuments, taking up the space of 4,564 hectares. There were 9,289 martyrs' monuments which were within management organizations and there were 11,365 scattered monuments.

In 2014, there were 28,000 retired military cadres (including demobilized sergeants), retirees military employees who had no military registration and demobilized officers. There were 185 management centers for the emeritus and retired personnel who were from troops and 2,000 employees worked in these management centers. There were 30 activity centers granted for the emeritus and retired personnel who were from troops and one thousand employees worked in these places.

8. Community Services

By the end of 2014, there were 311 thousand community service institutions, and the coverage rate of community service institutions was 45.5 percent. Among these institutions, 918 were community service instruction centers and 23,088 were community service centers, an increase of 4,074 over the previous year. There were 120,188 community service stations which an increase of 11,811 over the previous year. There were 18,927 community welfare institutions and facilities for the aged, 40,357 mutual aid facilities, 107 thousand other community service institutions. There were 309 thousand convenience stations and 109 thousand community organizations of volunteers in urban areas.

Table 12: Community Service Institutions

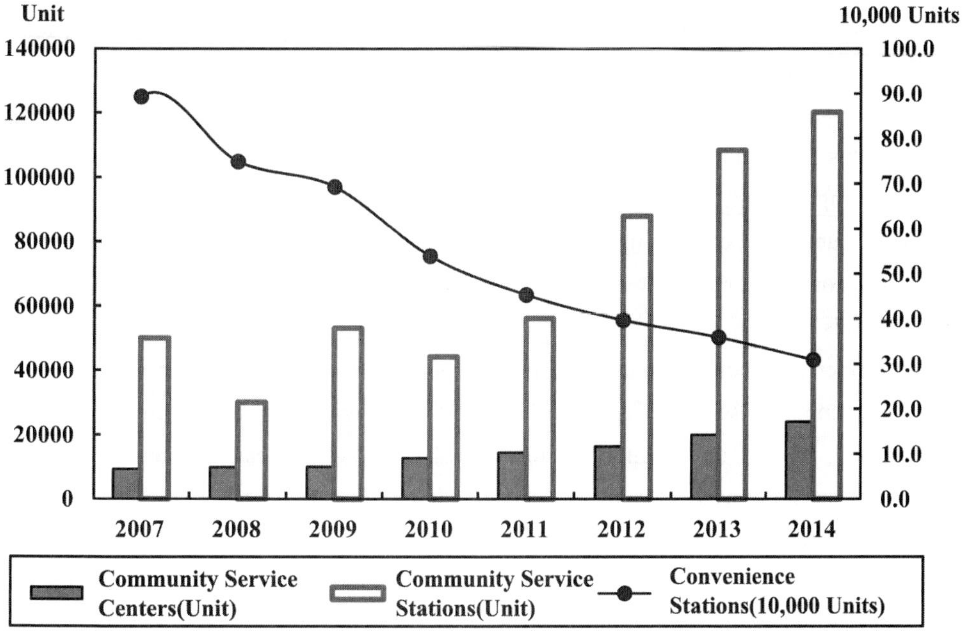

Table 12: Community Service Institutions

Indicators	2007	2008	2009	2010	2011	2012	2013	2014
Community Service Institutions (10,000 Units)	12.9	14.6	14.6	15.3	16.0	20.0	25.2	31.1
Community Service Centers (Unit)	9319	9873	10003	12720	14391	16306	19904	23088
Community Service Stations (Unit)	50116	30021	53170	44237	56156	87931	108377	120188
Convenience Stations (10,000 Units)	89.3	74.9	69.3	53.9	45.3	39.7	35.9	30.9

III. Member Organizations and Other Social Services

A. Member Organizations

1. Non-Government Organizations (NGOs)

By the end of 2014, there were altogether 606 thousand NGOs, an increase of 10.8 percent over that of the previous year. There were 6.823 million employees, an increase of 7.2 percent over the previous year. The total value of fixed assets was 156.06 billion yuan. The added value of NGOs was 63.86 billion yuan, an increase of 11.8 percent over the previous year and it accounted for 0.21 percent in the added value of tertiary industry. The NGOs received donations of 52.49 billion yuan. There were 4,246 law-breaking cases which concerned NGOs and were investigated and penalized. As a result, 46 illegal NGOs were banned and 4,200 administrative punishments took place.

There were 310 thousand social organizations, a growth of 7.2 percent over the previous year. Among these social organizations, 34,099 were engaged in industry and commercial services, 16,923 in science and technology services, 11,412 in education, 10,060 in health, 44,630 in social services, 30,101 in culture, 20,848 in sports, 6,964 in eco-environment, 3,270 in legal services, 4,898 in religion, 60,202 in agricultural and rural development, 19,867 in profession, 516 in international and other overseas affairs and 45,946 in other fields. In 2014, there were 2,312 law-breaking cases which concerned social organizations and were investigated and penalized. Thereinto, 4 illegal social organizations were banned and 2,308 administrative punishments took place.

In 2014, there were 4,117 foundations across the country, an increase of 568, rose by 16.0 percent over that of the previous year. Of this total, there were 1,470 public-raising foundations, 2,610 nonpublic raising foundations, 9 foundations concerning foreign affairs, 28 representative offices of overseas foundations. There were 227 foundations (including foundations concerning foreign affairs) registered in the Ministry of Civil Affairs. The public-raising foundations and non-public-raising foundations totally received donations of 37.43 billion yuan. In 2014, 13 administrative punishments took place and 1 was banned.

There were altogether 292 thousand non-governmental and non-commercial enterprises, a rise of 14.7 percent over the previous year. Among these enterprises, there were 15,110 engaged in science and technology services, 398 in ecological environment, 163,681 in education, 23,404 in health, 42,244 in social services, 14,148 in culture, 11,901 in sports, 5,915 in commercial services, 82 in religion, 4 in international and other overseas affairs and 15,308 in other fields. In 2014, there were 1,920 law-breaking cases which concerned non-governmental and non-commercial enterprises and were investigated and penalized. Thereinto, 41 illegal non-governmental and non-commercial enterprises were banned, and 1,879 administrative punishments took place.

Figure 13: Non-Governmental Organizations

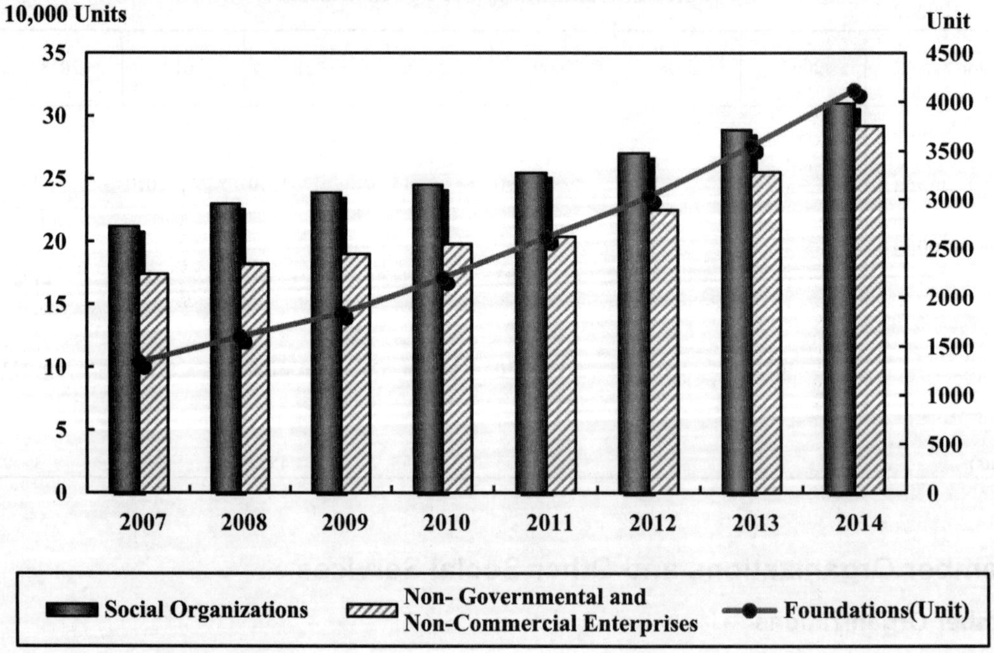

Figure 13: Non-Governmental Organizations

Indicators	2007	2008	2009	2010	2011	2012	2013	2014
Social Organizations (10,000 Units)	21.2	23	23.9	24.5	25.5	27.1	28.9	31.0
Foundations (Unit)	1340	1597	1843	2200	2614	3029	3549	4117
Non-Governmental and Non-Commercial Enterprises (10,000 Units)	17.4	18.2	19	19.8	20.4	22.5	25.5	29.2

2. Self-Governing Organizations

By the end of 2014, self-governing organizations at the grass-roots totaled 682 thousand. Of this total, there were 585 thousand village committees. The number of village groups was 4.704 million. There were 2.305 million members of village committees. There were 96,693 community neighborhood committees, a rise of 2.2 percent over that of the previous year. There were 1.358 million neighborhood groups. There were 497 thousand members of neighborhood committees, a rise of 2.7 percent over that in the previous year. In 2014, elections in 330 thousand neighborhood committees and village committees were completed. The registered number of residents and villagers who participated in the elections was 430 million. The number of voters was 340 million.

Figure14: Self-Governing Organizations

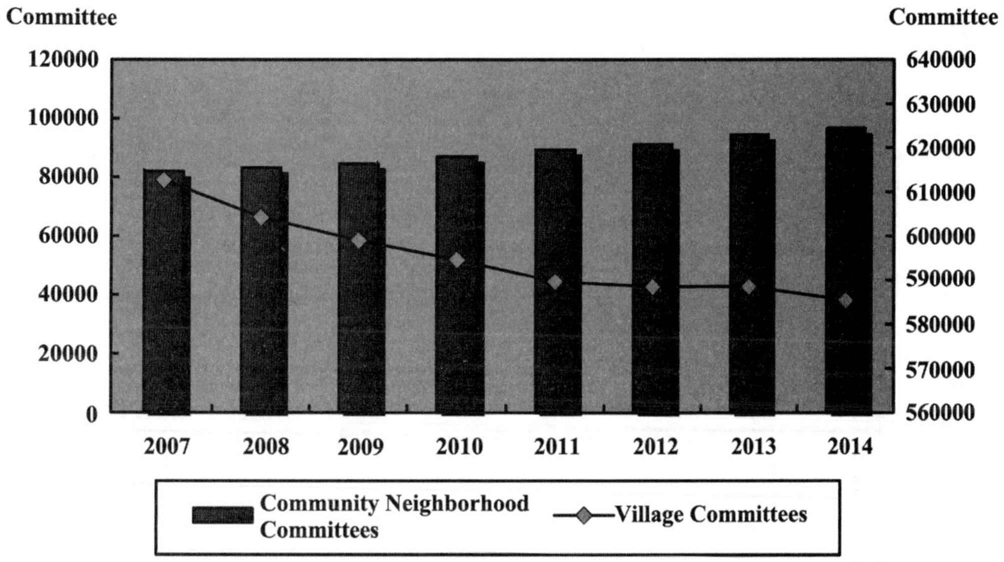

Figure14: Self-Governing Organizations

Indicators	2007	2008	2009	2010	2011	2012	2013	2014
Community Neighborhood Committees (committee)	82006	83413	84689	87057	89480	91153	94620	96693
Village Committees (committee)	612709	604285	599078	594658	589653	588475	588547	585451

B. Other Social Services

1. Marriage Service

In 2014, there were 2,236 service institutions of marriage registration (qualified as public institutions) and 6,797 service offices of marriage registration in China. The number of people that registered their marriage through civil affairs departments or marriage registration institutions reached 13.067 million couples. Of this total, 13.020 million couples were mainland Chinese residents. There were 47 thousand couples concerning foreigners, overseas Chinese, and residents of Hong Kong, Macau and Taiwan. The crude nuptiality was 9.6 per thousand. The proportion of people ranged from 25 to 29 years old accounted for 38.0 percent of all registered for marriage, taking the lead among other age groups and it increased by 2.8 percent over that of the previous year.

In 2014, there were 3.637 million couples handling divorce, which was an increase of 3.9 percent over the previous year. The crude divorce rate was 2.7 per thousand, which was an increase of 0.1 per thousand over that in 2013. Of this total, 2.957 million couples were registered through the civil affairs departments and those who divorced through courts were 679 thousand couples.

Figure 15: Crude Nuptiality and Divorce Rate

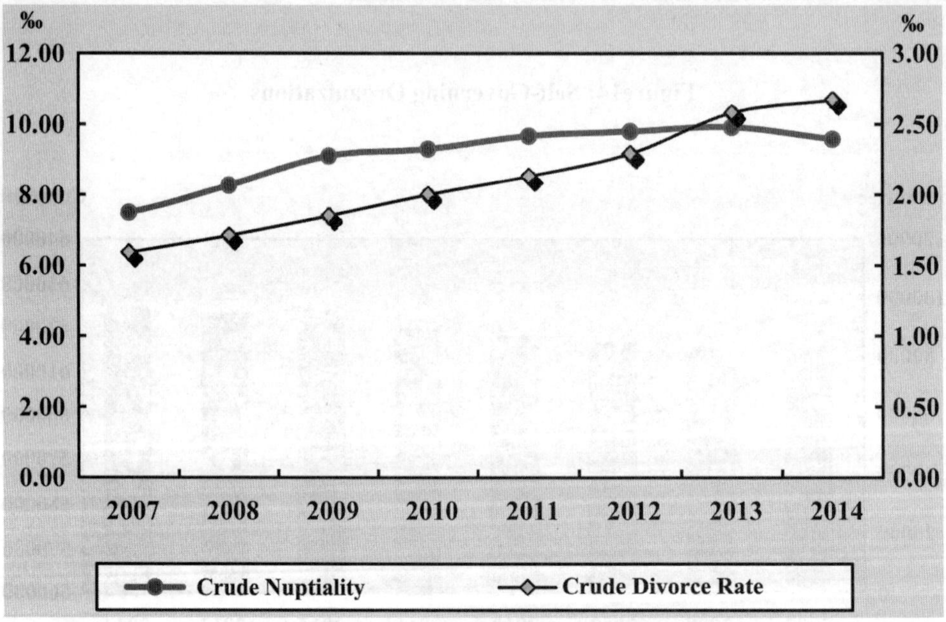

Figure 15: Crude Nuptiality and Divorce Rate

Indicators	2007	2008	2009	2010	2011	2012	2013	2014
Crude Nuptiality (‰)	7.50	8.27	9.10	9.30	9.67	9.80	9.92	9.58
Crude Divorce Rate (‰)	1.59	1.71	1.85	2.00	2.13	2.29	2.58	2.67

2. Funeral and Interment

By the end of 2014, there were 4,559 funeral and interment service institutions. Of this total, there were 1,801 funeral parlors, 1,141 funeral management organizations. There were 1,598 public cemeteries under the management of the civil affairs departments. There were 83 thousand employees in the funeral and interment service institutions. Among these institutions, 46 thousand people worked for funeral parlors. There were 5,908 cremators, which cremated

4.593 million remains. The cremation rate stood at 47.0 percent.

Figure 16: Cremation of Funeral Service

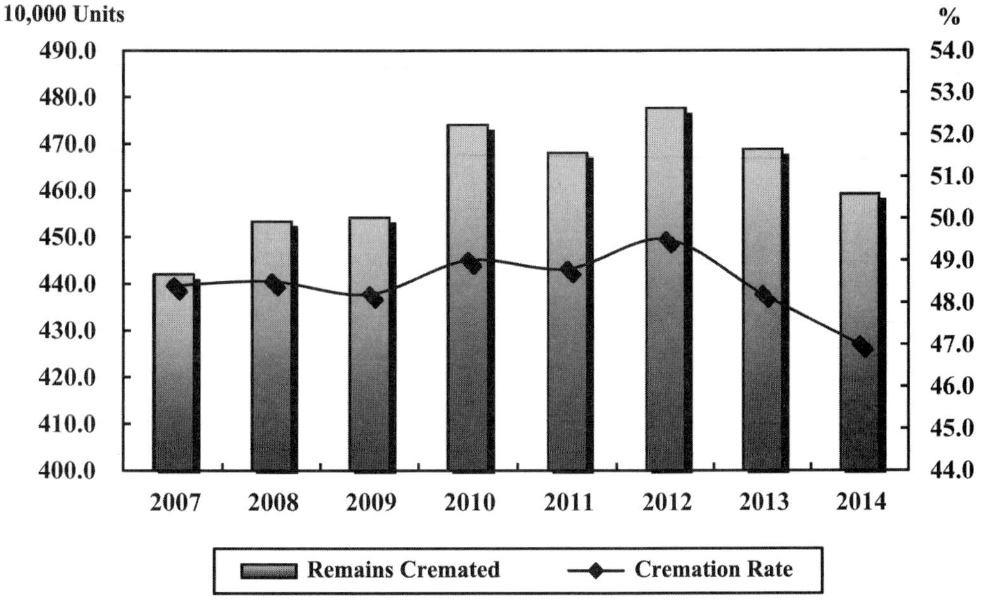

Figure 16: Cremation of Funeral Service

Indicators	2007	2008	2009	2010	2011	2012	2013	2014
Remains Cremated (10,000 Units)	442.1	453.4	454.2	474.1	468.1	477.7	468.9	459.3
Cremation Rate (%)	48.4	48.5	48.2	49.0	48.8	49.5	48.2	47.0

Notes:

[1] Townships in figure 1 and table 1 include ethnic townships, sumus and ethnic sumus.

[2] The relief funds allocated by the Ministry of Finance and the Ministry of Civil Affairs do not include the purchasing funds for central relief material and the relief funds that the central government allocated to Xinjiang Production and Construction Corps.

[3] The quantity of community service centers counted in 2014 contains community service instruction centers.

[4] The number of foundations under the management of the Civil Affairs Department contains the amount of foundations concerning foreign affairs and representative offices of overseas foundations.

[5] As the annual inspection of social organizations usually lags behind the annual bulletin release , the annual data of the previous year's donations(2013) was used.

[6] The statistics of judicial decisions and mediate divorces recorded in the divorce registration service comes from the supreme peoples' court.

[7] In this report, the numbers of people were the actual amount and the numbers of institutions were the numbers of authorized ones. These numbers should not be compared with approved numbers and predicted numbers.

[8] The itemized figures may not match the totalized ones in this report, this is because some of the statistics in the report were rounded off and no mechanical adjustments have been made for mending the error.

[9] Statistics of Hong Kong, Macau and Taiwan province were not included into the report.

社会服务
主要数据图表

02

图1-1 市、区、县

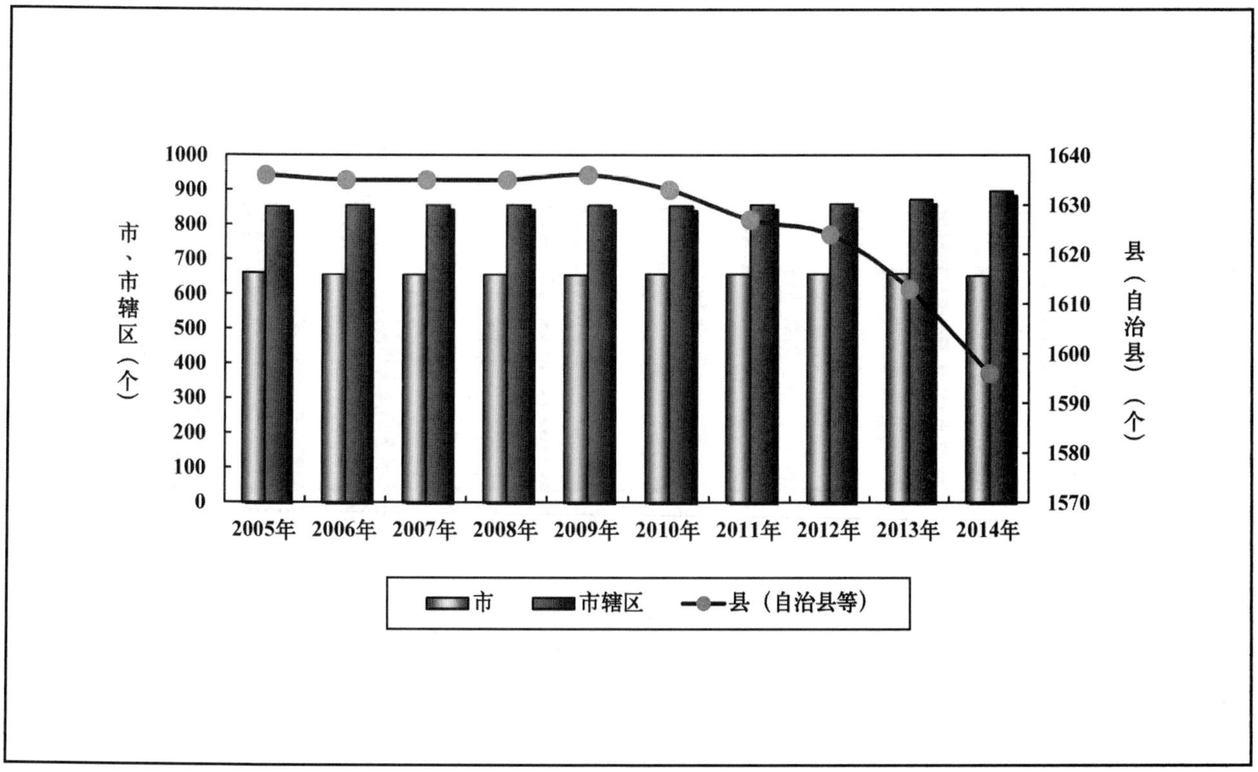

单位：个

指　标	2005年	2006年	2007年	2008年	2009年	2010年	2011年	2012年	2013年	2014年
市	661	656	655	655	654	657	657	657	658	653
市辖区	852	856	856	856	855	853	857	860	872	897
县（自治县等）	1636	1635	1635	1635	1636	1633	1627	1624	1613	1596

注释：市含直辖市、地级市及县级市。

图1-2　乡镇与街道

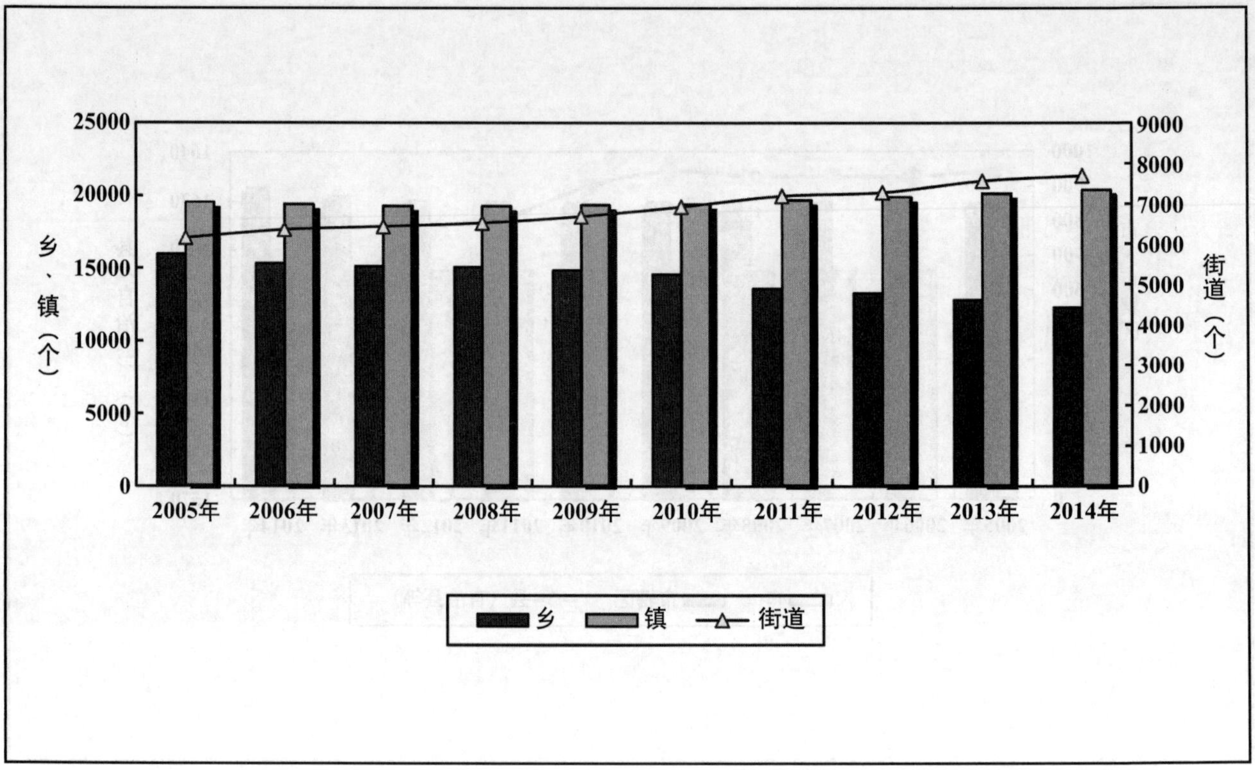

单位：个

指　标	2005年	2006年	2007年	2008年	2009年	2010年	2011年	2012年	2013年	2014年
乡	15951	15306	15120	15067	14848	14571	13587	13281	12812	12282
镇	19522	19369	19249	19234	19322	19410	19683	19881	20117	20401
街道	6152	6355	6434	6524	6686	6923	7194	7282	7566	7696

图1-3　60岁及以上老年人口占全国总人口比重

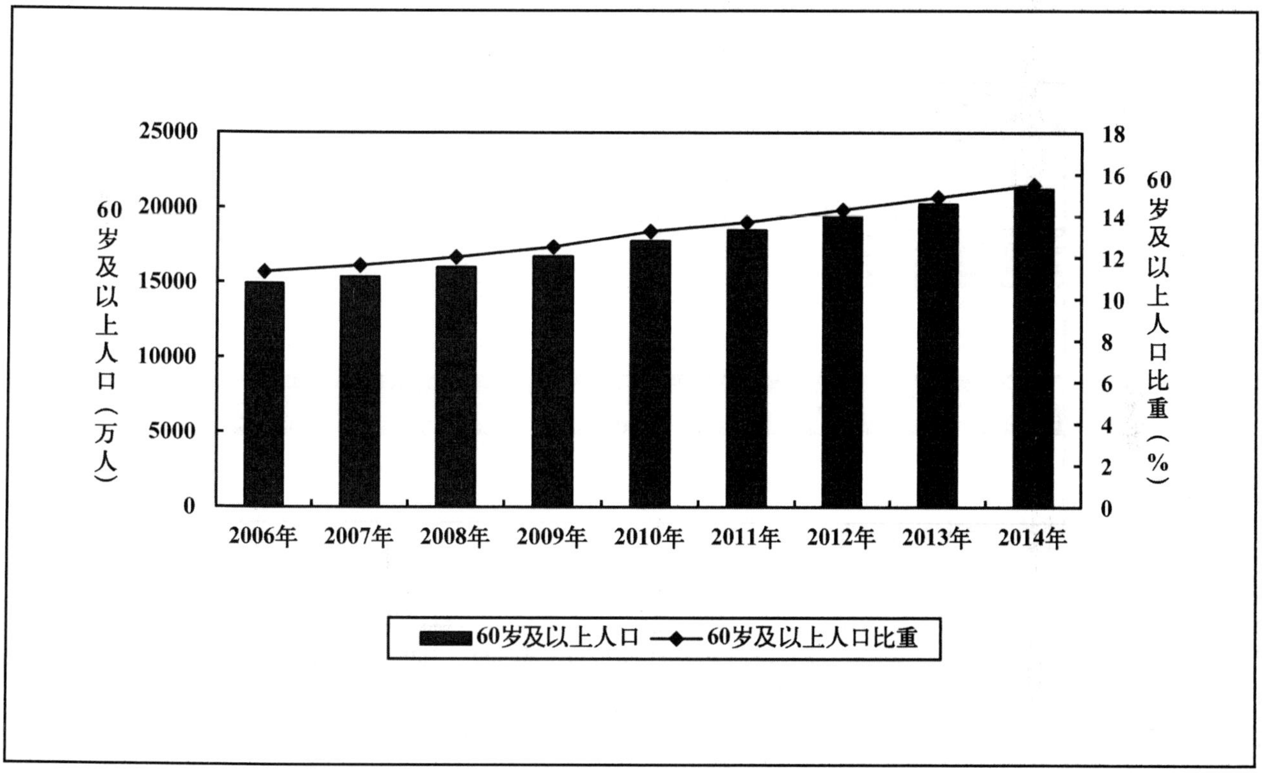

单位：万人、%

指　标	2006年	2007年	2008年	2009年	2010年	2011年	2012年	2013年	2014年
60岁及以上人口	14901	15340	15989	16714	17765	18499	19390	20243	21242
60岁及以上人口比重	11.3	11.6	12	12.5	13.26	13.7	14.3	14.9	15.5

注：本表数据来源于国家统计局。

图1-4 人口年龄结构

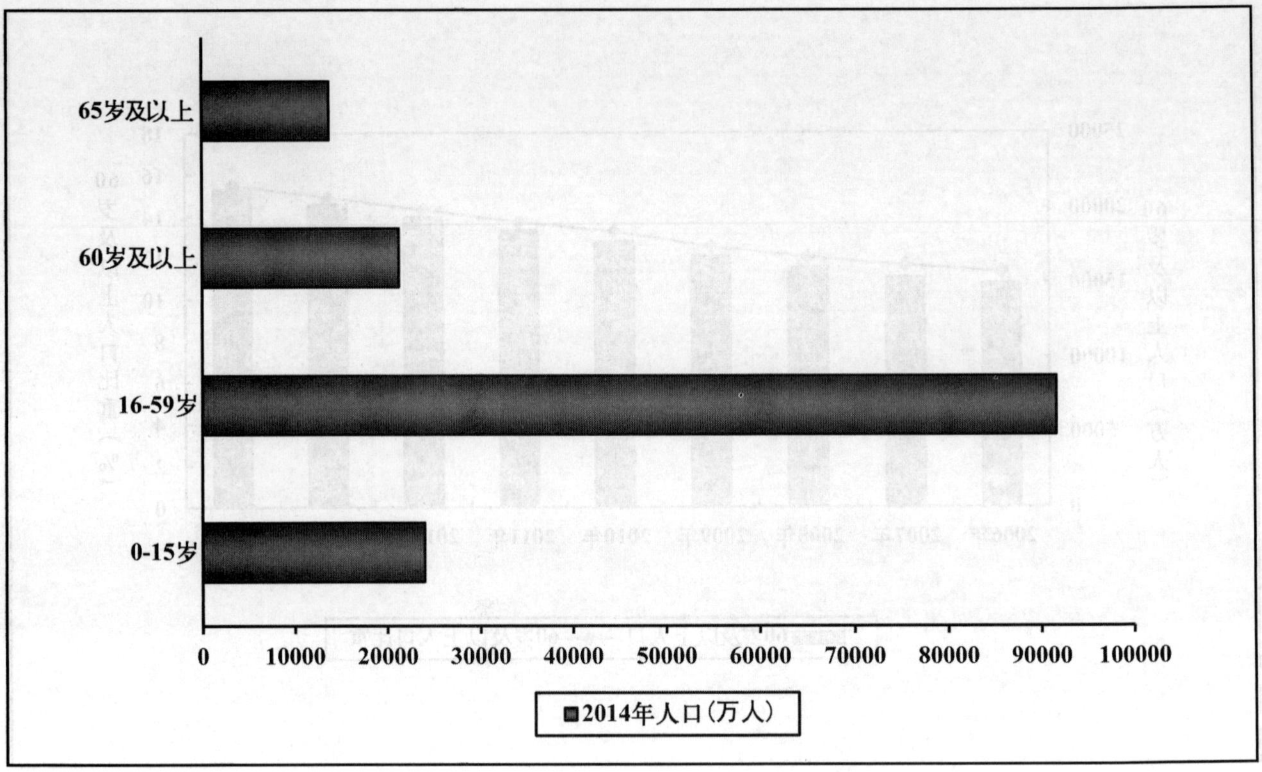

单位：万人、%

指　标	0–15岁	16–59岁	60岁及以上	65岁及以上
2014年人口	23957	91583	21242	13755
不同年龄段人口比重	17.5	67.0	15.5	10.1
比2013年增减百分点		-0.6	0.6	0.4

图1-5　社会服务机构设施和职工

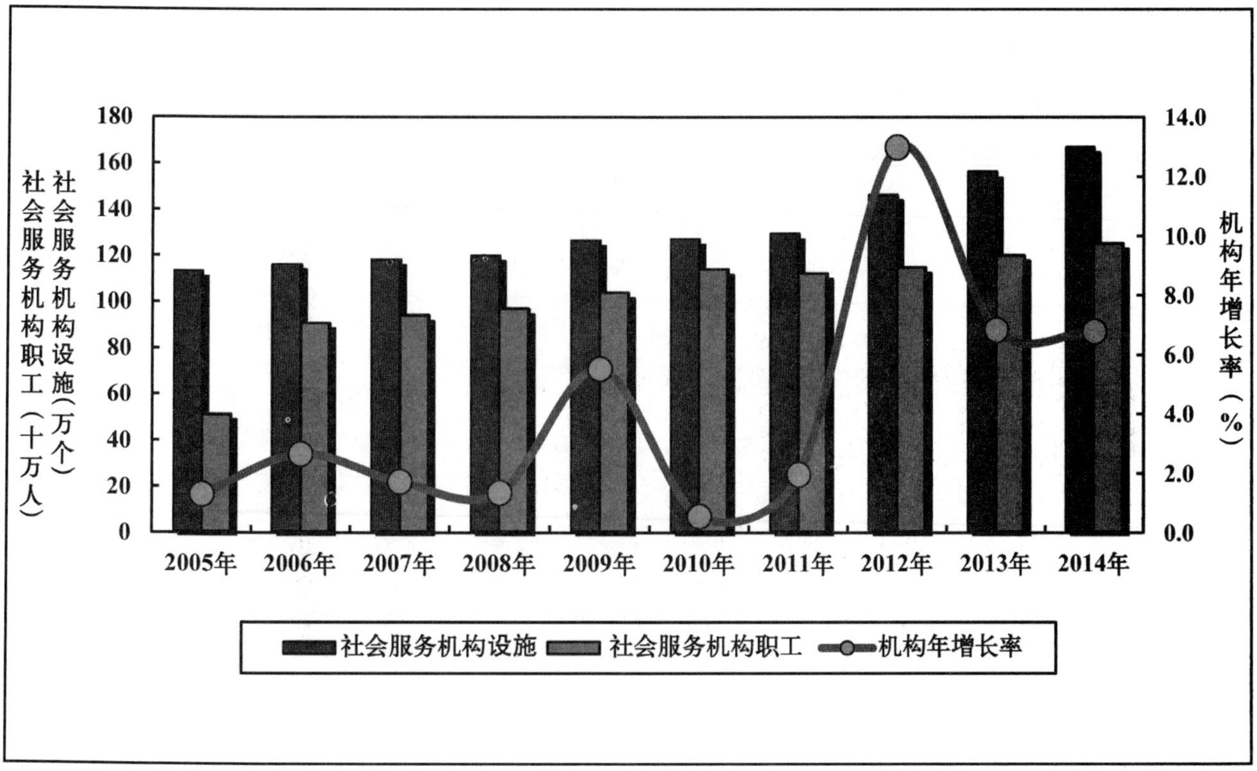

单位：万个、%、十万人

指　标	2005年	2006年	2007年	2008年	2009年	2010年	2011年	2012年	2013年	2014年
社会服务机构设施	113	116	118	119.6	126.2	126.9	129.4	146.2	156.2	166.8
社会服务机构职工	50.9	90.4	93.8	96.7	103.8	113.8	112.1	114.7	119.8	125.1
机构年增长率	1.3	2.7	1.7	1.4	5.5	0.6	2.0	13.0	6.8	6.8

图1-6 社会服务对象占全国总人口比重

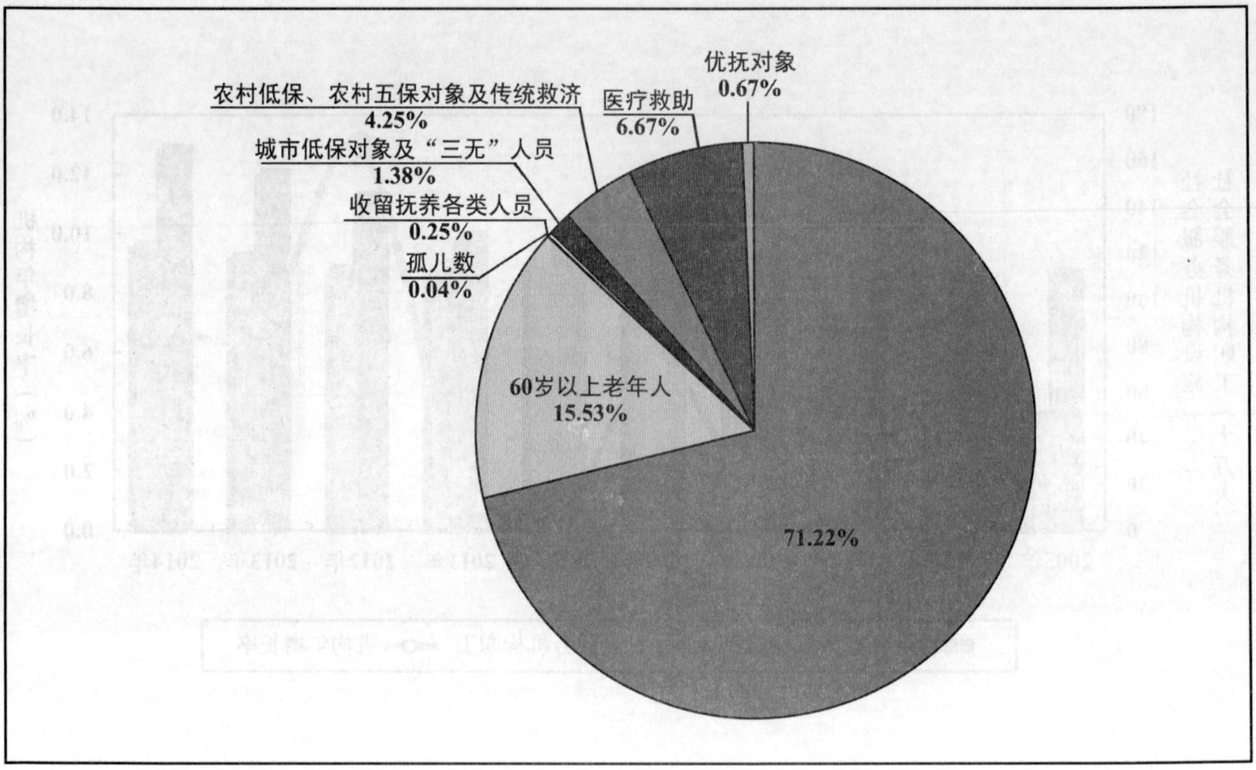

单位：万人、%

指　标	2014年	比　重
全国总人口	136782	100.0
社会服务对象	39363.1	28.78
# 60岁以上老年人	21242	15.53
孤儿数	52.5	0.04
收留抚养各类人员	336.8	0.25
城市低保对象及“三无”人员	1884.6	1.38
农村低保、农村五保对象及传统救济	5810.8	4.25
医疗救助	9119.1	6.67
优抚对象	917.3	0.67

图1-7　社会服务机构增加值占服务业增加值比重

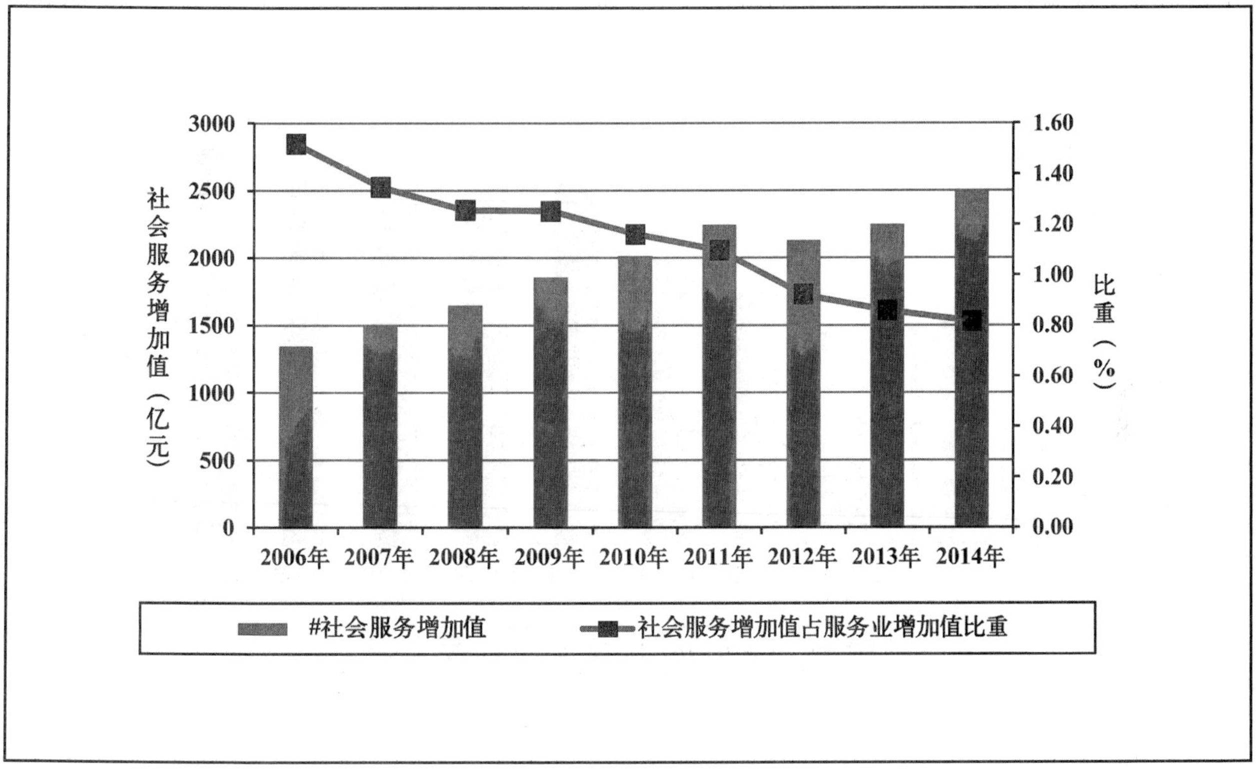

单位：亿元、%

指　标	2006年	2007年	2008年	2009年	2010年	2011年	2012年	2013年	2014年
服务业增加值	88554.9	111351.9	131340.0	148038.0	173596	204982.5	231626	262204	306739
# 社会服务增加值	1344.8	1501.2	1650.1	1856.2	2014.5	2246.9	2128.9	2251.9	2515.2
社会服务增加值占服务业增加值比重	1.52	1.35	1.26	1.25	1.16	1.10	0.92	0.86	0.82

图1-8 社会服务固定资产原值

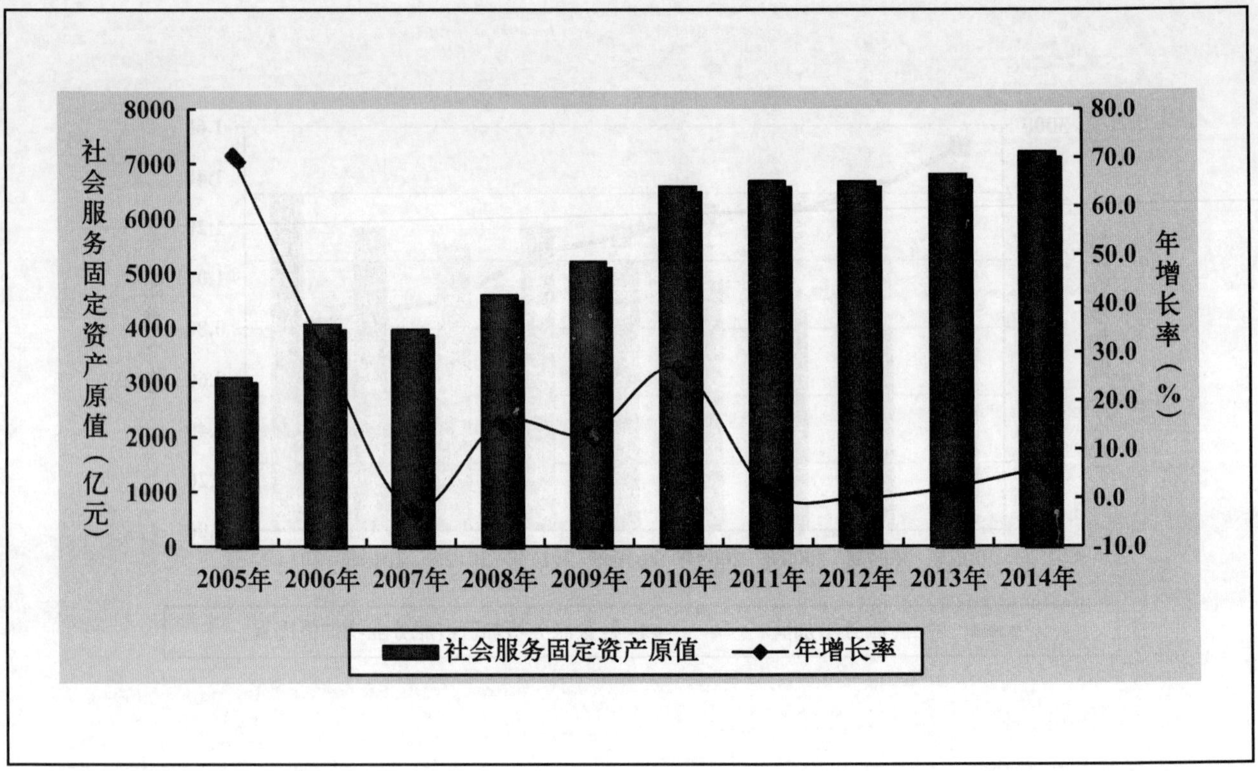

单位：亿元、%

指　标	2005年	2006年	2007年	2008年	2009年	2010年	2011年	2012年	2013年	2014年
社会服务固定资产原值	3097.8	4066.7	3973	4592.8	5198	6589.3	6676.7	6675.4	6810.2	7213.0
年增长率	70.4	31.3	-2.3	15.6	13.2	26.8	1.3		2.0	5.9

图1–9　社会服务基本建设投资

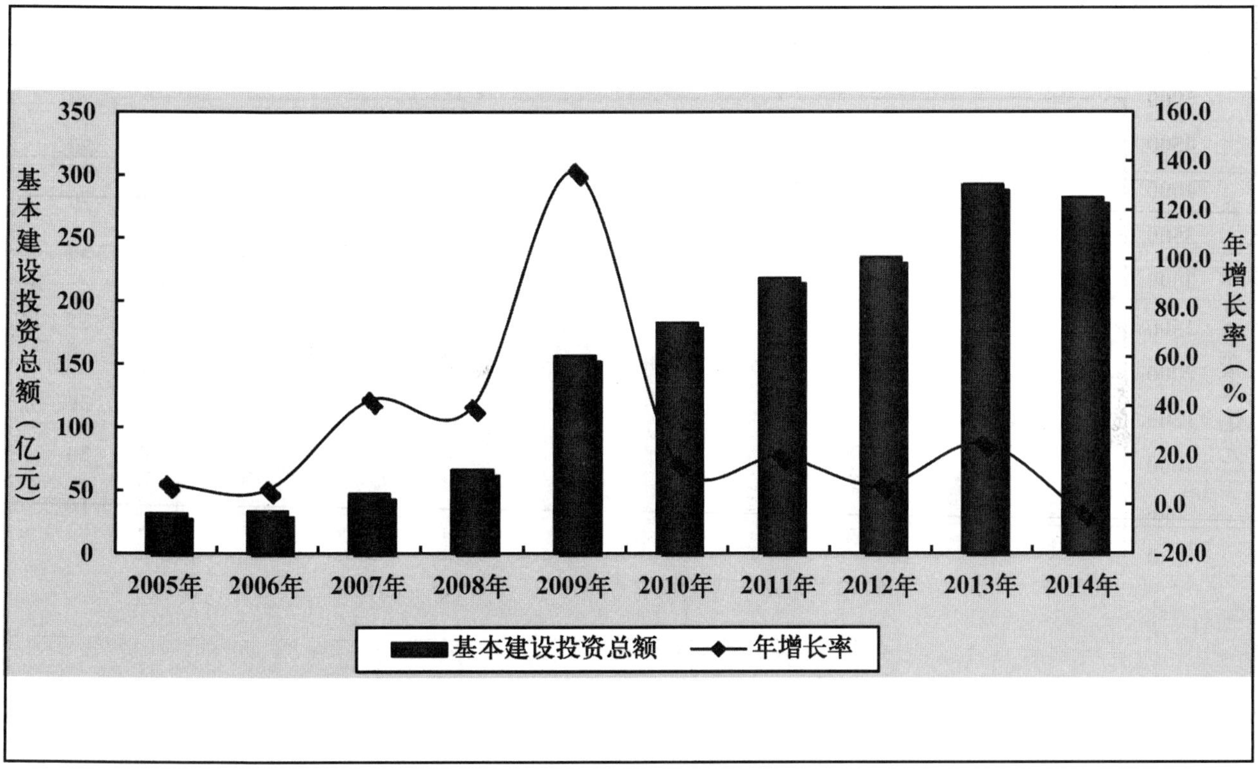

单位：亿元、%

指　标	2005年	2006年	2007年	2008年	2009年	2010年	2011年	2012年	2013年	2014年
基本建设投资总额	31.6	33.5	47.7	66.6	157	183	218.5	234.7	292.8	282.2
年增长率	8.2	6.0	42.4	39.6	135.7	16.6	19.4	7.4	24.8	-3.6

图1-10 社会服务经费

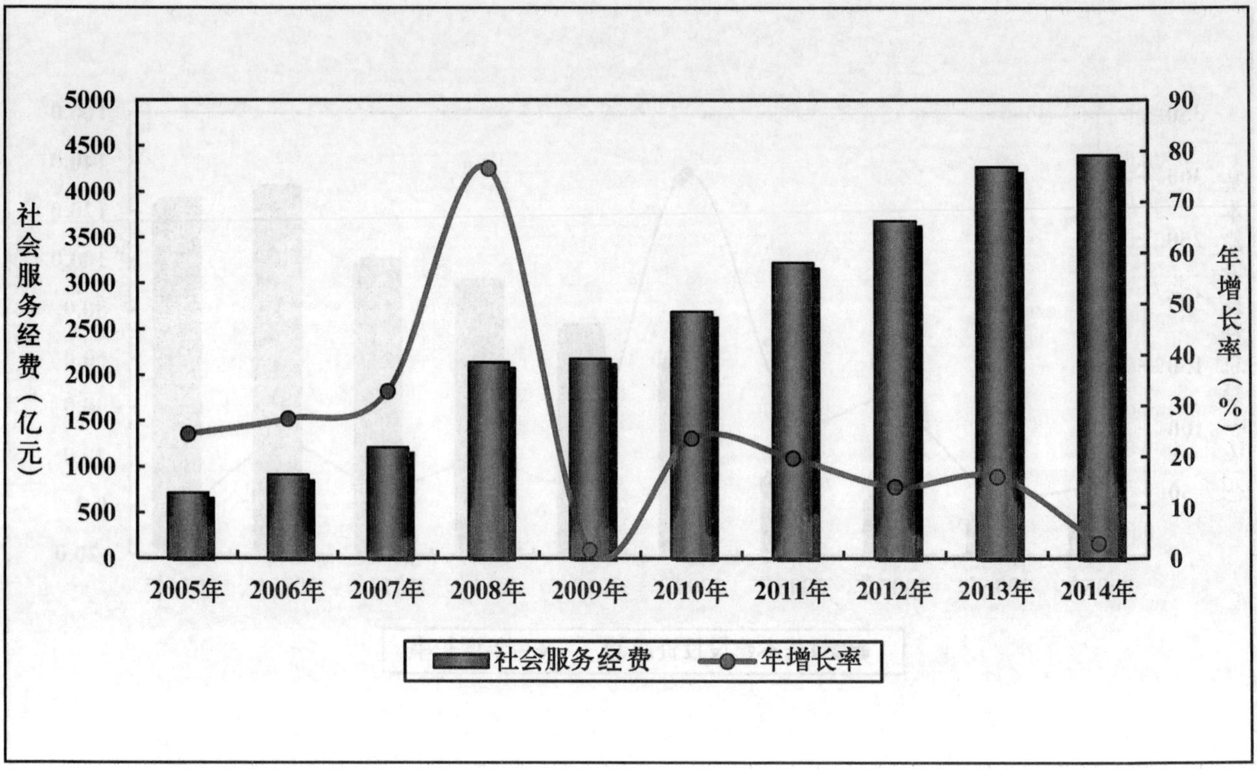

单位：亿元、%

指　标	2005年	2006年	2007年	2008年	2009年	2010年	2011年	2012年	2013年	2014年
社会服务经费	718.4	915.4	1215.5	2146.5	2181.9	2697.5	3229.1	3683.7	4276.5	4404.1
年增长率	24.4	27.4	32.8	76.6	1.6	23.6	19.7	14.1	16.1	3.0

图1-11 社会服务经费支出占国家财政支出的比重

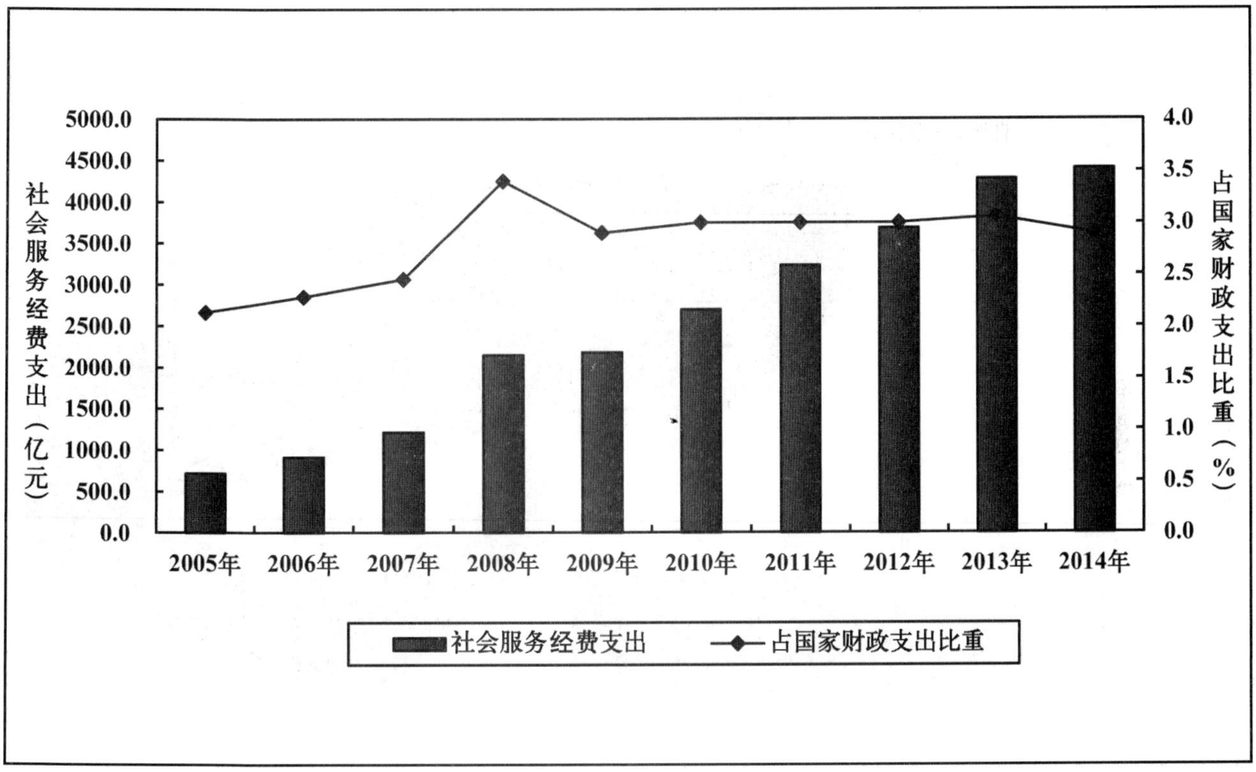

单位：亿元、%

指　标	2005年	2006年	2007年	2008年	2009年	2010年	2011年	2012年	2013年	2014年
社会服务经费支出	718.4	915.4	1215.5	2146.5	2181.9	2697.5	3229.1	3683.7	4276.5	4404.1
占国家财政支出比重	2.1	2.3	2.5	3.4	2.9	3.0	3.0	3.0	3.1	2.9

图1-12 社会服务经费按用项支出比重

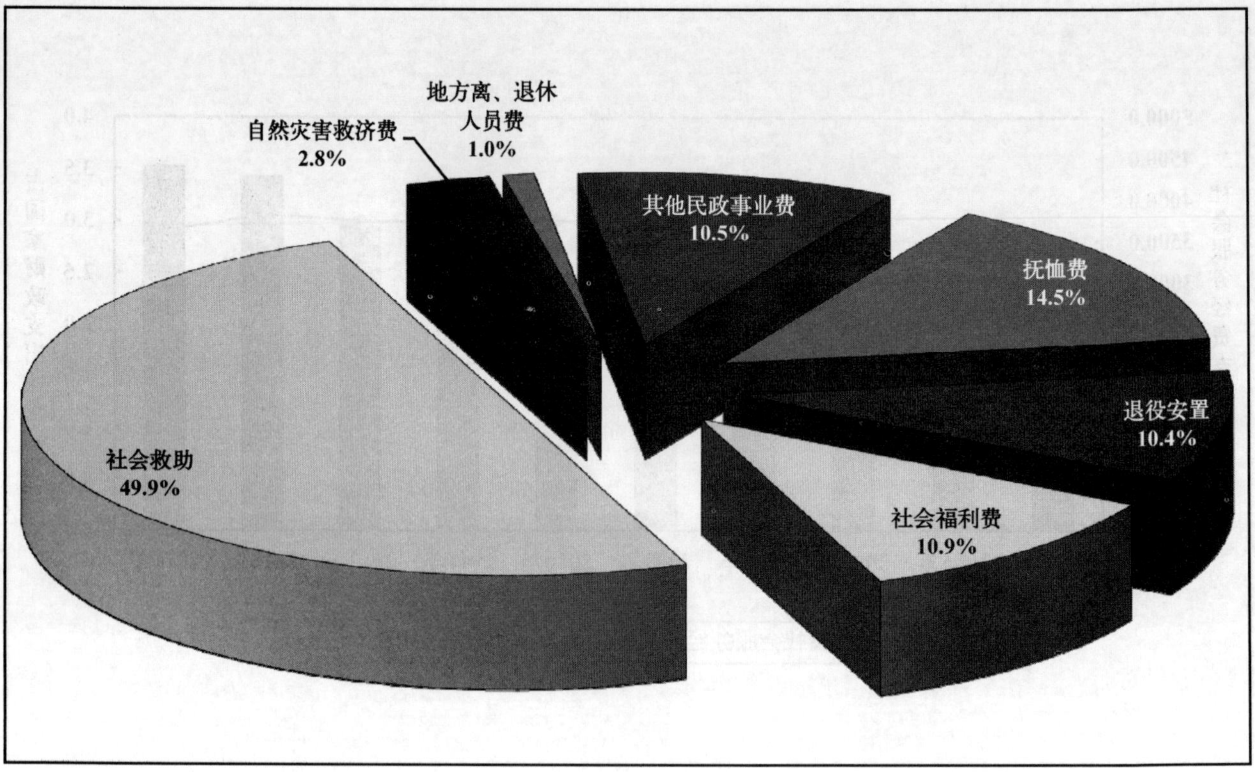

单位：亿元、%

指　标	社会服务经费总支出	抚恤费	退役安置	社会福利费	社会救助	自然灾害救济费	地方离、退休人员费	其他民政事业费
金　额	4404.1	636.6	456.8	480.9	2197.5	124.4	44.2	463.6
比　重	100.0	14.5	10.4	10.9	49.9	2.8	1.0	10.5

图1-13 中央转移支付社会服务经费

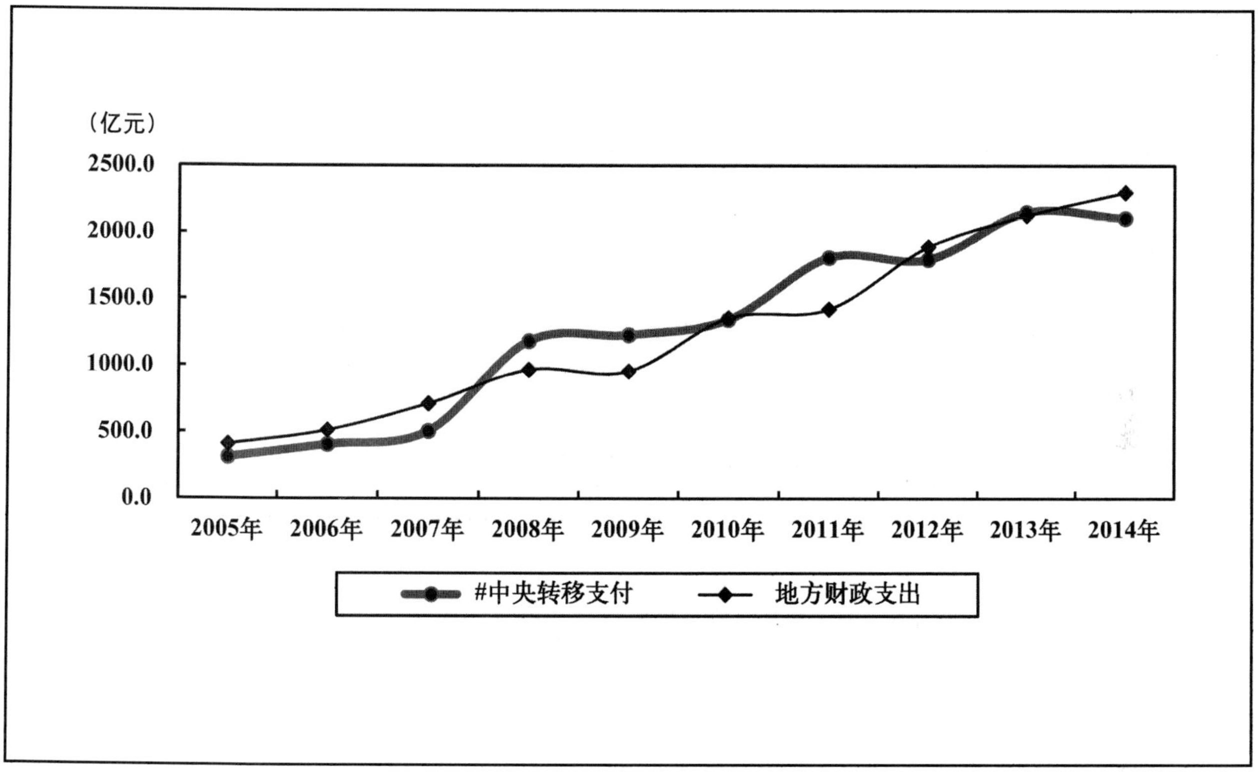

单位：亿元、%

指　标	2005年	2006年	2007年	2008年	2009年	2010年	2011年	2012年	2013年	2014年
社会服务经费支出	718.4	915.4	1215.5	2146.5	2181.9	2697.5	3229.1	3683.7	4276.5	4404.1
# 中央转移支付	310.3	404.0	504.4	1181.1	1227.0	1342.4	1808.0	1794.6	2149.7	2105.0
地方财政支出	408.1	511.4	711.1	965.4	954.9	1355.1	1421.1	1889.1	2126.8	2299.1
中央支付占社会服务经费支出比重	43.2	44.1	42.6	55.0	56.2	49.8	56.0	48.7	50.3	47.8

图1-14 基本建设预算内支出和中央转移支付情况

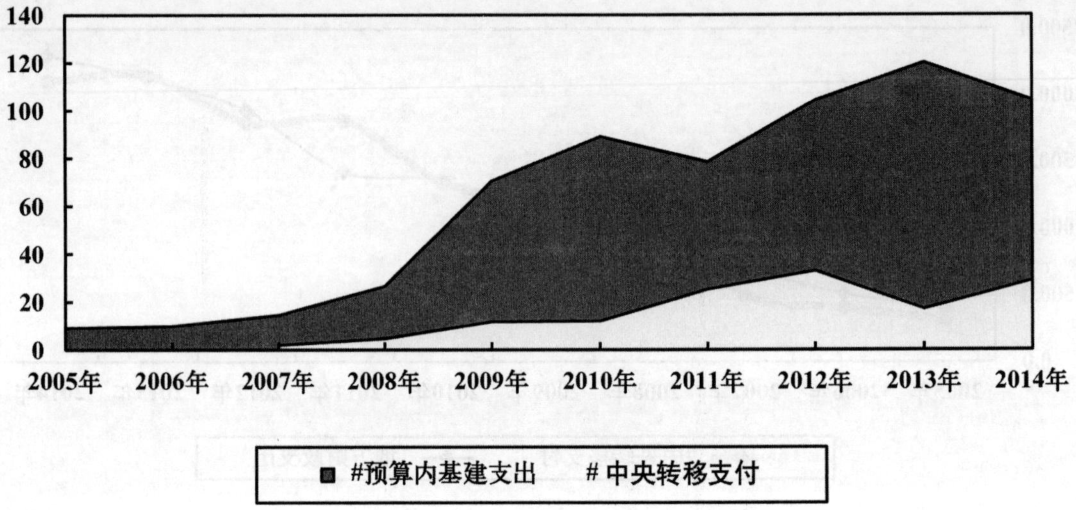

单位：亿元、%

指 标	2005年	2006年	2007年	2008年	2009年	2010年	2011年	2012年	2013年	2014年
社会服务经费支出	718.4	915.4	1215.5	2146.5	2181.9	2697.5	3229.1	3683.7	4276.5	4404.1
#预算内基建支出	9.1	9.9	14.5	26.6	70.6	89.1	78.5	104.2	120.1	104.3
#中央转移支付			2.0	4.7	11.7	12.0	25.3	33.0	17.0	29.0

图2-1　社会服务床位数

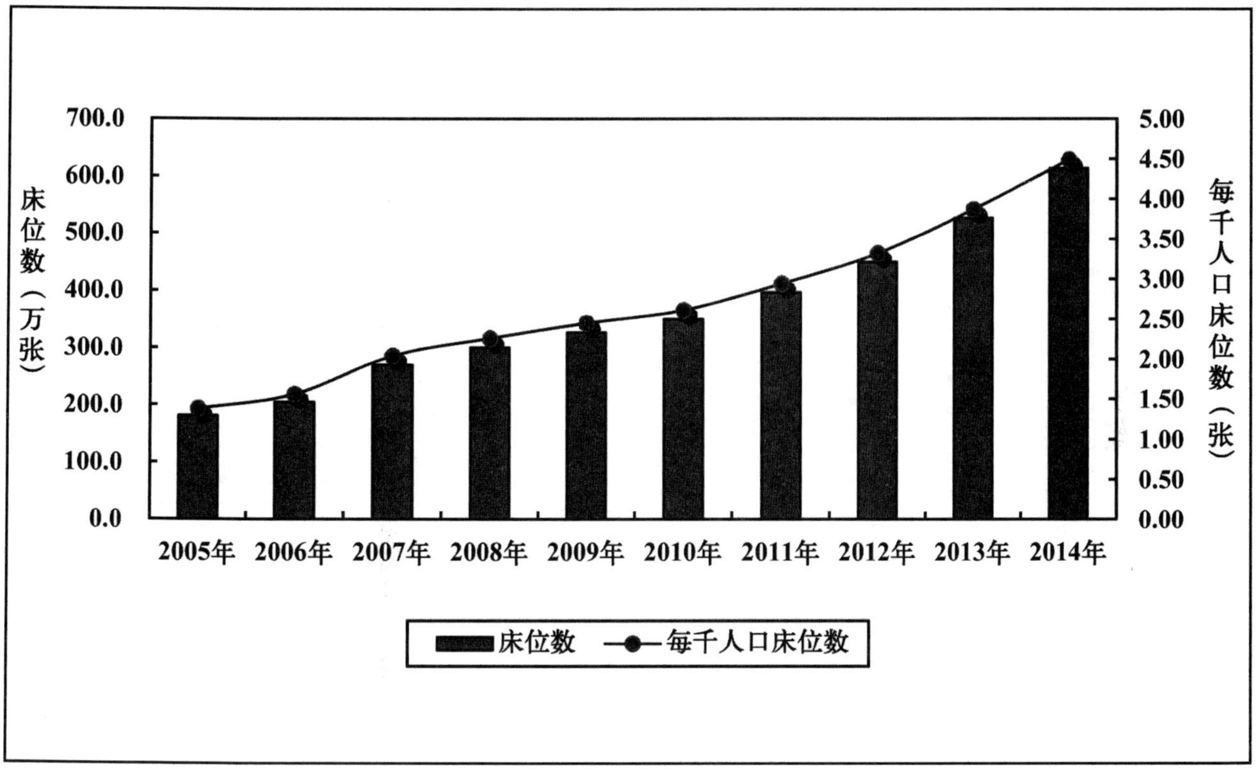

单位：万张、张

指　标	2005年	2006年	2007年	2008年	2009年	2010年	2011年	2012年	2013年	2014年
床位数	180.7	204.5	269.6	300.3	326.5	349.6	396.4	449.3	526.7	613.5
每千人口床位数	1.38	1.56	2.04	2.26	2.45	2.61	2.94	3.32	3.87	4.49

图2-2 养老服务床位数

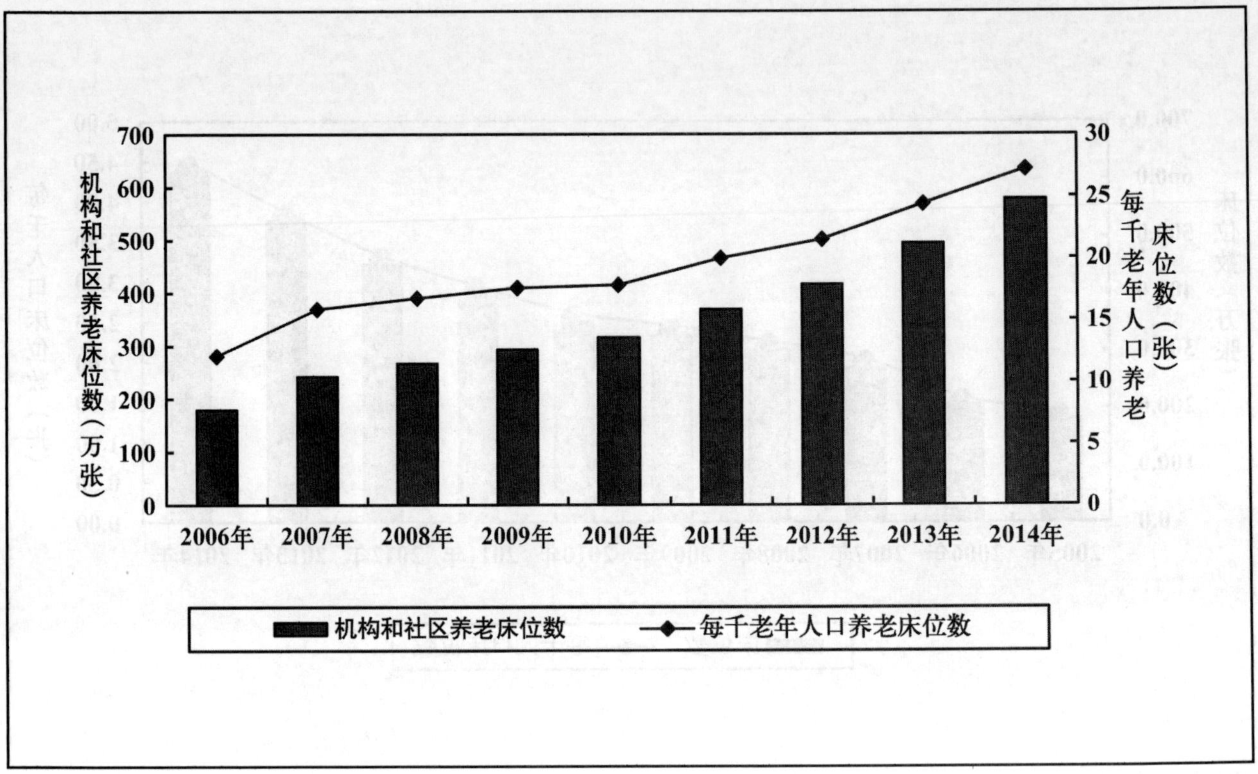

单位：万张、%、张

指 标	2006年	2007年	2008年	2009年	2010年	2011年	2012年	2013年	2014年
机构和社区养老床位数	179.6	242.9	267.4	293.5	316.1	369.2	416.5	493.7	577.7
增长率	13.6	35.2	10.1	9.8	7.7	16.8	12.8	18.5	17.0
每千老年人口养老床位数	12.05	15.83	16.72	17.56	17.79	19.96	21.48	24.39	27.2

图2-3　智障和精神病人服务床位数

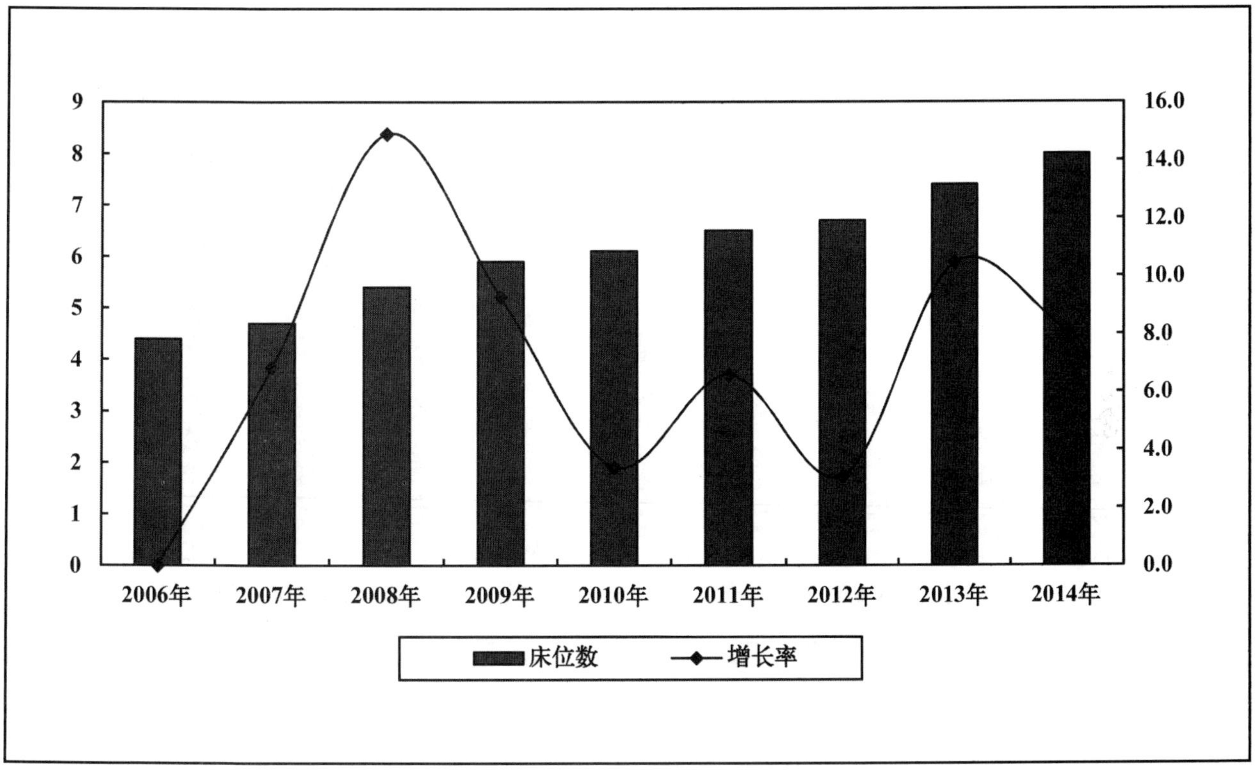

单位：万张、%

指　标	2006年	2007年	2008年	2009年	2010年	2011年	2012年	2013年	2014年
床位数	4.4	4.7	5.4	5.9	6.1	6.5	6.7	7.4	8.0
增长率		6.8	14.9	9.3	3.4	6.6	3.1	10.4	8.1

图2-4 儿童服务床位数

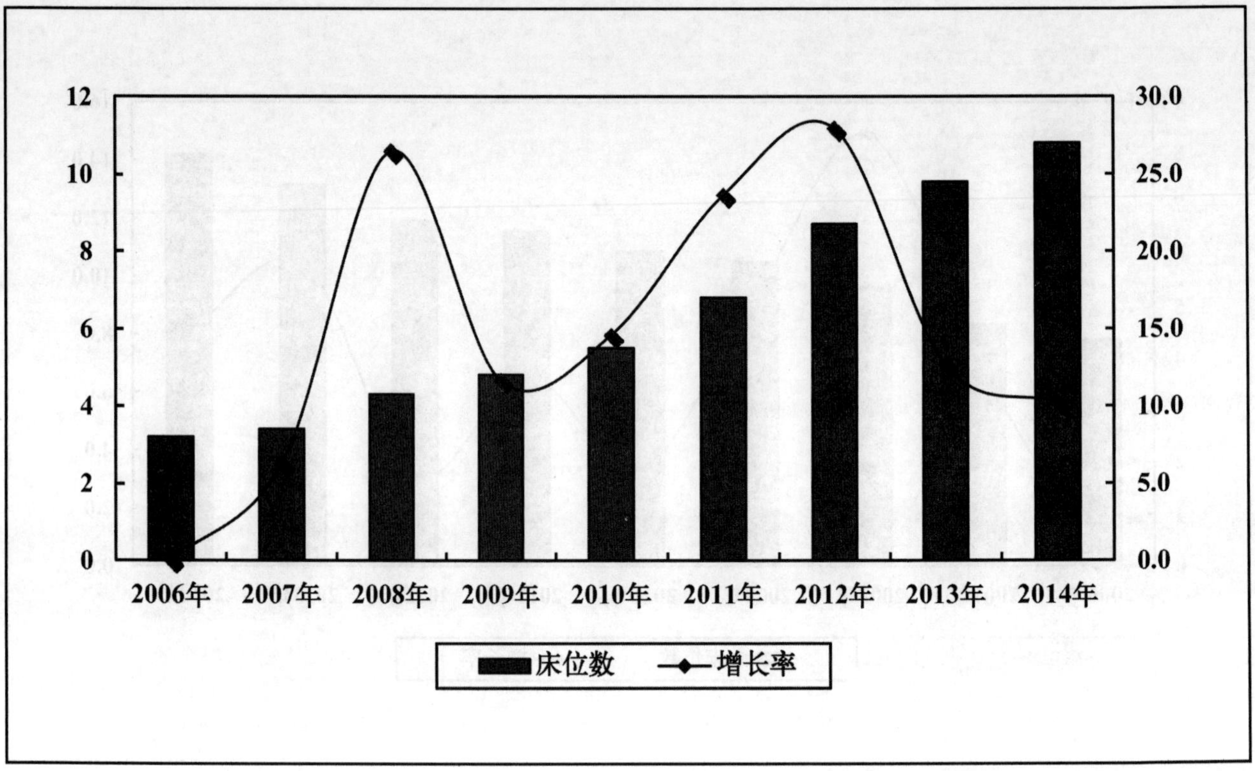

单位：万张、%

指　标	2006年	2007年	2008年	2009年	2010年	2011年	2012年	2013年	2014年
床位数	3.2	3.4	4.3	4.8	5.5	6.8	8.7	9.8	10.8
增长率		6.2	26.5	11.6	14.6	23.6	27.9	12.6	10.2

图2–5　社区服务机构和设施

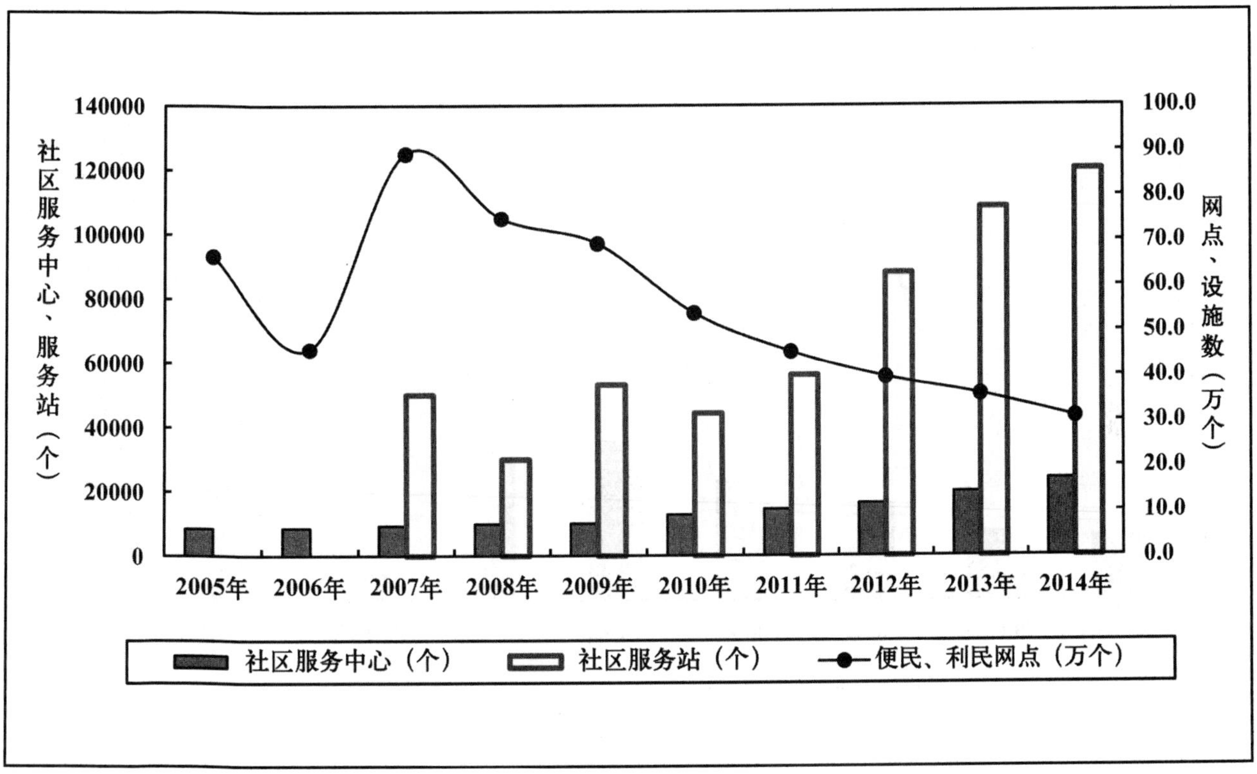

单位：万个

指　标	2005年	2006年	2007年	2008年	2009年	2010年	2011年	2012年	2013年	2014年
社区服务机构和设施	20.3	12.5	12.9	14.6	14.6	15.3	16.0	20.0	25.2	31.1
社区服务中心	0.8	0.9	0.9	1.0	1.0	1.3	1.4	1.6	2.0	2.4
社区服务站			5.0	3.0	5.3	4.4	5.6	8.8	10.8	12.0
便民、利民网点	66.5	45.8	89.3	74.9	69.3	53.9	45.3	39.7	35.9	30.9

注释：2014年社区服务中心里含社区服务指导中心。

图2-6 老年福利

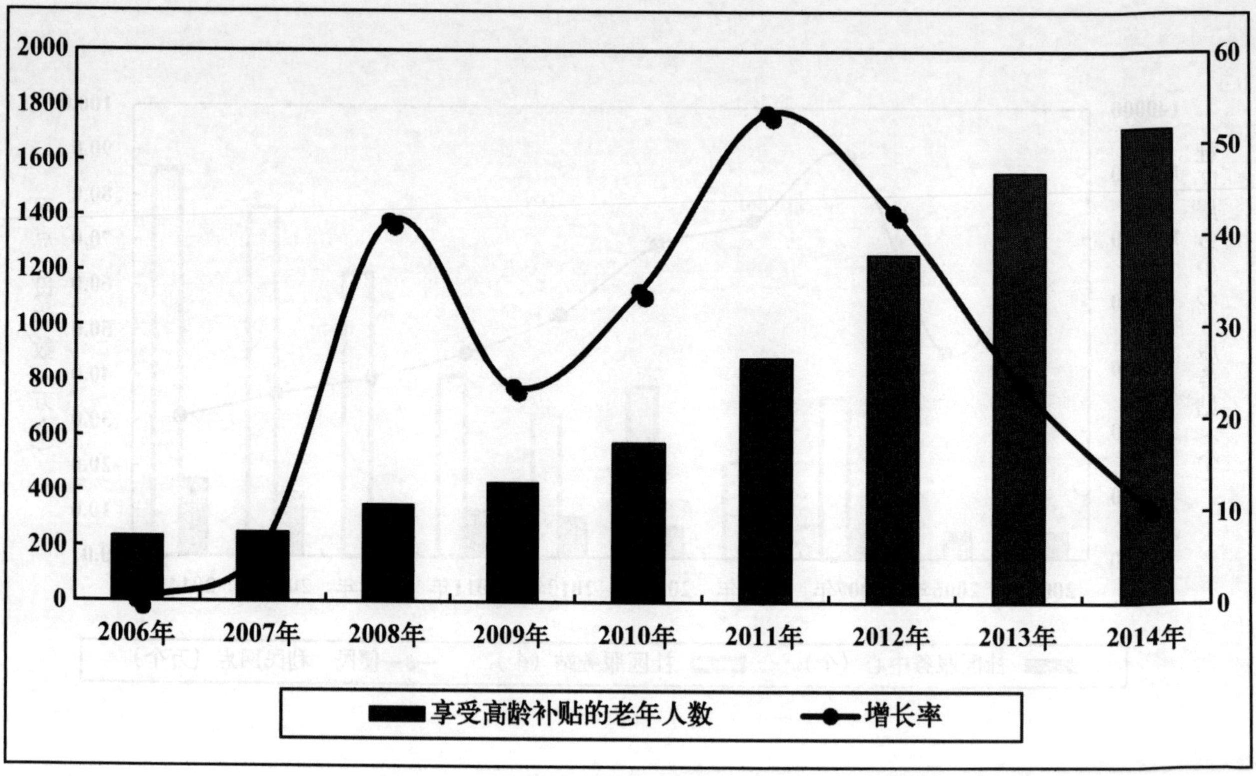

单位：万人

指标	2006年	2007年	2008年	2009年	2010年	2011年	2012年	2013年	2014年
享受高龄补贴的老年人数	233.5	247.1	349.3	430.9	576.4	883.1	1257.7	1557.9	1719.6
增长率		5.8	41.4	23.4	33.8	53.2	42.4	23.9	10.4

图2-7　家庭儿童收养

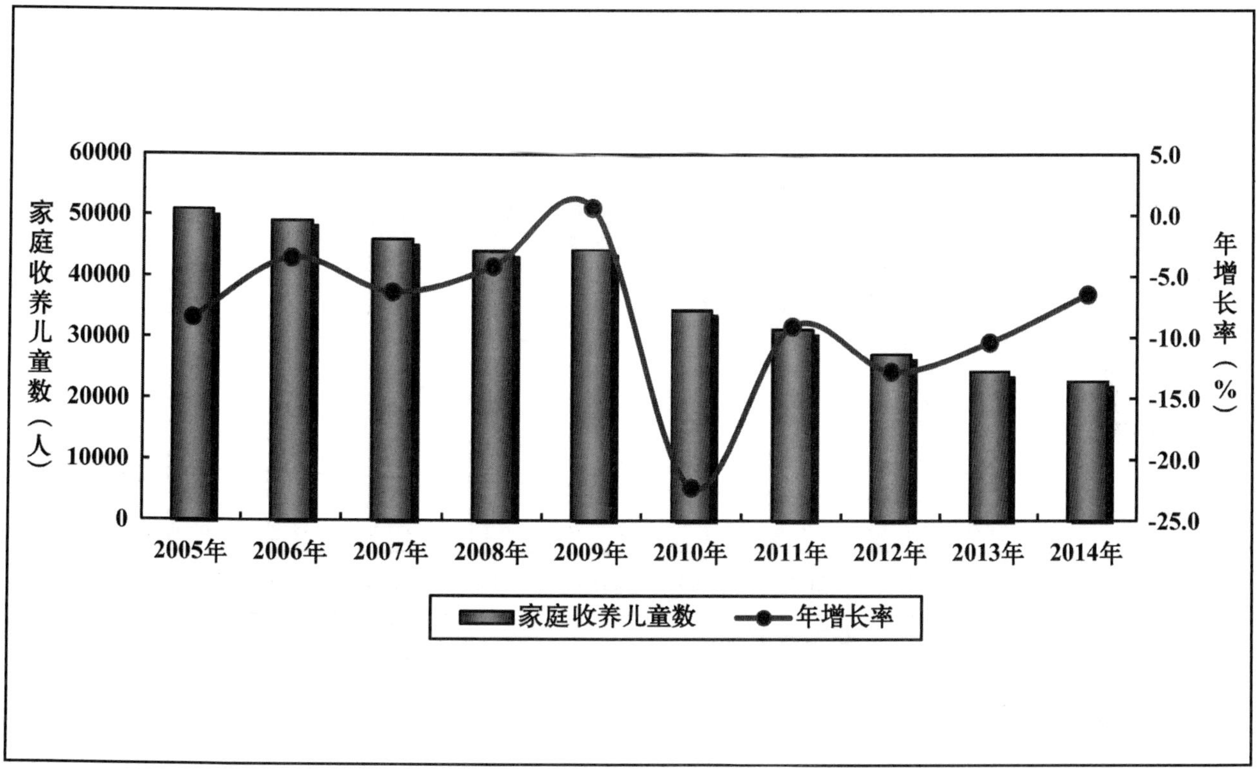

单位：人、%

指　标	2005年	2006年	2007年	2008年	2009年	2010年	2011年	2012年	2013年	2014年
家庭收养儿童数	50921	49148	46047	44115	44359	34473	31329	27310	24460	22876
年增长率	-8.4	-3.5	-6.3	-4.2	0.6	-22.3	-9.1	-12.8	-10.4	-6.5

图2-8　为残疾人提供服务机构中的残疾职工

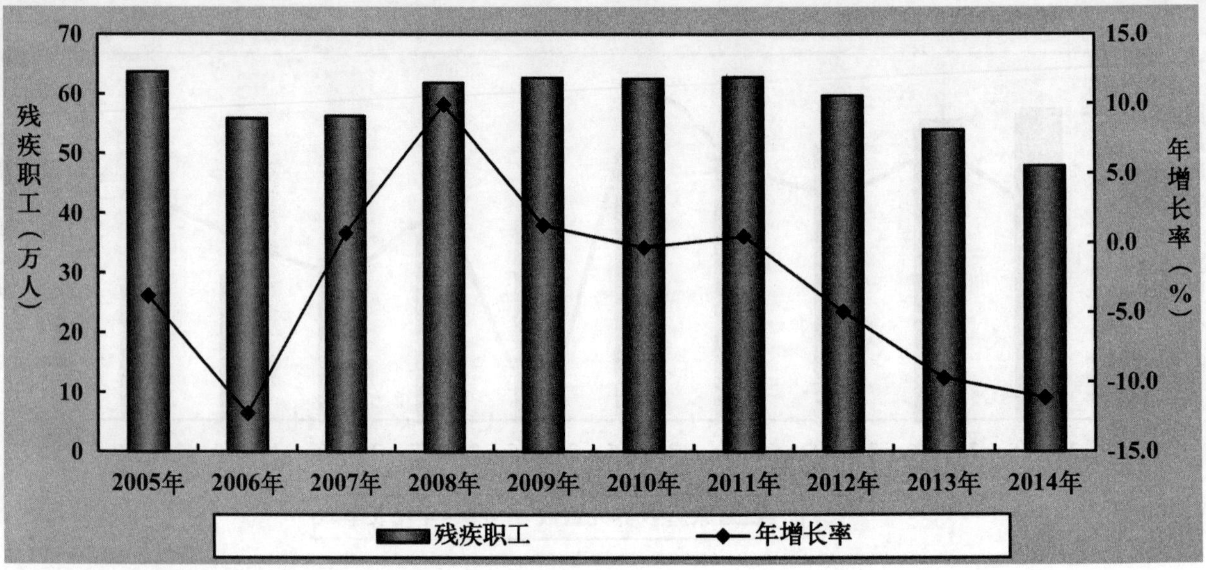

单位：万人、%

指　标	2005年	2006年	2007年	2008年	2009年	2010年	2011年	2012年	2013年	2014年
残疾职工	63.7	55.9	56.3	61.9	62.7	62.5	62.8	59.7	53.9	47.9
年增长率	-3.8	-12.2	0.7	9.9	1.3	-0.3	0.5	-4.9	-9.7	-11.1

图2-9 城市居民最低生活保障

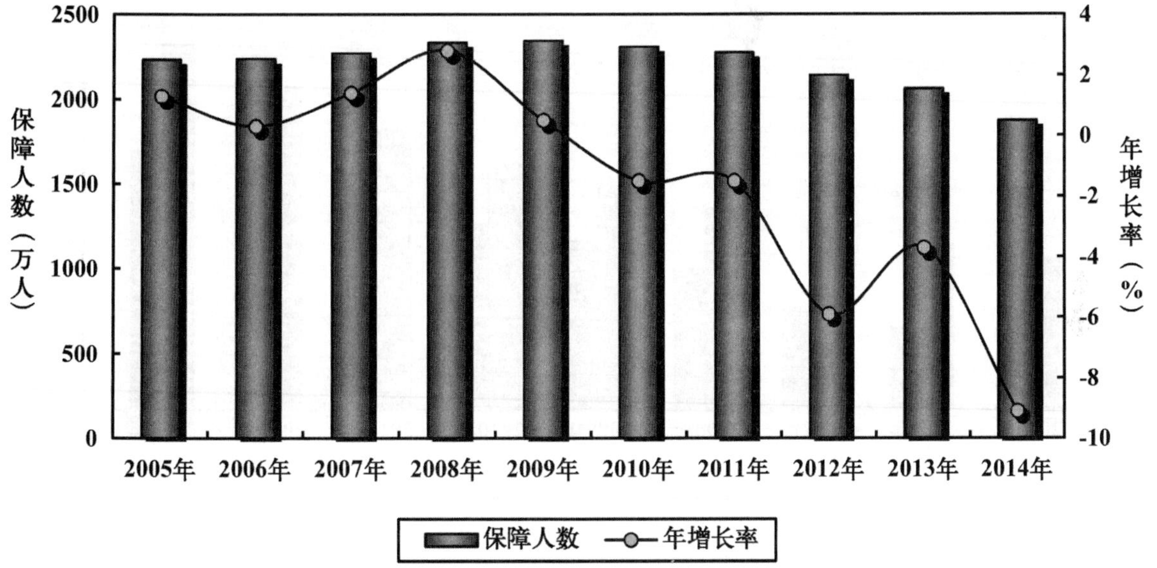

单位：万人、%

指 标	2005年	2006年	2007年	2008年	2009年	2010年	2011年	2012年	2013年	2014年
保障人数	2234.2	2240.1	2272.1	2334.8	2345.6	2310.5	2276.8	2143.5	2064.2	1877
年增长率	1.3	0.3	1.4	2.8	0.5	-1.5	-1.5	-5.9	-3.7	-9.1

图2-10　城市居民最低生活保障平均标准与平均支出水平

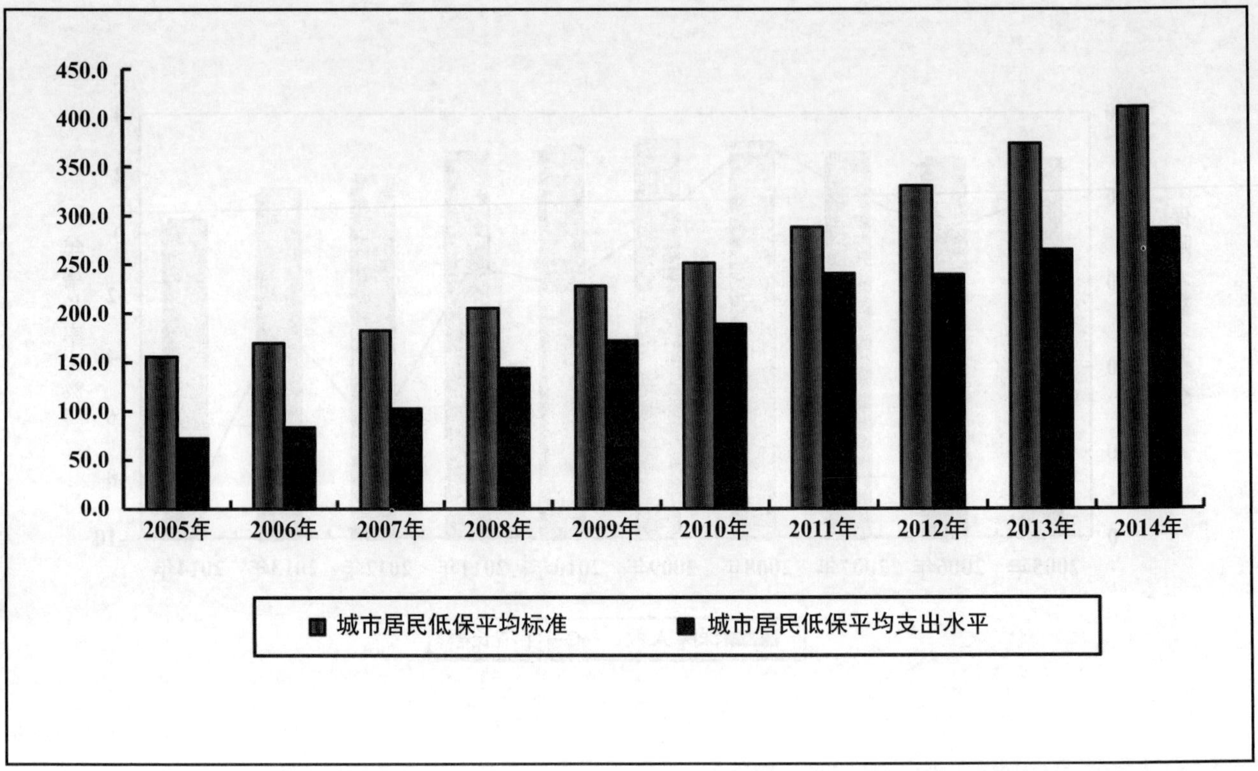

单位：元/人、月

指　标	2005年	2006年	2007年	2008年	2009年	2010年	2011年	2012年	2013年	2014年
城市居民低保平均标准	156.0	169.6	182.4	205.3	227.8	251.2	287.6	330.1	373.3	410.5
城市居民低保平均支出水平	72.3	83.6	102.7	143.7	172.0	189.0	240.3	239.1	264.2	285.6

图2-11　各省城市居民最低生活保障平均标准与支出水平

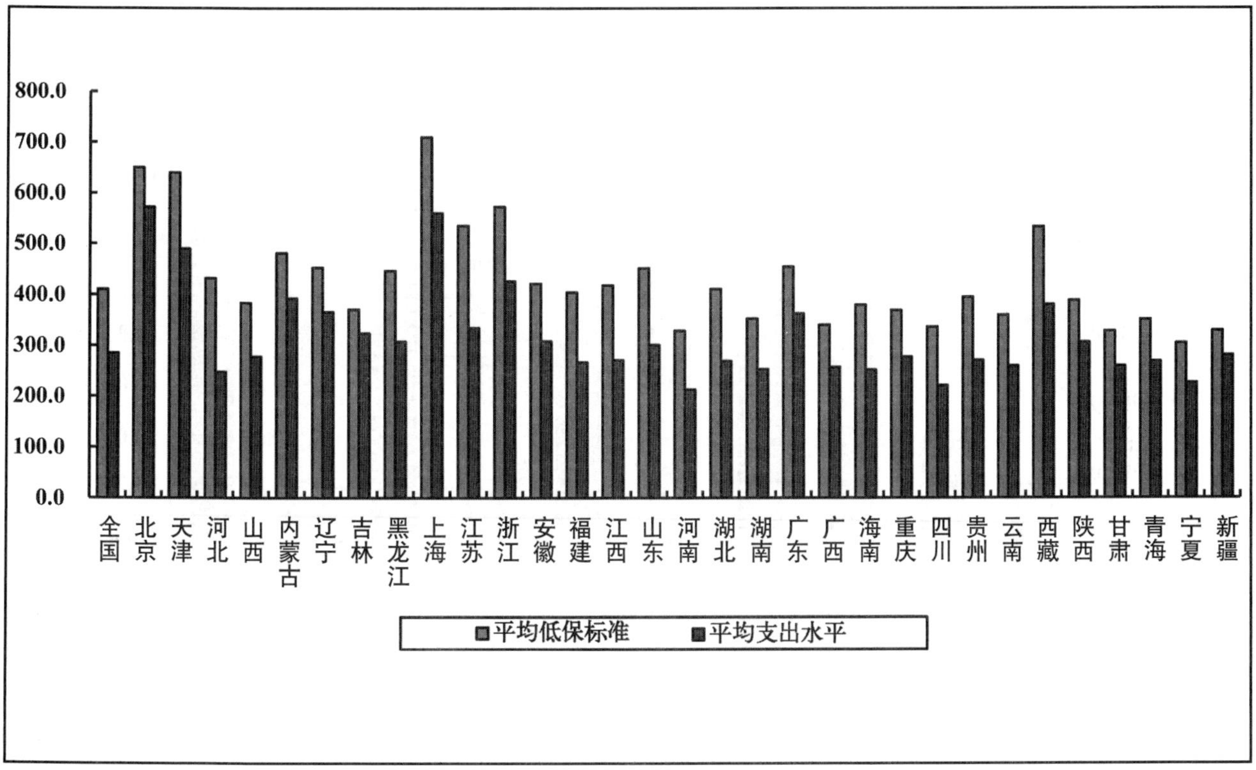

单位：元/人、月

地　区	平均低保标准	平均支出水平	地　区	平均低保标准	平均支出水平	地　区	平均低保标准	平均支出水平	地　区	平均低保标准	平均支出水平
全　国	**410.5**	**285.6**	黑龙江	446.8	307.7	河　南	328.8	212.5	贵　州	395.0	270.9
北　京	650.0	572.7	上　海	710.0	560.6	湖　北	411.0	269.5	云　南	359.6	260.3
天　津	640.0	490.0	江　苏	536.1	334.6	湖　南	352.8	253.2	西　藏	533.9	380.2
河　北	431.9	247.8	浙　江	573.3	426.5	广　东	454.5	362.7	陕　西	388.5	306.0
山　西	383.7	278.1	安　徽	421.5	308.4	广　西	340.1	257.3	甘　肃	328.3	259.6
内蒙古	481.4	392.4	福　建	404.4	267.3	海　南	379.6	251.9	青　海	351.0	269.1
辽　宁	452.8	365.8	江　西	418.3	271.6	重　庆	369.0	277.7	宁　夏	304.8	226.2
吉　林	371.1	323.7	山　东	451.9	301.2	四　川	336.2	220.5	新　疆	329.2	280.9

图2-12　农村最低生活保障

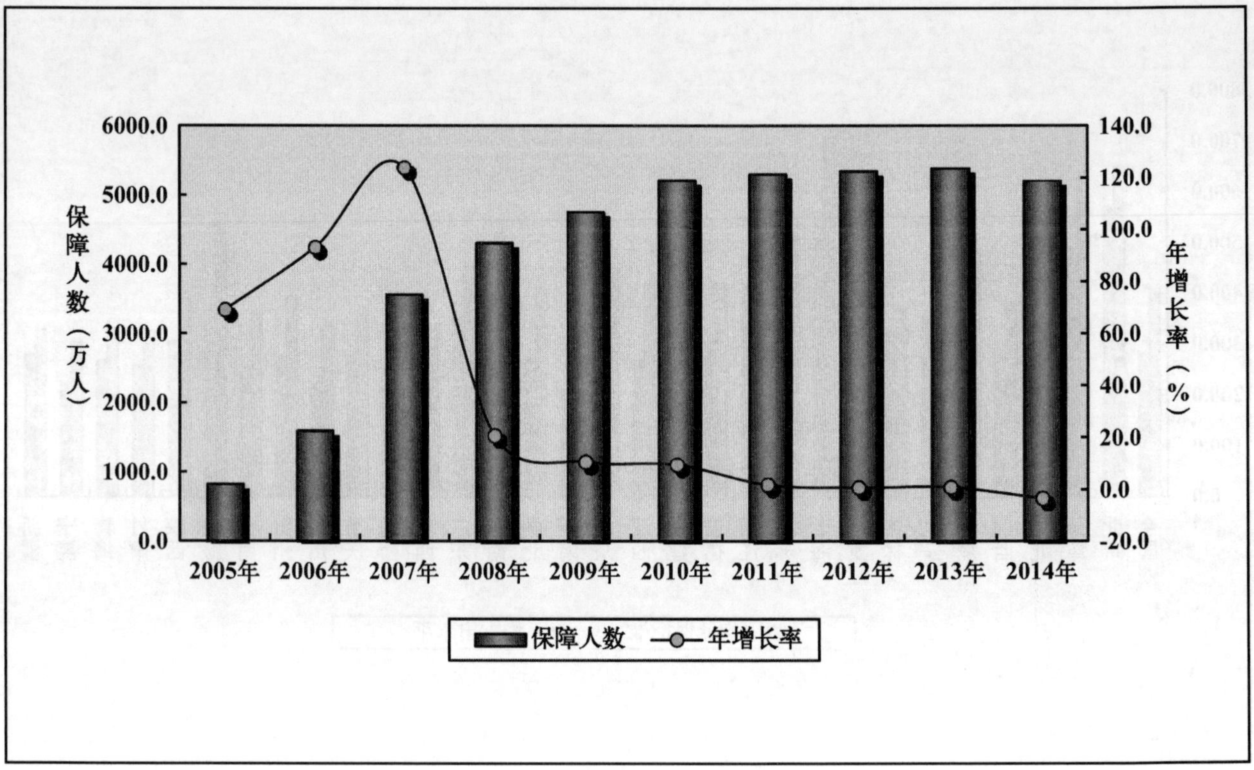

单位：万人、%

指　标	2005年	2006年	2007年	2008年	2009年	2010年	2011年	2012年	2013年	2014年
保障人数	825.0	1593.1	3566.3	4305.5	4760.0	5214.0	5305.7	5344.5	5388.0	5207.2
年增长率	69.1	93.1	123.9	20.7	10.6	9.5	1.8	0.7	0.8	-3.4

图2-13 农村最低生活保障平均标准与平均支出水平

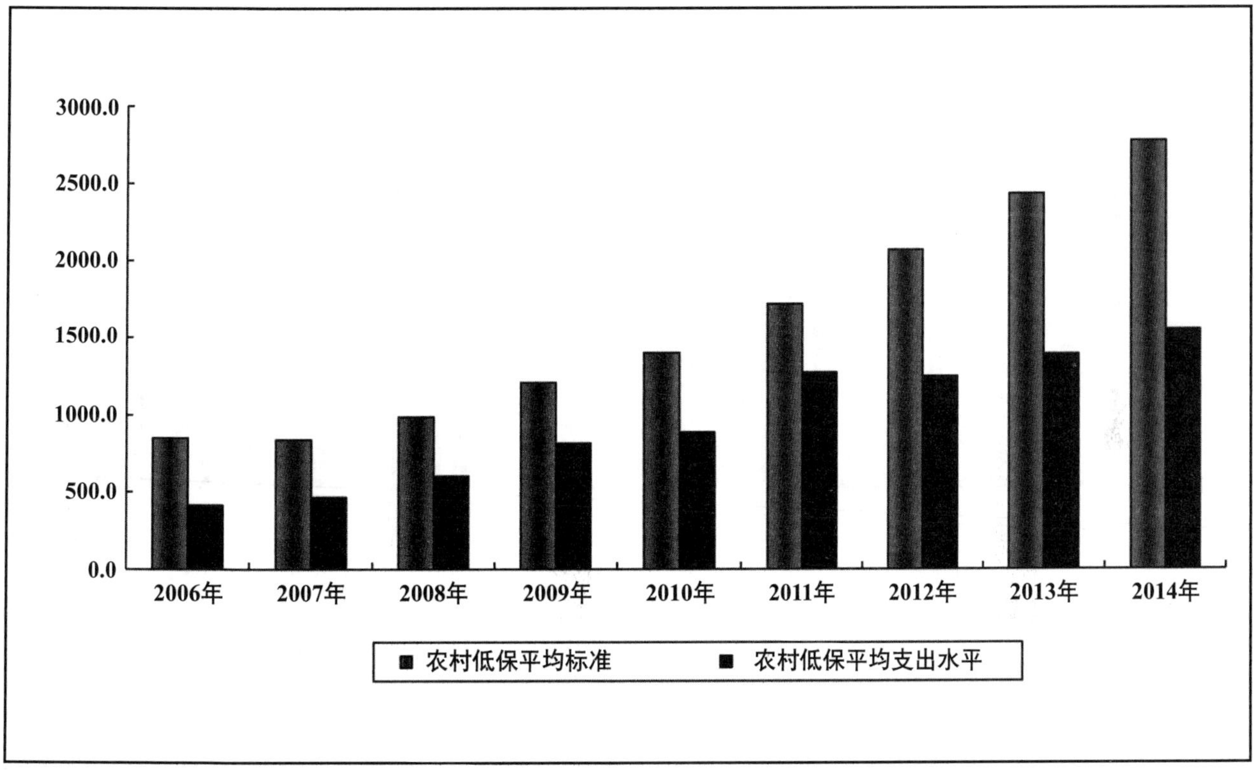

单位：元/人、年

指　标	2006年	2007年	2008年	2009年	2010年	2011年	2012年	2013年	2014年
农村低保平均标准	850.8	840.0	987.6	1209.6	1404.0	1718.4	2067.8	2433.9	2776.6
农村低保平均支出水平	414.0	465.6	604.8	816.0	888.0	1273.2	1247.9	1393.5	1552.3

图2-14 各省农村最低生活保障平均标准与支出水平

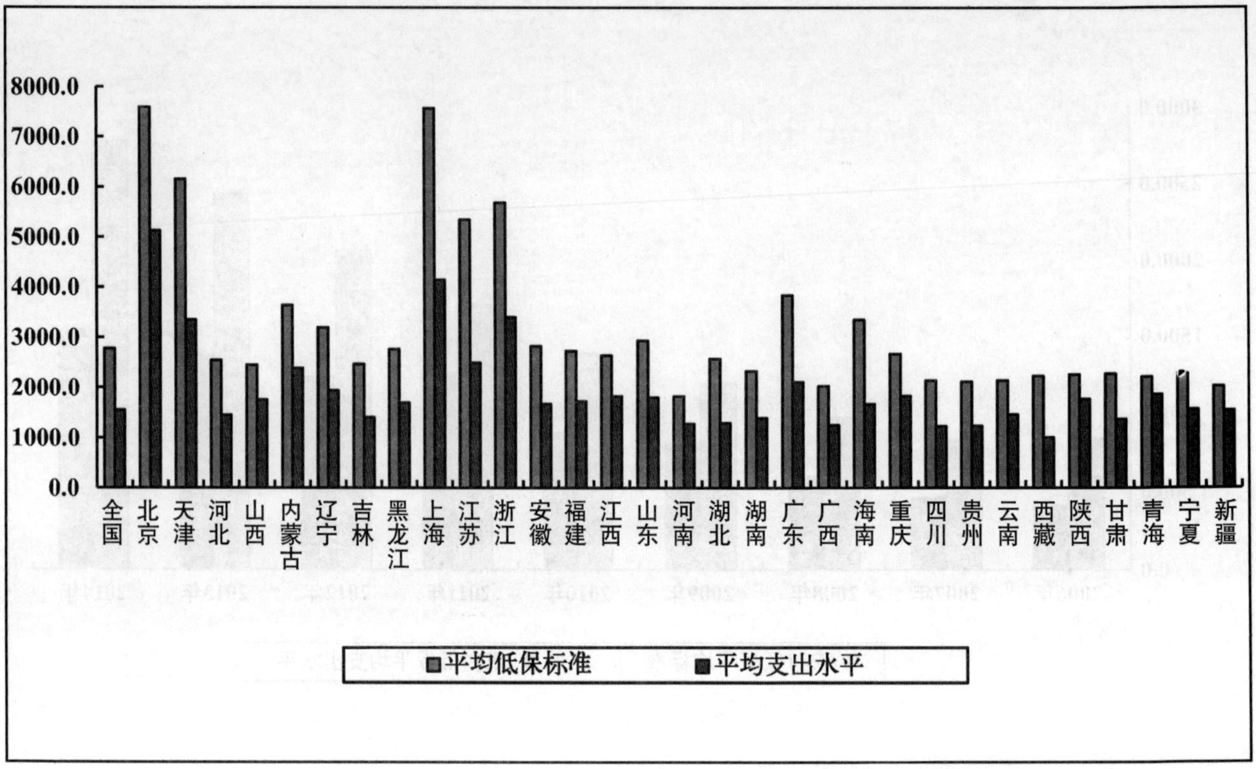

单位：元/人、年

地 区	平均低保标准	平均支出水平	地 区	平均低保标准	平均支出水平	地 区	平均低保标准	平均支出水平	地 区	平均低保标准	平均支出水平
全 国	**2776.6**	**1552.3**	黑龙江	2764.2	1693.8	河 南	1824.1	1271.4	贵 州	2116.1	1238.5
北 京	7587.7	5126.6	上 海	7560.0	4142.0	湖 北	2567.8	1290.4	云 南	2141.9	1464.7
天 津	6153.6	3350.1	江 苏	5345.5	2496.7	湖 南	2326.8	1392.1	西 藏	2230.9	1008.3
河 北	2543.5	1451.9	浙 江	5686.0	3398.7	广 东	3837.9	2107.1	陕 西	2262.8	1772.7
山 西	2454.8	1755.4	安 徽	2828.3	1667.8	广 西	2029.0	1250.0	甘 肃	2275.6	1371.1
内蒙古	3633.8	2387.8	福 建	2732.2	1725.1	海 南	3355.0	1667.1	青 海	2213.1	1862.9
辽 宁	3195.7	1936.6	江 西	2638.6	1820.8	重 庆	2667.2	1834.0	宁 夏	2281.8	1567.0
吉 林	2466.1	1406.7	山 东	2936.7	1794.8	四 川	2139.7	1232.1	新 疆	2029.4	1543.8

图2-15 农村五保供养

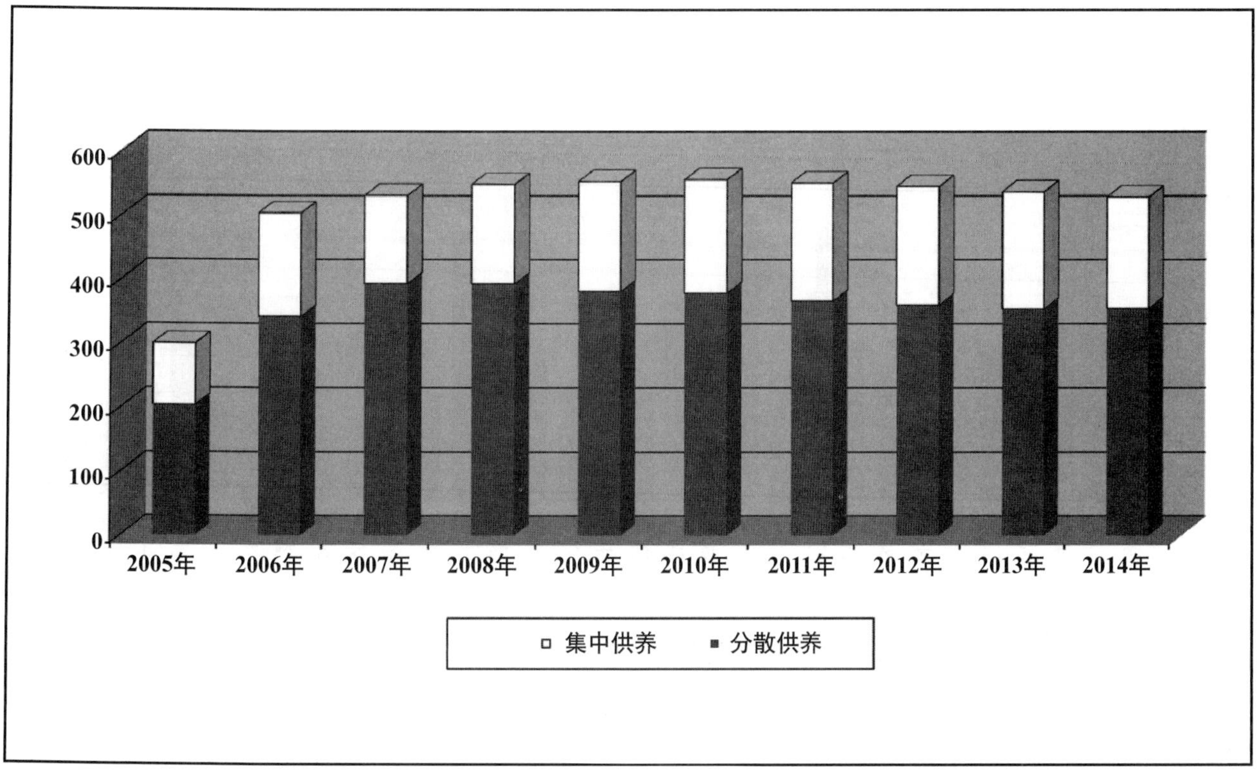

单位：万人

指　标	2005年	2006年	2007年	2008年	2009年	2010年	2011年	2012年	2013年	2014年
供养合计	300	503.3	531.3	548.6	553.4	556.3	551.0	545.6	537.3	529.1
分散供养	204.0	342.2	393.3	393.0	381.6	378.9	366.5	360.3	353.8	354.8
集中供养	96.0	161.1	138.0	155.6	171.8	177.4	184.5	185.3	183.5	174.3

图2-16　各省农村五保集中供养平均标准与支出水平

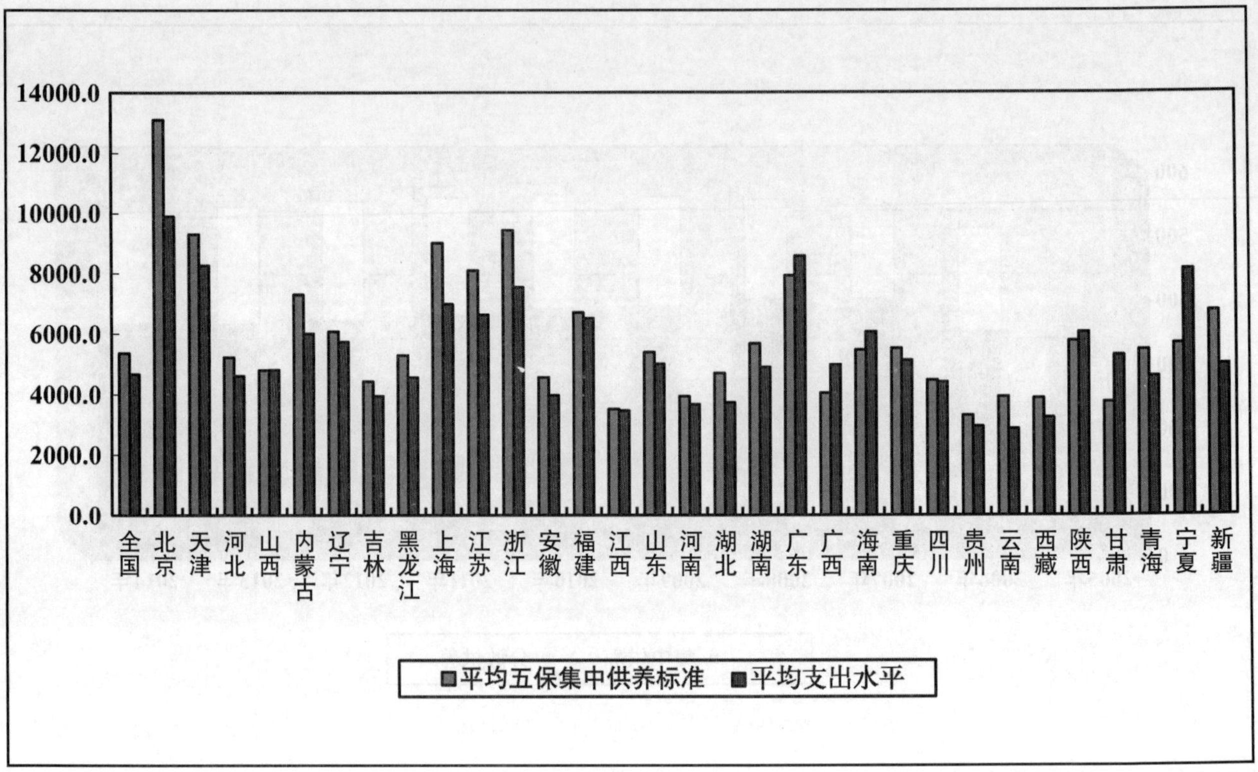

单位：元/人、年

地　区	平均五保集中供养标准	平均支出水平	地　区	平均五保集中供养标准	平均支出水平	地　区	平均五保集中供养标准	平均支出水平	地　区	平均五保集中供养标准	平均支出水平
全　国	**5371.3**	**4676.1**	黑龙江	5296.2	4558.7	河　南	3932.3	3663.9	贵　州	3297.7	2938.1
北　京	13085.1	9903.4	上　海	9000.0	6987.0	湖　北	4693.6	3728.2	云　南	3919.1	2848.4
天　津	9300.9	8260.7	江　苏	8096.8	6635.6	湖　南	5688.2	4889.6	西　藏	3872.6	3229.6
河　北	5230.5	4607.3	浙　江	9430.8	7542.1	广　东	7928.4	8573.9	陕　西	5777.7	6059.8
山　西	4810.5	4812.7	安　徽	4559.6	3971.5	广　西	4037.3	4979.1	甘　肃	3743.4	5309.1
内蒙古	7303.6	6006.6	福　建	6708.7	6516.6	海　南	5475.0	6071.7	青　海	5478.9	4587.7
辽　宁	6075.8	5744.2	江　西	3507.4	3454.9	重　庆	5522.6	5134.6	宁　夏	5687.1	8132.9
吉　林	4422.0	3942.7	山　东	5394.4	5009.6	四　川	4468.7	4404.1	新　疆	6749.9	4979.4

图2-17 各省农村五保分散供养平均标准与支出水平

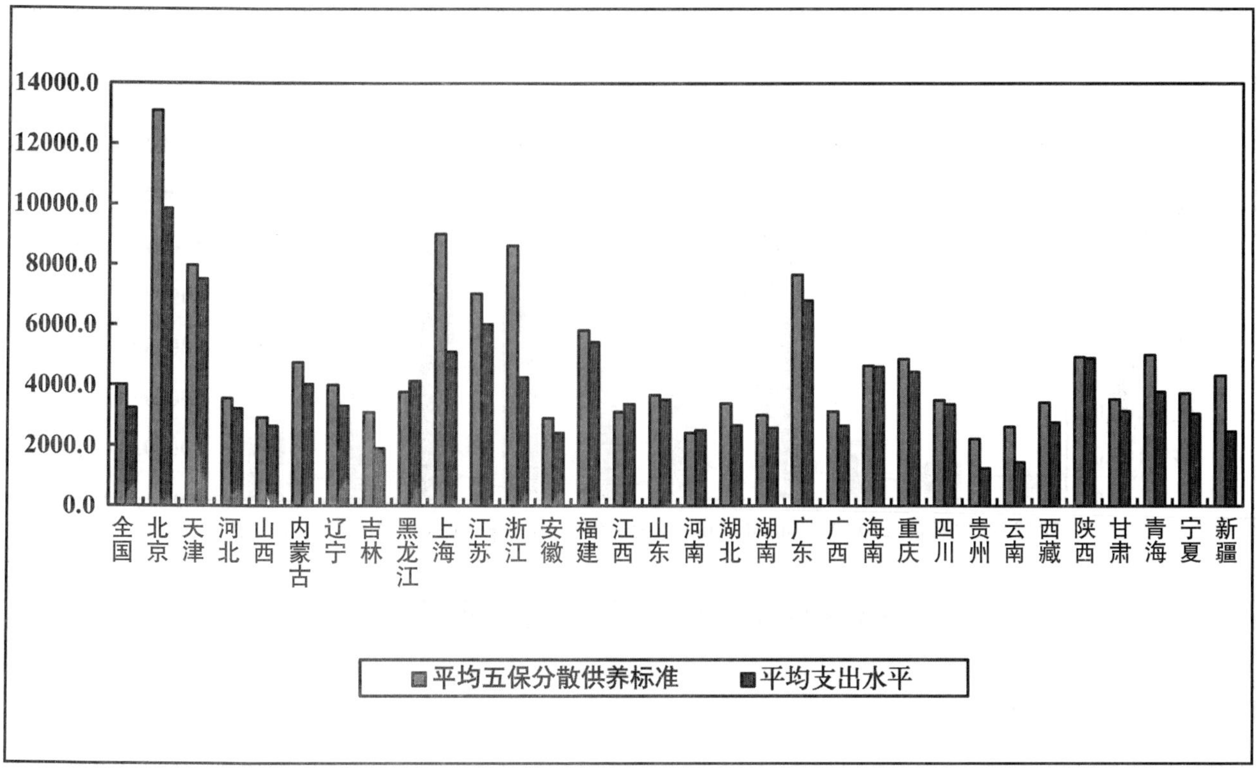

单位：元/人、年

地　区	平均五保分散供养标准	平均支出水平	地　区	平均五保分散供养标准	平均支出水平	地　区	平均五保分散供养标准	平均支出水平	地　区	平均五保分散供养标准	平均支出水平
全　国	**4005.9**	**3228.9**	黑龙江	3763.7	4126.4	河　南	2414.3	2497.4	贵　州	2206.1	1233.9
北　京	13085.1	9848.1	上　海	9000.0	5101.7	湖　北	3378.7	2653.1	云　南	2610.5	1436.9
天　津	7970.9	7515.1	江　苏	7021.0	6008.1	湖　南	2998.9	2569.2	西　藏	3413.0	2754.4
河　北	3548.1	3220.9	浙　江	8617.9	4240.1	广　东	7648.4	6792.7	陕　西	4919.0	4893.6
山　西	2908.9	2637.7	安　徽	2894.4	2415.9	广　西	3119.3	2647.0	甘　肃	3520.2	3123.0
内蒙古	4739.3	4020.9	福　建	5815.6	5418.9	海　南	4640.0	4603.6	青　海	5000.3	3768.7
辽　宁	3995.0	3308.5	江　西	3100.6	3363.7	重　庆	4858.2	4425.1	宁　夏	3709.9	3037.0
吉　林	3090.2	1897.0	山　东	3663.7	3507.4	四　川	3484.1	3348.4	新　疆	4301.0	2461.2

图2–18 社会捐赠

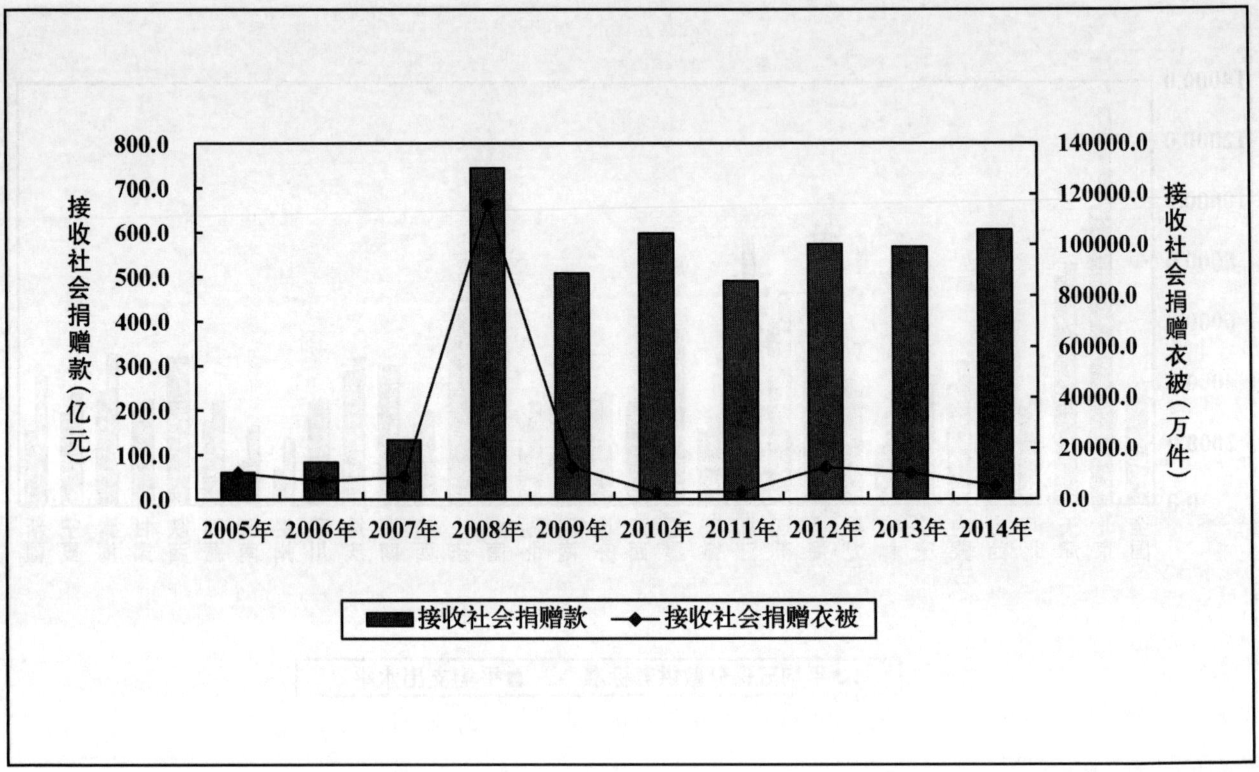

单位：亿元、万件

指 标	2005年	2006年	2007年	2008年	2009年	2010年	2011年	2012年	2013年	2014年
接收社会捐赠款	60.3	83.1	132.8	744.5	507.2	596.8	490.1	572.5	566.4	604.4
接收社会捐赠衣被	10355.0	7123.6	8756.8	115816.3	12476.6	2750.2	2918.5	12538.2	10405.0	5244.5

图2-19　福利彩票

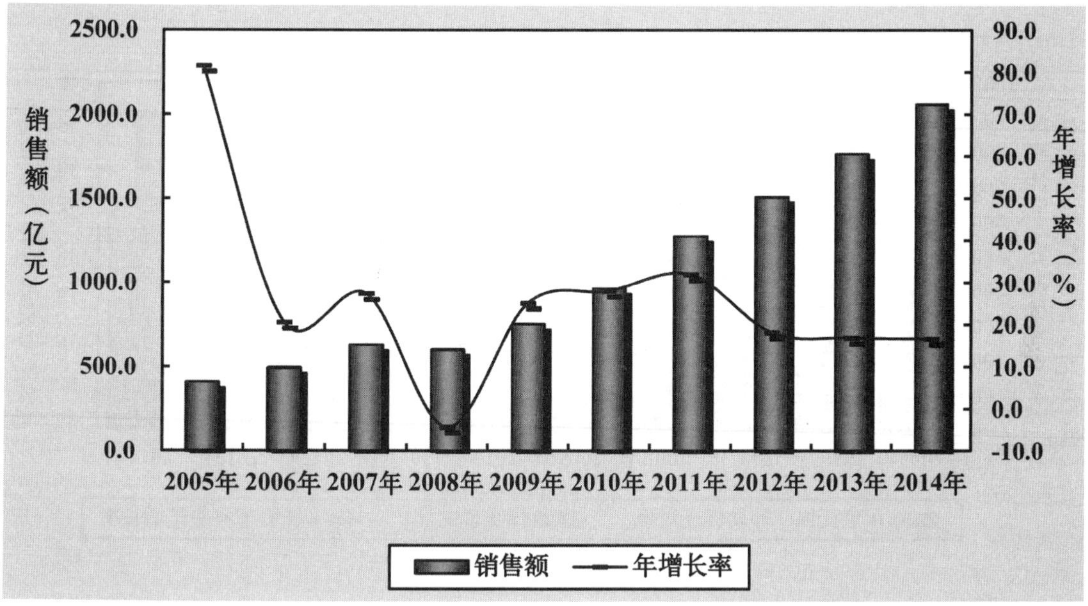

单位：亿元、%

指　标	2005年	2006年	2007年	2008年	2009年	2010年	2011年	2012年	2013年	2014年
销售额	411.2	495.7	631.6	604.0	756.0	968.0	1278.0	1510.3	1765.3	2059.7
年增长率	81.6	20.5	27.4	−4.4	25.2	28.0	32.0	18.2	16.9	16.7

图2-20 国家抚恤、补助优抚对象

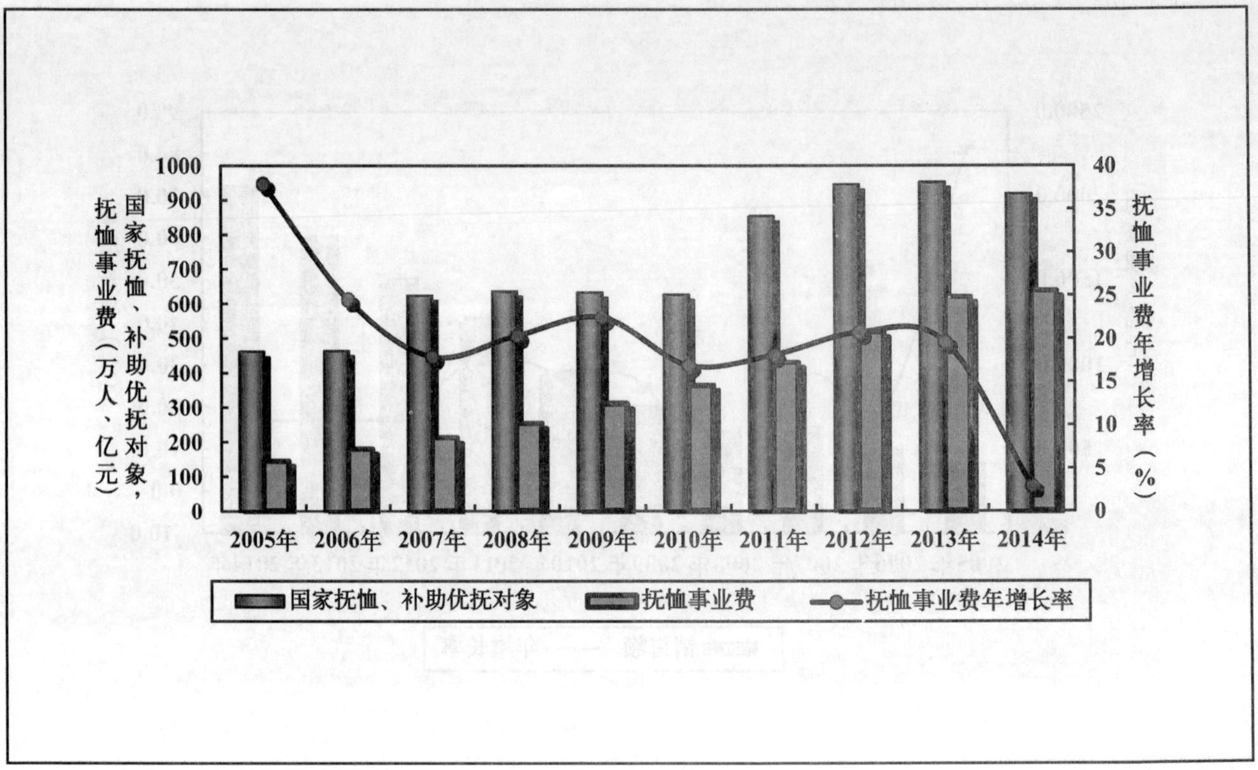

单位：万人、亿元、%

指　标	2005年	2006年	2007年	2008年	2009年	2010年	2011年	2012年	2013年	2014年
国家抚恤、补助优抚对象	460.3	462.6	622.4	633.2	630.7	625	852.5	944.4	950.5	917.3
抚恤事业费	143.6	178.8	210.8	253.6	310.3	362.7	428.3	517	618.4	636.6
抚恤事业费年增长率	37.9	24.5	17.9	20.3	22.4	16.9	18.1	20.7	19.6	2.9

图2-21 优抚对象分类

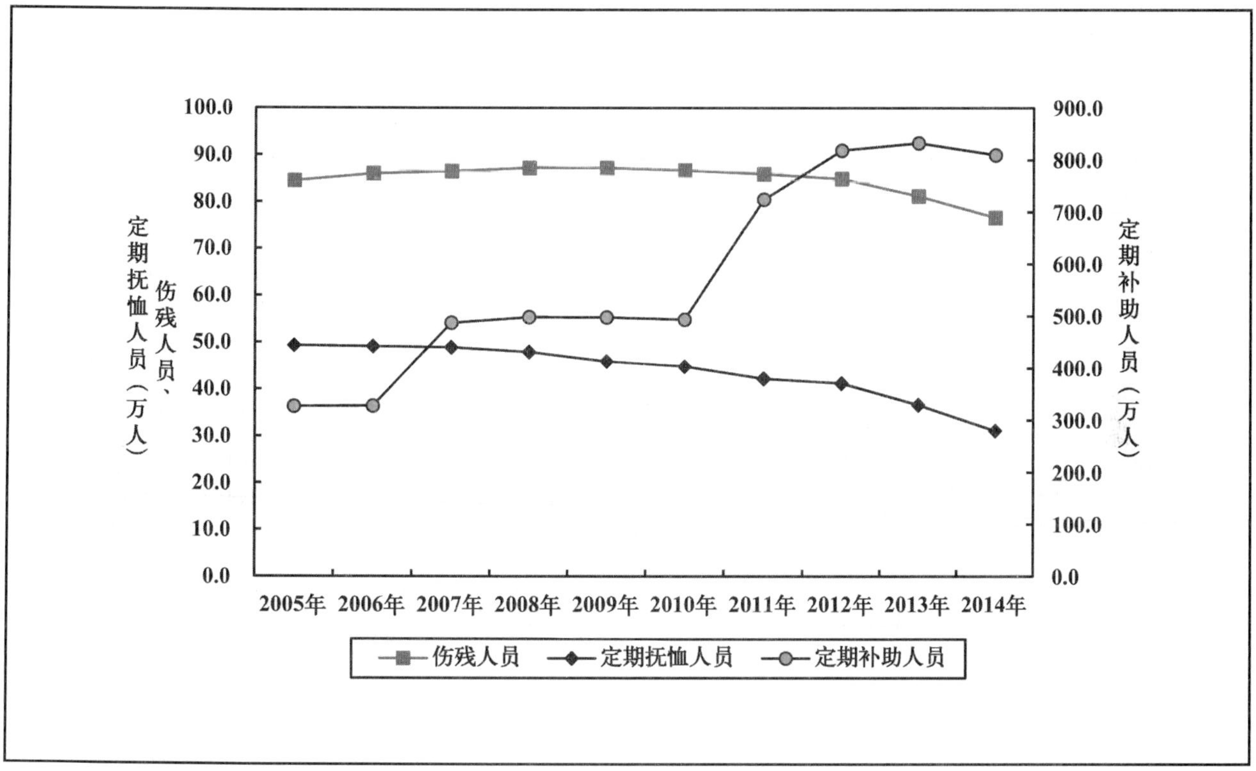

单位：万人

指　标	2005年	2006年	2007年	2008年	2009年	2010年	2011年	2012年	2013年	2014年
伤残人员	84.5	86.0	86.5	87.2	87.2	86.7	85.9	84.9	81.2	76.6
定期抚恤人员	49.3	49.1	48.9	47.9	45.9	44.8	42.2	41.2	36.6	31.1
定期补助人员	326.6	327.4	487.1	498.2	497.7	493.5	724.4	818.4	832.6	809.6

图2-22　接收安置军休干部、军休职工

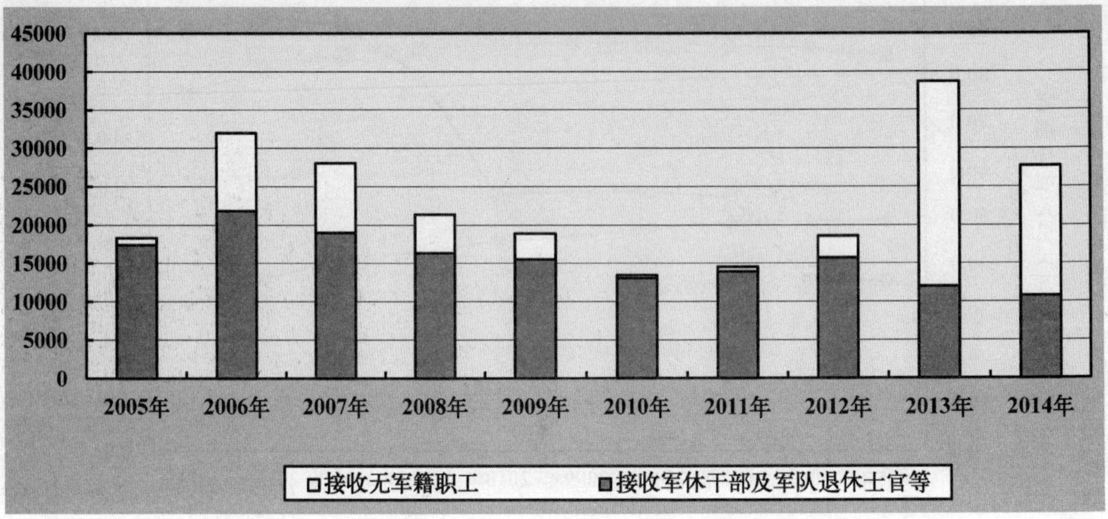

单位：人

指　标	2005年	2006年	2007年	2008年	2009年	2010年	2011年	2012年	2013年	2014年
接收军休干部及军队退休士官等	17416	21832	18997	16331	15492	13070	13901	15723	11997	10791
接收无军籍职工	904	10136	9061	5047	3412	381	629	2847	26709	16908

图2-23 烈士纪念建筑物管理机构和藏品量

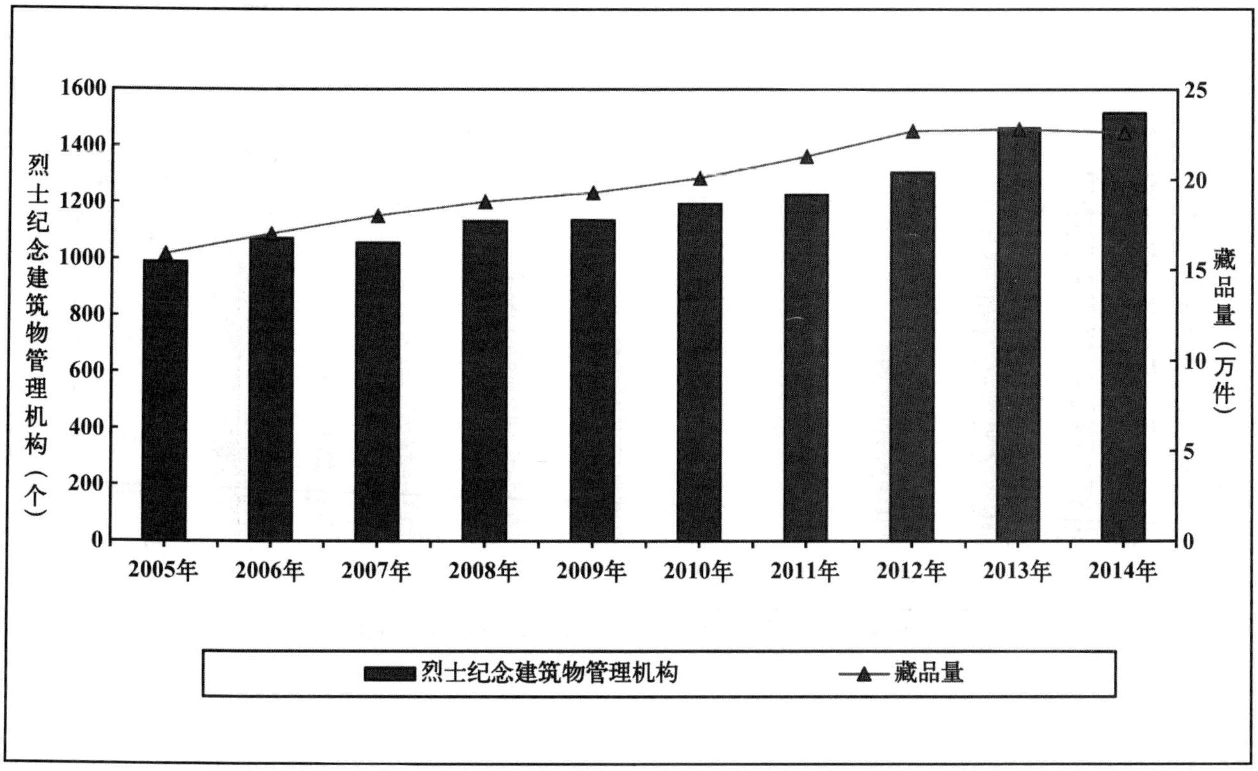

单位：个、万件

指　标	2005年	2006年	2007年	2008年	2009年	2010年	2011年	2012年	2013年	2014年
烈士纪念建筑物管理机构	989	1072	1056	1133	1137	1195	1227	1306	1463	1516
藏品量	15.9	17	18	18.8	19.3	20.1	21.3	22.7	22.8	22.6

图2-24　烈士褒扬和零散烈士纪念设施

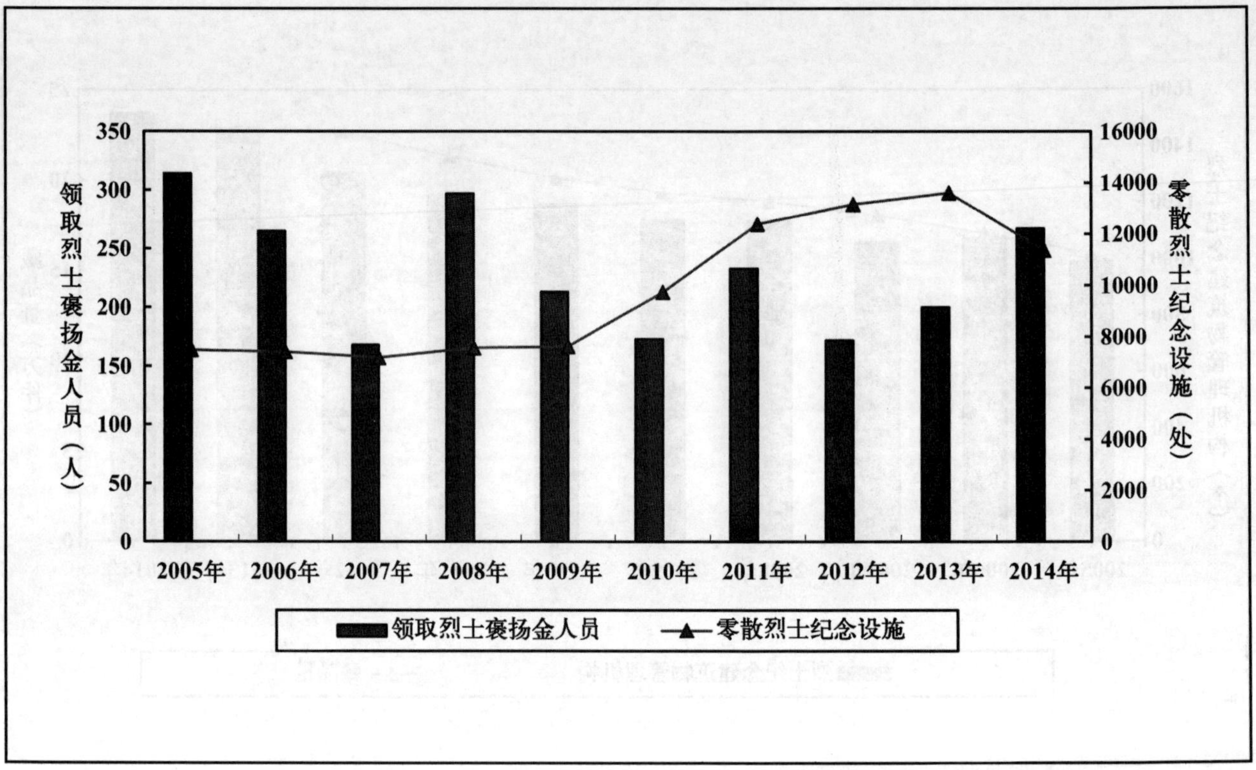

单位：人、处

指　标	2005年	2006年	2007年	2008年	2009年	2010年	2011年	2012年	2013年	2014年
领取烈士褒扬金人员	314	265	168	297	213	173	233	172	200	267
零散烈士纪念设施	7483	7414	7186	7569	7622	9729	12378	13151	13601	11365

图2-25 因灾死亡人口

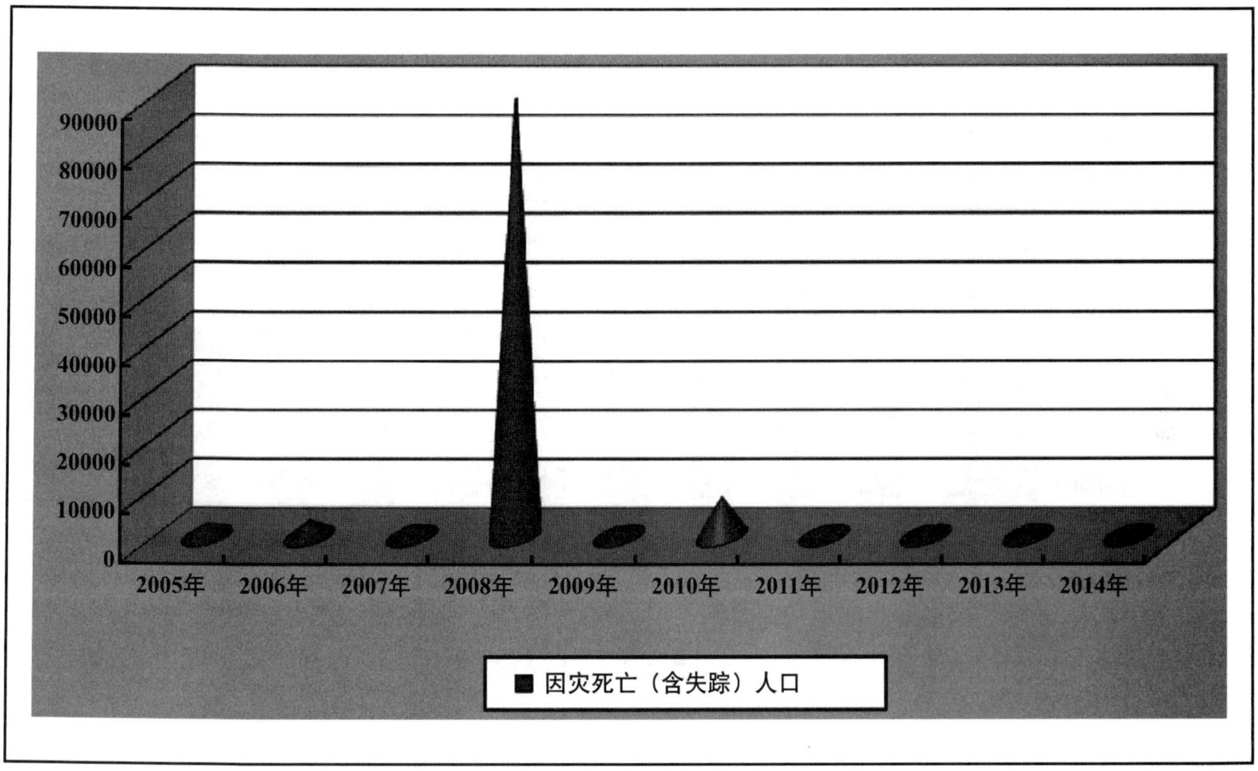

单位：人

指　标	2005年	2006年	2007年	2008年	2009年	2010年	2011年	2012年	2013年	2014年
因灾死亡(含失踪)人口	2475	3186	2325	88928	1528	7844	1126	1530	2284	1818

图2-26 受灾人口

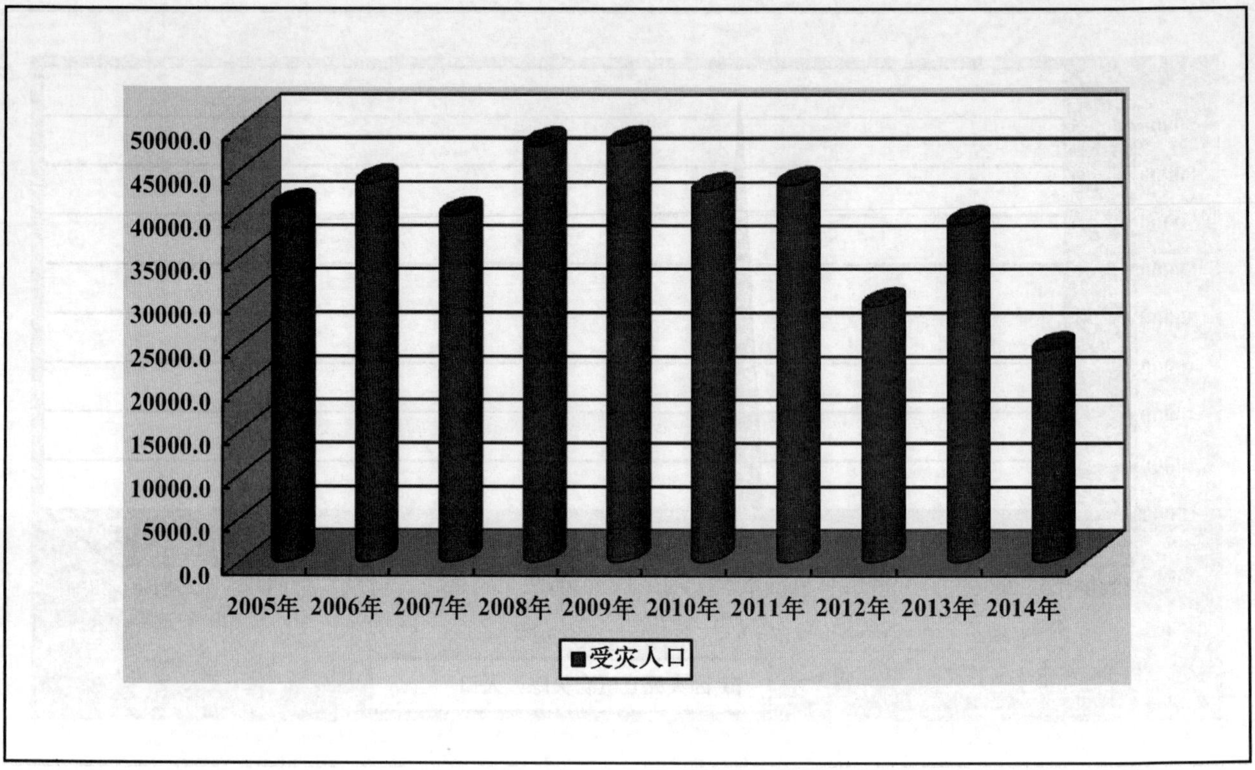

单位：万人次

指 标	2005年	2006年	2007年	2008年	2009年	2010年	2011年	2012年	2013年	2014年
受灾人口	40653.7	43453.3	39777.9	47795.0	47933.5	42610.2	43290.0	29421.7	38818.7	24353.7

图3-1　社会组织

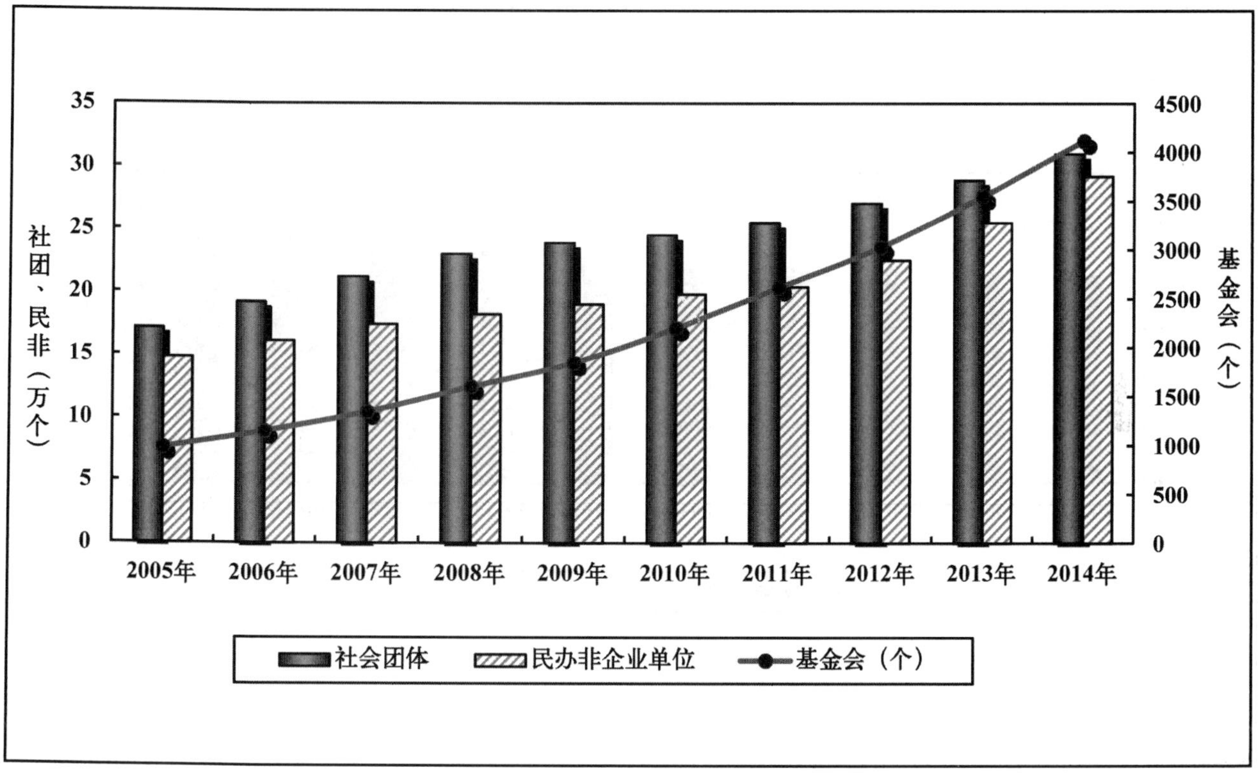

单位：万个

指　标	2005年	2006年	2007年	2008年	2009年	2010年	2011年	2012年	2013年	2014年
社会组织	32.0	35.4	38.7	41.4	43.1	44.6	46.2	49.9	54.7	60.6
社会团体	17.1	19.2	21.2	23	23.9	24.5	25.5	27.1	28.9	31.0
基金会(个)	975	1144	1340	1597	1843	2200	2614	3029	3549	4117
民办非企业单位	14.8	16.1	17.4	18.2	19	19.8	20.4	22.5	25.5	29.2

图3-2 自治组织

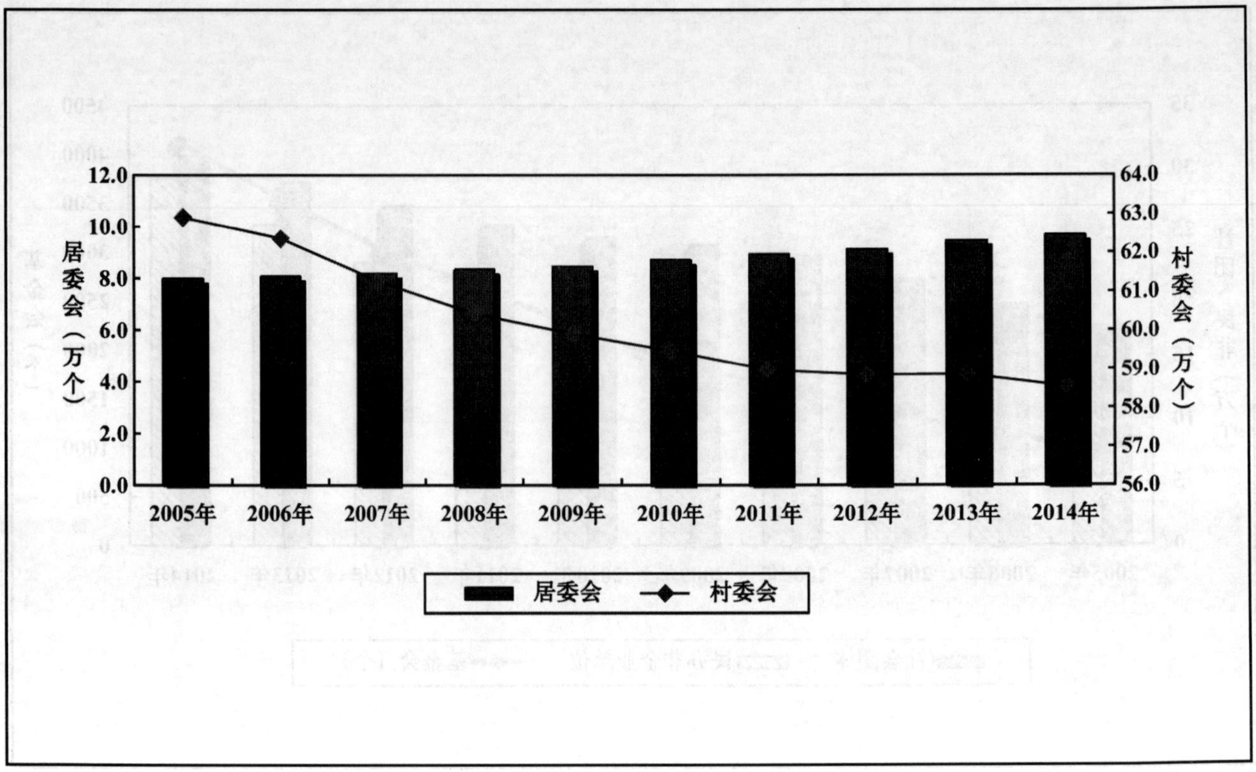

单位：万个

指 标	2005年	2006年	2007年	2008年	2009年	2010年	2011年	2012年	2013年	2014年
自治组织	70.9	70.4	69.5	68.8	68.4	68.2	67.9	68.0	68.3	68.2
居委会	8.0	8.1	8.2	8.3	8.5	8.7	8.9	9.1	9.5	9.7
村委会	62.9	62.4	61.3	60.4	59.9	59.5	59.0	58.8	58.9	58.5

图3-3 结婚登记情况

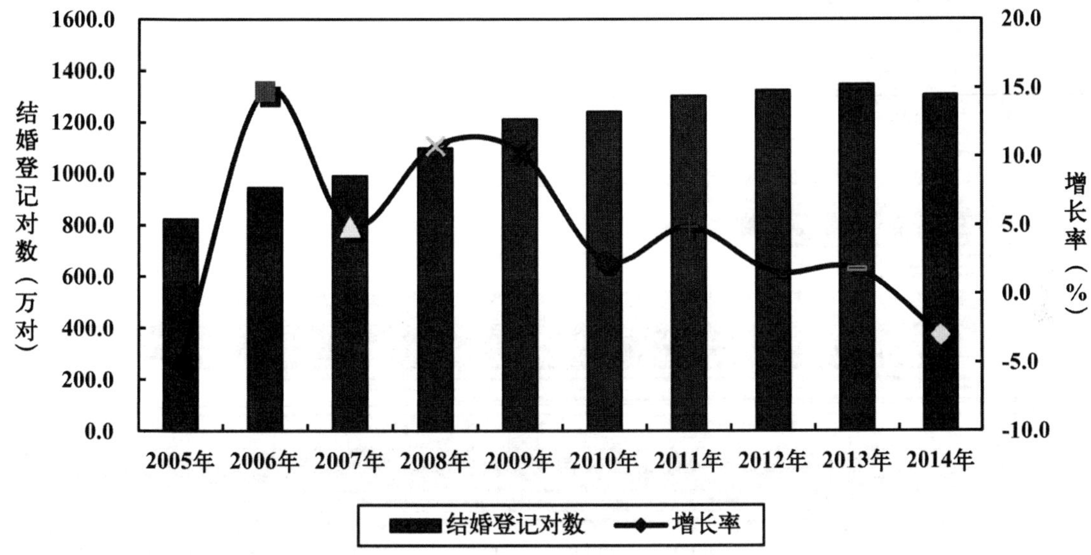

单位：万对、%

指 标	2005年	2006年	2007年	2008年	2009年	2010年	2011年	2012年	2013年	2014年
结婚登记对数	823.1	945.0	991.4	1098.3	1212.2	1241.0	1302.4	1323.6	1346.9	1306.7
增长率	-5.1	14.8	4.9	10.8	10.4	2.4	4.9	1.6	1.8	-3.0

图3-4　分年龄组结婚登记情况

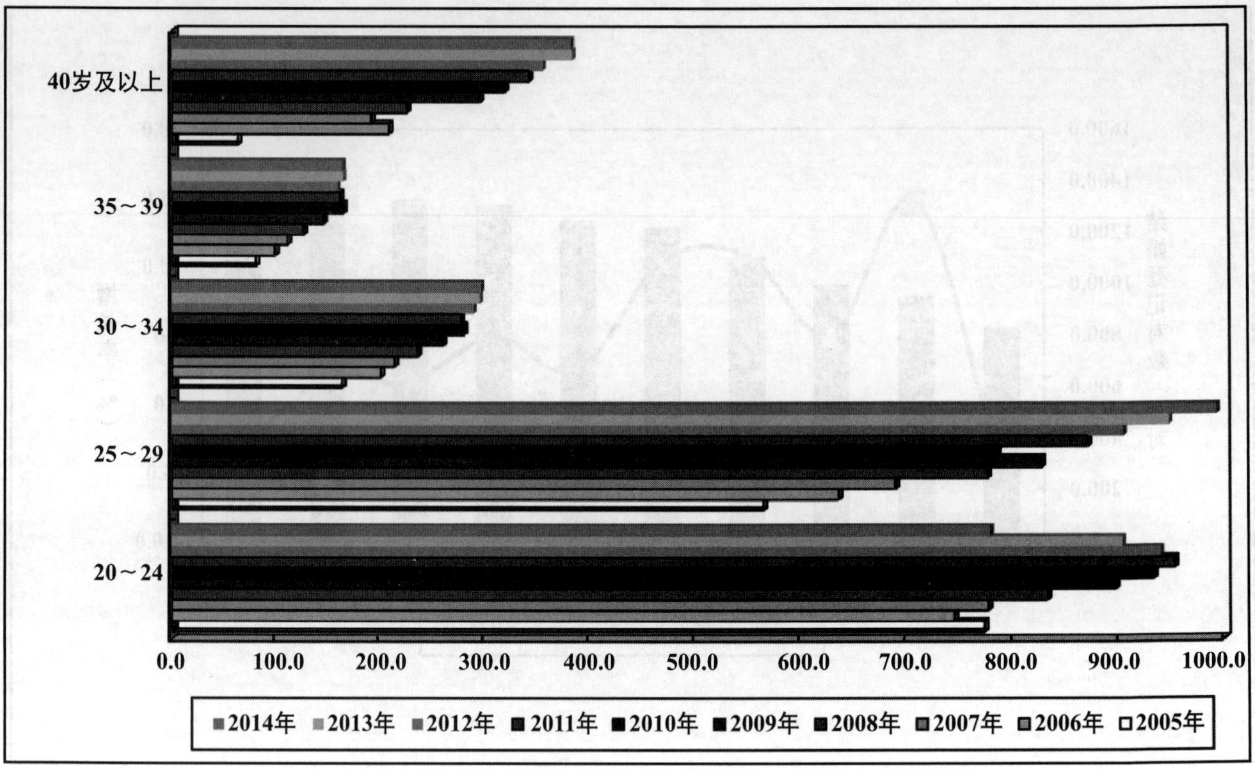

单位：万人

年　份	20～24岁	25～29岁	30～34岁	35～39岁	40岁及以上
2005	773.2	565.0	163.4	80.6	63.8
2006	744.8	636.3	200.8	99.0	209.1
2007	776.7	689.5	214.0	110.9	191.6
2008	832.3	775.7	236.1	126.5	226.2
2009	896.7	826.4	260.3	145.4	295.5
2010	933.4	784.6	279.9	164.5	319.6
2011	953.0	870.2	277.6	161.5	342.4
2012	939.6	904.1	289.0	158.9	355.6
2013	903.4	947.5	295.1	164.3	383.5
2014	778.2	993.1	296.5	163.5	382.2

图3-5 结婚率和离婚率

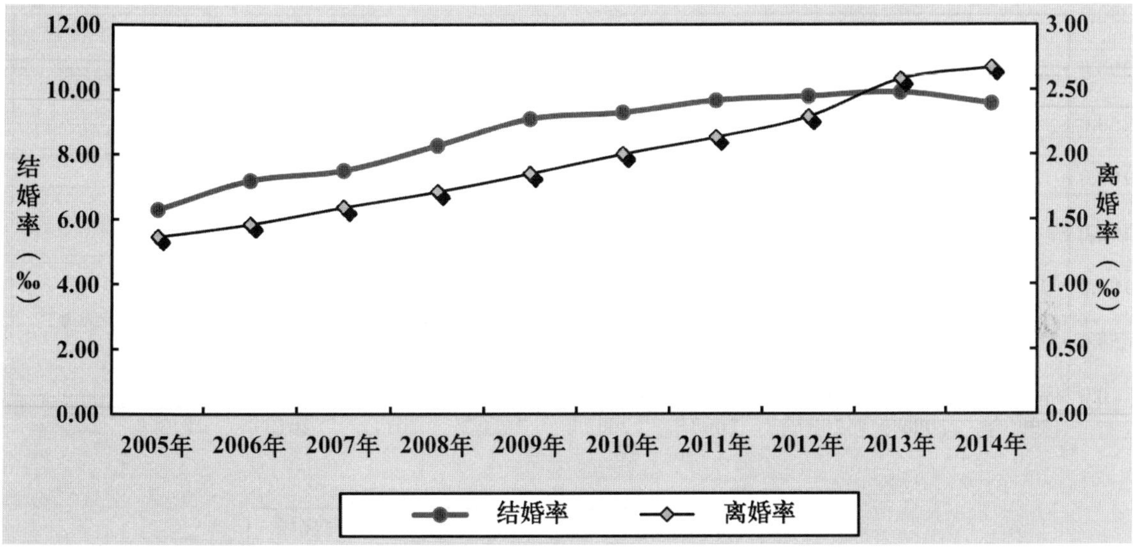

单位：‰

指　标	2005年	2006年	2007年	2008年	2009年	2010年	2011年	2012年	2013年	2014年
结婚率	6.30	7.19	7.50	8.27	9.10	9.30	9.67	9.80	9.92	9.58
离婚率	1.37	1.46	1.59	1.71	1.85	2.00	2.13	2.29	2.58	2.67

注释：结（离）婚率计算方法：结婚对数除以当期人口平均数。

图3-6 民政部门和法院办理离婚情况

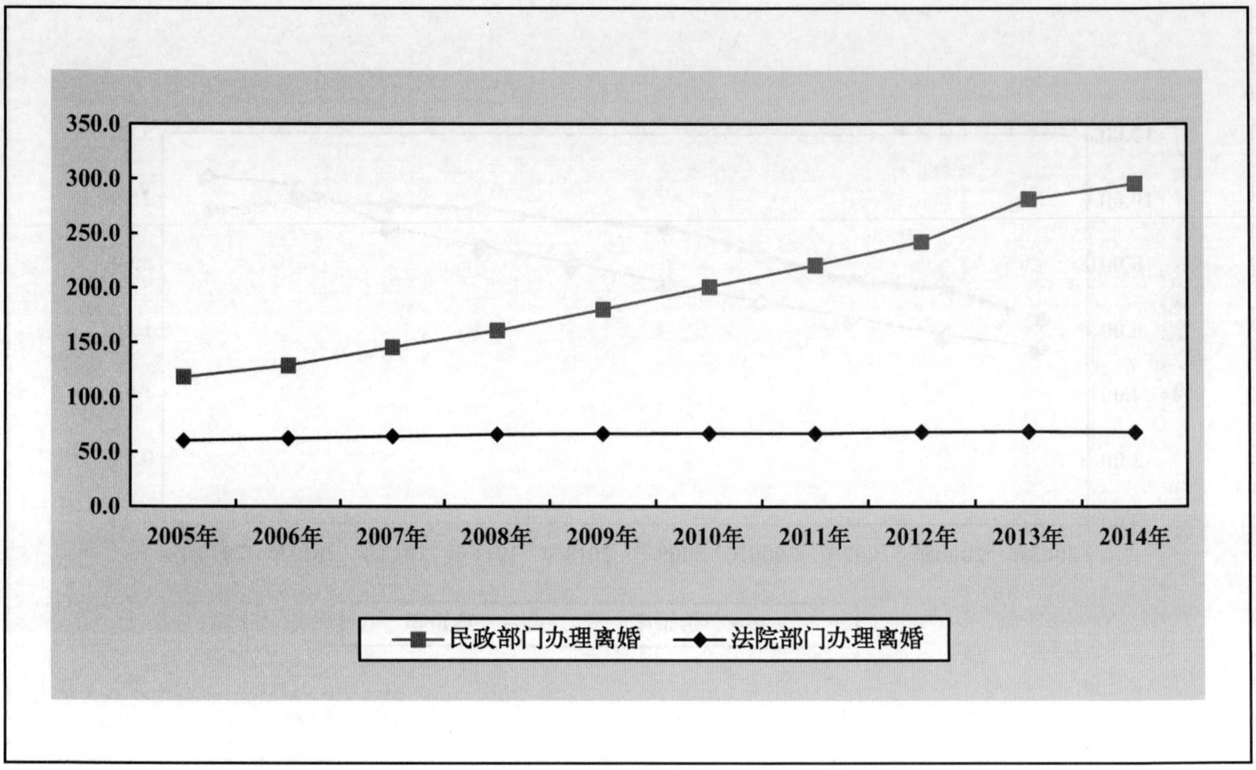

单位：万对

指 标	2005年	2006年	2007年	2008年	2009年	2010年	2011年	2012年	2013年	2014年
离婚总对数	178.5	191.3	209.8	226.9	246.8	267.8	287.4	310.4	350.0	363.6
民政部门办理离婚	118.4	129.1	145.7	161.0	180.2	201.0	220.7	242.3	281.5	295.7
法院部门办理离婚	60.1	62.2	64.1	65.9	66.6	66.8	66.7	68.1	68.5	67.9

图3-7　火化遗体情况

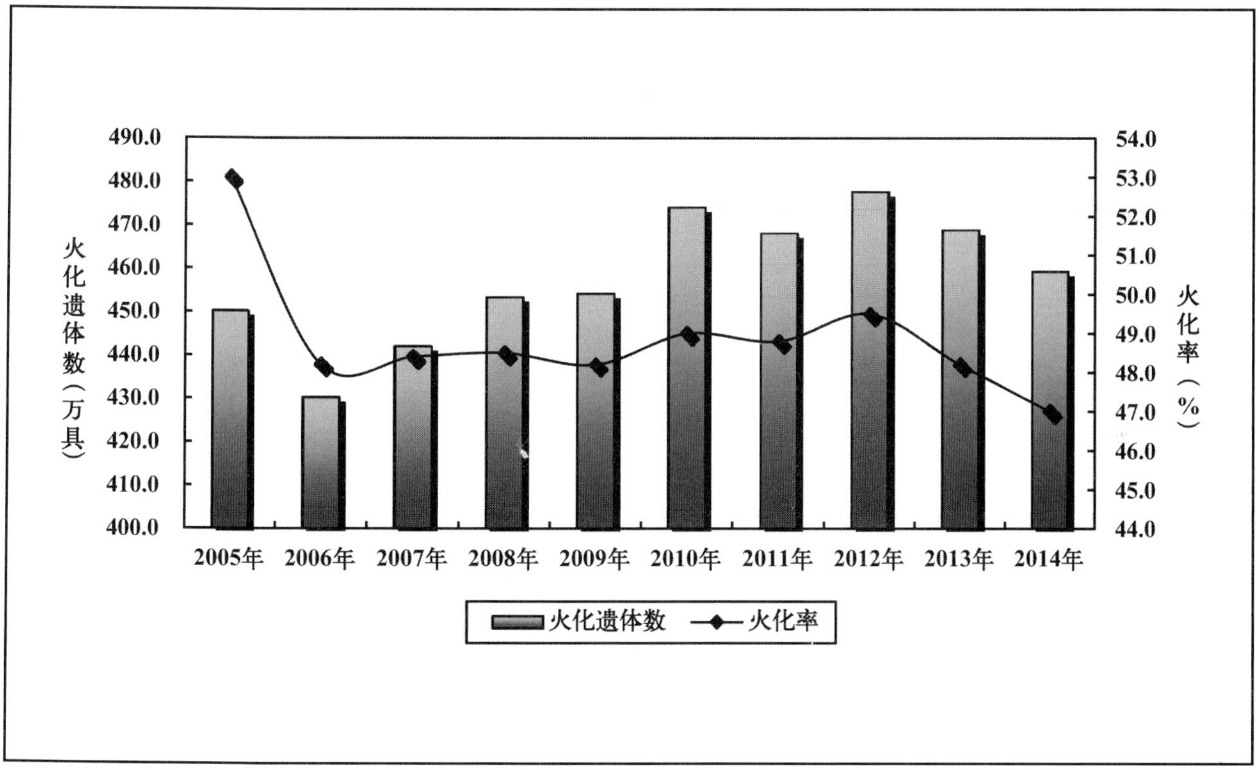

单位：万具、%

指　标	2005年	2006年	2007年	2008年	2009年	2010年	2011年	2012年	2013年	2014年
火化遗体数	450.2	430.2	442.1	453.4	454.2	474.1	468.1	477.7	468.9	459.3
火化率	53.0	48.2	48.4	48.5	48.2	49.0	48.8	49.5	48.2	47.0

社会服务
综合统计资料

03

A-1-1 “七五”—“十二五”时期社会服务发展速度

单位：%

指　标	“七五”时期平均增长速度	“八五”时期平均增长速度	“九五”时期平均增长速度	“十五”时期平均每年增长速度	“十一五”时期平均增长速度	“十二五”时期前4年平均增长速度
一、综合						
行政区划						
镇	5.7	7.7	3.0	-0.8	-0.1	1.2
乡	-11.6	-7.8	-4.7	-7.2	-1.8	-4.2
60岁及以上老年人口					4.3	4.4
事业费支出	11.9	14.8	17.3	25.6	30.3	16.6
固定资产	20.8	22.5	53.1	9.9	16.3	1.1
二、社会工作						
社会服务床位	9.7	4.6	3.0	7.7	13.8	14.6
#养老床位				5.0	15.3	16.0
智障和精神疾病床位				10.0	8.8	6.7
儿童床位				11.7	11.5	21.2
家庭儿童收养				-2.0	-7.5	-11.8
安置残疾人的福利企业	23.0	7.6	-7.6	-5.2	-6.6	-6.5
为弱势群体筹集资金的福利彩票		54.5	14.6	29.4	18.7	22.2
享受最低生活保障城市居民				40.9	0.7	-3.7
抚恤补助优抚对象	8.5	1.1	-0.3	0.8	6.3	15.0
伤残人员抚恤水平			27.1	18.2	18.5	13.6
烈属和牺牲病故军人家属抚恤水平			6.7	13.5	14.9	19.2
社区服务中心			8.0	5.6	8.2	16.1
三、成员组织和其他社会服务						
社会组织		75.5	-3.2	15.8	6.9	7.0
社会团体				5.6	7.5	5.7
基金会					17.7	17.3
民办非企业单位				45.5	6.1	8.8
自治组织						
村民委员会	1.1	-6.9	-4.7	-3.0	-1.1	-0.3
社区居委会	4.1	2.5	-0.6	-5.9	1.7	3.0
婚姻						
办理结婚登记	2.7	-0.4	-0.2	-0.6	8.6	2.8
办理离婚登记	11.7	5.7	2.8	8.0	8.5	9.3
殡葬						
处理遗体数	5.3	5.5	7.3	3.8	1	-0.4

A-1-2 社会服务发展主要指标预期值

指　标	单　位	2015年预期值	2020年预期值	2030年预期值
一、综合				
行政区划				
镇	万个	2.1	2.2	2.5
乡	万个	1.2	0.9	0.6
人口	万人	137408.9	140808.9	147863.4
60岁及以上老年人口	万人	22084.2	27453.5	42425.8
事业费支出	亿元	5814.4	12532.9	58229.3
固定资产	亿元	6961.6	7354.9	8209.4
二、社会工作				
社会服务床位	万张	642.4	1055.5	2849.0
# 养老床位	万张	601.2	984.0	2635.4
智障和精神疾病床位	万张	8.5	12.2	25.1
儿童床位	万张	11.8	18.9	48.5
家庭儿童收养	万件	1.9	1.0	0.3
安置残疾人的福利企业	万个	1.6	1.1	0.6
为弱势群体筹集资金的福利彩票	亿元	2635.0	7172.8	53149.2
享受最低生活保障城市居民	万人	1914.8	1586.8	1089.8
抚恤补助优抚对象	万人	1037.3	1290.7	1998.1
伤残人员抚恤水平	元/人、年	17033.2	32204.0	115116.8
烈属和牺牲病故军人家属抚恤水平	元/人、年	13692.4	32943.8	190706.6
社区服务中心	万个	2.7	5.7	25.2
三、成员组织和其他社会服务				
社会组织	万个	62.7	88.1	173.9
社会团体	万个	32.3	42.5	73.7
基金会	万个	0.5	1.1	5.3
民办非企业单位	万个	30.2	46.0	106.9
自治组织				
村民委员会	万个	58.5	57.5	55.6
社区居委会	万个	10.1	11.7	15.6
婚姻				
办理结婚登记	万对	1422.5	1630.5	2142.2
办理离婚登记	万对	418.4	653.6	1595.4
殡葬				
处理遗体数	万具	507.5	618.4	918.4

注：发展速度为“十二五”时期平均增长速度，其中床位数、抚恤补助优抚对象和处理遗体数用的是1978年至2012年的平均速度。

A-1-3 2010-2014年社会服务业发展主要指标数据

指　标	单　位	2010年	2011年	2012年	2013年	2014年
一、综合						
社会服务基本情况						
机构	万个	126.9	129.4	136.7	156.2	166.8
服务人员	万人	1138.4	1120.8	1144.7	1197.6	1251.0
固定资产	亿元	6589.3	6676.7	6675.4	6810.2	7213.0
增加值	亿元	2014.5	2246.9	2128.9	2251.9	2515.2
事业费	亿元	2697.5	3229.1	3683.7	4276.5	4404.1
# 抚恤	亿元	362.7	428.3	517.0	618.4	636.6
退役安置	亿元	269.0	302.3	372.1	435.3	456.8
社会福利	亿元	109.9	232.2	319.5	397.6	480.9
社会救助	亿元	1302.0	1766.3	1866.1	2172.4	2197.5
自然灾害生活救助	亿元	237.2	128.7	163.4	178.7	124.4
离退休人员经费	亿元	30.4	35.3	39.0	43.6	44.2
其他	亿元	386.3	336.0	406.7	430.6	463.6
# 公益金支出	亿元	121.2	127.9	159.0	195.5	231.3
* 中央转移支付的事业费占全国总事业费比重	%	49.8	56.0	48.7	50.3	47.8
全国总事业费占财政支出的比重	%	3.0	3.0	3.0	3.1	2.9
基本建设投资	亿元	183.0	218.5	234.7	292.8	282.2
# 预算内投资	亿元	89.1	78.5	104.2	120.1	104.3
公益金投资	亿元	32.3	53.4	51.1	64.7	57.5
预算内基本建设投资占事业费比重	%	3.3	2.4	2.8	2.8	2.4
公益金基本建设投资占公益金支出的比重	%	26.7	41.8	32.1	33.1	24.9
乡镇级行政区划						
镇	个	19410	19683	19881	20117	20401
乡	个	14571	13587	13281	12812	12282
# 民族乡	个	1096	1086	1064	1035	1020
街道办事处	个	6923	7194	7282	7566	7696
区公所	个	2	2	2	2	2
老龄人口						
60岁及以上老年人口	万人	17765	18499	19390	20243	21242
占全国总人口	%	13.3	13.7	14.3	14.9	15.5
二、社会工作						
提供住宿的社会服务机构						
单位数	万个	4.4	4.6	4.8	4.6	3.7
床位数	万张	349.6	396.4	449.4	526.7	613.5
# 养老床位	万张	316.1	369.2	416.6	493.7	577.7
智障和精神疾病床位	万张	6.1	6.5	6.7	7.4	8.0
儿童床位	万张	5.5	6.8	8.7	9.8	10.8
其他床位	万张	21.9	13.9	17.4	15.7	17.0
收养人数	万人	278.2	293.4	309.5	322.5	272.3
每千人口社会服务床位数	张	2.6	2.9	3.3	3.9	4.5
每千老年人口养老床位数	张	17.8	20.0	21.5	24.4	27.2

A-1-3续表1

指 标	单 位	2010年	2011年	2012年	2013年	2014年
不提供住宿的社会服务机构						
机构数	万个	8.8	10.0	13.3	27.7	33.4
儿童						
孤儿数	万人	25.2	49.1	57.0	54.9	52.5
家庭收养儿童	万人	3.5	3.1	2.7	2.4	2.3
流浪儿童救助	万人次	14.6	17.9	15.2	18.1	
残疾人						
为残疾人提供服务的机构数	万个	2.2	2.2	2.0	1.8	1.6
残疾职工数	万人	62.5	62.8	59.7	53.9	47.9
社会救助						
最低生活保障						
城市居民最低生活保障人数	万人	2310.5	2276.8	2143.5	2064.2	1877.0
城市居民最低生活保障户数	万户	1145.0	1145.7	1114.9	1097.2	1026.0
城市居民最低生活保障平均标准	元/人、月	251.2	287.6	330.1	373.3	410.5
*城市居民最低生活保障平均支出水平	元/人、月	189.0	240.3	239.1	264.2	285.6
农村最低生活保障人数	万人	5214.0	5305.7	5344.5	5388.0	5207.2
农村最低生活保障户数	万户	2528.7	2672.8	2814.9	2931.1	2943.6
农村最低生活保障平均标准	元/人、年	1404.0	1718.4	2067.8	2433.9	2776.6
*农村最低生活保障平均支出水平	元/人、年	888.0	1273.2	1247.9	1393.5	1552.3
五保供养						
农村五保集中供养人数	万人	177.4	184.5	185.3	183.5	174.3
农村五保集中供养平均标准	元/人、年	2951.4	3399.7	4060.9	4685.0	5371.3
农村五保集中供养平均支出水平	元/人、年	2460.0	3081.9	3496.6	4078.3	4676.1
农村五保分散供养人数	万人	378.9	366.5	360.3	353.8	354.8
农村五保分散供养平均标准	元/人、年	2102.1	2470.5	3008.0	3498.5	4005.9
农村五保分散供养平均支出水平	元/人、年	1416.0	1774.9	2237.3	2724.3	3228.9
医疗救助						
民政部门直接救助人次数	万人次	1479.3	2144.0	2173.7	2126.4	2395.3
民政部门资助参加医疗保险人数	万人	1461.2	1549.8	1387.1	1490.1	1702.0
民政部门资助参加合作医疗人数	万人	4615.4	4825.3	4490.4	4868.7	5021.7
生活无着人员救助						
生活无着人员救助	万人次	171.9	241.0	276.6	348.5	351.7
为弱势群体筹集资金的活动						
民政部门接收社会捐赠						
社会捐赠款数	亿元	179.8	96.6	101.7	107.6	79.6
捐赠衣被总数	亿件	0.3	0.3	1.3	1.0	0.5
捐赠其他物资价值	亿元	4.9	4.8	6.3	8.7	8.0
受益人次数	万人次	2514.7	1459.7	1325.0	1246.0	1694.9
社会捐赠接收站、点数	万个	3.2	3.4	3.1	3.1	3.2
销售福利彩票	亿元	968.0	1278.0	1510.3	1765.3	2059.7
筹集社会公益金	亿元	298.8	382.0	449.4	510.7	585.7

A-1-3续表2

指　标	单　位	2010年	2011年	2012年	2013年	2014年
优抚安置						
国家抚恤、补助各类优抚对象	万人	625.0	852.5	944.4	950.5	917.3
接收军队离退休人员人数	万人	1.3	1.5	1.9	3.9	2.8
社区服务						
社区服务机构和设施	万个	15.3	16.0	20.0	25.2	31.1
# 社区服务中心	个	12720	14391	16306	19904	24006
社区服务站	个	44237	56156	87931	108377	120188
社区服务机构和设施覆盖率	%	22.4	23.6	29.5	36.9	45.5
便民、利民网点	万个	53.9	45.3	39.7	35.9	30.9
自然灾害情况						
受灾人口	万人次	42610.2	43290.0	29421.7	38818.7	24353.7
因灾死亡（含失踪）人口	人	7844	1126	1530	2284	1818
直接经济损失	亿元	5339.9	3096.4	4185.5	5808.4	3373.8
三、成员组织和其他社会服务						
社会组织	万个	44.6	46.2	49.9	54.7	60.6
社会团体	万个	24.5	25.5	27.1	28.9	31.0
基金会	个	2200	2614	3029	3548	4117
民办非企业单位	万个	19.8	20.4	22.5	25.5	29.2
自治组织	万个	68.2	67.9	67.9	68.4	68.2
村委会	万个	59.5	59.0	58.8	58.9	58.5
社区居委会	万个	8.7	8.9	9.1	9.5	9.7
婚姻服务						
结婚登记	万对	1241.0	1302.4	1323.6	1346.9	1306.7
# 涉外及华侨、港澳台	万对	4.9	4.9	5.3	5.5	4.7
每千居民之结婚宗数	‰	9.3	9.7	9.8	9.9	9.6
离婚办理	万对	267.8	287.4	310.4	350.0	363.7
每千居民之离婚宗数	‰	2.0	2.1	2.3	2.6	2.7
殡葬服务						
火化遗体数	万具	474.1	468.1	477.7	468.9	459.3
火化率	%	49.0	48.8	49.5	48.2	47.0

A-1-4 社会服务发展主要数据与上年比较

指标	单位	2014年	2013年	比上年增长(%)
一、综合				
行政区划				
镇	个	20401	20117	1.4
乡	个	12282	12812	-4.1
#民族乡	个	1020	1035	-1.4
街道办事处	个	7696	7566	1.7
区公所	个	2	2	
老龄人口				
60岁及以上老年人口	万人	21242	20243	4.9
占全国总人口	%	15.5	14.9	0.6 (百分点)
65岁及以上老年人口	万人	13755	13161	4.5
占全国总人口	%	10.1	9.7	0.4(百分点)
资产				
民政事业费总支出	亿元	4404.1	4276.5	3.0
#抚恤	亿元	636.6	618.4	2.9
退役安置	亿元	456.8	435.3	4.9
社会福利	亿元	481.0	397.6	21.0
社会救助	亿元	2197.5	2172.4	1.2
自然灾害生活救助	亿元	124.4	178.7	-30.4
离退休人员经费	亿元	44.2	43.6	1.4
其他	亿元	133.1	430.6	-69.1
基本建设支出	亿元	282.2	292.8	-3.6
固定资产	亿元	7213.0	6810.2	5.9
二、社会工作				
提供住宿的社会服务机构				
单位数	万个	3.7	4.6	-19.6
床位数	万张	613.5	526.7	16.5
收养人数	万人	334.0	322.5	3.6
每千人口社会服务床位数	张	4.5	3.9	15.1

A-1-4续表1

指　标	单　位	2014年	2013年	比上年增长(%)
社会救助				
城市				
城市居民最低生活保障人数	万人	1877.0	2064.2	-9.1
城市居民最低生活保障户数	万户	1026.1	1097.2	-6.5
城市居民最低生活保障平均标准	元/人、月	410.5	373.3	10.0
城市居民最低生活保障平均支出水平	元/人、月	285.6	264.2	8.1
农村				
农村最低生活保障人数	万人	5207.2	5388.0	-3.4
农村最低生活保障户数	万户	2943.6	2931.1	0.4
农村最低生活保障平均标准	元/人、年	2776.6	2433.9	14.1
农村最低生活保障平均支出水平	元/人、年	1552.3	1393.5	11.4
农村五保集中供养人数	万人	174.3	183.5	-5.0
农村五保集中供养平均标准	元/人、年	5371.3	4685.0	14.6
农村五保集中供养平均支出水平	元/人、年	4676.1	4078.3	14.7
农村五保分散供养人数	万人	354.8	353.8	0.3
农村五保分散供养平均标准	元/人、年	4005.9	3498.5	14.5
农村五保分散供养平均支出水平	元/人、年	3228.9	2724.3	18.5
医疗救助				
民政部门直接救助人次数	万人次	2395.3	2126.4	12.6
民政部门资助参加医疗保险人数	万人	1702.0	1490.1	14.2
农村资助参加合作医疗人数	万人	5021.7	4868.7	3.1
儿童收养				
家庭收养儿童	万人	2.3	2.4	-4.2
为残疾人提供服务的机构				
为残疾人提供服务的机构数	万个	1.6	1.8	-11.1
残疾职工人数	万人	47.9	53.9	-11.1
福利彩票				
销售福利彩票	亿元	2059.7	1765.3	16.7
筹集社会公益金	亿元	585.7	510.7	14.7
优抚安置				
国家抚恤、补助各类优抚对象	万人	917.3	950.5	-3.5
安置义务兵、士官人数	万人	44.1	44.0	0.2
接收军队离退休人员人数	万人	2.8	3.9	-28.2

A-1-4续表2

指　标	单　位	2014年	2013年	比上年增长(%)
社会捐赠				
社会捐赠款数	亿元	79.6	107.6	-26.0
捐赠衣被总数	亿件	0.5	1.0	-50.0
捐赠其他物资价值	亿元	8.0	8.7	-8.0
受益人次数	万人次	1694.9	1246.0	36.0
社会捐赠接收站、点数	万个	3.2	3.1	3.2
社区服务机构和设施				
社区服务指导中心	个	918	890	3.1
社区服务中心	个	23088	19014	21.4
社区服务站	个	120188	108377	10.9
养老等其他社区服务机构	个	160420	123658	29.7
社区服务机构和设施覆盖率	%	45.5	36.9	8.6(百分点)
便民利民网点	个	30.9	35.9	-13.9
三、成员组织和其他社会服务				
社会组织				
社会组织总数	万个	60.6	54.7	10.8
社会团体	万个	31.0	28.9	7.3
基金会	个	4116	3549	16.0
民办非企业	万个	29.2	25.5	10.1
自治组织				
村委会	万个	58.5	58.9	-0.7
居委会	万个	9.7	9.5	2.1
婚姻				
结婚登记	万对	1306.7	1346.9	-3.0
# 涉外及华侨、港澳台	万对	4.7	5.5	-14.5
每千居民之结婚宗数	‰	9.6	9.9	-0.3 (千分点)
离婚办理	万对	363.7	350.0	3.9
每千居民之离婚宗数	‰	2.7	2.6	0.3 (千分点)
殡葬				
火化遗体数	万具	459.3	468.9	-2.0
火化率	%	47.0	48.2	-1.3 (百分点)

A-1-5 行政区划与上年比较

单位:个

指 标	2014年	2013年	比上年增长(%)
地级行政区划合计	**333**	**333**	
# 地级市	288	286	0.7
地区	12	14	-14.3
自治州	30	30	
盟	3	3	
县级行政区划合计	**2854**	**2853**	
# 市辖区	897	872	2.9
县级市	361	368	-1.9
县	1425	1442	-1.2
自治县	117	117	
旗	49	49	
自治旗	3	3	
特区	1	1	
林区	1	1	
乡镇、街道级行政区划合计	**40381**	**40497**	**-0.3**
# 镇	20401	20117	1.4
乡	12282	11626	5.6
苏木	151	151	
民族乡	1020	1034	-1.4
民族苏木	1	1	
街道办事处	7696	7566	1.7
区公所	2	2	

A-1-6 社会服务机构和设施与上年比较

单位：个

指 标	2014年	2013年	比上年增长(%)
社会服务	**1668143**	**1562298**	**6.8**
一、社会工作	**370893**	**323061**	**14.8**
提供住宿的社会服务机构	**36810**	**45977**	**-19.9**
老年人与残疾人服务机构	**33043**	**42475**	**-22.2**
城市养老服务机构	7642	7077	8.0
农村养老服务机构	20261	30247	-33.0
社会福利院	1864	1825	2.1
光荣院	1411	1425	-1.0
荣誉军人康复医院	44	42	4.8
复员军人疗养院	38	38	
军休所	1783	1821	-2.1
智障与精神疾病服务机构	**254**	**261**	**-2.7**
社会福利医院	156	155	0.6
复退军人精神病院	98	106	-7.5
儿童收养救助服务机构	**890**	**803**	**10.8**
儿童福利机构	545	529	3.0
未成年人救助保护中心	345	274	25.9
其他提供住宿的服务机构	**2623**	**2438**	**7.6**
生活无着人员救助管理站	1949	1891	3.1
安置农场	13	26	-50.0
军供站	327	325	0.6
其他提供住宿的机构	334	196	70.4

A–1–6续表

单位：个

指 标	2014年	2013年	比上年增长(%)
不提供住宿的社会服务机构	**334083**	**277084**	**20.6**
老龄机构	2558	2571	-0.5
为残疾人提供服务的机构	16389	18227	-10.1
救助低保服务机构	992	987	0.5
救灾储备单位	868	784	10.7
福利彩票发行机构	893	940	-5.0
军队离退休人员管理中心	185	145	27.6
军队离退休人员活动中心	30	28	7.1
烈士纪念建筑物管理机构	1516	1463	3.6
社区服务机构和设施	310652	251939	23.3
二、成员组织和其他社会服务	**1294987**	**1236853**	**4.7**
成员组织	**1288192**	**1230412**	**4.7**
社会组织	**606048**	**547245**	**10.7**
社会团体	309736	289026	7.2
基金会	4117	3549	16.0
民办非企业	292195	254670	14.7
自治组织	**682144**	**683167**	**-0.1**
居委会	96693	94620	2.2
村委会	585451	588547	-0.5
其他社会服务	**6795**	**6441**	**5.5**
婚姻服务机构	**2236**	**2059**	**6.9**
殡葬服务机构	**4559**	**4382**	**4.0**
殡仪馆	1801	1784	1.0
公墓	1598	1506	6.1
骨灰堂	19	29	-34.5
殡葬管理单位	1141	1063	7.3
三、其他事业单位	**2263**	**2384**	**-5.1**
行政机关	**3491**	**3492**	

A-1-7 社会服务机构职工与上年比较

单位：万人

指　标	2014年	2013年	比上年增长(%)
社会服务	**1251.0**	**1197.8**	**4.4**
一、社会工作	**277.3**	**269.3**	**3.0**
提供住宿的社会服务机构	**40.3**	**42.4**	**-5.0**
老年人与残疾人服务机构	**33.4**	**35.6**	**-6.2**
城市养老服务机构	12.2	11.0	10.9
农村养老服务机构	13.0	16.4	-20.7
社会福利院	4.5	4.5	
光荣院	1.2	1.2	
荣誉军人康复医院	0.5	0.5	
复员军人疗养院	0.3	0.3	
军休所	1.7	1.7	
智障与精神疾病服务机构	**2.6**	**2.5**	**4.0**
社会福利医院	1.4	1.4	
复退军人精神病院	1.2	1.1	9.1
儿童收养救助服务机构	**1.5**	**1.4**	**7.1**
儿童福利机构	1.3	1.2	8.3
未成年人救助保护中心	0.2	0.2	
其他提供住宿的服务机构	**2.9**	**2.9**	
生活无着人员救助管理站	1.8	1.8	
安置农场	0.1	0.1	
军供站	0.5	0.6	-16.7
其他提供住宿的机构	0.5	0.4	25.0

A-1-7续表

单位：万人

指　标	2014年	2013年	比上年增长(%)
不提供住宿的社会服务机构	**237.0**	**226.9**	**4.5**
老龄机构	1.0	1.0	
为残疾人提供服务的机构	125.4	137.3	-8.7
救助低保服务机构	0.7	0.7	
救灾储备单位	0.2	0.2	
福利彩票发行机构	1.1	1.1	
军队离退休人员管理中心	0.2	0.2	
军队离退休人员活动中心	0.1	0.1	
烈士纪念建筑物管理机构	1.0	1.0	
社区服务机构和设施	107.1	85.3	25.6
二、成员组织和其他社会服务	**971.8**	**926.5**	**4.9**
成员组织	**962.5**	**917.4**	**4.9**
社会组织	**682.3**	**636.7**	**7.2**
社会团体	373.6	353.2	5.8
基金会	2.0	1.9	5.3
民办非企业	306.6	281.6	8.9
自治组织	**280.2**	**280.7**	**-0.2**
居委会	49.7	48.4	2.7
村委会	230.5	232.3	-0.8
其他社会服务	**9.3**	**9.1**	**2.2**
婚姻服务机构	**1.0**	**1.0**	
殡葬服务机构	**8.3**	**8.1**	**2.5**
殡仪馆	4.6	4.6	
公墓	2.7	2.5	8.0
骨灰堂	0.1	0.1	
殡葬管理单位	1.0	0.9	11.1
三、其他事业单位	**2.0**	**2**	
行政机关	**9.5**	**9.4**	**1.1**

A-1-8 社会服务机构中社会工作师人员情况

单位：人

指 标	社会工作师			助理社会工作师		
	2014年	2013年	比上年增长(%)	2014年	2013年	比上年增长(%)
社会服务	**25782**	**21917**	**17.6**	**50770**	**43301**	**17.2**
一、社会工作	**10252**	**8014**	**27.9**	**18295**	**15736**	**16.3**
提供住宿的社会服务机构	**3795**	**3256**	**16.6**	**4070**	**3510**	**16.0**
老年人与残疾人服务机构	**2567**	**2250**	**14.1**	**2839**	**2491**	**14.0**
城市养老服务机构	650	603	7.8	926	712	30.1
农村养老服务机构	407	383	6.3	397	429	-7.5
社会福利院	867	694	24.9	968	864	12.0
光荣院	149	115	29.6	164	120	36.7
荣誉军人康复医院	69	62	11.3	47	44	6.8
复员军人疗养院	42	28	50.0	13	19	-31.6
军休所	383	365	4.9	324	303	6.9
智障与精神疾病服务机构	**218**	**183**	**19.1**	**265**	**209**	**26.8**
社会福利医院	117	106	10.4	124	103	20.4
复退军人精神病院	101	77	31.2	141	106	33.0
儿童收养救助服务机构	**466**	**382**	**22.0**	**394**	**338**	**16.6**
儿童福利机构	421	332	26.8	334	294	13.6
未成年人救助保护中心	45	50	-10.0	60	44	36.4
其他提供住宿的服务机构	**544**	**441**	**23.4**	**572**	**472**	**21.2**
生活无着人员救助管理站	464	372	24.7	455	381	19.4
安置农场				6	11	-45.5
军供站	46	42	9.5	56	53	5.7
其他提供住宿的机构	34	27	25.9	55	27	103.7

A-1-8续表

单位：人

指标	社会工作师			助理社会工作师		
	2014年	2013年	比上年增长(%)	2014年	2013年	比上年增长(%)
不提供住宿的社会服务机构	**6457**	**4758**	**35.7**	**14255**	**11961**	**19.2**
老龄机构	140	113	23.9	92	84	9.5
为残疾人提供服务的机构		749	-100.0		1900	-100.0
救助低保服务机构	136	114	19.3	112	96	16.7
救灾储备单位	38	22	72.7	29	17	70.6
福利彩票发行机构	104	100	4.0	152	137	10.9
军队离退休人员管理中心	72	48	50.0	45	32	40.6
军队离退休人员活动中心	4	6	-33.3	6	5	20.0
烈士纪念建筑物管理机构	172	150	14.7	117	103	13.6
社区服务机构和设施	4946	3456	43.1	11802	9587	23.1
二、成员组织和其他社会服务机构	**14442**	**13554**	**6.6**		**27565**	**13.8**
成员组织	**14442**	**12994**	**11.1**	**31381**	**26871**	**16.8**
社会组织	**9324**	**8561**	**8.9**	**16651**	**13399**	**24.3**
社会团体	3537	3556	-0.5	7360	5437	35.4
基金会	76	78	-2.6	90	151	-40.4
民办非企业	5711	4927	15.9	9201	7811	17.8
自治组织	**5118**	**4433**	**15.5**	**14730**	**13472**	**9.3**
居委会	4602	3964	16.1	13151	11852	11.0
村委会	516	469	10.0	1579	1620	-2.5
其他社会服务	**681**	**560**	**21.6**	**803**	**694**	**15.7**
婚姻服务机构	**200**	**162**	**23.5**	**173**	**135**	**28.1**
殡葬服务机构	**481**	**398**	**20.9**	**630**	**559**	**12.7**
殡仪馆	239	204	17.2	367	308	19.2
公墓	107	97	10.3	161	150	7.3
骨灰堂					1	
殡葬管理单位	135	97	39.2	102	100	2.0
三、其他事业单位	**407**	**349**	**16.6**	**291**	**265**	**9.8**
行政机关	**1475**	**1280**	**15.2**	**1404**	**1264**	**11.1**

A-1-9 性别统计情况

指　标	人员总数（人）	#女性	占总人数的比重（%）	比上年增长（百分点）
社会服务	**12509814**	**3847483**	**30.8**	
一、社会工作	**2772513**	**1037987**	**37.4**	
提供住宿的社会服务机构	**402905**	**220419**	**54.7**	**1.6**
老年人与残疾人服务机构	**333615**	**184568**	**55.3**	**1.7**
城市养老服务机构	121743	76167	62.6	-1.6
农村养老服务机构	130119	63388	48.7	2.4
社会福利院	44840	27502	61.3	1.1
光荣院	11833	5568	47.1	0.4
荣誉军人康复医院	5405	2969	54.9	0.8
复员军人疗养院	2837	1564	55.1	-1.0
军休所	16838	7410	44.0	0.5
智障与精神疾病服务机构	**25972**	**15036**	**57.9**	**1.7**
社会福利医院	14300	8096	56.6	1.2
复退军人精神病院	11672	6940	59.5	2.2
儿童收养救助服务机构	**14817**	**9540**	**64.4**	**1.2**
儿童福利机构	12768	8730	68.4	0.6
未成年人救助保护中心	2049	810	39.5	2.3
其他提供住宿的服务机构	**28501**	**11275**	**39.6**	**0.3**
生活无着人员救助管理站	17848	5977	33.5	-0.2
安置农场	370	109	29.5	-9.9
军供站	5344	2085	39.0	-1.5
其他提供住宿的机构	4939	3104	62.8	-1.1

A-1-9续表

指　标	人员总数（人）	#女性	占总人数的比重（%）	比上年增长（百分点）
不提供住宿的社会服务机构	**2369608**	**817568**	**34.5**	
老龄机构	10044	4410	43.9	0.3
为残疾人提供服务的机构	1254051	403316	32.2	0.2
救助低保服务机构	7424	3283	44.2	-0.8
救灾储备单位	2321	713	30.7	0.6
福利彩票发行机构	11206	4610	41.1	0.6
军队离退休人员管理中心	2426	1128	46.5	1.0
军队离退休人员活动中心	661	258	39.0	-4.6
烈士纪念建筑物管理机构	10201	4031	39.5	-0.4
社区服务机构和设施	1071274	395819	36.9	-1.4
二、成员组织和其他社会服务	**9718097**	**2800977**	**28.8**	
成员组织	**9624685**	**2770933**	**28.8**	
社会组织	**6822623**	**2003785**	**29.4**	**-0.2**
社会团体	3736265	815873	21.8	-0.7
基金会	20394	5420	26.6	-1.3
民办非企业	3065964	1182492	38.6	0.2
自治组织	**2802062**	**767148**	**27.4**	**0.3**
居委会	497038	240739	48.4	
村委会	2305024	526409	22.8	0.2
其他社会服务	**93412**	**30044**	**32.2**	**0.6**
婚姻服务机构	**10761**	**7064**	**65.6**	**-1.2**
殡葬服务机构	**82651**	**22980**	**27.8**	**0.6**
殡仪馆	45767	11637	25.4	0.5
公墓	26895	8813	32.8	0.7
骨灰堂	100	20		
殡葬管理单位	9889	2510	25.4	-0.3
三、其他事业单位	**19204**	**8519**	**44.4**	**-0.5**
行政机关	**95372**	**30559**	**32.0**	**-0.1**

A-1-10 社会服务机构固定资产与上年比较

单位：亿元

指　标	2014年	2013年	比上年增长(%)
社会服务	**7213.0**	**6810.2**	**5.9**
一、社会工作	**3273.0**	**3030.7**	**8.0**
提供住宿的社会服务机构	**859.2**	**843.7**	**1.8**
老年人与残疾人服务机构	**719.0**	**724.1**	**-0.7**
城市养老服务机构	233.7	200.8	16.4
农村养老服务机构	269.8	313.0	-13.8
社会福利院	123.7	119.9	3.2
光荣院	25.1	24.7	1.6
荣誉军人康复医院	21.4	19.8	8.1
复员军人疗养院	8.7	10.1	-13.9
军休所	36.6	35.8	2.2
智障与精神疾病服务机构	**46.9**	**40.1**	**17.0**
社会福利医院	24.9	20.5	21.5
复退军人精神病院	22.0	19.6	12.2
儿童收养救助服务机构	**38.2**	**33.0**	**15.8**
儿童福利机构	34.1	30.3	12.5
未成年人救助保护中心	4.1	2.7	51.9
其他提供住宿的服务机构	**55.4**	**46.5**	**19.1**
生活无着人员救助管理站	33.7	27.6	22.1
安置农场	0.3	0.5	-40.0
军供站	13.8	13.0	6.2
其他提供住宿的机构	7.5	5.4	38.9

A-1-10续表

单位：亿元

指 标	2014年	2013年	比上年增长(%)
不提供住宿的社会服务机构	**2413.8**	**2187.0**	**10.4**
老龄机构	7.9	8.4	-6.0
为残疾人提供服务的机构	1789.5	1760.1	1.7
救助低保服务机构	1.5	1.3	15.4
救灾储备单位	12.0	11.5	4.3
福利彩票发行机构	69.7	68.5	1.8
军队离退休人员管理中心	14.2	12.9	10.1
军队离退休人员活动中心	7.0	6.7	4.5
烈士纪念建筑物管理机构	51.2	49.1	4.3
社区服务机构和设施	460.8	268.5	71.6
二、成员组织和其他社会服务	**3893.1**	**3732.7**	**4.3**
成员组织	**3609.3**	**3465.7**	**4.1**
社会组织	**1560.6**	**1496.6**	**4.3**
社会团体	337.7	325.8	3.7
基金会	24.5	14.3	71.3
民办非企业	1198.4	1156.5	3.6
自治组织	**2048.6**	**1969.1**	**4.0**
居委会	372.2	349.8	6.4
村委会	1676.4	1619.3	3.5
其他社会服务	**283.8**	**267.0**	**6.3**
婚姻服务机构	**9.4**	**9.4**	
殡葬服务机构	**270.5**	**257.6**	**5.0**
殡仪馆	166.1	165.0	0.7
公墓	82.3	72.1	14.1
骨灰堂		0.4	
殡葬管理单位	22.1	20.1	10.0
三、其他事业单位	**46.8**	**46.8**	
行政机关	**168.3**	**185.4**	**-9.2**

A-1-11 社会服务机构增加值（按国民经济行业分类）

单位：亿元

指　标	2014年	2013年	比上年增长(%)
合计	**2734.4**	**2463.6**	**11.0**
社会服务	**2515.2**	**2251.9**	**11.7**
一、社会工作	**1314.4**	**1167.1**	**12.6**
提供住宿的社会服务机构	**354.7**	**332.7**	**6.6**
老年人与残疾人服务机构	**289.9**	**273.3**	**6.1**
城市养老服务机构	27.8	26.5	4.9
农村养老服务机构	30.9	36.8	-16.0
社会福利院	44.3	30.7	44.3
光荣院	5.3	5.1	3.9
荣誉军人康复医院	7.0	7.1	-1.4
复员军人疗养院	3.2	3.1	3.2
军休所	171.4	164.0	4.5
智障与精神疾病服务机构	**28.7**	**26.2**	**9.5**
社会福利医院	16.6	15.0	10.7
复退军人精神病院	12.1	11.2	8.0
儿童收养救助服务机构	**12.4**	**11.8**	**5.1**
儿童福利机构	11.2	10.6	5.7
未成年人救助保护中心	1.2	1.2	
其他提供住宿的服务机构	**23.7**	**21.4**	**10.7**
生活无着人员救助管理站	16.3	15.0	8.7
安置农场	0.4	0.8	-50.0
军供站	4.9	4.7	4.3
其他提供住宿的机构	2.1	0.9	133.3

A-1-11续表

单位：亿元

指　标	2014年	2013年	比上年增长(%)
不提供住宿的社会服务机构	**959.7**	**834.4**	**15.0**
老龄机构	7.4	6.6	12.1
为残疾人提供服务的机构	757.0	693.2	9.2
救助低保服务机构	2.8	2.7	3.7
救灾储备单位	1.5	1.3	15.4
福利彩票发行机构	17.7	17.6	0.6
军队离退休人员管理中心	39.8	24.1	65.1
军队离退休人员活动中心	1.0	0.9	11.1
烈士纪念建筑物管理机构	8.4	8.0	5.0
社区服务机构和设施	124.1	80.0	55.1
二、成员组织和其他社会服务	**1181.1**	**1064.7**	**10.9**
成员组织	**1081.7**	**972.9**	**11.2**
社会组织	**650.3**	**571.1**	**13.9**
社会团体	179.3	155.5	15.3
基金会	23.2	16.2	43.2
民办非企业	447.8	399.4	12.1
自治组织	**431.4**	**401.8**	**7.4**
居委会	109.9	107.0	2.7
村委会	321.5	294.8	9.1
其他社会服务	**99.4**	**91.8**	**8.3**
婚姻服务机构	**3.5**	**3.3**	**6.1**
殡葬服务机构	**95.8**	**88.5**	**8.3**
殡仪馆	48.3	48.2	0.2
公墓	39.4	33.5	17.6
骨灰堂		0.1	-80.0
殡葬管理单位	8.1	6.7	20.9
三、其他事业单位	**19.7**	**20.1**	**-2.0**
行政机关	**219.2**	**211.7**	**3.5**

A-1-12 社会服务机构增加值（按登记类型分类）

单位：亿元

指　标	2014年	2013年	比上年增长(%)
民政管理单位增加值合计	**2734.4**	**2463.6**	**11.0**
一、事业单位	**676.3**	**585.8**	**15.5**
收养类	160.9	147.8	8.9
城市老年福利机构	27.8	26.5	4.9
农村老年福利机构	30.9	36.8	-16.0
社会福利院	44.3	30.7	44.3
光荣院	5.3	5.1	3.9
荣誉军人康复医院	7.0	7.1	-1.4
复员军人疗养院	3.2	3.1	3.2
复退军人精神病院	12.1	11.2	8.0
社会福利医院	16.6	15.0	10.7
儿童福利机构	11.2	10.6	5.7
安置农场	0.4	0.8	-50.0
其他提供住宿的机构	2.1	0.9	133.3
救助类	17.5	16.2	8.0
生活无着人员救助管理站	16.3	15.0	8.7
未成年人救助保护中心	1.2	1.2	
救灾储备类	1.5	1.3	15.4
救灾储备单位	1.5	1.3	15.4
筹集资金类	17.7	17.6	0.6
福利彩票发行单位	17.7	17.6	0.6

A-1-12续表

单位：亿元

指　标	2014年	2013年	比上年增长(%)
优抚安置类	225.5	201.7	11.8
军休所	171.4	164.0	4.5
军供站	4.9	4.7	4.3
军队离退休人员管理中心	39.8	24.1	65.1
军队离退休人员活动中心	1.0	0.9	11.1
烈士纪念建筑物管理单位	8.4	8.0	5.0
社区服务类	124.2	80.0	55.3
社区服务指导中心	3.7	3.1	19.4
社区服务中心	20.6	17.5	17.7
社区服务站	54.3	40.1	35.4
养老等其他社区服务机构	45.6	19.3	
婚姻登记服务类	3.3	3.3	
殡葬服务类	95.8	88.5	8.3
殡仪馆	48.3	48.2	0.2
公墓	39.4	33.5	17.6
骨灰堂		0.1	
殡葬管理机构	8.1	6.7	20.9
其他	29.9	29.4	1.7
老龄行政机构	7.4	6.6	12.1
救助低保服务机构	2.8	2.7	3.7
其他事业单位	19.7	20.1	-2.0
二、成员组织			
社会组织	650.3	571.1	13.9
社会团体	179.3	155.5	15.3
基金会	23.2	16.2	43.2
民办非企业	447.8	399.4	12.1
自治组织	431.4	401.8	7.4
居委会	109.9	107.0	2.7
村委会	321.5	294.8	9.1
三、企业	**757.0**	**693.2**	**9.2**
为残疾人提供服务的机构	757.0	693.2	9.2
四、行政机关	**219.2**	**211.7**	**3.5**

A-1-13 基本建设投资与上年比较

单位：亿元、个

指 标	2014年	2013年	比上年增长(%)
计划总投资	**915.2**	**1036.1**	**-11.7**
本年计划投资	**266.0**	**311.9**	**-14.7**
提供住宿的社会工作机构	**147.4**	**195.3**	**-24.5**
老年人与残疾人服务机构	128.5	173.0	-25.7
智障与精神疾病服务机构	6.2	6.6	-6.1
儿童收养救助服务机构	8.1	11.1	-27.0
其他提供住宿的服务机构	4.6	4.6	
不提供住宿的社会工作机构	**36.1**	**55.4**	**-34.8**
其他	**35.3**	**61.2**	**-42.3**
自开始建设至本年底累计完成投资	**501.3**	**549.2**	**-8.7**
本年完成投资	**282.2**	**292.8**	**-3.6**
提供住宿的社会工作机构	**156**	**188.8**	**-17.4**
老年人与残疾人服务机构	134.2	167.3	-19.8
智障与精神疾病服务机构	6.5	6.4	1.6
儿童收养救助服务机构	10.4	10.5	-1.0
其他提供住宿的服务机构	4.9	4.6	6.5
不提供住宿的社会工作机构	**41.5**	**49.2**	**-15.7**
其他	**84.7**	**54.8**	**54.6**
国家投资	104.3	120.1	-13.2
国内贷款	3.5	1.4	150.0
利用外资	1.7	1.7	
福利彩票公益金	57.5	64.7	-11.1
其他	115.3	104.8	10.0
本年完工项目个数	**11355**	**15328**	**-25.9**

A-1-14 社会服务经费与上年比较

单位：亿元

指　标	2014年	2013年	比上年增长(%)
社会服务经费合计	**4404.0**	**4276.6**	**3.0**
占国家财政支出比重（%）	2.9	3.1	-0.2(百分点)
# 中央转移支付的事业费	2105.0	2149.7	-2.1
占社会服务经费的比重（%）	47.8	50.3	-2.5
# 国家基本建设投资	104.3	120.1	-13.2
# 公益金支出	231.3	195.5	18.3
按支出性质分			
抚恤	636.6	618.4	2.9
退役安置	456.8	435.3	4.9
社会福利	480.9	397.6	21.0
社会救助	2197.5	2172.4	1.2
# 城市居民最低生活保障	721.7	756.7	-4.6
农村最低生活保障	870.3	866.9	0.4
其他社会救助	321.5	291.4	10.3
医疗救助	284.0	257.4	10.3
自然灾害生活救助	124.4	178.7	-30.4
离退休人员经费	44.2	43.6	1.4
其他	463.6	430.6	7.7

A-1-15 中央级社会服务费和转移支付的社会服务费与上年比较

单位：万元

指　标	2014年	2013年	比上年增长(%)
合计	**21179140.0**	**21634580.4**	**-2.1**
中央级民政事业费	**128646.0**	**137419.9**	**-6.4**
民政管理事务	59927.8	46609.8	28.6
# 行政运行	5991.9	6043.8	-0.9
一般行政管理政务	12358.7	3431.9	260.1
机关服务	249.4	244.4	2.0
拥军优属	298.4	298.7	-0.1
老龄事务	980.5	1030.6	-4.9
民间组织管理	20761.4	19691.7	5.4
行政区划和地名管理	1247.8	807.2	54.6
基层政权和社区建设	341.0	443.8	-23.2
其他民政管理政务支出	17698.7	14617.7	21.1
自然灾害生活救助	23137.0	43506.0	-46.8
其他款项用于民政支出	45581.2	47304.1	-3.6
中央财政转移支付的民政经费	**21050494.04**	**21497160.48**	**-2.1**
# 抚恤	3380102.18	3697979	-8.6
退役安置	2887631.82	2774042	4.1
社会福利	634277.74	543649.48	16.7
最低生活保障	11012786.5	11687897	-5.8
医疗救助	1650084.8	1566688	5.3
自然灾害生活救助	963211	1019248	-5.5
其他	522400	207657	151.6

A-1-16 按支出形式分类的社会服务经费支出情况

单位：万元

指　标	2014年	2013年	占全部(%)	比上年增减额	比上年增长(%)
总计	**44041244.2**	**42765370.8**	**100.0**	**1275873.4**	**2.98**
直接发放	**35424060.4**	**33690680.3**	**80.4**	**1733380.1**	**5.14**
按标准发放和报销	26740287.4	25426105.1	60.7	1314182.3	5.17
发放数	26191173.3	24938318.7	59.5	1252854.6	5.02
定期发放	25908016.0	24705123.8	58.8	1202892.2	4.87
军队干部离休金	303946.6	287951.3	0.7	15995.3	5.55
军队干部退休金	1672077.7	1662363.8	3.8	9713.9	0.58
军队无军籍退休金	423724.2	316383.0	1.0	107341.2	33.93
地方干部、人员退休金、退职金	122568.9	128819.7	0.3	-6250.8	-4.85
离休、退休、退职金小计	2522317.4	2395517.8	5.7	126799.6	5.29
烈属和牺牲病故定期抚恤金	348231.3	353112.6	0.8	-4881.3	-1.38
伤残抚恤金	1066942.3	1010354.1	2.4	56588.2	5.6
在乡退伍红军老战士生活费	1641.8	2474.0		-832.2	-33.64
红军失散人员补助费	17446.7	27460.8		-10014.1	-36.47
复员退伍军人定期定量补助费	1564600.5	1593219.6	3.6	-28619.1	-1.8
"参战"退伍军人补助费	571973.5	547642.4	1.3	24331.1	4.44
"涉核"退伍军人补助费	89848.9	84506.7	0.2	5342.2	6.32
抚恤、补助费小计	3660685.0	3618770.2	8.3	41914.8	1.16
军队离休干部遗属、退休人员遗属定期定量补助费	16406.7	13433.6		2973.1	22.13
农村五保供养救济费	1898245.9	1723213.1	4.3	175032.8	10.16
农村最低生活保障金	8182245.5	7440641.9	18.6	741603.6	9.97
城市居民最低生活保障金	7217471.5	7567087.0	16.4	-349615.5	-4.62
传统救济	305192.9	303280.7	0.7	1912.2	0.63
定期定量救济费小计	17619562.5	17047656.3	40.0	571906.2	3.35
分散安置伤残军人护理费	27833.8	24257.9	0.1	3575.9	14.74
军队离休、退休人员护理费	36444.1	31162.3	0.1	5281.8	16.95
儿童福利支出	524454.6	512724.7	1.2	11729.9	2.29
老年人福利	1516718.6	1075034.6	3.4	441684.0	41.09
非定期发放	283157.3	233194.9	0.6	49962.4	21.43
烈士和牺牲病故人员一次性抚恤金	225984.4	203231.1	0.5	22753.3	11.2
企事业退休人员一次性抚恤金	7535.1	7600.7		-65.6	-0.86
离休、退休干部死亡丧葬补助费	49637.8	22363.1	0.1	27274.7	121.96
城市居民最低生活保障对象临时补助	496649.4	921889.5	1.1	-425240.1	-46.13
农村最低生活保障对象临时补助	520354.9	1228397.2	1.2	-708042.3	-57.64
报销数	549114.1	487786.4	1.3	61327.7	12.57
伤残补助费	70951.2	61431.8	0.2	9519.4	15.5
离休、退休干部其他费用	478162.9	426354.6	1.1	51808.3	12.15

A-1-16续表

单位：万元

指　标	2014年	2013年	占全部(%)	比上年增减额	比上年增长(%)
临时性发放	8683773.0	8264575.2	19.7	419197.8	5.07
烈军属复员退伍军人临时补助费	2364119.5	2260265.7	5.4	103853.8	4.59
退伍军人建房补助费	19940.9	20198.2	0.1	-257.3	-1.27
义务兵优待金	1131325.6	964378.5	2.6	166947.1	17.31
退役士兵自谋职业金	881878.6	830837.0	2.0	51041.6	6.14
城镇退役士兵生活补助	143759.8	132257.2	0.3	11502.6	8.7
优抚对象临时补助费小计	4541024.4	4207936.6	10.3	333087.8	7.92
灾民生活救济费	726829.5	1009445.7	1.7	-282616.2	-28
医疗救助	2839871.8	2574119.1	6.5	265752.7	10.32
其他对象临时救助	576047.3	473073.8	1.3	102973.5	21.77
单位拨款	**2961289.7**	**2812021.9**	**6.7**	**149267.8**	**5.31**
民政部门举办事业单位经费	2401955.6	2293641.8	5.5	108313.8	4.72
优抚事业单位	481858.3	435144.3	1.1	46714.0	10.74
荣誉军人康复医院	73310.5	68539.2	0.2	4771.3	6.96
复员军人慢性病疗养院	42299.4	32160.6	0.1	10138.8	31.53
复员退伍军人精神病院	100705.9	93801.9	0.2	6904.0	7.36
光荣院	87159.7	80831.4	0.2	6328.3	7.83
烈士纪念建筑物管理机构	94185.9	91133.4	0.2	3052.5	3.35
其他优抚事业单位	84196.9	68677.8	0.2	15519.1	22.6
社会福利事业单位	998606.2	928043.8	2.3	70562.4	7.6
社会福利院	518412.0	495319.7	1.2	23092.3	4.66
儿童福利院	154128.1	133016.6	0.4	21111.5	15.87
精神病人福利院	162598.4	132519.6	0.4	30078.8	22.7
流浪乞讨人员救助站	163467.7	167187.9	0.4	-3720.2	-2.23
军队离退休干部管理机构	307126.6	375917.5	0.7	-68790.9	-18.3
殡葬事业单位	614364.5	554536.2	1.4	59828.3	10.79
火葬场	253373.7	243437.4	0.6	9936.3	4.08
其他殡葬事业单位	360990.8	311098.8	0.8	49892.0	16.04
集体办事业单位补贴	377312.3	285014.9	0.9	92297.4	32.38
优抚事业单位	2570.2	2117.0		453.2	21.41
社会福利事业单位	374742.1	282897.9	0.9	91844.2	32.47
生产单位拨款	18649.6	18563.6		86.0	0.46
假肢厂、站	9661.6	8118.9		1542.7	19
安置农场	8988.0	10444.7		-1456.7	-13.95
灾民紧急抢救、转移、安置费	82393.8	110119.6	0.2	-27725.8	-25.18
救灾储备	80978.4	104682.0	0.2	-23703.6	-22.64
其他支出	**5655894.1**	**6262668.6**	**12.8**	**-606774.5**	**-9.69**

A-1-17 按支出性质分类的社会服务经费支出情况

单位：万元

指　标	2014年	2013年	占全部(%)	比上年增减额	比上年增长(%)
总计	**44041244.2**	**42765370.8**	**100.0**	**1275873.4**	**3.0**
优待抚恤支出合计	**6365744.2**	**6184310.6**	**14.5**	**181433.6**	**2.9**
死亡抚恤	618219.8	596955.5	1.4	21264.3	3.6
伤残抚恤	1137893.5	1071785.9	2.6	66107.6	6.2
在乡复员、退伍军人生活补助	2245511.4	2255303.5	5.1	-9792.1	-0.4
优抚事业单位	691267.1	699863.5	1.6	-8596.4	-1.2
义务兵优待金	1131325.6	964378.5	2.6	166947.1	17.3
其他优抚支出	541526.8	596023.7	1.2	-54496.9	-9.1
退役安置	**4567849.2**	**4352600.2**	**10.4**	**215249.0**	**5.0**
退伍军人安置	1171583.3	1098342.4	2.7	73240.9	6.7
军队移交政府的离退休人员安置	2877911.4	2693052.7	6.5	184858.7	6.9
军队移交政府离退休干部管理机构	307126.6	375917.5	0.7	-68790.9	-18.3
其他退役安置支出	211227.9	185287.6	0.5	25940.3	14.0
社会福利	**4809479.7**	**3975669.6**	**10.9**	**833810.1**	**21.0**
儿童福利	524454.6	512724.7	1.2	11729.9	2.3
老年人福利	1516718.6	1075034.6	3.4	441684.0	41.1
假肢矫形	20807.0	14227.7	0.1	6579.3	46.2
殡葬	614364.5	554536.2	1.4	59828.3	10.8
社会福利事业单位	1218868.6	1054198.5	2.8	164670.1	15.6
其他社会福利支出	914266.4	764947.9	2.1	149318.5	19.5
社会救助	**21975319.6**	**21724118.2**	**49.9**	**251201.4**	**1.2**
最低生活保障	15920071.9	16236126.1	36.2	-316054.2	-2.0
城市居民最低生活保障	7217471.5	7567087.0	16.4	-349615.5	-4.6
农村最低生活保障	8702600.4	8669039.1	19.8	33561.3	0.4

A-1-17续表

单位：万元

指　标	2014年	2013年	占全部(%)	比上年增减额	比上年增长(%)
其他社会救助	3215375.9	2913873.0	7.3	301502.9	10.4
医疗救助	2839871.8	2574119.1	6.5	265752.7	10.3
民政部门资助参合	322959.9	300427.0	0.7	22532.9	7.5
民政部门资助参保	161507.9	144061.2	0.4	17446.7	12.1
直接医疗救助	2041295.0	1804596.5	4.6	236698.5	13.1
优抚对象医疗补助	314109.0	325034.4	0.7	-10925.4	-3.4
自然灾害生活救助	**1244362.2**	**1786987.6**	**2.8**	**-542625.4**	**-30.4**
生活救济费	726829.5	1009445.7	1.7	-282616.2	-28.0
紧急抢救、安置、转移灾民支出	82393.8	110119.6	0.2	-27725.8	-25.2
救灾储备	80978.4	104682.0	0.2	-23703.6	-22.6
自然灾害灾后重建补助	252276.2	436158.1	0.6	-183881.9	-42.2
其他救助	101884.3	126582.2	0.2	-24697.9	-19.5
民政管理事务	**3305417.4**	**2967378.9**	**7.5**	**338038.5**	**11.4**
行政运行	768472.8	703821.7	1.7	64651.1	9.2
一般行政管理事务	145644.0	140587.2	0.3	5056.8	3.6
机关服务	22755.7	21345.4	0.1	1410.3	6.6
拥军优属	212913.0	204454.4	0.5	8458.6	4.1
老龄事务	287730.3	263798.2	0.7	23932.1	9.1
民间组织管理	72527.1	57838.9	0.2	14688.2	25.4
行政区划和地名管理	50244.3	54308.6	0.1	-4064.3	-7.5
基层政权和社区建设	895866.8	758420.3	2.0	137446.5	18.1
部队供应	57750.3	40981.0	0.1	16769.3	40.9
其他民政管理事务支出	791513.1	721823.2	1.8	69689.9	9.7
行政事业单位离退休	**442370.8**	**435817.7**	**1.0**	**6553.1**	**1.5**
地方离退休人员经费	135669.0	143243.2	0.3	-7574.2	-5.3
行政单位离退休	167520.1	159588.6	0.4	7931.5	5.0
事业单位离退休	123365.0	111312.1	0.3	12052.9	10.8
离退休人员管理机构	2008.3	2522.8		-514.5	-20.4
其他行政事业单位离退休支出	13808.4	19151.0		-5342.6	-27.9
其他	**1330701.1**	**1338488.0**	**3.0**	**-7786.9**	**-0.6**

A-2-1 社会工作类机构财务状况

单位：万元

指　标	2014年	2013年	比上年增长(%)
执行企业会计制度单位情况			
固定资产原价	18272589.6	17819100.0	2.54
本年折旧	1918752.3	1770212.0	8.39
营业收入	47465545.4	52462724.8	-9.53
营业成本	20169413.8	20749655.3	-2.80
营业税金及附加	830669.3	1082070.2	-23.23
销售费用	1899756.3	2554860.8	-25.64
管理费用	2344568.5	2236730.0	4.82
# 税金	257835.7	269064.9	-4.17
差旅费	90625.2	89652.4	1.09
财务费用	1558746.9	1014560.9	53.64
# 利息支出	1183391.4	706436.7	67.52
公允价值变动收益	13881.9	15392.8	-9.82
投资收益	29325.9	24948.6	17.55
营业利润	1270512.4	1596719.6	-20.43
营业外收入	261314.5	165738.3	57.67
# 政府补助	53777.7	20078.2	167.84
应付职工薪酬	3386388.0	2275714.5	48.81

A-2-1续表

单位：万元

指　标	2014年	2013年	比上年增长(%)
执行行政事业单位会计制度情况			
固定资产原价	10530176.0	9487436.7	10.99
上年结转和结余	829170.0	940370.5	-11.83
本年收入合计	8311246.1	8240070.7	0.86
#事业收入	3332713.6	3687462.0	-9.62
经营收入	204722.3	173418.9	18.05
本年支出合计	8152083.5	8066596.6	1.06
#工资福利支出	1732467.0	1447814.4	19.66
商品和服务支出	1626295.0	1585510.2	2.57
#取暖费	57652.2	50429.3	14.32
差旅费	24381.5	24857.0	-1.91
因公出国（境）费用	740.5	680.3	8.85
劳务费	112498.1	106408.1	5.72
工会经费	8213.1	6830.4	20.24
福利费	27581.5	29917.2	-7.81
对个人和家庭的补助	2630196.4	2327616.2	13.00
#抚恤金	28193.6	24940.0	13.05
生活补助	397172.1	342933.4	15.82
救济费	130495.9	102462.2	27.36
助学金	2635.0	2852.6	-7.63
奖励金	6374.0	5823.3	9.46
生产补贴	692.7	398.8	73.70
经营支出	63868.9	45952.7	38.99
收支结余	646756.5	437944.9	47.68
销售税金	9640.3	4669.1	106.47
执行民间非营利组织单位会计制度情况			
固定资产原价	3927116.6	3000559.9	30.88
上年结余	74842.0	53953.7	38.72
本年收入合计	1399974.9	1187693.9	17.87
# 捐赠收入	109196.5	94629.9	15.39
会费收入	107999.0	90566.1	19.25
本年费用合计	1315556.6	1117084.4	17.77
# 业务活动成本	777037.6	557800.1	39.30
# 人员费用	396229.1	263059.8	50.62
日常费用	149793.8	119702.1	25.14
固定资产折旧	100590.9	76876.5	30.85
税费	2708.1	2045.2	32.41
管理费用	399369.6	297372.7	34.30
# 人员费用	175921.6	134034.0	31.25
日常费用	88394.4	73135.5	20.86
固定资产折旧	43420.7	34124.9	27.24
税费	24826.3	1450.9	1611.10
净资产变动额	63155.7	43329.3	45.76

A-2-2 提供住宿的社会服务机构和社区养老情况与上年比较

指　标	机构与设施数（万张、%）			工作人员数（万张、%）		
	2014年	2013年	比上年增长(%)	2014年	2013年	比上年增长(%)
合计	**96094**	**45977**	**109.0**	**54.7**	**42.4**	**29.0**
老年人与残疾人服务机构	**92327**	**42475**	**117.4**	**47.7**	**35.6**	**34.0**
机构类	**33043**	**42475**	**-22.2**	**33.4**	**35.6**	**-6.2**
城市养老服务机构	7642	7077	8.0	12.2	11.0	10.9
农村养老服务机构	20261	30247	-33.0	13.0	16.4	-20.7
社会福利院	1864	1825	2.1	4.5	4.5	
光荣院	1411	1425	-1.0	1.2	1.2	
荣誉军人康复医院	44	42	4.8	0.5	0.5	
复员军人疗养院	38	38		0.3	0.3	
军休所（万户）	1783	1821	-2.1	1.7	1.7	
社区机构和设施类	**59284**			**14.3**		
社区养老机构和设施	18927			7.0		
社区互助型的养老设施	40357			7.3		
智障与精神疾病服务机构	**254**	**261**	**-2.7**	**2.6**	**2.5**	**4.0**
社会福利医院	156	155	0.6	1.4	1.4	
复退军人精神病院	98	106	-7.5	1.2	1.1	9.1
儿童收养救助服务机构	**890**	**803**	**10.8**	**1.5**	**1.4**	**7.1**
儿童福利院	545	529	3.0	1.3	1.2	8.3
流浪儿童救助保护中心	345	274	25.9	0.2	0.2	
其他提供住宿的服务机构	**2623**	**2438**	**7.6**	**2.9**	**2.9**	
生活无着人员救助管理站	1949	1891	3.1	1.8	1.8	
军供站	327	325	0.6	0.5	0.6	-16.7
其他	347	222	56.3	0.6	0.5	20.0

A-2-2续表

指 标	床位数（万张、%）			收养救助人数（万人、%）			年末床位利用率（%）
	2014年	2013年	比上年增长（%）	2014年	2013年	比上年增长（%）	
合计	**613.5**	**462.5**	**32.6**	**337.0**	**313.3**	**7.6**	**54.9**
老年人与残疾人服务机构	**577.8**	**429.6**	**34.5**	**320.4**	**298.2**	**7.4**	**55.5**
机构类	**390.3**	**429.6**	**-9.1**	**255.9**	**298.2**	**-14.2**	**65.6**
城市养老服务机构	108.5	97.1	11.7	57.7	53.5	7.9	53.2
农村养老服务机构	219.6	272.9	-19.5	155.7	201.2	-22.6	70.9
社会福利院	37.0	34.6	6.9	21.7	21.1	2.8	58.6
光荣院	9.4	8.8	6.8	5.4	5.5	-1.8	57.4
荣誉军人康复医院	0.9	0.9		0.6	0.5	20.0	66.7
复员军人疗养院	0.7	0.7		0.5	0.5		71.4
军休所（万户）	14.2	14.6	-2.7	14.3	15.9	-10.1	100.7
社区机构和设施类	**187.5**			**64.5**			**34.4**
社区养老机构和设施	71.1			35.4			49.8
社区互助型的养老设施	50.1			18.5			36.9
其他社区机构和设施	66.3			10.6			16.0
智障与精神疾病服务机构	**8.0**	**7.4**	**8.1**	**6.5**	**6.0**	**8.3**	**81.3**
社会福利医院	4.9	4.5	8.9	4.0	3.7	8.1	81.6
复退军人精神病院	3.1	2.9	6.9	2.5	2.3	8.7	80.6
儿童收养救助服务机构	**10.8**	**9.8**	**10.2**	**5.9**	**5.6**	**5.4**	**54.6**
儿童福利院	9.6	8.7	10.3	5.7	5.4	5.6	59.4
流浪儿童救助保护中心	1.2	1.1	9.1	0.2	0.2		16.7
其他提供住宿的服务机构	**16.9**	**15.7**	**7.6**	**4.2**	**3.5**	**20.0**	**24.9**
生活无着人员救助管理站	9.9	9.7	2.1	1.5	2.2	-31.8	15.2
军供站	3.7	3.7		1.0			27.0
其他	3.3	2.3	43.5	1.7	1.3	30.8	51.5

A-2-3 社区服务与上年比较

单位：万个、个、人、张

指 标	2014年	2013年	比上年增长(%)
社区服务机构和设施总数	**31.1**	**25.2**	**23.4**
社区服务指导中心	918	890	3.1
社区服务中心	23088	19014	21.4
社区服务站	120188	108377	10.9
社区养老机构和设施	18927		
社区互助型的养老设施	40357		
其他机构和设施	107114		
社区服务机构和设施覆盖率	**45.5**	**36.9**	**23.3**
便民利民网点数（万个）	**30.9**	**35.9**	**-13.9**
社区养老床位数	**1875053**	**641443**	**192.3**
日间照料床位	759655	417686	81.9
留宿照料床位	1115398	223757	398.5
社区服务志愿者组织数（万个）	**10.9**	**12.8**	**-14.8**

A-2-4 儿童收养与上年比较

单位：人、%

指　标	2014年	2013年	比上年增长(%)
孤儿数	**525179**	**548845**	**-4.31**
集中供养孤儿	93522	93899	-0.40
社会散居孤儿	431657	454946	-5.12
儿童收养服务			
收养登记合计(人)	22772	24460	-6.90
中国公民收养登记	19885	21230	-6.34
# 香港居民	120	139	-13.67
澳门居民	12	6	100.00
台湾居民	39	28	39.29
华侨	20	24	-16.67
外国人收养登记	2887	3230	-10.62
被收养人合计（人）	22876	24491	-6.59
# 女性	16158	17164	-5.86
残疾儿童	2637	2632	0.19
社会福利机构抚养的儿童	10336	9657	7.03
# 被外国人收养	2608	2695	-3.23
社会福利机构抚养的弃婴	6802	7814	-12.95
# 被外国人收养	184	524	-64.89
社会弃婴	1375	2466	-44.24
父母无力抚养的儿童	527	640	-17.66
# 被外国人收养	29	11	163.64
其他	3836	3914	-1.99

A-2-5 社会救助与上年比较

指　标	2014年	2013年	比上年增长(%)
救助总人数	**17679.0**	**17602.9**	**0.43**
城市			
城市居民最低生活保障人数（万人）	1877.0	2064.2	-9.1
# 女性	792.4	867.0	-8.6
残疾人	161.1	169.2	-4.8
三无对象	50.0	58.0	-13.8
# 老年人	315.8	330.3	-4.4
在职人员	37.5	45.1	-16.8
灵活就业	425.8	462.1	-7.9
登记失业	312.5	365.5	-14.5
未登记失业	398.7	416.8	-4.3
在校生	266.0	303.2	-12.3
其他未成年人	120.7	141.3	-14.6
城市居民最低生活保障家庭数（万户）	1026.1	1097.2	-6.5
城市居民最低生活保障费（亿元）	721.7	756.7	-4.6
城市居民最低生活保障平均标准（元/人、月）	410.5	373.3	10.0
城市居民最低生活保障平均支出水平（元/人、月）	285.6	264.2	8.1
城市“三无”救助人数（万人）	**7.6**	**8.6**	**-12.0**
城市临时救助户次数（万户次）	**202.0**	**323.0**	**-37.5**
农村			
农村最低生活保障人数（万人）	5207.2	5388.0	-3.35
农村最低生活保障家庭数（万户）	2943.6	2931.1	0.43
农村最低生活保障费（亿元）	870.3	866.9	0.39
农村最低生活保障平均标准（元/人、年）	2776.6	2433.9	14.08
农村最低生活保障平均支出水平（元/人、年）	129.4	1393.5	-90.71

A-2-5续表

指　标	2014年	2013年	比上年增长(%)
五保供养			
农村五保集中供养人数（万人）	174.3	183.5	-5.04
农村五保集中供养救济费（亿元）	79.8	74.7	6.78
农村五保集中供养平均标准(元/人、年)	5371.3	4685.0	14.65
农村五保集中供养平均支出水平(元/人、年)	4676.1	4078.3	14.66
农村五保分散供养人数（万人）	354.8	353.8	0.29
农村五保分散供养救济费（亿元）	110.1	97.6	12.76
农村五保分散供养平均标准(元/人、年)	4005.9	3498.5	14.50
农村五保分散供养平均支出水平(元/人、年)	3228.9	2724.3	18.52
传统救济人数（万人）	**74.5**	**73.0**	**2.07**
农村临时救助户次数（万户次）	**310.9**	**375.1**	**-17.12**
医疗救助			
民政部门直接救助人次数（万人次）	2395.3	2126.4	12.65
民政部门直接救助平均支出水平（元/人、次）	852.2	848.7	0.41
民政部门资助参加医疗保险人数（万人）	1702.0	1490.1	14.22
民政部门资助加医疗保险平均支出水平（元/人）	94.9	96.7	-1.86
民政部门资助参加合作医疗人数（万人）	5021.7	4868.7	3.14
民政部门资助参加合作医疗平均支出水平（元/人）	64.3	61.7	4.21
生活无着人员救助（万人次）	**351.7**	**348.5**	**0.92**

A-2-6 各省城市居民最低生活保障平均标准与上年比较

单位：元/人、月

地 区	2014年	2013年	比上年增长(%)
全 国	**410.5**	**373.3**	**10.0**
北 京	650.0	580.0	12.1
天 津	640.0	600.0	6.7
河 北	431.9	378.5	14.1
山 西	383.7	351.1	9.3
内蒙古	481.4	460.3	4.6
辽 宁	452.8	411.5	10.0
吉 林	371.1	322.5	15.1
黑龙江	446.8	387.7	15.2
上 海	710.0	640.0	10.9
江 苏	536.1	485.1	10.5
浙 江	573.3	515.5	11.2
安 徽	421.5	380.5	10.8
福 建	404.4	363.3	11.3
江 西	418.3	395.7	5.7
山 东	451.9	417.7	8.2
河 南	328.8	309.2	6.4
湖 北	411.0	375.1	9.6
湖 南	352.8	356.1	-0.9
广 东	454.5	380.4	19.5
广 西	340.1	334.7	1.6
海 南	379.6	353.3	7.4
重 庆	369.0	346.8	6.4
四 川	336.2	306.4	9.7
贵 州	395.0	347.6	13.6
云 南	359.6	323.9	11.0
西 藏	533.9	432.4	23.5
陕 西	388.5	374.7	3.7
甘 肃	328.3	279.0	17.6
青 海	351.0	330.8	6.1
宁 夏	304.8	287.6	6.0
新 疆	329.2	300.4	9.6

A-2-7 各省城市居民最低生活保障支出水平与上年比较

单位：元/人、月

地区	2014年	2013年	比上年增长(%)
全国	**269.1**	**264.2**	**1.8**
北京	820.7	510.9	60.6
天津	626.3	433.4	44.5
河北	268.4	231.9	15.7
山西	219.8	240.7	-8.7
内蒙古	335.1	367.5	-8.8
辽宁	275.7	312.7	-11.8
吉林	158.1	321.7	-50.9
黑龙江	343.9	290.3	18.5
上海	425.1	500.9	-15.1
江苏	500.7	296.5	68.9
浙江	353.3	400.4	-11.8
安徽	201.3	271.5	-25.8
福建	451.6	240.4	87.8
江西	280.3	226.5	23.8
山东	292.3	286.4	2.1
河南	208.1	207.2	0.4
湖北	221.1	246.6	-10.3
湖南	214.1	244.4	-12.4
广东	566.1	253.6	123.2
广西	220.6	228.3	-3.4
海南	383.6	237.1	61.8
重庆	368.8	257.9	43.0
四川	279.0	206.9	34.9
贵州	102.8	245.9	-58.2
云南	119.7	224.2	-46.6
西藏	229.5	384.4	-40.3
陕西	407.8	308.3	32.3
甘肃	260.3	268.9	-3.2
青海	314.1	267.9	17.2
宁夏	253.1	202.5	25.0
新疆	205.1	266.7	-23.1

A-2-8 社会捐赠与上年比较

指　标	2014年	2013年	比上年增长(%)
社会捐赠合计（万元）	**6065621.2**	**5750775.5**	**5.5**
民政部门直接接收的捐赠（万元）	**817062.0**	**1163269.0**	**-29.8**
直接接收捐赠情况			
捐赠款数额（万元）	795542.9	1076179.2	-26.1
捐赠衣被合计（万件）	5244.5	10405.0	-49.6
捐赠其他物资价值（万元）	80053.2	87089.8	-8.1
间接接收捐赠情况			
捐赠款数额（万元）	21519.1	50195.9	-57.1
捐赠衣被合计（万件）	105.6	739.1	-85.7
捐赠其他物资价值（万元）	39011.6	35081.4	11.2
受益人次数（万人次）	1695.0	1246.0	36.0
社会捐赠接收工作站、点数（个）	32061	30703	4.4
# 社会捐赠接收工作站数（个）	14126	15149	-6.8
慈善超市数（个）	10174	9492	7.2
各类社会组织接收捐赠（万元）	**5248559.2**	**4587506.5**	**14.4**

注：由于社会组织年检工作滞后于年报汇总工作，社会组织捐赠数据为2013年。

A-2-9 自然灾害与上年比较

指　标	2014年	2013年	比上年增长(%)
农作物受灾情况总计(千公顷)			
受灾	24890.7	31349.8	-20.6
绝收	3090.3	3844.4	-19.6
旱灾			
受灾	12271.7	14100.4	-13.0
绝收	1484.7	1416.1	4.8
洪涝(含山体滑坡和泥石流)			
受灾	4738.9	8765.8	-45.9
绝收	628.2	1539.4	-59.2
风雹			
受灾	3225.4	3387.3	-4.8
绝收	457.7	412.4	11.0
台风			
受灾	2483.1	2670.1	-7.0
绝收	348.7	289.5	20.4
地震			
受灾	36.4	115.1	-68.4
绝收	2.8	6.3	-55.6
雪灾、低温冷冻			
受灾	2132.5	2320.1	-8.1
绝收	168.2	180.7	-6.9
人口受灾情况			
受灾（万人次）	24353.7	38818.7	-37.3
死亡人口（含失踪）（人）	1818	2284	-20.4
紧急转移人口（万人次）	601.7	1215.0	-50.5
损失情况			
倒塌房屋（万间）	45.0	87.5	-48.6
损坏房屋（万间）	354.2	770.3	-54.0
直接经济损失（亿元）	3373.8	5808.4	-41.9

A-2-10 国家优抚、安置对象与上年比较

单位：人

指　标	2014年	2013年	比上年增长(%)
重点优抚对象人数	**9173281**	**9504555**	**-3.5**
抚恤	1077331	1178219	-8.6
烈士家属抚恤	197955	240375	-17.6
因公牺牲抚恤	48179	55734	-13.6
病故军人家属抚恤	65076	70291	-7.4
伤残人员抚恤	766121	811819	-5.6
补助	8095950	8326336	-2.8
在乡红军老战士	341	647	-47.3
在乡西路军红军老战士	87	117	-25.6
红军失散人员	11269	18976	-40.6
在乡复员军人	993204	1260945	-21.2
带病回乡退伍军人	1242020	1306479	-4.9
60岁以上农村籍退伍军人	3748039	3566766	
参战退役人员	1448018	1523763	-5.0
参试退役人员	188072	199215	-5.6
部分60周岁以上烈士(含错杀被平反)人员子女	229308	222838	
其他补助人数	235592	226590	4.0
本年接收离退休人员和安置复原干部数	**30237**	**39343**	**-23.1**
军队干部（含地方）	10288	11427	-10.0
军队退休士官	503	570	-11.8
军队无军籍职工	16908	26709	-36.7
复员干部	2538	637	298.4
当年批准的烈士	**267**	**200**	**33.5**
零散烈士纪念建筑物	**11365**	**13601**	**-16.4**
优待			
优待优抚对象（万户）	335.5	340.3	-1.4
# 军属（万户）	88.3	95.8	-7.8
优待金（亿元）	151.0	135.1	11.8
# 军属（亿元）	69.3	64.6	7.3

A-3-1 社会组织财务状况

单位：万元

指　标	2014年	2013年	比上年增长(%)
执行行政事业单位会计制度情况			
固定资产原价	259575.3	230469.3	12.6
上年结转和结余	21959.1	21577.4	1.8
本年收入合计	378379.6	360143.7	5.1
# 事业收入	33507.6	25508.0	31.4
经营收入	27056.1	22245.2	21.6
本年支出合计	89551.3	76056.5	17.7
# 工资福利支出	37714.3	25773.6	46.3
商品和服务支出	19563.9	14702.8	33.1
# 取暖费	253.3	390.0	-35.1
差旅费	834.1	967.2	-13.8
因公出国（境）费用			
劳务费	692.1	660.6	4.8
工会经费	399.4	351.3	13.7
福利费	778.1	962.1	-19.1
对个人和家庭的补助	5507.5	6087.2	-9.5
# 抚恤金	11.0	12.0	-8.3
生活补助	245.2	142.1	72.6
救济费	14.6	16.6	-12.0
助学金	163.4	127.5	28.2
奖励金	230.0	235.0	-2.1
生产补贴	273.3	232.0	17.8
经营支出	176.4	197.6	-10.7
收支结余	1492.5	1053.5	41.7
销售税金	1040.30	1373.8	-24.3

A-3-1续表

单位：万元

指　标	2014年	2013年	比上年增长(%)
执行民间非营利组织单位会计制度情况			
固定资产原价	15346719.3	14735831.8	4.1
上年结余	7923623.1	5849439.7	35.5
本年收入合计	20059288.4	18488799.5	8.5
# 捐赠收入	5248559.2	4587506.5	14.4
会费收入	1819941.6	2290481.7	-20.5
本年费用合计	19122330.6	16676894.8	14.7
# 业务活动成本	12099571.8	10519432.3	15.0
# 人员费用	3383741.8	3065213.8	10.4
日常费用	1771261.0	1915178.4	-7.5
固定资产折旧	847865.7	589198.6	43.9
税费	162677.6	153772.2	5.8
管理费用	4217260.2	3894350.8	8.3
# 人员费用	1630606.3	1458542.1	11.8
日常费用	610696.1	577864.5	5.7
固定资产折旧	308281.6	278985.0	10.5
税费	87410.1	99149.8	-11.8
净资产变动额	9806108.6	4398132.3	123.0

A-3-2 社会组织分类情况与上年比较

单位：个

指　标	2014年	2013年	比上年增长(%)
社会组织合计	**606048**	**547245**	**10.7**
社会团体	**309736**	**289026**	**7.2**
按活动区域分			
中央级	1941	1908	1.7
省级	27973	26569	5.3
地级	76211	72075	5.7
县级	203611	188474	8.0
基金会	**4117**	**3549**	**16.0**
按性质分类			
公募性	1470	1378	6.7
非公募性	2610	2137	22.1
涉外基金会	9	8	
境外代表机构	28	26	7.7
民办非企业	**292195**	**254670**	**14.7**
按性质分类			
法人	228366	194827	17.2
合伙	7033	6951	1.2
个体	56796	52892	7.4

A-3-3 自治组织财务状况

单位：万元

指　标	2014年	2013年	比上年增长(%)
执行企业会计制度单位情况			
固定资产原价	2863527.7	2710492.8	5.6
本年折旧	154016.3	97026.5	58.7
营业收入	1362536.0	1170136.8	16.4
营业成本	1057966.8	597710.7	77.0
营业税金及附加	20949.6	17664.6	18.6
销售费用	39664.3	34488.4	15.0
管理费用	262901.7	298542.1	-11.9
# 税金	4113.0	3606.1	14.1
差旅费	566.7	1130.1	-49.9
财务费用	-8149.7	-26013.1	43.2
# 利息支出	-21569.3	-44993.2	2.4
公允价值变动收益	30.1	33.1	-9.1
投资收益	41995.8	34940.6	20.2
营业利润	24846.5	15205.5	63.4
营业外收入	141390.6	64087.7	120.6
#政府补助	48597.7	40936.3	18.7
应付职工薪酬	99631.6	100144.0	-0.5

A-3-3续表

单位：万元

指　标	2014年	2013年	比上年增长(%)
执行行政事业单位会计制度情况			
固定资产原价	15128537.8	14761875.6	2.5
上年结转和结余	878930.5	782291.3	12.4
本年收入合计	8366917.6	7356717.6	13.7
#事业收入	2100182.4	2054096.4	2.2
经营收入	633541.5	495967.9	27.7
本年支出合计	11373307.6	6948677.2	63.7
#工资福利支出	1936016.0	1862284.5	4.0
商品和服务支出	1860147.8	1742872.7	6.7
#取暖费	75776.8	44509.3	70.2
差旅费	65561.3	63052.8	4.0
因公出国（境）费用	1102.1	1087.9	1.3
劳务费	167477.6	167196.7	0.2
工会经费	14159.3	14104.7	0.4
福利费	152721.0	129752.6	17.7
对个人和家庭的补助	308360.0	284576.1	8.4
#抚恤金	3489.9	3249.3	7.4
生活补助	85213.6	66111.3	28.9
救济费	5162.0	1745.6	195.7
助学金	8173.2	9155.5	-10.7
奖励金	6149.4	6210.2	-1.0
生产补贴	9790.9	2604.9	275.9
经营支出	49546.2	28273.5	75.2
收支结余	30651.1	12307.2	
销售税金	13423.3	18291.0	-26.6
执行民间非营利组织单位会计制度情况			
固定资产原价	2494387.5	2218317.5	12.4
上年结余	90812.2	78777.9	15.3
本年收入合计	2246029.9	2277945.9	-1.4
# 捐赠收入	27275.8	27077.5	0.7
会费收入	95641.6	97933.6	-2.3
本年费用合计	833931.8	840258.8	-0.8
# 业务活动成本	461111.6	468877.2	-1.7
# 人员费用	143556.9	146171.0	-1.8
日常费用	87746.0	76432.4	14.8
固定资产折旧	79719.1	88263.4	-9.7
税费	8888.2	8037.7	10.6
管理费用	216370.0	219837.9	-1.6
# 人员费用	86798.0	88616.2	-2.1
日常费用	46458.5	45350.9	2.4
固定资产折旧	19475.2	19105.3	1.9
税费	5709.0	5913.3	-3.5
净资产变动额	86599.9	107540.8	-19.5

A-3-4 自治组织主要指标与上年比较

单位：个、人

指　标	2014年	2013年	比上年增长(%)
城市			
社区居委会	96693	94620	2.2
居民小组	1357913	1356954	0.1
居民委员会成员人数	497038	484015	2.7
# 中共党员	265098	258341	2.6
# 女性	240739	234413	2.7
居委会选举情况			
当年进行选举的居委会数	27337	19674	38.9
当年参选人口数	60995065	47359318	28.8
# 登记选民数	54530894	41752811	30.6
# 参选人数	42225351	33317825	26.7
农村			
村民委员会	585451	588547	-0.5
村民小组	4704267	4664307	0.9
村民委员会成员人数	2305024	2323113	-0.8
# 中共党员	1315790	1344643	-2.1
# 女性	526409	526435	
村委会选举情况			
当年进行选举的村委会数	302832	130763	131.6
当年参选村人口数	368872058	169057485	118.2
# 登记选民数	343801097	157432303	118.4
# 参选人数	301390325	139419135	116.2

A-3-5 其他社会服务机构财务状况

单位：万元

指　标	2014年	2013年	比上年增长(%)
执行企业会计制度单位情况			
固定资产原价	922067.8	767595.3	20.1
本年折旧	80285.4	71829.7	11.8
营业收入	909193.5	650281.3	39.8
营业成本	364205.6	211523.7	72.2
营业税金及附加	10265.4	5339.6	92.3
销售费用	74504.2	79569.2	-6.4
管理费用	158282.6	128439.2	23.2
# 税金	5032.9	5116.3	-1.6
差旅费	2335.3	1478.3	58.0
财务费用	6675.4	7413.6	-10.0
# 利息支出	2044.0	3069.0	-33.4
公允价值变动收益			
投资收益	418.0	396.2	5.5
营业利润	171638.9	159947.2	7.3
营业外收入	5814.7	6575.1	-11.6
#政府补助	1840.3	4195.2	-56.1
应付职工薪酬	69787.5	54139.4	28.9

A-3-5续表

单位：万元

指　标	2014年	2013年	比上年增长(%)
执行行政事业单位会计制度情况			
固定资产原价	1858650.8	1875873.8	-0.9
上年结转和结余	109889.2	87091.2	26.2
本年收入合计	1462109.8	1410394.2	3.7
#事业收入	702973.6	688144.0	2.2
经营收入	262144.2	248893.1	5.3
本年支出合计	1367846.6	1363074.6	0.4
#工资福利支出	331822.0	310350.7	6.9
商品和服务支出	515119.2	513727.7	0.3
#取暖费	6955.2	7598.5	-8.5
差旅费	4548.5	4824.8	-5.7
因公出国（境）费用	59.2	78.3	-24.4
劳务费	38679.6	32503.7	19.0
工会经费	2226.7	2061.8	8.0
福利费	7453.4	10034.0	-25.7
对个人和家庭的补助	63470.1	61841.9	2.6
#抚恤金	1408.2	1407.2	0.1
生活补助	3429.2	3113.0	10.2
救济费	593.0	285.1	108.0
助学金	134.1	136.9	-2.0
奖励金	1360.8	1143.3	19.0
生产补贴	1386.3	1760.3	-21.2
经营支出	131134.0	122128.3	7.4
收支结余	63252.4	38633.2	
销售税金	3790.3	3254.3	16.5
执行民间非营利组织单位会计制度情况			
固定资产原价	57747.2	26728.9	116.0
上年结余	2992.7	2144.3	39.6
本年收入合计	13247.5	8069.1	64.2
# 捐赠收入	611.7	424.9	44.0
会费收入	1184.6	209.0	466.8
本年费用合计	10394.6	6377.1	63.0
# 业务活动成本	7104.3	3582.0	98.3
# 人员费用	1930.0	995.7	93.8
日常费用	1784.0	917.4	94.5
固定资产折旧	1640.4	355.4	361.6
税费	159.0	37.4	325.1
管理费用	2895.9	1615.9	79.2
# 人员费用	912.5	556.8	63.9
日常费用	1091.6	430.7	153.4
固定资产折旧	213.3	184.1	15.9
税费	25.0	3.9	541.0
净资产变动额	1080.6	620.0	74.3

A-3-6 其他社会服务主要指标与上年比较

指 标	2014年	2013年	比上年增长(%)
婚姻服务			
结婚登记	13067426	13469267	-3.0
内地居民登记结婚对数（对）	13020405	13414255	-2.9
初婚人数（人）	22868064	23859646	-4.2
再婚人数（人）	3266788	3078888	6.1
其中：女性	1686629	1565397	7.7
恢复结婚（对）	348285	298766	16.6
涉外及华侨、港澳台居民登记结婚（对数）	47021	55012	-14.5
每千居民之结婚宗数（‰）	9.6	9.9	-0.3(千分点)
办理离婚登记（对）	3636754	3500111	3.9
民政部门办理离婚对数（对）	2957295	2815369	5.0
内地居民办理离婚	2950581	2808831	5.0
华侨、港澳台居民登记离婚	6714	6538	2.7
各级法院办理离婚件数（件）	679459	684742	-0.8
每千居民之离婚宗数（‰）	2.7	2.6	0.1(千分点)
办理婚姻登记业务的处数（处）	6797	6780	0.3
殡葬服务			
火化炉数(台)	5908	5743	2.9
全年处理遗体数（具）	4593037	4688910	-2.0
火化率(%)	47.0	48.2	-1.2(百分点)
穴位数（个）	14318347	13039598	9.8
安葬数（具）	8963554	8932865	0.3

社会服务
历年统计资料

04

B-1-1 县及以上行政区划

单位：个

年 份	省 级	地 级（不含地级市）	县级（不含县级市、市辖区）	市			市辖区	县级合计
					地 级	县 级		
1978	30	212	2153	193	98	92	408	2653
1979	30	211	2153	216	104	109	428	2690
1980	30	211	2151	223	107	113	511	2775
1981	30	208	2144	233	108	122	514	2780
1982	30	210	2140	245	112	130	527	2797
1983	30	178	2091	289	144	142	552	2785
1984	30	175	2069	300	147	150	595	2814
1985	30	165	2046	324	162	159	621	2826
1986	30	159	2017	353	166	184	629	2830
1987	30	156	1986	381	170	208	632	2826
1988	31	151	1936	434	183	248	647	2831
1989	31	151	1919	450	185	262	648	2829
1990	31	151	1903	467	185	279	651	2833
1991	31	151	1894	479	187	289	650	2833
1992	31	148	1848	517	191	323	662	2833
1993	31	139	1795	570	196	371	669	2835
1994	31	127	1735	622	206	413	697	2845
1995	31	124	1716	640	210	427	706	2849
1996	31	117	1696	666	218	445	717	2858
1997	33	110	1693	668	222	442	727	2862
1998	33	104	1689	668	227	437	737	2863
1999	34	95	1682	667	236	427	749	2858
2000	34	74	1674	663	259	400	787	2861
2001	34	67	1660	662	265	393	808	2861
2002	34	57	1649	660	275	381	830	2860
2003	34	51	1642	660	282	374	845	2861
2004	34	50	1636	661	283	374	852	2862
2005	34	50	1636	661	283	374	852	2862
2006	34	50	1635	656	283	369	856	2860
2007	34	50	1635	655	283	368	856	2859
2008	34	50	1635	655	283	368	856	2859
2009	34	50	1636	654	283	367	855	2858
2010	34	50	1633	657	283	370	853	2856
2011	34	48	1627	657	284	369	857	2853
2012	34	48	1624	657	285	368	860	2852
2013	34	47	1613	658	286	368	872	2853
2014	34	45	1596	649	288	361	897	2854

B-1-2 乡镇级行政区划

单位：个

年份	乡镇级区划数	镇数	乡数	#民族乡	街道办事处	区公所
1978	6195	2173				4022
1979	10424	2361			4444	3619
1980						
1981	11434	2678			4965	3791
1982						
1983	49695	2968	35514		5304	5909
1984	106439	7186	85290		5844	8119
1985	104900	9140	82450	3144	5402	7908
1986	83954	10718	61353	2936	5718	6165
1987	81025	11103	58739	3020	5680	5503
1988	65345	11481	45195	1571	5099	3570
1989	65419	11873	44624	1755	5420	3502
1990	65188	12084	44397	1980	5269	3438
1991	63391	12455	42654	1403	5186	3096
1992	54830	14539	33827	1348	5233	1231
1993	54863	15805	32445	1351	5470	1143
1994	54605	16702	31463	1322	5372	1068
1995	53360	17532	29502	1330	5596	730
1996	51336	18171	27056	1383	5565	544
1997	50967	18925	25966	1545	5678	398
1998	50999	19216	25712	1517	5732	339
1999	50750	19756	24745	1222	5904	345
2000	51024	20312	24555	1356	5902	255
2001	46369	20358	20012	1165	5972	27
2002	44822	20600	18640	1162	5516	66
2003	44067	20226	18064	1149	5751	26
2004	43275	19892	17534	1127	5829	20
2005	41636	19522	15951	1093	6152	11
2006	41040	19369	15306	1089	6355	10
2007	40813	19249	15120	1094	6434	10
2008	40828	19234	15067	1097	6524	3
2009	40858	19322	14848	1098	6686	2
2010	40906	19410	14571	1096	6923	2
2011	40466	19683	13587	1086	7194	2
2012	40446	19881	13281	1064	7282	2
2013	40497	20117	12812	1035	7566	2
2014	40381	20401	12282	1020	7696	2

B-1-3 全国人口情况

单位：万人、%

年份	总人口	城镇	乡村	农村贫困人口	65岁及以上老年人口	65岁及以上人口比重	60岁及以上老年人口	60岁及以上人口比重	出生人口	死亡人口	当年净增人口
1978	96259	17245	79014	25000							
1979	97542	18495	79047								1283
1980	98705	19140	79565								1163
1981	100072	20171	79901								1367
1982	101654	21480	80174		4991	4.9					1469
1983	103008	22274	80734								954
1984	104357	24017	80340	12800							
1985	105851	25094	80757	12500							1164
1986	107507	26366	81141	13100							1476
1987	109300	27674	81626	12200	5968	5.4					1500
1988	111026	28661	82365	9600							1541
1989	112704	29540	83164	10200							1577
1990	114333	30195	84138	8500	6368	5.6			2391	762	1629
1991	115823	31203	84260						2258	768	1490
1992	117171	32175	84996	8000					2119	771	1348
1993	118517	33173	85344						2126	780	1346
1994	119850	34169	85681	7000					2104	771	1333
1995	121121	35174	85947	6540	7510	6.2			2063	792	1271
1996	122389	37304	85085		7833	6.4			2067	799	1268
1997	123626	39449	84177	4962	8085	6.5			2038	801	1237
1998	124761	41608	83153	4210	8359	6.7			1942	807	1135
1999	125786	43748	82038	3412	8679	6.9			1834	809	1025
2000	126743	45906	80837	3209	8821	7.0			1771	814	957
2001	127627	48064	79563	2927	9062	7.1			1702	818	884
2002	128453	50212	78241	2820	9377	7.3			1647	821	826
2003	129227	52376	76851	2900	9692	7.5			1599	825	774
2004	129988	54283	75705	2610	9857	7.6			1593	832	761
2005	130756	56212	74544	2365	10055	7.7	14408	11.03	1617	849	768
2006	131448	57706	73742	2148	10419	7.9	14901	11.3	1584	892	692
2007	132129	59379	72750	4320	10636	8.1	15340	11.6	1594	913	681
2008	132802	60667	72135	4007	10956	8.3	15989	12	1608	935	673
2009	133450	62186	71288	3597	11309	8.5	16714	12.5	1615	943	672
2010	134091	66558	67415	2688	11883.2	8.9	17764.9	13.26	1596	953	642
2011	134735	69079	65656	12238	12288	9.1	18499	13.7	1604	960	644
2012	135404	71182	64222	9899	12714	9.4	19390	14.3	1635	966	669
2013	136072	73111	62961	8249	13161	9.7	20243	14.9	1640	972	668
2.14	136782	74916	61866	7017	13755	10.1	21242	15.5	1687	977	710

注：本表资料来源于国家统计局。

B-1-4 社会服务机构（按登记类型分类）

单位：万个

年 份	合 计	事业单位	福利企业	社会组织	自治组织	行政机关
1978	1.1	1.1	0.1			
1979	1.3	1.2	0.1			
1980	1.4	1.3	0.1			
1981	1.5	1.3	0.2			
1982	1.7	1.6	0.2			
1983	40.2	1.9	0.6		37.7	
1984	103.6	2.6	0.7		100.3	
1985	107.7	3.3	1.5		103.0	
1986	101.2	3.9	2.0		95.3	
1987	100.1	4.2	2.8		93.2	
1988	106.7	4.3	4.0	0.4	97.8	
1989	111.8	4.4	4.2	0.5	102.8	
1990	119.8	4.5	4.2	1.1	110.0	
1991	129.2	4.7	4.4	8.3	111.9	
1992	136.1	4.8	5.0	15.5	110.8	
1993	139.7	5.3	5.7	16.8	112.0	
1994	140.3	5.2	6.0	17.4	111.7	
1995	133.7	5.2	6.0	18.1	104.4	
1996	133.9	5.3	5.9	18.5	104.2	
1997	131.4	5.3	5.6	18.1	102.4	
1998	122.2	5.4	5.1	16.6	95.2	
1999	115.7	5.4	4.5	14.3	91.6	
2000	109.5	6.1	4.1	15.3	84.0	
2001	110.4	5.7	3.8	21.1	79.2	0.6
2002	111.0	5.8	3.6	24.5	76.7	0.5
2003	110.3	5.8	3.4	26.7	74.0	0.4
2004	111.5	6.7	3.2	28.9	72.2	0.4
2005	113.0	6.6	3.1	32.0	70.9	0.4
2006	116.0	6.7	3.0	35.4	70.5	0.4
2007	118.0	7.0	2.5	38.7	69.5	0.3
2008	119.6	6.6	2.4	41.4	68.8	0.4
2009	126.2	12.1	2.3	43.1	68.4	0.3
2010	126.9	11.6	2.2	44.6	68.2	0.3
2011	129.8	13.1	2.2	46.2	67.9	0.3
2012	146.5	26.3	2	49.9	68	0.3
2013	156.5	31.4	1.8	54.7	68.3	0.3
2014	166.8	36.0	1.7	60.6	68.2	0.3

B-1-5 社会服务机构（按行业分类分）

单位：万个

年 份	合 计	社会工作	成员组织			其他社会服务	其他事业单位	民政系统行政机关
				社会组织	自治组织			
1978	1.1	0.8				0.3		
1979	1.3	1.0				0.3		
1980	1.4	1.1				0.3		
1981	1.5	1.2				0.3		
1982	1.7	1.4				0.3		
1983	40.2	2.2	37.7		37.7	0.3		
1984	103.6	3.0	100.3		100.3	0.3		
1985	107.7	4.5	103.0		103.0	0.3		
1986	101.2	5.6	95.3		95.3	0.3		
1987	100.1	6.6	93.2		93.2	0.3		
1988	106.7	8.1	98.3	0.4	97.8	0.3		
1989	111.8	8.3	103.3	0.5	102.8	0.3		
1990	119.8	8.4	111.1	1.1	110.0	0.3		
1991	129.2	8.7	120.2	8.3	111.9	0.3		
1992	136.1	9.5	126.3	15.5	110.8	0.3		
1993	139.7	10.7	128.7	16.8	112.0	0.3		
1994	140.3	10.9	129.1	17.4	111.7	0.3		
1995	133.6	10.9	122.4	18.1	104.4	0.3		
1996	133.9	10.9	122.7	18.5	104.2	0.3		
1997	131.4	10.6	120.5	18.1	102.4	0.3		
1998	122.2	10.2	111.8	16.6	95.2	0.3		
1999	115.7	9.5	105.9	14.3	91.6	0.3		
2000	109.5	9.8	99.3	15.3	84.0	0.3		
2001	110.4	9.2	100.3	21.1	79.2	0.3		0.6
2002	111.0	9.1	101.2	24.5	76.7	0.3		0.5
2003	110.3	8.9	100.7	26.7	74.0	0.3		0.4
2004	111.5	9.6	101.1	28.9	72.2	0.3		0.4
2005	113.0	9.5	102.9	32.0	70.9	0.3		0.4
2006	116.0	9.2	105.9	35.4	70.5	0.5		0.4
2007	118.0	9.0	108.2	38.7	69.5	0.5		0.3
2008	119.6	8.4	110.2	41.4	68.8	0.6		0.4
2009	126.2	13.8	111.5	43.1	68.4	0.6		0.3
2010	126.9	13.2	112.8	44.6	68.2	0.6		0.3
2011	129.8	14.6	114.1	46.2	67.9	0.7		0.3
2012	146.5	27.5	117.9	49.9	68	0.6	0.2	0.3
2013	156.5	32.3	123.0	54.7	68.3	0.6	0.2	0.3
2014	166.8	37.1	128.8	60.6	68.2	0.7	0.2	0.3

注：2012年开始社会工作中包含其他社区服务机构。

B-1-6 社会服务机构职工

单位：万人

年 份	合 计	社会工作	成员组织	社会组织	自治组织	其他社会服务	其他事业单位	行政机关	乡、镇民政助理员
1978	19.7	19.7							
1979	21.9	21.9							
1980	25.3	25.3							
1981	27.8	27.8							
1982	29.1	29.1							
1983	41.5	41.5							
1984	48.0	48.0							
1985	497.9	83.4	414.5		414.5				
1986	506.2	104.1	402.1		402.1				
1987	529.1	132.2	396.9		396.9				
1988	569.6	166.9	402.7		402.7				
1989	587.5	171.5	416.0		416.0				
1990	631.8	179.3	452.5		452.5				
1991	661.2	192.7	468.5		468.5				
1992	691.3	213.9	477.4		477.4				
1993	733.9	230.0	503.9		503.9				
1994	749.6	243.1	506.5		506.5				
1995	694.2	245.7	448.5		448.5				
1996	676.0	229.2	446.8		446.8				
1997	681.1	238.2	428.6		428.6			14.3	
1998	649.2	225.0	409.4		409.4			14.8	
1999	629.9	213.7	401.4		401.4			14.8	5.9
2000	580.3	203.4	363.4		363.4			13.5	5.7
2001	577.3	202.4	362.8		362.8			12.1	4.6
2002	537.4	192.4	333.8		333.8			11.2	4.1
2003	562.6	193.0	358.8		358.8			10.8	3.7
2004	543.7	197.8	334.6		334.6			11.3	3.9
2005	509.0	189.5	311.1		311.1			8.4	5.5
2006	903.8	183.0	712.5	425.2	287.3			8.3	4.6
2007	938.4	190.4	739.6	456.9	282.7			8.4	4.7
2008	967.4	206.9	751.8	475.8	276.0			8.7	4.5
2009	1038.1	207.5	821.8	544.7	277.1			8.8	4.7
2010	1138.4	234.0	895.5	618.2	277.3			8.9	5.0
2011	1129.8	235.7	876.6	599.3	277.3	8.5		9.0	4.9
2012	1154.0	241.4	892.5	613.3	279.2	8.6	2.2	9.3	5.2
2013	1207.0	269.2	917.3	636.6	280.7	9.1	2.0	9.4	5.2
2014	1260.4	277.3	962.5	682.3	280.2	9.3	1.9	9.5	5.4

注：合计数不含乡镇助理员。

B-1-7 社会工作师

单位：人

年　份	报考人数	考试通过人数	社会服务行业现在人数	行政机关	社会工作	成员组织	其他社会服务	其他事业单位
2008	77698	4192	3144	286	1496	1191	171	
2009	46015	4227	7360	758	3809	2544	249	
2010	25547	2664	9901	922	5176	3473	330	
2011	25500	2338	11604	854	5165	5247	338	
2012	34245	6104	18215	1114	6276	10056	443	326
2013	48287	11658	23197	1280	8014	12994	560	349
2014	62881	7427	27257	1475	10252	14442	681	407

B-1-8 助理社会工作师

单位：人

年　份	报考人数	考试通过人数	社会服务行业现在人数	行政机关	社会工作	成员组织	其他社会服务	其他事业单位
2008	60139	20648	17574	609	4727	11840	398	
2009	38204	6611	24095	798	5530	17388	379	
2010	46047	5428	24700	969	6724	16517	490	
2011	54515	8068	29626	963	10686	17419	558	
2012	92621	23846	37599	1163	11998	23513	645	280
2013	121937	27300	44565	1264	15471	26871	694	265
2014	144813	28431	52174	1404	18295	31381	803	291

B-1-9 社会服务职业技能人员情况

单位：人

年 份	合格总人数	养老护理员	假肢类技能人员	孤残儿童护理员	灾害信息员	殡葬类技能人员
2007	114		21			93
2008	1027		139			888
2009	3575	24	302	23	1397	1829
2010	16809	171	252	196	14554	1636
2011	33240	1538	164	1270	27842	2426
2012	34931	4220	219	2590	25608	2294
2013	17612	4072	193	2216	8989	2142
2014	13246	5934	338	2093	2765	2116

说明：1.以上数据为民政部职业技能鉴定指导中心及分布在全国31个省、自治区、直辖市76个鉴定站鉴定人数和竞赛晋级人数（不含地方自行组织的鉴定人数）。

2.殡葬类职业包括：殡仪服务员（初中高技师4个级别）、遗体接运工（初中高3个级别）、遗体防腐师（初中高技师高级技师5个级别）、遗体整容师（初中高技师高级技师5个级别）、遗体火化师（初中高技师高级技师5个级别）、墓地管理员（初中高技师4个级别）。

3.假肢类职业包括：假肢师（初中高技师高级技师5个级别）、矫形器师（初中高技师高级技师5个级别）。

B-1-10 社会服务增加值

单位：亿元

年 份	合计	民政系统行政机关	社会工作	成员组织			其他社会服务	其他事业单位
					社会组织	自治组织		
2006	1344.8	72.2	833.6	385.3	112.2	273.1	53.7	
2007	1501.2	83.7	776.7	588.6	307.6	281.0	52.2	
2008	1650.1	108.7	780.8	701.0	372.4	328.6	59.6	
2009	1849.4	141.1	777.7	864.1	493.1	371.0	66.5	
2010	2014.5	190.8	912.4	841.1	531.2	309.9	70.2	
2011	2459.8	212.9	1152.2	1023.3	660.0	363.3	71.4	
2012	2321.6	192.7	1125.2	900.7	525.6	375.1	84.2	18.8
2013	2463.6	211.7	1167.1	972.9	571.1	401.8	91.8	20.1
2014	2734.4	219.2	1314.6	1081.7	650.3	431.4	99.4	19.7

B-1-11 历年性别情况统计

单位：万人

年份	城市居民最低生活保障人数	女	农村最低生活保障人数	女	农村供养集中五保人数	女	农村供养分散五保人数	女	本年在站救助人次数	女	年末残疾职工人数	女
1996	84.9											
1997	87.9											
1998	184.1											
1999	256.9										79.0	19.2
2000	402.6										72.9	26.8
2001	1170.7		304.6								69.9	25.2
2002	2064.7		407.8								68.3	25.1
2003	2246.8		367.1						634528		67.9	24.0
2004	2205.0		488.0						820254		66.2	23.0
2005	2234.2	592.4	825.0	235.1					1196305	209632	63.7	21.8
2006	2240.1	787.5	1593.1	455.1					1295506	221164	55.9	18.3
2007	2272.1	922.5	3566.3	1169.2	138.0	38.3	393.3	99.2	1544492	281987	56.3	16.9
2008	2334.8	947.7	4305.5	1337.0	155.6	36.4	393.0	91.1	1573484	269609	61.9	19.3
2009	2345.6	961.4	4760.0	1502.4	171.8	38.0	381.6	85.9	1680532	281387	62.7	19.8
2010	2310.5	943.4	5214.0	1673.4	177.4	36.9	378.9	83.8	1719008	314866	62.5	19.6
2011	2276.8	920.2	5305.7	1700.6	184.5	37.7	366.5	77.9	2409701	373103	62.8	19.7
2012	2143.5	889.9	5344.5	1814.5	185.3	36.1	360.3	73.3	2765761	383262	59.7	18.4
2013	2064.2	867.0	5388.0	1866.5	183.5	34.1	353.8	67.9	3479536	609333	53.9	16.6
2014	1877.0	792.4	5207.2	1826.4	174.3	30.6	354.8	63.5	2953359	568551	47.9	15.0

B-1-11续表

单位：万人

年 份	社团负责人数	女	基金会负责人数(人)	女	民办非企业单位负责人数	女	居委会主任数	女	村委会主任数	女
1996										
1997										
1998										
1999	47.6	6.0			0.9	0.2				
2000	45.4	6.1			3.2	0.7				
2001	43.3	5.7			10.1	3.6				
2002	45.5	6.1			14.4	5.1				
2003	51.8	6.2			16.6	5.8				
2004	56.0	6.6			19.1	6.5				
2005	64.0	6.9	2940	450	23.1	7.0				
2006	36.4	7.0	3014	738	20.9	6.5				
2007	39.2	7.9	3113	925	25.9	7.4	8.2	3.7	61.1	9.1
2008	49.5	10.2	3231	600	30.6	8.9	7.8	3.4	57.6	5.9
2009	49.4	9.4	3856	637	31.1	9.6	7.8	3.4	56.3	6.2
2010	56.9	9.1	4797	1019	35.7	10.1	8.1	3.5	56.3	5.9
2011	59.4	8.2	6257	1388	33.6	11.0	8.0	3.5	54.5	6.1
2012	61.6	9.1	6896	1167	35.9	11.9	9.1	3.8	58.7	6.9
2013	61.0	10.0	7331	1429	37.7	12.6	9.4	3.9	58.7	7.0
2014	63.9	10.7	8952	1687	41.3	13.9	9.6	3.9	58.4	7.2

B-1-12 社会服务机构固定资产原值

单位：亿元

年份	合计							
		社会工作	成员组织			其他社会服务	其他事业单位	行政机关
				社会组织	自治组织			
1978								
1979								
1980								
1981								
1982								
1983	13.0	13.0						
1984	14.9	14.9						
1985	20.1	20.1						
1986	24.2	24.2						
1987	28.7	28.7						
1988	40.8	40.8						
1989	44.1	44.1						
1990	51.7	51.7						
1991	63.6	63.6						
1992	75.6	75.6						
1993	100.3	100.3						
1994	119.0	119.0						
1995	142.6	142.6						
1996	168.1	168.1						
1997	211.5	211.5						
1998	962.4	962.4						
1999	1017.3	1017.3						
2000	1199.3	1199.3						
2001	1317.0	1317.0						
2002	1394.9	1394.9						
2003	1644.3	1644.3						
2004	1818.4	1755.6						62.8
2005	3097.8	1858.0	1174.9		1174.9			64.9
2006	4066.7	2103.0	1869.4	423.0	1446.4			94.3
2007	3973.0	1934.3	1905.9	682.0	1223.9			132.8
2008	4592.8	2186.8	2273.1	805.8	1467.3			132.9
2009	5198.0	2326.4	2752.4	1030	1722.4			119.2
2010	6589.3	2671.9	3795.6	1864.1	1931.5			121.8
2011	6989.8	2790.4	3684.2	1885.0	1799.2	231		284.2
2012	7019.5	2898.9	3477.7	1425.4	2052.3	251.8	47	344.1
2013	6995.5	3030.7	3465.7	1496.6	1969.1	267	46.8	185.4
2014	7382.2	3273.0	3609.3	1560.6	2048.64	283.8	46.8	169.3

B-1-13 历年财政支出和社会服务经费支出情况

单位：亿元

年 份	国家财政支出	社会服务经费支出	占财政支出%	年 份	国家财政支出	社会服务经费支出	占财政支出%
1950	68.04	1.32	1.94	1981	1138.41	19.23	1.69
1951	122.32	1.37	1.12	1982	1229.98	19.19	1.56
1952	175.78	2.83	1.61	1983	1409.52	21.61	1.53
1953	220.5	3.55	1.61	1984	1701.02	24.24	1.43
1954	280.93	6.04	2.15	1985	2004.25	29.58	1.48
1955	474.29	4.98	1.05	**“七五”时期**	**12865.67**	**208.49**	**1.62**
“一五”时期	**1367.89**	**25.99**	**1.90**	1986	2204.91	34.41	1.56
1956	536.79	5.69	1.06	1987	2262.18	35.93	1.59
1957	303.43	5.31	1.75	1988	2491.21	39.56	1.59
1958	408.75	3.27	0.80	1989	2823.78	46.65	1.65
1959	553.09	4.48	0.81	1990	3083.59	51.94	1.68
1960	652.25	7.24	1.11	**“八五”时期**	**24387.46**	**386.59**	**1.59**
“二五”时期	**3760.99**	**53.03**	**1.41**	1991	3386.62	62.54	1.85
1961	367.66	9.89	2.69	1992	3742.2	63.71	1.70
1962	305.33	7.45	2.44	1993	4642.3	69.87	1.51
1963	339.15	8.75	2.58	1994	5792.62	87.02	1.50
1964	398.77	16.15	4.05	1995	6823.72	103.45	1.52
1965	467.1	10.79	2.31	**“九五”时期**	**57043.46**	**840.90**	**1.47**
“三五”时期	**2523.24**	**35.83**	**1.42**	1996	7937.55	121.15	1.53
1966	540.49	8.81	1.63	1997	9233.56	133.52	1.45
1967	441.4	8.21	1.86	1998	10798.18	161.84	1.50
1968	359.62	5.61	1.56	1999	13187.67	194.70	1.48
1969	525.2	6.67	1.27	2000	15886.5	229.69	1.45
1970	646.53	6.53	1.01	**“十五”时期**	**127800.69**	**2471.74**	**1.93**
“四五”时期	**3924.37**	**46.70**	**1.19**	2001	18902.58	284.75	1.51
1971	734.41	6.83	0.93	2002	22053.15	392.27	1.78
1972	768.87	8.15	1.06	2003	24649.95	498.92	2.02
1973	810.57	9.97	1.23	2004	28486.89	577.39	2.03
1974	792.98	9.04	1.14	2005	33708.12	718.41	2.13
1975	820	12.71	1.55	**“十一五”时期**	**317654.99**	**9156.70**	**2.88**
“五五”时期	**5198.77**	**84.22**	**1.62**	2006	40213.16	915.35	2.28
1976	804.48	16.17	2.01	2007	49565.4	1215.49	2.45
1977	842.27	18.53	2.20	2008	62427.03	2146.45	3.44
1978	1122.09	13.71	1.22	2009	75874	2181.90	2.88
1979	1281.79	18.33	1.43	2010	89575.4	2697.51	3.01
1980	1228.83	17.48	1.42	**“十二五”时期**	**374385.92**	**11189.38**	**2.99**
“六五”时期	**7483.18**	**113.85**	**1.52**	2011	108930	3229.1	2.96
				2012	125712	3683.7	2.93
				2013	139744	4276.5	3.06
				2014	151662	4414.1	2.91

B-1-14 按科目分的社会服务经费

单位：亿元

年份	社会服务经费总支出	抚恤费	离休费	社会福利及其他社会救济费		自然灾害救济费	退休费	其他社会服务经费
					最低生活保障费			
1978	13.7	2.8		4.4		4.2	2.3	
1979	18.4	3.5		5.2		6.8	2.9	
1980	17.5	4.4		5.2		4.5	3.4	
“六五”时期	**114.2**	**27.3**	**0.9**	**32.1**		**35.2**	**16.8**	**1.7**
1981	19.2	4.4		5.1		6.3	3.4	
1982	19.6	4.8		5.1		6.0	3.5	
1983	21.6	5.3		6.5		6.4	3.4	
1984	24.2	6.1	0.2	8.0		6.9	3.0	
1985	29.6	6.7	0.7	7.4		9.6	3.5	1.7
“七五”时期	**208.4**	**59.2**	**11.4**	**46.7**		**56.4**	**22.0**	**12.8**
1986	34.4	8.4	1.2	8.3		10.7	3.8	1.9
1987	35.9	9.6	1.8	8.6		9.9	4.1	2
1988	39.6	11	2.3	9		10.4	4.3	2.5
1989	46.6	14	2.9	10		12.3	4.6	2.9
1990	51.9	16.2	3.2	10.8		13.1	5.2	3.5
“八五”时期	**386.6**	**107.8**	**23.2**	**75.6**		**94.1**	**45.5**	**40.5**
1991	62.5	16.8	3.6	11.7		20.9	5.4	4.2
1992	63.7	18	4.2	12.4		17.1	6.6	5.4
1993	69.9	20.1	3.6	14.5		14.9	8.3	8.4
1994	87	24.4	5.5	17.3		17.7	12.1	10.1
1995	103.5	28.5	6.3	19.7		23.5	13.1	12.4

年份	社会服务经费总支出	抚恤费	军队离退休、退职费	社会福利及其他社会救济费		自然灾害救济费	地方离、退休人员费	其他社会服务经费
					最低生活保障费			
“九五”时期	**840.9**	**220.6**	**76.9**	**201.8**	**48.7**	**171.5**	**58.0**	**112.2**
1996	121.2	31.9	6.2	22.8	3	30.8	13.9	15.5
1997	133.5	36.1	12.4	27.1	2.9	28.7	10.3	19
1998	161.8	39.4	15.2	34	7.1	41.2	10.9	21.3
1999	194.7	49.7	18.4	52.5	13.8	35.6	11.2	27.2
2000	229.7	63.5	24.7	65.4	21.9	35.2	11.7	29.2

年份	社会服务经费总支出	抚恤费	退役安置	社会福利	社会救助				自然灾害生活救助	离退休人员经费	其他
						城市低保及其他城市社会救济	农村低保及其他农村社会救济	医疗救助			
“十五”时期	**2471.8**	**479.8**	**302.7**	**444.7**		**668**	**127.6**	**11**	**247.6**	**66.9**	**273.7**
2001	284.8	69.5	31.2	90.6		41.6			41	13	39.5
2002	392.3	74.7	49.5	167.5		108.7			40	13.2	47.3
2003	498.9	87.9	59	78.9	153.1	153.1			52.9	13.1	54
2004	577.4	104.1	74.1	52.1	223.6	172.7	47.7	3.2	51.1	13.9	58.5
2005	718.4	143.6	88.9	55.6	279.6	191.9	79.9	7.8	62.6	13.7	74.4
“十一五”时期	**9156.8**	**1316.2**	**956**	**490**	**3673.6**	**1941.7**	**1710.7**	**436.1**	**1205**	**125.7**	**975.4**
2006	915.4	178.8	115.7	65.3	372	224.2	126.6	21.2	79	14	90.6
2007	1215.5	210.8	165	87.6	509.7	277.4	189.8	42.5	79.8	24.8	137.8
2008	2146.5	253.6	180.6	103.1	806.7	393.4	326.8	86.5	609.8	26.5	166.2
2009	2181.9	310.3	225.7	124.1	1098.1	482.1	487.9	128.1	199.2	30	194.5
2010	2697.5	362.7	269	109.9	1302	564.6	579.6	157.8	237.2	30.4	386.3

年份	社会服务经费总支出	抚恤费	退役安置	社会福利	社会救助				自然灾害生活救助	离退休人员经费	其他
						城乡低保	其他社会救助	医疗救助			
“十二五”时期	**15593.4**	**2200.3**	**1566.5**	**1430.3**	**8002.3**	**5935.5**	**1078.5**	**988.3**	**595.2**	**162.1**	**1306.4**
2011	3229.1	428.3	302.3	232.2	1766.3	1327.6	222.4	216.3	128.7	35.3	336.0
2012	3683.7	517	372.1	319.5	1866.1	1392.3	243.2	230.6	163.4	39	406.7
2013	4276.5	618.4	435.3	397.6	2172.4	1623.6	291.4	257.4	178.7	43.6	430.6
2014	4404.1	636.6	456.8	481	2197.5	1592.0	321.5	284.0	124.4	44.2	133.1

B-1-15 中央转移支付的社会服务经费

单位：万元

年 份	合 计	中央级民政事业费	中央专项转移支付	抚恤、退休、救济费	救 灾	社会福利救济费	其 他
1978	11	11					
1979	44	44					
1980	103	103					
“六五”时期	**335594**	**1108**	**334486**	**63306**	**270745**	**220**	**215**
1981	138	138					
1982	74120	78	74042	14247	59795		
1983	74368	163	74205	14205	60000		
1984	78872	286	78586	18586	60000		

年 份	合 计	中央级民政事业费	中央专项转移支付	抚 恤	安 置	救 灾	社会福利救济费	其 他
1985	108096	443	107653	9698	6570	90950	220	215
“七五”时期	**778310**	**9267**	**769043**	**148718**	**105230**	**512500**		
1986	132802	2526	130276	16396	9285	102000		
1987	133877	2742	131135	21726	19409	90000		
1988	158355	1297	157058	24110	21948	111000		
1989	174374	1185	173189	43206	26483	103500		
1990	178902	1517	177385	43280	28105	106000		
“八五”时期	**1488090**	**15897**	**1472193**	**328272**	**315101**	**828820**		
1991	309432	1792	307640	49010	34210	224420		
1992	209360	3217	206143	52156	40587	113400		
1993	238083	3108	234975	60494	53481	121000		
1994	353831	4077	349754	79084	90670	180000		
1995	377384	3703	373681	87528	96153	190000		
“九五”时期	**2943934**	**104302**	**2839632**	**749824**	**773058**	**1122750**	**190000**	**4000**
1996	426354	6371	419983	102394	102589	215000		
1997	455309	5954	449355	110430	114925	220000		4000
1998	568049	50783	517266	120000	149516	247750		

年 份	合 计（亿元）	中央级民政事业费(亿元)	中央专项转移支付（亿元）	抚恤（亿元）	安置（亿元）	救灾（亿元）	低保（亿元）	临时救助（亿元）	医疗救助（亿元）	福利（亿元）	其他（亿元）
1999	62.8	1.2	61.6	18.0	17.6	22.0	4.0				
2000	86.6	2.9	83.7	23.7	23.0	22.0	15.0				
“十五”时期	**1004.3**	**11.9**	**992.4**	**212.1**	**217.3**	**170.1**	**373.1**		**12.0**		**7.9**
2001	109.6	1.4	108.2	26.3	28.7	30.2	23.0				
2002	140.2	1.8	138.4	31.6	37.0	24.3	45.5				
2003	213.6	1.8	211.8	37.1	39.2	40.5	92.0		3.0		0.1
2004	227.7	3.9	223.8	40.7	47.4	32.0	100.6		3.0		0.1
2005	313.2	2.9	310.3	76.4	65.0	43.1	112.0		6.0		7.7
“十一五”时期	**4761.3**	**89.3**	**4658.9**	**767.6**	**699.9**	**856.1**	**1941.6**		**319.6**		**74.2**
2006	406.8	2.8	404.0	111.7	73.9	49.4	136.0		14.3		18.7
2007	523.1	5.6	504.4	110.9	117.4	49.9	189.9		36.3		0.1
2008	1207.7	26.6	1181.1	142.1	142.9	478.4	363.1		54.5		0.1
2009	1232.5	5.5	1227.0	187.3	160.2	174.7	620		84.5		0.3
2010	1391.2	48.8	1342.4	215.6	205.5	103.7	632.6		130		55
“十二五”时期	**7903.2**	**45.9**	**7857.3**	**1318.5**	**1038.0**	**394.9**	**4145.3**	**32.0**	**621.7**	**185.0**	**122.0**
2011	1817.4	9.4	1808.0	277.4	206.4	84	1004.7		150	25.2	60.3
2012	1804.6	10	1794.6	333.3	265.4	112.7	870.5		150	42	20.7
2013	2163.4	13.7	2149.7	369.8	277.4	101.9	1168.8		156.7	54.4	20.8
2014	2117.8	12.8	2105.0	338	288.8	96.3	1101.3	32	165	63.4	20.2

B-1-16 彩票公益金使用情况

单位：亿元

年 份	合计	抚恤	退役安置	社会福利	低保及其他社会救济	医疗救助	自然灾害生活救助	其他
2001								
2002								
2003								
2004								
2005								
“十一五”时期	**485.3**	**17.6**	**6**	**204.9**	**26.2**	**48.8**		**175.6**
2006	52.6	2.6	1	24.1	3.3			21.6
2007	77.6	3	0.9	35.5	4.3			33.9
2008	119.2	3.7	1.3	44.9	7.2	17.5		38.5
2009	113.4	3.4	1.2	49.3	5.9	15.5		38
2010	122.5	4.9	1.6	51.1	5.5	15.8		43.6
“十二五”时期	**713.7**	**23.6**	**2.4**	**414.3**	**33.4**	**69.7**	**6.9**	**163.1**
2011	127.9	4.8	0.4	61.4	7.4	16.3	0.8	36.6
2012	159.0	5.4	0.5	92.2	7.3	16.8	1.3	35.6
2013	195.5	7.5	0.6	117.1	8.7	17.5	2.6	41.5
2014	231.3	5.9	0.9	143.6	10.0	19.1	2.2	49.4

B-1-17 中央彩票公益金使用情况

单位：万元

年 份	合 计	中央级	转移支付					
				养老	残疾人	儿童	社会公益	医疗救助
“十五”时期	**14.91**		**14.91**	**0.70**		**2.06**	**0.15**	**12.00**
2001								
2002								
2003	3.00		3.00					3.00
2004	5.91		5.91	0.70		2.06	0.15	3.00
2005	6.00		6.00					6.00
“十一五”时期	**112.29**	**2.47**	**109.82**	**21.64**		**16.37**	**1.81**	**70.00**
2006	14.03	0.10	13.93	1.59		3.24	0.10	9.00
2007	16.98	0.88	16.10	1.53		1.24	0.33	13.00
2008	28.14	0.10	28.04	4.79		6.67	0.58	16.00
2009	26.61	0.09	26.52	7.79		2.05	0.68	16.00
2010	26.53	1.30	25.23	5.94		3.17	0.12	16.00
“十二五”时期	**145.47**	**1.30**	**144.17**	**50.89**	**5.94**	**16.88**	**6.46**	**64.00**
2011	30.03	1.30	28.73	7.86		3.48	1.39	16.00
2012	33.68		33.68	10.67	0.99	4.35	1.67	16.00
2013	46.91		46.91	22.16	1.98	5.08	1.69	16.00
2014	34.85		34.85	10.20	2.97	3.97	1.71	16.00

B-1-18 社会服务基本建设投资（按投资来源分）

单位：亿元、个

年 份	计划总投资	本年完成投资	国家投资	国内贷款	自 筹	福利彩票公益金	其 他	本年完工项目个数
1988								
1989	5.8	2.0	0.7	0.1	0.8		0.2	
1990	6.9	2.4	0.8	0.1	1.0		0.3	
“八五”时期	**63.4**	**27.6**	**10.3**	**1.2**	**13.4**		**2.8**	
1991	7.0	3.0	1.0	0.1	1.5		0.3	
1992	7.3	3.2	1.0	0.1	1.9		0.4	
1993	12.8	5.6	1.4	0.2	3.4		0.7	
1994	15.5	6.2	2.3	0.5	2.9		0.6	
1995	20.9	9.6	4.6	0.3	3.8		0.9	
“九五”时期	**237.9**	**89.8**	**21.3**	**5.9**	**54.3**	**6.8**	**8.3**	**2793**
1996	29.8	10.1	2.1	0.4	6.4		1.1	
1997	35.7	13.8	2.7	0.8	8.6		1.6	
1998	41.0	16.6	2.8	0.8	11.1		1.9	
1999	63.2	24.7	6.0	2.3	14.6	3.5	1.8	1456
2000	68.2	24.7	7.7	1.6	13.6	3.3	1.9	1337
“十五”时期	**376.9**	**151.7**	**47.9**	**8.8**	**78.4**	**21.0**	**16.6**	**22117**
2001	77.5	30.8	10.4	2.2	15.1	3.6	3.1	1360
2002	88.7	30.1	9.5	1.4	15.9	3.3	3.3	3659
2003	87.3	30.0	9.9	1.7	15.1	3.5	3.3	3867
2004	89.7	29.2	8.9	2.4	14.4	4.7	3.5	8982
2005	33.8	31.6	9.1	1.0	17.9	5.8	3.5	4249
“十一五”时期	**485.6**	**487.8**	**210.7**	**12.4**	***148.8***	**96.8**	**82.3**	**62453**
2006	34.8	33.5	9.9	0.9	19.9	8.4	2.5	3626
2007	47.6	47.7	14.5	3.0	26.9	13.0	2.9	2446
2008	63.5	66.6	26.6	1.9	34.6	16.5	3.2	3906
2009	166.5	157.0	70.6	3.7	67.4	26.6	15.3	6457

年 份	计划总投资	本年完成投资	国家投资	国内贷款	利用外资	福利彩票公益金	其 他	本年完工项目个数
2010	173.2	183.0	89.1	2.9	0.2	32.3	58.5	46018
“十二五”时期	**1017.5**	**1028.2**	**407.1**	**14.9**	**5**	**226.6**	**374.6**	**37311**
2011	217.3	218.5	78.5	6.2	0.5	53.4	79.9	4533
2012	222.3	234.7	104.2	3.8	1.1	51	74.6	6095
2013	311.9	292.8	120.1	1.4	1.7	64.7	104.8	15328
2014	266	282.2	104.3	3.5	1.7	57.5	115.3	11355

B-1-19 国家对社会服务基本建设投资

单位：亿元

年　份	国家基本建设投资	#优抚安置单位	#社区服务设施	#收养性福利机构	#殡仪	#救助	#其他
1989	0.7						
1990	0.8			0.2	0.1		
“八五”时期	**10.3**	**4.2**		**1.4**	**1.1**	**0.2**	
1991	1.0	0.1		0.2	0.1		
1992	1.0			0.2			
1993	1.4			0.2	0.4		
1994	2.3	1.2		0.3	0.3		
1995	4.6	2.9		0.5	0.3	0.2	
“九五”时期	**21.3**	**2.0**	**1.6**	**6.6**	**6.5**		**2.6**
1996	2.1	0.1		0.5	0.5		
1997	2.7			0.7	1.1		
1998	2.8	0.2		1.8	0.8		
1999	6.0	0.9	0.6	1.5	1.7		1.2
2000	7.7	0.8	1.0	2.1	2.4		1.4
“十五”时期	**47.9**	**5.0**	**9.4**	**14.3**	**9.2**		**9.8**
2001	10.4	0.7	1.5	3.1	2.1		3.0
2002	9.5	0.7	2.1	2.8	1.9		1.9
2003	9.9	1.2	2.4	3.3	1.5		1.5
2004	9.0	1.1	2.3	2.5	1.1		1.9
2005	9.1	1.3	1.1	2.6	2.6		1.5
“十一五”时期	**210.8**	**27.8**	**31.5**	**85.2**	**19.2**	**8.1**	**39.0**
2006	9.9	1.8	0.8	3.9	1.4	0.3	1.6
2007	14.5	2.5	0.9	6.5	2.4	0.4	1.8
2008	26.6	8.2	1.9	8.5	3.7	1.1	3.2
2009	70.6	7.4	14.0	30.1	5.7	2.5	11.0
2010	89.2	7.9	13.9	36.2	6.0	3.8	21.4
“十二五”时期	**407.1**	**163.4**	**154.0**	**82.1**	**22.0**	**48.3**	**76.8**
2011	78.5	9.5	11.1	31.1	5.8	3.8	17.2
2012	104.2	11.3	18.3	45.1	7.1	6.1	16.2

年　份	国家基本建设投资	#提供住宿的社会工作机构	#为老年人与残疾人提供服务的机构	#为智障与精神病提供服务的机构	#为儿童提供收养救助服务的机构	#不提供住宿的社会工作机构	#其他
2013	120.1	76.2	66.5	3.2	4.6	22.2	21.7
2014	104.3	66.4	58.1	2.7	4.5	16.2	21.7

B-1-20 中央预算内

年份	项目合计（个）	投资合计	本级情况：本级项目数	本级情况：本级投资	地方项目小计	补助地方投资小计	养老：项目数	养老：资金额
1989								
1990		0.1		0.1				
“八五”时期		**0.2**		**0.2**				
1991		0.2		0.2				
1992								
1993								
1994								
1995								
“九五”时期								
1996								
1997								
1998								
1999								
2000								
“十五”时期	**24**	**0.8**	**24**	**0.8**				
2001	3	0.3	3	0.3				
2002	10	0.2	10	0.2				
2003	6	0.1	6	0.1				
2004	3	0.1	3	0.1				
2005	2	0.1	2	0.1				
“十一五”时期	**2088**	**35.9**	**18**	**5.5**	**2070**	**30.37**	**189**	**5.0**
2006	2	0.2	2	0.2				
2007	218	2.8	5	0.8	213	2.0		
2008	575	6.8	3	2.1	572	4.7		
2009	774	13.0	4	1.3	770	11.7	63	2.0
2010	519	13.1	4	1.1	515	12.0	126	3
“十二五”时期	**1860**	**76.0**	**4**	**0.7**	**1856**	**75.3**	**1364**	**55.0**
2011	433	26.0	4	0.7	429	25.3	338	9
2012	692	33.0			692	33.0	669	31
2013	735	17.0			735	17.0	357	15

年份	建设规模（平方米）	投资合计	本级情况：建设规模	本级情况：本级投资	建设规模	补助地方投资小计	养老：建设规模	养老：资金额	精神：建设规模
2014	383.28	29.0			383.28	29.0	330	24.39	

基本建设投资情况

单位：亿元、个、平方米

地方情况									
精神卫生		儿童		流浪		社区		烈建	
项目数	资金额	项目数	资金额	项目数	资金额	项目数	资金额	项目数	资金额
26	**4.4**	**134**	**5.0**	**254**	**5.0**	**1334**	**6.0**	**133**	**5.0**
		15	0.5	28	0.8	170	0.7		
		32	1.3	65	1.4	475	2.0		
		33	1.3	78	1.4	463	2.0	133	5.0
26	4.37	54	1.9	83	1.4	226	1.3		
91.0	**16.3**					**401.0**	**4.0**		
91	16.3								
						23	2		
						378	2		

地方情况								
卫生	儿童		社会事务		社区		烈建	
资金额	建设规模	资金额	建设规模	资金额	建设规模	资金额	建设规模	资金额
	22.33	2	5.37	0.65	25.58	1.96		

B-2-1 按收养人员分类的提供住宿的社会服务机构

单位：个

年 份	单位数	老年及残疾人	智障和精神疾病	儿童	其他	#救助管理站	#安置农场	#军供站
1978	8571	8365	139	67				
1979	8988	8801	135	52				
1980	9669	9460	150	59				
1981	10031	9813	155	63				
1982	12275	12046	165	64				
1983	15807	15582	165	60				
1984	22796	22566	167	63				
1985	29100	28852	161	59	28			
1986	35008	34750	166	58	34			
1987	37372	37109	170	60	33			
1988	39030	38767	173	62	28			
1989	39743	39472	180	64	27			
1990	40583	40340	181	62				
1991	42264	42013	188	63				
1992	43319	43063	189	67				
1993	43681	43375	190	67	49			
1994	43240	42911	188	73	68			
1995	43074	42735	190	77	72			
1996	42829	42518	155	84	72			
1997	42385	42027	192	91	75			
1998	42131	41755	195	105	76			
1999	40430	40030	191	110	99			
2000	40491	39321	201	126	843			
2001	38785	38106	200	160	319			
2002	38200	37591	200	178	231			
2003	37294	36224	205	192	1587			
2004	38593	37880	211	208	1320			
2005	42487	40641	226	224	1396			
2006	43187	40964	219	249	1755			
2007	44958	42713	234	269	1742			
2008	41099	38674	244	290	1891			
2009	43944	39671	266	419	3588			
2010	44482	39904	251	480	3847			
2011	45973	42828	251	638	2256	1547		327
2012	48078	44304	257	724	2793	1770	27	328
2013	45977	42475	261	803	2438	1891	26	325
2014	36810	33044	254	890	2622	1949	13	327

B-2-2 按收养人员分类的提供住宿的社会服务床位

单位：万张

年 份	床位数合计	老年及残疾人床位	智障和精神疾病床位	儿童床位	其他床位	#救助管理站	#军供站	每千人口拥有社会服务床位数	每千老年人口拥有养老床位数
1978	16.3	15.7	0.6					0.17	
1979	22.6	20.1	2.1	0.4				0.23	
1980	24.2	21.3	2.4	0.5				0.25	
1981	25.3	22.2	2.5	0.6				0.25	
1982	28.2	24.8	2.8	0.6				0.28	
1983	32.4	29.0	2.8	0.6				0.31	
1984	42.5	39.0	2.9	0.6				0.41	
1985	49.1	45.7	2.9	0.5	0.2			0.46	
1986	58.7	55.0	3.1	0.6	0.3			0.55	
1987	64.9	61.0	3.3	0.6	0.3			0.59	
1988	69.5	65.5	3.4	0.6	0.2			0.63	
1989	73.8	69.5	3.6	0.7	0.2			0.65	
1990	78.0	73.5	3.7	0.8				0.68	
1991	82.8	78.3	3.8	0.7				0.71	
1992	89.8	85.2	3.8	0.8				0.77	
1993	92.7	87.8	4.0	0.9	0.4			0.78	
1994	95.5	90.6	4.0	0.9	0.5			0.80	
1995	97.6	92.5	4.0	1.1	0.6			0.81	
1996	100.8	95.6	4.0	1.2	0.6			0.82	
1997	103.1	97.8	4.0	1.3	0.6			0.83	
1998	105.8	100.2	4.1	1.5	0.6			0.85	
1999	108.9	102.4	4.1	1.6	0.8			0.87	
2000	113.0	104.5	4.1	1.8	2.6			0.89	
2001	140.7	114.6	4.2	2.3	19.6			1.10	
2002	141.5	114.9	4.3	2.5	19.8			1.10	
2003	142.9	120.6	4.5	2.7	15.1			1.11	
2004	157.2	139.5	4.5	3.0	10.2			1.21	
2005	180.7	158.1	4.4	3.2	15.0			1.38	10.97
2006	204.5	179.6	4.4	3.2	17.3			1.56	12.05
2007	269.6	242.9	4.7	3.4	18.6			2.04	15.83
2008	300.3	267.4	5.4	4.3	23.2			2.26	16.72
2009	326.5	293.5	5.9	4.8	22.3			2.45	17.56
2010	349.6	316.1	6.1	5.5	21.9			2.61	17.79
2011	396.4	369.2	6.5	6.8	13.9	7.1	3.8	2.94	19.96
2012	449.3	416.5	6.7	8.7	17.4	9.0	3.8	3.32	21.48
2013	526.7	493.7	7.4	9.8	15.7	9.7	3.7	3.87	24.39
2014	613.5	577.7	8.0	10.8	17.0	9.9	3.7	4.49	27.20

注：老年及残疾人床位含社区服务床位（含日间照料床位）。

B-2-3 提供住宿的社会服务机构收养人员情况

单位：万人

年 份	总人数	老年及残疾人	智障和精神疾病人	儿童	其他
1978	16.3	14.0	1.9	0.4	
1979	18.6	16.3	1.9	0.4	
1980	19.1	16.7	2.0	0.4	
1981	19.7	17.0	2.2	0.5	
1982	22.5	19.7	2.3	0.5	
1983	25.9	23.0	2.4	0.5	
1984	34.1	31.0	2.6	0.5	
1985	40.8	37.5	2.6	0.5	0.2
1986	47.4	43.9	2.8	0.5	0.2
1987	51.8	48.2	2.9	0.5	0.2
1988	54.8	51.1	3.0	0.6	0.1
1989	56.9	53.0	3.1	0.6	0.2
1990	59.9	56.1	3.2	0.6	
1991	64.6	60.8	3.2	0.6	
1992	69.6	65.6	3.3	0.7	
1993	72.4	68.0	3.4	0.7	0.3
1994	73.6	69.2	3.3	0.8	0.3
1995	74.7	70.1	3.2	1.0	0.4
1996	76.9	72.3	3.1	1.1	0.4
1997	78.5	73.7	3.2	1.2	0.4
1998	80.0	74.9	3.2	1.4	0.5
1999	82.7	77.6	3.2	1.4	0.5
2000	85.4	78.6	3.2	1.8	1.8
2001	88.5	82.0	3.3	2.1	1.1
2002	91.6	85.0	3.4	2.2	1.0
2003	96.5	89.1	3.5	2.5	1.4
2004	110.9	103.9	3.6	2.8	0.6
2005	123.6	116.2	3.7	2.9	0.8
2006	147.0	138.5	3.8	3.2	1.5
2007	200.0	191.3	4.1	3.0	1.6
2008	240.0	211.5	4.5	3.4	20.6
2009	256.0	227.5	5.0	3.7	19.8
2010	278.2	247.0	5.3	4.2	21.7
2011	293.4	279.7	5.5	4.6	3.6
2012	309.5	293.6	5.8	5.4	4.7
2013	322.5	307.4	6.0	5.6	3.5
2014	337.0	320.4	6.5	5.9	4.2

B-2-4 按城乡分类的提供住宿的社会服务机构情况

年 份	单位数（个）	城市	农村	床位数（万张）	城市	农村	收养人数（万人）	城市	农村
1978	8571	728	7843	16.3	0.1	16.2	16.3	5.7	10.6
1979	8988	1518	7470	22.6	6.4	16.2	18.6	8	10.6
1980	9669	1407	8262	24.2	7.1	17.1	19.1	7.9	11.2
1981	10031	1487	8544	25.3	7.4	17.9	19.7	8.2	11.5
1982	12275	1689	10586	28.2	7.6	20.6	22.5	8.7	13.8
1983	15807	1760	14047	32.4	7.7	24.7	25.9	9	16.9
1984	22796	1925	20871	42.5	8.5	34	34.1	10	24.1
1985	29100	5478	23622	49.1	18.2	30.9	40.8	14.6	26.2
1986	35008	8330	26678	58.7	23.6	35.1	47.4	18.9	28.5
1987	37372	9358	28014	64.9	25.8	39.1	51.8	20.5	31.3
1988	39030	10498	28532	69.5	28.4	41.1	54.8	22.3	32.5
1989	39743	10118	29625	73.8	28.7	45.1	56.9	22.3	34.6
1990	40583	12697	27886	78	34.5	43.5	59.9	26.8	33.1
1991	42264	13197	29067	82.8	36.7	46.1	64.6	28.5	36.1
1992	43319	16847	26472	89.8	44.6	45.2	69.6	34.5	35.1
1993	43681	17400	26281	92.7	47	45.7	72.4	37.2	35.2
1994	43240	18035	25205	95.5	50	45.5	73.6	39.1	34.5

年 份	单位数（个）	国有社会福利院	社会办敬老院	床位数（万张）	国有社会福利院	社会办敬老院	收养人数（万人）	国有社会福利院	社会办敬老院
1995	43074	11184	31890	97.6	18.6	79	74.7	14.4	60.3
1996	42829	11216	31613	100.8	19.2	81.6	76.9	14.8	62.1
1997	42385	10417	31968	103.1	19.9	83.2	78.5	15.4	63.1
1998	42131	9895	32236	105.8	21	84.8	80	16.1	63.9
1999	40430	3086	37344	108.9	23.6	85.3	82.7	17.9	64.8

年 份	单位数（个）	城 市	农 村	床位数（万张）	城 市	农 村	收养人数（万人）	城 市	农 村
2000	40491	14915	25576	113	57.4	55.6	85.4	42.6	42.8
2001	38785	12135	26650	140.7	72.3	68.4	88.5	39.6	48.9
2002	38200	12503	25697	141.5	75.3	66.2	91.6	42.2	49.4
2003	37294	12951	24343	142.9	75.3	67.6	96.5	46.1	50.4
2004	38593	12151	26442	157.2	79.7	77.5	110.9	51.5	59.4
2005	42487	12806	29681	180.7	91.2	89.5	123.6	55.7	67.9
2006	43187	11814	31373	204.5	90.9	113.6	147.0	55.0	92.0
2007	44958	10274	34684	269.6	89.8	179.8	200.0	43.9	149.3
2008	41099	10731	30368	300.3	107.2	193.1	240.0	79.5	160.5
2009	43944	12658	31286	326.5	117.7	208.8	256.0	83.0	173.0
2010	44482	13010	31472	349.6	124.7	224.9	278.2	95.7	182.5
2011	45973	13833	32140	396.4	154.5	241.9	293.4	100.9	192.5
2012	48078	15291	32787	449.3	188.3	261	309.5	109.5	200.0
2013	45977	15730	30247	526.7	253.9	272.8	322.5	121.3	201.2
2014	36810	16549	20261	613.5	265.4	348.1	334.0	127.6	155.7

B-2-5 社区服务机构和设施

单位：个

年　份	城乡各类服务机构和设施合计	社区服务中心	其他社区服务机构和设施	便民利民网点	社区服务机构和设施覆盖率(%)
1987					
1988	69699		69699		7.1
1989	71357		71357		6.9
1990	84757		84757		7.7
1991	89918		89918		8.0
1992	112171		112171		10.1
1993	92946	3711	89235	169503	8.3
1994	98679	4034	94645	204229	8.8
1995	115175	4380	110795	234024	11.0
1996	132309	5055	127254	259201	12.7
1997	138366	5113	133253	307226	13.5
1998	154196	6154	148042	345075	16.2
1999	164962	7623	157339	405740	18.0
2000	187888	6444	181444	451567	22.4
2001	201758	6179	195579	539544	25.5
2002	206743	7898	198845	622986	27.0
2003	203945	7520	196425	668418	27.5
2004	205926	7804	198122	703760	28.5
2005	203275	8479	194796	664764	28.7
2006	160007	8565	151442	457896	22.7

年　份	城乡各类服务机构和设施合计	社区指导中心	社区服务中心	社区服务站	其他社区服务机构和设施	便民利民网点	社区服务机构和设施覆盖率(%)
2007	134852		9319	50116	75417	892656	19.4
2008	146322		9873	30021	106428	748684	21.3
2009	146341		10003	53170	83168	692625	21.4
2010	152941		12720	44237	95984	539136	22.4
2011	160352		14391	56156	89805	452868	23.6
2012	200162	809	15497	87931	95925	397222	29.5
2013	251939	890	19014	108377	123658	358518	36.9

年　份	城乡各类服务机构和设施合计	社区指导中心	社区服务中心	社区服务站	社区养老机构和设施	互助型的养老设施	其他社区服务设施
2014	310652	918	23088	120188	18927	40357	107174

注：社区服务机构和设施覆盖率=(社区服务中心+社区服务站+其他社区服务机构和设施)/村居委会。

B-2-6 老年福利与福利企业

单位：万人

年　份	老年福利			福利企业		
	享受高龄补贴的老年人数	享受护理补贴的老年人数	享受养老服务补贴的老年人数	单位数（个）	残疾职工人数（万人）	利润额（亿元）
1978				920	3.5	0.8
1979				1106	4.8	0.8
1980				1309	5.5	0.9
1981				1574	6.1	0.7
1982				1704	6.4	0.8
1983				5930	9.6	0.9
1984				6710	11.6	1.3
1985				14872	23.2	5.1
1986				19865	31.4	4.2
1987				27793	43.3	8.8
1988				40496	55.9	16.5
1989				41565	60.5	16.1
1990				41827	63.8	17.8
1991				43805	70.1	21.3
1992				49836	77.8	32.6
1993				56881	84.5	44.7
1994				60233	90.9	44.1
1995				60237	93.9	49.1
1996				59397	93.6	45.1
1997				55509	91.0	66.3
1998				50514	85.6	63.9
1999				44628	79.0	76.7
2000				40670	72.5	99.0
2001				37980	69.9	119.5
2002				35758	68.3	148.3
2003				33976	67.9	189.9
2004				32410	66.2	219
2005				31211	63.7	225.2
2006	233.5			30199	55.9	237.8
2007	247.1			24974	56.3	169.3
2008	349.3			23780	61.9	119.2
2009	430.9			22783	62.7	125.4
2010	576.4			22226	62.5	150.8
2011	883.1			21507	62.8	140.1
2012	1257.7			20205	59.7	118.4
2013	1557.9	11.7	101.9	18227	53.9	106.9
2014	1719.6	20	154.7	16389	47.9	95.2

B-2-7 孤儿和收养

单位：件、人

年 份	孤儿数	收养登记总数	中国公民收养登记	外国公民收养登记	被收养人合计	福利机构抚养的儿童	被中国公民收养	被外国人收养
1996		18896	14804	4092	20389	2201		
1997		21548	17193	4355	21548	975		
1998		26498	20611	5887	26498	677		
1999		38074	31916	6158	38019	1670	31882	6137
2000		55802	49037	6765	56191	1847	49500	6691
2001		44706	36089	8617	45844	1908	37200	8644
2002		45336	35372	9964	47860	2404	37642	10218
2003		54159	44884	9275	54159	3427	44884	9275
2004		52603	40084	12519	55572	3189	44708	10864
2005		49506	35470	14036	50921	3564	38057	12864
2006		48178	38393	9785	49148	2867	39424	9724
2007		45192	36893	8299	46047	1146	37790	8257
2008	67921	42550	37009	5541	44115	1846	38617	5498
2009	127599	44260	39801	4459	44359	1605	39964	4395
2010	252110	34529	29618	4911	34473	1878	29978	4495
2011	509695	31424	27579	3845	31329	1679	28117	3212
2012	570075	27278	23157	4121	27310	1760	23169	4141
2013	548845	24460	21230	3230	24491	9657	21261	3230
2014	525179	22772	19885	2887	22876	10336	20055	2821

注：福利机构抚养的儿童2012年以前是孤儿，2013年以后含弃婴。

B-2-8 城市社会救济和城市居民最低生活保障

单位：万人

年　份	城市居民传统救济总人数	城市居民传统定救人数	城市精简退职老职工人数	享受40%人数	定量救济人数
1978					
1979	33.6	23.7	*9.9*		
1980	32.9	22.9	*10*		
1981	31.5	21.5	*10*		
1982	34.7	21.4	*13.3*		
1983	47.1	22.6	*24.5*		
1984	*207.4*	*160.6*	*46.8*	*25.3*	
1985	30.0	18.2	11.8	6.4	5.4
1986	49.0	35.6	13.4	7.1	6.3
1987	29.8	16.2	13.6	7.2	6.4
1988	32.9	17.6	15.3	7.7	7.6
1989	30.5	16.2	14.3	7.1	7.2
1990	41.8	16.4	25.4	16.4	9.0
1991	33.7	16.1	17.6	8.5	9.0
1992	39.5	19.2	20.3	9.7	10.6
1993	24.6	13.8	10.8	5	5.8
1994	23.0	12.4	10.6	4.9	5.7
1995	109.0	55.2	53.8	23.9	29.9
1996	120.1	66.5	53.6	23.6	30.0

年　份	城市居民最低生活保障人数	在职人员	下岗人员	退休人员	失业人员	“三无”人员	其他人员
1996	84.9						
1997	87.9						
1998	184.1						
1999	256.9						
2000	402.6						
2001	1170.7						
2002	2064.7	186.8	554.5	90.8	358.3	91.9	783.1
2003	2246.8	179.3	518.4	90.7	409	99.9	949.3
2004	2205	141	468.9	73.1	423.1	95.4	1003.5
2005	2234.2	114.1	430.7	61.3	410.1	95.8	1122.1
2006	2240.1	97.6	350	53.2	420.8	93.1	1225.3

年　份	城市居民最低生活保障人数	残疾人	三无人员	老年人	成年人				未成年人	
					在职人员	灵活就业	登记失业	未登记失业	在校生	其他
2007	2272.1	161.0	125.8	298.4	93.9	343.8	627.2	364.3	321.6	223
2008	2334.8	169.1	106.9	316.7	82.2	381.7	564.3	402.2	358.1	229.6
2009	2345.6	181.0	94.1	333.5	79.0	432.2	510.2	410.9	369.1	210.7
2010	2310.5	180.7	89.3	338.6	68.2	432.4	492.8	420.0	357.3	201.2
2011	2276.8	184.1	80.3	346.9	61.5	429.7	472.5	426.7	348.5	191
2012	2143.5	174.5	64.9	339.3	49.6	459.3	400.4	422.1	318.3	154.5
2013	2064.2	169.2	58	330.3	45.1	462.1	365.5	416.8	303.2	141.3
2014	1877.0	161.1	50	315.8	37.5	425.8	312.5	398.7	266	120.7

注：1984年的精简退职老职工人数含农村的数据。

B-2-9 农村社会救济和农村最低生活保障

单位：万人、万户

年 份	农村社会救济总人数	农村定期定量救济人数	农村精简退职老职工人数	享受40%人数	定量救济人数
1978					
1979	6847.6	*6837.7*	*9.9*		
1980	4651.8	*4641.8*	*10*		
1981	4265.1	*4255.1*	*10*		
1982	4270.7	*4257.4*	*13.3*		
1983	3526.7	*3502.2*	*24.5*		
1984	3842.7	*3795.9*	*46.8*	*25.3*	
1985	116.7	75.1	41.6	18.1	23.5
1986	103	63.1	39.9	18.1	21.7
1987	92.2	53.2	39	17.7	21.3
1988	93	54.1	38.9	17.6	21.4
1989	75.7	35.0	40.7	18.3	22.3
1990	100.2	46.7	53.5	23.6	29.9
1991	97	43.8	53.2	23.5	29.8
1992	97.5	45.6	51.9	23.3	28.6
1993	80.1	36.3	43.8	19.5	24.3
1994	82.1	38.5	43.6	19.2	24.3
1995	98.3	55.2	43.1	19	24.1
1996	109.2	66.5	42.7	18.6	24.1
1997	104.5	51.4	53.1	23.2	29.8
1998	120.5	65.6	54.9	24.9	30
1999	107.1	55.6	51.5	22.5	28.7
2000	112.2	62.5	49.7	22.1	27.6
2001	130.5	80.7	49.8	21.3	27.8
2002	138.7	*90*	48.7	20.9	27.8

年 份	农村困难群众救助总人数	农村最低生活保障人数	农村特困户救助人数	农村困难群众救助总户数	农村最低生活保障户数	困难户	其 他	农村特困户救助户数	困难户	其 他	五保户供养户数	农村传统救济人数
2001	385.3	304.6	80.7									
2002	497.8	407.8	*90.0*	156.7	156.7							
2003	1160.5	367.1	793.4	632.8	146.5	114.5	32	282.1	192.7	89.3	204.2	
2004	1402.1	488	914.1	780.8	197.9	165.2	33.6	317.1	260.4	56.6	265.8	
2005	1891.8	825	1066.8	1061	356.5	298.8	57.7	354.8	290.4	64.4	349.7	
2006	2987.8	1593.1	775.8	1606.3	777.2			325.8			503.3	115.6

年 份	农村救助总人数	农村最低生活保障人数	农村集中供养五保人数	农村分散供养五保人数	传统救济人数	农村临时救济人数
2007	4818.6	3566.3	138	393.3	75	646
2008	5757.3	4305.5	155.6	393	72.2	831
2009	5922	4760	171.8	381.6	62.2	546.4
2010	6443.5	5214	177.4	378.9	59.5	613.7
2011	6522.2	5305.7	184.5	366.5	68.7	596.8
2012	5969.7	5344.5	185.3	360.3	79.6	
2013	5998.3	5388	183.5	353.8	73	
2014	5810.8	5207.2	174.3	354.8	74.5	

注：1984年以前含应保未保的农村救济人数。

B-2-10 最低生活保障和社会救济平均标准

年　份	城市居民最低生活保障平均标准（元/人、月）	农村最低生活保障平均标准（元/人、年）	农村五保集中供养平均标准（元/人、年）	农村五保分散供养平均标准（元/人、年）
1999	149.0			
2000	157.0			
2001	147.0			
2002	148.0			
2003	149.0			
2004	152.0			
2005	156.0			
2006	169.6	850.8	1608.2	1224.5
2007	182.4	840.0	1953.0	1432.0
2008	205.3	987.6	2176.1	1624.4
2009	227.8	1210.1	2587.5	1842.7
2010	251.2	1404.0	2951.4	2102.1
2011	287.6	1718.4	3399.7	2470.5
2012	330.1	2067.8	4060.9	3008.0
2013	373.3	2433.9	4685.0	3498.5
2014	410.5	2776.6	5371.3	4005.9

B-2-11 最低生活保障和社会救济平均支出水平

年　份	城市居民最低生活保障平均支出水平（元/人、月）	农村最低生活保障平均支出水平（元/人、年）	农村五保集中供养平均支出水平（元/人、年）	农村五保分散供养平均支出水平（元/人、年）
1999	44.8			
2000	45.3			
2001	29.6			
2002	43.9			
2003	58.0			
2004	65.0			
2005	72.3			
2006	83.6	414.0		
2007	102.7	465.6		
2008	143.7	604.8	2055.7	1121.0
2009	172.0	816.0	2316.0	1284.0
2010	189.0	888.0	2460.0	1416.0
2011	240.3	1273.2	3081.9	1774.9
2012	239.1	1247.9	3496.6	2237.3
2013	264.2	1393.5	4078.3	2724.3
2014	285.6	1552.3	4676.1	3228.9

B-2-12 医疗救助

单位：万人次、万人

年　份	民政部门资助参加城市医疗保险人数	民政部门资助参加农村合作医疗人数	民政部门直接医疗救助人次数	住院救助	门诊救助
2004		552.6	121.1		
2005		654.9	199.6		
2006		1317.1	201.3		
2007		2517.3	819.1		
2008	642.6	3432.4	1203.1		
2009	1095.9	4059.1	1140.4		
2010	1461.2	4615.4	1479.3		
2011	1549.8	4825.3	2144		
2012	1387.1	4490.4	2173.7	1141.4	1032.3
2013	1490.1	4868.7	2126.4	1074.0	1052.4
2014	1702	5021.7	2395.3	1106.6	1288.7

B-2-13 城市生活无着人员救助

年 份	救助站（个）	未成年人救助保护中心（个）	生活无着人员救助（人次）	#未成年人救助	救助类单位床位数（张）	#未成年人救助保护中心床位
1978	783					
1979	845					
1980	665					
1981	598					
1982	610					
1983	615					
1984	628					
1985	636					
1986	647					
1987	639					
1988	644					
1989	669					
1990	666					
1991	691					
1992	692					
1993	719					
1994	712					
1995	722					
1996	720					
1997	728					
1998	742					
1999	800					
2000	857					
2001	838					
2002	861					
2003	864		634528	60257		
2004	977		820254	104455	47086	
2005	1079	40	1196305	120487	45603	1849
2006	1189	50	1295506	129337	45661	1133
2007	1261	90	1544492	159989	46800	3621
2008	1334	88	1573484	155794	50642	3543
2009	1372	116	1680532	167283	51049	3670
2010	1448	145	1719008	146329	55562	5221
2011	1547	241	2409701	178705	71109	8165
2012	1770	261	2765761	152070	99901	10038
2013	1891	274	3484727	183802	108360	11499
2014	1949	345	3474544	128033	110806	11584

B-2-14 社会捐赠

单位：亿元、亿件

年 份	社会捐赠款物合计	社会捐赠款	民政部门	各类社会组织	社会捐赠其他物资折款	接收社会捐赠衣被数量
1997	14.0	4.2			9.9	0.9
1998	113.2	50.2	50.2		63.0	2.9
1999	17.8	6.9	5.0	2.0	10.8	0.6
2000	16.3	9.3	5.4	3.9	7.0	0.8
2001	20.0	11.7	7.6	4.1	8.3	1.3
2002	20.8	19.0	11.1	7.9	1.8	2.3
2003	43.4	41.0	29.2	11.9	2.4	2.0
2004	35.1	34.0	17.1	16.9	1.2	0.9
2005	61.9	60.3	31.3	29.0	1.6	1.0
2006	89.5	83.1	43.0	40.1	6.4	0.7
2007	148.3	132.8	50.9	81.9	15.6	0.9
2008	764.1	744.5	479.3	265.2	19.6	11.6
2009	485.9	483.7	66.5	417.2	2.2	1.2
2010	601.7	596.8	179.8	417.0	4.9	0.3
2011	494.9	490.1	96.6	393.5	4.8	0.3
2012	578.8	572.5	101.7	470.8	6.3	1.3
2013	575.1	566.4	107.6	458.8	8.7	1
2014	612.4	604.4	79.6	524.9	8.0	0.5

B–2–15 中国福利彩票销售

年 份	福利彩票发行单位（个）	福利彩票销售额（亿元）	提取公益金（亿元）	公益金支出（亿元）
1978				
1979				
1980				
“六五”时期				
1981				
1982				
1983				
1984				
1985				
“七五”时期		**14.2**	**4.6**	
1986				
1987		0.2	0.1	
1988		3.8	1.2	
1989		3.8	1.3	
1990		6.5	2.0	
“八五”时期		**115.2**	**34.3**	
1991		7.7	2.5	
1992		13.8	4.1	
1993		18.4	5.5	
1994		18.0	5.3	
1995		57.3	16.9	
“九五”时期		**358.7**	**103.5**	**72.7**
1996		64.8	19.1	
1997		36.4	10.1	
1998		63.2	19.6	14.1
1999	1169	104.4	30.5	19.9
2000	1253	89.9	24.2	38.7
“十五”时期		**1145.2**	**377.1**	**161.9**
2001	1185	139.6	41.9	19.7
2002	1121	168.0	52.3	25.5
2003	1145	200.1	67.2	30.6
2004	1128	226.4	79.4	33.8
2005	1113	411.2	136.3	52.3
“十一五”时期		**3455.3**	**1127.4**	**484.0**
2006	989	495.7	168.8	52.6
2007	985	631.6	211.0	77.6
2008	999	604.0	205.4	119.2
2009	988	756.0	243.4	113.4
2010	993	968.0	298.8	121.2
“十二五”时期		**6613.6**	**1927.8**	**713.7**
2011	974	1278.0	382.0	127.9
2012	955	1510.3	449.4	159
2013	940	1765.3	510.7	195.5
2014	893	2060.0	585.7	231.3

B-2-16 定期抚恤优抚对象

单位：人

年 份	抚恤补助总人数（万人）	定期抚恤人数	烈属	牺牲、病故军人家属	伤残人员（万人）
1978	205.9				73.4
1979	173.6				75.6
1980	222.4				78.6
1981	233.6				79.6
1982	240.8	590104	541516	48588	81.6
1983	251.2	577791	526826	50965	83.0
1984	267.3	585403	536523	48880	84.4
1985	283.3	518566	440000	78566	85.3
1986	339.8	533245	446209	87036	86.5
1987	366.3	548063	453480	94583	88.0
1988	378.5	537472	429271	108201	88.7
1989	411.7	525134	422656	102478	89.1
1990	425.7	516638	407276	109362	87.4
1991	434.8	614945	504462	110483	87.5
1992	433.7	602163	492457	109706	87.6
1993	441.2	495994	383924	112070	88.3
1994	442.0	487256	372850	114406	88.5
1995	448.8	486250	370685	115565	88.8
1996	447.0	484270	366216	118054	89.3
1997	448.3	480464	362086	118378	89.5
1998	447.0	473901	357492	116409	89.2
1999	445.1	458079	336587	121492	88.7
2000	442.4	448276	325116	123160	88.1

年 份	抚恤补助总人数（万人）	定期抚恤人数	烈 属	牺牲军人家属	病故军人家属	伤残人员（万人）
2001	450.7	480852	348521	60081	72250	85.5
2002	459.0	480466	341109	63953	75404	85.8
2003	464.9	488820	345141	65303	78376	86.0
2004	462.0	485733	339817	65695	80221	85.6
2005	460.3	492517	349253	63603	79661	84.5
2006	462.6	491320	346089	64248	80983	86.0
2007	622.4	488675	342101	64478	82096	86.5
2008	633.2	478880	332390	65001	81489	87.2
2009	630.7	458578	317675	62304	78599	87.2
2010	625.0	447824	307587	62338	77899	86.7
2011	852.5	422439	286449	60534	75456	85.9
2012	944.4	411711	277712	59478	74521	84.9
2013	950.5	366400	240375	55734	70291	81.2
2014	917.3	311210	197955	48179	65076	76.6

B-2-17 定期补助优抚对象

单位：人

年 份	定期补助总人数	红军老战士合计	在乡红军老战士	西路军	红军失散人员	在乡复员军人	带病回乡退伍军人	60岁及以上农村籍退伍军人	其 他
1978	9251	9251	9251						
1979	7872	7872	7872						
1980	6922	6922	6922						
1981	6567	6567	6567						
1982	1002181	6383	6383			859055	136743		
1983	1104586	6142	6142			952993	145451		
1984	1243633	6159	6159			1081350	156124		
1985	1461180	6329	6329			1185502	183129		86220
1986	1999872	6315	6315			1673990	210445		109122
1987	2230873	7466	7466			1833402	241290		148715
1988	2360462	7415	7415			1950641	247009		155397
1989	2715258	6628	6628			2272639	283075		152916
1990	2866579	7514	7514			2373873	305045		180147
1991	2939074	7015	7015			2419453	346021		166585
1992	2975175	6599	6599			2402869	373989		191718
1993	2947209	113728	5531	2997	105200	2424984	408497		
1994	2963965	112054	5058	2430	104566	2424435	427476		
1995	2987751	108484	4659	2318	101507	2423191	456076		
1996	3018047	115317	4480	2303	108534	2421517	481213		
1997	3037367	122115	4195	2214	115706	2396017	519235		
1998	3033826	118245	3996	2157	112092	2367266	548315		
1999	3056727	111096	3687	2106	105303	2363466	582165		
2000	3057257	105632	3326	1997	100309	2320739	630886		
2001	3170877	98345	3325	1889	93131	2246954	782802		42776
2002	3251971	94848	3136	1691	90021	2274657	882090		376
2003	3300232	90767	2893	1610	86264	2262264	919349		27852
2004	3277914	87521	2701	1454	83366	2214467	950428		25498
2005	3265797	79639	2681	1370	75588	2145421	977424		63313
2006	3274059	71707	2417	1220	68070	2064713	1072684		64955
2007	4870800	66220	2049	966	63205	1988977	1134414		1681189
2008	4981893	49198	1622	440	47136	1920235	1193622		1818838
2009	4976839	42945	1351	322	41272	1809019	1219752		1905123
2010	4935399	38630	1226	273	37131	1703396	1265664		1927709
2011	7243706	30309	911	190	29208	1587006	1321786	2373772	1930833
2012	8183693	26882	757	164	25961	1474790	1324325	3210986	2146710
2013	8326336	19740	647	117	18976	1260945	1306479	3566766	2172406
2014	8095950	11697	341	87	11269	993204	1242020	3748039	2100990

B-2-18 接收军队离退休、退职人员

单位：人

年份	合计	军队离退休干部	地方(含军队职工)人员
1978			
1979			
1980			
1981			
1982	21993	801	21192
1983	20038	1507	18531

年份	合计	军队离退休干部	#离休	地方人员	军队职工
1984	9916	1873	117	6228	1815
1985	12429	6137	3327	4472	1820
1986	29260	21564	15598	4236	3460
1987	14146	10035	6224	1719	2392
1988	6050	4242	2329	1287	521
1989	4858	3441	1530	994	423
1990	6214	4988	2573	1008	218
1991	6558	5568	2703	806	184
1992	4420	3551	1516	693	176
1993	5578	916	283	543	4318
1994	5773	1016	447	566	4190
1995	3531	1056	323	476	1999
1996	9346	3210	371	282	5854
1997	6311	3246	401	230	2835
1998	8156	5868	785	691	1597

年份	合计	军队离退休干部	地方离退休干部	军队无军籍职工
1999	12380	9464	305	2611
2000	15238	10197	219	4822
2001	13738	6236	373	7129

年份	合计	军队离退休干部(含地方)	#离休	军队退休士官	军队无军籍职工
2002	14428	3640		161	10627
2003	11057	5055	143	140	6312
2004	10794	8884	200	90	1820

年份	合计	军队离退休干部	#离休	地方离退休干部	#离休	军队退休士官	军队无军籍职工
2005	18512	17280	223	136	14	192	904
2006	31968	20794	259	673	85	365	10136
2007	28058	18534	258	303	23	160	9061
2008	21378	15829	78	205	15	297	5047
2009	18904	13836	143	348	5	1308	3412
2010	13451	11775	148	183	4	1112	381
2011	14530	12355	140	141	8	1405	629
2012	18570	14341	416	335	45	1047	2847
2013	38762	10927	108	500	29	570	26709
2014	27699	10067	246	221	9	503	16908

B-2-19 烈士褒扬和优待

年 份	烈士纪念建筑物管理机构（个）	本年领取烈士褒扬金人数（人）	零散烈士纪念建筑物（个）	优待优抚对象户数（户）	#优待军属户数	优待总金额（万元）	#固定优待军属总额
1978			5347				
1979			3779			20393	
1980			2825			31459	
1981			2915			47255	
1982	965	8601	3592	4730756		58750	
1983	928	11024	3826	4387292		59588	
1984	786	8478	3953	4102419		62263	
1985	579	5887	3716	3567165	2884906	71655	577018
1986	582	11758	3871	3355694	2710272	75243	62205
1987	587	10644	4121	3223550	2562036	80915	66321
1988	632	9035	4236	3225253	2477699	87160	71735
1989	637	3960	4466	3086285	2423418	92169	77764
1990	632	3067	6065	2941486	2522476	99535	86739
1991	630	1556	6474	2967881	2540714	106354	93069
1992	684	1338	6957	2967002	2535037	116573	102008
1993	696	1467	6956	3009163	2470099	131555	113330
1994	718	1215	7279	3027420	2462671	155627	133070
1995	715	1277	7067	3051322	2476261	194379	166414
1996	740	1187	7020	3040439	2449077	251798	217527
1997	737	888	7048	3334000	2427586	321741	261865
1998	752	749	7322	3250395	2415838	356413	292305
1999	774	616	7252	3818210	2380675	402998	305386
2000	795	468	7427	3855797	2282584	469054	363675
2001	845	460	7802	3973085	2086464	385859	275456
2002	873	403	8051	4130817	1929011	374819	251854
2003	918	461	7781	3962425	1672205	391581	239410
2004	938	316	7425	3632630	1430630	418499	267458
2005	989	314	7483	3393218	1224036	379631	213968
2006	1072	265	7414	3220933	1183674	421010	224354
2007	1056	168	7186	3277318	1145223	454090	233479
2008	1133	297	7569	3301682	1108878	666011	267750
2009	1137	213	7622	3280522	1190816	751065	297448
2010	1195	173	9729	3308766	1169833	671536	340382
2011	1227	233	12378	3330859	1050918	968175	555402
2012	1306	172	13151	3471611	1008477	1121135	520520
2013	1463	200	13601	3402629	958255	1351368	646023
2014	1516	267	11365	3354536	883066	1510252	693201

注：2011年由于部分省份指标理解错误，数据有调整。

B-2-20 自然灾害情况

年 份	受灾人口（万人次）	因灾死亡人口（含失踪）（人）	紧急转移人口（万人）	直接经济损失（亿元）	倒塌房屋（万间）	农作物受灾面积（万公顷）
1978		4965			73.1	4844
1979		6962			152.1	3937
1980		6821			137.3	5003
1981	26710.0	7422			261.5	3979
1982	22900.7	7935			320.3	3313
1983	22439.0	10952		260.9	345.4	3471
1984	20894.0	6927			274.7	3189
1985	26446.0	4394	290.5	410.4	224.9	4437
1986	29928.0	5410	345.8		209.7	4714
1987	23512.0	5495	348.0	326.3	180.0	4207
1988	36169.0	7306	582.9		258.0	5087
1989	34569.0	5952	365.3	525.0	194.1	4699
1990	29348.0	7338	579.2	616.0	247.4	3847
1991	41941.0	7315	1308.5	1215.1	581.5	5547
1992	37174.0	5741	303.6	853.9	196.6	5133
1993	37541.0	6125	307.7	933.2	271.6	4867
1994	43799.0	8549	1054.0	1876.0	512.1	5504
1995	24215.0	5561	1064.0	1863.0	439.3	4587
1996	32305.0	7273	1216.0	2882.0	809.0	5975
1997	47886.0	3212	511.3	1975.0	288.0	5343
1998	35216.0	5511	2082.4	3007.4	821.4	2229
1999	35319.0	2966	664.8	1962.4	174.5	4998
2000	45652.3	3014	467.1	2045.3	147.3	5469
2001	37255.9	2583	211.1	1942.0	92.2	5215
2002	37841.8	2840	471.8	1717.4	175.7	4711.9
2003	49745.9	2259	707.3	1884.2	343.0	5438.6
2004	33920.6	2250	563.2	1602.3	155.0	3710.6
2005	40653.7	2475	1570.3	2042.1	226.4	3881.8
2006	43453.3	3186	1384.5	2528.1	193.3	4109.1
2007	39777.9	2325	1499.1	2363.0	146.7	4899.3
2008	47795.0	88928	2682.2	11752.4	1097.7	3999.0
2009	47933.5	1528	709.9	2523.7	83.8	4721.4
2010	42610.2	7844	1858.4	5339.9	273.3	3742.6
2011	43290.0	1126	939.4	3096.4	93.5	3247.1
2012	29421.7	1530	1109.6	4185.5	90.6	2496.2
2013	38818.7	2284	1215.0	5808.4	87.5	3135
2014	24353.7	1818	601.7	3373.8	45.0	2489.1

B-3-1 社会组织

单位：个

年 份	社会组织合计	社会团体	基金会	民办非企业
1978				
1979				
1980				
1981				
1982				
1983				
1984				
1985				
1986				
1987				
1988	4446	4446		
1989	4544	4544		
1990	10855	10855		
1991	82814	82814		
1992	154502	154502		
1993	167506	167506		
1994	174060	174060		
1995	180583	180583		
1996	184821	184821		
1997	181318	181318		
1998	165600	165600		
1999	142665	136764		5901
2000	153322	130668		22654
2001	210939	128805		82134
2002	244509	133297		111212
2003	266612	141167	954	124491
2004	289432	153359	892	135181
2005	319762	171150	975	147637
2006	354393	191946	1144	161303
2007	386916	211661	1340	173915
2008	413660	229681	1597	182382
2009	431069	238747	1843	190479
2010	445631	245256	2200	198175
2011	461971	254969	2614	204388
2012	499268	271131	3029	225108
2013	547245	289026	3549	254670
2014	606048	309736	4117	292195

注：2001年以前的基金会含在社会团体内。

B-3-2 自治组织

年　份	基层群众性自治组织合计（万个）	居民委员会（个）	居民小组（万个）	居民委员会成员（万人）	村民委员会（万个）	村民小组（万个）	村民委员会成员（万人）
1978							
1979		46810					
1980							
1981		57169					
1982							
1983	37.7	65519			31.2		
1984	100.3	75609			92.7		
1985	103.0	80943		34.9	94.9		379.6
1986	95.3	86824		36.2	86.6		365.9
1987	93.2	86799		37.0	84.5		359.9
1988	97.8	95684		36.1	88.3		366.6
1989	102.8	93691		36.6	93.4		379.4
1990	110.0	98814		43.1	100.1		409.4
1991	111.9	100347		44.1	101.9		424.4
1992	110.8	104136		46.5	100.4		430.9
1993	112.0	107173		47.9	101.3		456.0
1994	111.7	110112		48.0	100.7		458.5
1995	104.4	111860		48.0	93.2		400.5
1996	104.2	113690		49.3	92.8		397.5
1997	102.4	117915	108.3	49.8	90.6	535.8	378.8
1998	95.2	119042	117.2	50.8	83.3	537.1	358.6
1999	91.6	114815	124.7	50.1	80.1	555.7	351.3
2000	84.0	108424	127.2	48.4	73.2	553.4	315.0
2001	79.2	91893	125.9	46.4	70.0	541.9	316.4
2002	76.7	86087	124.4	39.6	68.1	528.6	294.2
2003	74.1	77431	122.2	39.7	66.3	519.2	319.1
2004	72.2	77884	129.6	42.5	64.4	507.9	292.1
2005	70.9	79947	123.3	45.4	62.9	490.5	265.7
2006	70.4	80717	123.5	44.3	62.4	453.3	243.0
2007	69.5	82006	122.3	41.6	61.3	466.9	241.1
2008	68.8	83413	128.7	42.2	60.4	480.9	233.9
2009	68.4	84689	129.5	43.1	59.9	480.5	234.0
2010	68.2	87057	130.7	43.9	59.5	479.1	233.4
2011	67.9	89480	134.0	45.4	59.0	476.4	231.9
2012	68.0	91153	133.5	46.9	58.8	469.4	232.3
2013	68.3	94620	135.7	48.4	58.9	466.4	232.3
2014	68.2	96693	135.8	49.7	58.5	470.4	230.5

B-3-3 结婚

年　份	结婚登记总数（万对）	内地居民登记结婚数（万对）	涉外华侨港澳台登记结婚数（万对）	登记结婚人数（万人）
1978	597.8	597.8		
1979	637.1	636.3	0.8	
1980	720.9	719.8	1.1	
1981	1041.7	1040.3	1.4	
1982	836.9	835.5	1.4	
1983	765.4	764.2	1.3	
1984	784.8	783.4	1.4	
1985	831.3	829.1	2.2	
1986	884.0	882.3	1.7	
1987	926.7	924.7	2.0	
1988	899.2	897.2	2.0	
1989	937.2	935.2	2.0	
1990	951.1	948.7	2.4	
1991	953.6	951.0	2.6	
1992	957.5	954.5	3.0	
1993	915.4	912.2	3.3	
1994	932.4	929.0	3.4	
1995	934.1	929.7	4.4	
1996	938.7	934.0	4.7	1877.4
1997	914.1	909.1	5.1	1828.3
1998	891.7	886.7	5.0	1783.4
1999	885.3	879.9	5.4	1770.6
2000	848.5	842.0	6.5	1697.0
2001	805.0	797.1	7.9	1610.0
2002	786	778.8	7.3	1572.0
2003	811.4	803.5	7.8	1622.8
2004	867.2	860.8	6.4	1734.4
2005	823.1	816.6	6.4	1646.2
2006	945	938.2	6.8	1890.0
2007	991.4	986.3	5.1	1982.8
2008	1098.3	1093.2	5.1	2196.6
2009	1212.4	1207.5	4.9	2424.8
2010	1241	1236.1	4.9	2482.0
2011	1302.4	1297.5	4.9	2604.8
2012	1323.6	1318.3	5.3	2647.2
2013	1346.9	1341.4	5.5	2693.8
2014	1306.7	1302.0	4.7	2613.5

每千居民之结婚宗数（结婚率）计算方法：

$$每千居民之结婚宗数=\frac{结婚宗数}{（当年期初人口数+当年期末人口数）/2}\times 1000‰$$

登记

初婚人数（万人）	再婚人数（万人）			每千居民之结婚宗数（结婚率）（‰）
		#女（万人）	#恢复结婚（对数）	
				6.2
				6.7
				7.3
				10.4
				8.3
				7.5
				7.5
				7.9
				8.2
				8.6
				8.3
				8.4
				8.2
				8.3
				8.3
				7.8
				7.8
				7.7
1781.7	86.2	41.1	48044	7.7
1726.0	92.2	46.3	62752	7.4
1675.4	97.9	49.8	69160	7.2
1659.4	100.5	50.0	57815	7.1
1581.4	102.6	50.8	56324	6.7
1481.7	112.5	58.0	63442	6.3
1440.3	117.2	60.2	68081	6.1
1483.9	123.3	60.7	68204	6.3
1569.6	152.0	77.1	84799	6.7
1483.0	163.1	74.3	115003	6.3
1705.6	184.4	86.7	107113	7.2
1779.7	203.1	97.3	138967	7.5
1972.5	224.1	108.0	162244	8.3
2168.8	256.0	124.7	181162	9.1
2200.9	281.1	138.8	190356	9.3
2309.9	294.9	146.5	209781	9.7
2361.2	286.0	145.8	229607	9.8
2386.0	307.9	156.5	298766	9.9
2286.8	326.7	168.7	348285	9.6

B-3-4 离婚办理

年 份	离婚总数（万对）	民政部门登记离婚数（万对）	内地居民登记离婚数（万对）	涉外华侨港澳台登记离婚数（对）	法院部门办理离婚数（万对）	每千居民之离婚宗数（离婚率）（‰）
1978	28.5	17.0	17		11.5	0.18
1979	31.9	19.3	19.3	82	12.6	0.33
1980	34.1	18.0	18	330	16.1	0.35
1981	38.9	18.7	18.7	46	20.2	0.39
1982	42.8	21.1	21.1	116	21.7	0.42
1983	41.8	19.7	19.7	126	22.1	0.42
1984	45.4	19.9	19.9	110	25.5	0.40
1985	45.8	19.6	19.6	108	26.2	0.44
1986	50.6	21.4	21.4	205	29.2	0.47
1987	58.1	23.6	23.6	220	34.5	0.55
1988	65.5	26.4	26.4	310	39.1	0.60
1989	75.3	28.8	28.7	518	46.5	0.68
1990	80.0	30.1	30	602	49.9	0.69
1991	83.1	30.1	30	588	53	0.72
1992	85.0	31.6	31.5	833	53.4	0.74
1993	91.0	33.6	33.5	968	57.4	0.77
1994	98.2	35.5	35.4	737	62.7	0.82
1995	105.6	36.8	36.7	813	68.8	0.88
1996	113.4	39.4	39.3	1175	74	0.93
1997	119.9	44.0	43.9	1385	75.9	0.97
1998	119.2	46.6	46.5	948	72.6	0.96
1999	120.2	47.8	47.7	975	72.4	0.96
2000	121.3	48.9	48.8	1075	72.4	0.96
2001	125.0	52.8	52.5	2856	72.2	0.98
2002	117.7	57.3	56.8	5221	60.4	0.90
2003	133.0	69	68.7	3333	64	1.05
2004	166.5	104.6	104.0	5830	61.9	1.28
2005	178.5	118.4	117.5	8267	60.1	1.37
2006	191.3	129.1	128.3	8414	62.2	1.46
2007	209.8	145.7	144.8	8852	64.1	1.59
2008	226.9	161.0	160.0	9470	65.9	1.71
2009	246.8	180.2	179.6	5608	66.6	1.85
2010	267.8	201.0	200.4	5783	66.8	2.00
2011	287.4	220.7	220.2	5761	66.7	2.13
2012	310.4	242.3	241.7	6161	68.1	2.29
2013	350.0	281.5	280.9	6538	68.5	2.58
2014	363.9	295.7	295.1	6714	67.9	2.67

每千居民之离婚宗数（离婚率）计算方法：

$$每千居民之离婚宗数=\frac{离婚宗数}{（当年期初人口数+当年期末人口数）/2}\times 1000‰$$

B-3-5 殡葬服务

年份	殡仪馆（个）	公墓（个）	骨灰堂	殡葬管理机构（个）	火化炉数（台）	火化遗体数（万具）	火化率（%）
1978					1712	117.5	
1979					2300	102.1	
1980					2510	98.7	
1981					2586	85.4	
1982					2622	96.2	
1983					2622	108.0	
1984					2686	128.2	
1985	9	24		122	2729	155.2	
1986	5	25		143	2745	155.5	26.2
1987	6	29		195	2752	162.0	27.0
1988	14	37		219	2729	180.9	29.5
1989	17	50		217	2768	182.3	30.1
1990	1260	73		211	2795	201.3	31.5
1991	1283	84		234	2714	215.6	34.0
1992	1288	88		228	2852	242.6	31.2
1993	1264	136		296	2891	247.6	31.6
1994	1272	163		284	2882	257.1	33.4
1995	1281	209		302	2927	262.7	33.2
1996	1283	256		313	3005	282.7	35.2
1997	1289	359		340	2959	295.0	36.8
1998	1310	425		374	3157	319.7	39.6
1999	1318	624		402	*3340*	336.4	41.5
2000	1363	692		466	*3565*	373.7	46.0
2001	1415	757		540	4299	386.7	47.3
2002	1486	854		542	3945	415.2	50.6
2003	1515	855		599	4159	434.9	52.7
2004	1549	937		633	4792	436.9	52.5
2005	1594	1009		681	5037	450.2	53
2006	1635	1109		805	5649	430.2	48.2
2007	1708	1162		799	4838	442.1	48.4
2008	1692	1209		853	4789	453.4	48.5
2009	1729	1266		901	5123	454.2	48.2
2010	1724	1308		919	5229	474.1	49
2011	1745	1406		952	5209	468.1	48.8
2012	1782	1597		978	5539	477.7	49.5
2013	1784	1506	29	1063	5743	468.9	48.2
2014	1801	1598	19	1141	5908	459.3	47

注：斜体下划线数据经过修正。1989年以前部分数据统计不完全。

社会服务当年
分省统计资料

05

C-1-1 省级行政区划

地 区	面积（万平方千米）	省级合计（个）	直辖市	省	自治区	特别行政区
全 国	**960**	**34**	**4**	**23**	**5**	**2**
北 京	1.68	1	1			
天 津	1.1	1	1			
河 北	19	1		1		
山 西	15	1		1		
内蒙古	110	1			1	
辽 宁	15	1		1		
吉 林	18	1		1		
黑龙江	46	1		1		
上 海	0.58	1	1			
江 苏	10	1		1		
浙 江	10	1		1		
安 徽	13	1		1		
福 建	12	1		1		
江 西	16	1		1		
山 东	15	1		1		
河 南	16	1		1		
湖 北	18	1		1		
湖 南	21	1		1		
广 东	18	1		1		
广 西	23	1			1	
海 南	3.4	1		1		
重 庆	8.23	1	1			
四 川	48	1		1		
贵 州	17	1		1		
云 南	38	1		1		
西 藏	120	1			1	
陕 西	19	1		1		
甘 肃	39	1		1		
青 海	72	1		1		
宁 夏	6.6	1			1	
新 疆	160	1			1	
香 港		1				1
澳 门		1				1
台 湾		1		1		

C-1-2 地级与县级行政区划

单位:个

地 区	地级合计	地级市	地区	自治州	盟	县级合计	市辖区	县级市	县	自治县	旗	自治旗	特区	林区
全 国	**333**	**288**	**12**	**30**	**3**	**2854**	**897**	**361**	**1425**	**117**	**49**	**3**	**1**	**1**
北 京						16	14		2					
天 津						16	13		3					
河 北	11	11				171	39	20	106	6				
山 西	11	11				119	23	11	85					
内蒙古	12	9			3	102	22	11	17		49	3		
辽 宁	14	14				100	56	17	19	8				
吉 林	9	8		1		60	21	20	16	3				
黑龙江	13	12	1			128	65	17	45	1				
上 海						17	16		1					
江 苏	13	13				99	55	23	21					
浙 江	11	11				90	35	20	34	1				
安 徽	16	16				105	43	6	56					
福 建	9	9				85	28	13	44					
江 西	11	11				100	20	10	70					
山 东	17	17				137	51	28	58					
河 南	17	17				158	50	21	87					
湖 北	13	12		1		103	39	24	37	2				1
湖 南	14	13		1		122	35	16	64	7				
广 东	21	21				119	61	21	34	3				
广 西	14	14				110	36	7	55	12				
海 南	3	3				24	8	6	4	6				
重 庆						38	21		13	4				
四 川	21	18		3		183	49	14	116	4				
贵 州	9	6		3		88	14	7	55	11			1	
云 南	16	8		8		129	13	13	74	29				
西 藏	7	3	4			74	3		71					
陕 西	10	10				107	25	3	79					
甘 肃	14	12		2		86	17	4	58	7				
青 海	8	2		6		43	5	3	28	7				
宁 夏	5	5				22	9	2	11					
新 疆	14	2	7	5		103	11	24	62	6				

C-1-3　乡镇级行政区划

单位:个

地　区	乡镇级合计	镇	乡	#民族乡	街道办事处	区公所	村	居
全　国	**40381**	**20401**	**12282**	**1020**	**7696**	**2**	**585451**	**96693**
北　京	329	144	38	5	147		3937	2932
天　津	240	121	6	1	113		3698	1575
河　北	2246	1050	907	50	288	1	48636	3835
山　西	1398	564	632		202		28072	2282
内蒙古	1010	495	275	18	240		11192	2235
辽　宁	1530	645	217	56	668		11558	4105
吉　林	900	434	184	28	282		9313	1995
黑龙江	1231	513	380	53	338		8902	2839
上　海	209	107	2		100		1605	4122
江　苏	1274	780	79	1	415		14428	6972
浙　江	1321	629	258	14	434		27997	4321
安　徽	1505	938	315	9	252		14786	3257
福　建	1104	628	301	19	175		14440	2308
江　西	1548	816	587	8	145		17011	3308
山　东	1826	1114	81		631		73388	6627
河　南	2420	1103	718	12	599		46938	4404
湖　北	1233	761	170	10	302		25448	4187
湖　南	2414	1153	902	97	359		41523	5100
广　东	1587	1128	11	7	448		19347	6586
广　西	1243	773	350	59	120		14291	1892
海　南	218	176	21		21		2561	475
重　庆	1023	610	207	14	206		8255	2775
四　川	4648	1937	2382	98	329		46318	6805
贵　州	1396	762	500	208	134		16747	2016
云　南	1389	665	561	140	163		12035	2203
西　藏	694	140	544	9	10		5255	209
陕　西	1420	1142	74		204		26608	2153
甘　肃	1351	526	702	34	123		15957	1340
青　海	399	140	225	28	34		4157	451
宁　夏	237	102	91		44		2274	467
新　疆	1038	305	562	42	170	1	8774	2917

C-1-4 民政部门

地 区	单位数	年末职工人数	女性	受教育程度 大学专科人数	大学本科及以上人数	职业资 助理社会工作师人数
全 国	**3491**	**95372**	**30559**	**36872**	**39516**	**1404**
中央级	1	368	109	7	360	
北 京	18	1121	438	197	853	63
天 津	18	618	158	147	360	
河 北	196	6119	2272	2297	1984	111
山 西	131	2596	806	1162	949	22
内蒙古	117	3153	1069	1413	1351	4
辽 宁	121	2959	920	1058	1673	23
吉 林	70	2871	317	432	671	12
黑龙江	146	2575	943	1072	1198	58
上 海	19	743	299	150	528	39
江 苏	121	3437	912	1022	2032	187
浙 江	102	2500	664	930	1335	29
安 徽	122	2705	724	1063	1258	88
福 建	97	1734	364	663	690	22
江 西	117	3155	936	1116	1072	26
山 东	180	6438	2009	2408	3136	117
河 南	182	8139	2968	3617	2518	132
湖 北	119	4083	1300	1861	1462	27
湖 南	146	6416	2217	2359	2372	49
广 东	141	3868	1176	1404	1802	100
广 西	127	2335	744	970	974	13
海 南	23	637	196	252	232	22
重 庆	41	1186	347	419	706	6
四 川	209	5403	1863	2232	2231	70
贵 州	100	3131	960	1424	1243	11
云 南	149	4374	1454	1855	1710	21
西 藏	83	947	399	382	325	2
陕 西	119	3666	1033	1561	1300	18
甘 肃	101	3102	929	1201	1174	65
青 海	55	765	288	304	284	44
宁 夏	28	721	256	272	366	2
新 疆	292	3507	1489	1622	1367	21

行政机构

单位:个、人、人次、时

格水平	年龄结构				志愿服务	
社会工作师人数	35岁及以下人数	36岁至45岁人数	46岁至55岁人数	56岁及以上人数	志愿者服务人次数	志愿服务时间
1475	**24560**	**34986**	**28648**	**7178**	**309512**	**682153.0**
	143	113	71	41		
24	288	363	378	92	100	100.0
	120	177	247	74	2042	4100.0
87	1791	2286	1697	345	1068	4869.0
17	643	931	851	171	225	507.0
13	858	1128	952	215		
30	617	937	1092	313	830	1515.0
22	725	1059	986	101		
35	633	975	839	128	50	106.0
79	173	217	238	115	33	264.0
208	528	1176	1310	423	33012	63599.0
42	446	737	984	333	52906	65930.0
85	481	1027	929	268	25475	65262.0
47	280	595	675	184	38018	116600.0
28	608	1259	986	302	540	1691.0
138	2069	2367	1651	351		
144	2883	2931	1821	504	36	125.0
29	810	1412	1353	508	328	1105.0
42	2019	2394	1525	478	7796	29072.0
102	916	1348	1234	370	5579	27048.0
28	277	836	976	246	216	632.0
5	114	250	210	63	309	722.0
15	202	397	464	123	1431	3992.0
65	1252	2167	1624	360	135142	282129.0
5	779	1293	904	155	589	2459.0
32	908	1650	1524	292	713	1008.0
4	451	341	140	15	4	28.0
55	1077	1284	1038	267	1652	6001.0
56	1043	1135	776	148	182	244.0
19	195	377	174	19	855	1856.0
6	178	276	212	55	29	69.0
13	1053	1548	787	119	352	1120.0

C-1-4续表

地区	职工按行政级别分				乡、镇、街道民政助理员
	中央级	省级	地级	县级	
全 国	**368**	**3711**	**13845**	**77448**	**53813**
中央级	368				
北 京		219		902	710
天 津		131	92	395	398
河 北		114	660	5345	3482
山 西		98	386	2112	1458
内蒙古		82	471	2600	1662
辽 宁		89	736	2134	1069
吉 林		119	247	2505	249
黑龙江		17	634	1924	394
上 海		173		570	417
江 苏		168	668	2601	1733
浙 江		105	408	1987	1858
安 徽		106	510	2089	2011
福 建		120	304	1310	1604
江 西		79	391	2685	1094
山 东		140	846	5452	4507
河 南		144	784	7211	2442
湖 北		101	593	3389	1524
湖 南		185	730	5501	5449
广 东		139	932	2797	733
广 西		111	430	1794	2804
海 南		83	99	455	308
重 庆		195		991	2930
四 川		128	756	4519	3713
贵 州		109	402	2620	3030
云 南		142	686	3546	1931
西 藏		100	238	609	66
陕 西		149	513	3004	3676
甘 肃			636	2466	1361
青 海			173	592	393
宁 夏		153	95	473	230
新 疆		212	425	2870	577

单位：人、万元

执行行政事业单位会计制度财务指标					
固定资产原价	上年结转和结余	本年收入合计	本年支出合计	收支结余	行政事业单位增加值
1692760.4	**735985.8**	**6907744.8**	**6889363.0**	**430693.5**	**2191856.9**
132478.2	28334.7	185979.8	148102.3	66030.1	25687.6
44531.8	56715.7	364313.9	355144.3	61373.1	84268.9
12778.2	10280.7	128112.1	122407.3	638.3	49473.5
56056.3	11850.9	325150.6	320004.1	7061.5	79166.0
52866.8	10849.1	112812.6	123507.2	5926.4	41276.1
41883.2	15990.3	84789.8	83014.1	7023.1	39216.0
60766.3	22198.2	160144.9	168795.3	9278.7	59101.5
32549.2	2910.0	71592.3	57277.2	662.0	29490.9
26322.8	1162.7	92255.3	93915.5		22790.6
27898.6	44369.2	354303.4	355801.6	24370.7	140525.0
73275.8	31973.6	382031.8	381316.2	9000.3	147050.6
65133.7	38991.7	694549.8	689529.2	8167.8	193508.8
62289.1	10073.2	250518.7	240778.9	3750.5	74297.0
33086.0	32902.6	274876.2	282780.7	22704.6	102951.2
36715.2	12492.3	65951.2	55991.6	22481.5	21664.2
90912.6	10694.5	237524.0	238736.3		105556.9
38007.8	19312.8	170181.2	166760.4	2513.4	67064.8
89362.2	951.7	116039.4	115853.0	1801.7	54251.4
62647.2	3336.1	328501.6	336463.8	247.4	144423.2
117072.9	29110.1	560586.8	552947.8	15576.6	186828.4
67859.7	94631.9	379716.8	495825.0	24691.4	87572.6
12235.8	23036.0	126714.0	122674.3	6545.5	11244.9
36510.7	4872.6	102382.8	101564.8	5690.6	44541.0
78179.4	18358.2	247155.6	237213.9	18685.9	107676.4
44791.7	33148.5	163528.4	170306.1	13601.3	33523.6
101397.0	94632.2	405123.7	364329.9	46368.5	87508.6
30812.0	1890.0	45096.9	16266.4		4470.3
46666.4	6518.2	150904.0	151431.1	7492.0	55696.9
11973.9	27318.8	37829.7	51673.8	12923.9	25070.1
15483.2	279.5	53707.6	53718.7	28.9	7035.4
22859.1	17026.1	62878.2	61431.9	9957.7	13205.0
67357.6	19773.7	172491.7	173800.3	16100.1	45719.4

C-1-5 社会服务

地　区	机构和设施数	按登记类型分				按行业	
		工商登记	编制登记	民政登记	设施	社会工作	成员组织
全　国	**1668143**	**17422**	**29455**	**645153**	**976106**	**370893**	**1288192**
中央级	2283		31	2252		2	2252
北　京	28556	583	823	9727	17423	12461	15952
天　津	12527	226	162	5257	6882	2461	10002
河　北	103729	623	1080	18437	83589	33309	70113
山　西	47819	385	850	13124	33460	4915	42684
内蒙古	29242	160	645	12094	16343	3831	25217
辽　宁	46533	1787	909	21699	22138	10228	35800
吉　林	24189	350	1172	10668	11999	2111	21829
黑龙江	28505	454	734	13948	13369	4013	24220
上　海	23803	986	291	13737	8789	5507	18092
江　苏	131794	2790	1728	87006	40269	38410	92971
浙　江	106707	2007	1235	41626	61839	34077	72162
安　徽	50117	371	768	23271	25707	9228	40592
福　建	44503	310	642	21566	21985	6123	38105
江　西	41026	302	1760	16784	22180	5794	34555
山　东	151665	1244	1295	43000	106126	30142	121180
河　南	86957	843	1135	29139	55840	7593	78914
湖　北	68874	559	1897	27395	39023	12329	56195
湖　南	81576	523	2133	24229	54691	10481	70634
广　东	131630	220	1673	48654	81083	57527	73613
广　西	47697	147	722	20540	26288	10946	36504
海　南	9882	23	88	5140	4631	1950	7883
重　庆	32538	794	654	14698	16392	6933	25417
四　川	110569	754	3362	39083	67368	19080	90923
贵　州	49151	94	736	9686	38631	20567	28187
云　南	36739	282	636	19528	16293	2967	33445
西　藏	6447	5	57	835	5550	356	6064
陕　西	52156	228	735	19112	32081	5125	46811
甘　肃	39050	82	444	14595	23929	7099	31697
青　海	8711	44	67	3470	5130	678	7970
宁　夏	8219	77	149	4714	3279	1065	7065
新　疆	24949	169	842	10139	13799	3585	21144

总表

单位:个、人

分类分		年末职工人数	女性	按登记类型分			
其他社会服务	其他事业单位			工商登记	编制登记	民政登记	设施
6795	**2263**	**12509814**	**3847483**	**1274639**	**351217**	**7111518**	**3772440**
	29	34817	15374		1716	33101	
68	75	221523	93974	26530	14109	112921	67963
43	21	97029	43407	16021	3460	44180	33368
254	53	567970	150507	35020	17050	269583	246317
146	74	318899	86868	36026	8882	153043	120948
169	25	172671	57675	8906	7659	91244	64862
398	107	432819	155603	89918	15117	216382	111402
215	34	127112	35104	17132	14493	56775	38712
229	43	235084	85228	14606	11322	148153	61003
93	111	313247	106660	77182	8508	186445	41112
345	68	1095220	340314	251029	22374	622637	199180
299	169	782178	252190	205529	13872	367367	195410
269	28	378531	111585	17798	10166	238145	112422
209	66	376788	88642	19335	6256	261852	89345
236	441	311834	92516	24963	11932	192624	82315
288	55	896913	260157	92332	19416	361533	423632
305	145	539051	160005	55396	18525	231700	233430
275	75	565643	177199	34907	21107	361050	148579
348	113	489892	158716	31526	19859	243635	194872
448	42	891410	346962	16034	25277	584378	265721
171	76	443470	104888	8746	9593	325110	100021
31	18	72766	24510	1696	1035	46954	23081
167	21	297098	118009	69087	6377	149829	71805
426	140	859866	249218	55169	23407	522810	258480
316	81	364816	90316	4108	9305	175543	175860
299	28	569994	191379	32636	6161	450708	80489
27		38625	10701	203	452	13059	24911
177	43	402830	96698	13109	9544	258491	121686
221	33	263658	53420	3966	4707	170809	84176
49	14	39893	9908	2122	881	17181	19709
81	8	82974	21109	4918	1931	62349	13776
193	27	225193	58641	8689	6724	141927	67853

C-1-5续表1

地区	受教育程度		职业资格水平	
	大学专科人数	大学本科及以上人数	助理社会工作师人数	社会工作师人数
全　国	**2085424**	**1214588**	**50770**	**25782**
中央级	601	25251	762	1510
北　京	47905	57819	6383	2900
天　津	22722	24042	1416	420
河　北	68561	39800	1584	1004
山　西	54710	27392	286	332
内蒙古	38782	16371	415	246
辽　宁	82017	53640	1844	926
吉　林	17961	6856	1067	553
黑龙江	39207	13852	735	422
上　海	73616	27063	1818	1113
江　苏	201493	115501	7447	2539
浙　江	138028	71881	3313	1986
安　徽	77671	40148	3150	937
福　建	35687	26229	1277	807
江　西	33114	10873	892	314
山　东	206038	118557	1586	896
河　南	93652	45392	731	561
湖　北	101187	36537	957	498
湖　南	91575	48027	1212	511
广　东	183091	121785	7130	4243
广　西	55337	33948	1102	452
海　南	10684	4620	99	42
重　庆	56402	45040	1465	622
四　川	131774	74499	2105	1015
贵　州	54285	45655	243	103
云　南	49977	26999	659	233
西　藏	1316	697	2	3
陕　西	42363	17226	325	181
甘　肃	24841	11385	285	157
青　海	3619	1178	101	44
宁　夏	9364	5573	65	34
新　疆	37844	20752	314	178

单位:个、人、人次、时

年龄结构				志愿服务	
35岁及以下人数	36岁至45岁人数	46岁至55岁人数	56岁及以上人数	志愿者服务人次数	志愿服务时间
3770961	**4836176**	**2831952**	**1070739**	**10959002**	**27110872.4**
10935	11930	6977	4975		
58977	77238	60035	25273	5366192	13575953.0
27715	30783	26332	12199	99222	183519.0
173683	227242	130666	36379	66378	298384.0
94058	114372	79825	30644	10487	22880.4
52566	66286	40245	13574	29102	68112.0
114913	165144	99112	53650	57751	87473.0
28244	77225	15943	5700	426	680.0
83132	91078	48291	12597	55646	129093.0
87515	105634	82869	37229	523443	1161718.0
310106	415158	276237	93719	662543	1564960.5
230423	288776	173144	89835	674797	1250975.1
106599	149159	93803	28970	180256	388128.0
91114	130097	96835	58742	145931	396027.0
96099	141416	58180	16139	7151	21774.7
275996	366694	197385	56838	632013	1544661.4
185072	213529	107450	33000	1114	2423.0
171431	205255	161590	27367	54405	121386.0
153141	204848	101235	30668	193557	656114.5
366264	291266	175895	57985	48918	123111.0
111676	167007	115933	48854	8931	22982.8
24222	32935	11842	3767	8860	15319.0
101407	106286	63650	25755	667519	1774863.0
287884	322942	161164	87876	162593	457713.0
106373	153592	79242	25609	1198346	2937902.0
165654	196729	117632	89979	1846	4065.0
8792	14083	10463	5287	213	663.5
102669	145717	123431	31013	27814	75659.5
58778	132148	58944	13788	12112	61906.0
10443	16693	10346	2411	24195	46141.0
12509	52439	13761	4265	1925	2679.0
62571	122475	33495	6652	35316	113605.0

C-1-5续表2

地区	增加值合计	执行企业会计制度单位财务指标					执行行政	
		固定资产原价	营业收入	费用合计	营业利润	企业单位增加值	固定资产原价	上年结转和结余
全 国	**25154677.6**	**22107074.9**	**49765149.3**	**6356498.6**	**1464313.3**	**8127297.0**	**28196380.0**	**1907150.4**
中央级	227981.9	38641.5	21386.9	13778.6	-2236.5	4571.1	133150.3	24075.5
北 京	1448183.6	2946294.3	1950534.3	379783.8	45158.3	340676.9	1046484.3	394604.3
天 津	253516.1	236954.6	352568.1	87783.9	5172.7	61740.7	400755.1	40433.2
河 北	745856.4	485919.3	1235290.4	104962.8	7681.6	177164.6	1159231.7	47462.2
山 西	353990.3	333583.5	444806.7	41830.6	-15511.6	44474.1	701868.9	28299.5
内蒙古	192192.1	81694.0	65973.2	14969.4	2019.2	16553.9	311722.0	18894.9
辽 宁	975986.8	1470690.2	1933784.1	221125.5	63072.4	365696.8	610628.0	55122.7
吉 林	118403.9	128732.1	241794.9	28455.4	445.2	20743.9	336727.8	8141.6
黑龙江	306516.2	127332.3	165828.4	40161.1	6482.7	38267.9	728137.1	46727.5
上 海	1877152.4	1910954.4	3585961.6	424229.7	270342.2	926534.3	1329414.1	156174.8
江 苏	3242731.8	3581587.7	11210310.6	1275012.9	262492.5	1347592.4	3455855.1	107492.6
浙 江	3893761.6	5362327.2	15665433.6	2283768.0	501836.4	2542243.8	4393801.3	174967.0
安 徽	537460.5	147857.2	941220.4	63859.4	19032.8	68683.5	845559.1	23109.0
福 建	338112.6	228099.8	341746.0	58705.9	4521.9	66549.0	303051.3	23681.7
江 西	344375.4	120571.2	2191623.5	21254.9	3100.9	17847.7	362925.1	8830.8
山 东	2562613.6	1038452.6	1720885.3	323275.2	141021.9	599244.0	2027677.6	9774.2
河 南	449617.5	414007.0	778213.8	94379.9	20152.7	119206.4	619234.5	17355.9
湖 北	687440.7	231512.6	380493.2	99713.9	11361.7	82979.7	1116129.5	3905.4
湖 南	564202.6	322362.8	590637.6	67851.7	9876.9	85483.8	789631.7	10319.3
广 东	2127235.4	344471.9	341536.1	50698.9	11642.2	83963.5	2782445.8	159609.9
广 西	364759.1	96386.0	368271.2	20276.0	-863.9	32063.5	447068.6	37663.2
海 南	90902.8	31088.3	54964.9	11115.4	-393.7	8242.3	85425.6	13361.8
重 庆	666350.3	752080.1	1967228.6	232656.3	44206.3	341586.9	436012.9	34658.0
四 川	965424.7	513402.7	1451806.3	109823.2	26255.1	329969.4	1082433.4	228081.2
贵 州	274480.0	98727.3	57461.3	22135.1	4757.2	20230.9	283119.3	28489.5
云 南	402721.7	546658.4	1064002.7	160205.4	-10919.0	52922.5	913553.9	112329.7
西 藏	6868.4	13130.4	398.0	222.5	26.0	68.3	69043.7	3250.0
陕 西	679120.9	166052.7	361385.0	53446.2	21307.2	268470.6	546019.2	34866.2
甘 肃	134215.0	33909.8	16049.6	3349.7	1358.9	6134.5	314889.5	7475.0
青 海	27812.5	10723.5	16436.0	3895.6	426.2	5106.4	40975.1	980.8
宁 夏	67593.2	106477.5	49238.3	12055.4	3801.1	16124.4	199431.9	13672.3
新 疆	227088.8	186392.0	197878.7	31716.3	6685.8	36159.5	323976.6	33340.7

单位：万元

事业单位会计制度财务指标				执行民间非营利组织单位会计制度财务指标				
本年收入合计	本年支出合计	收支结余	行政事业单位增加值	固定资产原价	上年结余	本年收入合计	本年费用合计	社会组织增加值
18920362.5	**21362952.6**	**817999.2**	**9514074.2**	**21825970.6**	**8092270.0**	**23718540.7**	**21282213.6**	**7513306.4**
176113.4	121727.6	77432.7	22988.7	760245.7		4300338.0	3583248.7	200422.1
1275636.5	1323218.5	228431.8	879161.9	799569.5	942170.5	1342197.5	1052042.3	228344.9
330012.8	346972.4	19433.8	140534.5	123965.9	21918.0	229027.0	196110.8	51240.8
739824.0	716950.3	30970.2	320068.9	1337271.0	449288.5	372464.5	407580.5	248623.2
341364.8	339689.8	16318.5	195205.5	276091.0	12772.3	178778.2	175951.6	114311.0
243419.8	230415.9	33496.7	129888.8	119294.7	272.4	83436.2	84674.2	45749.6
592255.0	734641.6	14830.8	402534.8	548160.6	385669.4	440904.9	534332.7	207755.5
165626.7	162307.2	5070.7	83968.4	14512.0	375.3	18258.1	24079.6	13691.7
504895.4	237495.3	629.3	171256.5	155179.3	4031.0	35932.3	194292.4	96992.5
795918.8	702672.4	22089.4	365561.4	428325.2	2161842.1	2740286.8	2197456.3	585056.8
1602863.8	1718392.0	72127.7	1034575.5	2819141.6	1638673.7	2987978.4	2429900.7	860564.0
2156793.8	1665548.9	28555.7	930245.1	2341690.7	595565.6	1473216.9	1332422.5	421272.9
377371.0	361708.5	5148.3	232907.4	988306.1	12560.7	457677.9	462114.1	235870.1
331150.0	323636.2	15745.2	141623.7	448947.3	152457.7	243667.5	260984.6	129939.9
184990.6	168927.7	11048.6	104320.7	335558.0	7033.8	251073.4	927155.6	222207.1
1836609.8	1846482.4		1068906.7	1550081.4	72.0	1260395.5	1261402.3	894462.9
512022.3	500995.0	17595.1	211280.6	538023.5	40569.3	266185.8	214545.1	119130.8
656995.2	653816.7	5127.4	376991.1	590534.7	18346.5	525261.9	490548.8	227469.9
690118.0	658746.9	10490.9	324124.2	437580.4	67318.3	320841.1	325178.2	154595.0
1580330.2	1539168.5	42460.3	766564.0	2834954.6	241020.5	2535655.1	2149982.4	1276708.3
309749.1	364530.0	20139.3	265207.8	202074.7	73671.6	97035.6	99979.1	67487.9
79716.1	76929.0	9094.2	35158.6	155772.3	1619.2	62460.1	60001.7	47501.9
291217.4	286494.4	36417.3	168133.8	785997.0	190699.9	704807.7	636461.6	156629.7
1780998.8	1741060.3	24151.6	334955.2	962633.7	656867.0	740723.0	892627.6	300500.2
166809.5	171476.6	8193.6	129204.5	545221.2	50245.0	190259.4	187298.9	125044.9
263907.1	241971.4	11435.5	164046.5	775214.8	243228.0	260801.8	325693.4	185753.4
15818.9	15034.4		5392.3	6620.8	13056.5	3086.8	2688.6	1407.9
368005.3	356577.4	22518.8	245639.3	555054.9	5390.3	61509.8	226497.1	165011.2
172062.3	127938.1	2022.2	85510.5	136138.1	3002.0	1385164.4	60716.1	42570.0
18959.4	17973.5	1241.2	11390.5	78594.3	1410.7	34302.2	29877.4	11315.6
124895.7	39855.4	8220.0	29102.9	57331.5	23174.0	39537.5	377716.8	22365.9
233911.0	3569598.3	17562.4	137620.8	117884.1	77948.2	75275.4	78651.9	53308.8

C-1-6 社会服务发展

地 区	社会服务综合指数(%)	每万人口社会服务机构数(个/万人)	每万人口社会服务职工人员(人/万人)	每百万人口社工助工师(人/百万人)	每千人口社会服务业增加值(万元/千人)	每千人口固定资产原值(万元/千人)
全 国	**100.0**	**12.2**	**91.5**	**56.0**	**18.3**	**52.7**
北 京	240.4	13.3	103.0	431.4	67.3	222.7
天 津	110.9	8.3	64.0	121.0	16.7	50.2
河 北	91.6	14.0	76.9	35.0	10.1	40.4
山 西	79.8	13.1	87.4	16.9	9.7	36.0
内蒙古	91.4	11.7	68.9	26.4	7.7	20.5
辽 宁	112.4	10.6	98.6	63.1	22.2	59.9
吉 林	67.9	8.8	46.2	58.9	4.3	17.4
黑龙江	73.8	7.4	61.3	30.2	8.0	26.4
上 海	148.9	9.8	129.1	120.8	74.9	151.2
江 苏	164.5	16.6	137.6	125.5	40.7	123.8
浙 江	182.0	19.4	142.0	96.2	70.7	219.6
安 徽	95.9	8.2	62.2	67.2	8.8	32.6
福 建	100.3	11.7	99.0	54.8	8.9	25.8
江 西	72.9	9.0	68.7	26.6	7.6	18.0
山 东	111.9	15.5	91.6	25.4	26.2	47.2
河 南	69.1	9.2	57.1	13.7	4.8	16.7
湖 北	100.6	11.8	97.3	25.0	11.8	33.3
湖 南	83.0	12.1	72.7	25.6	8.2	23.0
广 东	123.2	12.3	83.1	106.1	19.8	55.6
广 西	77.6	10.0	93.3	32.7	7.7	15.7
海 南	81.0	10.9	80.5	15.6	10.1	30.1
重 庆	109.9	10.9	99.3	69.8	22.3	66.0
四 川	90.8	13.6	105.6	38.3	11.8	31.4
贵 州	90.2	14.0	104.0	9.9	7.8	26.4
云 南	79.2	7.8	120.9	18.9	8.5	47.4
西 藏	39.0	20.3	121.6	1.6	2.2	28.0
陕 西	94.8	13.8	106.7	13.4	18.0	33.6
甘 肃	80.8	15.1	101.8	17.1	5.2	18.7
青 海	49.0	14.9	68.4	24.9	4.8	22.3
宁 夏	78.5	12.4	125.4	15.0	10.2	54.9
新 疆	68.9	10.9	98.0	21.4	9.9	27.3

综合评估指数

社会服务事业费占财政支出的比重(‰)	每千人口社会服务事业费(万元/千人)	每百万人口乡镇街道数(个/百万人)	万人口社会服务床位(张/万人)	千老年人口养老床位(张/千人)	每十万人口孤儿数(人/十万人)	每百万人口家庭收养数(件/百万人)
29.0	**32.2**	**29.5**	**44.9**	**27.2**	**38.4**	**16.6**
38.3	74.4	15.3	66.8	45.7	10.6	9.2
23.2	39.0	15.8	41.6	20.9	5.8	8.5
37.5	22.4	30.4	61.4	38.9	21.2	5.4
37.8	31.4	38.3	24.4	16.5	42.1	6.9
38.2	56.3	40.3	75.5	49.0	23.5	9.0
32.6	38.6	34.8	50.4	24.3	17.7	4.2
34.3	34.2	32.7	34.8	17.8	19.6	1.6
40.8	35.8	32.1	36.9	21.8	20.6	1.2
18.9	35.3	8.6	53.2	33.5	8.5	10.5
31.6	30.9	16.0	71.8	38.6	23.2	25.4
31.8	27.3	24.0	80.1	52.9	9.2	76.4
39.1	27.9	24.7	56.4	34.9	44.5	16.6
25.3	20.4	29.0	32.7	25.7	16.9	33.8
42.4	32.4	34.1	41.0	28.4	54.7	13.4
40.5	27.6	18.7	58.1	31.0	18.4	24.7
36.8	21.8	25.6	37.7	25.2	48.0	4.7
42.4	31.9	21.2	47.7	27.3	46.4	12.3
44.5	31.0	35.8	30.1	16.8	67.5	11.9
26.6	20.9	14.8	20.7	15.3	38.9	16.7
43.4	29.3	26.1	32.5	21.9	49.9	34.2
28.5	31.9	24.1	20.0	16.6	23.8	17.9
33.6	34.4	34.2	54.9	25.0	41.5	9.9
46.9	35.8	57.1	56.7	24.5	37.1	13.2
45.1	39.7	39.8	33.6	22.4	61.7	12.1
48.3	42.0	29.5	17.3	11.2	48.8	26.3
13.5	43.1	218.5	33.7	27.7	184.8	10.1
45.8	44.5	37.6	31.4	17.8	34.5	8.7
52.6	46.9	52.1	35.6	24.8	84.9	5.0
31.1	65.4	68.4	33.1	26.7	274.1	7.2
28.7	40.0	35.8	19.9	15.1	107.0	7.3
36.7	49.0	45.2	27.8	21.0	111.1	15.0

C-1-6续表

地 区	每万人口流浪救助人次数（人次/万人）	每十万人口福利企业残疾职工人数（人/十万人）	城市低保平均标准（十元/人、月）	农村低保平均标准（十元/人、月）	五保集中供养平均标准（十元/人、月）	五保分散供养平均标准（十元/人、月）	每万人口优抚对象人数（人/万人）
全 国	**25.7**	**35.1**	**41.1**	**23.1**	**44.8**	**33.4**	**67.1**
北 京	273.7	48.5	65.0	63.2	109.0	109.0	20.7
天 津	7.7	42.3	64.0	51.3	77.5	66.4	30.5
河 北	11.2	18.4	43.2	21.2	43.6	29.6	76.7
山 西	28.4	40.6	38.4	20.5	40.1	24.2	49.8
内蒙古	24.8	19.2	48.1	30.3	60.9	39.5	19.1
辽 宁	12.4	89.0	45.3	26.6	50.6	33.3	53.6
吉 林	22.4	25.2	37.1	20.6	36.8	25.8	46.4
黑龙江	8.2	20.5	44.7	23.0	44.1	31.4	32.3
上 海	11.9	101.1	71.0	63.0	75.0	75.0	16.7
江 苏	12.9	109.0	53.6	44.5	67.5	58.5	62.2
浙 江	11.0	122.5	57.3	47.4	78.6	71.8	50.2
安 徽	27.4	11.4	42.2	23.6	38.0	24.1	78.1
福 建	29.6	21.0	40.4	22.8	55.9	48.5	49.3
江 西	25.4	22.2	41.8	22.0	29.2	25.8	71.0
山 东	13.1	35.6	45.2	24.5	45.0	30.5	98.0
河 南	21.4	25.8	32.9	15.2	32.8	20.1	79.8
湖 北	51.7	22.7	41.1	21.4	39.1	28.2	82.4
湖 南	48.1	23.4	35.3	19.4	47.4	25.0	130.3
广 东	18.6	5.3	45.4	32.0	66.1	63.7	40.4
广 西	17.5	6.7	34.0	16.9	33.6	26.0	62.0
海 南	39.3	8.8	38.0	28.0	45.6	38.7	29.8
重 庆	21.7	87.1	36.9	22.2	46.0	40.5	93.6
四 川	28.6	26.4	33.6	17.8	37.2	29.0	105.7
贵 州	27.8	2.7	39.5	17.6	27.5	18.4	66.3
云 南	14.1	25.6	36.0	17.8	32.7	21.8	74.6
西 藏	25.0	3.1	53.4	18.6	32.3	28.4	14.6
陕 西	25.7	11.9	38.9	18.9	48.1	41.0	71.0
甘 肃	14.7	5.2	32.8	19.0	31.2	29.3	46.6
青 海	26.7	16.3	35.1	18.4	45.7	41.7	25.2
宁 夏	16.1	35.3	30.5	19.0	47.4	30.9	17.4
新 疆	12.6	17.8	32.9	16.9	56.2	35.8	14.8

每千人口福利彩票销售（万元/千人）	社区服务设施覆盖率（%）	城市社区服务中心（站）覆盖率（%）	每十万人口社会组织（个/十万人）	每十万人口村居委会个数（个/十万人）	每万人口结婚对数（对/万人）	每万人口离婚对数（对/万人）	火化率（%）
15.1	**36.9**	**75.4**	**44.3**	**49.9**	**95.5**	**26.6**	**47.0**
24.8	154.0	99.7	42.2	31.9	79.0	30.5	75.5
28.1	33.1	79.0	31.2	34.8	65.5	29.3	66.6
10.8	48.0	51.7	23.9	71.1	89.6	25.2	38.9
11.2	10.1	67.7	33.8	83.2	96.1	18.0	8.9
19.8	15.8	70.9	47.1	53.6	86.5	35.3	41.1
24.3	34.6	97.4	45.9	35.7	78.6	34.8	89.8
16.8	5.6	23.7	38.2	41.1	85.5	44.4	37.8
13.5	18.4	61.0	32.6	30.6	91.9	48.9	59.1
19.9	57.4	63.6	51.0	23.6	58.5	25.3	88.0
17.5	110.9	105.7	89.9	26.9	104.8	27.4	74.3
25.0	73.9	80.3	72.3	58.7	79.3	24.7	87.8
11.4	30.1	78.0	37.1	29.7	131.3	28.1	63.3
13.1	17.4	83.9	56.1	44.0	98.6	22.9	73.2
13.5	15.7	40.7	31.3	44.7	81.7	19.7	27.2
15.1	29.5	82.3	42.1	81.7	85.0	23.9	75.5
6.9	5.7	27.9	29.2	54.4	124.6	24.5	29.3
15.3	28.5	100.7	45.7	51.0	106.9	27.1	45.2
10.8	18.6	46.1	35.6	69.2	92.3	26.1	15.5
19.3	175.1	127.6	44.5	24.2	83.1	16.6	81.8
14.9	47.0	33.6	42.7	34.0	99.3	21.2	22.7
18.3	51.7	57.4	53.6	33.6	99.7	15.6	5.0
20.7	44.4	73.0	48.1	36.9	101.8	44.3	32.9
9.6	10.5	48.5	46.4	65.3	95.1	33.8	31.7
6.1	91.9	116.0	26.9	53.5	124.6	27.3	24.9
12.4	8.9	48.6	40.7	30.2	98.6	21.3	17.6
22.9	0.6	13.1	18.9	172.1	61.6	8.3	4.1
20.1	10.0	102.8	47.8	76.2	101.0	22.6	19.8
18.0	29.8	137.4	55.6	66.8	77.9	16.3	10.0
19.5	3.7	36.3	57.6	79.0	92.6	21.5	18.7
23.3	28.2	109.0	65.4	41.4	84.6	23.9	12.2
16.1	18.7	70.9	41.1	50.9	121.5	47.0	14.1

C-1-7 社会工作师、助理

地　区	社会工作师和助理社会工作师累计合格人数	社会工作师		
		累计合格人数	当年考试通过人数	当年报考人数
全　国	**158942**	**38610**	**7427**	**62881**
北　京	17963	4168	701	3911
天　津	3370	658	152	1406
河　北	2951	1057	124	1265
山　西	1633	683	102	1218
内蒙古	794	262	69	1031
辽　宁	5393	1524	279	2593
吉　林	3063	633	173	1757
黑龙江	2779	690	115	1262
上　海	7384	2347	399	3261
江　苏	21155	4604	983	7038
浙　江	12753	3867	701	4944
安　徽	4229	941	262	1948
福　建	4929	1288	330	2773
江　西	2075	504	52	445
山　东	6949	2283	440	3691
河　南	3719	1080	144	1075
湖　北	4140	722	174	1644
湖　南	3386	908	133	1447
广　东	33369	6553	1276	11504
广　西	2184	475	48	643
海　南	207	49	11	141
重　庆	2468	654	166	1578
四　川	4968	1051	255	2170
贵　州	627	108	18	347
云　南	1252	311	39	752
西　藏	10	4	1	7
陕　西	2666	453	164	850
甘　肃	742	167	27	313
青　海	268	55	4	140
宁　夏	322	121	12	311
新　疆	864	281	63	1115
兵　团	330	109	10	301

社工师人员情况

单位:人

	助理社会工作师			
当年实考人数	累计合格人数	当年考试通过人数	当年报考人数	当年实考人数
49490	**120332**	**28431**	**144813**	**117067**
3418	13795	1833	9425	7970
1215	2712	814	5117	4563
1007	1894	330	1407	1159
934	950	170	759	621
764	532	140	1024	689
2190	3869	701	5889	4874
1465	2430	371	3368	2757
990	2089	301	2205	1751
2344	5037	1042	5471	3927
5796	16551	4217	19585	16397
3792	8886	1933	7422	5801
1559	3288	965	4326	3496
2199	3641	1047	5941	4771
347	1571	211	1067	860
2388	4666	1000	4182	3010
922	2639	558	1553	1338
1360	3418	881	5522	4706
1008	2478	515	3712	2753
9043	26816	7466	35892	28949
508	1709	311	1289	1135
117	158	52	724	579
1251	1814	489	2846	2297
1760	3917	1261	7188	5899
194	519	109	660	449
534	941	157	992	731
7	6	1	44	38
715	2213	1133	2780	2348
236	575	127	444	353
93	213	24	473	329
271	201	49	442	377
831	583	178	2533	1745
232	221	45	531	395

C-1-8 社会服务职业

地 区	累计鉴定合格人数	2014年鉴定合格人数	养老护理员		假肢类技能人员	
			累计鉴定合格人数	2014年鉴定合格人数	累计鉴定合格人数	2014年鉴定合格人数
全 国	**120554**	**13246**	**15959**	**5934**	**1628**	**338**
中央级	6110	1479	2232	748	461	106
北 京	12461	30	238		58	
天 津	616	39	144		2	
河 北	672	42	360	42	10	
山 西	2406	347	652	262		
内蒙古	1981	243	149	69	21	8
辽 宁	2682	272	346	62	128	44
吉 林	2906	350	87		5	
黑龙江	3245	44	454	8	4	
上 海	2689	48	8		154	23
江 苏	3076	236	41		161	35
浙 江	31474	972	22		61	17
安 徽	2267	88	182		24	
福 建	1513	1415	562	560	4	
江 西	2476	193	69	15	24	13
山 东	5132	586	655	164	62	37
河 南	4648	832	1805	702	63	
湖 北	2581	106	360		13	
湖 南	4675	448	124		26	6
广 东	6112	1570	3013	1235	135	19
广 西	1981	446	882	269	108	15
海 南	243	171	137	123		
重 庆	3817	345	7		39	15
四 川	3722	1089	2011	1000	1	
贵 州	2427	186	280	33	8	
云 南	2673	369	147	89	23	
西 藏	136	112	71	71		
陕 西	577	120	73			
甘 肃	1001	94	201		19	
青 海	267	68	198	53		
宁 夏	3207	612	243	225		
新 疆	781	294	206	204	14	

说明：1.以上数据为民政部职业技能鉴定指导中心及分布在全国31个省、自治区、直辖市76个鉴定站鉴定人数和竞赛晋级人数（不含地方自行组织的鉴定人数）。

2.殡葬类职业包括：殡仪服务员（初中高技师4个级别）、遗体接运工（初中高3个级别）、遗体防腐师（初中高技师高级技师5个级别）、遗体整容师（初中高技师高级技师5个级别）、遗体火化师（初中高技师高级技师5个级别）、墓地管理员（初中高技师4个级别）。

3.假肢类职业包括：假肢师（初中高技师高级技师5个级别）、矫形器师（初中高技师高级技师5个级别）。

技能人员情况

单位：人

孤残儿童护理员		灾害信息员		殡葬类技能人员	
累计鉴定合格人数	2014年鉴定合格人数	累计鉴定合格人数	2014年鉴定合格人数	累计鉴定合格人数	2014年鉴定合格人数
8388	**2093**	**81155**	**2765**	**13424**	**2116**
705	184	982	126	1730	315
184	30	10651		1330	
109	39	246		115	
164		11		127	
261	85	1493			
370	92	1072		369	74
219	59	1573		416	107
148	24	2666	326		
214	36	2440		133	
96	25	2420		11	
499	112	1869		506	89
363	58	30671	794	357	103
176	88	1498		387	
46		901	855		
313	104	1840	31	230	30
454	152	3052		909	233
567	130	2041		172	
302	46	1691	28	215	32
291	31	2157		2077	411
575	101	1238		1151	215
267	95	177		547	67
68	19	30	29	8	
143		2858	271	770	59
278	89	1245		187	
257	89	1603		279	64
296	99	1517		690	181
49	41			16	
497	120	7			
128	61	479		174	33
64	15	5			
103	39	2611	305	250	43
182	30	111		268	60

C-1-9 各省、自治区、直辖市

地 区	1952年	1953年	1954年	1955年	1956年	1957年
全 国	**28265**	**35484**	**60390**	**49842**	**56906**	**53119**
中央级	6	443	20619	8736	270	85
北 京	198	237	276	247	584	302
天 津	208	315	131	157	217	240
河 北	2849	4558	4764	4526	9681	6640
山 西	1253	1398	1531	1373	2096	1953
内蒙古	912	370	306	364	625	417
辽 宁	611	1434	1392	1298	1638	1339
吉 林	346	595	880	856	1331	1610
黑龙江	640	831	912	952	1442	1336
上 海	550	306	411	729	1121	1073
江 苏	1980	1993	2051	3003	4052	5051
浙 江	398	426	505	757	1430	988
安 徽	2051	4061	3382	3453	4748	4306
福 建	828	732	789	933	1473	866
江 西	1519	1040	1368	2253	1889	1802
山 东	2624	3993	5082	3975	3664	5261
河 南	1440	2745	2307	2494	4360	5539
湖 北	2719	1058	2765	2664	1306	1505
湖 南	1255	1089	3381	2205	2259	2177
广 东	1762	1454	1270	1407	2725	2729
广 西	516	645	735	700	1414	1589
海 南						
重 庆						
四 川	1583	2035	2052	2646	3570	2606
贵 州	368	686	633	567	618	494
云 南	630	695	875	740	908	599
西 藏			43	207	91	
陕 西	519	1023	984	1135	1794	1250
甘 肃	390	1074	675	1171	1083	871
青 海	52	134	140	154	281	237
宁 夏						
新 疆	58	114	131	140	236	254

社会服务经费历年支出情况

单位：万元

1958年	1959年	1960年	1961年	1962年	1963年
32693	**44786**	**72444**	**98912**	**74475**	**87533**
82	192	262	39		
376	751	824	658	542	638
194					
2494	4148	5070	10807	5780	15681
2279	1656	2659	2896	2556	2640
505	873	525	785	1468	1124
1098	1249	4475	4392	3933	3467
1126	764	1055	1271	1660	2138
948	782	991	1485	2151	2362
464	475	471	422	539	874
2617	2956	4843	4107	4873	7282
672	874	857	1414	1597	1166
1642	3169	3161	4704	3530	5431
823	4141	2823	2798	1493	1687
1717	1691	2179	3224	3168	2273
3795	4494	8141	11332	6963	7201
2990	2672	10271	11417	8107	10099
1210	2466	4428	4569	3767	3468
1344	967	1690	4299	2697	2834
1223	2982	4608	3475	2830	3146
582	903	997	2687	1505	2125
1982	2583	6315	9758	5918	4227
331	613	750	2390	1429	1792
514	675	880	1692	773	1250
2	1	25	48	117	
588	1109	1113	1530	1422	1640
539	681	1778	4522	2464	2988
164	447	576	1028	1005	
92	239	428	303	365	
300	233	249	860	1823	

C-1-9续表1

地 区	1964年	1965年	1966年	1967年	1968年	1969年
全 国	**161510**	**107869**	**88112**	**81887**	**56154**	**66683**
中央级	31	2325	454	534	308	11
北 京	816	1047	914	939	868	820
天 津				473	439	572
河 北	31433	18545	12395	6983	4443	5333
山 西	2361	2899	4447	2692	2478	2579
内蒙古	1360	1440	2182	2401	1194	842
辽 宁	3382	2942	2572	2781	2473	3542
吉 林	2235	1798	1704	1745	1579	1890
黑龙江	2796	2611	2548	2169	1775	2355
上 海	1074	1220	1472	1654	1410	1359
江 苏	11070	5506	7298	5400	3756	3839
浙 江	1152	1351	1142	1366	1486	1481
安 徽	10567	3347	4119	6861	4025	4246
福 建	1394	1463	1673	1738	1727	1922
江 西	3081	1989	2145	2318	1637	1924
山 东	11079	15807	9458	9844	5878	7622
河 南	48554	17841	9303	8611	4105	6983
湖 北	3319	2790	2579	3177	2651	3509
湖 南	4522	2482	2141	2562	1848	2019
广 东	3056	2664	2454	2644	2046	2639
广 西	4006	1983	1997	2541	1641	1607
海 南						
重 庆						
四 川	4495	5179	4774	4067	3374	3439
贵 州	1808	1726	1730	1926	1224	1314
云 南	1494	1596	1772	1412	807	1018
西 藏	133	192	374			96
陕 西	1918	3137	3623	1874	1477	1733
甘 肃	2310	1611	1161	1963	671	989
青 海	465	695	409	185	190	246
宁 夏	378	284	272	287	200	238
新 疆	1212	1399	1000	740	444	516

单位：万元

1970年	1971年	1972年	1973年	1974年	1975年
65349	**68269**	**81549**	**99675**	**90406**	**127082**
		8	10		
895	974	1192	1506	1284	1461
405	407	546	762	937	881
2054	3591	5482	8727	5925	5960
4777	4563	4025	4696	3587	3420
891	649	1020	1914	1575	1559
2867	3922	4574	5590	3902	18731
1837	1968	1753	2174	2500	2448
2247	2317	2768	3701	3884	3701
1442	1554	1676	1885	2088	2263
4191	4969	7368	6988	7258	8001
1496	1517	2399	2103	1973	1984
5547	3365	4639	4625	3981	5828
1463	1481	1721	2142	2150	1991
2047	2357	2357	4039	3220	2964
6442	9034	8801	8110	8601	10417
4947	4699	4799	5474	4190	24152
4197	3116	3462	4747	3487	4471
1668	1602	2272	3321	2580	2942
2734	2410	2800	4041	5051	3836
1555	1827	1713	1597	1669	1653
3678	4518	5615	6780	5936	6061
1646	1535	2116	3574	1955	2352
2460	1454	1746	1509	2245	2242
100	104	173	228	195	206
1778	2099	2415	3435	2986	2579
952	968	2206	3421	4183	2603
207	291	366	311	342	521
242	354	810	1369	1813	600
584	651	727	896	909	1255

C-1-9续表2

地区	1976年	1977年	1978年	1979年	1980年	1981年
全国	**161690**	**185288**	**137135**	**183279**	**174769**	**192267**
中央级			11	44	103	138
北京	1742	3068	1990	2238	2802	3167
天津	933	13670	1061	1482	1474	1670
河北	7041	36568	11605	9140	11165	13597
山西	4111	4813	5437	8154	6749	7893
内蒙古	2502	1873	2040	5922	5714	6218
辽宁	14705	7427	6103	5607	6671	8073
吉林	2834	3677	3869	3477	4482	4970
黑龙江	4176	5463	5545	5149	5370	6562
上海	2469	2581	2777	3290	3375	3381
江苏	7719	8031	9208	10019	11269	12914
浙江	2424	2641	2853	3475	3703	3897
安徽	15690	6300	6756	13263	9385	9550
福建	2432	2826	2730	3272	3625	4268
江西	3606	3981	3953	8610	6289	5309
山东	9746	10599	12292	15169	16327	14126
河南	40056	21437	14140	19495	12007	10921
湖北	5463	5160	6149	9597	9265	12458
湖南	3442	3550	4380	6747	7026	8924
广东	4884	5546	5435	8146	8337	7767
广西	1963	2355	2073	4019	3213	3674
海南						
重庆						
四川	9037	12602	8511	12722	12063	15429
贵州	2748	3296	2740	4767	4123	4718
云南	3428	3783	2948	3478	4172	4599
西藏	289	270	379	1366	1704	1208
陕西	3174	4575	4834	5780	5390	8198
甘肃	2240	5485	4030	5204	4801	4338
青海	407	514	696	853	862	915
宁夏	1150	1780	1090	1040	1385	1118
新疆	1279	1417	1500	1754	1918	2267

单位：万元

1982年	1983年	1984年	1985年	1986年	1987年
191874	**216116**	**242371**	**295841**	**344064**	**359278**
78	163	286	443	2526	2742
3416	4063	4904	5719	7287	8906
1669	2194	3101	3583	4113	4531
10179	9692	12427	16654	16581	20578
7854	7015	7924	10683	10193	11833
5135	7379	7909	9030	11684	10867
10591	11727	11741	18341	22112	18104
4951	6300	5952	8391	13570	14016
8005	9546	8782	10119	13791	13686
3215	3170	3540	4467	5503	5603
11991	14750	16403	16254	20586	21208
4070	4808	6480	8174	10211	12353
7521	12093	14059	14340	13524	12942
4773	5506	5601	8298	7657	9238
6183	7093	8360	8364	9768	11546
18998	17811	17413	22757	22496	29017
12862	15216	13710	18456	20939	2260
7956	10798	10760	11860	14581	14846
7546	10428	10373	12357	15013	15167
9550	9035	12337	14516	15526	17076
3897	4779	6382	9438	9634	9054
14542	13943	17823	20667	24973	25524
4354	5211	5833	9182	8657	9092
4231	5251	7025	10137	13752	12712
1151	1357	1821	1391	1789	1828
6271	5820	6313	7545	8586	9299
5778	4902	8983	6541	7655	7238
1068	1270	1674	1918	2134	1837
1819	2329	1497	1826	1990	1780
2220	2467	2958	4395	4768	4896

C-1-9续表3

地 区	1988年	1989年	1990年	1991年	1992年	1993年
全 国	**395646**	**466492**	**519383**	**625359**	**637097**	**698708**
中央级	1297	1185	1517	1792	3217	3108
北 京	11355	12805	14738	16249	19073	26105
天 津	5209	5861	6585	7176	8173	9218
河 北	24272	26484	32162	30785	33344	38161
山 西	13977	15845	15976	17378	19264	19515
内蒙古	11254	10975	13510	13449	14250	15314
辽 宁	19595	22233	26318	26380	29561	32903
吉 林	10692	11439	14155	14619	16553	18461
黑龙江	14205	15127	15982	18411	19734	19377
上 海	3965	4741	5364	6270	7742	10368
江 苏	23816	27647	33150	50604	48290	47590
浙 江	16113	18710	21111	22094	22124	26924
安 徽	14854	16444	19755	80611	39002	26982
福 建	10332	11213	13935	15070	18423	20141
江 西	13240	15076	15791	16915	21249	21410
山 东	31890	39382	44965	46744	52525	62616
河 南	21784	26566	24275	27675	31304	34498
湖 北	17804	20704	21092	23318	23677	28918
湖 南	19110	22384	24981	23436	24712	29096
广 东	16675	20206	21863	25022	29602	43983
广 西	9757	11955	11313	12728	14317	16760
海 南	2338	3659	3366	3843	4270	4630
重 庆						
四 川	28123	32186	36228	39004	42563	49037
贵 州	9408	11568	12079	11043	11761	15154
云 南	14934	31640	33901	38725	41026	30502
西 藏	1795	2116	2909	3499	2647	2598
陕 西	10602	12277	13688	13412	16805	20107
甘 肃	8346	7681	8813	9124	11256	12186
青 海	1750	1802	2086	2036	2387	2965
宁 夏	2609	1805	2000	2206	2456	2464
新 疆	4549	4776	5775	5741	5790	7617

单位：万元

1994年	1995年	1996年	1997年	1998年	1999年
870194	**1034502**	**1211500**	**1335202**	**1618445**	**1946843**
4077	3703	6371	5954	50783	11856
36146	44073	54012	61184	74406	97748
11970	15023	17254	19738	20952	20611
48303	58804	74364	71151	79064	88202
22995	31008	37882	37150	39519	45466
18378	20470	26012	26773	35484	35659
44239	60067	59580	65370	74946	85394
24648	30876	31416	33928	52337	53311
26195	28798	30459	33020	55977	60566
15557	19773	23984	30860	37336	54151
59349	69907	80163	93383	108862	121349
40044	43610	50852	60657	65733	88269
26883	37348	43979	50559	56473	72895
25502	31904	34498	46134	49421	50996
23815	30354	33883	35962	47177	45334
71995	76826	88009	101613	112960	131746
44163	52458	59353	64155	68311	80338
39148	40291	50385	58511	85285	75622
35093	42680	53778	48234	54533	73272
53653	64806	75354	88748	96993	112133
30480	28730	36280	28944	30995	31950
6163	7210	8828	8274	9472	10818
			25048	35054	51123
59629	70257	77059	63016	72283	89492
15641	20528	26419	27866	27126	30834
31529	36916	46048	52043	53384	63169
5304	4466	5228	6987	11749	6824
20404	26336	32108	31702	25791	43230
13897	17748	21484	20366	20554	26371
3454	4342	6473	8088	8669	23784
3244	3458	4279	4397	5442	8651
8297	11732	15706	25387	22690	55676

C-1-9续表4

地区	2000年	2001年	2002年	2003年	2004年	2005年
全国	**2296954**	**2847548**	**3922695**	**4989171.81**	**5773906.5**	**7184146**
中央级	29338	13965	18467	18027.2	39289.8	37423
北京	150746	196540	233429	303795.3	327957	370918
天津	30547	41580	58202	62682.2	71091.4	92462
河北	113381	125698	153525	185640.8	216769.6	283480
山西	56815	71776	105897	124002.5	147569.6	192257
内蒙古	44674	55328	70606	99367.7	126236.7	141727
辽宁	131675	180547	227704	279736.9	304551.2	368476
吉林	51153	76026	118392	166702.2	182133.4	218688
黑龙江	61753	80658	177852	167487.2	193823.3	222865
上海	87021	121538	167719	222539.6	228764.3	282196
江苏	159691	170800	205763	256062.56	309196	419996
浙江	97755	124023	159432	189645.4	294720.4	354320
安徽	72568	89476	138918	208605.9	195411.9	250782
福建	67797	68897	85353	94060.8	139539.3	157015
江西	49521	57966	92013	149217.2	176371.5	225667
山东	159315	180470	233918	283989.3	311522.3	408419
河南	102698	117574	159157	221712.8	251438.9	337872
湖北	113381	122382	167653	229233.85	270653.4	345556
湖南	80343	104818	158443	210815.4	252891.5	326694
广东	144461	198362	278022	341821	386221.4	483430
广西	35135	49819	82929	109901	113722.5	156841
海南	13568	15372	18032	24304.1	27949.8	38103
重庆	55934	70571	117114	125112.4	145713	174682
四川	105249	139493	194774	244374.4	302566.3	376043
贵州	36085	51264	67973	82093.5	102696.6	151257
云南	78944	98782	115945	150814	183854.7	202346
西藏	9920	14979	15358	17912.7	23199.7	22574
陕西	54365	72136	103474	147038.8	149120.1	186935
甘肃	35251	42851	58315	75346	91876.1	111530
青海	16159	19790	24812	36616	39139.1	47402
宁夏	13775	21289	28724	30448.1	34071.3	35346
新疆	56940	52768	104762	130065	133844.4	160847

单位：万元

2006年	2007年	2008年	2009年	2010年	2011年	2012年	2013年	2014年
9153527	**12154874**	**21464484**	**21819430.2**	**26975149**	**32291356**	**36837379.4**	**42765370.8**	**44041244.2**
27907	32841	263213	55240.2	488035.9	93505.4	100110.8	137419.9	128646.0
450229	575756	575302	745435.4	982144.3	1031493	1260515.9	1555734.8	1600353.6
121917	149046	196893	244982.6	313824.7	375011.5	444250.9	552118	591814.0
356510	488387	678036	843485.2	969269.1	1244217.3	1438698.1	1672465.7	1653297.9
236469	339210	457567	562518.4	634004.6	876097.5	936468.5	1130400.3	1144649.5
187147	283105	420111	575897.9	768526.2	968084.5	1127395.6	1236610	1409253.2
437608	575209	724799	887386.5	1066504.6	1347428.2	1567755.2	1672890.8	1694087.8
284676	341920	470519	642777.6	750632.3	801698.3	765275	986245.5	942015.8
376619	478896	643011	800947.6	854398.8	1050480.9	1152380.1	1589618.1	1373441.2
316864	406118	515828	557187.9	572521.7	662862.5	727872.8	832211.6	857287.8
502744	632560	811832	996449.2	1265312.3	1711513.8	1970955.5	2335259.9	2460508.3
415110	508925	610800	704117.9	884859.5	1061597.3	1253870.2	1428845.7	1502557.1
312519	490974	659432	804010.6	971558.4	1263090.4	1421837.3	1601142.2	1699609.2
226313	247500	282403	322487.9	422187.8	503195.6	614533.8	729824.6	775607.4
340990	434664	596019	693704.1	847650.9	986614.7	1075144.7	1224409.1	1472214.2
526836	715079	885720	1122739	1437374.8	1691804.7	2183629.3	2502270.9	2706751.9
425038	598726	785189	1035342.8	1230796.6	1586875.1	1740800.2	2097496	2054924.0
440298	514067	748412	897367.7	1082788.8	1408483.1	1531263.7	1849392.5	1852790.6
422998	521304	771404	997685.9	1165255.4	1545645.5	2003252.4	1996276.3	2085354.4
635940	720130	834465	1021108.9	1154286.9	1480652.6	1668953.2	1981669	2237116.3
175928	247212	410162	492763.3	731162.4	971372.9	1173997.1	1292515.6	1391271.4
49003	65929	96527	142315.6	190264.1	223849.3	240254.6	254400.4	287775.5
216847	307697	435014	514479.6	674873.3	783120.4	907587.4	999446.7	1027739.5
500440	734868	4848630	2289514.1	2408738.2	2168767.6	2375722.4	2880631.2	2917857.6
181266	264299	443051	560108.4	728242.8	1116447.6	1248670.9	1341494.8	1391678.3
228950	420914	687354	930167.6	1224026.2	1432131.1	1730472.3	1845730.7	1979476.0
30224	38363	69982	82169.4	85017.8	130279.7	155073.7	156074.8	136789.5
244342	365358	849627	867024.3	1139380.6	1356364.3	1424205.1	1838401.7	1679000.3
149598	226791	1063855	577204.8	740624.8	1000902.5	1051754.7	1299304.5	1214834.5
51844	81455	123508	189659.7	330701.5	359785.5	341516.9	377594.3	381598.0
57593	79705	110375	143479.2	161335.6	195226.4	220055.6	266258.2	264662.5
222762	267867	395446	519670.9	698848.1	862756.8	983105.5	1101217	1126280.9

C-1-10 社会服务经费预算

地 区	预算指标		
	2014年	2013年	增长 (%)
全 国	**45130767.7**	**43268489.6**	**4.3**
中央级	160968.3	132229.8	21.7
北 京	1584025.2	1429615.9	10.8
天 津	613841.0	561715.2	9.3
河 北	1732833.6	1658617.9	4.5
山 西	1207672.5	1145199.4	5.5
内蒙古	1416401.6	1274677.4	11.1
辽 宁	1684919.2	1667135.5	1.1
吉 林	1055354.4	982109.1	7.5
黑龙江	1404905.7	1629434.3	-13.8
上 海	994656.3	952375.6	4.4
江 苏	2463224.8	2277104.5	8.2
浙 江	1514614.1	1449943.3	4.5
安 徽	1659327.3	1588794.1	4.4
福 建	812657.2	732793.1	10.9
江 西	1459303.5	1260784.9	15.7
山 东	2702182.5	2542119.4	6.3
河 南	2137429.4	2089771.4	2.3
湖 北	2051670.0	1837118.4	11.7
湖 南	2121593.7	1995947.6	6.3
广 东	2230664.5	1982305.0	12.5
广 西	1381693.7	1350210.3	2.3
海 南	361912.9	294076.0	23.1
重 庆	1072614.3	1007108.9	6.5
四 川	2969415.3	2909798.8	2.0
贵 州	1516174.5	1458130.4	4.0
云 南	1957799.1	1854957.0	5.5
西 藏	210770.9	166015.3	27.0
陕 西	1769283.1	1996633.1	-11.4
甘 肃	1221824.8	1292279.6	-5.5
青 海	357353.5	351399.8	1.7
宁 夏	272324.5	285516.1	-4.6
新 疆	1031356.3	1112572.5	-7.3

指标地方安排情况

单位：万元

地方预算安排预算指标		
2014年	2013年	增长 (%)
24023782.4	**21610000.3**	**11.2**
976640.2	866453.9	12.7
472402.0	421625.2	12.0
835564.6	716433.9	16.6
590413.5	517245.4	14.1
841676.6	700058.4	20.2
830428.2	764356.5	8.6
419342.4	318734.1	31.6
572905.7	788714.3	-27.4
871216.3	834706.6	4.4
1988514.8	1753758.5	13.4
1313343.1	1229097.3	6.9
839501.3	726851.1	15.5
580091.2	484266.1	19.8
695115.5	474373.9	46.5
1714136.5	1457377.4	17.6
854706.4	765640.4	11.6
956153.0	723950.4	32.1
900103.7	755067.6	19.2
1786459.5	1518665.0	17.6
652565.7	618515.3	5.5
204446.9	159519.0	28.2
521997.3	470061.9	11.0
1332462.3	1257946.8	5.9
426446.5	393433.4	8.4
881657.1	751076.0	17.4
85571.9	46825.3	82.7
861078.1	1055311.1	-18.4
387905.8	383462.6	1.2
134415.5	136929.8	-1.8
100366.5	122015.1	-17.7
396154.3	397528.0	-0.3

C-1-11 中央专项

地 区	合计	抚恤合计	财社 [2013]157号	财社 [2013]158号	财社 [2014]9号	财社 [2014]10号
全 国	**21050494.04**	**3380102.18**	**2179863**	**15323**	**500**	**500**
北 京	607385	21753	12940	133		
天 津	141439	15187	9858	82		
河 北	899269	216055	135489	4376		
山 西	617259	119172	62492	1172		
内蒙古	574725	39230	26470	198		
辽 宁	854491	72136	59433	265		
吉 林	636012	62194	37137	188		
黑龙江	832000	65945	48132	242		
上 海	123440	12570	7871	2		
江 苏	474710	144399	99865	1541		
浙 江	201535	60365	38345	280		
安 徽	819826	149354	102645	158		
福 建	232566	53262	33978	17		
江 西	764188	158091	90038	9		
山 东	988046	358271	250262	5034		
河 南	1282723	234499	158333	1008		
湖 北	1095517	190406	131381	60		
湖 南	1221490	287144	181724	35		
广 东	442205	102153	63099	20		
广 西	729128	89309	55502	6	500	
海 南	157466	15693	9530	39		
重 庆	550617	105826	69914	22		
四 川	1636953	335284	211022	44		
贵 州	1089728	104474	62896	8		
云 南	1076142	128076	84879	29		500
西 藏	125199	7002	3011			
陕 西	910564	134724	84605	289		
甘 肃	833919	41704	25931	49		
青 海	222938	9743	5329	2		
宁 夏	173958	6121	4007	4		
新 疆	735056.04	39960.18	13745	11		

拨款对账单

单位：万元

财社[2014]38号		财社[2014]47号	财社[2014]90号	财社[2014]141号	财社[2014]142号	新疆兵团
抚恤补助资金	老党员生活补贴补助资金					
714466	**3530**	**289728**	**11311**	**157191**	**559**	**7131.18**
6550	43	720	279	1083	5	
4029	17	400	74	724	3	
32265	996	31728	639	10405	157	
18196	253	32307	222	4487	43	
8548	35	1964	213	1795	7	
4941	49	3630	148	3662	8	
15856	38	5654	295	3019	7	
6529	42	8060		2932	8	
3721	1	180	148	647		
21221	486	13143	574	7507	62	
15903	76	2331	148	3271	11	
33759	36	6093	148	6510	5	
10019	5	6422	213	2607	1	
34937	3	25640		7464		
51552	1097	31012	1302	17829	183	
54204	205	7405	795	12512	37	
42785	24	6014	426	9714	2	
86473	8	4550	140	14213	1	
27180	9	7037	344	4463	1	
16831	1	12705	148	3616		
2446	11	2881	74	711	1	
27684	1	3213	287	4704	1	
79246	12	29472	925	14561	2	
26108	2	11523	205	3732		
33363	9	3708	270	5317	1	
1413		2261		317		
26899	59	17134	132	5595	11	
10189	5	3221	295	2012	2	
2548		1367	74	423		
919	1	920		270		
8152	6	7033	2793	1089		7131.18

C-1-11续表1

地 区	安置合计	财社[2013]159号	财社[2013]160号	财社[2014]39号	财社[2014]40号	财社[2014]42号	财社[2014]44号
全 国	**2887631.82**	**1852784**	**73742**	**69015**	**742684**	**33732**	**2170**
北 京	556524	330899	14238	118	149601	6210	10
天 津	67787	46954	1698	215	16305	644	10
河 北	159624	108177	4612	4016	38672	1804	60
山 西	54015	35795	1280	986	14385	683	90
内蒙古	33640	22246	1231	1231	7958	461	50
辽 宁	279474	186893	6945	3222	73042	3127	90
吉 林	60289	39358	1734	1325	15698	812	50
黑龙江	49277	31142	1583	2527	12540	680	100
上 海	92940	58338	2424	261	24274	1094	20
江 苏	155590	102250	4095	5042	38496	1912	70
浙 江	56966	35790	1553	1975	15215	711	60
安 徽	42859	26367	1265	3877	9850	526	90
福 建	46863	31144	1319	1367	11275	504	30
江 西	26565	15368	626	2818	6659	348	80
山 东	235118	160779	5625	5435	57108	1823	220
河 南	90338	56046	2427	5949	22100	1071	250
湖 北	111912	71653	2416	4352	28953	1349	160
湖 南	65930	40168	1635	4875	17309	959	120
广 东	121509	79426	2584	2348	30225	1458	60
广 西	28001	16822	839	2155	6767	388	80
海 南	13745	7590	341	399	4913	300	30
重 庆	48238	32260	1116	1459	11652	474	40
四 川	121448	78515	3002	5193	30529	1365	210
贵 州	17700	11500	582	1498	3608	229	80
云 南	79650	54546	2234	1581	19053	1043	50
西 藏	12142	7566	154	185	3542	370	
陕 西	128201	83294	3032	1812	35521	1410	30
甘 肃	49984	30586	1266	1575	14639	887	
青 海	13962	8974	315	170	3962	227	
宁 夏	8701	5397	267	590	2142	148	30
新 疆	58639.82	36941	1304	459	16691	715	

单位：万元

财社[2014]43号	新疆兵团	社会福利合计	财社[2013]165号	财社[2014]54号	彩票公益金	财综[2014]94号	财综[2014]84号
112963	**541.82**	**634277.74**	**169674**	**46137**	**405948**	**98832**	**50000**
55448		6293.00	449	115	5729	1011	
1961		3782.00	164	37	3581	984	
2283		19565.00	4343	1158	14064	5292	2000
796		15329.00	4244	1589	9496	3036	2000
463		14201.00	2496	822	10883	1944	3000
6155		9684.00	1489	372	7823	2673	
1312		11237.00	1650	448	9139	1500	3000
705		13214.00	2375	536	10303	2211	3000
6529		3711.00	402	112	3197		
3725		20401.00	3551	1116	15734	4335	3000
1662		9837.00	1082	173	8582	3630	
884		24422.00	7631	2152	14639	4578	3000
1224		11601.00	1211	384	10006	2664	2000
666		21387.00	8208	362	12817	3264	3000
4128		22204.00	3334	926	17944	7308	2000
2495		36522.00	13916	3465	19141	6102	2000
3029		26414.00	8318	2565	15531	4035	3000
864		34373.00	14762	4204	15407	5280	2000
5408		20777.00	8114	2507	10156	3213	
950		21745.00	7953	2848	10944	3870	
172		4914.00	841	-8	4081	1416	
1237		17271.00	7066	-561	10766	3063	2000
2634		35478.00	11640	2937	20901	7341	3000
203		72994.00	7888	3456	61650	3741	
1143		26387.00	12933	3841	9613	3492	
325		10440.00	2009	846	7585	948	
3102		17851.00	5039	1440	11372	3735	2000
1031		21657.00	8270	2459	10928	3054	3000
314		17407.00	5892	1960	9555	1467	3000
127		10205.00	2571	822	6812	1251	2000
1988	541.82	52974.74	9833	3054	27569	2394	2000

C-1-11续表2

地 区	财综[2014]50号	财综[2014]52号	财社[2014]170号	新疆兵团	城市低保合计	财社[2013]163号	财社[2014]55号
全 国	**52000**	**16600**	**188516**	**12518.74**	**5186786.5**	**3336507**	**1802934**
北 京			4718				
天 津			2597		40799	27999	12800
河 北			6772		182582	125301	57281
山 西			4460		196268	130095	66173
内蒙古			5939		228382	151956	76426
辽 宁			5150		331560	214084	117476
吉 林			4639		304717	194941	109776
黑龙江			5092		436485	272803	163682
上 海			3197				
江 苏			8399				
浙 江			4952				
安 徽			7061		231550	144719	86831
福 建			5342		25502	15939	9563
江 西			6553		216667	148693	67974
山 东			8636		86130	53831	32299
河 南			11039		333441	215250	118191
湖 北			8496		363862	227414	136448
湖 南			8127		344176	226046	118130
广 东			6943				
广 西			7074		127648	81673	45975
海 南			2665		36014	24716	11298
重 庆			5703		176536	110335	66201
四 川			10560		435478	272174	163304
贵 州	52000		5909		127994	84089	43905
云 南			6121		174467	113644	60823
西 藏			6637		13783	8614	5169
陕 西			5637		199226	136724	62502
甘 肃			4874		204054	140037	64017
青 海			5088		61002	41864	19138
宁 夏			3561		48086	33000	15086
新 疆		16600	6575	12518.74	260377.5	140566	72466

单位：万元

新疆兵团	农村低保合计	财社[2013]164号	财社[2014]56号	临时救助合计	财社[2014]96号	新疆兵团	医疗救助支出合计
47345.5	**5826000**	**3543958**	**2282042**	**320000**	**311969**	**8031**	**1650084.8**
				5260	5260		4147
				5587	5587		6242
	210133	132334	77799	11034	11034		57596
	147639	87824	59815	9509	9509		44503
	162790	97473	65317	9629	9629		47400
	80818	49797	31021	9451	9451		35552
	96679	61133	35546	8991	8991		61286
	146786	85625	61161	11144	11144		75642
				8250	8250		3457
	100872	60270	40602	10817	10817		26040
	43287	28057	15230	8807	8807		12688
	255229	155660	99569	11664	11664		73458
	60368	37626	22742	8788	8788		16598
	196063	119132	76931	10506	10506		77719
	198775	116655	82120	12216	12216		54260
	433511	259003	174508	13451	13451		96389
	252436	147707	104729	11268	11268		74924
	286468	167106	119362	12285	12285		108229
	123068	74699	48369	10324	10324		24428
	343730	200509	143221	11396	11396		61395
	30184	19564	10620	7217	7217		19319
	98323	63728	34595	8425	8425		47435
	457255	266732	190523	13704	13704		148743
	592826	384239	208587	11557	11557		81377
	506440	295423	211017	12119	12119		92273
	35852	23237	12615	9161	9161		17518
	292876	189289	103587	9637	9637		76051
	373856	242314	131542	11768	11768		82314
	61350	39764	21586	9079	9079		29917
	49324	28772	20552	8918	8918		22544
47345.5	189062	110286	78776	18038	10007	8031	70640.8

C-1-11续表3

地 区	城乡医疗救助合计	财社[2013]178号	财社[2014]52号	新疆兵团	优抚医疗补助合计	财社[2013]162号	财社[2014]41号
全 国	**1411665.8**	**1044470**	**357583**	**9612.8**	**238419**	**177937**	**59230**
北 京	2183	1638	545		1964	1446	518
天 津	3247	2432	815		2995	2194	801
河 北	45471	33790	11681		12125	9476	2649
山 西	38418	27589	10829		6085	4636	1449
内蒙古	44208	31728	12480		3192	2372	820
辽 宁	29792	22381	7411		5760	4825	935
吉 林	55848	41925	13923		5438	4004	1434
黑龙江	70165	52674	17491		5477	4175	1302
上 海	2099	1571	528		1358	989	369
江 苏	14751	11117	3634		11289	8623	2666
浙 江	7163	5408	1755		5525	4103	1422
安 徽	62031	46855	15176		11427	8483	2944
福 建	11639	8785	2854		4959	3657	1302
江 西	69520	49960	19560		8199	6073	2126
山 东	30783	23216	7567		23477	18528	4949
河 南	80656	60854	19802		15733	11857	3876
湖 北	61432	45860	15572		13492	10000	3492
湖 南	89286	67248	22038		18943	13956	4987
广 东	14564	10983	3581		9864	7286	2578
广 西	55450	40484	14966		5945	4338	1607
海 南	17280	12399	4881		2039	1454	585
重 庆	39070	28070	11000		8365	6179	2186
四 川	129220	97403	31817		19523	14378	5145
贵 州	74447	56236	18211		6930	5182	1748
云 南	82848	62553	20295		9425	6959	2466
西 藏	16506	12426	4080		1012	714	298
陕 西	67899	51175	16724		8152	6026	2126
甘 肃	79354	59846	19508		2960	2149	811
青 海	28171	20232	7939		1746	1206	540
宁 夏	21228	15247	5981		1316	943	373
新 疆	66936.8	42385	14939	9612.8	3704	1726	726

单位：万元

新疆兵团	流浪乞讨救助合计	财社[2013]156号	财社[2014]32号	新疆兵团	救灾合计	财社[2014]1号
1252	**200000**	**139835**	**60094**	**71**	**963211**	**144100**
	12730	7858	4872		678	200
	1706	1680	26		349	
	7940	4667	3273		34740	6500
	4244	3326	918		26580	4900
	2803	1960	843		36650	5800
	5774	3533	2241		30042	5600
	3139	2800	339		27480	5500
	2803	2557	246		30704	7100
	2512	2512				
	8851	5578	3273		7740	2300
	5545	4281	1264		4040	1400
	10195	7273	2922		21095	4600
	4198	3389	809		5386	1700
	7100	5673	1427		50090	6700
	7132	5809	1323		13940	3700
	11248	7293	3955		33324	4000
	16000	10044	5956		48295	7100
	17881	10323	7558		65004	7000
	11326	7030	4296		28620	1900
	5125	4292	833		40779	4900
	2000	1400	600		28380	800
	4283	3645	638		44280	5200
	19833	12516	7317		69730	10100
	6216	4210	2006		74590	9100
	3268	3103	165		53462	8100
	862	857	5		18439	3100
	6414	4379	2035		45584	6400
	2947	2881	66		45635	8700
	1878	1610	268		18600	3400
	779	700	79		19280	3300
1252	3268	2656	541	71	39695	5000

C-1-11续表4

地 区	财社[2014]28号	财社[2014]29号	财社[2014]30号	财社[2014]31号	财社[2014]61号	财社[2014]74号	财社[2014]75号
全 国	**9000**	**8000**	**10000**	**8800**	**5000**	**5000**	**5000**
北 京							
天 津							
河 北							
山 西							
内蒙古							
辽 宁							
吉 林							
黑龙江							
上 海							
江 苏							
浙 江							
安 徽							
福 建							
江 西	9000					5000	
山 东							
河 南							
湖 北							
湖 南			10000				5000
广 东		8000					
广 西							
海 南							
重 庆					5000		
四 川							
贵 州				8800			
云 南							
西 藏							
陕 西							
甘 肃							
青 海							
宁 夏							
新 疆							

单位：万元

财社[2014]91号	财社[2014]92号	财社[2014]93号	财社[2014]94号	财社[2014]95号	财社[2014]97号	财社[2014]108号	财社[2014]109号
13000	**14000**	**12000**	**15000**	**17000**	**1400**	**6000**	**6000**
						6000	
							6000
13000							
		12000					
			15000				
				17000			
	14000						
					1400		

C-1-11续表5

地 区	财社[2014]110号	财社[2014]111号	财社[2014]119号	财社[2014]112号	财社[2014]121号	财社[2014]122号	财社[2014]123号
全 国	**7500**	**6000**	**12000**	**2600**	**5000**	**11000**	**12000**
北 京							
天 津							
河 北							
山 西							
内蒙古							
辽 宁							
吉 林							
黑龙江							
上 海							
江 苏							
浙 江							
安 徽							
福 建							
江 西							
山 东							
河 南	7500						
湖 北		6000			5000		
湖 南							
广 东							
广 西							
海 南							
重 庆			12000				
四 川						11000	
贵 州							
云 南							
西 藏							
陕 西							12000
甘 肃							
青 海							
宁 夏				2600			
新 疆							

单位：万元

财社[2014]153号	财社[2014]189号	财社[2014]196号	财社[2014]197号	财社[2014]201号	财社[2014]228号	新疆兵团	民政管理事务（新疆兵团）
8000	**7331**	**4100**	**32430**	**5000**	**560000**	**10950**	**2400**
	78				400		
	349						
			1920		26320		
			1680		20000		
			1650		23200		
	522				17920		
			540		21440		
	744		1260		21600		
					5440		
					2640		
	265		1350		14880		
	166				3520		
			1710		27680		
					10240		
	744		1320		19760		
	455		1020		28720		
	404		1440		28160		
					6720		
	279		1560		19040		
			180		10400		
			480		21600		
	460		2610	5000	40560		
		4100	1950		36640		
8000	282		2400		33280		
	139		2160		13040		
	924		1860		24400		
	425		1710		34800		
	530		990		13680		
			180		13200		
	565		2460		20720	10950	2400

C-1-12 收入支出情况

单位：万元

地　区	收入合计	上年结余	本年收入合计	本年实际支出	收支结余	用事业基金弥补收支差额	结余分配	年末净结余
全　国	**48022690.0**	**2501991.5**	**45520698.5**	**44926560.0**	**3096130.0**	**33211.5**	**152236.4**	**2977105.1**
中央级	214132.5	28334.6	185797.9	148102.4	66030.1	83.0	2176.9	63936.2
北　京	2156284.3	304996.7	1851287.6	1828820.7	327463.6	10679.8	10330.9	327812.5
天　津	708923.6	61475.7	647447.9	609917.3	99006.3	2127.7	14368.9	86765.1
河　北	1760987.0	70604.9	1690382.1	1655026.9	105960.1	520.5	182.4	106298.2
山　西	1284582.3	105192.8	1179389.5	1154729.6	129852.7	203.5	1026.3	129029.9
内蒙古	1493210.5	69205.1	1424005.4	1419805.9	73404.6	583.4	1359.9	72628.1
辽　宁	1816197.9	37492.3	1778705.6	1728448.6	87749.3		859.6	86889.7
吉　林	964116.9	1866.8	962250.1	942898.2	21218.7	1059.9	746.5	21532.1
黑龙江	1395468.9	18009.6	1377459.3	1373997.1	21471.8		652.6	20819.2
上　海	1086809.2	160975.4	925833.8	900729.9	186079.3	172.9	5135.5	181116.7
江　苏	2534901.4	33792.3	2501109.1	2491036.9	43864.5	886.8	9001.1	35750.2
浙　江	1699309.5	92971.4	1606338.1	1592495.1	106814.4	210.5	9321.9	97703.0
安　徽	1730326.0	18704.5	1711621.5	1700544.8	29781.2	98.0	21159.3	8719.9
福　建	867273.9	68864.9	798409.0	786110.9	81163.0	854.8	1110.6	80907.2
江　西	1475023.1	1163.3	1473859.8	1474554.9	468.2			468.2
山　东	2747424.5	21488.3	2725936.2	2726841.3	20583.2	180.2	971.3	19792.1
河　南	2128601.0	45407.8	2083193.2	2056538.3	72062.7	47.0	5336.2	66773.5
湖　北	1900157.0	8222.9	1891934.1	1874861.3	25295.7	575.5	2718.3	23152.9
湖　南	2179771.2	20244.1	2159527.1	2150165.1	29606.1	5742.3	6487.0	28861.4
广　东	2466641.3	84639.4	2382001.9	2358028.3	108613.0	2407.6	24441.6	86579.0
广　西	1640703.9	220229.4	1420474.5	1417236.9	223467.0	2594.5	5450.9	220610.6
海　南	406496.3	96667.3	309829.0	293343.4	113152.9	286.7	172.4	113267.2
重　庆	1097514.5	50698.9	1046815.6	1034119.1	63395.4	291.1	5165.6	58520.9
四　川	3166347.1	173508.0	2992839.1	2968248.0	198099.1	491.3	2285.5	196304.9
贵　州	1776779.1	305548.0	1471231.1	1399481.7	377297.4		591.1	376706.3
云　南	2176965.5	179925.1	1997040.4	1990463.4	186502.1	2726.7	12006.6	177222.2
西　藏	206379.8	32012.6	174367.2	136909.5	69470.3		375.8	69094.5
陕　西	1779251.6	42576.2	1736675.4	1709355.6	69896.0		7968.6	61927.4
甘　肃	1261566.0	49101.1	1212464.9	1214844.3	46721.7	75.5	520.8	46276.4
青　海	404870.2	13845.8	391024.4	395351.6	9518.6			9518.6
宁　夏	331059.7	48968.5	282091.2	267272.1	63787.6	312.3	312.3	63787.6
新　疆	1164614.3	35257.8	1129356.5	1126280.9	38333.4			38333.4

C-1-13 行政事业性收费收入情况

单位：万元

地　区	行政事业性收费	婚姻登记收费	收养登记收费	殡葬收费
全　国	**373939.5**	**12058.6**	**453.4**	**361427.5**
中央级				
北　京	24716.1	74.7	6.4	24635.0
天　津	12488.0	134.7		12353.3
河　北	13388.6	507.4	31.6	12849.6
山　西	16966.0	476.0	5.1	16484.9
内蒙古	11779.3	490.7	4.4	11284.2
辽　宁	12813.0	219.7	68.7	12524.6
吉　林	2478.2	51.8		2426.4
黑龙江	25280.4	191.3	1.5	25087.6
上　海				
江　苏	28377.1		20.9	28356.2
浙　江	8496.6	195.1	44.7	8256.8
安　徽	18312.6	813.7	13.7	17485.2
福　建	16791.1	369.9	24.1	16397.1
江　西	4.3		4.3	
山　东	19911.2	696.1	52.5	19162.6
河　南	2508.5	850.8		1657.7
湖　北	45775.5	315.5	15.7	45444.3
湖　南	1638.5	232.6	8.1	1397.8
广　东	31601.7	716.4	43.5	30841.8
广　西	16668.8	942.1	41.9	15684.8
海　南	19.3	19.3		
重　庆	1004.8	997.4	7.4	
四　川	35892.2	1992.8	22.8	33876.6
贵　州	447.2	420.3	6.8	20.1
云　南	1910.2	219.8	14.3	1676.1
西　藏	0.3	0.3		
陕　西	514.3	128.1	3.4	382.8
甘　肃	6350.7	324.6	2.7	6023.4
青　海	57.4	57.0	0.4	
宁　夏	144.6	63.9	0.8	79.9
新　疆	17603.0	556.6	7.7	17038.7

C-1-14 财政性资金

地区	上年结余合计	抚恤	退役安置	社会福利
全 国	**2223511.4**	**264806.6**	**283878.7**	**348344.6**
中央级	18458.8	563.7		8464.9
北 京	238803.8	12739.2	119972.4	38498.2
天 津	56347.8	3718.7	7238.9	16110.5
河 北	70713.9	12197.3	16421.2	12278.2
山 西	101943.3	16810.1	6753.5	14077.9
内蒙古	68054.2	7840.1	4185.2	10567.9
辽 宁	38486.8	913.9	409.7	2736.6
吉 林	1866.8			
黑龙江	18009.6	1516.0	406.4	101.4
上 海	101806.2	12983.3	10358.5	12848.4
江 苏	29395.6	1699.0	2027.6	5505.8
浙 江	87062.3	17130.1	6823.8	18990.7
安 徽	17977.0	190.2	794.8	1912.3
福 建	64593.1	10937.8	10389.5	8616.8
江 西	1163.3	18.2	248.0	546.5
山 东	16118.6	7609.1	2019.3	1291.1
河 南	45247.1	3726.9	2290.5	5544.3
湖 北	7232.0	98.1	2251.1	158.7
湖 南	6024.6	1911.7	531.2	39.6
广 东	67202.8	8561.4	8408.5	19375.4
广 西	206451.7	41990.8	9978.9	37839.9
海 南	88409.5	11199.6	7167.1	11846.9
重 庆	49875.7	3306.2	1395.4	27690.5
四 川	153619.2	8877.3	8149.4	12594.2
贵 州	297078.5	41758.6	12901.7	35584.6
云 南	176472.7	25634.5	27264.7	17624.3
西 藏	32069.7	312.8	3.0	7.0
陕 西	18769.0	1462.5	1331.2	4820.4
甘 肃	49101.1	1298.7	2018.5	2511.3
青 海	13845.8	992.9	2281.8	3069.5
宁 夏	46053.1	1692.0	7304.0	2663.2
新 疆	35257.8	5115.9	2552.9	14427.6

收、支、余情况

单位：万元

社会救助	自然灾害 生活救助	民政管理 事务	行政事业单位 离退休	其他款项用于 民政支出
690346.6	**178502.9**	**195357.0**	**7934.9**	**215895.2**
	0.8	7430.2		1999.2
21609.3	3701.7	19953.3	350.8	21978.9
8647.0	1078.5	15344.1	366.2	3843.7
16289.6	4134.3	4459.6	53.0	4803.5
56511.7	3538.4	2872.8	26.8	1352.1
13326.5	5697.4	6709.3	17.2	19278.5
18390.1	520.8	1023.2	402.7	14089.8
1377.8	489.0			
14121.5	602.0	1246.7		15.6
34826.4	618.4	23820.3	144.8	5730.2
840.3	298.0	4668.3	5.4	14350.9
21564.1	3661.5	11715.2	1538.7	5638.2
3612.7	37.5			30.6
12614.7	3051.2	9724.9	1073.9	2979.7
348.4	2.2			
950.2	4.7	4244.1		
30076.8	537.6	264.7	20.3	2136.7
2793.6	121.1	792.4		580.0
2812.8	521.9	221.7		-15.2
18108.2	1815.9	6525.6	2336.0	1364.8
72077.5	15162.2	11744.9	369.7	6588.6
26388.9	4651.3	9385.4	22.8	12383.6
8514.8	5567.8	1232.9	89.6	2078.5
46814.8	55246.9	4298.9	325.4	17280.3
153391.1	27948.3	15483.2	1.7	10009.3
42167.1	19878.0	18170.8	783.3	23695.5
10010.4	777.2			20902.2
6509.2	573.7	2281.7		562.4
14930.0	13672.5	2028.8	3.9	12637.4
1413.1	925.0	518.3		4266.9
21578.8	3006.2	6387.0	1.4	3380.1
7729.2	660.9	2808.7	1.3	1953.2

C-1-14续表1

地区	本年收入合计	抚恤	退役安置	社会福利
全国	**44174734.2**	**6348199.4**	**4550523.8**	**4943197.9**
中央级	160968.3	10063.0		33760.0
北京	1566277.6	104130.1	696193.2	230870.8
天津	615414.4	66416.4	92592.4	57353.9
河北	1682625.7	351386.4	266819.5	155251.0
山西	1167667.8	219112.7	80796.0	91131.9
内蒙古	1364675.8	97305.3	65519.7	150460.2
辽宁	1724092.1	186973.7	342262.8	123610.9
吉林	950672.3	113278.4	86887.9	51595.9
黑龙江	1344105.2	105207.0	71755.8	79757.4
上海	865065.3	95033.5	151632.7	150114.1
江苏	2401691.3	406681.1	305579.7	421244.2
浙江	1500822.4	238942.7	116022.5	335412.2
安徽	1709939.8	268562.8	152653.5	169734.1
福建	785800.2	129737.4	90093.6	116100.5
江西	1471465.5	237554.6	49971.2	139837.5
山东	2705418.1	718641.6	379574.3	368505.2
河南	2081520.1	415666.8	176035.1	147481.6
湖北	1850996.4	317619.6	161833.3	162976.0
湖南	2095297.7	410297.3	106458.9	151814.9
广东	2238604.4	319215.5	230040.5	344894.6
广西	1386942.5	150400.4	47468.1	155671.6
海南	299962.1	28549.1	26277.9	36926.8
重庆	1011956.2	171263.2	90742.8	109591.8
四川	2935290.5	478593.9	224984.2	365007.3
贵州	1461393.7	140255.6	38008.1	140749.6
云南	1981881.1	173106.5	112727.9	105502.6
西藏	141283.9	12340.5	3231.5	12406.8
陕西	1700980.3	235945.5	181867.6	179679.0
甘肃	1206888.1	56856.9	75907.7	82578.1
青海	359311.3	17211.0	22777.5	56606.8
宁夏	276375.2	11269.0	19898.7	15424.5
新疆	1129348.9	60581.9	83909.2	201146.1

单位：万元

社会救助	自然灾害生活救助	民政管理事务	行政事业单位离退休	其他款项用于民政支出
22053760.4	**1224548.0**	**3250221.3**	**439509.5**	**1364773.9**
	28604.0	58994.5	4761.6	24785.2
169201.3	3439.6	176978.7	53557.5	131906.4
228561.3	969.5	116409.9	3865.2	49245.8
738308.3	38157.8	80931.7	21523.0	30248.0
661022.0	28661.6	64965.2	9930.6	12047.8
861989.1	37020.0	71757.0	15051.1	65573.4
738160.3	54931.4	181153.1	20922.1	76077.8
560954.6	35746.8	52432.6	5912.7	43863.4
1006215.9	13834.0	52529.0	10104.3	4701.8
317694.6	1800.0	122714.4	11106.9	14969.1
852699.7	16454.6	227318.2	26590.6	145123.2
477442.2	23121.3	220204.1	21874.1	67803.3
946231.7	28258.9	69445.4	14395.5	60657.9
312380.3	17730.2	63684.6	23617.2	32456.4
924055.1	59292.8	39594.1	11166.9	9993.3
978186.9	20604.6	169537.5	13372.0	56996.0
1160215.7	18973.1	99025.0	20122.8	44000.0
1002054.2	31414.7	132400.5	16698.2	25999.9
1224923.7	50828.5	115374.4	8735.0	26865.0
885423.6	50966.7	250143.4	37075.1	120845.0
820995.9	59452.6	109764.3	13971.8	29217.8
134760.0	22247.9	34113.4	4818.5	12268.5
476226.4	35193.0	90598.5	10326.1	28014.4
1511918.5	124174.4	163676.7	20806.0	46129.5
947269.6	89188.3	72979.0	2386.6	30556.9
1189732.5	154330.5	132396.4	13183.5	100901.2
68489.8	27446.0	16691.2	644.1	34.0
902510.8	34166.1	133288.7	8909.7	24612.9
903691.0	49048.1	27242.1	5494.5	6069.7
208449.0	21468.9	18539.7	2413.1	11845.3
163837.8	22627.5	18667.4	2024.2	22626.1
680158.6	24394.6	66670.6	4149.0	8338.9

C-1-14续表2

地 区	本年支出合计	抚恤	退役安置	社会福利
全 国	**44041244.2**	**6365744.2**	**4567849.2**	**4809479.7**
中央级	128646.0	2166.0		
北 京	1600353.6	107558.6	724662.4	225668.2
天 津	591814.0	66835.9	92687.2	56445.7
河 北	1653297.9	349994.0	255298.0	149277.7
山 西	1144649.5	211508.0	80063.2	79829.0
内蒙古	1409253.2	97170.7	61802.4	151283.7
辽 宁	1694087.8	184824.0	337923.7	132829.0
吉 林	942015.8	113342.3	78741.7	49320.4
黑龙江	1373441.2	105906.5	71615.6	79242.4
上 海	857287.8	94994.7	147881.8	146537.4
江 苏	2460508.3	423763.2	335953.8	424389.9
浙 江	1502557.1	238431.3	116663.3	331852.9
安 徽	1699609.2	284993.5	152501.8	168348.4
福 建	775607.4	130093.4	88560.5	111201.5
江 西	1472214.2	239898.3	50440.9	139507.2
山 东	2706751.9	723769.0	379751.4	364226.8
河 南	2054924.0	415921.9	174654.0	145683.8
湖 北	1852790.6	322408.2	156196.7	164422.0
湖 南	2085354.4	411076.4	105284.9	153669.5
广 东	2237116.3	320673.1	229139.4	349232.9
广 西	1391271.4	148375.4	48840.2	148070.1
海 南	287775.5	31562.1	23680.6	29281.1
重 庆	1027739.5	169469.5	92065.4	128084.2
四 川	2917857.6	477657.1	224381.1	308904.4
贵 州	1391678.3	134549.8	36898.1	110102.2
云 南	1979476.0	170978.0	115255.4	104660.8
西 藏	136789.5	7712.9	9814.1	15856.6
陕 西	1679000.3	236078.2	182025.6	179999.5
甘 肃	1214834.5	57501.5	74595.5	77144.8
青 海	381598.0	17019.7	23176.9	65199.6
宁 夏	264662.5	11245.0	16909.3	15125.9
新 疆	1126280.9	58266.0	80384.3	204082.1

单位：万元

社会救助	自然灾害生活救助	民政管理事务	行政事业单位离退休	其他款项用于民政支出
21975319.6	**1244362.2**	**3305417.4**	**442370.8**	**1330701.1**
	23137.0	59927.8	3966.6	39448.6
167609.7	6195.7	186222.1	55100.1	127336.8
216315.6	869.6	113669.6	3877.5	41112.9
727204.0	37851.4	80110.0	21769.4	31793.4
660396.3	27198.8	63732.5	9934.4	11987.3
859741.8	48219.3	90301.8	14738.4	85995.1
740673.8	40718.5	194035.6	20390.5	42692.7
571910.6	31255.0	52288.6	5912.7	39244.5
1034755.9	13887.6	53687.0	10112.3	4233.9
312486.0	1607.5	127537.2	11305.2	14938.0
853526.6	16524.1	229400.1	26638.2	150312.4
481116.2	22835.6	218983.9	21657.1	71016.8
947406.1	26592.6	71484.6	14425.6	33856.6
311489.7	18906.3	60316.1	23306.8	31733.1
923129.3	58542.9	39779.3	11159.2	9757.1
978667.7	20589.3	169379.7	13372.0	56996.0
1137122.2	19320.4	99605.5	20269.2	42347.0
999986.0	31596.9	133907.1	16736.9	27536.8
1222781.2	51680.8	114913.2	8964.7	16983.7
880137.6	51645.7	247091.2	37507.2	121689.2
824000.4	55855.7	110122.2	14097.6	41909.8
133925.9	22510.2	30870.7	4820.7	11124.2
473314.1	35457.6	93733.2	10407.6	25207.9
1500628.8	159210.9	166204.5	21906.0	58964.8
915379.7	85394.1	78526.6	2268.4	28559.4
1185535.6	157347.7	137135.5	13123.2	95439.8
81798.5	8498.2	9921.2	968.8	2219.2
878774.9	34977.8	135655.4	8918.8	22570.1
901129.3	63562.1	27739.9	5324.6	7836.8
209303.2	28251.5	19545.6	2465.1	16636.4
164163.2	19500.1	21902.9	2817.7	12998.4
680909.7	24621.3	67686.8	4108.3	6222.4

C-1-14续表3

地 区	年末结余合计	抚恤	退役安置	社会福利
全 国	**2633518.2**	**296696.5**	**290631.3**	**502121.5**
中央级	50781.1	8460.7		20769.2
北 京	204742.8	9283.5	91523.8	44532.6
天 津	80429.0	3349.7	7124.6	15194.3
河 北	100916.6	14956.4	28575.9	16205.0
山 西	125041.3	24414.8	7486.3	25445.6
内蒙古	72326.8	6936.4	6149.2	11894.8
辽 宁	84151.0	2817.5	6654.7	3262.6
吉 林	20659.0	-87.5	-69.5	1725.5
黑龙江	20819.2	963.3	366.7	1220.6
上 海	135209.3	14491.7	15117.7	23665.4
江 苏	30461.9	1607.3	3158.9	6850.5
浙 江	87239.8	16760.7	6347.7	27567.1
安 徽	8719.9	230.0	849.0	1982.3
福 建	77077.7	11115.0	13365.1	14953.1
江 西	468.2	18.2		74.2
山 东	14784.8	2481.7	1842.2	5569.5
河 南	66012.2	3725.2	3938.9	5952.1
湖 北	22164.3	22.3	7834.4	9159.7
湖 南	7857.9	1642.0	339.7	63.9
广 东	71455.7	8927.0	12435.3	14747.6
广 西	205133.5	41986.3	9632.0	47841.4
海 南	110375.2	9673.5	9764.5	16456.4
重 庆	57696.4	5472.2	436.5	29316.7
四 川	178197.0	10519.0	10067.9	47798.7
贵 州	366793.9	47464.4	14011.7	66232.0
云 南	169096.5	27528.1	20157.7	15104.7
西 藏	69094.5	7567.9	112.6	1708.1
陕 西	52309.5	2235.0	1691.9	5677.6
甘 肃	45743.0	1599.2	2798.1	5012.6
青 海	9518.6	1162.9	1544.4	2651.6
宁 夏	49908.2	1792.0	1252.3	3195.5
新 疆	38333.4	7580.1	6121.1	10290.6

单位：万元

社会救助	自然灾害生活救助	民政管理事务	行政事业单位离退休	其他款项用于民政支出
831839.9	**174903.9**	**222216.8**	**9859.4**	**242022.2**
	5558.8	10463.3	795.1	4374.0
24306.4	945.6	8975.0	569.0	24606.2
21350.3	4365.1	16964.4	353.9	11726.6
26788.4	4474.7	8755.3	55.5	906.9
57137.4	5001.2	4105.5	23.0	1427.5
18246.2	2935.9	7954.5	25.8	17246.9
30868.4	2227.0	8171.5	973.6	21766.0
1969.0	4903.4	112.5		1329.0
16795.7	550.4	344.3		143.3
46143.6	800.0	28264.3	148.6	6250.2
949.5	54.0	1691.5		16150.1
18338.7	3689.3	10071.8	1791.8	2118.4
4737.8	506.0			414.8
14434.4	2138.8	13600.7	1443.7	4191.9
375.8				
469.4	20.0	4401.9		
46632.0	485.0	750.8		4329.2
1548.5	206.9	2511.6		443.9
5248.9	244.6	281.5		29.9
22205.2	1222.4	6666.9	2384.3	2511.4
59380.3	13893.9	13731.1	247.2	14800.3
29912.1	4621.0	12292.0	51.2	10909.1
10249.4	5302.8	3227.5	82.4	3608.9
57357.5	23098.8	4212.9	151.3	24694.7
185281.0	31742.5	9935.6	119.9	12006.8
45286.3	19097.7	16309.5	485.2	24268.5
15392.1	20918.0	9582.8		12828.8
23678.8	345.6	1842.6	1.7	659.7
17332.8	6021.2	5534.5	93.6	7155.2
1465.1	1754.3	938.7		1.6
20028.0	7344.8	5992.5	40.5	9751.0
7930.9	434.2	4529.8	22.1	1371.4

C-1-15 预算指标

地　区	本年预算指标合计	上年结转预算指标	本级财政安排预算指标	本年上级下达预算指标	本年下达所属地方预算指标	本年抚恤预算指标
全　国	**47738611.2**	**2772266.2**	**45288833.6**	**67407513.0**	**67730001.6**	**6570940.9**
中央级	160968.3		21106985.3		20946017.0	10063.0
北　京	1950905.5	366880.3	976640.2	1341035.9	733650.9	120048.3
天　津	628408.9	14567.9	472402.0	272570.2	131131.2	67115.7
河　北	1826233.1	87979.4	836599.5	3134818.2	2233164.0	374852.8
山　西	1270201.0	62528.5	590413.5	2230075.5	1612816.5	240815.7
内蒙古	1467021.6	75572.2	841795.5	2292978.9	1743325.0	99522.8
辽　宁	1787766.2	47372.3	855682.7	2657423.3	1772712.1	192473.5
吉　林	976950.1	34934.1	420425.6	1345802.5	824212.1	113189.5
黑龙江	1390247.6	20462.9	574142.7	3095954.1	2300312.1	106533.3
上　海	910207.1	42511.8	871216.3	123440.0	126961.0	95033.5
江　苏	2572945.9	130198.5	2014907.3	1984733.8	1556893.7	418827.0
浙　江	1635024.4	120410.3	1313343.1	627090.0	425819.0	251386.9
安　徽	1737497.9	44464.5	858034.7	1840523.8	1005525.1	271626.4
福　建	884102.8	71445.4	580091.2	977263.6	744697.4	137367.9
江　西	1500005.5	40702.0	695115.5	2646468.4	1882280.4	237554.6
山　东	2778164.4	75981.3	1714136.5	3843103.4	2855056.8	721422.6
河　南	2179281.9	44700.7	868195.6	4182297.1	2915911.5	416550.5
湖　北	2087256.4	35589.2	956153.0	2514128.5	1418614.3	318472.7
湖　南	2136083.7	15609.2	904863.5	4212384.6	2996773.6	411811.5
广　东	2342688.2	94467.1	1805818.3	2615190.3	2172787.5	328715.7
广　西	1596441.1	212143.4	655169.7	2116564.2	1387436.2	183120.3
海　南	398288.8	46279.0	211770.9	368288.5	228049.6	33437.9
重　庆	1158421.8	86497.0	521997.3	1241934.9	692007.4	172225.1
四　川	3031627.0	59579.2	1335667.8	5610253.2	3973873.2	482893.1
贵　州	1773357.0	257182.5	426446.5	3483400.3	2393672.3	152228.0
云　南	2002252.6	22240.7	903869.9	4069939.9	2993797.9	175440.2
西　藏	165015.1	34036.6	85571.9	188869.6	143463.0	13253.8
陕　西	2208088.5	421719.2	872076.5	3315819.2	2401526.4	277910.8
甘　肃	1255066.4	32782.6	388364.8	1893612.8	1059693.8	57399.0
青　海	383930.1	22465.0	134415.5	650555.0	423505.4	17211.0
宁　夏	304341.9	37910.3	100366.5	365776.8	199711.7	11448.7
新　疆	1239820.4	113053.1	396154.3	2165216.5	1434603.5	60989.1

收入情况

单位：万元

上年结转预算指标	本级财政安排预算指标	本年上级下达预算指标	本年下达所属地方预算指标	本年退役安置预算指标	上年结转预算指标	本级财政安排预算指标
209627.0	**6387642.1**	**10410581.2**	**10436909.4**	**5201206.0**	**582724.9**	**4824294.5**
	3384455.0		3374392.0			2887046.0
7902.4	90392.9	36416.3	14663.3	1037921.0	286672.3	194724.7
902.7	51026.0	29871.1	14684.1	97832.4	4865.8	25179.6
9419.4	149377.9	727776.9	511721.4	281368.2	11390.4	110350.5
11762.6	109881.1	360803.3	241631.3	88824.3	3525.4	31283.9
2258.5	57108.7	139491.9	99336.3	73821.7	5419.2	40757.5
2986.3	115627.0	245263.6	171403.4	349120.1	5675.4	93065.6
501.7	52445.8	147126.7	86884.7	86818.4	151.0	54129.8
1597.3	40797.8	233566.8	169428.6	73265.7	1128.2	25231.4
	95033.5	12570.0	12570.0	193080.1	35296.4	157783.7
8421.9	270437.6	522801.6	382834.1	323188.2	14302.3	178973.7
16249.1	174772.8	142499.3	82134.3	120882.3	4198.4	59981.9
6908.2	121824.3	309692.1	166798.2	154720.6	1468.7	110393.0
5886.3	78219.6	201278.5	148016.5	103244.0	18424.6	37956.4
	79463.6	516527.7	358436.7	49971.2		23406.2
4907.6	357644.0	1174370.8	815499.8	396276.5	16101.0	145057.4
433.5	184222.7	762749.0	530854.7	179023.1	3060.6	86990.0
2558.6	125508.1	428023.2	237617.2	164835.5	2034.4	50889.1
2790.5	120924.2	916780.9	628684.1	106752.9	558.0	44640.5
11238.9	216402.1	464231.8	363157.1	275929.0	49397.5	105272.9
24361.3	69450.0	256653.0	167344.0	56327.1	5275.7	23050.4
3936.1	12680.3	35149.0	18327.5	28554.1	1927.4	11696.4
3414.3	63008.8	230671.0	124869.0	91701.0	2020.8	41442.2
4105.8	143499.3	1059922.7	724634.7	235728.0	8316.3	106108.7
6952.1	40801.9	327029.8	222555.8	39683.9	1080.4	20903.5
3308.5	44055.7	414360.2	286284.2	114517.4	998.3	33869.1
562.1	9200.9	10763.6	7272.8	3231.5		1355.6
64766.7	78980.0	458379.5	324215.4	265050.7	91599.3	44985.9
12.0	15683.0	88361.8	46657.8	81512.6	1886.2	29642.4
532.0	7600.9	27088.6	18010.5	23326.5		8952.2
508.8	5276.5	12646.4	6983.0	20787.4	5950.9	14048.8
441.8	21840.1	117714.1	79006.9	83910.6		25125.5

C-1-15续表1

地 区	本年上级下达预算指标	本年下达所属地方预算指标	本年社会福利预算指标	上年结转预算指标	本级财政安排预算指标	本年上级下达预算指标
全 国	**6896696.6**	**7102510.0**	**5587452.8**	**564576.4**	**5063330.0**	**4003576.2**
中央级		2887046.0	33760.0		622585.0	
北 京	1132312.3	575788.3	245250.4	23906.0	215051.4	92849.3
天 津	135812.1	68025.1	62462.8	3963.2	54717.6	4982.9
河 北	454436.8	294809.5	191903.1	23864.8	149984.6	150744.7
山 西	140426.5	86411.5	105195.2	6706.6	83159.6	76303.1
内蒙古	78765.7	51120.7	176694.9	18136.7	117814.9	165726.8
辽 宁	611959.9	361580.8	126558.1	3923.2	114286.2	60293.1
吉 林	99189.0	66651.4	56545.4	4912.4	60214.9	35927.1
黑龙江	109714.1	62808.0	91121.9	4089.1	76404.6	51654.2
上 海	92940.0	92940.0	153311.1	1983.0	150114.1	3711.0
江 苏	461204.1	331291.9	441740.6	19118.3	419084.4	175437.6
浙 江	118668.7	61966.7	417232.1	71192.1	336316.8	91980.1
安 徽	100128.3	57269.4	173732.1	10753.6	131532.2	81319.3
福 建	116129.3	69266.3	173614.8	26378.9	135634.7	135957.2
江 西	74406.9	47841.9	140697.5	10615.0	108695.5	136606.1
山 东	628077.9	392959.8	392280.5	22151.6	359004.5	408017.0
河 南	242716.8	153744.3	162019.0	15790.2	122320.8	159116.2
湖 北	251368.6	139456.6	176198.3	8853.6	140930.7	82574.0
湖 南	182849.7	121295.3	159953.9	11314.0	125616.5	220026.5
广 东	382941.7	261683.1	364231.7	10789.2	330711.1	226321.5
广 西	69401.0	41400.0	219269.4	57144.4	140380.0	163574.3
海 南	27523.1	12592.8	41214.7	4926.0	40801.4	19230.4
重 庆	114664.0	66426.0	120435.8	15181.8	90941.3	54432.7
四 川	376643.6	255340.6	391516.4	18405.1	349045.4	446225.7
贵 州	52887.2	35187.2	184844.0	28030.5	83819.5	257513.9
云 南	228394.8	148744.8	107901.0	2535.1	82470.9	119492.5
西 藏	15405.3	13529.4	13667.1	51.9	8596.6	11733.3
陕 西	346707.0	218241.5	209805.7	20926.1	170190.2	202448.2
甘 肃	105198.0	55214.0	86875.4	58.3	65160.1	79947.0
青 海	35541.9	21167.6	64694.8	7013.0	40895.3	61740.2
宁 夏	14759.5	13971.8	16208.1	1689.2	9179.9	8934.7
新 疆	95522.8	36737.7	286517.0	110173.5	127669.3	218755.6

单位：万元

本年下达所属地方预算指标	本年社会救助预算指标				
		上年结转预算指标	本级财政安排预算指标	本年上级下达预算指标	本年下达所属地方预算指标
4044029.8	**23465758.6**	**964815.2**	**22503739.3**	**42266144.2**	**42268940.1**
588825.0			13086359.0		13086359.0
86556.3	175756.4	6024.1	147595.3	34645.0	12508.0
1200.9	229182.8	2862.0	171986.8	101555.1	47221.1
132691.0	785761.2	33470.2	279530.9	1673468.0	1200707.9
60974.1	700148.6	28950.0	278544.6	1531131.3	1138477.3
124983.5	878117.7	8234.4	414411.9	1729753.5	1274282.1
51944.4	780111.8	23893.8	225177.4	1525601.0	994560.4
44509.0	580184.2	11036.6	124539.9	975659.7	531052.0
41026.0	1014565.4	12229.5	356756.8	2619139.7	1973560.6
2497.0	318192.0	497.4	317694.6	14219.0	14219.0
171899.7	964605.8	69083.9	759925.2	731658.2	596061.5
82256.9	498117.9	15331.4	412409.5	250000.3	179623.3
49873.0	961032.0	21379.6	374287.4	1244333.2	678968.2
124356.0	323360.8	12990.8	194916.0	465096.4	349642.4
115219.1	924055.1	100.0	415900.1	1760833.8	1252778.8
396892.6	989862.8	10295.5	619952.6	1545513.1	1185898.4
135208.2	1199926.7	10142.4	325450.2	2908273.4	2043939.3
56160.0	1183512.2	14439.5	450585.5	1629822.7	911335.5
197003.1	1225021.7	168.2	454937.7	2693378.3	1923462.5
203590.1	908707.2	15991.7	723923.4	1346837.6	1178045.5
141829.3	874638.5	88496.7	236847.8	1495800.1	946506.1
23743.1	175663.7	25701.3	65864.8	204464.4	120366.8
40120.0	582095.5	57493.0	189664.7	766164.2	431226.4
422159.8	1545726.0	8505.6	462826.9	3443163.1	2368769.6
184519.9	1177180.7	206743.3	150467.4	2571201.8	1751231.8
96597.5	1197474.5	7643.9	401263.6	2854093.4	2065526.4
6714.7	88733.1	11724.9	26693.3	125866.9	75552.0
183758.8	1202206.4	229799.7	388637.3	2091333.5	1507564.1
58290.0	919485.8	13734.6	230812.2	1525181.5	850242.5
44953.7	208750.8	1220.0	41861.0	475841.1	310171.3
3595.7	172357.7	15043.2	36489.4	266884.9	146059.8
170081.4	681223.6	1588.0	137426.1	1665230.0	1123020.5

C-1-15续表2

地 区	本年城市最低生活保障预算指标	上年结转预算指标	本级财政安排预算指标	本年上级下达预算指标	本年下达所属地方预算指标	本年农村最低生活保障预算指标	上年结转预算指标
全 国	**7847965.1**	**351317.8**	**7520617.0**	**15569708.2**	**15593677.9**	**9380204.4**	**420646.3**
中央级			5154107.0		5154107.0		
北 京	71756.2	1217.7	70538.5	409.3	409.3	33267.8	
天 津	128303.1	2823.6	79093.5	92756.8	46370.8	44817.1	
河 北	236082.3	18291.1	35209.2	558912.2	376330.2	338304.7	6777.4
山 西	290435.1	15635.6	78531.5	703533.0	507265.0	266053.3	4332.0
内蒙古	384175.5	3215.2	153090.9	873492.1	645622.7	318742.4	180.9
辽 宁	446280.2	12833.0	72146.8	1005427.5	644127.1	170979.0	3005.3
吉 林	341589.6	6484.3	51912.1	610035.2	326842.0	124324.2	3037.0
黑龙江	546177.3	7173.3	129310.0	1501992.6	1092298.6	226871.1	976.4
上 海	135884.6	398.8	135485.8			13375.2	95.3
江 苏	146179.9	859.7	145471.7	68984.9	69136.4	451531.1	67412.2
浙 江	43569.3	1006.2	42457.1	7691.0	7585.0	217690.3	6293.5
安 徽	299713.9	6140.9	61967.0	489279.2	257673.2	375610.3	3372.2
福 建	54619.7	372.1	28745.6	85051.5	59549.5	139249.4	933.9
江 西	327218.9		110551.9	653102.0	436435.0	302143.6	
山 东	189765.3	4835.2	163731.6	293421.9	272223.4	506851.2	3872.0
河 南	376518.1	7159.0	36708.8	1045049.6	712399.3	521096.9	355.5
湖 北	539727.1	8486.2	167378.9	799699.6	435837.6	382801.6	4340.9
湖 南	450039.9	38.3	104165.2	1118960.3	773123.9	455627.7	31.9
广 东	159217.6	432.0	158795.7	191655.4	191665.5	391632.7	7444.0
广 西	172849.6	35430.0	9771.6	311195.9	183547.9	429122.2	20807.1
海 南	69233.8	10441.0	27438.8	83788.0	52434.0	53193.4	4097.6
重 庆	217730.1	37848.5	3345.6	348791.7	172255.7	151219.4	14524.6
四 川	508846.6	2588.9	63014.0	1367667.7	924424.0	560084.3	1758.0
贵 州	178342.4	12840.1	37508.3	416332.2	288338.2	844978.4	180883.1
云 南	326028.2	1342.7	134162.4	721810.7	531287.6	690357.7	2905.7
西 藏	17611.4	92.2	6154.3	26812.8	15447.9	41430.0	-22.0
陕 西	441304.2	130876.0	110693.5	655460.1	455725.4	489633.8	80444.1
甘 肃	282090.1	9022.0	69014.1	450619.0	246565.0	468387.7	2484.9
青 海	78010.0		8814.4	192063.7	122868.1	79240.4	
宁 夏	58490.6	12566.9	10361.6	87365.1	51803.0	70448.7	253.6
新 疆	330174.5	867.3	60939.6	808347.2	539979.6	221138.8	49.2

本级财政安排预算指标	本年上级下达预算指标	本年下达所属地方预算指标	本年其他社会救济预算指标	上年结转预算指标	本级财政安排预算指标	本年上级下达预算指标	本年下达所属地方预算指标
8876425.5	**18903402.9**	**18820270.3**	**3312183.6**	**69684.9**	**3303963.6**	**2584850.8**	**2646315.7**
5837122.0		5837122.0			462989.0		462989.0
28007.8	5260.0		51895.6	3942.0	35223.6	19476.7	6746.7
44817.1			23275.2	38.4	21530.8	2556.3	850.3
121394.3	793557.7	583424.7	118763.0	3049.3	93264.7	126911.9	104462.9
114082.3	589187.6	441548.6	62002.8	1934.8	55824.0	72144.6	67900.6
155776.6	602614.9	439830.0	93715.4	2327.6	72562.4	91145.1	72319.7
72560.7	345300.7	249887.7	87188.3	2466.0	62619.5	58621.0	36518.2
31932.4	204135.8	114781.0	41838.3	34.0	30272.4	34374.9	22843.0
80308.2	589659.9	444073.4	104528.7	911.1	86158.8	167768.4	150309.6
13279.9			141069.3	3.3	141066.0	10762.0	10762.0
289040.5	488499.0	393420.6	234077.6	379.1	216395.5	60151.1	42848.1
159408.8	166563.3	114575.3	132795.7	4902.0	122298.7	20891.4	15296.4
117009.1	561521.5	306292.5	165377.6	1707.3	150816.9	39974.8	27121.4
93177.5	213923.6	168785.6	73494.0	450.0	44828.1	87815.2	59599.3
106080.6	611644.3	415581.3	123960.2		106354.2	200198.0	182592.0
239272.5	920199.6	656492.9	160797.1	311.1	139491.6	113845.9	92851.5
90296.3	1410076.9	979631.8	182009.9	2116.9	174672.3	158994.0	153773.3
126024.7	569694.4	317258.4	117875.3	368.6	90241.5	98577.8	71312.6
159613.1	1075476.4	779493.7	177667.9	98.0	158315.9	160132.2	140878.2
261317.6	723429.4	600558.3	217460.2	3602.4	192343.1	228983.5	207468.8
64585.1	898552.4	554822.4	176129.3	15277.5	144330.8	120994.1	104473.1
21639.9	68499.9	41044.0	27388.5	7972.6	12687.3	13983.4	7254.8
38372.0	231882.5	133559.7	122941.5	3229.2	106600.3	69598.0	56486.0
98990.4	1448840.4	989504.5	246783.4	2753.9	218890.5	122145.5	97006.5
71269.3	1839581.8	1246755.8	53343.1	2345.3	33224.8	66447.6	48674.6
148815.3	1783852.9	1245216.2	66893.3	2242.9	99077.5	51658.3	86085.4
13790.9	58178.8	30517.7	8337.3	15.0	1717.2	15300.6	8695.5
116838.7	974791.0	682440.0	146267.8	4288.3	127000.8	211106.9	196128.2
92046.8	833485.0	459629.0	74702.2	257.4	59729.8	78889.5	64174.5
17032.2	186322.8	124114.6	16909.3	1220.0	10686.6	12672.8	7670.1
20610.1	110482.0	60897.0	17799.6	809.9	2149.5	25458.0	10617.8
31912.8	598188.4	409011.6	44896.2	631.0	30599.5	43271.3	29605.6

C-1-15续表3

地 区	本年医疗救助预算指标	上年结转预算指标	本级财政安排预算指标	本年上级下达预算指标	本年下达所属地方预算指标
全 国	**2925405.5**	**123166.2**	**2802733.2**	**5208182.3**	**5208676.2**
中央级			1632141.0		1632141.0
北 京	18836.8	864.4	13825.4	9499.0	5352.0
天 津	32787.4		26545.4	6242.0	
河 北	92611.2	5352.4	29662.7	194086.2	136490.1
山 西	81657.4	7047.6	30106.8	166266.1	121763.1
内蒙古	81484.4	2510.7	32982.0	162501.4	116509.7
辽 宁	75664.3	5589.5	17850.4	116251.8	64027.4
吉 林	72432.1	1481.3	10423.0	127113.8	66586.0
黑龙江	136988.3	3168.7	60979.8	359718.8	286879.0
上 海	27862.9		27862.9	3457.0	3457.0
江 苏	132817.2	432.9	109017.5	114023.2	90656.4
浙 江	104062.6	3129.7	88244.9	54854.6	42166.6
安 徽	120330.2	10159.2	44494.4	153557.7	87881.1
福 建	55997.7	11234.8	28164.8	78306.1	61708.0
江 西	170732.4	100.0	92913.4	295889.5	218170.5
山 东	132449.2	1277.2	77456.9	218045.7	164330.6
河 南	120301.8	511.0	23772.8	294152.9	198134.9
湖 北	143108.2	1243.8	66940.4	161850.9	86926.9
湖 南	141686.2		32843.5	338809.4	229966.7
广 东	140396.7	4513.3	111467.0	202769.3	178352.9
广 西	96537.4	16982.1	18160.3	165057.7	103662.7
海 南	25848.0	3190.1	4098.8	38193.1	19634.0
重 庆	90204.5	1890.7	41346.8	115892.0	68925.0
四 川	230011.7	1404.8	81932.0	504509.5	357834.6
贵 州	100516.8	10674.8	8465.0	248840.2	167463.2
云 南	114195.3	1152.6	19208.4	296771.5	202937.2
西 藏	21354.4	11639.7	5030.9	25574.7	20890.9
陕 西	125000.6	14191.3	34104.3	249975.5	173270.5
甘 肃	94305.8	1970.3	10021.5	162188.0	79874.0
青 海	34591.1		5327.8	84781.8	55518.5
宁 夏	25618.8	1412.8	3368.2	43579.8	22742.0
新 疆	85014.1	40.5	13974.2	215423.1	144423.7

单位：万元

本年自然灾害生活救助预算指标	上年结转预算指标	本级财政安排预算指标	本年上级下达预算指标	本年下达所属地方预算指标
1658396.3	**199029.9**	**1505592.3**	**2488870.1**	**2535096.0**
28604.0		980865.0		952261.0
4659.6	920.0	3061.6	2378.0	1700.0
969.5		620.5	349.0	
55688.2	8258.2	12290.0	113891.0	78751.0
45138.6	9189.0	9369.6	78264.0	51684.0
54378.9	22011.8	6163.1	94621.0	68417.0
57571.0	3862.9	24035.0	94114.1	64441.0
36718.5	18024.4	21257.5	56461.6	59025.0
36850.8	966.2	7102.0	50063.0	21280.4
1800.0		1800.0		
22499.1	2899.2	11854.5	20702.2	12956.8
28698.6	6929.7	17728.9	11508.0	7468.0
30575.1	3455.0	6025.1	44902.6	23807.6
22015.9	3574.5	13055.4	11942.0	6556.0
86972.8	27000.0	9882.8	148044.0	97954.0
26994.6	2681.2	9283.4	42793.0	27763.0
41329.0	947.9	7791.1	58591.0	26001.0
61371.0	2714.9	10361.1	70644.3	22349.3
81147.5	710.7	15036.6	141768.2	76368.0
52702.6	2105.2	22051.4	109783.7	81237.7
90038.0	18019.0	31240.0	88014.3	47235.3
63195.3	2775.3	32732.9	80167.1	52480.0
60949.4	6204.5	10444.9	68340.0	24040.0
140221.4	12801.9	58628.0	235726.7	166935.2
109869.8	11921.4	23358.4	234718.3	160128.3
157627.8	3755.1	100410.7	279729.9	226267.9
28565.0	795.5	23527.0	23626.4	19383.9
63439.4	6478.4	11144.5	96252.2	50435.7
55788.1	1946.0	8207.1	93926.5	48291.5
37148.9	13700.0	4848.9	35559.0	16959.0
27174.3	3532.2	3326.5	40654.0	20338.4
47693.6	849.8	8088.8	61335.0	22580.0

C-1-15续表4

地　区	本年民政管理事务预算指标	上年结转预算指标	本级财政安排预算指标	本年上级下达预算指标	本年下达所属地方预算指标	本年行政事业单位离退休预算指标	上年结转预算指标
全　国	**3324624.1**	**38937.8**	**3268981.6**	**775285.4**	**758580.7**	**440032.9**	**1240.9**
中央级	58994.5		71995.5		13001.0	4761.6	
北　京	176978.7	15.0	176963.7	372.6	372.6	53557.5	
天　津	116934.9	667.9	116267.0			3865.2	
河　北	84588.6	1504.4	83083.7	14468.7	14468.2	21523.0	
山　西	67646.5	1204.3	56933.2	42862.3	33353.3	9930.6	
内蒙古	75965.2	5492.1	65348.8	31257.3	26133.0	15051.1	
辽　宁	183466.4	1301.1	195796.4	95782.7	109413.8	20922.1	571.1
吉　林	52564.0		51855.1	11785.9	11077.0	5912.7	
黑龙江	53104.4	452.6	53165.3	31695.0	32208.5	10104.3	
上　海	122714.4		122714.4			11106.9	
江　苏	228088.7	719.6	227142.7	29021.6	28795.2	26690.6	
浙　江	228521.1	4299.7	224221.4	12014.9	12014.9	21884.4	40.3
安　徽	69638.6	403.4	67835.2	11067.1	9667.1	14426.3	12.0
福　建	65166.4	907.3	64259.1	19650.2	19650.2	23868.9	602.1
江　西	39594.1		39594.1	6507.0	6507.0	11166.9	
山　东	169723.5	1484.0	166223.6	26668.6	24652.7	13372.0	
河　南	99112.5	85.0	96048.2	10535.0	7555.7	20122.8	
湖　北	138205.2	2144.7	136060.5	42695.7	42695.7	16809.8	
湖　南	115796.2	67.8	110593.1	54625.0	49489.7	8735.0	
广　东	253652.0	938.2	252713.8	63857.5	63857.5	37075.1	0.3
广　西	118852.5	4292.4	114560.1	25122.1	25122.1	13986.6	12.9
海　南	36954.2	2663.5	34347.9	482.2	539.4	4818.5	
重　庆	91864.1	444.6	89232.5	7513.0	5326.0	10326.1	
四　川	166664.6	684.0	165976.5	21797.0	21792.9	20810.2	0.8
贵　州	74046.0	961.6	73084.4	18177.8	18177.8	2386.6	
云　南	133761.5	1989.9	128279.6	81487.3	77995.3	13183.5	
西　藏	16691.2		15768.7	1030.5	108.0	644.1	
陕　西	152294.4	5294.7	143063.8	98895.5	94959.6	8909.7	
甘　肃	27295.8		27295.8	998.0	998.0	5494.5	
青　海	18539.7		17796.3	7924.9	7181.5	2413.1	
宁　夏	20533.6	920.0	15380.6	4473.0	240.0	2024.2	1.4
新　疆	66670.6		65380.6	2517.0	1227.0	4149.0	

单位：万元

本级财政安排预算指标	本年上级下达预算指标	本年下达所属地方预算指标	本年其他款项用于民政支出预算指标	上年结转预算指标	本级财政安排预算指标	本年上级下达预算指标	本年下达所属地方预算指标
436848.5	**2160.8**	**217.3**	**1490199.6**	**211314.1**	**1298405.3**	**564198.5**	**583718.3**
4761.6			24785.2		68918.2		44133.0
53557.5			136733.6	41440.5	95293.1	42062.4	42062.4
3865.2			50045.6	1306.3	48739.3		
21520.9	2.1		30548.0	72.0	30461.0	30.0	15.0
9930.6			12501.5	1190.6	11310.9	285.0	285.0
15051.1			93469.3	14019.5	125139.5	53362.7	99052.4
19693.7	657.3		77543.2	5158.5	68001.4	23751.6	19368.3
5447.6	465.1		45017.4	308.0	50535.0	19187.4	25013.0
10104.3			4701.8		4580.5	121.3	
11106.9			14969.1	4735.0	14969.1		4735.0
26566.6	248.0	124.0	147305.9	15653.3	120922.6	43660.5	32930.5
21844.1			68301.1	2169.6	66067.7	418.7	354.9
14414.3			61746.8	84.0	31723.2	49081.2	19141.6
23266.8			35464.1	2680.9	32783.2	27210.0	27210.0
11166.9			9993.3	2987.0	7006.3	3542.9	3542.9
13372.0			68231.9	18360.4	43599.0	17663.0	11390.5
20122.8			61198.3	14241.1	25249.8	40315.7	18608.3
16809.8			27851.7	2843.5	25008.2	9000.0	9000.0
8719.0	70.8	54.8	26865.0		24395.9	2885.2	416.1
37074.8			121674.9	4006.1	117668.8	21216.5	21216.5
13973.7			40208.7	14541.0	25667.7	17999.4	17999.4
4818.5			14450.4	4349.4	8828.7	1272.3	
10326.1			28824.8	1738.0	26936.8	150.0	
20809.4			48067.3	6759.7	28773.6	26774.4	14240.4
2386.6			33118.0	1493.2	31624.8	21871.5	21871.5
13183.5	38.5	38.5	102346.7	2009.9	100336.8	92343.3	92343.3
401.3	242.8		229.3	20902.2	28.5	200.8	20902.2
8803.7	106.0		28471.4	2854.3	26271.1	21697.3	22351.3
5494.5			21215.2	15145.5	6069.7		
2413.1			11845.3		10047.8	6859.3	5061.8
1692.6	330.2		33807.9	10264.6	14972.2	17094.1	8523.0
4149.0			8666.9		6474.9	4142.0	1950.0

C-1-15续表5

地区	本年预算指标结余	抚恤	退役安置	社会福利
全 国	**3563877.0**	**222741.5**	**650682.2**	**644254.9**
中央级				
北 京	384627.9	15918.2	341727.8	14379.6
天 津	12994.5	699.3	5240.0	5108.9
河 北	143607.4	23466.4	14548.7	36652.1
山 西	102533.2	21703.0	8028.3	14063.3
内蒙古	102345.8	2217.5	8302.0	26234.7
辽 宁	63674.1	5499.8	6857.3	2947.2
吉 林	26277.8	-88.9	-69.5	4949.5
黑龙江	46142.4	1326.3	1509.9	11364.5
上 海	45141.8		41447.4	3197.0
江 苏	171254.6	12145.9	17608.5	20496.4
浙 江	134202.0	12444.2	4859.8	81819.9
安 徽	27558.1	3063.6	2067.1	3998.0
福 建	98302.6	7630.5	13150.4	57514.3
江 西	28540.0			860.0
山 东	72746.3	2781.0	16702.2	23775.3
河 南	97761.8	883.7	2988.0	14537.4
湖 北	236260.0	853.1	3002.2	13222.3
湖 南	40786.0	1514.2	294.0	8139.0
广 东	104083.8	9500.2	45888.5	19337.1
广 西	209498.6	32719.9	8859.0	63597.8
海 南	98326.7	4888.8	2276.2	4287.9
重 庆	146465.6	961.9	958.2	10844.0
四 川	96336.5	4299.2	10743.8	26509.1
贵 州	311963.3	11972.4	1675.8	44094.4
云 南	20371.5	2333.7	1789.5	2398.4
西 藏	23731.2	913.3		1260.3
陕 西	507108.2	41965.3	83183.1	30126.7
甘 肃	48178.3	542.1	5604.9	4297.3
青 海	24618.8		549.0	8088.0
宁 夏	27966.7	179.7	888.7	783.6
新 疆	110471.5	407.2	1.4	85370.9

单位：万元

社会救助	自然灾害生活救助	民政管理事务	行政事业单位离退休	其他款项用于民政支出
1411998.2	**433848.3**	**74402.8**	**523.4**	**125425.7**
6555.1	1220.0			4827.2
621.5		525.0		799.8
47452.9	17530.4	3656.9		300.0
39126.6	16477.0	2681.3		453.7
16128.6	17358.9	4208.2		27895.9
41951.5	2639.6	2313.3		1465.4
19229.6	971.7	131.4		1154.0
8349.5	23016.8	575.4		
497.4				
111906.1	6044.5	770.5	100.0	2182.7
20675.7	5577.3	8317.0	10.3	497.8
14800.3	2316.2	193.2	30.8	1088.9
10980.5	4285.7	1481.8	251.7	3007.7
	27680.0			
11675.9	6390.0	186.0		11235.9
39711.0	22355.9	87.5		17198.3
181458.0	29956.3	5804.7	111.6	1851.8
98.0	30319.0	421.8		
23283.6	1735.9	3508.6		829.9
53642.6	30585.4	9088.2	14.8	10990.9
40903.7	40947.4	2840.8		2181.9
105869.1	25756.4	1265.6		810.4
33807.5	16047.0	2987.9	4.2	1937.8
229911.1	20681.5	1067.0		2561.1
7742.0	3297.3	1365.1		1445.5
20243.3	1119.0			195.3
299695.6	29273.3	19005.7		3858.5
15794.8	6740.0	53.7		15145.5
301.8	15680.0			
8519.9	4546.8	1866.2		11181.8
1065.0	23299.0			328.0

C-1-16 当年预算

地 区	全国预算安排合计	中央安排合计	全省安排合计	省 级	市 级	县级及以下	抚 恤	中央安排
全 国	**45130767.7**	**21106985.3**	**24023782.4**	**7682992.9**	**3803714.6**	**12537074.9**	**6364371.2**	**3384455.0**
中央级	160968.3	160968.3					10063.0	10063.0
北 京	1584025.2	607385.0	976640.2	400266.2		576374.0	112145.9	21753.0
天 津	613841.0	141439.0	472402.0	67278.2		405123.8	66213.0	15187.0
河 北	1732833.6	897269.0	835564.6	319719.6	143740.4	372104.6	365320.3	216055.0
山 西	1207672.5	617259.0	590413.5	214973.5	168066.2	207373.8	229053.1	119172.0
内蒙古	1416401.6	574725.0	841676.6	324861.5	172976.2	343838.9	96332.4	39230.0
辽 宁	1684919.2	854491.0	830428.2	185536.3	275684.0	369207.9	180777.5	72136.0
吉 林	1055354.4	636012.0	419342.4	212036.9	61279.4	146026.1	114035.6	61974.0
黑龙江	1404905.7	832000.0	572905.7	306795.2	71739.1	194371.4	106700.4	65945.0
上 海	994656.3	123440.0	871216.3	96248.3		774968.0	107603.5	12570.0
江 苏	2463224.8	474710.0	1988514.8	411692.0	258023.3	1318799.5	411762.5	144399.0
浙 江	1514614.1	201271.0	1313343.1	220823.7	150707.8	941811.6	235137.8	60365.0
安 徽	1659327.3	819826.0	839501.3	143291.1	122680.3	573529.9	269317.4	149354.0
福 建	812657.2	232566.0	580091.2	179590.2	94373.8	306127.2	131481.6	53262.0
江 西	1459303.5	764188.0	695115.5	223249.5	59386.7	412479.3	237554.6	158091.0
山 东	2702182.5	988046.0	1714136.5	482253.3	338731.9	893151.3	717915.0	360271.0
河 南	2137429.4	1282723.0	854706.4	312839.7	124418.2	417448.5	414340.6	234499.0
湖 北	2051670.0	1095517.0	956153.0	215441.0	197657.5	543054.5	315914.1	190406.0
湖 南	2121593.7	1221490.0	900103.7	366428.3	101701.4	431974.0	406927.9	287144.0
广 东	2230664.5	444205.0	1786459.5	618989.1	474543.6	692926.8	317922.7	102153.0
广 西	1381693.7	729128.0	652565.7	281874.9	121986.0	248704.8	158506.1	89309.0
海 南	361912.9	157466.0	204446.9	88115.2	24842.7	91489.0	28373.3	15693.0
重 庆	1072614.3	550617.0	521997.3	212944.6		309052.7	168834.8	105826.0
四 川	2969415.3	1636953.0	1332462.3	380280.3	183380.5	768801.5	478350.9	335284.0
贵 州	1516174.5	1089728.0	426446.5	116157.2	90147.9	220141.4	145275.9	104474.0
云 南	1957799.1	1076142.0	881657.1	438577.4	145880.2	297199.5	169467.5	128076.0
西 藏	210770.9	125199.0	85571.9	47657.3	2801.5	35113.1	16202.9	7002.0
陕 西	1769283.1	908205.0	861078.1	301265.5	275883.4	283929.2	212153.4	134365.0
甘 肃	1221824.8	833919.0	387905.8	258579.4	49843.3	79483.1	57277.0	41704.0
青 海	357353.5	222938.0	134415.5	71680.1	6006.0	56729.4	17343.9	9743.0
宁 夏	272324.5	171958.0	100366.5	41210.5	15751.4	43404.6	11397.5	6121.0
新 疆	1031356.3	635202.0	396154.3	142336.9	71481.9	182335.5	54669.1	32829.0

安排情况

单位：万元

全省安排	省 级	市 级	县级及以下	退役安置	中央安排	全省安排	省 级
2979916.2	**718190.2**	**303466.2**	**1958259.8**	**4808593.6**	**2887046.0**	**1921547.6**	**558097.0**
90392.9	2258.0		88134.9	751248.7	556524.0	194724.7	161203.0
51026.0	5894.7		45131.3	92966.6	67787.0	25179.6	155.7
149265.3	56834.0	18379.0	74052.3	269974.5	159624.0	110350.5	46621.2
109881.1	14006.3	22394.7	73480.1	85298.9	54015.0	31283.9	13465.8
57102.4	12284.0	5925.2	38893.2	74317.6	33640.0	40677.6	15825.0
108641.5	20831.4	20761.1	67049.0	370017.3	279474.0	90543.3	8370.0
52061.6	29494.3	969.4	21597.9	114467.8	60509.0	53958.8	7863.9
40755.4	19376.5	2897.9	18481.0	74503.1	49277.0	25226.1	3156.8
95033.5	6751.9		88281.6	250723.7	92940.0	157783.7	13673.2
267363.5	58507.9	19061.7	189793.9	333056.2	155590.0	177466.2	39061.4
174772.8	18971.1	7815.1	147986.6	116683.9	56702.0	59981.9	1900.0
119963.4	13555.9	6461.0	99946.5	151503.6	42859.0	108644.6	6847.5
78219.6	19969.8	8811.2	49438.6	84819.4	46863.0	37956.4	5317.4
79463.6	25896.7	1324.9	52242.0	49971.2	26565.0	23406.2	8499.0
357644.0	63381.7	52271.0	241991.3	380175.4	235118.0	145057.4	28863.0
179841.6	42767.1	17621.2	119453.3	175954.3	90338.0	85616.3	20135.0
125508.1	31281.0	15772.7	78454.4	162801.1	111912.0	50889.1	13305.0
119783.9	36456.5	12627.3	70700.1	109867.0	65930.0	43937.0	14080.3
215769.7	69691.8	39199.1	106878.8	221458.5	121509.0	99949.5	25405.3
69197.1	38946.3	7454.5	22796.3	51001.2	28001.0	23000.2	8314.6
12680.3	2767.9	975.5	8936.9	24884.1	13745.0	11139.1	3202.7
63008.8	21131.8		41877.0	89680.2	48238.0	41442.2	17292.7
143066.9	34921.9	8867.0	99278.0	227321.0	121448.0	105873.0	20119.0
40801.9	8120.7	6362.4	26318.8	38603.5	17700.0	20903.5	3542.8
41391.5	18358.2	2391.7	20641.6	112215.5	79650.0	32565.5	3729.4
9200.9	7254.8	337.0	1609.1	13497.6	12142.0	1355.6	1150.7
77788.4	19599.4	18924.8	39264.2	173102.2	128201.0	44901.2	27858.2
15573.0	5649.8	2833.2	7090.0	79592.0	49984.0	29608.0	20500.0
7600.9	2238.7	170.3	5191.9	22914.2	13962.0	8952.2	8221.5
5276.5	932.0	956.8	3387.7	22749.8	8701.0	14048.8	5379.2
21840.1	10058.1	1900.5	9881.5	83223.5	58098.0	25125.5	5037.7

C-1-16续表1

地　区	市级	县级及以下	社会福利	中央安排	全省安排	省级	市级	县级及以下
全　国	**318648.0**	**1044802.6**	**5038022.8**	**622585.0**	**4415437.8**	**1673159.6**	**1129558.4**	**1612719.8**
中央级			33760.0	33760.0				
北　京		33521.7	221344.4	6293.0	215051.4	132954.5		82096.9
天　津		25023.9	58499.6	3782.0	54717.6	17711.5		37006.1
河　北	23652.3	40077.0	167495.3	17565.0	149930.3	42474.3	45772.0	61684.0
山　西	7111.3	10706.8	98488.6	15329.0	83159.6	26533.2	43999.1	12627.3
内蒙古	5314.7	19537.9	126069.6	8262.0	117807.6	42763.0	32021.0	43023.6
辽　宁	37397.0	44776.3	121890.0	9684.0	112206.0	28129.6	48174.4	35902.0
吉　林	36501.6	9593.3	71451.9	11237.0	60214.9	34342.7	12600.4	13271.8
黑龙江	10246.8	11822.5	92361.0	16017.0	76344.0	39878.2	23508.8	12957.0
上　海		144110.5	153825.1	3711.0	150114.1	37949.8		112164.3
江　苏	23773.1	114631.7	437098.6	20401.0	416697.6	92026.0	103350.4	221321.2
浙　江	6029.2	52052.7	346153.8	9837.0	336316.8	77884.8	59347.4	199084.6
安　徽	17293.9	84503.2	138699.0	9783.0	128916.0	23469.8	42487.2	62959.0
福　建	7537.0	25102.0	147235.7	11601.0	135634.7	62645.4	36099.2	36890.1
江　西	1185.1	13722.1	130082.5	21387.0	108695.5	62010.8	11751.1	34933.6
山　东	35041.2	81153.2	379208.5	20204.0	359004.5	171791.8	93567.2	93645.5
河　南	20005.0	45476.3	157943.3	36522.0	121421.3	58184.3	23553.8	39683.2
湖　北	10718.0	26866.1	167344.7	26414.0	140930.7	29772.0	55309.9	55848.8
湖　南	9570.8	20285.9	159457.8	34373.0	125084.8	73044.5	20804.6	31235.7
广　东	19846.7	54697.5	347766.8	22777.0	324989.8	58449.6	159925.9	106614.3
广　西	7247.7	7437.9	161818.7	21745.0	140073.7	69480.1	45134.0	25459.6
海　南	3478.5	4457.9	44902.7	6914.0	37988.7	19207.6	4863.8	13917.3
重　庆		24149.5	108212.3	17271.0	90941.3	43801.0		47140.3
四　川	7095.0	78659.0	383920.3	35478.0	348442.3	187425.2	77475.7	83541.4
贵　州	3571.8	13788.9	156813.5	72994.0	83819.5	33389.7	23530.8	26899.0
云　南	11537.2	17298.9	101025.6	22895.0	78130.6	23346.4	22604.1	32180.1
西　藏		204.9	16181.6	7585.0	8596.6	3521.9	788.0	4286.7
陕　西	7449.6	9593.4	183156.8	15851.0	167305.8	61061.2	65232.7	41011.9
甘　肃	2902.1	6205.9	86814.6	21657.0	65157.6	39417.9	19158.4	6581.3
青　海	324.5	406.2	58302.3	17407.0	40895.3	30495.0	1316.5	9083.8
宁　夏	3405.5	5264.1	12572.9	3393.0	9179.9	4229.3	3312.6	1638.0
新　疆	412.4	19675.4	168125.3	40456.0	127669.3	45768.5	53869.4	28031.4

单位：万元

社会救助	中央安排合计	全省安排合计				城市最低生活保障	中央安排	全省安排
			省级	市级	县级及以下			
22440101.8	**13086359.0**	**9353742.8**	**3418060.8**	**939446.5**	**4996235.5**	**7500896.5**	**5154107.0**	**2346789.5**
169732.3	22137.0	147595.3	11056.2		136539.1	70538.5		70538.5
226320.8	54334.0	171986.8	26125.4		145861.4	125479.5	46386.0	79093.5
748020.8	469285.0	278735.8	128030.0	29770.2	120935.6	217766.7	182582.0	35184.7
671198.6	392654.0	278544.6	148258.2	62104.7	68181.7	274799.5	196268.0	78531.5
865390.5	451004.0	414386.5	137068.6	101229.5	176088.4	381469.2	228382.0	153087.2
678429.2	463155.0	215274.2	74703.0	29653.8	110917.4	397125.2	331560.0	65565.2
599111.9	474812.0	124299.9	56310.0	383.0	67606.9	356589.1	304717.0	51872.1
1025807.5	670057.0	355750.5	207974.0	17949.0	129827.5	565006.3	436485.0	128521.3
331913.6	14219.0	317694.6	11643.4		306051.2	135485.8		135485.8
891605.2	146580.0	745025.2	193752.8	34039.8	517232.6	142881.4		142881.4
482736.5	70327.0	412409.5	96142.6	24359.4	291907.5	42457.1		42457.1
928779.9	563353.0	365426.9	69660.7	30071.7	265694.5	291581.0	231550.0	60031.0
310370.0	115454.0	194916.0	51085.0	15655.1	128175.9	54247.6	25502.0	28745.6
923955.1	508055.0	415900.1	115468.4	33110.8	267320.9	327218.9	216667.0	110551.9
978465.6	358513.0	619952.6	204164.2	84439.7	331348.7	249861.6	86130.0	163731.6
1208617.9	888040.0	320577.9	161916.4	26035.8	132625.7	370129.8	333441.0	36688.8
1169075.5	718490.0	450585.5	94127.0	59295.5	297163.0	531240.9	363862.0	167378.9
1223107.4	769039.0	454068.4	203528.4	23995.1	226544.9	447793.4	344176.0	103617.4
886663.6	169146.0	717517.6	410383.4	67227.7	239906.5	157939.0		157939.0
784803.3	549294.0	235509.3	123452.7	7566.9	104489.7	137111.8	127648.0	9463.8
156344.5	92734.0	63610.5	28584.9	6444.4	28581.2	61198.5	36014.0	25184.5
524666.7	335002.0	189664.7	99172.6		90492.1	179881.6	176536.0	3345.6
1536269.0	1075013.0	461256.0	97538.0	43965.0	319753.0	498416.2	435478.0	62938.2
970437.4	819970.0	150467.4	45320.0	29072.8	76074.6	165502.3	127994.0	37508.3
1183553.0	788567.0	394986.0	218756.3	54851.8	121377.9	306401.6	174467.0	131934.6
106724.3	80031.0	26693.3	55.0	152.4	26485.9	19937.3	13783.0	6154.3
968736.5	584204.0	384532.5	124370.5	143164.9	116997.1	308518.0	199226.0	109292.0
905537.7	674939.0	230598.7	182822.3	12848.7	34927.7	273004.1	204054.0	68950.1
205087.0	163226.0	41861.0	13553.9	479.1	27828.0	78895.4	70081.0	8814.4
166140.4	129651.0	36489.4	13983.0	214.7	22291.7	58447.6	48086.0	10361.6
612500.1	475074.0	137426.1	69053.9	1365.0	67007.2	273971.6	213032.0	60939.6

C-1-16续表2

地区	省级	市级	县级及以下	农村最低生活保障	中央安排	全省安排	省级	市级
全 国	**740317.9**	**297028.2**	**1309443.4**	**8863959.7**	**5837122.0**	**3026837.7**	**1388733.4**	**304919.9**
中央级								
北 京	409.3		70129.2	33267.8	5260.0	28007.8		
天 津	3017.8		76075.7	44817.1		44817.1		
河 北	3546.0	8609.2	23029.5	331442.2	210133.0	121309.2	81191.0	9991.7
山 西	51055.0	12700.9	14775.6	261721.3	147639.0	114082.3	58054.0	30162.6
内蒙古	75467.6	39298.8	38320.8	318566.6	162790.0	155776.6	36845.0	40559.6
辽 宁	15000.0	9132.4	41432.8	152737.9	80818.0	71919.9	48016.0	4244.7
吉 林	22125.0		29747.1	128411.4	96679.0	31732.4	18102.0	
黑龙江	59858.0	10422.3	58241.0	226924.8	146786.0	80138.8	37136.0	3551.3
上 海			135485.8	13279.9		13279.9		
江 苏	31423.5	7139.9	104318.0	386421.0	100872.0	285549.0	138063.3	814.7
浙 江	6276.0	3251.1	32930.0	211502.8	52094.0	159408.8	57673.3	1391.2
安 徽	6310.0	6279.7	47441.3	370078.5	255229.0	114849.5	42650.0	6620.1
福 建	3685.0	2740.5	22320.1	138315.5	45138.0	93177.5	36783.0	5320.6
江 西	300.0	6084.5	104167.4	302143.6	196063.0	106080.6	11790.0	2703.3
山 东	74141.2	17221.1	72369.3	438047.5	198775.0	239272.5	82496.0	27132.2
河 南	25751.0	5279.2	5658.6	522418.2	433511.0	88907.2	53244.0	10906.3
湖 北	9480.0	27924.1	129974.8	378460.7	252436.0	126024.7	44000.0	13975.2
湖 南	46872.1	5949.0	50796.3	458340.8	298753.0	159587.8	93436.9	9414.9
广 东	90084.2	15395.7	52459.1	382691.3	123068.0	259623.3	170879.5	13031.1
广 西	149.3	2098.3	7216.2	407894.4	343730.0	64164.4	52205.7	989.7
海 南	16420.0	1903.0	6861.5	51823.9	30184.0	21639.9	10860.0	2442.0
重 庆	-4280.3		7625.9	136695.0	98323.0	38372.0	35236.7	
四 川	20000.0	6499.1	36439.1	556225.4	457255.0	98970.4	27000.0	22686.0
贵 州	12400.0	8557.9	16550.4	664095.3	592826.0	71269.3	22500.0	17613.4
云 南	72410.2	22801.0	36723.4	653679.3	506440.0	147239.3	84809.9	26633.6
西 藏	30.0	17.0	6107.3	49642.9	35852.0	13790.9	10.0	5.0
陕 西	11109.1	69300.9	28882.0	409120.7	292876.0	116244.7	24608.8	52643.3
甘 肃	42511.0	8051.7	18387.4	465902.8	373856.0	92046.8	85773.0	1923.4
青 海	2772.0	268.8	5773.6	78382.2	61350.0	17032.2	8310.0	6.0
宁 夏	2000.0		8361.6	69934.1	49324.0	20610.1	11573.0	
新 疆	39994.9	102.1	20842.6	220974.8	189062.0	31912.8	15486.3	158.0

单位：万元

县级及以下	其他社会救助	中央安排	全省安排	省级	市级	县级及以下	医疗救助	中央安排
1333184.4	**3281428.5**	**462989.0**	**2818439.5**	**870914.9**	**212015.4**	**1735509.2**	**2793817.1**	**1632141.0**
28007.8	47953.6	12730.0	35223.6	9441.9		25781.7	17972.4	4147.0
44817.1	23236.8	1706.0	21530.8	779.1		20751.7	32787.4	6242.0
30126.5	111612.2	18974.0	92638.2	32560.0	8638.2	51440.0	87199.7	57596.0
25865.7	60068.0	4244.0	55824.0	26322.2	10781.6	18720.2	74609.8	44503.0
78372.0	84994.4	12432.0	72562.4	16808.0	11881.7	43872.7	80360.3	47400.0
19659.2	75312.7	15225.0	60087.7	5630.0	12233.0	42224.7	53253.4	35552.0
13630.4	42402.4	12130.0	30272.4	10783.0	383.0	19106.4	71709.0	61286.0
39451.5	97255.8	11144.0	86111.8	56246.0	3791.6	26074.2	136620.6	75642.0
13279.9	151828.0	10762.0	141066.0	11506.3		129559.7	31319.9	3457.0
146671.0	230564.9	19668.0	210896.9	3266.0	18093.3	189537.6	131737.9	26040.0
100344.3	127843.7	5545.0	122298.7	5899.2	12714.4	103685.1	100932.9	12688.0
65579.4	156979.5	10195.0	146784.5	12224.0	13158.3	121402.2	110140.9	66379.0
51073.9	73044.1	28216.0	44828.1	2600.0	6379.0	35849.1	44762.8	16598.0
91587.3	123960.2	17606.0	106354.2	73369.4	8314.6	24670.2	170632.4	77719.0
129644.3	158839.6	19348.0	139491.6	21406.0	27806.9	90278.7	131716.9	54260.0
24756.9	196734.2	24699.0	172035.2	79821.4	8419.5	83794.3	119335.7	96389.0
68049.5	117509.5	27268.0	90241.5	36012.0	8969.7	45259.8	141864.4	74924.0
56736.0	176115.7	17881.0	158234.7	56777.4	4823.8	96633.5	140857.5	108229.0
75712.7	212152.5	21650.0	190502.5	86767.7	18672.5	85062.3	133880.8	24428.0
10969.0	160307.4	16521.0	143786.4	60499.7	2880.5	80406.2	79489.7	61395.0
8337.9	19904.3	7217.0	12687.3	1004.9	1199.4	10483.0	23417.8	19319.0
3135.3	119308.3	12708.0	106600.3	45958.5		60641.8	88781.8	47435.0
49284.4	251250.3	33537.0	217713.3	20672.0	6220.7	190820.6	230377.1	148743.0
31155.9	50997.8	17773.0	33224.8	7420.0	2289.3	23515.5	89842.0	81377.0
35795.8	112447.4	15387.0	97060.4	52742.3	3450.3	40867.8	111024.7	92273.0
13775.9	14595.2	12878.0	1717.2	15.0	32.0	1670.2	22548.9	17518.0
38992.6	141637.1	16051.0	125586.1	80172.7	17266.3	28147.1	109460.7	76051.0
4350.4	74358.3	14715.0	59643.3	49469.5	2248.7	7925.1	92272.5	82314.0
8716.2	12564.6	1878.0	10686.6	458.0	204.3	10024.3	35244.8	29917.0
9037.1	11846.5	9697.0	2149.5	210.0	122.9	1816.6	25912.2	22544.0
16268.5	43803.5	13204.0	30599.5	4072.7	1039.9	25486.9	73750.2	59776.0

C-1-16续表3

地 区	全省安排	省级	市级	县级及以下	自然灾害生活救助	中央安排	全省安排	省级
全 国	**1161676.1**	**418094.6**	**125483.0**	**618098.5**	**1503497.5**	**980865.0**	**522632.5**	**279929.4**
中央级					28604.0	28604.0		
北 京	13825.4	1205.0		12620.4	3739.6	678.0	3061.6	2500.0
天 津	26545.4	22328.5		4216.9	969.5	349.0	620.5	540.0
河 北	29603.7	10733.0	2531.1	16339.6	47030.0	34740.0	12290.0	6410.0
山 西	30106.8	12827.0	8459.6	8820.2	35949.6	26580.0	9369.6	4300.0
内蒙古	32960.3	7948.0	9489.4	15522.9	42813.1	36650.0	6163.1	2450.0
辽 宁	17701.4	6057.0	4043.7	7600.7	53997.0	30042.0	23955.0	5724.0
吉 林	10423.0	5300.0		5123.0	48717.5	27480.0	21237.5	15335.2
黑龙江	60978.6	54734.0	183.8	6060.8	37806.0	30704.0	7102.0	3858.7
上 海	27862.9	137.1		27725.8	1800.0		1800.0	1800.0
江 苏	105697.9	21000.0	7991.9	76706.0	19040.3	7740.0	11300.3	4000.0
浙 江	88244.9	26294.1	7002.7	54948.1	21768.9	4040.0	17728.9	5000.0
安 徽	43761.9	8476.7	4013.6	31271.6	27110.1	21095.0	6015.1	2612.9
福 建	28164.8	8017.0	1215.0	18932.8	18441.4	5386.0	13055.4	6500.0
江 西	92913.4	30009.0	16008.4	46896.0	59972.8	50090.0	9882.8	1980.0
山 东	77456.9	26121.0	12279.5	39056.4	23223.4	13940.0	9283.4	1806.8
河 南	22946.7	3100.0	1430.8	18415.9	41096.1	33324.0	7772.1	3469.9
湖 北	66940.4	4635.0	8426.5	53878.9	58656.1	48295.0	10361.1	2000.0
湖 南	32628.5	6442.0	3807.4	22379.1	80031.9	65004.0	15027.9	4482.4
广 东	109452.8	62652.0	20128.4	26672.4	50671.4	28620.0	22051.4	14013.3
广 西	18094.7	10598.0	1598.4	5898.3	72014.2	40779.0	31235.2	15895.4
海 南	4098.8	300.0	900.0	2898.8	61112.9	28380.0	32732.9	25082.2
重 庆	41346.8	22257.7		19089.1	54724.9	44280.0	10444.9	2345.0
四 川	81634.1	29866.0	8559.2	43208.9	128356.0	69730.0	58626.0	21350.0
贵 州	8465.0	3000.0	612.2	4852.8	97948.4	74590.0	23358.4	6737.0
云 南	18751.7	8793.9	1966.9	7990.9	153051.6	53462.0	99589.6	84871.5
西 藏	5030.9		98.4	4932.5	41966.0	18439.0	23527.0	20392.6
陕 西	33409.7	8479.9	3954.4	20975.4	56198.5	45584.0	10614.5	
甘 肃	9958.5	5068.8	624.9	4264.8	53797.1	45635.0	8162.1	2983.5
青 海	5327.8	2013.9		3313.9	23448.9	18600.0	4848.9	4259.0
宁 夏	3368.2	200.0	91.8	3076.4	22606.5	19280.0	3326.5	2000.0
新 疆	13974.2	9500.0	65.0	4409.2	36833.8	28745.0	8088.8	5230.0

单位：万元

市级	县级及以下	民政管理事务	中央安排	全省安排	省级	市级	县级及以下
50022.7	**192680.4**	**3251070.8**	**71995.5**	**3179075.3**	**552980.4**	**684843.5**	**1941251.4**
		58994.5	58994.5				
	561.6	176963.7		176963.7	52056.7		124907.0
	80.5	116267.0		116267.0	14270.1		101996.9
3190.5	2689.5	83072.1		83072.1	12010.2	15368.3	55693.6
1808.9	3260.7	66442.2	9509.0	56933.2	4341.1	23283.3	29308.8
721.5	2991.6	65348.8		65348.8	18003.0	13155.8	34190.0
3828.5	14402.5	192808.2		192808.2	35408.9	77432.5	79966.8
10.0	5892.3	51587.1		51587.1	23901.9	6699.4	20985.8
49.5	3193.8	53042.9		53042.9	27109.0	10246.4	15687.5
		122714.4		122714.4	19828.8		102885.6
427.0	6873.3	225896.1		225896.1	21564.1	39059.1	165272.9
2983.1	9745.8	224221.4		224221.4	18285.2	36900.5	169035.7
143.0	3259.2	65597.3		65597.3	8299.9	17609.2	39688.2
1747.2	4808.2	64259.1		64259.1	20270.7	11933.0	32055.4
820.0	7082.8	39594.1		39594.1	5791.4	6834.5	26968.2
2069.0	5407.6	166223.6		166223.6	7632.7	58595.3	99995.6
1118.5	3183.7	94575.2		94575.2	8966.8	25231.7	60376.7
481.3	7879.8	136060.5		136060.5	28956.0	47047.7	60056.8
2152.0	8393.5	109136.3		109136.3	22131.0	29109.3	57896.0
2034.0	6004.1	251755.5		251755.5	21240.9	97008.2	133506.4
7232.7	8107.1	114020.0		114020.0	11930.4	38737.5	63352.1
823.4	6827.3	32648.2		32648.2	6031.2	5359.4	21257.6
	8099.9	89232.5		89232.5	18959.4		70273.1
2413.2	34862.8	165699.6		165699.6	15788.6	24639.6	125271.4
3254.7	13366.7	73084.4		73084.4	8047.3	21584.3	43452.8
7347.5	7370.6	129284.8	3492.0	125792.8	37245.6	23065.0	65482.2
674.0	2460.4	15768.7		15768.7	14881.0	850.1	37.6
3880.5	6734.0	140947.7		140947.7	44298.1	32910.3	63739.3
631.2	4547.4	27267.4		27267.4	6120.0	7410.6	13736.8
116.5	473.4	17796.3		17796.3	9028.9	1191.8	7575.6
65.0	1261.5	15380.6		15380.6	5198.0	2842.8	7339.8
	2858.8	65380.6		65380.6	5383.5	10737.9	49259.2

C-1-16续表4

地 区	行政事业单位离退休	中央安排	全省安排	省级	市级
全 国	**433780.4**	**4761.6**	**429018.8**	**65364.9**	**87750.6**
中央级	4761.6	4761.6			
北 京	53557.5		53557.5	2443.1	
天 津	3865.2		3865.2		
河 北	21459.6		21459.6	4232.3	4525.6
山 西	9930.6		9930.6	2199.9	3086.3
内蒙古	15051.1		15051.1	770.7	5333.1
辽 宁	18998.6		18998.6	2605.7	6667.4
吉 林	5447.6		5447.6	654.1	1102.5
黑龙江	10104.3		10104.3	5442.0	3270.1
上 海	11106.9		11106.9	4335.8	
江 苏	26397.7		26397.7	1155.9	4046.2
浙 江	21844.1		21844.1	1166.5	6479.6
安 徽	13756.9		13756.9	1914.6	3880.6
福 建	23266.8		23266.8	2002.0	3961.2
江 西	11166.9		11166.9	1655.7	2181.0
山 东	13372.0		13372.0	4213.1	3369.5
河 南	19842.7		19842.7	3312.1	5666.4
湖 北	16809.8		16809.8	3832.0	2371.6
湖 南	8697.3		8697.3	904.3	1394.4
广 东	37037.1		37037.1	5142.3	14505.0
广 西	13870.8		13870.8	802.0	3378.5
海 南	4818.5		4818.5	2546.2	472.8
重 庆	10326.1		10326.1	3056.7	
四 川	20724.9		20724.9	2731.2	4670.1
贵 州	2386.6		2386.6		298.0
云 南	12337.0		12337.0	1869.1	1800.7
西 藏	401.3		401.3	401.3	
陕 西	8716.9		8716.9	2705.6	1998.6
甘 肃	5469.3		5469.3	878.0	1490.0
青 海	2413.1		2413.1	866.9	552.7
宁 夏	1692.6		1692.6		697.7
新 疆	4149.0		4149.0	1525.8	551.0

单位：万元

县级及以下	其他款项用于民政支出	中央安排	全省安排	省级	市级	县级及以下
275903.3	**1291329.6**	**68918.2**	**1222411.4**	**417210.6**	**289978.7**	**515222.1**
	24785.2	24785.2				
51114.4	95293.1		95293.1	35794.7		59498.4
3865.2	48739.3		48739.3	2580.8		46158.5
12701.7	30461.0		30461.0	23107.6	3082.5	4270.9
4644.4	11310.9		11310.9	1869.0	4277.9	5164.0
8947.3	131078.5	5939.0	125139.5	95697.2	9275.4	20166.9
9725.5	68001.4		68001.4	9763.7	51769.3	6468.4
3691.0	50535.0		50535.0	44134.8	3013.1	3387.1
1392.2	4580.5		4580.5		3570.6	1009.9
6771.1	14969.1		14969.1	265.4		14703.7
21195.6	118368.2		118368.2	1623.9	34266.0	82478.3
14198.0	66067.7		66067.7	1473.5	6793.5	57800.7
7961.7	64563.1	33382.0	31181.1	16929.8	4733.7	9517.6
17303.6	32783.2		32783.2	11799.9	8629.9	12353.4
7330.2	7006.3		7006.3	1947.5	2179.3	2879.5
5789.4	43599.0		43599.0	400.0	9379.0	33820.0
10864.2	25059.3		25059.3	14088.1	5185.8	5785.4
10606.2	25008.2		25008.2	12168.0	6660.8	6179.4
6398.6	24368.1		24368.1	11800.9	2047.9	10519.3
17389.8	117388.9		117388.9	14662.5	74797.0	27929.4
9690.3	25659.4		25659.4	13053.4	5234.2	7371.8
1799.5	8828.7		8828.7	692.5	2424.9	5711.3
7269.4	26936.8		26936.8	7185.4		19751.4
13323.6	28773.6		28773.6	406.4	14254.9	14112.3
2088.6	31624.8		31624.8	10999.7	2473.1	18152.0
8667.2	96864.1		96864.1	50400.9	22282.2	24181.0
	28.5		28.5			28.5
4012.7	26271.1		26271.1	21372.5	2322.0	2576.6
3101.3	6069.7		6069.7	207.9	2569.1	3292.7
993.5	10047.8		10047.8	3016.2	1854.6	5177.0
994.9	19784.2	4812.0	14972.2	9489.0	4256.3	1226.9
2072.2	6474.9		6474.9	279.4	2645.7	3549.8

C-1-17 预算资金

地　区	民政预算内经费实际支出	抚恤	死亡抚恤				伤残抚恤
				一次性抚恤金	定期抚恤金	其他	
全　国	**44041244.2**	**6365744.2**	**618219.8**	**225984.4**	**348231.3**	**44004.1**	**1137893.5**
中央级	128646.0	2166.0					
北　京	1600353.6	107558.6	35314.9	31202.6	3991.0	121.3	15242.6
天　津	591814.0	66835.9	6600.1	4898.2	1578.3	123.6	12654.7
河　北	1653297.9	349994.0	27870.8	10350.5	17317.1	203.2	67379.2
山　西	1144649.5	211508.0	13277.8	4694.1	8191.9	391.8	32395.3
内蒙古	1409253.2	97170.7	4856.7	2115.7	2519.7	221.3	18271.7
辽　宁	1694087.8	184824.0	24681.6	12254.5	8443.0	3984.1	40034.2
吉　林	942015.8	113342.3	10634.0	3023.3	7315.8	294.9	31679.1
黑龙江	1373441.2	105906.5	9107.2	2184.6	6738.7	183.9	23252.3
上　海	857287.8	94994.7	14036.3	7335.9	5055.2	1645.2	16063.5
江　苏	2460508.3	423763.2	46804.8	14991.9	26972.9	4840.0	87479.1
浙　江	1502557.1	238431.3	18799.4	8160.3	10124.0	515.1	38208.4
安　徽	1699609.2	284993.5	17748.0	4959.6	11311.5	1476.9	44367.8
福　建	775607.4	130093.4	16019.1	4221.8	11473.0	324.3	17080.1
江　西	1472214.2	239898.3	36581.6	4314.9	27724.9	4541.8	33253.4
山　东	2706751.9	723769.0	56567.7	18630.8	35136.3	2800.6	167415.7
河　南	2054924.0	415921.9	29510.8	10957.7	17175.5	1377.6	84853.5
湖　北	1852790.6	322408.2	40354.0	7013.5	31867.2	1473.3	45027.5
湖　南	2085354.4	411076.4	46799.7	11554.6	26417.4	8827.7	78041.6
广　东	2237116.3	320673.1	28049.7	14445.3	11711.1	1893.3	39764.0
广　西	1391271.4	148375.4	7489.4	2388.4	4522.5	578.5	13865.3
海　南	287775.5	31562.1	4047.2	974.7	2900.5	172.0	7422.5
重　庆	1027739.5	169469.5	13743.3	3901.6	7455.4	2386.3	30711.6
四　川	2917857.6	477657.1	39829.1	10393.0	27825.0	1611.1	82705.5
贵　州	1391678.3	134549.8	9459.9	4931.6	3866.9	661.4	18937.9
云　南	1979476.0	170978.0	14987.5	6543.5	7635.7	808.3	26811.0
西　藏	136789.5	7712.9	3094.5	593.2	2068.7	432.6	2292.7
陕　西	1679000.3	236078.2	21536.5	7920.6	13032.0	583.9	30778.8
甘　肃	1214834.5	57501.5	8518.1	4252.7	3544.3	721.1	14143.3
青　海	381598.0	17019.7	3390.4	1976.9	995.0	418.5	3771.6
宁　夏	264662.5	11245.0	1894.5	938.7	945.3	10.5	2266.6
新　疆	1126280.9	58266.0	6615.2	3859.7	2375.5	380.0	11723.0

总体支出情况

单位：万元

伤残抚恤金	在乡伤残抚恤金	在职保健金	伤残补助费	分散安置残疾军人护理费	在乡复员、退伍军人生活补助	在乡复退军人定期定量补助费	在乡红军老战士定期定量补助费	红军失散人员定期定量补助费
1066942.3	**804271.3**	**262671.0**	**70951.2**	**27833.8**	**2245511.4**	**1564600.5**	**1641.8**	**17446.7**
14453.6	7629.1	6824.5	789.0	328.0	11071.8	8053.3	4.3	
11680.9	5608.7	6072.2	973.8	449.1	22661.4	16078.0		
64571.7	63139.0	1432.7	2807.5	773.2	110141.0	80558.3	7.6	
31177.6	19530.1	11647.5	1217.7	778.2	41453.9	34978.5	25.1	1.7
16804.7	7818.5	8986.2	1467.0	100.5	22309.2	21099.3	16.9	3.3
36957.1	27678.8	9278.3	3077.1	686.7	58254.4	53428.6	28.0	
28897.0	20080.8	8816.2	2782.1	939.3	25636.8	23217.5		7.6
22512.0	17115.6	5396.4	740.3	536.8	37900.3	35665.1	44.8	23.3
14988.9		14988.9	1074.6	306.1	11256.3	8446.5		
80670.6	62350.2	18320.4	6808.5	3116.9	112015.4	94852.9		1.9
35860.7	24381.3	11479.4	2347.7	734.9	72474.8	57282.2		116.6
42980.7	30702.7	12278.0	1387.1	1059.0	118260.4	92839.1	13.0	3091.7
16518.3	13258.4	3259.9	561.8	381.6	42858.9	23564.4		418.5
30873.8	27389.8	3484.0	2379.6	1023.5	95471.0	63404.3	32.8	7221.4
155466.9	110538.2	44928.7	11948.8	6384.3	197002.8	159645.9		
81122.0	60395.5	20726.5	3731.5	1927.6	147102.6	99167.8	27.5	607.3
42716.4	38008.1	4708.3	2311.1	867.3	129169.0	96536.4	10.0	605.1
71968.7	61611.6	10357.1	6072.9	1342.8	178232.6	112672.4	11.3	2603.7
35736.6	28224.7	7511.9	4027.4	794.3	148525.8	62550.5		100.5
13109.3	11001.1	2108.2	756.0	131.6	67416.3	30311.4	46.0	515.2
6852.7	6698.9	153.8	569.8	6.3	8556.5	5937.9		32.9
28931.0	21340.5	7590.5	1780.6	1245.6	84427.3	58308.5		
78192.0	64651.3	13540.7	4513.5	1827.1	239162.0	181974.7	235.2	993.7
17069.0	13842.4	3226.6	1868.9	331.4	67586.7	34922.3	5.0	8.8
25281.9	16983.5	8298.4	1529.1	532.1	69242.5	29844.3		5.8
1924.1	1668.1	256.0	368.6		565.4	283.3	273.0	
29649.8	22397.2	7252.6	1129.0	491.7	86240.5	54062.6	739.0	1074.9
12951.7	9125.3	3826.4	1191.6	617.4	19796.0	9816.0	92.7	9.9
3736.7	2954.8	781.9	34.9	9.6	3934.8	2114.2		
2193.3	1943.8	249.5	73.3	27.8	2526.9	1825.8	7.8	1.5
11092.6	6203.3	4889.3	630.4	83.1	14258.1	11158.5	21.8	1.4

C-1-17续表1

地 区	“参战”退伍军人生活补助	“涉核”退伍军人生活补助	优抚事业单位	烈士纪念建筑物管理维修经费
全 国	**571973.5**	**89848.9**	**691267.1**	**301024.5**
中央级			2166.0	2166.0
北 京	2110.0	904.2	6122.9	2923.6
天 津	6438.8	144.6	10400.0	2603.1
河 北	20897.4	8677.7	60660.5	27742.5
山 西	3782.9	2665.7	47564.9	18636.9
内蒙古	1107.6	82.1	11122.0	3965.6
辽 宁	3212.6	1585.2	14108.1	4917.3
吉 林	1680.2	731.5	11939.0	4307.5
黑龙江	2086.3	80.8	16310.3	5288.7
上 海	2315.3	494.5	9684.4	7248.0
江 苏	14689.6	2471.0	43160.0	18146.5
浙 江	13659.0	1417.0	18888.3	10968.3
安 徽	16456.3	5860.3	33203.6	10385.8
福 建	18648.0	228.0	13588.2	6437.4
江 西	22539.4	2273.1	33891.6	22075.6
山 东	30693.2	6663.7	93053.8	37537.3
河 南	36916.8	10383.2	31949.4	12319.6
湖 北	28181.9	3835.6	33694.9	7295.8
湖 南	56439.1	6506.1	33330.7	11606.9
广 东	81270.4	4604.4	21829.9	10298.2
广 西	34732.3	1811.4	22824.5	8406.8
海 南	2410.2	175.5	2960.0	1755.0
重 庆	23278.2	2840.6	8253.9	2965.6
四 川	47454.6	8503.8	40590.3	22683.3
贵 州	32544.3	106.3	10590.4	4828.7
云 南	39317.7	74.7	9363.8	4728.3
西 藏	9.1		1026.3	441.1
陕 西	19917.6	10446.4	26669.2	15650.0
甘 肃	6494.6	3382.8	6478.8	4407.0
青 海	1148.2	672.4	1682.5	248.4
宁 夏	502.8	189.0	603.0	353.0
新 疆	1039.1	2037.3	13555.9	7686.7

单位：万元

烈士纪念建筑物管理单位经费	荣誉军人康复医院经费	在院人员生活费	复员军人疗养院经费	在院人员生活费
94185.9	**73310.5**	**4450.8**	**42299.4**	**2692.4**
2166.0				
907.0				
1918.8			2096.4	47.8
5564.2	1989.2		10948.2	169.3
5832.8	1708.7	261.1	4896.2	
994.5	1301.5		40.0	
2014.3	1696.5	367.4		
1083.1	4482.6			
872.5	5009.0	33.0		
6636.6	1240.7	27.2		
8512.9	3332.0		1679.1	388.7
3570.5	5836.5		6.0	
4417.4	2170.6			
2417.7	512.9	170.0		
3223.4	3089.6	800.0	181.1	64.7
11363.0	12532.1	180.0	17150.1	814.1
4545.3	6546.6	379.0	1372.7	262.7
2331.0	3693.6		9.0	
3083.9	960.1		310.0	
2961.1	886.7	230.0	1754.7	400.0
1492.9	3039.9			
2.7				
431.0	2640.3	220.0		
6645.7	3192.2	1282.8	170.5	92.9
736.3	2513.8	176.0		
1405.8	660.0			
134.8				
3375.4	2081.4	302.3	1685.4	452.2
3431.6	687.1			
50.0				
50.3				
2013.4	1506.9	22.0		

C-1-17续表2

地区	复退军人精神病院经费	在院人员生活费	光荣院经费	在院人员生活费
全 国	**100705.9**	**10537.2**	**87159.7**	**23074.7**
中央级				
北 京			2938.1	400.3
天 津	1938.7	133.4	2754.2	276.0
河 北	5939.8	141.0	12696.2	2988.0
山 西	7002.5	466.1	6936.4	1765.8
内蒙古	966.5	90.0	3885.3	916.0
辽 宁	2168.6	735.1	4067.4	1734.2
吉 林	659.6	217.0	994.8	498.1
黑龙江	1644.0	144.0	1973.1	636.0
上 海	89.4	89.4		
江 苏	8515.9		635.1	273.7
浙 江	476.3	28.1	759.6	185.2
安 徽	3357.0		3654.0	859.1
福 建	2589.1	799.0	2450.8	552.5
江 西	23.0	7.3	5213.6	2305.5
山 东	17838.0	1935.6	4477.8	1604.6
河 南	5732.1	435.0	2921.6	527.6
湖 北	14658.4	2327.9	6819.3	2046.6
湖 南	6382.3	441.0	9775.9	2189.4
广 东	4672.8	1114.4	2732.2	1020.9
广 西	6655.4	25.0	1150.4	224.4
海 南			441.1	82.9
重 庆			1477.7	358.1
四 川	5089.5	610.5	2430.1	744.3
贵 州	193.0	193.0	1414.5	392.0
云 南	666.5		6.0	
西 藏				
陕 西	2732.8	604.4	2059.8	328.7
甘 肃	590.7		60.0	
青 海			104.0	4.0
宁 夏			250.0	55.0
新 疆	124.0		2080.7	105.8

单位：万元

其他优抚事业单位经费	集体办优抚事业单位补助费	义务兵优待金	城市义务兵优待金	农村义务兵优待金	其他优抚支出
84196.9	**2570.2**	**1131325.6**	**555710.1**	**575615.5**	**541526.8**
261.2		18703.0	14393.4	4309.6	21103.4
1007.6		9868.5	6156.0	3712.5	4651.2
1344.6		72602.5	32579.8	40022.7	11340.0
8384.2		64103.9	37725.9	26378.0	12712.2
613.2	349.9	29770.1	17209.2	12560.9	10841.0
1258.3		31827.1	16419.8	15407.3	15918.6
1494.5		28701.5	18341.6	10359.9	4751.9
2395.5		12609.5	9287.5	3322.0	6726.9
1106.3		37107.6	32137.3	4970.3	6846.6
10400.4	451.0	77927.6	44069.5	33858.1	56376.3
816.6	25.0	70888.2	28907.0	41981.2	19172.2
13581.0	55.2	56943.7	20638.8	36304.9	14470.0
1598.0		28544.2	10426.5	18117.7	12002.9
3291.7	17.0	22758.3	11654.5	11103.8	17942.4
3518.5		120701.3	39423.6	81277.7	89027.7
2916.8	140.0	100539.7	49219.1	51320.6	21965.9
1198.8	20.0	54932.0	26275.9	28656.1	19230.8
3586.5	709.0	54056.2	31677.1	22379.1	20615.6
1358.2	127.1	46870.2	18528.0	28342.2	35633.5
3572.0		18464.4	5848.8	12615.6	18315.5
763.9		1525.2	882.8	642.4	7050.7
1170.3		20580.0	9283.5	11296.5	11753.4
6448.7	576.0	53350.9	22749.9	30601.0	22019.3
1640.4		16504.2	9079.7	7424.5	11470.7
3303.0		10911.9	3655.9	7256.0	39661.3
585.2		512.2	145.6	366.6	221.8
2459.8		51120.7	27195.1	23925.6	19732.5
734.0		5755.3	2419.8	3335.5	2810.0
1230.1	100.0	2789.1	1868.2	920.9	1451.3
		3064.6	1789.4	1275.2	889.4
2157.6		7292.0	5720.9	1571.1	4821.8

C-1-17续表3

地 区	退役安置	退伍军人安置	一次性建房补助费	退役士兵自谋职业金	城镇退役士兵生活补助	军队移交政府的离退休人员安置	军队离休干部离休金	军队退休干部退休金
全 国	**4567849.2**	**1171583.3**	**19940.9**	**881878.6**	**143759.8**	**2877911.4**	**303946.6**	**1672077.7**
中央级								
北 京	724662.4	19724.6		18551.8	289.0	608600.9	19368.2	379298.8
天 津	92687.2	15562.2	756.9	13797.4	125.9	64765.9	5163.5	39369.9
河 北	255298.0	85727.3	2539.0	62189.9	13349.8	148104.0	16805.6	97741.6
山 西	80063.2	15279.3	543.8	6717.8	5699.3	50829.2	5459.1	21185.9
内蒙古	61802.4	19009.9	413.5	12315.7	4841.2	33264.6	3438.7	21110.5
辽 宁	337923.7	51908.9	678.8	32789.2	7014.2	263177.0	69763.4	112432.0
吉 林	78741.7	22329.1	230.2	10670.6	3518.9	41544.2	507.1	2676.9
黑龙江	71615.6	20459.4	166.9	17246.7	2474.0	44433.7	4230.7	28062.7
上 海	147881.8	27182.0	17.0	21635.5	1710.4	102735.8	5084.6	56384.0
江 苏	335953.8	103001.0	194.7	89952.8	5849.6	185278.4	17418.8	100271.1
浙 江	116663.3	47260.3	446.1	37117.9	4183.5	55650.4	7764.9	32127.0
安 徽	152501.8	101732.0	331.7	91015.2	6377.4	42471.9	7468.0	23851.8
福 建	88560.5	28906.2	165.5	25172.0	2008.3	43241.6	6278.1	29484.1
江 西	50440.9	23257.6	787.0	14698.6	5349.7	20776.3	5734.3	6920.8
山 东	379751.4	100373.4	1149.2	70402.7	14966.9	237185.1	33683.5	144207.8
河 南	174654.0	75801.8	919.1	49458.3	18445.6	82391.2	10542.8	53578.9
湖 北	156196.7	38519.2	930.6	27499.9	7633.1	105033.9	10961.6	62567.4
湖 南	105284.9	31897.5	1720.3	17392.2	6580.9	58379.4	6538.9	33475.7
广 东	229139.4	69753.2	2406.1	57983.1	4627.8	124104.6	11878.6	74937.1
广 西	48840.2	18328.0	243.0	14162.2	1315.2	25830.5	2085.8	15827.1
海 南	23680.6	6693.8	30.0	4326.8	1152.3	12352.3	451.3	8940.6
重 庆	92065.4	36121.7	675.4	31962.6	929.8	49498.3	2847.9	32194.9
四 川	224381.1	93296.5	1515.7	73548.5	6371.8	112975.2	9262.7	75579.0
贵 州	36898.1	16080.4	229.5	13266.0	1704.3	17749.8	2957.6	9129.4
云 南	115255.4	20799.8	1240.4	14338.6	1717.9	84543.0	20511.4	44212.4
西 藏	9814.1	2415.7	155.0	891.5	402.0	6691.6	253.6	5690.5
陕 西	182025.6	26809.1	986.0	17153.0	7119.2	132827.5	10229.0	86044.2
甘 肃	74595.5	23128.6	437.0	11269.0	5742.6	44989.9	3172.6	26224.0
青 海	23176.9	5495.2		3717.7	327.2	15789.2	8.4	8470.1
宁 夏	16909.3	11089.3		8622.6	998.7	1389.2	97.4	499.6
新 疆	80384.3	13640.3	32.5	12012.8	933.3	61306.8	3978.5	39581.9

单位：万元

军队无军籍职工退休金	军队离退休人员其他费用	死亡丧葬费	护理费	遗属生活困难补助费	定期定量补助费	其他费用	军队移交政府离退休干部管理机构	其他退役安置支出
423724.2	**478162.9**	**49637.8**	**36444.1**	**16406.7**	**6141.8**	**375674.3**	**307126.6**	**211227.9**
79999.7	129934.2	4692.1	5372.9	284.0	27.0	119585.2	73808.7	22528.2
6922.5	13310.0	490.5	1232.5	186.7	35.0	11400.3	11259.7	1099.4
16125.0	17431.8	1775.6	1422.0	3762.8	499.4	10471.4	18587.8	2878.9
8070.2	16114.0	505.8	1032.7	696.5	363.3	13879.0	5861.9	8092.8
4475.5	4239.9	271.1	1808.7	277.5	152.7	1882.6	2973.9	6554.0
27582.2	53399.4	22231.2	2126.3	753.9	495.8	28288.0	17411.2	5426.6
7155.9	31204.3	269.9	38.3	54.1	37.4	30842.0	13995.4	873.0
8375.7	3764.6	417.3	499.2	197.0	77.7	2651.1	5118.2	1604.3
17157.9	24109.3	731.5	1054.7	87.5	75.4	22235.6	13627.9	4336.1
37520.1	30068.4	4044.8	1880.6	1185.5	504.5	22957.5	22954.1	24720.3
10476.3	5282.2	276.4	854.8	187.6	86.0	3963.4	8126.9	5625.7
4039.0	7113.1	772.9	973.5	767.6	236.4	4599.1	6363.6	1934.3
4278.8	3200.6	508.6	501.4	228.8	126.0	1961.8	6290.3	10122.4
3746.4	4374.8	75.7	291.3	226.0	44.6	3781.8	2082.7	4324.3
24126.7	35167.1	3574.7	6215.0	1343.0	647.5	24034.4	15546.1	26646.8
11029.5	7240.0	1915.2	1472.7	817.9	359.2	3034.2	7795.3	8665.7
20566.7	10938.2	974.7	1860.7	474.8	215.2	7628.0	9403.5	3240.1
13679.3	4685.5	682.8	865.0	750.9	179.9	2386.8	9174.5	5833.5
22925.4	14363.5	564.6	620.6	408.0	226.1	12770.3	11834.9	23446.7
5020.0	2897.6	163.1	264.2	133.1	78.1	2337.2	3522.0	1159.7
1446.5	1513.9	14.2	213.2	127.4	13.2	1159.1	1213.8	3420.7
7292.5	7163.0	445.8	491.6	146.9	71.0	6078.7	5228.0	1217.4
15978.1	12155.4	1381.1	1569.8	930.4	372.6	8274.1	10563.0	7546.4
3105.8	2557.0	368.8	991.8	73.0	32.1	1123.4	1046.2	2021.7
10734.6	9084.6	498.8	544.4	240.8	131.6	7800.6	5048.4	4864.2
677.1	70.4	50.0		20.4			601.6	105.2
20029.9	16524.4	1210.6	1623.8	1295.5	568.6	12394.5	8797.9	13591.1
10454.0	5139.3	431.4	560.4	269.7	84.4	3877.8	2286.4	4190.6
7024.7	286.0			6.8		279.2	1629.5	263.0
743.5	48.7	32.6	10.1	6.0			222.8	4208.0
12964.7	4781.7	266.0	51.9	466.6	401.1	3997.2	4750.4	686.8

C-1-17续表4

地 区	社会福利	儿童福利	老年人福利	假肢矫形
全 国	**4809479.7**	**524454.6**	**1516718.6**	**20807.0**
中央级				
北 京	225668.2	13857.0	109390.1	375.2
天 津	56445.7	1286.8	29094.2	2056.0
河 北	149277.7	12945.3	51151.5	654.0
山 西	79829.0	11765.8	14894.4	603.1
内蒙古	151283.7	8630.7	66444.8	1477.3
辽 宁	132829.0	12496.9	23764.4	71.4
吉 林	49320.4	3972.4	12542.7	210.2
黑龙江	79242.4	6128.2	14636.4	879.8
上 海	146537.4	7356.5	46465.6	
江 苏	424389.9	23397.2	155698.0	492.4
浙 江	331852.9	8400.0	107437.6	1251.3
安 徽	168348.4	21824.9	47204.4	106.2
福 建	111201.5	5645.3	21844.2	
江 西	139507.2	30795.1	48136.2	1380.6
山 东	364226.8	20194.1	136429.3	1606.0
河 南	145683.8	35411.3	30043.2	604.8
湖 北	164422.0	22654.0	25600.0	151.8
湖 南	153669.5	41129.8	30219.4	378.8
广 东	349232.9	43893.9	106878.0	20.2
广 西	148070.1	20612.4	57292.7	3218.8
海 南	29281.1	2604.3	18561.9	
重 庆	128084.2	11863.0	31057.0	3010.5
四 川	308904.4	31802.1	66548.9	514.1
贵 州	110102.2	19889.0	23616.6	50.0
云 南	104660.8	24640.6	33624.6	126.1
西 藏	15856.6	9295.4	1656.2	
陕 西	179999.5	12577.9	98235.9	285.4
甘 肃	77144.8	18241.7	16028.5	295.8
青 海	65199.6	12525.5	18695.9	185.2
宁 夏	15125.9	5151.9	1575.9	
新 疆	204082.1	23465.6	71950.1	802.0

单位：万元

假肢厂(站)专项拨款	其他经费	殡葬	补贴火化场经费	补贴殡葬类单位经费
9661.6	**11145.4**	**614364.5**	**253373.7**	**360990.8**
375.2		25762.9	17121.5	8641.4
	2056.0	9205.1	780.0	8425.1
654.0		28955.1	12205.4	16749.7
400.0	203.1	18837.7	17520.8	1316.9
843.8	633.5	16061.7	4493.8	11567.9
53.0	18.4	40239.0	21891.1	18347.9
	210.2	7714.2	3320.1	4394.1
829.8	50.0	5796.9	3036.1	2760.8
100.0	392.4	60195.8	32729.9	27465.9
330.0	921.3	66170.8	33197.6	32973.2
90.0	16.2	27091.5	15349.2	11742.3
		25410.9	13287.3	12123.6
1180.0	200.6	5262.4	2312.4	2950.0
1606.0		16163.0	8546.2	7616.8
604.8		17844.2	11782.2	6062.0
145.8	6.0	35447.9	2531.1	32916.8
372.8	6.0	10961.9	2388.9	8573.0
20.0	0.2	62095.2	10634.2	51461.0
	3218.8	18058.4	1092.0	16966.4
		1895.0	4.5	1890.5
	3010.5	15037.6	11160.2	3877.4
510.2	3.9	34114.2	7597.8	26516.4
50.0		7646.0	3014.5	4631.5
120.0	6.1	16443.9	7801.1	8642.8
		575.1	278.3	296.8
280.4	5.0	8756.5	3054.3	5702.2
295.8		8509.5	1741.5	6768.0
	185.2	221.3	13.3	208.0
		391.8	210.6	181.2
800.0	2.0	23499.0	4277.8	19221.2

C-1-17续表5

地区	社会福利事业单位	社会福利院经费	在院人员生活费	儿童福利院经费	在院人员生活费	精神病人福利院经费
全 国	**1218868.6**	**518412.0**	**83362.3**	**154128.1**	**52256.0**	**162598.4**
中央级						
北 京	17625.1	6403.3	1161.2	1967.6	547.1	4252.9
天 津	11967.2	1637.4	390.8	3066.2	709.5	3059.0
河 北	29838.6	11083.9	1956.9	596.4	246.9	
山 西	15200.0	7853.0	2331.7	1403.6	536.2	400.0
内蒙古	31274.6	14837.4	3692.0	4043.2	1655.3	4683.9
辽 宁	33169.2	19731.0	2525.0	4268.2	2844.0	
吉 林	19002.5	8284.7	2383.9	2450.9	965.2	5233.9
黑龙江	44968.7	12102.7	2225.5	4672.9	1664.4	16360.7
上 海	49362.9	28961.4	2388.2	5990.7	3929.0	10731.5
江 苏	105908.4	46928.0	8324.0	8490.0	4017.6	22907.7
浙 江	116673.1	45302.7	2525.1	10138.0	553.7	3716.9
安 徽	44579.7	10952.4	2504.3	12265.4	3597.7	76.2
福 建	38066.0	13420.8	2911.9	2673.5	776.2	11304.2
江 西	19974.2	8404.9	2181.2	879.4	283.7	8261.0
山 东	70175.8	18594.9	4437.3	13220.9	4815.3	3992.4
河 南	27959.5	9932.6	2864.7	5332.5	1757.8	2154.5
湖 北	60365.5	40260.2	4503.7	10162.3	2464.6	3387.2
湖 南	34692.0	17821.4	1566.3	3076.6	1915.6	2012.3
广 东	95385.1	64175.6	15368.1	9290.0	3789.0	7040.0
广 西	32288.1	16823.0	1366.3	2772.6	809.6	9860.9
海 南	2473.3	2153.7	3.0	83.0	28.8	
重 庆	46464.9	17509.0	1692.7	5162.0	2231.4	12462.7
四 川	119648.5	39635.3	5083.5	8031.8	2457.7	5171.2
贵 州	23065.1	4629.6	951.4	3276.0	1462.1	3669.4
云 南	12193.6	4511.6	616.8	1800.9	534.5	1816.9
西 藏	2065.0	1178.6	428.2	882.4	776.6	
陕 西	25108.4	10414.4	2765.1	7727.2	1769.1	1332.9
甘 肃	12584.6	4990.6	540.8	3229.2	1010.4	1593.5
青 海	8664.9	7779.7	95.0	756.2	82.0	60.0
宁 夏	6125.6	1898.9	276.0	1431.5	367.2	500.0
新 疆	61998.5	20199.3	3301.7	14987.0	3657.8	16556.6

单位：万元

在院人员生活费	补贴安置农场经费	其他社会福利单位	其他社会福利支出	社会救助	最低生活保障	城市最低生活保障	城市最低生活保障金
15890.3	**8988.0**	**374742.1**	**914266.4**	**21975319.6**	**15920071.9**	**7217471.5**	**6720822.1**
253.7		5001.3	58657.9	167609.7	100206.6	71168.9	67626.7
334.7		4204.6	2836.4	216315.6	166174.9	119809.6	88625.1
	107.5	18050.8	25733.2	727204.0	528680.0	208723.0	201517.3
		5543.4	18528.0	660396.3	522877.8	266264.0	260960.8
630.6		7710.1	27394.6	859741.8	686686.0	369794.3	348747.6
		9170.0	23088.1	740673.8	594678.9	420934.0	379695.2
620.9		3033.0	5878.4	571910.6	456824.5	331870.5	306168.3
2119.9	2429.0	9403.4	6832.4	1034755.9	816440.1	587269.1	493613.2
89.0		3679.3	43352.4	312486.0	150292.7	136752.8	131606.3
2334.1		27582.7	78698.1	853526.6	485140.4	143732.6	130193.2
233.9	439.0	57076.5	31920.1	481116.2	244170.1	42048.6	34883.0
28.3	309.5	20976.2	27541.7	947406.1	659280.6	289567.6	279430.9
1723.1	479.0	10188.5	20235.1	311489.7	192471.0	52929.2	48475.1
78.0		2428.9	33958.7	923129.3	626041.1	325365.2	318456.4
746.5		34367.6	119658.6	978667.7	688750.8	183589.5	165755.7
12.0		10539.9	33820.8	1137122.2	844637.6	331863.0	318785.8
113.4		6555.8	20202.8	999986.0	740194.7	415013.7	373882.4
100.0	75.0	11706.7	36287.6	1222781.2	894568.0	445206.0	421635.7
1518.4	113.8	14765.7	40960.5	880137.6	532682.2	154578.9	141378.2
480.0	244.1	2587.5	16599.7	824000.4	581602.0	149629.9	146114.3
		236.6	3746.6	133925.9	82300.8	41032.6	40221.2
907.8		11331.2	20651.2	473314.1	259828.3	151390.5	142755.9
1124.1		66810.2	56276.6	1500628.8	1021218.3	477673.6	468791.9
634.5	3541.9	7948.2	35835.5	915379.7	777983.8	167700.6	158225.5
17.5	33.1	4031.1	17632.0	1185535.6	1007216.8	324793.2	321313.6
		4.0	2264.9	81798.5	62717.0	25202.0	21869.1
229.0		5633.9	35035.4	878774.9	631424.2	258022.0	230016.5
58.7	67.7	2703.6	21484.7	901129.3	736682.3	269833.7	264348.9
		69.0	24906.8	209303.2	157252.3	76056.5	69279.5
	1090.0	1205.2	1880.7	164163.2	121850.8	50946.3	46390.7
1502.2	58.4	10197.2	22366.9	680909.7	549197.3	328710.1	300058.1

C-1-17续表6

地 区	城市最低生活保障对象临时补助	农村最低生活保障	农村最低生活保障金	农村最低生活保障对象临时补助	其他社会救助	五保供养	五保集中供养	五保集中供养保障金
全 国	**496649.4**	**8702600.4**	**8182245.5**	**520354.9**	**3215375.9**	**1898245.9**	**797672.7**	**766822.5**
中央级								
北 京	3542.2	29037.7	28586.3	451.4	44137.0	3753.1	1807.8	1790.3
天 津	31184.5	46365.3	35894.9	10470.4	17368.4	9177.6	1038.7	1004.5
河 北	7205.7	319957.0	310185.7	9771.3	112410.2	85309.0	37134.8	35344.6
山 西	5303.2	256613.8	253835.5	2778.3	62505.1	46131.4	12571.2	12041.4
内蒙古	21046.7	316891.7	296209.2	20682.5	95056.4	39222.3	14783.6	14204.7
辽 宁	41238.8	173744.9	162943.1	10801.8	77103.4	52904.6	19454.3	18060.4
吉 林	25702.2	124954.0	114180.0	10774.0	42697.2	27650.4	10953.6	10534.4
黑龙江	93655.9	229171.0	199872.9	29298.1	90078.9	58182.6	27318.7	26210.8
上 海	5146.5	13539.9	12920.4	619.5	136319.0	1689.8	801.3	755.4
江 苏	13539.4	341407.8	314477.2	26930.6	234174.6	121599.3	70026.0	67814.0
浙 江	7165.6	202121.5	181644.2	20477.3	140159.3	27393.2	27069.2	25429.7
安 徽	10136.7	369713.0	353519.2	16193.8	169085.8	120369.8	59199.1	58663.0
福 建	4454.1	139541.8	127508.8	12033.0	67048.5	45720.4	5653.1	5530.8
江 西	6908.8	300675.9	295416.7	5259.2	123575.6	74483.9	40030.7	38606.7
山 东	17833.8	505161.3	453614.8	51546.5	159649.0	102285.9	81506.5	77095.6
河 南	13077.2	512774.6	497402.4	15372.2	171444.3	134018.0	65439.5	64401.3
湖 北	41131.3	325181.0	294655.7	30525.3	124555.9	76955.8	28689.3	25983.4
湖 南	23570.3	449362.0	418137.5	31224.5	187697.2	148991.7	49434.4	48217.6
广 东	13200.7	378103.3	337129.6	40973.7	222196.5	164614.9	26309.5	24137.4
广 西	3515.6	431972.1	426302.8	5669.3	141908.9	77124.7	10277.4	9988.9
海 南	811.4	41268.2	39806.4	1461.8	23218.8	16538.5	1694.6	1299.1
重 庆	8634.6	108437.8	99322.9	9114.9	126855.5	74542.7	31121.2	29861.3
四 川	8881.7	543544.7	531593.7	11951.0	251320.7	184467.0	108336.7	106732.6
贵 州	9475.1	610283.2	542694.1	67589.1	45596.1	19703.7	8329.9	7788.8
云 南	3479.6	682423.6	677947.0	4476.6	64442.5	34095.9	9765.1	9397.0
西 藏	3332.9	37515.0	32967.3	4547.7	5561.1	4754.3	2720.1	2420.2
陕 西	28005.5	373402.2	338790.1	34612.1	131585.1	70578.1	29309.4	26896.2
甘 肃	5484.8	466848.6	465080.1	1768.5	69637.3	38348.3	5330.2	5245.2
青 海	6777.0	81195.8	73602.8	7593.0	18259.5	8611.0	1887.5	1833.9
宁 夏	4555.6	70904.5	59851.4	11053.1	13600.8	6027.1	3054.3	3003.4
新 疆	28652.0	220487.2	206152.8	14334.4	46127.3	23000.9	6625.0	6529.9

单位：万元

五保集中供养对象临时补助	五保分散供养	五保分散供养保障金	五保分散供养对象临时补助	城市“三无”救助	流浪乞讨人员救助	流浪乞讨人员救助单位经费	流浪乞讨人员救助经费	临时救助	传统救济
30850.2	**1100573.2**	**1059994.4**	**40578.8**	**51193.9**	**384695.9**	**163467.7**	**221228.2**	**576047.3**	**305192.9**
17.5	1945.3	1942.8	2.5	295.5	20170.7	3435.1	16735.6	17543.6	2374.1
34.2	8138.9	7709.3	429.6		3298.1	1435.4	1862.7	4379.9	512.8
1790.2	48174.2	46174.2	2000.0	178.4	11500.8	4137.6	7363.2	14101.9	1320.1
529.8	33560.2	32754.5	805.7	193.1	8288.9	2803.8	5485.1	5732.9	2158.8
578.9	24438.7	22998.5	1440.2	10241.0	5688.6	3654.2	2034.4	21046.6	18857.9
1393.9	33450.3	31675.7	1774.6	599.7	10804.6	4486.6	6318.0	7752.9	5041.6
419.2	16696.8	15863.8	833.0	394.8	6340.8	2269.7	4071.1	6936.9	1374.3
1107.9	30863.9	29452.4	1411.5	486.0	7835.4	4611.8	3223.6	22862.8	712.1
45.9	888.5	753.8	134.7		15022.8	11754.6	3268.2	96780.2	22826.2
2212.0	51573.3	49724.8	1848.5	2463.0	22022.3	9751.9	12270.4	39675.0	48415.0
1639.5	324.0	309.3	14.7	1103.2	17338.4	9487.4	7851.0	34380.2	59944.3
536.1	61170.7	60590.9	579.8	862.4	21613.2	8234.8	13378.4	14938.2	11302.2
122.3	40067.3	38625.4	1441.9	839.6	8765.4	4031.0	4734.4	5991.2	5731.9
1424.0	34453.2	33438.3	1014.9	1612.9	11188.1	3470.3	7717.8	20853.6	15437.1
4410.9	20779.4	19186.6	1592.8	1636.8	19733.1	8616.2	11116.9	34709.4	1283.8
1038.2	68578.5	67165.7	1412.8	250.2	18911.2	8899.8	10011.4	8633.5	9631.4
2705.9	48266.5	45044.2	3222.3	1946.1	19983.6	7915.5	12068.1	18648.6	7021.8
1216.8	99557.3	95614.9	3942.4	1423.2	20384.7	5367.7	15017.0	13330.7	3566.9
2172.1	138305.4	133420.9	4884.5	4325.9	36667.3	20086.4	16580.9	13035.6	3552.8
288.5	66847.3	65947.0	900.3	470.7	12207.5	5709.2	6498.3	18522.7	33583.3
395.5	14843.9	12786.0	2057.9	2.3	4304.8	220.9	4083.9	2092.2	281.0
1259.9	43421.5	41169.4	2252.1	8279.3	8311.1	3166.1	5145.0	28510.3	7212.1
1604.1	76130.3	75547.9	582.4	2737.5	28583.7	8926.0	19657.7	18728.3	16804.2
541.1	11373.8	10684.0	689.8	5848.9	8640.9	3702.1	4938.8	5701.0	5701.6
368.1	24330.8	23526.9	803.9	422.6	5243.0	1549.1	3693.9	17529.5	7151.5
299.9	2034.2	1903.4	130.8	4.6	478.9	214.5	264.4	290.3	33.0
2413.2	41268.7	37972.7	3296.0	2667.0	12598.1	5329.4	7268.7	42080.7	3661.2
85.0	33018.1	32458.5	559.6	1066.2	4199.9	1927.7	2272.2	21945.3	4077.6
53.6	6723.5	6498.9	224.6	250.0	5544.1	3558.7	1985.4	3661.9	192.5
50.9	2972.8	2938.9	33.9	115.6	836.8	270.8	566.0	6616.2	5.1
95.1	16375.9	16114.8	261.1	477.4	8189.1	4443.4	3745.7	9035.2	5424.7

C-1-17续表7

地　区	医疗救助	资助参加合作医疗	资助参加医疗保险	医疗救助	门诊救助	住院救助
全　国	**2839871.8**	**322959.9**	**161507.9**	**2041295.0**	**239709.1**	**1801585.9**
中央级						
北　京	23266.1	350.9	4598.8	13425.1	6028.2	7396.9
天　津	32772.3		6017.0	19023.4	429.9	18593.5
河　北	86113.8	13620.0	1913.7	48288.6	4896.0	43392.6
山　西	75013.4	8240.3	4495.0	53796.0	4820.5	48975.5
内蒙古	77999.4	6757.4	4639.5	60320.8	5930.9	54389.9
辽　宁	68891.5	7635.8	14799.2	38717.6	5349.2	33368.4
吉　林	72388.9	11233.6	4710.8	50701.1	10630.3	40070.8
黑龙江	128236.9	9102.4	11262.4	100694.9	13147.5	87547.4
上　海	25874.3	106.1	3500.9	20006.0	1567.3	18438.7
江　苏	134211.6	12924.5	7685.5	96686.9	17947.1	78739.8
浙　江	96786.8	10043.8	1167.0	71627.0	17082.2	54544.8
安　徽	119039.7	16284.1	3568.5	87955.0	7691.5	80263.5
福　建	51970.2	5984.6	341.7	39189.8	6713.6	32476.2
江　西	173512.6	8646.8	10449.6	142260.6	16551.0	125709.6
山　东	130267.9	18707.1	5499.6	67756.4	1767.4	65989.0
河　南	121040.3	20558.7	6492.8	78595.2	3127.1	75468.1
湖　北	135235.4	18080.3	4537.8	99531.9	10723.4	88808.5
湖　南	140516.0	16073.3	8120.6	96172.9	17053.9	79119.0
广　东	125258.9	11514.9	13371.7	80974.3	12487.2	68487.1
广　西	100489.5	13229.2	1530.4	79795.7	4627.5	75168.2
海　南	28406.3	1756.9	1070.0	23060.0	1865.2	21194.8
重　庆	86630.3	6237.3	4051.8	63868.3	12366.2	51502.1
四　川	228089.8	33963.9	12925.8	160568.3	17338.7	143229.6
贵　州	91799.8	14650.9	1222.8	69201.2	3068.9	66132.3
云　南	113876.3	28279.5	9294.6	67424.7	8730.9	58693.8
西　藏	13520.4	509.9	318.4	12348.8	887.5	11461.3
陕　西	115765.6	6695.3	1138.1	100358.7	11722.5	88636.2
甘　肃	94809.7	9534.6	2847.9	79007.4	3533.0	75474.4
青　海	33791.4	2432.0	1688.3	28168.0	1767.3	26400.7
宁　夏	28711.6	1532.8	1064.7	25087.6	5534.9	19552.7
新　疆	85585.1	8273.0	7183.0	66682.8	4322.3	62360.5

单位：万元

优抚对象医疗补助	自然灾害生活救助	生活救济费	紧急抢救、安置、转移灾民支出	救灾储备	自然灾害灾后重建补助	其他救助
314109.0	**1244362.2**	**726829.5**	**82393.8**	**80978.4**	**252276.2**	**101884.3**
	23137.0			21323.0	1814.0	
4891.3	6195.7	3731.5		821.3	1000.0	642.9
7731.9	869.6	25.1		531.7		312.8
22291.5	37851.4	35924.4	290.0	750.5	676.5	210.0
8482.1	27198.8	21891.5	460.2	3308.9	595.7	942.5
6281.7	48219.3	31997.6	7195.8	2948.8	3391.1	2686.0
7738.9	40718.5	29854.7	106.0	1920.3	4229.2	4608.3
5743.4	31255.0	11159.0	521.2	447.5	18562.9	564.4
7177.2	13887.6	11315.3	1071.2	839.3	290.8	371.0
2261.3	1607.5					1607.5
16914.7	16524.1	11365.1	656.3	284.8	1346.7	2871.2
13949.0	22835.6	11307.8	998.3	6232.2	1288.4	3008.9
11232.1	26592.6	22653.8	374.0	385.2	1512.7	1666.9
6454.1	18906.3	7074.3	490.7	656.6	1553.2	9131.5
12155.6	58542.9	35013.8	7605.2	956.7	9816.1	5151.1
38304.8	20589.3	17651.8	35.2	956.5	70.0	1875.8
15393.6	19320.4	16512.8		1583.5	817.8	406.3
13085.4	31596.9	18552.9	1827.1	2898.6	4454.7	3863.6
20149.2	51680.8	33861.0	4744.2	739.4	7782.9	4553.3
19398.0	51645.7	21191.4	4777.9	5300.4	14213.7	6162.3
5934.2	55855.7	32180.5	1589.7	2905.2	15611.9	3568.4
2519.4	22510.2	10502.5	798.0	1140.7	7549.1	2519.9
12472.9	35457.6	18982.5	4535.5	2048.5	9338.8	552.3
20631.8	159210.9	71004.6	4308.4	5237.6	69344.4	9315.9
6724.9	85394.1	55117.1	4496.4	3663.6	15608.3	6508.7
8877.5	157347.7	82303.1	29369.4	3075.9	36096.5	6502.8
343.3	8498.2	1617.8	283.1	2004.7	4144.5	448.1
7573.5	34977.8	18261.9	2775.8	1240.8	9610.5	3088.8
3419.8	63562.1	42820.4	1834.9	936.6	1871.0	16099.2
1503.1	28251.5	18581.2	105.9	1466.6	6839.1	1258.7
1026.5	19500.1	16967.9	318.2	135.5	1266.6	811.9
3446.3	24621.3	17406.2	825.2	4237.5	1579.1	573.3

C-1-17续表8

地 区	民政管理事务	行政运行	一般行政管理事务	机关服务	拥军优属
全 国	**3305417.4**	**768472.8**	**145644.0**	**22755.7**	**212913.0**
中央级	59927.8	5991.9	12358.7	249.4	298.4
北 京	186222.1	29646.1	4508.7	2275.4	6280.8
天 津	113669.6	16096.8	975.8	50.9	2360.6
河 北	80110.0	37178.2	3144.3	387.4	4025.8
山 西	63732.5	16171.4	2190.8	99.3	2781.6
内蒙古	90301.8	24595.8	2333.4	975.6	3301.0
辽 宁	194035.6	20901.2	8692.4	373.7	7159.3
吉 林	52288.6	9844.8	2534.4	171.8	1765.5
黑龙江	53687.0	10923.8	3893.2	492.9	1352.1
上 海	127537.2	19610.3			16470.8
江 苏	229400.1	60191.1	7761.3	750.6	19026.1
浙 江	218983.9	50128.4	9046.7	1262.0	15246.1
安 徽	71484.6	18071.2	7111.7	681.8	5641.7
福 建	60316.1	17828.2	2354.6	234.9	7267.4
江 西	39779.3	13103.4	3110.6	667.6	1389.7
山 东	169379.7	41747.0	7761.7	1752.7	16256.6
河 南	99605.5	32347.1	5504.3	2162.8	10313.3
湖 北	133907.1	29147.5	7184.8	1319.0	4762.8
湖 南	114913.2	37595.6	8914.6	1559.1	3285.2
广 东	247091.2	48531.7	8642.3	1905.5	28819.3
广 西	110122.2	23198.6	5497.0	369.4	14045.1
海 南	30870.7	6414.9	1264.3	74.9	4589.9
重 庆	93733.2	16125.4	2661.3	530.3	3718.7
四 川	166204.5	46143.6	7432.1	1128.3	7956.8
贵 州	78526.6	31506.3	2302.5	56.4	5117.3
云 南	137135.5	32051.9	4461.4	737.6	6338.2
西 藏	9921.2	4253.7	360.7		714.8
陕 西	135655.4	19929.2	2786.4	1343.4	3643.5
甘 肃	27739.9	12383.0	2321.1	265.5	938.3
青 海	19545.6	5019.1	551.2	233.1	630.1
宁 夏	21902.9	6401.0	4399.1	7.3	562.5
新 疆	67686.8	25394.6	3582.6	637.1	6853.7

单位：万元

老龄事务	民间组织管理	行政区划和地名管理	基层政权和社区建设	部队供应	其他民政管理事务支出
287730.3	**72527.1**	**50244.3**	**895866.8**	**57750.3**	**791513.1**
980.5	20761.4	1247.8	341.0	13732.2	3966.5
10046.1	6005.1	736.1	68149.0	4063.3	54511.5
978.1	244.6	312.5	66246.7	1292.2	25111.4
3235.3	485.1	4096.1	11585.6	1038.4	14933.8
2538.6	157.1	1394.0	21173.0	1039.6	16187.1
2223.1	5818.9	1650.5	11107.4	1177.0	37119.1
4133.7	766.5	1822.0	103626.5	1502.5	45057.8
2400.6	428.8	754.4	18402.0	269.0	15717.3
1396.7	147.6	543.4	19441.6	1204.8	14290.9
22413.3	6548.6	192.4	6248.2	1244.9	54808.7
24922.4	3891.4	2372.3	52249.6	1826.9	56408.4
25716.8	6497.3	9560.0	49363.7	2592.2	49570.7
6964.1	1151.0	884.6	15406.1	1148.6	14423.8
3157.4	311.1	1456.7	11337.3	1113.2	15255.3
6458.7	274.5	770.9	6542.1	801.3	6660.5
3712.8	2316.6	3194.4	55690.9	2192.9	34754.1
6155.9	871.4	1568.0	16961.0	2237.1	21484.6
4043.4	785.4	847.7	49729.4	2645.6	33441.5
5987.1	1402.9	2362.4	33105.8	1201.3	19499.2
18483.9	7964.7	2295.5	64661.3	3565.7	62221.3
8425.5	249.7	1126.5	28221.4	2146.3	26842.7
2151.3	523.6	872.0	3565.8	1164.4	10249.6
3906.0	378.1	1142.8	38966.6	692.7	25611.3
21026.8	2743.7	2322.2	43229.1	1151.4	33070.5
4241.3	231.1	1021.9	13756.9	1402.4	18890.5
45352.9	160.5	854.5	11627.0	2072.6	33478.9
100.6	15.0	1125.9	285.5	120.0	2945.0
33002.7	412.9	1058.0	53025.1	922.0	19532.2
1975.1	252.8	331.6	1600.4	275.2	7396.9
1005.0	94.5	175.9	8257.8	209.8	3369.1
1211.4	175.1	276.2	4819.4	1.0	4049.9
9383.2	460.1	1875.1	7143.6	1703.8	10653.0

C-1-17续表9

地 区	行政事业单位离退休	地方离退休人员经费	离休人员离休金	退休人员退休金	退职人员退职金	离退休人员其他费用
全 国	**442370.8**	**135669.0**	**8167.0**	**112322.8**	**2079.1**	**13100.1**
中央级	3966.6					
北 京	55100.1	40107.7	246.4	35965.5	656.5	3239.3
天 津	3877.5	2186.4	78.5	1510.3	18.7	578.9
河 北	21769.4	6016.5	769.6	4747.6	57.7	441.6
山 西	9934.4	1940.2	172.3	1610.3	16.9	140.7
内蒙古	14738.4	2137.7	138.1	1845.0		154.6
辽 宁	20390.5	3851.0	598.5	3001.0		251.5
吉 林	5912.7	1770.9	252.6	1425.1		93.2
黑龙江	10112.3	123.5	15.3	99.0	9.2	
上 海	11305.2	1304.2	84.7	918.7		300.8
江 苏	26638.2	13778.5	2021.5	9496.8	170.2	2090.0
浙 江	21657.1	6660.8	304.0	5705.8	37.0	614.0
安 徽	14425.6	3325.5	641.0	1841.0	359.3	484.2
福 建	23306.8	11994.0	115.7	11154.4	142.9	581.0
江 西	11159.2	4493.2	223.0	3786.2	157.9	326.1
山 东	13372.0	3565.9	208.5	2743.9	24.0	589.5
河 南	20269.2	5302.8	785.5	3786.5	159.3	571.5
湖 北	16736.9	6078.9	474.2	4901.5	18.4	684.8
湖 南	8964.7	3802.2	162.8	3439.5	53.0	146.9
广 东	37507.2	2500.5	162.3	2100.6	13.0	224.6
广 西	14097.6	742.4	23.0	664.6		54.8
海 南	4820.7	372.4	8.4	364.0		
重 庆	10407.6	521.0	8.3	491.1		21.6
四 川	21906.0	5125.8	177.8	4360.0	98.8	489.2
贵 州	2268.4	1653.5	81.6	1398.8	2.0	171.1
云 南	13123.2	2169.3	155.9	1618.8		394.6
西 藏	968.8	316.8		148.0		168.8
陕 西	8918.8	1334.6	88.0	1137.3	30.0	79.3
甘 肃	5324.6	1480.1	135.1	1161.1	8.8	175.1
青 海	2465.1	550.1	4.4	506.2	39.5	
宁 夏	2817.7	35.3		35.3		
新 疆	4108.3	427.3	30.0	358.9	6.0	32.4

单位：万元

一次性抚恤金	行政单位离退休	事业单位离退休	离退休人员管理机构	其他行政事业单位离退休支出	其他
7535.1	**167520.1**	**123365.0**	**2008.3**	**13808.4**	**1330701.1**
	2745.0	810.6	411.0		39448.6
2224.4	8242.7	3271.4	198.0	3280.3	127336.8
143.3	425.2	483.0		782.9	41112.9
355.2	7205.1	8058.0	19.4	470.4	31793.4
93.1	3598.7	4332.5		63.0	11987.3
19.7	7687.1	4913.6			85995.1
176.9	8313.9	7633.9	40.6	551.1	42692.7
89.0	2728.2	1322.6		91.0	39244.5
	2838.2	7087.7		62.9	4233.9
158.7	6070.4	3918.2		12.4	14938.0
956.6	8483.9	3872.1	14.0	489.7	150312.4
146.0	8990.7	5121.8	96.5	787.3	71016.8
406.0	7031.5	3910.0	53.5	105.1	33856.6
431.1	6349.8	4092.5	8.0	862.5	31733.1
144.4	4125.2	2198.8	216.5	125.5	9757.1
168.4	3222.3	6574.0		9.8	56996.0
382.2	7503.1	7075.9	42.6	344.8	42347.0
452.4	5539.0	2842.4	380.0	1896.6	27536.8
79.1	4026.4	887.8	1.5	246.8	16983.7
60.4	17007.7	17128.4	21.0	849.6	121689.2
49.3	6003.9	7239.3		112.0	41909.8
	2213.1	1842.2	385.6	7.4	11124.2
20.0	6290.7	2073.8		1522.1	25207.9
323.7	10084.0	6072.1	6.0	618.1	58964.8
32.6	329.9	285.0			28559.4
382.4	7563.0	3076.1	52.0	262.8	95439.8
	610.1	41.9			2219.2
53.3	3195.1	4210.5	20.0	158.6	22570.1
154.5	2781.7	1020.7	42.1		7836.8
	1359.3	542.4		13.3	16636.4
	2030.1	669.9		82.4	12998.4
32.4	2925.1	755.9			6222.4

C-1-18 支出水

地区	优抚对象整体抚恤水平	定期抚恤水平	伤残抚恤	定期补助水平	在乡复退军人定期定量补助水平
全国	**6185.88**	**11189.59**	**14852.66**	**2773.62**	**2614.96**
中央级					
北京	22775.60	23366.51	13327.45	3526.95	3189.43
天津	12218.74	19509.27	18044.63	5906.64	5760.87
河北	5108.70	12211.48	14537.04	2177.46	1989.98
山西	9033.03	9948.87	13453.20	2778.80	2975.12
内蒙古	17945.51	13438.40	15413.95	6519.15	6753.94
辽宁	7255.86	11659.99	13437.45	2938.49	3449.34
吉林	7939.69	14478.13	16937.98	2466.00	2404.81
黑龙江	7233.02	11979.91	12881.45	3782.65	3829.97
上海	21114.84	8771.82	22659.75	4085.62	3452.91
江苏	7681.43	16370.03	17944.43	2603.45	2823.04
浙江	7947.09	20673.88	17175.40	2909.31	2639.27
安徽	5298.26	10198.81	13214.53	2746.63	2522.93
福建	6204.44	11758.74	14527.60	2577.78	1902.50
江西	6390.74	9972.99	14100.58	3523.32	3676.02
山东	6573.35	10201.29	15454.38	2412.09	2341.33
河南	5097.44	9579.20	13353.92	2189.70	1853.13
湖北	6025.78	10062.27	14428.19	3103.14	3013.13
湖南	4303.99	9823.15	15369.18	2227.92	1887.67
广东	6902.82	14941.44	16533.89	3703.51	3056.57
广西	4262.51	10250.45	13020.28	2412.15	2501.87
海南	10627.61	7877.51	40186.79	4001.36	4305.95
重庆	5756.10	13263.48	14577.37	3331.92	3196.21
四川	5081.96	9730.72	13866.76	3098.76	3038.13
贵州	5326.16	10588.44	12795.01	3154.07	2749.31
云南	4593.56	11168.20	14557.75	2120.27	2046.86
西藏	14401.46	9559.61	12967.76	7952.18	5643.43
陕西	7812.17	11568.58	13711.77	3680.10	3597.65
甘肃	4222.48	13359.59	13514.86	1837.76	1212.99
青海	10429.92	13355.70	11076.65	3727.90	3275.80
宁夏	9228.23	19058.47	10844.98	2824.61	3095.63
新疆	13156.22	13175.26	15986.64	5738.13	6212.63

平情况

单位：元/人、年、元/个、年

在乡红军老战士定期定量补助费水平	红军失散人员定期定量补助水平	“参战”退伍军人生活补贴水平	“涉核”退伍军人生活补助水平	烈士纪念建筑物管理单位补助水平
38359.81	**15482.03**	**3950.04**	**4777.37**	**621279.02**
43000.00		6704.80	11108.11	1814000.00
		8449.87	8033.33	2132000.00
		4154.39	4463.38	524924.53
35857.14	17000.00	4320.85	4012.19	988610.17
33800.00	16500.00	6009.77	7396.40	765000.00
35000.00		4602.58	4529.14	437891.30
	76000.00	4570.73	4632.68	361033.33
37333.33	15533.33	4219.86	3689.50	349000.00
		9415.62	9401.14	6033272.73
	19000.00	4445.33	5369.40	967375.00
	18806.45	5560.80	6052.97	892625.00
32500.00	15427.64	4673.36	5258.23	866156.86
	17081.63	5975.97	6705.88	447722.22
32800.00	14624.14	5113.06	6934.41	481104.48
		4030.94	4179.44	979568.97
34375.00	15335.86	3917.48	4313.21	459121.21
33333.33	16808.33	4210.09	4268.89	416250.00
37666.67	15544.48	3149.78	8333.67	734261.90
	20510.20	5378.30	5209.19	257486.96
30666.67	19664.12	3998.98	5623.72	649086.96
	8225.00	3656.80	8200.93	3375.00
		3704.42	4659.78	215500.00
35636.36	16561.67	3587.33	4124.25	402769.70
50000.00	14666.67	3758.09	4041.83	133872.73
	19333.33	2247.52	6790.91	219656.25
30333.33		7583.33		269600.00
44787.88	17885.19	3931.62	4111.78	823268.29
42136.36	16500.00	3630.70	5719.02	434379.75
		11125.97	4231.59	500000.00
39000.00	15000.00	4570.91	6539.79	55888.89
36333.33	14000.00	5844.21	5117.56	1438142.86

C-1-18续表1

地 区	荣誉军人康复医院补助水平	荣誉军人康复医院在院人员补助水平	复员军人疗养院补助水平	复员军人疗养院在院人员补助水平	复退军人精神病院补助水平
全 国	**16661477.27**	**10392.28**	**11131421.05**	**7225.74**	**10276112.24**
中央级					
北 京					
天 津			20964000.00	4473.59	19387000.00
河 北	19892000.00		13685250.00	1280.49	29699000.00
山 西	3417400.00	18501.91	48962000.00		10003571.43
内蒙古	13015000.00		400000.00		4832500.00
辽 宁	16965000.00	36672.68			4337200.00
吉 林	22413000.00				942285.71
黑龙江	50090000.00	16038.62			16440000.00
上 海	12407000.00	18133.33			
江 苏	33320000.00		4197750.00	10352.10	85159000.00
浙 江	58365000.00		60000.00		4763000.00
安 徽	21706000.00				33570000.00
福 建	5129000.00	11333.33			8630333.33
江 西	30896000.00	12480.50	905500.00	9618.56	230000.00
山 东	62660500.00	9385.71	24500142.86	11065.43	14865000.00
河 南	21822000.00	16311.74	6863500.00	26009.90	57321000.00
湖 北	36936000.00		90000.00		13325818.18
湖 南	9601000.00		3100000.00		7977875.00
广 东	4433500.00	7031.64	8773500.00	15011.62	5192000.00
广 西	15199500.00				16638500.00
海 南					
重 庆	6600750.00	9093.17			
四 川	7980500.00	103019.14	568333.33	7110.34	5655000.00
贵 州	6284500.00	6267.32			
云 南	6600000.00				3332500.00
西 藏					
陕 西	20814000.00	20297.92	4213500.00	14552.37	9109333.33
甘 肃	6871000.00				1969000.00
青 海					
宁 夏					
新 疆	15069000.00	23288.86			310000.00

单位：元/个、年、元/人、年

复退军人精神病院在院人员补助水平	光荣院补助水平	光荣院在院人员补助水平	军队离休干部支出水平	军队退休干部支出水平	军队无军籍职工支出水平	孤儿补助水平
5090.42	**617715.80**	**5958.93**	**144557.50**	**84454.34**	**39364.21**	**9986.21**
	2938100.00	24542.61	101351.13	89389.80	41300.83	60590.29
7133.69	4590333.33	9791.04	99489.40	83446.16	43130.84	14556.56
1713.46	894098.59	6337.62	134015.95	83668.55	32867.92	8264.89
3605.22	762241.76	12193.41	115658.90	62476.85	33115.31	7665.52
1744.80	1339758.62	9271.02	109512.74	87887.18	45070.49	14670.58
6215.78	1768434.78	19028.56	360907.40	55629.11	38399.28	16104.25
1730.84	216260.87	3380.80	105645.83	89828.86	39535.36	7354.93
419808.31	379442.31	7152.52	115277.93	87915.73	43307.65	7772.96
			85169.18	83892.28	42916.21	35815.48
	577363.64	10067.67	130575.71	87550.07	68082.20	12684.85
1405.00	422000.00	12140.01	116941.27	88382.39	50561.29	16509.43
	794347.83	7376.80	114892.31	87754.97	30575.32	8061.50
11979.01	490160.00	7174.10	127087.04	91850.78	39508.77	8770.08
4297.58	256827.59	2888.80	131822.99	86726.82	25677.86	12387.41
9769.04	758949.15	5436.98	112503.34	89497.80	42679.46	11204.63
7250.00	301195.88	2334.21	108913.22	79956.57	31548.91	7812.58
6355.10	774920.45	5450.77	106423.30	94655.67	42704.94	8393.48
3502.00	769755.91	5573.65	95737.92	68766.84	31011.79	9041.70
7064.20	471068.97	16600.52	150171.93	104953.92	51973.25	10523.34
222.27	155459.46	2731.31	127182.93	86866.63	35628.11	8696.85
	441100.00	11162.61	92102.04	151792.87	13544.01	12101.77
	1847125.00	18287.02	169517.86	87391.15	39762.81	9549.99
3001.50	441836.36	6090.83	117696.32	82609.03	28945.83	10539.57
	321477.27	6867.92	158160.43	79802.45	44752.16	9188.30
	30000.00		260627.70	73859.67	22966.62	10715.63
				111578.43	9855.90	15838.13
11409.67	1084105.26	8111.93	111670.31	94429.54	37481.10	9665.64
	150000.00		107545.76	93390.31	31002.37	8292.06
	173333.33	1748.50	42000.00	107080.91	51275.18	7832.84
	625000.00	31925.89	20723.40	8613.79	31504.24	7279.78
	717482.76	1639.31	239668.67	112512.51	43725.80	9190.30

C-1-18续表2

地 区	康复辅具机构(站)专项拨款支出水平	补贴火化场人员水平	补贴殡葬类单位补助水平	社会福利院补助水平	社会福利院在院人员生活费补助水平
全 国	**3578370.37**	**551.65**	**791820.14**	**2781180.26**	**5238.39**
中央级					
北 京	3752000.00	1890.12	1600259.26	7114777.78	4607.81
天 津		117.07	3008964.29	8187000.00	11170.09
河 北	6540000.00	591.66	915284.15	2842025.64	5947.62
山 西	4000000.00	7874.52	202600.00	3739523.81	8401.11
内蒙古	8438000.00	682.94	896736.43	2853346.15	7853.34
辽 宁	530000.00	786.73	626208.19	3587454.55	4141.37
吉 林		439.27	300965.75	1479410.71	4623.23
黑龙江	4149000.00	183.60	185288.59	1921063.49	5666.36
上 海				13164272.73	5975.11
江 苏	1000000.00	688.49	1064569.77	8232982.46	8998.40
浙 江	3300000.00	1080.26	1465475.56	4719031.25	2499.09
安 徽	900000.00	591.43	624590.43	1888344.83	6540.19
福 建		672.56	767316.46	1945043.48	8386.86
江 西	11800000.00	257.60	212230.22	618007.35	2915.70
山 东	16060000.00	146.97	440277.46	6887000.00	13629.13
河 南	3024000.00	529.05	234054.05	1482477.61	5373.95
湖 北	486000.00	121.65	1849258.43	3327289.26	3562.96
湖 南	3728000.00	290.03	369525.86	1916279.57	1588.97
广 东	100000.00	224.26	1633682.54	4087617.83	6900.80
广 西		141.56	1585644.86	1633300.97	3035.63
海 南		15.05	1112058.82	3589500.00	59.82
重 庆		1412.49	334258.62	4863611.11	3067.71
四 川	5102000.00	368.61	869390.16	2733468.97	4520.71
贵 州	500000.00	417.83	312939.19	826714.29	5100.84
云 南	1200000.00	1266.80	411561.90	1100390.24	2915.43
西 藏		3357.06	1484000.00	149189.87	2760.04
陕 西	2804000.00	572.21	513711.71	2975542.86	6880.18
甘 肃		969.98	902400.00	959730.77	3449.33
青 海		17.77	59428.57	7072454.55	1657.36
宁 夏		574.00	67111.11	1726272.73	4799.54
新 疆	8000000.00	2325.65	1208880.50	2269584.27	6878.94

单位：元/个、年、元/人、年、元/人次

儿童福利院补助水平	儿童福利院在院人员生活费补助水平	精神病人福利院补助水平	精神病人福利院在院人员生活费补助水平	城市居民最低生活保障补助水平（不含春节补助）	农村最低生活保障补助水平（不含春节补助）	农村集中五保供养救助水平
2828038.53	**11311.01**	**10422974.36**	**4887.26**	**3580.53**	**1571.32**	**4577.54**
1788727.27	3872.53	21264500.00	5932.54	7587.00	5569.77	9204.68
15331000.00	11669.41	30590000.00	5254.32	6528.07	3538.29	8369.86
497000.00	12962.96			3222.92	1477.82	5559.85
2005142.86	8990.24	4000000.00		3592.99	1804.05	4966.30
5054000.00	19086.24	9367800.00	6909.60	4940.94	2424.96	5934.81
4268200.00	10246.93			4731.92	2019.86	5777.59
1361611.11	21140.63	7477000.00	4836.01	4035.12	1444.45	4575.06
3115266.67	18548.39	23372428.57	23187.47	3876.20	1704.28	5361.97
19969000.00	18665.30	35771666.67	521.62	7026.87	4341.09	7004.37
6064285.71	19475.04	20825181.82	6096.17	4243.68	2640.54	6856.89
6336250.00	3623.30	18584500.00	5685.88	5426.73	3577.22	7769.35
2920333.33	11844.97	254000.00	2640.53	3859.27	1692.11	3677.67
2227916.67	10429.92	8074428.57	6122.69	3306.33	1724.98	6114.76
1758800.00	11722.34	27536666.67	3971.87	3238.74	1736.50	3318.50
7344944.44	14927.94	19962000.00	23249.70	3715.50	1756.77	4854.21
2962500.00	6541.63	3077857.14	94.55	2680.92	1249.93	3500.95
1954288.46	8064.36	11290666.67	2262.04	3491.22	1329.39	4092.98
1709222.22	10351.33	2012300.00	795.87	3146.22	1323.10	4777.10
2510810.81	17474.55	23466666.67	11169.23	4474.43	2123.50	9596.05
1980428.57	12113.15	24652250.00	3771.81	3261.36	1295.87	4650.41
415000.00	3995.74			3628.34	1853.56	7144.18
5735555.56	23217.25	13847444.44	4637.10	3483.22	1977.02	4851.47
1673291.67	10794.08	2872888.89	1980.44	2702.88	1249.83	4018.98
1638000.00	10569.20	1595391.30	3382.75	3322.91	1301.97	2122.27
667000.00	4860.74	3633800.00	211.09	3185.27	1477.20	2485.58
588266.67	4615.07			4649.74	1019.27	3309.12
6439333.33	9290.96	13329000.00	5111.61	3982.23	1865.09	6019.10
1899529.41	8257.23	7967500.00	2425.62	3247.94	1371.96	4139.64
1080285.71	1415.30	600000.00		3412.55	1978.54	3979.55
2863000.00	12104.04	5000000.00		2756.15	1528.35	7575.15
2938627.45	10353.82	20695750.00	8401.15	3405.44	1553.64	4822.04

C-1-18续表3

地区	农村分散五保供养补助水平	流浪乞讨人员救助单位补助水平	救助流浪乞讨人员每次补助水平	临时救助户次补助水平	资助参加合作医疗补助水平	资助参加医疗保险补助水平
全　国	**3101.84**	**712588.06**	**629.11**	**885.27**	**64.31**	**94.89**
中央级						
北　京	8723.32	1561409.09	284.17	2539.68	58.30	872.82
天　津	7370.19	1104153.85	1590.15	492.48	69.26	200.77
河　北	2934.71	492571.43	891.21	1240.23	69.26	116.54
山　西	2485.81	301483.87	529.97	504.12	59.95	76.03
内蒙古	3815.63	913550.00	327.74	1252.65	61.96	76.14
辽　宁	3192.52	659794.12	1161.46	247.43	77.13	196.01
吉　林	1821.22	436480.77	661.44	332.28	116.71	52.73
黑龙江	3591.87	606815.79	1029.58	926.39	69.75	85.25
上　海	5659.24	5877300.00	1127.82	612.03	106.68	421.40
江　苏	5361.89	928752.38	1194.09	1135.59	109.20	328.23
浙　江	3843.42	1232129.87	1290.46	2463.74	147.90	244.58
安　徽	2268.79	968800.00	802.89	1602.69	68.62	66.40
福　建	5319.26	584202.90	420.20	956.92	73.12	100.17
江　西	3172.34	330504.76	669.62	1607.98	34.41	103.20
山　东	3576.18	1325569.23	869.36	977.80	84.22	167.80
河　南	2283.26	881168.32	495.73	705.84	63.23	101.62
湖　北	2587.96	520756.58	401.45	515.89	68.58	33.15
湖　南	2487.74	301556.18	463.05	486.66	61.36	69.54
广　东	6539.32	2642947.37	830.99	802.71	79.13	155.88
广　西	2499.99	704839.51	779.41	2267.27	52.12	71.09
海　南	5111.01	276125.00	1151.63	699.71	64.02	94.72
重　庆	4366.34	719568.18	793.61	1428.38	54.88	65.40
四　川	3236.72	413240.74	844.00	655.19	71.46	83.20
贵　州	1451.31	493613.33	505.61	619.82	45.84	36.38
云　南	1414.02	148951.92	555.46	573.12	62.32	87.42
西　藏	2679.75	306428.57	333.17	492.70	277.48	103.93
陕　西	4902.49	585648.35	749.01	2036.64	82.52	110.22
甘　肃	3005.69	344232.14	597.71	2063.67	27.97	36.87
青　海	3600.07	1186233.33	1275.80	1153.86	53.17	80.96
宁　夏	2876.72	180533.33	532.10	1459.79	58.25	68.75
新　疆	2397.22	516674.42	1288.42	553.95	63.03	84.25

单位：元/个、年、元/人、年、元/人次

直接医疗救助补助水平	门诊救助人次补助水平	住院救助人次补助水平	优抚对象医疗补助支出水平	救灾物资储备中心补助水平	老龄机构补助水平	军供站补助水平
852.20	**186.01**	**1627.97**	**661.78**	**932930.88**	**1124825.25**	**1127935.55**
1510.59	905.41	3318.04	2983.77	410650.00	5287421.05	1231303.03
919.81	32.49	2496.04	3233.35	2658500.00	698642.86	6461000.00
1861.59	721.97	2264.99	1037.98	682272.73	414782.05	314666.67
2448.89	1056.29	2814.05	892.24	441186.67	228702.70	1299500.00
1998.16	708.64	2492.80	1859.76	2457333.33	585026.32	1961666.67
521.14	113.88	1221.24	1171.76	711222.22	616970.15	653260.87
645.45	235.23	1201.12	1139.68	279687.50	510765.96	244545.45
1600.15	382.99	3061.06	1237.49	839300.00	135601.94	926769.23
1996.97	281.55	4142.04	1572.31		11206650.00	1556125.00
311.33	72.56	1245.50	636.36	406857.14	3665058.82	1014944.44
466.22	155.75	1240.93	1519.38	989238.10	2735829.79	1080083.33
928.54	513.60	1006.46	481.94	296307.69	669625.00	267116.28
490.32	123.02	1280.96	801.30	262640.00	501174.60	654823.53
918.14	151.89	2734.11	1183.10	597937.50	598027.78	572357.14
2516.76	562.17	2775.19	691.97	1594166.67	247520.00	843423.08
917.38	184.28	1098.45	442.64	1218076.92	603519.61	699093.75
978.39	380.01	1208.09	380.15	603875.00	481357.14	2035076.92
981.81	420.35	1378.76	272.31	528142.86	450157.89	667388.89
820.40	183.38	2237.75	888.91	779470.59	1665216.22	1876684.21
1886.14	1174.40	1959.24	484.19	1452600.00	1428050.85	1262529.41
2712.91	473.21	4649.51	1355.24	3802333.33	2689125.00	3881333.33
245.67	63.03	807.62	518.74	539078.95	1260000.00	769666.67
911.02	295.57	1218.05	606.44	534448.98	987173.71	411214.29
2289.67	1060.91	2419.73	460.90	2616857.14	437247.42	1274909.09
819.78	437.98	941.92	527.26	768975.00	3571094.49	609588.24
3135.65	4304.07	3071.09	1304.33	501175.00	251500.00	400000.00
2577.43	1028.17	3218.90	803.63	620400.00	3235558.82	658571.43
1931.52	303.67	2578.56	887.20	228439.02	195554.46	275200.00
986.31	128.44	1783.96	3326.91	190467.53	239285.71	419600.00
758.19	271.24	1541.66	1824.56	123181.82	465923.08	5000.00
594.42	53.02	2033.61	2399.60	2230263.16	400991.45	1135866.67

C-1-19 中央专项基本

地 区	建设规模(平方米)	地方配套资金合计	中央对地方投资合计	社区发改投资[2014] 1325号				养老发改	
				建设规模	小计	中央投资	地方投资	建设规模	小计
全 国	**3832772**	**509033**	**290000**	**255806**	**48414**	**19600**	**28814**	**3300038**	**691813**
北 京	20881	16067	1000					20881	17067
天 津									
河 北	182229	26122	15400	10540	3590	1200	2390	165039	36652
山 西	142973	26166	10200	9939	2170	800	1370	130434	33666
内蒙古	86038	8748	10800	12451	2672	800	1872	66567	15472
辽 宁	141027	20541	11100	8477	2001	800	1201	126050	28300
吉 林	118175	14932	11100	10528	2533	800	1733	101840	21953
黑龙江	130750	16120	12700	15350	3070	800	2270	108800	21760
上 海	26271	14303	1200					26271	15503
江 苏	118337	24659	4400					106237	25959
浙 江	108755	29651	5100					99447	31289
安 徽	359796	36079	15500	27176	4011	1200	2811	315110	44388
福 建	83258	13276	4700					77663	16785
江 西	262023	27683	13000	16330	2980	1200	1780	234593	35483
山 东	170152	39272	4700					154592	40860
河 南	180779	14131	16200	25806	2616	1200	1416	146873	26385
湖 北	227428	18417	16200	17359	2601	1200	1401	198209	29636
湖 南	255213	38755	16200	18540	3746	1200	2546	214991	46869
广 东	138438	28791	4400					133338	31896
广 西	88462	4187	11200	6670	1189	800	389	74552	12850
海 南	39486	5072	4800	2800	700	400	300	34186	8547
重 庆	97814	17200	10600	7758	1531	800	731	84056	25069
四 川	149569	14925	15500	11000	2315	1200	1115	130769	26550
贵 州	127915	9854	11200	7990	1416	800	616	110820	18180
云 南	88404	6238	11200	7744	1333	800	533	73460	14665
西 藏	21740		4400	1600	400	400		20140	4000
陕 西	168840	17221	10600	11600	1761	800	961	146540	24020
甘 肃	92000	3603	10600	8000	1200	800	400	76000	11403
青 海	32070	2893	5700	2400	742	400	342	25050	6650
宁 夏	51678	8158	4800	10248	2782	400	2382	38430	9426
新 疆	68600	1785	10600	5500	1055	800	255	59100	10530
兵 团		4184	4900						

建设投资对账单

单位：平方米、万元

投资[2014]1337号		儿童发改 投资[2014] 1341号				社会事务发改 投资[2014]544号			
中央投资	地方投资	建设规模	小计	中央投资	地方投资	建设规模	小计	中央投资	地方投资
243900	**447913**	**223257**	**47052**	**20000**	**27052**	**53671**	**11754**	**6500**	**5254**
1000	16067								
13500	23152	6650	1280	700	580				
9000	24666	2600	530	400	130				
9000	6472	7020	1404	1000	404				
9500	18800	6500	1340	800	540				
9500	12453	5807	1546	800	746				
9500	12260	6600	1320	800	520	18960	2670	1600	1070
1200	14303								
4000	21959	12100	3100	400	2700				
4600	26689	9308	3462	500	2962				
13500	30888	17510	3180	800	2380				
4000	12785	5595	1191	700	491				
11000	24483	11100	2220	800	1420				
4300	36560	15560	3112	400	2712				
14000	12385	8100	1330	1000	330				
14000	15636	11860	2380	1000	1380				
14000	32869	21682	4340	1000	3340				
4000	27896	5100	1295	400	895				
9500	3350	7240	1348	900	448				
4000	4547	2500	625	400	225				
9000	16069	6000	1200	800	400				
13500	13050	7800	1560	800	760				
9400	8780	9105	1458	1000	458				
9400	5265	7200	1440	1000	440				
4000									
9000	15020	10700	2040	800	1240				
9000	2403	8000	1600	800	800				
4500	2150	4620	1201	800	401				
4000	5426	3000	750	400	350				
9000	1530	4000	800	800					
						34711	9084	4900	4184

C-1-20 民政事业基本

地 区	在建项目数	#使用彩票公益金项目数	在建项目总投资	开工累计完成投资	本年计划投资	本年实际完成投资
全 国	**14001**	**7373**	**9151903.8**	**5012875.8**	**2659804.7**	**2822436.1**
中央级	8		38567.0	56760.5	13000.0	12210.3
北 京	76		465603.4	332254.5	64364.3	83248.8
天 津	5	4	77463.0	23242.6	12817.1	14429.6
河 北	428	281	129118.2	76185.8	32856.8	39207.0
山 西	50	33	42273.7	9598.5	9398.2	4831.5
内蒙古	61	52	112561.8	59173.9	16512.2	26968.4
辽 宁	147	117	87412.7	65039.0	20104.0	28437.8
吉 林	340	8	21542.7	11646.3	6289.4	6565.4
黑龙江	3	2	43373.6	36723.9	4378.1	4833.2
上 海	9	4	37833.1	28497.8	5906.0	12823.6
江 苏	2575	393	1914183.1	1063799.3	742700.2	661464.6
浙 江	90	61	495053.7	221996.0	75659.2	83139.4
安 徽	445	207	187623.6	119633.6	126481.8	101318.0
福 建	125	103	226385.3	88216.0	33631.4	31540.6
江 西	1553	1303	482210.6	234922.8	128038.3	186887.8
山 东	2117	1270	1116144.1	535475.6	284122.9	307322.2
河 南	188	140	168836.4	91931.9	34217.4	44439.9
湖 北	554	178	525601.2	321792.9	122853.9	147206.6
湖 南	382	299	218026.3	127555.7	48901.6	57064.1
广 东	184	123	558623.4	203781.9	95277.7	88695.2
广 西	1777	1263	242229.3	104966.9	65073.5	69119.6
海 南	44	13	40057.7	14357.0	22776.1	14024.5
重 庆	742	490	289814.1	146654.0	88634.1	98018.7
四 川	204	83	165640.3	97413.1	71691.1	77364.5
贵 州	525	356	429000.2	257476.8	177784.2	189916.1
云 南	476	149	160598.4	104316.0	55222.5	85480.8
西 藏	66	1	63319.3	49237.0	38929.0	45693.0
陕 西	159	103	216057.3	153931.7	73723.8	72658.3
甘 肃	85	50	116744.5	47633.5	22038.0	29837.5
青 海	207	63	69855.4	57774.1	40867.1	56089.1
宁 夏	28	4	153184.5	87051.6	33896.1	33836.9
新 疆	348	220	256965.9	183835.6	91658.7	107763.1

建设投资情况总表

单位：万元、个、平方米、张

国家预算内投资	国内贷款	利用外资	福利彩票公益金	其他	本年完工项目数	未投入使用项目建设床位数
1042891.7	**34708.2**	**16680.0**	**575015.5**	**1153140.7**	**11355**	**379057**
12210.3					3	
50997.0				32251.8	12	4471
5800.2			8629.4		2	150
16719.7	100.0		13456.8	8930.5	456	10861
2834.5			1407.0	590.0	27	2184
13970.1			8928.5	4069.8	20	5428
4617.6	57.0		19875.6	3887.6	145	3436
3449.6			2197.0	918.8	16	2252
172.0			4661.2		5	150
9993.0			1402.0	1428.6	5	948
203292.8			45658.9	412512.9	2034	39424
50373.8			21958.1	10807.5	28	16140
68311.9	1870.0	340.0	8813.8	21982.3	407	21629
9579.6	29.8		12434.1	9497.1	133	7407
47141.2	10.0	5000.0	62979.1	71757.5	1359	22105
106626.9			62072.4	138622.9	1782	67607
15547.9			8131.4	20760.6	136	9172
44056.8		10460.0	27688.1	65001.7	432	18227
12339.7	240.0		14255.9	30228.5	364	11733
55325.8	310.0	80.0	21851.8	11127.6	128	17440
25660.6			27892.9	15566.1	1471	20558
4861.8	314.7		1859.6	6988.4	23	1637
32037.7	1400.0		33709.2	30871.8	757	13239
21999.5	1551.7		25004.0	28809.3	182	11995
76904.3	3345.0	800.0	26976.9	81889.9	343	27179
19645.7	24200.0		13407.1	28228.0	370	7949
38775.0			720.0	6198.0	64	4187
17380.4			15202.3	40075.6	132	6492
19816.7			7234.8	2786.0	63	4238
21587.5			12344.6	22157.0	147	5533
4412.0			106.8	29318.1	28	1197
26450.1	1280.0		64156.2	15876.8	281	14089

C-1-21 提供住宿的机构

地 区	在建项目数	#使用彩票公益金项目数	在建项目总投资	开工累计完成投资	本年计划投资	本年实际完成投资
全 国	**6319**	**3745**	**5820157.0**	**2960674.5**	**1474442.5**	**1560077.4**
中央级						
北 京	72		337571.4	274555.5	51780.9	51122.1
天 津	1		3200.0	3194.9	3200.0	3194.9
河 北	197	107	78963.8	50764.1	20156.1	24269.7
山 西	19	13	35121.7	6059.9	5529.2	2119.9
内蒙古	38	37	84119.9	43658.4	11319.7	21586.6
辽 宁	46	42	45163.2	26777.0	10478.0	11588.0
吉 林	15	7	16807.9	8531.5	3038.1	4093.1
黑龙江	1		42992.6	36663.9	4378.1	4773.2
上 海	6	2	32734.7	24359.7	3415.0	10796.2
江 苏	1021	135	1173407.7	474902.5	292972.9	234939.6
浙 江	63	43	363773.0	162555.7	56254.7	61417.0
安 徽	269	167	104946.4	78259.0	78783.0	70105.4
福 建	116	102	161066.0	68881.2	22607.9	19750.4
江 西	1062	897	423908.0	202214.0	109571.0	165487.0
山 东	753	399	816109.4	334551.7	185218.9	196337.2
河 南	146	112	139013.7	69036.9	29233.9	33953.2
湖 北	229	79	341723.3	197518.6	75871.7	93537.1
湖 南	208	175	159563.6	100531.9	31882.8	40244.3
广 东	82	58	289279.5	95802.5	50099.9	46059.4
广 西	718	600	147196.6	47844.4	36096.0	29580.4
海 南	21	6	12301.6	4966.3	8017.1	4633.8
重 庆	359	240	132690.2	80094.2	38811.1	47459.5
四 川	129	78	109010.9	61018.7	42121.1	46045.5
贵 州	273	156	214688.4	130810.3	94739.2	100516.7
云 南	82	63	54257.3	28190.8	18823.4	24950.6
西 藏	22		52710.0	42309.0	33249.0	39959.0
陕 西	36	9	98789.9	57770.8	35267.4	33244.2
甘 肃	62	38	46785.5	20863.3	6881.5	11830.3
青 海	50	20	24643.0	21695.5	18405.5	20010.5
宁 夏	13	3	85317.4	75520.7	31195.0	30009.0
新 疆	210	157	192300.4	130771.6	65044.4	76463.6

基本建设投资情况

单位：万元、个、平方米、张

国家预算内投资	国内贷款	利用外资	福利彩票公益金	其他	本年完工项目数	未投入使用项目建设床位数
664061.7	**7038.7**	**10420.0**	**394262.5**	**484294.5**	**5066**	**344819**
50422.1				700.0	11	4271
3194.9						150
6914.3			8668.4	8687.0	223	10336
1328.9			791.0		9	2118
13393.9			5723.4	2469.3	17	5418
2358.2	57.0		7132.8	2040.0	44	3153
1677.3			1497.0	918.8	11	2252
172.0			4601.2		5	150
9406.2				1390.0	3	948
134688.1			26930.0	73321.5	690	35446
33150.9			18750.4	9515.7	27	16120
48551.5	1870.0	340.0	7163.8	12180.1	259	20556
8161.1			7775.2	3814.1	104	7387
39169.0	10.0	5000.0	54888.0	66420.0	904	21167
51523.4			42766.3	102047.5	668	55236
9946.0			5916.5	18090.7	105	9082
33970.0		5000.0	18949.5	35617.6	185	17565
6688.7	240.0		11878.1	21437.5	216	9806
27376.4	310.0	80.0	12987.3	5305.7	45	17410
14343.1			12967.7	2269.6	588	15814
1799.9			1294.6	1539.3	16	1437
13570.4			27172.2	6716.9	317	12842
13504.2	1551.7		15063.0	15926.6	110	11809
53077.4	3000.0		20396.1	24043.2	138	26434
9265.5			7879.3	7805.8	48	7648
35559.0			150.0	4250.0	11	4176
11434.8			11116.3	10693.1	41	5317
6700.4			4613.9	516.0	51	4188
3598.5			4443.0	11969.0	28	2578
3197.0			83.0	26729.0	12	1162
15918.6			52664.5	7880.5	180	12843

C-1-22 不提供住宿的机构

地 区	在建项目数	#使用彩票公益金项目数	在建项目总投资	开工累计完成投资	本年计划投资	本年实际完成投资
全 国	**5578**	**2525**	**905670.4**	**568960.3**	**361097.1**	**415055.6**
中央级						
北 京	2		89131.9	30280.9	6644.9	28054.7
天 津						
河 北	207	156	13904.1	8051.7	5422.2	6100.1
山 西	28	18	3197.0	1479.6	2027.0	1144.6
内蒙古	8	2	3869.6	2431.1	895.4	895.4
辽 宁	44	37	17848.1	14852.6	3187.6	4435.4
吉 林	323		2008.8	1414.8	772.3	772.3
黑龙江						
上 海	1	1	179.8	161.1		92.4
江 苏	1388	243	165989.2	108334.6	97272.6	94862.6
浙 江	10	8	11378.0	7933.0	3018.0	1542.7
安 徽	92	31	26941.6	15591.0	17277.8	13989.0
福 建	3		9530.5	2116.1	610.5	676.5
江 西	300	230	26935.6	17608.8	12902.3	14548.8
山 东	983	529	147833.7	110187.9	53185.3	69530.3
河 南	22	13	15860.3	11270.6	672.1	2158.6
湖 北	219	71	44404.9	32960.3	16398.2	20857.5
湖 南	151	107	42034.7	18188.8	9525.8	10278.8
广 东	51	35	18647.5	17675.3	5563.9	5554.9
广 西	679	460	18608.2	15034.3	12147.4	12935.2
海 南	9	4	8495.4	1892.7	6342.7	1892.7
重 庆	345	237	26630.9	17906.7	16406.7	17846.7
四 川	66	3	30388.4	19757.1	16794.4	17265.1
贵 州	210	186	47646.2	22137.2	16625.3	17465.7
云 南	123	46	13256.8	7732.7	8363.9	6840.8
西 藏	41		6654.3	5350.0	4322.0	4156.0
陕 西	54	39	11582.9	7278.9	4722.4	6504.9
甘 肃	11	8	39174.0	15901.2	12086.5	13304.2
青 海	120	22	20521.0	19863.0	10343.0	19863.0
宁 夏	9		9362.1	9362.1	2501.1	2959.1
新 疆	79	39	33654.9	26206.2	15065.8	18527.6

基本建设投资情况

单位：万元、个、平方米、张

国家预算内投资	国内贷款	利用外资	福利彩票公益金	其他	本年完工项目数	未投入使用项目建设床位数（社区社施）
162020.7	**1280.0**	**300.0**	**65427.2**	**186027.7**	**4656**	**34238**
574.9				27479.8	1	200
4205.0			1819.4	75.7	220	525
796.6			250.0	98.0	18	66
195.2			600.0	100.2	2	10
270.0			2461.8	1703.6	47	283
772.3					4	
53.8				38.6	1	
38338.3			7089.7	49434.6	1265	3978
347.7			1120.0	75.0		20
10494.6			861.2	2633.2	88	1073
170.5			456.0	50.0	26	20
6198.2			3578.1	4772.5	282	938
31097.4			12206.0	26226.9	748	12371
1438.1			420.6	299.9	15	90
4768.8			2291.0	13797.7	169	662
4351.0			1450.8	4477.0	136	1927
1650.0			2018.3	1886.6	48	30
4825.4			7703.8	406.0	634	4744
855.7			354.0	683.0	3	200
7474.1			3368.3	7004.3	318	397
5139.8			580.0	11545.3	66	186
3593.7		300.0	3746.5	9825.5	187	745
2642.6			1650.0	2548.2	117	301
1966.0			242.0	1948.0	51	11
3052.4			1208.5	2244.0	29	1175
10088.3			1445.9	1770.0	7	50
8478.0			2440.0	8945.0	93	2955
570.0				2389.1	15	35
7612.3	1280.0		6065.3	3570.0	66	1246

C-1-23 其他社会服务机构

地 区	在建项目数	#使用彩票公益金项目数	在建项目总投资	开工累计完成投资	本年计划投资
全 国	**876**	**379**	**1516314.4**	**824896.0**	**353360.1**
中央级					
北 京	2		38900.10	27418.10	5938.50
天 津	4	4	74263.0	20047.7	9617.1
河 北	14	10	10031.3	6963.9	971.5
山 西					
内蒙古	4	3	7041.0	4285.0	861.8
辽 宁	49	38	24006.6	23014.6	6043.6
吉 林	1	1	1700.0	1700.0	1700.0
黑龙江					
上 海					
江 苏	86	7	220289.2	159462.2	64436.2
浙 江	11	6	74328.6	42104.2	13793.0
安 徽	7	3	29888.0	19467.0	12226.0
福 建	3		17588.8	9360.8	4058.0
江 西	184	169	14156.0	5739.0	2354.0
山 东	26	14	103516.0	52919.7	28632.1
河 南	7	5	11656.8	10173.8	2870.8
湖 北	28	11	107737.0	70553.0	24155.0
湖 南	9	4	14620.0	7521.0	6185.0
广 东	33	17	202165.7	65882.1	29896.5
广 西	27	21	37275.6	17144.7	4290.6
海 南	5	2	17027.6	5268.7	6183.2
重 庆	30	13	129384.0	47544.1	32307.3
四 川	8	1	4788.0	2982.3	1406.0
贵 州	22	5	141151.0	82241.0	49287.0
云 南	245	19	74198.1	54022.7	23117.8
西 藏					
陕 西	12	3	69073.0	59888.0	10635.0
甘 肃	2		4100.0	3510.0	1500.0
青 海	7	4	3223.4	2891.6	2951.6
宁 夏	4		58300.0	1500.0	200.0
新 疆	46	19	25905.6	21290.8	7742.5

基本建设投资情况

单位：万元、个、平方米

本年实际完成投资	国家预算内投资	国内贷款	利用外资	福利彩票公益金	其他	本年完工项目数
377871.5	**132695.0**	**26389.5**	**5960.0**	**56778.5**	**156048.5**	**569**
4072.00					4072.00	
11234.7	2605.3			8629.4		2
2689.9	1239.4	100.0		1312.0	38.5	8
1003.0	381.0			475.0	147.0	
12019.6	1594.6			10281.0	144.0	46
1700.0	1000.0			700.0		1
44881.2	21452.4			7891.0	15537.8	23
17876.3	15747.2			929.1	1200.0	1
10907.0	3528.0			660.0	6719.0	4
4215.8	748.0	29.8		40.0	3398.0	2
3491.0	1474.0			1473.0	544.0	167
22900.1	13742.1			4898.0	4260.0	16
6877.5	4163.8			343.7	2370.0	5
26070.0	4710.0		5460.0	4891.0	11009.0	12
5227.0	620.0			355.0	4252.0	4
27346.5	24357.8			355.3	2633.4	24
10007.2	589.9			1856.8	7560.5	13
5268.7		314.7		211.0	4743.0	3
31603.5	10748.2	1400.0		3168.7	16286.6	10
2882.3	1484.9			60.0	1337.4	2
53825.0	11170.0	345.0	500.0	471.0	41339.0	5
48759.7	5995.2	24200.0		2111.5	16453.0	182
10198.0	2836.0			374.0	6988.0	8
1310.0	700.0			110.0	500.0	2
2891.6	1063.0			1698.6	130.0	3
200.0					200.0	
8413.9	744.2			3483.4	4186.3	26

C-1-24 其他基本

地 区	在建项目数	#使用彩票公益金项目数	在建项目总投资	开工累计完成投资	本年计划投资
全 国	**1228**	**724**	**909762.0**	**658345.0**	**470905.0**
中央级	8		38567.00	56760.50	13000.00
北 京					
天 津					
河 北	10	8	26219.0	10406.1	6307.0
山 西	3	2	3955.0	2059.0	1842.0
内蒙古	11	10	17531.3	8799.4	3435.3
辽 宁	8		394.8	394.8	394.8
吉 林	1		1026.0		779.0
黑龙江	2	2	381.0	60.0	
上 海	2	1	4918.6	3977.0	2491.0
江 苏	80	8	354497.0	321100.0	288018.5
浙 江	6	4	45574.1	9403.1	2593.5
安 徽	77	6	25847.6	6316.6	18195.0
福 建	3	1	38200.0	7857.9	6355.0
江 西	7	7	17211.0	9361.0	3211.0
山 东	355	328	48685.0	37816.3	17086.6
河 南	13	10	2305.6	1450.6	1440.6
湖 北	78	17	31736.0	20761.0	6429.0
湖 南	14	13	1808.0	1314.0	1308.0
广 东	18	13	48530.7	24422.0	9717.4
广 西	353	182	39148.9	24943.5	12539.5
海 南	9	1	2233.1	2229.3	2233.1
重 庆	8		1109.0	1109.0	1109.0
四 川	1	1	21453.0	13655.0	11369.6
贵 州	20	9	25514.6	22288.3	17132.7
云 南	26	21	18886.2	14369.8	4917.4
西 藏	3	1	3955.0	1578.0	1358.0
陕 西	57	52	36611.5	28994.0	23099.0
甘 肃	10	4	26685.0	7359.0	1570.0
青 海	30	17	21468.0	13324.0	9167.0
宁 夏	2	1	205.0	668.8	
新 疆	13	5	5105.0	5567.0	3806.0

建设投资情况

单位：万元、个、平方米

本年实际完成投资	国家预算内投资	国内贷款	利用外资	福利彩票公益金	其他	本年完工项目数
469431.6	**84114.3**			**58547.3**	**326770.0**	**1064**
12210.30	12210.30					3
6147.3	4361.0			1657.0	129.3	5
1567.0	709.0			366.0	492.0	
3483.4				2130.1	1353.3	1
394.8	394.8					8
60.0				60.0		
1935.0	533.0			1402.0		1
286781.2	8814.0			3748.2	274219.0	56
2303.4	1128.0			1158.6	16.8	
6316.6	5737.8			128.8	450.0	56
6897.9	500.0			4162.9	2235.0	1
3361.0	300.0			3040.0	21.0	6
18554.6	10264.0			2202.1	6088.5	350
1450.6				1450.6		11
6742.0	608.0			1556.6	4577.4	66
1314.0	680.0			572.0	62.0	8
9734.4	1941.6			6490.9	1301.9	11
16596.8	5902.2			5364.6	5330.0	236
2229.3	2206.2				23.1	1
1109.0	245.0				864.0	112
11171.6	1870.6			9301.0		4
18108.7	9063.2			2363.3	6682.2	13
4929.7	1742.4			1766.3	1421.0	23
1578.0	1250.0			328.0		2
22711.2	57.2			2503.5	20150.5	54
3393.0	2328.0			1065.0		3
13324.0	8448.0			3763.0	1113.0	23
668.8	645.0			23.8		1
4358.0	2175.0			1943.0	240.0	9

C-2-1 社会

地　区	机构和设施数	工商登记	编制登记	民政登记	设施
全　国	**370893**	**16685**	**23158**	**38364**	**292686**
中央级	2		2		
北　京	12461	579	684	644	10554
天　津	2461	224	107	522	1608
河　北	33309	619	817	784	31089
山　西	4915	374	689	783	3069
内蒙古	3831	145	494	300	2892
辽　宁	10228	1753	566	1455	6454
吉　林	2111	318	985	141	667
黑龙江	4013	440	528	1435	1610
上　海	5507	930	216	1300	3061
江　苏	38410	2734	1428	15392	18856
浙　江	34077	1951	870	1769	29487
安　徽	9228	348	573	701	7606
福　建	6123	280	439	206	5198
江　西	5794	296	1169	2504	1825
山　东	30142	1225	992	1829	26096
河　南	7593	813	756	1549	4475
湖　北	12329	541	1628	813	9347
湖　南	10481	492	1831	211	7947
广　东	57527	168	1390	942	55027
广　西	10946	123	537	219	10067
海　南	1950	17	48	291	1594
重　庆	6933	768	538	285	5342
四　川	19080	709	2965	1261	14145
贵　州	20567	38	577	230	19722
云　南	2967	261	448	284	1974
西　藏	356	5	54	211	86
陕　西	5125	197	575	1050	3303
甘　肃	7099	65	352	173	6509
青　海	678	35	42	102	499
宁　夏	1065	74	121	336	534
新　疆	3585	163	737	642	2043

工作总表

单位:个、人

年末职工人数					
	女性	工商登记	编制登记	民政登记	设施
2772513	**1037987**	**1260442**	**262217**	**290030**	**965494**
300	168		300		
80470	37734	26407	11610	8818	33680
32424	15375	15934	2417	5934	8164
117922	45092	34976	12784	9015	61244
57619	17069	35870	7422	4498	9941
29992	13069	8752	5580	3459	12308
150099	61218	89385	9824	11120	40007
31545	10807	15695	11200	1085	3831
39346	15744	14589	7512	9251	8177
124328	55963	74653	7230	28646	13843
445430	157636	250537	17894	88616	88649
294983	107138	204806	10122	10425	69787
66243	26652	18011	6663	6818	35313
43945	16010	18297	4175	2813	18804
50341	17737	25188	7723	12853	4877
229195	84527	92314	14663	19640	102872
97668	37698	55148	10716	11021	21399
92420	38592	34842	16879	5961	34976
77341	28475	31082	16275	2323	27932
185065	64146	14863	18419	10347	141697
37899	14644	8367	6827	3870	19089
11341	3563	1577	761	1504	7539
94487	35517	68286	5108	3632	17531
126491	48273	54135	19135	8330	45110
97575	25180	2071	7302	1638	86659
48061	14538	32784	4376	2062	9172
1457	819	207	372	611	272
39142	16130	12184	7185	6244	13663
24747	8100	3784	3548	1331	16214
4578	1887	2071	777	296	1462
10877	5335	4909	1713	1808	2458
29182	13151	8718	5705	6061	8824

C-2-1续表1

地区	受教育程度		职业资格水平	
	大学专科人数	大学本科及以上人数	助理社会工作师人数	社会工作师人数
全国	**403215**	**194878**	**18295**	**10252**
中央级	76	224		2
北京	14453	12370	2528	994
天津	5461	3002	554	182
河北	10068	4288	185	267
山西	6120	2956	122	145
内蒙古	7241	4138	284	198
辽宁	20911	12990	577	453
吉林	4788	2277	481	300
黑龙江	7741	3294	356	224
上海	7175	4337	609	531
江苏	57009	25847	2137	1050
浙江	26927	12079	1301	920
安徽	12312	3921	594	316
福建	3809	2259	460	371
江西	4149	1283	167	120
山东	51428	25300	668	455
河南	15515	6606	300	320
湖北	14625	6683	493	197
湖南	12616	5400	656	283
广东	29251	18296	3662	1269
广西	5364	3213	311	242
海南	1401	568	64	35
重庆	12178	6359	358	271
四川	24758	7871	645	556
贵州	20602	6831	110	62
云南	4095	2117	110	109
西藏	240	102	2	3
陕西	8321	2841	198	120
甘肃	4485	2439	148	104
青海	713	361	47	32
宁夏	1423	925	34	24
新疆	7960	3701	134	97

单位：人、人次、时

年龄结构				志愿服务	
35岁及以下人数	36岁至45岁人数	46岁至55岁人数	56岁及以上人数	志愿者服务人次数	志愿服务时间
874724	**1083964**	**629649**	**184190**	**8128354**	**19437485.9**
198	48	40	14		
22222	30083	22529	5636	5203476	13053908.0
11266	11349	8064	1745	76930	120443.0
38936	43946	27048	7992	15464	59860.0
16682	22196	15289	3452	6015	16038.4
8947	11956	7746	1343	18509	37359.0
42485	62139	34349	11126	16593	32359.0
8272	15039	5645	2589	405	650.0
12889	16401	8090	1980	35108	74876.0
34037	42518	35372	12401	51497	154602.0
127924	175074	112474	29958	378853	869619.0
84144	102425	72092	36322	503017	870359.1
18437	28458	15948	3400	79876	153105.0
14032	17823	9048	3042	125830	355695.0
16622	21689	9648	2382	4518	13722.7
85630	87212	44763	11590	380165	898340.4
39472	38839	15989	3368	955	2240.0
26743	41907	19570	4200	31095	46616.0
20021	36780	17208	3332	40269	134665.5
63487	71352	39361	10865	12125	24913.0
12333	12045	9521	4000	1569	5258.8
3350	4799	2460	732	8860	15319.0
28602	38102	22221	5562	300274	704437.0
44504	51547	24609	5831	74016	166016.0
36100	37028	19474	4973	702797	1425584.0
19194	19163	8418	1286	521	1321.0
794	489	130	44	213	663.5
13869	14336	8991	1946	23909	62663.5
8833	9300	4991	1623	12024	61826.0
1871	1956	636	115	576	1630.0
3222	5106	2066	483	1660	2329.0
9606	12859	5859	858	21235	71067.0

C-2-1续表2

地　区	增加值合计	执行企业会计制度单位财务指标					执行行政	
		固定资产原价	营业收入	费用合计	营业利润	企业单位增加值	固定资产原价	上年结转和结余
全　国	**13146320.5**	**18272589.6**	**47465545.4**	**5803071.7**	**1270512.4**	**7573425.8**	**10530176.0**	**829170.0**
中央级	6338.7						34585.8	14746.3
北　京	729576.2	460511.5	590860.4	99641.0	5005.8	133038.0	366031.1	169689.0
天　津	156544.1	230348.0	349152.1	85839.5	5048.4	60513.9	180632.7	8926.3
河　北	398655.6	481863.6	1231791.4	101582.8	8285.2	176957.7	481202.6	27910.2
山　西	128585.3	324806.5	442043.7	40859.6	-15471.6	43010.6	206556.7	25354.9
内蒙古	96498.8	67104.9	60340.3	11843.9	1939.2	15370.6	192001.1	17593.9
辽　宁	617553.9	1430476.3	1905819.6	205563.4	61681.0	352048.9	319695.5	39266.9
吉　林	77989.2	109584.8	240973.7	28409.7	417.5	20323.2	192764.4	6763.7
黑龙江	139374.9	104535.6	157916.0	35190.2	4946.7	34144.8	298403.8	10925.6
上　海	953798.8	1334692.3	3150967.7	321068.7	179064.7	758086.5	274586.6	15719.5
江　苏	1843041.6	3542804.0	11151191.9	1264869.1	232264.2	1311545.7	1087089.4	45204.8
浙　江	2871922.4	5325008.2	15610875.1	2272443.9	495001.9	2530399.2	862455.5	70291.3
安　徽	214583.6	130735.1	930882.5	59405.8	17996.2	63888.7	445485.3	11841.4
福　建	143584.7	171544.6	315398.0	48138.1	1520.7	54377.2	138518.9	16791.1
江　西	76768.0	100414.0	2186710.8	19408.8	2946.9	16564.5	209767.0	8513.9
山　东	1243965.8	1031158.7	1716258.9	321268.3	140644.8	597521.1	530157.1	9727.5
河　南	254681.6	388638.0	769078.4	90857.8	19358.2	115817.6	309928.8	11644.2
湖　北	311262.1	217345.8	370849.5	95605.6	10275.1	79820.9	563091.7	3514.8
湖　南	233220.3	288785.6	579202.4	62613.6	9349.1	82310.4	370306.5	8201.1
广　东	404342.8	268212.4	303000.8	38342.5	5921.2	61939.0	777875.2	68349.8
广　西	225721.6	62014.8	297312.4	11543.7	-2029.5	22130.2	216305.0	26896.8
海　南	26213.2	24001.8	51071.8	9153.7	-1506.3	5923.7	50134.7	10417.4
重　庆	451415.9	724281.3	1944807.4	226656.2	43417.2	338634.0	224223.6	28054.2
四　川	548868.2	471632.5	1418256.4	98232.5	24663.0	322406.7	711257.6	45512.1
贵　州	130010.1	6908.5	18872.8	2915.1	917.5	2559.8	217371.4	23516.6
云　南	162135.6	503433.6	1059401.6	158287.6	-11500.5	49531.6	481800.7	24642.2
西　藏	4269.1	5250.6	398.0	222.5	26.0	67.9	45885.0	3098.0
陕　西	448295.1	147931.1	340976.7	44261.7	19440.4	264048.5	336637.0	27050.9
甘　肃	61959.6	29969.5	9953.7	2432.3	84.8	3465.9	147893.7	6968.1
青　海	16576.8	9282.5	16223.0	3682.6	426.2	5041.4	33290.8	980.8
宁　夏	34792.0	104486.5	48836.3	11731.4	3794.1	16053.1	50453.5	12619.5
新　疆	133773.2	174827.0	196122.1	31000.1	6584.3	35884.6	173787.3	28437.2

单位：万元

事业单位会计制度财务指标				执行民间非营利组织单位会计制度财务指标				
本年收入合计	本年支出合计	收支结余	行政事业单位增加值	固定资产原价	上年结余	本年收入合计	本年费用合计	社会组织增加值
8311246.1	**8152083.5**	**646756.5**	**4829198.0**	**3927116.6**	**74842.0**	**1399974.9**	**1315556.6**	**743696.7**
109187.4	71243.4	52690.2	6338.7					
838466.7	806892.2	201182.5	578475.7	125927.4	3611.2	49573.6	51252.8	18062.5
139914.5	147440.5	7004.7	87046.5	27704.4	1008.3	38607.1	25670.4	8983.7
364099.2	345426.4	27658.2	209377.0	295255.6	2295.0	21269.2	23240.5	12320.9
155825.5	142616.5	16321.9	82038.4	22897.7	317.4	3584.0	6423.6	3536.3
157211.0	144143.8	29526.7	77603.9	30535.4	4.0	7203.7	7040.9	3524.3
387025.7	469338.3	6893.2	257182.0	69367.8	655.0	77009.5	18708.9	8323.0
117186.4	117640.1	4026.0	57031.8	3450.2		3391.5	1677.2	634.2
142574.0	135456.4	545.8	102440.7	20930.2	3228.4	3613.7	4118.4	2789.4
300358.4	279255.5	14018.2	138193.5	132991.0	23543.6	210327.4	139171.3	57518.8
607112.4	605453.8	57019.1	429782.7	510135.8	2089.2	213304.4	208133.7	101713.2
820933.6	523085.8	13636.5	301809.1	283522.9	3030.3	98479.1	96865.5	39714.1
201135.7	191228.8	3308.9	121161.1	172226.0	309.5	30012.6	45515.4	29533.8
153592.0	138357.2	12628.0	84941.1	86861.6	2540.9	8726.3	10328.2	4266.4
95120.9	82661.1	7780.9	52620.5	67745.5	2.2	9909.5	11887.9	7583.0
579562.5	589340.8		345491.3	894136.3		414512.1	414457.1	300953.4
338304.1	323449.8	9294.3	128964.1	81115.0	1766.1	12472.9	16920.8	9899.9
361823.1	358528.7	4608.0	216278.0	53344.7	70.0	25859.6	25610.5	15163.2
288439.3	265025.5	9148.2	146722.0	24129.8	473.7	12355.8	10876.2	4187.9
541436.6	769601.3	34775.1	318187.2	164559.3	11442.0	40760.0	45580.7	24216.6
180997.8	274015.0	18096.1	195676.6	46447.1	1284.1	5028.9	11376.9	7914.8
46172.6	47694.2	5234.3	19693.1	5675.3	1408.0	1961.5	2120.9	596.4
177147.6	173784.3	29878.5	102852.7	124237.1	366.2	30164.2	29357.5	9929.2
333390.0	311496.4	16914.7	198342.5	150140.2	5781.0	39363.6	44975.9	28119.0
125449.5	131545.0	8034.2	94928.3	203698.1	8559.6	28602.7	44273.3	32522.0
164523.3	152550.4	10339.4	110629.7	228959.0	138.3	777.4	2874.4	1974.3
14523.8	13688.4		4201.2	754.0		10.0		
269382.5	260032.4	21205.4	181278.5	33304.1	-53.4	4914.9	5984.2	2968.1
88606.1	87237.2	1999.2	55419.4	29455.8	113.4	1638.4	4180.0	3074.3
17046.8	16233.8	1241.2	10298.6	20241.0	778.0	1092.8	1573.4	1236.8
35598.6	30959.0	7730.5	18240.2	2313.6		1244.7	1293.5	498.7
159098.5	146661.5	14016.6	95950.1	15054.7	80.0	4203.8	4066.6	1938.5

C-2-2 提供住宿的社会

地区	机构数	工商登记	编制登记	民政登记	一个机构多个牌子	0~99张
全国	**36810**	**151**	**16196**	**12618**	**7837**	**21391**
中央级	1		1			
北京	631	5	382	220	24	216
天津	364	1	56	276	31	169
河北	1467	4	564	531	368	732
山西	952		358	432	162	676
内蒙古	797		368	278	151	476
辽宁	1797	4	377	1125	291	1196
吉林	893		784	70	39	571
黑龙江	1124		287	714	123	705
上海	665	2	69	591	3	236
江苏	2477	16	1198	1125	137	1038
浙江	2030	18	681	591	740	983
安徽	1002	7	306	556	133	468
福建	494	3	313	121	57	329
江西	2033		903	1029	101	1441
山东	2235	4	612	1175	444	860
河南	2698		465	960	1273	1638
湖北	2265	8	1273	341	643	1208
湖南	1836	1	1534	136	165	1536
广东	1637	30	1045	262	300	1153
广西	614		345	163	106	475
海南	232	4	33	85	110	192
重庆	966	23	406	221	316	562
四川	3786	17	2336	401	1030	1997
贵州	519		309	136	69	363
云南	666	1	296	122	247	420
西藏	253	2	27	179	45	217
陕西	877		348	368	161	491
甘肃	432		170	123	139	295
青海	189		28	9	152	143
宁夏	106		60	38	8	54
新疆	772	1	262	240	269	551

服务机构总表

单位:个、人

100～299张	300～499张	500张以上	年末职工人数	女性	工商登记	编制登记
12940	**1621**	**858**	**402905**	**220419**	**4397**	**199624**
1			165	115		165
287	64	64	15080	9563	277	7910
156	14	25	6880	4665	75	1891
544	122	69	21283	11675	84	9910
233	22	21	9142	4188		4781
260	45	16	7996	4004		4009
482	82	37	19585	11071	26	8234
269	39	14	9843	3795		8865
322	55	42	11529	5423		5880
334	64	31	23760	16792	124	3714
1186	169	84	32210	18541	492	16015
866	113	68	20337	11892	654	8598
458	60	16	11326	5577	172	4558
116	37	12	6064	2888	75	3364
543	33	16	13042	4993		6324
1136	173	66	30396	16624	58	10751
974	54	32	22544	11467		8021
956	63	38	21970	12240	256	13967
253	29	18	16138	8221	135	13218
369	69	46	26199	16083	1150	15252
113	18	8	8917	6049		5317
21	13	6	1538	881	318	641
348	33	23	9419	4513	394	4106
1641	107	41	24386	11636	76	15382
139	13	4	4358	2070		2803
212	23	11	5443	2934	3	3445
33	2	1	897	575	2	284
297	69	20	9368	4752		5095
117	13	7	3818	1732		2263
36	3	7	1268	669		656
40	6	6	1311	878		965
198	14	9	6693	3913	26	3240

C-2-2续表1

地区	年末职工人数		受教育程度		职业资格水平	
	民政登记	一个机构多个牌子	大学专科人数	大学本科及以上人数	助理社会工作师人数	社会工作师人数
全　国	**153706**	**44946**	**76930**	**48414**	**4070**	**3795**
中央级			66	99		1
北　京	6596	297	2561	2495	161	109
天　津	4709	204	1344	813	54	75
河　北	7671	3584	3276	2056	102	122
山　西	3037	1319	1921	1163	22	85
内蒙古	3273	714	1917	1037	61	84
辽　宁	9484	1841	3951	3194	111	154
吉　林	483	495	1606	1306	70	42
黑龙江	4916	723	2112	1261	195	162
上　海	19861	61	1735	1304	196	261
江　苏	15049	650	5581	4080	375	357
浙　江	7128	3945	2617	1817	177	185
安　徽	5648	936	1860	923	127	124
福　建	2342	280	1132	951	112	111
江　西	6329	389	1469	652	92	65
山　东	15565	3997	7737	5142	288	211
河　南	8420	6084	4401	1939	135	166
湖　北	3598	4143	4611	2835	151	108
湖　南	1668	1087	4040	2203	191	157
广　东	7949	1840	4430	3127	562	379
广　西	3145	449	2340	1524	147	154
海　南	316	263	282	169	13	23
重　庆	3294	1625	1592	1107	92	85
四　川	3737	5178	5650	2496	219	272
贵　州	960	595	1491	813	52	24
云　南	910	1071	1344	895	50	67
西　藏	452	159	98	35	2	1
陕　西	3441	807	2169	961	88	75
甘　肃	941	609	965	653	109	50
青　海	92	520	347	193	25	22
宁　夏	300	46	283	354	26	17
新　疆	2392	1035	2002	817	65	47

单位：个、人、人次

年龄结构				按人员性质		志愿服务
35岁及以下人数	36岁至45岁人数	46岁至55岁人数	56岁及以上人数	管理人员	专业技术技能人员	志愿者服务人次数
111985	**154983**	**108256**	**27695**	**167075**	**235093**	**468780**
122	27	12	4	16	149	
3717	5339	4671	1353	5023	10057	25807
1566	2406	2436	472	2762	4118	13995
7339	8185	4797	962	6360	14923	6057
2730	3857	2129	426	3980	5162	4941
1936	3110	2402	548	3513	4483	388
4284	7867	6012	1422	9146	10439	5981
2957	4366	2128	392	5262	4581	105
3112	4862	3048	521	6044	4748	954
4555	7979	8279	2947	12053	11707	10049
7779	11085	10071	3275	8698	23512	77027
4545	6859	6788	2145	7287	13050	52099
2912	4076	3354	984	5666	5660	19002
1744	2361	1506	453	2543	3521	19699
2626	5872	3948	596	7105	5937	3499
10781	11504	6673	1438	8676	21720	122682
7389	8354	5493	1308	12046	10498	820
5895	9133	5571	1371	7889	14081	26313
4886	6935	3482	835	6609	9529	21509
6630	11183	7061	1325	10787	15412	7375
3208	3063	2157	489	2788	6129	1150
507	638	299	94	627	911	300
2000	3333	3080	1006	4781	4638	14175
6888	9514	6011	1973	13077	11309	15156
1440	1758	1014	146	2576	1782	7048
1772	2273	1152	246	2745	2698	514
502	292	73	30	482	415	213
3369	3380	2100	519	3733	5635	6420
1417	1431	787	183	1782	2036	381
573	468	179	48	585	683	571
450	543	254	64	501	810	1629
2354	2930	1289	120	1933	4760	2921

C-2-2续表2

地区	志愿服务	年末床位数				
	志愿服务时间		工商登记	编制登记	民政登记	一个机构多块牌子
全　国	**1173933.2**	**6135358**	**37607**	**1943082**	**1654960**	**2499709**
中央级		150		150		
北　京	78204.6	143689	963	79948	54536	8242
天　津	25570.0	63124	1010	11856	43450	6808
河　北	21744.0	453002	1172	85629	79078	287123
山　西	13754.0	89080		23746	36335	28999
内蒙古	841.0	189088		38915	37580	112593
辽　宁	14060.0	221111	346	72073	99451	49241
吉　林	300.0	95763		81805	7559	6399
黑龙江	3286.0	141322		55002	67025	19295
上　海	29992.0	129003	478	17534	101195	9796
江　苏	225890.0	571327	2949	206755	206119	155504
浙　江	101381.3	441321	6572	109737	98515	226497
安　徽	52422.0	342848	1240	34316	80917	226375
福　建	29712.0	124573	739	27947	22433	73454
江　西	11273.0	186293		75890	99076	11327
山　东	310886.0	569184	436	104154	184927	279667
河　南	1746.0	355961		44934	108733	202294
湖　北	37496.0	277345	6293	156307	41707	73038
湖　南	75093.5	202859	800	104816	17203	80040
广　东	14791.0	222242	5494	102268	48901	65579
广　西	3892.8	154567		21694	18058	114815
海　南		18034	4604	3209	4270	5951
重　庆	35132.0	164353	3023	49367	32628	79335
四　川	27765.0	461725	1167	267618	51516	141424
贵　州	15797.0	117765	1	23914	10733	83117
云　南	1308.0	81745	193	34609	13729	33214
西　藏	663.5	10698	57	4094	4936	1611
陕　西	18002.5	118485		46734	43445	28306
甘　肃	1240.0	92296	3	17410	10246	64637
青　海	1618.0	19308		5442	4845	9021
宁　夏	2321.0	13194		7544	4325	1325
新　疆	17751.0	63903	67	27665	21489	14682

单位：张、人天、人、人次、时、%

年末收养人数	工商登记	编制登记	民政登记	一个机构多块牌子	年末在院(站)人天数	年末床位利用率
3368331	**19191**	**1298801**	**954500**	**1095839**	**787400003**	**54.9**
149		149			47998	99.3
79542	276	56009	20440	2817	27054876	55.4
30924	18	8357	21572	977	7056162	49.0
139215	450	49861	37078	51826	37416428	30.7
44156		15292	19845	9019	11584390	49.6
116853		23576	21576	71701	32568953	61.8
123066	145	49978	55773	17170	29540144	55.7
52381		48346	3082	953	11536556	54.7
102866		39107	51313	12446	22601163	72.8
81901	201	14741	66069	890	24629543	63.5
252193	1800	135743	80006	34644	66928997	44.1
161515	3725	48093	41753	67944	34414209	36.6
178925	917	16636	47916	113456	26234623	52.2
35051	316	13416	10286	11033	7773826	28.1
162985		62097	92756	8132	34660586	87.5
345885	194	70741	107770	167180	89249764	60.8
268964		27969	83805	157190	48927474	75.6
183173	1123	115509	27621	38920	48445031	66.1
152693	308	82256	10263	59866	27445959	75.3
91011	4058	51923	24693	10337	26851749	41.0
66858		13670	9990	43198	9594743	43.3
7738	3105	1666	1285	1682	1128233	42.9
99475	1854	34359	19665	43597	26734114	60.5
332616	481	215563	30616	85956	82881204	72.0
43722		10955	3823	28944	5214719	37.1
49146	111	23202	7543	18290	11229499	60.1
7717	57	2811	3723	1126	1772429	72.1
77508		30171	31491	15846	18651073	65.4
23638		10136	5255	8247	3448538	25.6
7277		2747	823	3707	1523844	37.7
8603		5448	2808	347	1896277	65.2
40585	52	18274	13861	8398	8356899	63.5

C-2-2续表3

地区	增加值合计	执行企业会计制度单位财务指标					执行行政	
		固定资产原价	营业收入	费用合计	营业利润	企业单位增加值	固定资产原价	上年结转和结余
全　国	**3547838.7**	**208784.9**	**23682.0**	**12947.2**	**-1371.6**	**2106.0**	**6350904.7**	**413092.9**
中央级	2549.9						1910.3	28.0
北　京	376481.5	54847.7	4837.4	731.3	200.6	1624.7	182786.9	23556.2
天　津	77735.3	1308.7	140.0	43.0		63.0	59954.6	8094.3
河　北	169877.4	6656.1	338.0	198.6	-9.3	39.8	348325.9	21540.5
山　西	71769.3						161224.7	22070.2
内蒙古	55324.8						134126.0	9517.5
辽　宁	223335.3	300.5	130.0		25.0	25.5	234207.0	22404.5
吉　林	48531.0						155774.8	4092.8
黑龙江	57524.8	92.0					217508.9	6433.2
上　海	130470.5	120.1	208.0	1721.6	1.0	4.2	143100.3	10018.1
江　苏	312488.3	47240.2	1181.5	2259.9	-1197.2	-980.4	614157.9	21694.8
浙　江	126555.2	20857.8	6623.8	2698.0	1024.4	1661.9	318611.0	24414.3
安　徽	71172.0	2457.0	476.0	108.0			181732.0	4794.7
福　建	71537.6	1563.7	60.0	86.0		41.4	81570.0	12166.9
江　西	46055.0						179696.7	5039.1
山　东	337049.2	120.0	729.6	657.3	71.1	74.9	361559.1	6668.7
河　南	104338.1	201.0	14.0	2.0		20.0	194694.1	7094.6
湖　北	171739.7	7847.0	550.0	200.0		90.0	404632.5	2552.3
湖　南	111820.6	13701.0	650.0	650.0		68.0	252536.8	4187.5
广　东	229017.4	5024.3	5528.0	1428.5	100.9	569.8	487814.2	54349.7
广　西	164370.5						108227.1	25522.6
海　南	12356.4	2497.2	1228.5	1687.0	-1860.7	-1521.1	33021.0	8467.2
重　庆	77285.2	18961.8	866.1	291.6	265.0	311.3	122892.3	2578.9
四　川	144293.3	19245.0	70.2	94.6	6.6	11.2	573188.5	32407.5
贵　州	46418.2						89779.8	9591.1
云　南	52449.0	2053.0		9.0			166678.9	16940.6
西　藏	2317.0	1835.8					30593.0	2268.0
陕　西	133219.6						237307.9	13735.6
甘　肃	44900.0	200.0					99557.7	6257.4
青　海	10435.7						15527.7	980.7
宁　夏	14726.8	1200.0					38812.6	8425.8
新　疆	49694.0	455.0	50.9	80.8	1.0	2.0	119394.5	15199.6

单位：万元

事业单位会计制度财务指标				执行民间非营利组织单位会计制度财务指标				
本年收入合计	本年支出合计	收支结余	行政事业单位增加值	固定资产原价	上年结余	本年收入合计	本年费用合计	社会组织增加值
4762705.5	**4811344.7**	**251569.9**	**3333715.5**	**2032602.3**	**43428.2**	**589846.9**	**471834.8**	**212017.2**
4921.2	4946.2	3.0	2549.9					
475723.3	472005.6	22472.5	357871.2	123664.5	2835.5	46230.5	47759.2	16985.6
75616.3	85762.3	5011.6	71015.6	25127.7	795.6	35307.9	21944.5	6656.7
238614.4	227789.8	20306.0	164873.0	247816.6	1421.3	12963.2	12559.8	4964.6
111568.3	107503.6	11497.2	70399.7	17312.4	295.5	1426.6	2113.8	1369.6
89982.7	84882.9	13684.9	52553.0	26461.4	4.0	5883.8	5752.0	2771.8
285936.2	361109.1	5413.9	218594.2	57678.4	216.7	70424.6	11177.5	4715.6
86978.6	86171.8	2614.3	48323.3	2650.0		880.7	528.7	207.7
86226.1	78168.4	491.6	55337.8	17858.9	2228.4	2431.4	3181.5	2187.0
160727.6	154198.0	7568.8	90408.1	112777.9	11249.7	158299.8	107323.9	40058.2
390577.2	381048.4	25538.0	298133.1	161154.8	1668.6	34191.8	32312.2	15335.6
202837.6	186497.2	5636.0	112439.3	127199.6	1468.6	30806.1	28741.3	12454.0
93547.3	87366.4	835.0	63118.8	84479.9	129.5	14289.2	14501.4	8053.2
115320.4	102941.6	9265.0	70081.7	52291.2	2488.2	3314.6	2988.6	1414.5
70423.8	61691.1	7841.9	43719.1	55618.4	2.2	3979.2	4576.5	2335.9
398035.7	404704.4		283817.1	471507.8		88288.4	88233.4	53157.2
148052.9	145195.8	6522.0	97571.5	68011.3	1014.5	10484.3	11815.6	6746.6
262291.1	259994.4	4102.0	165585.2	34244.8	4.0	9601.5	9834.5	6064.5
184038.9	176124.2	3008.4	111219.0	8673.7	421.1	3370.9	2441.9	533.6
324908.7	321225.8	19675.8	223713.1	61704.7	9693.2	7959.9	10548.7	4734.5
100888.9	203886.1	15049.0	162674.5	14479.5	1215.7	3209.4	3787.6	1696.0
18471.6	20122.0	2457.2	13672.9	4120.8	1408.0	1228.9	1046.2	204.6
108420.3	105713.6	3924.3	71045.2	86551.7	358.2	22104.4	21723.4	5928.7
228655.3	211538.2	13062.0	139041.2	54208.6	3381.5	10931.8	12400.9	5240.9
52589.5	66693.8	3749.9	44914.5	30747.4	155.0	1103.1	2158.7	1503.7
84217.2	75899.4	6263.4	51878.2	10053.7	135.3	582.9	919.4	570.8
4047.7	3333.4		2317.0	726.0		10.0		
171007.6	158316.5	15090.8	130582.2	29593.0	-55.1	4785.2	5314.5	2637.4
68001.2	64869.0	1212.9	44510.5	17642.0	35.0	184.4	542.2	389.5
15742.8	15004.8	1241.2	9394.8	12837.0	778.0	934.9	1211.3	1040.9
24305.8	20117.3	8209.9	14421.8	1641.6		556.5	556.0	305.0
80029.3	76523.6	9821.4	47938.7	13767.0	80.0	4081.0	3839.6	1753.3

C-2-3 养老机构和

地区	单位数	工商登记	编制登记	民政登记	设施	0~99张	100~299张
全国	**92327**	**151**	**13558**	**14739**	**63879**	**77999**	**12154**
中央级							
北京	815	5	345	228	237	421	275
天津	389	1	38	276	74	201	153
河北	22305	4	490	493	21318	21629	492
山西	1150		260	429	461	897	213
内蒙古	1296		313	275	708	994	246
辽宁	1865	4	282	1097	482	1298	455
吉林	854		700	126	28	566	244
黑龙江	1031		181	712	138	647	295
上海	675	2	42	590	41	256	330
江苏	6071	16	1096	3089	1870	4678	1156
浙江	8184	18	602	609	6955	7166	844
安徽	2372	7	184	568	1613	1888	418
福建	2366	3	225	132	2006	2235	90
江西	1923		801	1029	93	1354	525
山东	5738	4	512	1216	4006	4418	1105
河南	3062		338	967	1757	2051	941
湖北	2532	8	1142	350	1032	1534	920
湖南	3975	1	1383	133	2458	3725	218
广东	1852	30	921	245	656	1435	322
广西	9560		262	169	9129	9452	91
海南	240	4	22	85	129	204	17
重庆	1884	23	350	220	1291	1493	342
四川	4669	17	2137	401	2114	2993	1565
贵州	2571		204	160	2207	2453	109
云南	696	1	176	116	403	503	167
西藏	230	2	10	175	43	204	25
陕西	1417		235	402	780	1055	281
甘肃	1681		106	119	1456	1568	98
青海	200		14	63	123	165	29
宁夏	86		41	41	4	41	37
新疆	638	1	146	224	267	475	151

设施情况总表

单位:个、人

300～499张	500张以上	年末职工人数	女性	工商登记	编制登记	民政登记	设施
1435	**739**	**476117**	**231715**	**4397**	**139380**	**163282**	**169058**
60	59	14099	8849	277	6241	6617	964
13	22	6302	4414	75	1167	4709	351
119	65	54869	23357	84	8534	6899	39352
20	20	8347	3400		2968	3042	2337
42	14	7133	3487		2628	3262	1243
81	31	17952	10459	26	5933	9313	2680
37	7	7537	2716		6326	768	443
52	37	9047	4373		3363	4904	780
63	26	22142	15771	124	2050	19808	160
159	78	50327	23787	492	12765	26334	10736
108	66	27566	13640	654	7310	7246	12356
52	14	17223	6987	172	2236	5733	9082
30	11	9145	3322	75	1726	2415	4929
28	16	11874	4497		5201	6329	344
153	62	43396	21098	58	7830	15855	19653
46	24	22779	10941		4486	8551	9742
49	29	18707	10554	256	9812	3869	4770
19	13	20337	8308	135	9893	1396	8913
56	39	22742	14408	1150	11284	7405	2903
11	6	17002	6696		2734	3224	11044
13	6	1395	826	318	485	316	276
31	18	10193	4725	394	3001	3278	3520
81	30	20895	8884	76	11030	2552	7237
8	1	9187	3189		1322	1120	6745
17	9	4133	2198	3	1925	850	1355
1		627	424	2	89	397	139
65	16	9520	4727		3448	3498	2574
10	5	5002	1842		1224	906	2872
2	4	870	407		223	179	468
4	4	848	556		520	310	18
5	7	4921	2873	26	1626	2197	1072

C-2-3续表1

地区	受教育程度		职业资格水平		
	大学专科人数	大学本科及以上人数	助理社会工作师人数	社会工作师人数	35岁及以下人数
全国	**69907**	**36324**	**3626**	**2894**	**118963**
中央级					
北京	2298	1956	127	98	3184
天津	1226	637	49	57	1318
河北	3995	1688	90	111	14993
山西	1398	742	12	58	2172
内蒙古	1407	584	48	53	1543
辽宁	3358	2465	91	132	3694
吉林	1090	680	63	37	2271
黑龙江	1326	562	182	128	2321
上海	1239	854	137	183	3840
江苏	7560	3760	398	290	12292
浙江	3203	1734	175	153	6884
安徽	1862	658	119	122	3222
福建	874	584	97	114	1918
江西	1041	457	77	50	2315
山东	9867	5378	347	168	13804
河南	3501	1448	105	97	6679
湖北	3595	1483	114	67	4289
湖南	3782	2254	388	127	4885
广东	3135	2204	401	241	5258
广西	1676	850	93	147	2555
海南	246	132	10	19	465
重庆	1459	718	63	56	1689
四川	3946	1406	123	185	5338
贵州	1904	851	47	28	2938
云南	751	402	30	26	1257
西藏	58	10			354
陕西	1870	691	75	53	3257
甘肃	861	473	100	54	1956
青海	119	114	16	18	401
宁夏	122	158	10	3	252
新疆	1138	391	39	19	1619

单位：人、人次、时

年龄结构			按人员性质分		志愿服务	
36岁至45岁人数	46岁至55岁人数	56岁及以上人数	管理人员	专业技术技能人员	志愿者服务人次数	志愿服务时间
182144	**134972**	**40038**	**139314**	**194136**	**525240**	**1322056.8**
5062	4561	1292	4354	9019	27672	79722.0
2274	2288	422	2513	3643	11995	21570.0
19719	15094	5063	5643	13242	8097	33775.0
3718	1802	655	3315	3901	4801	13280.0
2943	2087	560	2954	3635	338	541.0
7359	5418	1481	7910	9043	5886	13904.0
3499	1525	242	4109	3143	5	
4003	2317	406	4817	4058	608	2430.0
7583	7922	2797	11513	10530	8415	24951.0
17720	15969	4346	7879	20873	107839	292093.0
9373	8244	3065	6612	12310	44616	81872.3
6255	5806	1940	4449	4182	19433	51523.0
3479	2483	1265	1816	2514	19629	29553.0
5396	3640	523	6299	5520	2963	9113.0
16645	10386	2561	7884	19393	153983	383282.2
8716	5947	1437	9825	8993	910	2066.0
7967	5247	1204	6480	10140	24414	32355.0
8737	5281	1434	5038	6978	19346	67124.0
9800	6311	1373	8382	13253	7375	14791.0
5259	6036	3152	1973	4147	880	3320.8
592	254	84	575	802	300	
3543	3677	1284	4240	3992	13533	33990.0
8667	5359	1531	10391	7608	14723	26265.0
3539	2024	686	1627	1011	6362	15511.0
1735	903	238	1929	1706	378	789.0
190	53	30	390	237	194	609.5
3415	2249	599	2974	4725	6387	17915.0
1974	859	213	1290	1350	10043	51040.0
322	121	26	430	341	41	160.0
366	187	43	329	494	1490	1538.0
2294	922	86	1374	3353	2584	16973.0

C-2-3续表2

地区	年末床位数	机构床位	工商登记	编制登记	民政登记	社区床位	留宿床位
全国	**5777288**	**3902235**	**37007**	**1641744**	**1527567**	**1875053**	**759655**
中央级							
北京	133015	125377	963	68148	53904	7638	5905
天津	59862	53180	1010	7954	41975	6682	4323
河北	436839	197469	780	79188	70157	239370	145451
山西	83126	66935		18522	33554	16191	10192
内蒙古	182883	84839		32658	37107	98044	7489
辽宁	206660	175555	346	58971	97898	31105	17309
吉林	81546	77132		68428	6989	4414	3239
黑龙江	129823	125285		43742	64421	4538	2036
上海	122162	110690	478	10302	98923	11472	3950
江苏	554479	364312	2949	191514	157565	190167	113960
浙江	432098	288963	6572	101128	96117	143135	107315
安徽	328417	112565	1220	22846	78555	215852	15327
福建	115015	43249	704	19082	21290	71766	15573
江西	179504	173256		69507	97558	6248	4063
山东	552549	326036	436	88976	174676	226513	88517
河南	338852	256712		30722	105989	82140	23919
湖北	256618	233065	6293	141527	35103	23553	14512
湖南	185723	112008	800	91488	15153	73715	9672
广东	201553	156787	5490	82648	44193	44766	20358
广西	144745	34287		14043	17218	110458	20079
海南	17279	14591	4604	2474	4270	2688	577
重庆	156763	100082	3023	41325	32324	56681	11977
四川	422246	385416	1167	241870	39181	36830	27222
贵州	107439	30218		14984	10161	77221	27496
云南	69306	52528	55	25351	11071	16778	5433
西藏	6943	6896	57	991	4577	47	
陕西	109784	93801		37110	41841	15983	7688
甘肃	84900	31496		11294	9575	53404	41581
青海	16411	12869		3126	2351	3542	1616
宁夏	10963	9665		5710	3626	1298	1252
新疆	49785	46971	60	16115	20245	2814	1624

单位：张、人天、人

日间照料床位	光荣间床位	机构和设施类年末在院总人数	机构类年末在院人数	女性	工商登记	编制登记	民政登记
1115398	**125982**	**3203265**	**2557988**	**594111**	**19133**	**1158954**	**919982**
1733	650	74897	71850	15815	276	50693	20215
2359	691	29008	28382	12482	18	6441	21303
93919	11430	132690	103120	14196	450	47427	33425
5999	4599	41249	38550	2993		12854	19464
90555	2162	114265	52089	7768		20999	21461
13796	3628	116105	109476	18995	145	43618	55150
1175	2509	47283	47230	8212		43440	3082
2502	4663	98832	97625	15312		35240	50236
7522	56	76414	74725	44536	201	9324	64747
76207	6664	243148	211548	57616	1800	127318	73276
35820	2767	158159	138809	47259	3725	45147	41676
200525	3515	173786	65705	15407	915	12539	46358
56193	1511	29912	19412	4626	316	8537	10048
2185	20225	161300	157439	38431		60414	92549
137996	9766	338773	204809	55601	194	63776	102364
58221	13569	261535	209155	37884		21905	82457
9041	12609	172189	170569	43716	1123	107260	26486
64043	6580	144340	87329	21462	308	74881	9277
24408	2940	82775	79589	33651	4058	44705	23660
90379	2165	62098	20170	6394		9563	9540
2111	252	7205	7162	2170	3105	1133	1285
44704	907	95766	70013	14670	1854	30847	19623
9608	4905	312282	307229	39120	481	201867	25871
49725	634	39795	12561	2500		7529	3717
11345	1429	44684	38551	6818	55	19786	6802
47		5245	5245	1503	57	849	3463
8295	2359	73500	68327	11006		25872	31039
11823	1001	20305	16810	3651		7489	5156
1926	32	5569	5055	844		1242	630
46	484	7670	7357	1478		4695	2493
1190	1280	32486	32097	7995	52	11564	13129

C-2-3续表3

地区	收养性机构年末						
	在院人员按性质分				在院人员按年龄分		
	优抚对象	“三无”和五保对象	自费人员	其他社会救济对象	老人	青壮年	少年儿童
全　国	**111728**	**1520127**	**743617**	**144555**	**2284860**	**83090**	**47147**
中央级							
北　京	264	2925	30865	1765	32509	2153	181
天　津	461	1262	23320	2949	24039	1248	66
河　北	5931	64977	27064	17914	94005	2412	1785
山　西	2516	28191	5520	4869	32212	2352	2155
内蒙古	2547	24791	21824	4682	48080	1973	588
辽　宁	4256	36974	46275	25748	85754	4451	940
吉　林	6370	30655	5571	1522	40003	3937	501
黑龙江	6712	61316	25471	1840	89920	4776	363
上　海	435	2186	67820	331	68786	2142	67
江　苏	6563	111953	83407	10406	194950	4519	2132
浙　江	1751	32863	100792	5730	133585	2572	1198
安　徽	1815	44123	17351	284	61189	1059	1313
福　建	756	4104	12491	87	15615	628	1195
江　西	11809	133181	10516	30894	145118	3672	6882
山　东	10950	112872	65578	3926	188708	2034	466
河　南	15582	166003	21250	7060	194002	6459	4231
湖　北	9239	123315	28120	708	155192	8012	1632
湖　南	6279	62941	11831	425	75117	3929	4133
广　东	1796	28138	43442	5688	67202	2449	6493
广　西	1870	5599	11954	233	16477	1036	1818
海　南	102	2529	861	430	5856	627	290
重　庆	855	39913	27030	566	65194	3142	124
四　川	8331	266573	21575	7356	291129	8475	3409
贵　州	272	7904	3358	560	10343	575	1130
云　南	405	30223	3105	5227	31847	1556	614
西　藏	19	4318	10		4835	52	358
陕　西	2056	52049	10552	1428	59796	4225	721
甘　肃	631	11561	2852	101	13362	615	1573
青　海	91	3718	906	1019	4489	320	80
宁　夏	179	5683	825	289	6051	649	39
新　疆	885	17287	12081	518	29495	1041	670

单位：张、人、人次、平方米

在院人数			社区类年末在院人数			年在院人天数	康复和医疗门诊人次数	机构建筑面积
在院人员按类型分				社区养老机构和设施	社区互助型养老设施			
自理（完全自理）	介助（半自理）	介护（不能自理）						
1720532	**458789**	**235776**	**645277**	**416485**	**184999**	**618076607**	**6451390**	**72443121**
12215	9829	12799	3047	1895	1152	10856512	285860	2000558
11048	7051	7254	626	529		5410351	99432	823339
71433	17849	8920	29570	7366	21487	30452343	108057	3569739
28544	4960	3215	2699	812	1154	9596794	55727	1742286
36658	10040	3943	62176	1580	60242	14412180	42573	1492463
68162	14507	8476	6629	3210	48	20732963	88801	3055765
30054	10052	4335	53	53		9270912	79071	940556
75576	14042	5441	1207	1124		20851538	60252	1171182
21599	20262	29134	1689	1684		20923379	128633	2541771
133491	40890	27220	31600	26990	1461	57534310	852933	8631176
94591	28600	14164	19350	9954	4480	32016974	816046	3582428
47723	11552	4286	108081	104292	1044	18698463	69539	2006516
8921	5163	3354	10500	7076	1171	5133862	71653	826107
121155	30380	4137	3861	273		33440380	41860	3481388
154960	26603	9645	133964	81084	44845	60645762	560446	8356475
166015	28717	9960	52380	49310	782	42379273	239884	4001976
115477	35263	14096	1620	726	80	42617461	584310	5186984
57564	18233	7382	57011	48218	7681	22719479	283664	2353585
34052	17982	24110	3186	2079		22593221	955228	3068650
8521	5034	5776	41928	10172	31487	4799050	140525	638860
5624	504	645	43	43		885861	350	239930
56434	7878	4148	25753	19115	2820	19341858	186866	2143379
240348	52511	10154	5053	1674	1203	75293239	477904	5403246
9030	2399	619	27234	26477	500	3176567	21584	532195
22919	8755	2343	6133	4757	250	6929393	15960	907738
4695	440	110				1157721	494	209116
44712	15420	4610	5173	3625	1438	15569427	70731	1392134
10708	3354	1488	3495	1328	1674	2255900	72268	431678
2574	2210	105	514	514		1146556	3794	202545
3815	2125	799	313	313		1439631	8748	482426
21914	6184	3108	389	212		5795247	28197	1026931

C-2-3续表4

地 区	增加值合计	执行企业会计制度单位财务指标					执行行政	
		固定资产原价	营业收入	费用合计	营业利润	企业单位增加值	固定资产原价	上年结转和结余
全 国	**3049522.1**	**213049.2**	**23885.0**	**13081.1**	**-1371.6**	**2654.1**	**5493807.7**	**283729.4**
中央级								
北 京	355426.5	54847.7	4837.4	731.3	200.6	1624.7	149118.3	20031.2
天 津	66861.5	1308.7	140.0	43.0		63.0	54198.0	5777.5
河 北	164970.3	6886.1	338.0	198.6	-9.3	62.8	338143.3	18438.0
山 西	57733.0						137494.3	16556.6
内蒙古	41814.3	2.0					114563.7	6846.9
辽 宁	204790.3	835.5	130.0	126.0	25.0	0.5	198435.2	8495.1
吉 林	32164.9						116114.2	3425.5
黑龙江	45822.1	92.0					164129.6	3991.8
上 海	100598.2	120.1	208.0	1721.6	1.0	4.2	80414.8	2710.6
江 苏	272550.3	47402.2	1332.5	2259.9	-1197.2	-851.4	567028.0	12327.1
浙 江	112094.7	20923.8	6623.8	2703.8	1024.4	1672.8	279990.7	21552.4
安 徽	74466.2	2479.5	476.0	108.0			236594.6	3732.2
福 建	56944.2	4297.4	112.0	87.0		485.6	82042.8	9162.6
江 西	39848.3						160207.5	3765.8
山 东	336647.6	120.0	729.6	657.3	71.1	74.9	300651.6	6668.7
河 南	82033.4	201.0	14.0	2.0		46.0	179361.6	4514.4
湖 北	135794.6	7847.5	550.0	200.0		90.0	313787.5	1958.4
湖 南	94371.1	14031.0	650.0	650.0		8.0	251586.1	5385.7
广 东	172023.8	5030.3	5528.0	1428.5	100.9	569.8	382465.0	48258.2
广 西	151527.0	30.0		1.1			127234.3	16409.7
海 南	9869.2	2497.2	1228.5	1687.0	-1860.7	-1521.1	29916.3	7526.3
重 庆	63586.3	19009.8	866.1	291.6	265.0	311.3	125868.8	1747.6
四 川	98022.7	19255.0	70.2	94.6	6.6	11.2	471222.8	16177.8
贵 州	29633.8						116340.2	5626.7
云 南	38568.9	2053.0		9.0			120215.7	9483.0
西 藏	1250.2	1835.8					20821.7	2212.0
陕 西	119720.1	3.6					190763.1	5636.7
甘 肃	38963.9	202.0					79207.3	1230.6
青 海	8562.4	57.0					7818.9	908.7
宁 夏	10456.0	1226.0					23082.9	5746.1
新 疆	32406.2	455.0	50.9	80.8	1.0	2.0	74988.9	7425.5

单位：万元

事业单位会计制度财务指标				执行民间非营利组织单位会计制度财务指标				
本年收入合计	本年支出合计	收支结余	行政事业单位增加值	固定资产原价	上年结余	本年收入合计	本年费用合计	社会组织增加值
3606527.1	**3723392.1**	**157860.2**	**2765913.9**	**2419724.4**	**47115.1**	**682803.2**	**568331.9**	**280954.1**
418898.9	417850.1	18488.1	336655.2	123603.4	2835.5	46372.6	47935.8	17146.6
58774.5	68823.8	3122.2	60137.1	25277.7	795.6	35312.0	21950.6	6661.4
218410.4	211189.8	14808.7	155624.2	271075.6	2284.8	16905.6	18122.1	9283.3
84333.6	78917.8	10125.8	56278.7	17518.4	301.5	1474.6	2309.1	1454.3
64828.8	62054.8	7973.6	38820.6	27172.1	4.0	6126.4	5995.6	2993.7
247960.9	320073.5	4574.2	200099.7	58351.2	222.2	70351.9	11126.0	4690.1
60091.2	60640.8	1042.9	31957.2	2650.0		880.7	528.7	207.7
57559.0	55333.3	180.5	44163.7	17781.7	2081.4	2613.3	2526.2	1658.4
107513.8	102239.7	2947.8	60494.9	112883.0	11249.7	158699.7	107401.0	40099.1
313891.1	315661.7	8527.4	251549.9	219797.7	1671.6	49643.5	42570.7	21851.8
162825.2	150876.6	4600.6	90466.9	151706.6	1704.0	38308.1	40309.2	19955.0
78358.7	75329.4	600.7	61438.4	125101.5	29.5	20475.6	21062.1	13027.8
71403.7	69983.2	3344.3	54184.1	74726.7	2515.8	5283.4	4839.3	2274.5
59142.7	51157.0	7483.2	37499.6	56498.4	2.2	3979.2	4589.3	2348.7
330383.3	337052.0		249310.8	616202.4		135173.3	135118.3	87261.9
110203.4	107374.1	1654.5	75010.9	69699.8	1017.5	10454.0	12087.0	6976.5
177356.4	176315.9	1428.3	127291.6	40509.8	4.0	13360.1	13653.1	8413.0
137715.3	132588.6	1538.5	91816.8	16865.5	421.1	7249.5	6700.3	2546.3
226921.3	229900.1	16271.4	166605.2	62122.8	9550.4	7618.6	10606.6	4848.8
52609.2	158196.2	11648.7	144982.7	41661.8	1202.1	4759.9	9813.8	6544.3
13760.6	16226.5	2054.4	11185.7	4120.8	1408.0	1228.9	1046.2	204.6
71095.5	71768.0	899.9	56966.2	91119.7	358.2	22574.8	22190.5	6308.8
136434.1	127236.4	7449.3	94113.2	43107.0	224.4	8950.9	7851.8	3898.3
28575.2	27010.9	1271.8	26612.9	59775.4	6258.4	3565.2	4595.4	3020.9
57121.4	49187.1	2852.3	37888.6	10569.7	135.3	682.9	1118.0	680.3
586.4	752.9		1250.2	726.0		10.0		
138718.4	132411.2	9503.0	116963.1	31277.4	-55.1	4810.3	5705.7	2757.0
56039.8	55131.2	480.0	38241.9	19704.7	35.0	410.8	976.8	722.0
8803.9	8454.1	1241.2	7524.7	12647.0	778.0	934.9	1208.1	1037.7
16534.4	13433.2	5606.3	10172.0	1581.6		511.5	511.0	284.0
39676.0	40222.2	6140.6	30606.9	13889.0	80.0	4081.0	3883.6	1797.3

C-2-4 养老

地区	机构数	工商登记	编制登记	民政登记	一个机构多个牌子	0~99张	100~299张
全　国	**33043**	**151**	**13558**	**12314**	**7020**	**18715**	**12154**
中央级							
北　京	592	5	345	219	23	198	275
天　津	346	1	38	276	31	158	153
河　北	1283	4	490	470	319	607	492
山　西	833		260	427	146	580	213
内蒙古	734		313	275	146	432	246
辽　宁	1663	4	282	1096	281	1096	455
吉　林	798		700	70	28	510	244
黑龙江	983		181	682	120	599	295
上　海	637	2	42	590	3	218	330
江　苏	2324	16	1096	1121	91	931	1156
浙　江	1919	18	602	590	709	901	844
安　徽	831	7	184	554	86	347	418
福　建	380	3	225	118	34	249	90
江　西	1906		801	1029	76	1337	525
山　东	2119	4	512	1175	428	799	1105
河　南	2540		338	953	1249	1529	941
湖　北	2008	8	1142	311	547	1010	920
湖　南	1603	1	1383	130	89	1353	218
广　东	1489	30	921	243	295	1072	322
广　西	492		262	158	72	384	91
海　南	220	4	22	85	109	184	17
重　庆	900	23	350	220	307	509	342
四　川	3409	17	2137	347	908	1733	1565
贵　州	387		204	136	47	269	109
云　南	495	1	176	115	203	302	167
西　藏	230	2	10	175	43	204	25
陕　西	759		235	368	156	397	281
甘　肃	342		106	118	118	229	98
青　海	143		14	6	123	108	29
宁　夏	80		41	35	4	35	37
新　疆	598	1	146	222	229	435	151

机构

单位：个、人

300～499张	500张以上	年末职工人数	女性	工商登记	编制登记	民政登记	一个机构多个牌子
1435	**739**	**333450**	**184453**	**4397**	**139380**	**149216**	**40457**
60	59	13373	8534	277	6241	6560	295
13	22	6156	4335	75	1167	4709	205
119	65	18885	10528	84	8534	6876	3391
20	20	7216	3257		2968	3014	1234
42	14	6589	3376		2628	3262	699
81	31	16953	9908	26	5933	9312	1682
37	7	7252	2716		6326	483	443
52	37	8875	4295		3363	4786	726
63	26	22043	15737	124	2050	19808	61
159	78	28752	16559	492	12765	15023	472
108	66	18922	11153	654	7310	7121	3837
52	14	8631	4190	172	2236	5620	603
30	11	4330	1988	75	1726	2321	208
28	16	11819	4497		5201	6329	289
153	62	27277	14863	58	7830	15565	3824
46	24	18818	9462		4486	8351	5981
49	29	16620	9273	256	9812	3216	3336
19	13	12016	6086	135	9893	1369	619
56	39	21635	13824	1150	11284	7381	1820
11	6	6120	4340		2734	3100	286
13	6	1377	817	318	485	316	258
31	18	8232	3896	394	3001	3278	1559
81	30	17999	8137	76	11030	2319	4574
8	1	2638	1233		1322	960	356
17	9	3635	2037	3	1925	849	858
1		627	424	2	89	397	139
65	16	7699	4039		3448	3441	810
10	5	2640	1237		1224	902	514
2	4	771	372		223	80	468
4	4	823	542		520	285	18
5	7	4727	2798	26	1626	2183	892

C-2-4续表1

地　区	受教育程度		职业资格水平		
	大学专科人数	大学本科及以上人数	助理社会工作师人数	社会工作师人数	35岁及以下人数
全　国	**54853**	**30082**	**2839**	**2566**	**86867**
中央级					
北　京	2116	1877	126	93	3016
天　津	1195	620	45	56	1318
河　北	2916	1505	90	102	6591
山　西	1373	742	11	58	2080
内蒙古	1351	576	45	53	1439
辽　宁	3218	2360	81	127	3556
吉　林	1090	680	63	37	2271
黑龙江	1310	560	177	128	2285
上　海	1230	851	134	182	3840
江　苏	4625	2739	289	237	6583
浙　江	2228	1337	136	145	4073
安　徽	1056	461	67	75	2103
福　建	558	477	70	70	1037
江　西	1040	435	57	48	2283
山　东	6725	3737	232	152	9501
河　南	2929	1125	100	84	5969
湖　北	3018	1180	102	60	3828
湖　南	2579	1438	132	115	3396
广　东	3009	2071	341	227	4991
广　西	1445	703	85	108	1954
海　南	246	132	10	19	462
重　庆	1153	674	61	50	1507
四　川	3390	1310	107	176	4515
贵　州	780	387	27	16	843
云　南	742	373	25	21	1194
西　藏	58	10			354
陕　西	1583	656	71	53	2760
甘　肃	564	421	90	34	1023
青　海	93	98	16	18	318
宁　夏	117	158	10	3	249
新　疆	1116	389	39	19	1528

单位：人、人次、时

年龄结构			按人员性质分		志愿服务	
36岁至45岁人数	46岁至55岁人数	56岁及以上人数	管理人员	专业技术技能人员	志愿者服务人次数	志愿服务时间
130623	**92593**	**23367**	**139314**	**194136**	**415643**	**1028142.6**
4792	4328	1237	4354	9019	25352	76682.0
2246	2209	383	2513	3643	11995	21570.0
7268	4201	825	5643	13242	5008	17445.0
3153	1653	330	3315	3901	4801	13280.0
2714	1975	461	2954	3635	338	541.0
6964	5194	1239	7910	9043	5886	13904.0
3214	1525	242	4109	3143	5	
3902	2282	406	4817	4058	608	2430.0
7560	7888	2755	11513	10530	8415	24951.0
10012	9149	3008	7879	20873	70357	204321.0
6348	6439	2062	6612	12310	41222	77190.3
3103	2661	764	4449	4182	16345	43854.0
1821	1113	359	1816	2514	19620	29502.0
5377	3636	523	6299	5520	2963	9113.0
10604	5907	1265	7884	19393	106238	268666.0
6894	4774	1181	9825	8993	800	1686.0
7236	4545	1011	6480	10140	24414	32355.0
5154	2786	680	5038	6978	18892	64770.0
9494	6076	1074	8382	13253	7375	14791.0
2283	1564	319	1973	4147	880	3320.8
577	254	84	575	802	300	
2973	2828	924	4240	3992	12446	31019.0
7430	4759	1295	10391	7608	14723	26265.0
1126	608	61	1627	1011	5700	13015.0
1523	753	165	1929	1706	378	789.0
190	53	30	390	237	194	609.5
2816	1704	419	2974	4725	5902	16242.0
977	523	117	1290	1350	371	1160.0
306	121	26	430	341	41	160.0
347	184	43	329	494	1490	1538.0
2219	901	79	1374	3353	2584	16973.0

C-2-4续表2

地 区	年末床位数	工商登记	编制登记	民政登记	一个机构多个牌子
全 国	**3902235**	**37007**	**1641744**	**1527567**	**695917**
中央级					
北 京	125377	963	68148	53904	2362
天 津	53180	1010	7954	41975	2241
河 北	197469	780	79188	70157	47344
山 西	66935		18522	33554	14859
内蒙古	84839		32658	37107	15074
辽 宁	175555	346	58971	97898	18340
吉 林	77132		68428	6989	1715
黑龙江	125285		43742	64421	17122
上 海	110690	478	10302	98923	987
江 苏	364312	2949	191514	157565	12284
浙 江	288963	6572	101128	96117	85146
安 徽	112565	1220	22846	78555	9944
福 建	43249	704	19082	21290	2173
江 西	173256		69507	97558	6191
山 东	326036	436	88976	174676	61948
河 南	256712		30722	105989	120001
湖 北	233065	6293	141527	35103	50142
湖 南	112008	800	91488	15153	4567
广 东	156787	5490	82648	44193	24456
广 西	34287		14043	17218	3026
海 南	14591	4604	2474	4270	3243
重 庆	100082	3023	41325	32324	23410
四 川	385416	1167	241870	39181	103198
贵 州	30218		14984	10161	5073
云 南	52528	55	25351	11071	16051
西 藏	6896	57	991	4577	1271
陕 西	93801		37110	41841	14850
甘 肃	31496		11294	9575	10627
青 海	12869		3126	2351	7392
宁 夏	9665		5710	3626	329
新 疆	46971	60	16115	20245	10551

单位：张、人

年在院总人天数	年末在院人数	女性	工商登记	编制登记	民政登记	一个机构多个牌子
618076607	**2557988**	**594111**	**19133**	**1158954**	**919982**	**459919**
10856512	71850	15815	276	50693	20215	666
5410351	28382	12482	18	6441	21303	620
30452343	103120	14196	450	47427	33425	21818
9596794	38550	2993		12854	19464	6232
14412180	52089	7768		20999	21461	9629
20732963	109476	18995	145	43618	55150	10563
9270912	47230	8212		43440	3082	708
20851538	97625	15312		35240	50236	12149
20923379	74725	44536	201	9324	64747	453
57534310	211548	57616	1800	127318	73276	9154
32016974	138809	47259	3725	45147	41676	48261
18698463	65705	15407	915	12539	46358	5893
5133862	19412	4626	316	8537	10048	511
33440380	157439	38431		60414	92549	4476
60645762	204809	55601	194	63776	102364	38475
42379273	209155	37884		21905	82457	104793
42617461	170569	43716	1123	107260	26486	35700
22719479	87329	21462	308	74881	9277	2863
22593221	79589	33651	4058	44705	23660	7166
4799050	20170	6394		9563	9540	1067
885861	7162	2170	3105	1133	1285	1639
19341858	70013	14670	1854	30847	19623	17689
75293239	307229	39120	481	201867	25871	79010
3176567	12561	2500		7529	3717	1315
6929393	38551	6818	55	19786	6802	11908
1157721	5245	1503	57	849	3463	876
15569427	68327	11006		25872	31039	11416
2255900	16810	3651		7489	5156	4165
1146556	5055	844		1242	630	3183
1439631	7357	1478		4695	2493	169
5795247	32097	7995	52	11564	13129	7352

C-2-4续表3

地区	在院人员按性质分				收养性机构年末在院人员按	
	优抚对象	“三无”和五保对象	自费人员	其他社会救济对象	老人	青壮年
全　国	**111728**	**1520127**	**743617**	**144555**	**2284860**	**83090**
中央级						
北　京	264	2925	30865	1765	32509	2153
天　津	461	1262	23320	2949	24039	1248
河　北	5931	64977	27064	17914	94005	2412
山　西	2516	28191	5520	4869	32212	2352
内蒙古	2547	24791	21824	4682	48080	1973
辽　宁	4256	36974	46275	25748	85754	4451
吉　林	6370	30655	5571	1522	40003	3937
黑龙江	6712	61316	25471	1840	89920	4776
上　海	435	2186	67820	331	68786	2142
江　苏	6563	111953	83407	10406	194950	4519
浙　江	1751	32863	100792	5730	133585	2572
安　徽	1815	44123	17351	284	61189	1059
福　建	756	4104	12491	87	15615	628
江　西	11809	133181	10516	30894	145118	3672
山　东	10950	112872	65578	3926	188708	2034
河　南	15582	166003	21250	7060	194002	6459
湖　北	9239	123315	28120	708	155192	8012
湖　南	6279	62941	11831	425	75117	3929
广　东	1796	28138	43442	5688	67202	2449
广　西	1870	5599	11954	233	16477	1036
海　南	102	2529	861	430	5856	627
重　庆	855	39913	27030	566	65194	3142
四　川	8331	266573	21575	7356	291129	8475
贵　州	272	7904	3358	560	10343	575
云　南	405	30223	3105	5227	31847	1556
西　藏	19	4318	10		4835	52
陕　西	2056	52049	10552	1428	59796	4225
甘　肃	631	11561	2852	101	13362	615
青　海	91	3718	906	1019	4489	320
宁　夏	179	5683	825	289	6051	649
新　疆	885	17287	12081	518	29495	1041

单位：张、人天、人、人次、平方米

在院人数 年龄分 少年儿童	在院人员按类型分 自理 （完全自理）	介助 （半自理）	介护 （不能自理）	康复和医疗门诊 人次数	机构建筑 面积
47147	**1720532**	**458789**	**235776**	**6451390**	**72443121**
181	12215	9829	12799	285860	2000558
66	11048	7051	7254	99432	823339
1785	71433	17849	8920	108057	3569739
2155	28544	4960	3215	55727	1742286
588	36658	10040	3943	42573	1492463
940	68162	14507	8476	88801	3055765
501	30054	10052	4335	79071	940556
363	75576	14042	5441	60252	1171182
67	21599	20262	29134	128633	2541771
2132	133491	40890	27220	852933	8631176
1198	94591	28600	14164	816046	3582428
1313	47723	11552	4286	69539	2006516
1195	8921	5163	3354	71653	826107
6882	121155	30380	4137	41860	3481388
466	154960	26603	9645	560446	8356475
4231	166015	28717	9960	239884	4001976
1632	115477	35263	14096	584310	5186984
4133	57564	18233	7382	283664	2353585
6493	34052	17982	24110	955228	3068650
1818	8521	5034	5776	140525	638860
290	5624	504	645	350	239930
124	56434	7878	4148	186866	2143379
3409	240348	52511	10154	477904	5403246
1130	9030	2399	619	21584	532195
614	22919	8755	2343	15960	907738
358	4695	440	110	494	209116
721	44712	15420	4610	70731	1392134
1573	10708	3354	1488	72268	431678
80	2574	2210	105	3794	202545
39	3815	2125	799	8748	482426
670	21914	6184	3108	28197	1026931

C-2-4续表4

地区	增加值合计	执行企业会计制度单位财务指标						执行行政
		固定资产原价	营业收入	费用合计	营业利润	企业单位增加值	固定资产原价	上年结转和结余
全　国	**2900025.7**	**208784.9**	**23682.0**	**12947.2**	**-1371.6**	**2106.0**	**4976848.1**	**276755.4**
中央级								
北　京	355039.7	54847.7	4837.4	731.3	200.6	1624.7	149039.9	19986.4
天　津	66451.7	1308.7	140.0	43.0		63.0	49769.8	5777.5
河　北	155222.7	6656.1	338.0	198.6	-9.3	39.8	291529.3	17743.4
山　西	57626.3						137302.3	16556.6
内蒙古	41308.3						111659.0	6846.9
辽　宁	203913.1	300.5	130.0		25.0	25.5	192751.4	8403.3
吉　林	32164.9						116114.2	3425.5
黑龙江	45781.1	92.0					164129.6	3991.8
上　海	100531.2	120.1	208.0	1721.6	1.0	4.2	80414.8	2707.1
江　苏	258379.1	47240.2	1181.5	2259.9	-1197.2	-980.4	514360.8	12306.1
浙　江	101129.5	20857.8	6623.8	2698.0	1024.4	1661.9	272937.9	21437.4
安　徽	54289.4	2457.0	476.0	108.0			131745.7	3079.1
福　建	51228.3	1563.7	60.0	86.0		41.4	55045.3	7426.9
江　西	39826.4						160205.5	3765.8
山　东	299888.7	120.0	729.6	657.3	71.1	74.9	289086.6	6668.7
河　南	74771.0	201.0	14.0	2.0		20.0	150254.4	3735.4
湖　北	133282.0	7847.0	550.0	200.0		90.0	313586.9	1958.4
湖　南	83955.9	13701.0	650.0	650.0		68.0	207333.1	3537.2
广　东	170509.5	5024.3	5528.0	1428.5	100.9	569.8	371573.5	48257.2
广　西	141484.3						62987.5	15939.1
海　南	9865.6	2497.2	1228.5	1687.0	-1860.7	-1521.1	29826.3	7526.3
重　庆	59547.0	18961.8	866.1	291.6	265.0	311.3	99702.5	1747.6
四　川	95301.3	19245.0	70.2	94.6	6.6	11.2	468555.5	16072.8
贵　州	21716.4						63448.9	5338.9
云　南	37915.3	2053.0		9.0			110816.0	9465.1
西　藏	1250.2	1835.8					20821.7	2212.0
陕　西	118270.4						184730.2	5599.7
甘　肃	38000.4	200.0					71244.8	1164.6
青　海	8562.4						7818.9	908.7
宁　夏	10456.0	1200.0					23082.9	5746.1
新　疆	32357.5	455.0	50.9	80.8	1.0	2.0	74972.9	7423.8

单位：万元

事业单位会计制度财务指标				执行民间非营利组织单位会计制度财务指标				
本年收入合计	本年支出合计	收支结余	行政事业单位增加值	固定资产原价	上年结余	本年收入合计	本年费用合计	社会组织增加值
3510764.1	**3626356.5**	**157582.6**	**2690670.2**	**2002751.4**	**39948.2**	**581984.3**	**460805.3**	**207249.5**
418656.9	417642.6	18443.6	336429.6	122304.3	2835.5	46230.5	47759.0	16985.4
58433.3	68479.2	3122.2	59732.0	25127.7	795.6	35307.9	21944.5	6656.7
210752.2	203308.1	14808.7	150945.7	238160.7	1547.8	11515.7	11013.7	4237.2
84278.3	78862.5	10125.8	56256.7	17301.4	295.5	1426.6	2113.8	1369.6
64516.8	61742.8	7973.6	38572.7	26335.1	4.0	5820.4	5688.6	2735.6
246542.2	318865.3	4566.2	199255.9	57183.4	216.7	70326.9	11005.6	4631.7
60091.2	60640.8	1042.9	31957.2	2650.0		880.7	528.7	207.7
57555.0	55329.3	180.5	44163.7	17781.7	2081.4	2392.3	2447.2	1617.4
107181.2	101908.0	2946.9	60468.8	112777.9	11249.7	158299.8	107323.9	40058.2
297656.4	300591.9	8527.4	244030.9	161152.8	1668.6	34191.1	32305.2	15328.6
157994.9	144245.8	4579.6	87038.6	127099.6	1468.6	30756.1	28691.3	12429.0
61184.7	57488.3	497.2	46296.2	84379.9	29.5	14289.2	14431.4	7993.2
66650.6	65184.9	3337.7	49772.4	52291.2	2488.2	3314.6	2988.6	1414.5
59142.7	50967.0	7468.2	37490.5	55618.4	2.2	3979.2	4576.5	2335.9
326414.7	333083.4		246656.6	471507.8		88288.4	88233.4	53157.2
102383.2	99619.8	1654.5	68005.1	67911.3	1014.5	10394.3	11810.6	6745.9
177212.2	176171.7	1428.3	127275.6	33991.8	4.0	9225.7	9458.7	5916.4
126696.0	122610.3	1463.5	83365.3	8669.7	418.1	3362.9	2426.9	522.6
226275.7	229254.3	16271.4	165765.0	61438.3	9523.4	6763.6	9440.7	4174.7
49089.8	154436.5	11641.3	139845.1	14105.5	1192.1	3176.1	3667.3	1639.2
13760.6	16226.5	2054.4	11182.1	4120.8	1408.0	1228.9	1046.2	204.6
67313.7	67986.0	899.9	53307.0	86551.7	358.2	22104.4	21723.4	5928.7
134911.7	125106.2	7449.3	92507.0	37532.7	218.4	6516.0	5686.6	2783.1
23521.1	21945.0	1251.0	20212.7	30747.4	155.0	1103.1	2158.7	1503.7
56799.3	48891.5	2852.3	37344.5	10053.7	135.3	582.9	919.4	570.8
586.4	752.9		1250.2	726.0		10.0		
136533.4	130195.7	9528.1	115633.0	29593.0	-55.1	4785.2	5314.5	2637.4
53635.6	52714.7	480.0	37610.9	17642.0	35.0	184.4	542.2	389.5
8803.9	8454.1	1241.2	7524.7	12647.0	778.0	934.9	1208.1	1037.7
16534.4	13433.2	5606.3	10172.0	1581.6		511.5	511.0	284.0
39656.0	40218.2	6140.6	30602.2	13767.0	80.0	4081.0	3839.6	1753.3

C-2-5 社区养老

地区	机构和设施数		年末职工人数		受教育程度		职业资格
		农村社区服务机构		女性	大学专科人数	大学本科及以上人数	助理社会工作师人数
全国	**18927**	**12073**	**69659**	**23185**	**9201**	**4640**	**670**
中央级							
北京	11	9	94	63	14	11	1
天津	43	43	146	79	31	17	4
河北	247	150	1114	473	154	37	
山西	38	37	111	24	5		
内蒙古	23	16	84	9	7	2	
辽宁	106	45	815	516	118	101	7
吉林	56		285				
黑龙江	48		172	78	16	2	5
上海	38	22	99	34	9	3	3
江苏	3194	2074	18691	6039	2648	973	102
浙江	5897	2613	7666	1792	956	392	39
安徽	1448	1266	8217	2607	751	186	52
福建	912	627	2861	805	261	86	27
江西	17	1	55		1	22	20
山东	640	474	5760	2484	913	866	46
河南	498	423	3937	1479	572	323	5
湖北	336	60	1485	925	337	221	3
湖南	1053	870	5304	1458	817	680	236
广东	363	253	1107	584	126	133	60
广西	1085	929	3232	783	83	21	8
海南	20	3	18	9			
重庆	473	391	1335	643	214	28	2
四川	386	105	1132	352	277	48	16
贵州	1372	1205	4151	1368	652	377	20
云南	192	156	489	161	9	29	5
西藏							
陕西	221	169	640	215	106	29	2
甘肃	107	66	341	81	71	35	7
青海	57	57	99	35	26	16	
宁夏	6		25	14	5		
新疆	40	9	194	75	22	2	

机构和设施

单位：个、人、时

水平	年龄结构				志愿服务	
社会工作师人数	35岁及以下人数	36岁至45岁人数	46岁至55岁人数	56岁及以上人数	志愿者服务人次数	志愿服务时间
265	**16455**	**25559**	**20061**	**7584**	**66684**	**153891.2**
5	11	20	49	14	2320	3040.0
1		28	79	39		
4	367	429	263	55		
	34	54	16	7		
	10	44	23	7		
2	105	318	167	225		
		285				
	36	101	35			
1		23	34	42		
47	5340	6387	5800	1164	37106	86216.0
7	2750	2850	1471	595	3394	4682.0
47	1034	3044	2997	1142	3028	7489.0
43	450	947	1062	402	9	51.0
2	32	19	4			
7	1264	2515	1649	332	18616	44867.2
13	704	1805	1172	256	110	380.0
2	289	558	478	160		
7	986	2072	1734	512	454	2354.0
14	267	306	235	299		
34	229	735	859	1409		
	3	15				
5	131	403	590	211	933	2043.0
5	419	482	168	63		
12	1433	1502	769	447	627	2388.0
5	63	203	150	73		
	150	187	199	104	86	381.0
2	171	117	34	19	1	
	83	16				
	3	19	3			
	91	75	21	7		

C-2-5续表1

地 区	床位数合计	日间照料床位数	#农村	住宿收养床位数	#农村
全 国	**710697**	**98542**	**51011**	**612155**	**466817**
中央级					
北 京	434			434	222
天 津	1355			1355	1355
河 北	12024	1006	247	11018	10007
山 西	569	133	123	436	406
内蒙古	662			662	408
辽 宁	5999	2893	2382	3106	2560
吉 林	570			570	
黑龙江	1434			1434	
上 海	6635			6635	3762
江 苏	57796	16037	9624	41759	13402
浙 江	40486	23536	3225	16950	6200
安 徽	171813	3045	964	168768	145971
福 建	45777	3139	2610	42638	25171
江 西	97	48		49	12
山 东	94976	2400	1520	92576	69931
河 南	66293	18165	15250	48128	42867
湖 北	10076	4111	519	5965	
湖 南	58286	1197	1118	57089	44137
广 东	6772	2517	837	4255	2907
广 西	26293	4030	3013	22263	19975
海 南	580			580	329
重 庆	29149	2168	1914	26981	22929
四 川	3968	3603	701	365	298
贵 州	50555	7012	5167	43543	41023
云 南	6884	772	604	6112	5912
西 藏					
陕 西	5284	321	111	4963	3725
甘 肃	3245	1785	734	1460	1257
青 海	2264	338	338	1926	1926
宁 夏	48	38		10	
新 疆	373	248	10	125	125

单位:张、人、人天、平方米

年末收养人数合计	日间照料人数	农村	住宿收养人数	农村	本年收养照料人天数	机构建筑面积
354496	**26049**	**21649**	**328447**	**262655**	**29914485**	**9983282**
331			331	134	24120	7843
260			260	260		19430
7194	264	209	6930	6762	1319524	182514
127	108		19	19	6935	7400
154			154	153	49468	5910
2250	752	566	1498	1382		97941
1092			1092			7550
2			2			182704
14007	1039	573	12968	4292	1222812	1014802
7737	667	370	7070	1370	1300	857834
90298	299	269	89999	79280	4468043	1676194
6801	417	246	6384	3011	104505	424197
						20625
63848	1410	797	62438	44530	13313885	2175871
48209	13553	12812	34656	30686	2274812	575850
438	38		400			91075
47354	12		47342	37173	584625	687189
1897	1366	214	531	230	270340	167783
10145	1326	1284	8819	8559	1029283	362021
43			43	43		4123
18076	1203	1175	16873	15571	3491988	556019
381	333	144	48	48	20194	254721
25222	2704	2573	22518	21588	421389	370430
4631	4	4	4627	4443	1008844	119986
2719	177	97	2542	2279	302418	82820
1279	377	316	902	841		18650
						7200
						600
1			1	1		4000

C-2-5续表2

地区	增加值合计	执行企业会计制度单位财务指标					执行行政	
		固定资产原价	营业收入	费用合计	营业利润	企业单位增加值	固定资产原价	上年结转和结余
全　国	**96306.8**	**4264.3**	**203.0**	**133.9**		**548.1**	**402436.0**	**5205.9**
中央级								
北　京	386.8						78.4	44.8
天　津	409.8						4428.2	
河　北	1215.3	230.0				23.0	6977.6	16.0
山　西	14.6						122.7	
内蒙古	71.7	2.0					393.0	
辽　宁	819.1	535.0		126.0		-25.0	5656.8	91.8
吉　林								
黑龙江	41.0							
上　海	67.0							3.5
江　苏	13088.4	162.0	151.0			129.0	45125.5	21.0
浙　江	10739.6	66.0		5.8		10.9	6648.3	115.0
安　徽	19122.6	22.5					100521.8	609.8
福　建	5034.0	2733.7	52.0	1.0		444.2	25783.9	1736.0
江　西	21.9						2.0	
山　东	13686.6						11565.0	
河　南	7236.0					26.0	29107.2	779.0
湖　北	1557.0	0.5					95.5	
湖　南	6168.3	330.0				-60.0	37521.3	905.0
广　东	1514.3	6.0					10891.5	1.0
广　西	2663.3	30.0		1.1			25806.1	448.6
海　南	3.6						90.0	
重　庆	3580.2	48.0					23840.1	
四　川	846.8	10.0					1583.1	97.0
贵　州	6598.8						50980.3	230.8
云　南	648.7						9277.7	17.9
西　藏								
陕　西	460.0	3.6					3266.0	37.0
甘　肃	262.6	2.0					2658.0	50.0
青　海		57.0						
宁　夏		26.0						
新　疆	48.7						16.0	1.7

单位：万元

事业单位会计制度财务指标				执行民间非营利组织单位会计制度财务指标				
本年收入合计	本年支出合计	收支结余	行政事业单位增加值	固定资产原价	上年结余	本年收入合计	本年费用合计	社会组织增加值
76038.6	**76562.1**	**256.7**	**59333.6**	**266856.8**	**6396.8**	**51839.4**	**54930.2**	**36425.1**
242.0	207.5	44.5	225.6	1299.1		142.1	176.8	161.2
341.2	344.6		405.1	150.0		4.1	6.1	4.7
1042.3	973.3		1025.9	5949.7		337.5	354.7	166.4
45.3	45.3		14.2	6.0			0.4	0.4
74.3	74.3		55.7	40.0		40.0	40.0	16.0
1298.7	1088.2	8.0	785.7	1157.8	5.5	25.0	120.4	58.4
4.0	4.0					221.0	79.0	41.0
332.6	331.7	0.9	26.1	105.1		399.9	77.1	40.9
15303.7	14138.0		7072.2	56855.5	3.0	14128.0	8979.2	5887.2
3949.3	5749.8	21.0	3310.1	16280.0	235.4	3424.0	10017.9	7418.6
15971.0	16715.4	84.2	14142.2	40384.2		6046.8	6490.9	4980.4
4479.5	4533.8	5.0	4253.1	15918.0	22.0	875.1	783.4	336.7
	190.0	15.0	9.1	880.0			12.8	12.8
3968.6	3968.6		2654.2	82969.6		16484.0	16484.0	11032.4
7820.2	7754.3		7005.8	1788.5	3.0	59.7	246.0	204.2
126.0	126.0		11.8	3871.0		2719.0	2740.0	1545.2
7969.8	6914.2	75.0	4856.0	7055.6		3178.0	3294.1	1372.3
645.6	645.8		840.2	684.5	27.0	855.0	1165.9	674.1
1496.5	1549.4	7.4	2024.0	4680.4		392.1	880.2	639.3
			3.6					
3138.7	3138.7		3258.4	2910.0		395.0	391.7	321.8
388.0	576.7		463.3	2671.9	1.0	804.9	747.2	383.5
4099.1	4249.3	20.8	5657.9	20536.9	6099.9	1180.2	1563.6	940.9
322.1	295.6		539.2	516.0		100.0	198.6	109.5
985.6	998.1	-25.1	460.0					
1974.5	1945.5		229.4	25.0		28.0	36.2	33.2
20.0	4.0		4.7	122.0			44.0	44.0

C-2-6 社区互助型

地区	设施数		年末职工人数		受教育程度		职业资格
		农村社区服务机构		女性	大学专科人数	大学本科及以上人数	助理社会工作师人数
全　国	**40357**	**34702**	**73008**	**24077**	**5853**	**1602**	**117**
中央级							
北　京	212	161	632	252	168	68	
天　津							
河　北	20775	17824	34870	12356	925	146	
山　西	279	137	1020	119	20		1
内蒙古	539	425	460	102	49	6	3
辽　宁	96	61	184	35	22	4	3
吉　林							
黑龙江							
上　海							
江　苏	553	228	2884	1189	287	48	7
浙　江	368	356	978	695	19	5	
安　徽	93	66	375	190	55	11	
福　建	1074	451	1954	529	55	21	
江　西							
山　东	2979	2416	10359	3751	2229	775	69
河　南	24		24				
湖　北	188	77	602	356	240	82	9
湖　南	1319	1188	3017	764	386	136	20
广　东							
广　西	7983	7841	7650	1573	148	126	
海　南							
重　庆	511	497	626	186	92	16	
四　川	874	694	1764	395	279	48	
贵　州	812	721	2398	588	472	87	
云　南	9	9	9				
西　藏							
陕　西	437	406	1181	473	181	6	2
甘　肃	1232	1144	2021	524	226	17	3
青　海							
宁　夏							
新　疆							

养老设施

单位:个、人、时

水平	年龄结构				志愿服务	
社会工作师人数	35岁及以下人数	36岁至45岁人数	46岁至55岁人数	56岁及以上人数	志愿者服务人次数	志愿服务时间
63	**15641**	**25962**	**22318**	**9087**	**42913**	**140023.0**
	157	250	184	41		
5	8035	12022	10630	4183	3089	16330.0
	58	511	133	318		
	94	185	89	92		
3	33	77	57	17		
6	369	1321	1020	174	376	1556.0
1	61	175	334	408		
	85	108	148	34	60	180.0
1	431	711	308	504		
9	3039	3526	2830	964	29129	69749.0
	6	17	1			
5	172	173	224	33		
5	503	1511	761	242		
5	372	2241	3613	1424		
1	51	167	259	149	154	928.0
4	404	755	432	173		
	662	911	647	178	35	108.0
		9				
	347	412	346	76	399	1292.0
18	762	880	302	77	9671	49880.0

C-2-6续表1

地 区	床位数合计	日间照料床位数	#农村	住宿收养床位数	#农村
全 国	**501462**	**210067**	**179676**	**291395**	**270463**
中央级					
北 京	1789	1789	1327		
天 津					
河 北	165135	104151	92654	60984	57163
山 西	5905	2117	1774	3788	843
内蒙古	88292	24		88268	88254
辽 宁	432	175	125	257	207
吉 林					
黑龙江					
上 海					
江 苏	5853	4028	1866	1825	1019
浙 江	7649	7057	6885	592	592
安 徽	2385	612	228	1773	1359
福 建	13676	2965	1284	10711	4788
江 西					
山 东	79240	41080	35996	38160	33945
河 南	1238	658		580	
湖 北	3258	3258	533		
湖 南	9637	4964	4491	4673	4189
广 东					
广 西	82693	15092	14403	67601	66891
海 南					
重 庆	4479	668	628	3811	3811
四 川	4176	3510	2782	666	456
贵 州	8284	5762	4157	2522	2100
云 南	250			250	250
西 藏					
陕 西	4536	3258	3052	1278	1268
甘 肃	12555	8899	7491	3656	3328
青 海					
宁 夏					
新 疆					

单位:张、人、人天、平方米

年末收养人数合计	日间照料人数	农村	住宿收养人数	农村	本年收养照料人天数	机构建筑面积
184999	**58618**	**53234**	**126381**	**122339**	**27838701**	**8116962**
1152	1152	890			172860	69098
21487	13945	13858	7542	7532	1645493	2528891
1154	1154	465				37077
60242	24		60218	60218	16357744	1480286
48			48	48	2739	10960
1461	302	169	1159	569	114890	72970
4480	4480	4480			672000	97655
1044	132	72	912	792	202815	43573
1171			1171	897		162306
44845	23540	20426	21305	19230	5466316	1623045
782	202		580			5858
80	80	80			15000	32740
7681	3669	3267	4012	3692	263750	214097
31487	7434	7329	24053	23980	1913639	1108972
2820	17		2803	2803	741050	134790
1203	1196	1000	7	7	217069	159189
500	440	440	60	60		96947
250			250	250		2611
1438	808	715	630	630	53336	82203
1674	43	43	1631	1631		153694

C-2-6续表2

地区	增加值合计	执行行政事业单位会计制度财务指标				
		固定资产原价	上年结转和结余	本年收入合计	本年支出合计	收支结余
全国	**53189.6**	**114523.6**	**1768.1**	**19724.4**	**20473.5**	**20.9**
中央级						
北京						
天津						
河北	8532.3	39636.4	678.6	6615.9	6908.4	
山西	92.1	69.3		10.0	10.0	
内蒙古	434.3	2511.7		237.7	237.7	
辽宁	58.1	27.0		120.0	120.0	
吉林						
黑龙江						
上海						
江苏	1082.8	7541.7		931.0	931.8	
浙江	225.6	404.5		881.0	881.0	
安徽	1054.2	4327.1	43.3	1203.0	1125.7	19.3
福建	681.9	1213.6	-0.3	273.6	264.5	1.6
江西						
山东	23072.3					
河南	26.4					
湖北	955.6	105.1		18.2	18.2	
湖南	4246.9	6731.7	943.5	3049.5	3064.1	
广东						
广西	7379.4	38440.7	22.0	2022.9	2210.3	
海南						
重庆	459.1	2326.2		643.1	643.3	
四川	1874.6	1084.2	8.0	1134.4	1553.5	
贵州	1318.6	1911.0	57.0	955.0	816.6	
云南	4.9	122.0				
西藏						
陕西	989.7	2766.9		1199.4	1217.4	
甘肃	700.9	5304.5	16.0	429.7	471.0	
青海						
宁夏						
新疆						

单位：万元

		执行民间非营利组织单位会计制度财务指标				
	行政事业单位增加值	固定资产原价	上年结余	本年收入合计	本年费用合计	社会组织增加值
	15910.1	**150116.2**	**770.1**	**48979.5**	**52596.4**	**37279.5**
	3652.6	26965.2	737.0	5052.4	6753.7	4879.7
	7.8	211.0	6.0	48.0	194.9	84.3
	192.2	797.0		266.0	267.0	242.1
	58.1	10.0				
	446.8	1789.4		1324.4	1286.3	636.0
	118.2	8327.0		4128.0	1600.0	107.4
	1000.0	337.4		139.6	139.8	54.2
	158.6	6517.5	5.6	1093.7	1067.3	523.3
		61725.0		30400.9	30400.9	23072.3
					30.4	26.4
	4.2	2647.0		1415.4	1454.4	951.4
	3595.5	1140.2	3.0	708.6	979.3	651.4
	3113.6	22875.9	10.0	1191.7	5266.3	4265.8
	400.8	1658.0		75.4	75.4	58.3
	1142.9	2902.4	5.0	1630.0	1418.0	731.7
	742.3	8491.1	3.5	1281.9	873.1	576.3
	4.9					
	870.1	1684.4		25.1	391.2	119.6
	401.6	2037.7		198.4	398.4	299.3

C-2-7 智障与精神疾病

地　区	单位数	单位数按登记类型分			单位数按床位数量分	
		编制登记	民政登记	一个机构多个牌子	0～99张	100～299张
全　国	**254**	**242**	**7**	**5**	**46**	**99**
中央级						
北　京	2	2				1
天　津	2	2				
河　北	2	2				
山　西	8	8				7
内蒙古	7	7				5
辽　宁	5	5			1	2
吉　林	14	14			2	5
黑龙江	8	8			1	1
上　海	3	3				
江　苏	12	11		1		5
浙　江	3	3				1
安　徽	4	4			2	1
福　建	17	17			1	9
江　西	4	4			3	1
山　东	14	14			1	6
河　南	8	8			3	2
湖　北	14	13	1		1	3
湖　南	18	17	1		5	4
广　东	12	12			2	6
广　西	8	8				2
海　南						
重　庆	9	9			5	1
四　川	27	25		2	5	9
贵　州	23	21		2	11	10
云　南	7	7				5
西　藏						
陕　西	4	4				2
甘　肃	5	4	1		1	3
青　海	1	1				1
宁　夏	1	1				
新　疆	12	8	4		2	7

服务机构总表

单位:个、人

		年末职工人数		年末职工人数按登记类型分		受教育程度	
300~499张	500张以上		女性	编制登记	民政登记	大学专科人数	大学本科及以上人数
57	**52**	**25972**	**15036**	**25364**	**608**	**8248**	**8154**
	1	354	255	354		88	81
1	1	364	165	364		65	69
1	1	517	259	517		50	313
	1	1078	609	1078		226	254
1	1	527	279	527		206	192
1	1	582	293	582		94	87
1	6	1210	587	1210		196	335
2	4	1230	460	1230		260	359
1	2	577	349	577		186	148
3	4	1791	1100	1791		474	813
1	1	157	102	157		22	70
	1	546	291	546		234	119
6	1	995	582	995		375	215
		162	94	162		52	55
7		1736	1067	1736		518	878
2	1	1090	644	1090		367	388
5	5	2789	1712	2587	202	792	1213
5	4	2009	1281	1782	227	676	436
2	2	1215	677	1215		401	404
4	2	1419	986	1419		494	423
	3	442	232	442		154	110
6	7	2422	1318	2422		1132	491
1	1	678	385	678		318	134
2		441	255	441		175	174
1	1	357	180	357		121	76
1		237	129	224	13	93	51
		212	151	212		117	55
1		113	85	113		50	63
2	1	722	509	556	166	312	148

C-2-7续表1

地区	职业资格水平		按人员性质分		年龄	
	助理社会工作师人数	社会工作师人数	管理人员	专业技术技能人员	35岁及以下人数	36岁至45岁人数
全　国	**265**	**218**	**6242**	**18993**	**10433**	**8397**
中央级						
北　京			140	214	195	85
天　津	3		137	227	114	72
河　北	4	3	87	430	141	182
山　西	3	5	196	882	372	400
内蒙古	1	8	117	410	180	129
辽　宁	6	2	189	393	69	245
吉　林	2		524	686	273	564
黑龙江	9	4	242	251	373	441
上　海	20	11	144	433	269	118
江　苏	17	20	218	1573	677	503
浙　江	3	2	30	127	55	65
安　徽		1	117	429	237	173
福　建	17	12	177	818	473	286
江　西	5	7	87	75	44	69
山　东	14	12	332	1404	729	455
河　南	6	23	663	427	463	382
湖　北	13	18	466	2323	1227	816
湖　南	20	9	414	1595	758	862
广　东	56	29	377	838	494	457
广　西	9	11	206	1213	759	335
海　南						
重　庆	5	10	82	360	158	139
四　川	21	14	625	1797	1281	679
贵　州	2		256	422	208	252
云　南	3	3	127	314	190	133
西　藏						
陕　西	5	4	45	312	118	104
甘　肃	1	3	39	198	76	107
青　海	3	2	42	170	132	39
宁　夏	6	2	53	60	51	58
新　疆	11	3	110	612	317	247

单位：个、人、人次、时

结构		志愿服务		年末床位数	光荣间床位	床位按登记类型分	
46岁至55岁人数	56岁及以上人数	志愿者服务人次数	志愿服务时间			编制登记	民政登记
5720	**1436**	**12015**	**29217.0**	**80340**	**3273**	**78992**	**1348**
56	18			654		654	
124	54			950		950	
146	48			919		919	
250	56			1860	515	1860	
181	37			1940	40	1940	
240	28			2293	25	2293	
314	59			7180	575	7180	
408	22	200	300.0	3783	425	3783	
114	76	965	1930.0	1800		1800	
483	128	1422	2975.0	5767	10	5767	
34	3	6100	16200.0	1110		1110	
76	60			765		765	
185	51			4309	67	4309	
46	3	132	528.0	396		396	
447	105	2232	4943.0	3376		3376	
209	36			1912	3	1912	
522	224			5734	250	5309	425
321	68	210	630.0	5365	261	4765	600
224	40			4134	21	4134	
271	54	50	110.0	3042	152	3042	
109	36	320	710.0	2314		2314	
377	85			10601	138	10601	
170	48	13		2965	217	2965	
92	26			1930		1930	
109	26	20	75.0	1110	360	1110	
41	13			891	110	851	40
24	17	14	42.0	260	38	260	
4				315		315	
143	15	337	774.0	2665	66	2382	283

C-2-7续表2

地 区	年在院总人天数	年末在院人数	女性	在院人数按登记类型分 编制登记	民政登记
全 国	**19423029**	**64506**	**18175**	**63885**	**621**
中央级					
北 京	156089	422	159	422	
天 津	300760	829	227	829	
河 北	300357	842	139	842	
山 西	525909	1562	147	1562	
内蒙古	521389	1433	400	1433	
辽 宁	431662	2115	150	2115	
吉 林	926237	3429	745	3429	
黑龙江	334951	2224	745	2224	
上 海	622768	1717	492	1717	
江 苏	1722899	5162	1695	5162	
浙 江	223150	630	246	630	
安 徽	218525	641	103	641	
福 建	1270669	3817	1004	3817	
江 西	77879	372	35	372	
山 东	840391	2632	422	2632	
河 南	682244	1714	546	1714	
湖 北	1519991	4286	1697	4018	268
湖 南	918253	4005	1351	3941	64
广 东	1071998	3722	1150	3722	
广 西	875028	2977	890	2977	
海 南					
重 庆	714557	2095	614	2095	
四 川	2814149	9745	2904	9745	
贵 州	684627	2074	434	2074	
云 南	370120	1568	447	1568	
西 藏					
陕 西	356870	1000	238	1000	
甘 肃	137162	402	132	376	26
青 海	57246	260	106	260	
宁 夏	63000	315	189	315	
新 疆	684149	2516	768	2253	263

单位:人天、人

在院人员按性质分				在院人员按年龄分		
优抚对象	“三无”和五保对象	自费人员	其他社会救济对象	老人	青壮年	少年儿童
11238	**18213**	**29497**	**4729**	**24514**	**38737**	**1255**
4	10	105	303	102	306	14
157	265	407		217	612	
507	10	306	19	411	429	2
627	263	671	46	567	978	17
92	455	905	154	313	1110	10
380	469	728	20	1222	891	2
795	1626	875	202	1915	1514	
170	1780	274		643	1578	3
51	116	903	647	532	1185	
925	2196	1894		2040	3099	23
95	47	488		212	413	5
325	62	254		163	474	4
366	1141	2239	71	1081	2688	48
25	247	100	50	139	233	
1545	310	777		1249	1332	51
217	179	1072	275	187	1458	69
501	663	2307	344	1116	3085	85
1129	963	1913		1619	2041	345
552	769	1183	1169	1167	2454	101
359	529	2017	106	870	1936	171
50	812	1233	368	1057	1026	12
1605	1778	5686	424	4390	5214	141
44	742	1256	8	950	1109	15
88	821	269	207	488	1065	15
484	329	187		500	462	38
100	215	45	43	151	243	8
2	6	257		118	140	2
14	215	86		79	194	42
29	1195	1060	273	1016	1468	32

C-2-7续表3

地区	在院人员按类型分 自理(完全自理)	介助(半自理)	介护(不能自理)	康复和医疗门诊人次数	家庭寄养儿童数量	机构建筑面积
全国	**35070**	**21748**	**7688**	**2762553**		**2853357**
中央级						
北京	168	190	64	152851		5768
天津	782	47		52259		11677
河北	348	457	37	37055		87308
山西	950	549	63	68679		89455
内蒙古	585	723	125	63773		92630
辽宁	1964	128	23			54798
吉林	1480	1641	308	96876		66578
黑龙江	1271	917	36	60870		42200
上海	733	984		5614		81648
江苏	2719	1595	848	77204		232091
浙江	373	201	56			56500
安徽	37	554	50	57291		28661
福建	2625	647	545	175765		114382
江西	275	71	26			8862
山东	2271	281	80	129250		150277
河南	892	395	427	283781		67577
湖北	2174	1605	507	511252		325404
湖南	1611	1215	1179	261547		182523
广东	2320	1096	306	73013		93675
广西	1324	1069	584	142985		382082
海南						
重庆	1206	623	266	51451		89840
四川	4608	3493	1644	202444		223939
贵州	827	1132	115	66061		80402
云南	661	784	123	33003		103299
西藏						
陕西	753	205	42	20130		59835
甘肃	126	246	30	85449		16482
青海	259	1				18000
宁夏	43	182	90	7000		1200
新疆	1685	717	114	46950		86263

单位：人、人次、平方米、万元

增加值合计	执行行政事业单位会计制度财务指标					
	固定资产原价	上年结转和结余	本年收入合计	本年支出合计	收支结余	行政事业单位增加值
287151.9	**468782.7**	**48192.9**	**573240.2**	**522833.7**	**43227.5**	**287151.9**
3803.6	7997.6	1050.8	21186.6	20865.2	1481.8	3803.6
6868.7	6197.1	346.2	9757.7	9032.7	1071.1	6868.7
5731.5	19928.3	345.5	10302.3	9337.3	855.0	5731.5
8609.3	16522.9	2815.5	16929.0	17958.3	345.8	8609.3
6220.0	3982.9	1074.9	11305.9	9765.3	3152.2	6220.0
5294.6	9709.9	3891.7	9159.3	10618.5		5294.6
9327.2	20742.7	350.0	15744.2	14251.5	1127.0	9327.2
2774.9	19308.0	1303.0	8868.0	9121.0		2774.9
11639.4	18294.5	1106.4	16371.5	16215.7	1241.5	11639.4
30869.3	53239.9	2187.1	55479.8	43951.9	11085.5	30869.3
4088.9	8868.2	272.2	9002.6	7169.6	592.4	4088.9
4196.0	3203.8	-35.1	8490.8	6655.4	31.6	4196.0
12589.3	14290.7	719.7	30988.2	24762.1	1693.6	12589.3
1156.3	670.8		1980.5	1522.4		1156.3
20424.5	31096.3		40037.3	40037.3		20424.5
16780.2	13071.8		21525.9	20869.2	1740.4	16780.2
22912.1	41426.5	302.1	53211.1	51992.0	1478.8	22912.1
15299.4	18096.9	300.0	30937.6	25999.7	1253.0	15299.4
19494.4	28524.2	1863.3	33872.0	29216.2	776.2	19494.4
12700.4	21467.8	5511.8	31128.7	29632.6	71.3	12700.4
8741.3	8273.9		18947.4	16664.4	1097.2	8741.3
28631.4	47255.8	6807.7	57435.4	48322.6	2845.6	28631.4
8598.9	10889.2	2360.5	10823.0	12385.3	1501.0	8598.9
4853.9	18013.0	4330.1	9037.1	9477.5	1424.6	4853.9
2969.7	7379.3	5158.1	4225.0	7817.4	4427.4	2969.7
1745.6	4491.6	2846.8	5753.7	4138.4	73.9	1745.6
1372.8	2748.0		5548.3	5153.6		1372.8
583.5	660.0	1271.0	2075.3	1355.4	1990.9	583.5
8875.0	12431.1	2013.6	23116.0	18545.2	1869.7	8875.0

C–2–8 福利类

地区	单位数	编制登记	一个机构多个牌子	0～99张	100～299张	300～499张	500张以上
全国	**156**	**151**	**5**	**36**	**56**	**28**	**36**
中央级							
北京	2	2			1		1
天津	1	1					1
河北							
山西	1	1			1		
内蒙古	5	5			4	1	
辽宁							
吉林	7	7		1	1		5
黑龙江	7	7		1		2	4
上海	3	3				1	2
江苏	11	10	1		5	3	3
浙江	2	2				1	1
安徽	3	3		2	1		
福建	14	14		1	7	5	1
江西	3	3		2	1		
山东	2	2			1	1	
河南	7	7		3	2	2	
湖北	3	3		1	1		1
湖南	10	10		3	4	1	2
广东	3	3		1	1		1
广西	4	4			1	1	2
海南							
重庆	9	9		5	1		3
四川	18	16	2	4	4	4	6
贵州	23	21	2	11	10	1	1
云南	5	5			3	2	
西藏							
陕西	1	1					1
甘肃	2	2			2		
青海	1	1			1		
宁夏	1	1				1	
新疆	8	8		1	4	2	1

精神病院和医院

单位:个、人

年末职工人数	女性	受教育程度：大学专科人数	受教育程度：大学本科及以上人数	职业资格水平：助理社会工作师人数	职业资格水平：社会工作师人数	按人员性质分：管理人员	按人员性质分：专业技术技能人员
14300	**8096**	**4991**	**4010**	**124**	**117**	**3757**	**9806**
354	255	88	81			140	214
247	108	65	69	3		47	200
95	47	34	31	1	1	38	57
324	153	136	89	1	6	81	243
744	399	122	73	1		265	479
1184	439	246	334	9	4	202	245
577	349	186	148	20	11	144	433
1507	931	423	650	17	17	203	1304
81	49	8	36			22	59
250	156	108	51		1	17	233
837	474	330	207	14	12	150	687
159	93	52	55	5	7	86	73
236	110	52	72	2	5	59	177
789	468	294	237	3	11	591	198
381	192	132	74			58	323
1086	651	371	255		1	240	846
636	412	209	310	7	3	203	433
732	480	257	266	3	3	139	593
442	232	154	110	5	10	82	360
1484	769	765	320	13	12	430	1054
678	385	318	134	2		256	422
324	190	132	135	2	2	107	217
138	51	46	32	5	3	8	130
134	77	50	17	1	1	11	123
212	151	117	55	3	2	42	170
113	85	50	63	6	2	53	60
556	390	246	106	1	3	83	473

C-2-8续表1

地区	年龄结构				志愿服务		年末床位数	光荣间床位
	35岁及以下人数	36岁至45岁人数	46岁至55岁人数	56岁及以上人数	志愿者服务人次数	志愿服务时间		
全　国	**5789**	**4566**	**3116**	**843**	**3360**	**7309.0**	**49356**	**1677**
中央级								
北　京	195	85	56	18			654	
天　津	75	65	70	37			650	
河　北								
山　西	16	33	40	6			150	
内蒙古	101	86	114	23			1338	7
辽　宁								
吉　林	180	320	208	36			4800	470
黑龙江	357	427	392	22	200	300.0	3583	425
上　海	269	118	114	76	965	1930.0	1800	
江　苏	594	406	393	114	1422	2975.0	4701	10
浙　江	35	22	21	3			910	
安　徽	141	47	18	44			265	
福　建	383	240	164	50			3623	67
江　西	44	69	43	3	132	528.0	371	
山　东	76	57	70	33	12	30.0	430	
河　南	391	258	115	25			1312	3
湖　北	50	137	121	73			666	
湖　南	385	524	146	31	210	630.0	2556	215
广　东	289	243	90	14			1924	6
广　西	386	168	148	30			1732	
海　南								
重　庆	158	139	109	36	320	710.0	2314	
四　川	802	394	238	50			7374	19
贵　州	208	252	170	48	13		2965	217
云　南	130	97	73	24			1530	
西　藏								
陕　西	74	29	28	7	20	75.0	500	200
甘　肃	28	74	22	10			251	
青　海	132	39	24	17	14	42.0	260	38
宁　夏	51	58	4				315	
新　疆	239	179	125	13	52	89.0	2382	

单位：张、人天、人、人次、时

年在院总人天数	年末在院人数		在院人员按性质分			
		女性	优抚对象	“三无”和五保对象	自费人员	其他社会救济对象
11867500	**39808**	**12294**	**2679**	**14633**	**18556**	**3909**
156089	422	159	4	10	105	303
232505	642	217		265	377	
54020	148	38	2	60	86	46
333115	963	255	80	450	454	154
468627	2296	468	396	1277	623	
333699	2115	739	81	1760	274	
622768	1717	492	51	116	903	647
1397510	4096	1212	606	2129	1214	
150150	430	221	60	47	323	
39119	141	56		37	104	
1027214	3165	804	273	919	1902	71
71679	347	30		247	100	50
117194	387	109	80	249	58	
463244	1114	410	4	179	656	275
182981	526	155		21	392	112
458616	2251	722	424	609	1218	
496199	1725	682	40	397	230	990
464498	1727	559	141	350	1169	101
714557	2095	614	50	812	1233	368
2071746	6714	2320	235	1365	4417	369
684627	2074	434	44	742	1256	8
302595	1194	363	8	723	181	99
163520	448	120	51	319	78	
88330	243	100	32	134	35	43
57246	260	106	2	6	257	
63000	315	189	14	215	86	
652652	2253	720	1	1195	825	273

C-2-8续表2

地区	在院人员按年龄分			在院人员按类型分			康复和医疗门诊人次数	机构建筑面积
	老人	青壮年	少年儿童	自理（完全自理）	介助（半自理）	介护（不能自理）		
全国	**14236**	**24707**	**865**	**20810**	**13713**	**5285**	**1377858**	**1607311**
中央级								
北京	102	306	14	168	190	64	152851	5768
天津	161	481		642			18875	2000
河北								
山西	46	102		128	15	5	426	8262
内蒙古	241	722		198	642	123	19414	62206
辽宁								
吉林	1033	1263		1329	789	178	92809	17750
黑龙江	534	1578	3	1162	917	36	60870	39800
上海	532	1185		733	984		5614	81648
江苏	1613	2466	17	2002	1312	782	77204	194350
浙江	156	269	5	209	171	50		35000
安徽	85	56		37	54	50	19322	15661
福建	669	2448	48	2307	620	238	162765	97290
江西	114	233		250	71	26		8362
山东	178	209		349	23	15	4788	23538
河南	120	925	69	292	395	427	258761	64577
湖北	56	467	3		466	60	16750	35727
湖南	956	1027	268	1114	539	598	101936	37895
广东	605	1120		1436	186	103	43934	44063
广西	495	1075	157	848	472	407	13397	305785
海南								
重庆	1057	1026	12	1206	623	266	51451	89840
四川	2875	3710	129	2527	2746	1441	127606	184004
贵州	950	1109	15	827	1132	115	66061	74782
云南	400	779	15	641	436	117	26933	46819
西藏								
陕西	137	285	26	400	48			24759
甘肃	39	196	8	87	145	11	8176	9824
青海	118	140	2	259	1			18000
宁夏	79	194	42	43	182	90	7000	1200
新疆	885	1336	32	1616	554	83	40915	78400

单位：人、人次、平方米

增加值合计	执行行政事业单位会计制度财务指标					
	固定资产原价	上年结转和结余	本年收入合计	本年支出合计	收支结余	行政事业单位增加值
166315.8	**249047.8**	**23556.4**	**334208.6**	**296390.5**	**33577.9**	**166315.8**
3803.6	7997.6	1050.8	21186.6	20865.2	1481.8	3803.6
4936.5	1957.6		7017.8	6462.3	555.5	4936.5
1459.8	472.8		2078.3	2078.3		1459.8
3233.5	1435.9	1074.9	6643.4	5102.8	3152.2	3233.5
5142.5	11278.2		8189.7	7364.7	298.0	5142.5
2739.4	18421.0	1303.0	8371.0	8624.0		2739.4
11639.4	18294.5	1106.4	16371.5	16215.7	1241.5	11639.4
22554.0	33567.2	1392.7	44906.5	34229.5	11082.1	22554.0
2674.9	6990.5		6838.1	5562.9		2674.9
2287.6	1025.3	-35.1	3511.3	3582.7	31.6	2287.6
11195.3	13852.9	719.7	25591.3	21496.6	1041.6	11195.3
1155.6	654.2		1975.0	1516.9		1155.6
3369.6	2854.0		5210.0	5210.0		3369.6
8425.4	8387.7		15271.9	14175.2	946.3	8425.4
1360.6	1575.0		3049.0	3049.0		1360.6
6013.8	9956.3	300.0	14496.1	11169.0	1253.0	6013.8
12344.1	16184.2	85.0	20907.1	18352.2		12344.1
7506.4	10948.2	2123.0	15501.2	15850.3	71.3	7506.4
8741.3	8273.9		18947.4	16664.4	1097.2	8741.3
20455.6	30441.3	3850.2	36993.6	31124.2	2511.1	20455.6
8598.9	10889.2	2360.5	10823.0	12385.3	1501.0	8598.9
3861.1	15293.6	1843.4	6654.1	7622.9	346.2	3861.1
1021.2	1789.9	2805.0	2106.8	1878.8	3033.0	1021.2
1140.4	1184.3	292.3	1446.9	1372.0	73.9	1140.4
1372.8	2748.0		5548.3	5153.6		1372.8
583.5	660.0	1271.0	2075.3	1355.4	1990.9	583.5
8699.3	11914.5	2013.6	22497.4	17926.6	1869.7	8699.3

C-2-9 复退军人

地区	单位数					年末职工人数	女性
		0～99张	100～299张	300～499张	500张以上		
全国	**98**	**10**	**43**	**29**	**16**	**11672**	**6940**
中央级							
北京							
天津	1			1		117	57
河北	2			1	1	517	259
山西	7		6		1	983	562
内蒙古	2		1		1	203	126
辽宁	5	1	2	1	1	582	293
吉林	7	1	4	1	1	466	188
黑龙江	1		1			46	21
上海							
江苏	1				1	284	169
浙江	1		1			76	53
安徽	1				1	296	135
福建	3		2	1		158	108
江西	1	1				3	1
山东	12	1	5	6		1500	957
河南	1				1	301	176
湖北	11		2	5	4	2408	1520
湖南	8	2		4	2	923	630
广东	9	1	5	2	1	579	265
广西	4		1	3		687	506
海南							
重庆							
四川	9	1	5	2	1	938	549
贵州							
云南	2		2			117	65
西藏							
陕西	3		2	1		219	129
甘肃	3	1	1	1		103	52
青海							
宁夏							
新疆	4	1	3			166	119

精神病院

单位：个、人

受教育程度		职业资格水平		按人员性质分	
大学专科人数	大学本科及以上人数	助理社会工作师人数	社会工作师人数	管理人员	专业技术技能人员
3257	**4144**	**141**	**101**	**2485**	**9187**
				90	27
50	313	4	3	87	430
192	223	2	4	158	825
70	103		2	36	167
94	87	6	2	189	393
74	262	1		259	207
14	25			40	6
51	163		3	15	269
14	34	3	2	8	68
126	68			100	196
45	8	3		27	131
				1	2
466	806	12	7	273	1227
73	151	3	12	72	229
660	1139	13	18	408	2000
305	181	20	8	174	749
192	94	49	26	174	405
237	157	6	8	67	620
367	171	8	2	195	743
43	39	1	1	20	97
75	44		1	37	182
43	34		2	28	75
66	42	10		27	139

C-2-9续表1

地区	年龄结构				志愿服务		年末床位数	
	35岁及以下人数	36岁至45岁人数	46岁至55岁人数	56岁及以上人数	志愿者服务人次数	志愿服务时间		光荣间床位
全　国	**4644**	**3831**	**2604**	**593**	**8655**	**21908.0**	**30984**	**1596**
中央级								
北　京								
天　津	39	7	54	17			300	
河　北	141	182	146	48			919	
山　西	356	367	210	50			1710	515
内蒙古	79	43	67	14			602	33
辽　宁	69	245	240	28			2293	25
吉　林	93	244	106	23			2380	105
黑龙江	16	14	16				200	
上　海								
江　苏	83	97	90	14			1066	
浙　江	20	43	13		6100	16200.0	200	
安　徽	96	126	58	16			500	
福　建	90	46	21	1			686	
江　西			3				25	
山　东	653	398	377	72	2220	4913.0	2946	
河　南	72	124	94	11			600	
湖　北	1177	679	401	151			5068	250
湖　南	373	338	175	37			2809	46
广　东	205	214	134	26			2210	15
广　西	373	167	123	24	50	110.0	1310	152
海　南								
重　庆								
四　川	479	285	139	35			3227	119
贵　州								
云　南	60	36	19	2			400	
西　藏								
陕　西	44	75	81	19			610	160
甘　肃	48	33	19	3			640	110
青　海								
宁　夏								
新　疆	78	68	18	2	285	685.0	283	66

单位：人、人次、时、张、人天

年在院总人天数	年末在院人数		在院人员按性质分			
		女性	优抚对象	“三无”和五保对象	自费人员	其他社会救济对象
7555529	**24698**	**5881**	**8559**	**3580**	**10941**	**820**
68255	187	10	157		30	
300357	842	139	507	10	306	19
471889	1414	109	625	203	585	
188274	470	145	12	5	451	
431662	2115	150	380	469	728	20
457610	1133	277	399	349	252	202
1252	109	6	89	20		
325389	1066	483	319	67	680	
73000	200	25	35		165	
179406	500	47	325	25	150	
243455	652	200	93	222	337	
6200	25	5	25			
723197	2245	313	1465	61	719	
219000	600	136	213		416	
1337010	3760	1542	501	642	1915	232
459637	1754	629	705	354	695	
575799	1997	468	512	372	953	179
410530	1250	331	218	179	848	5
742403	3031	584	1370	413	1269	55
67525	374	84	80	98	88	108
193350	552	118	433	10	109	
48832	159	32	68	81	10	
31497	263	48	28		235	

C-2-9续表2

地区	在院人员按年龄分			在院人员按类型分			康复和医疗门诊人次数	机构建筑面积
	老人	青壮年	少年儿童	自理（完全自理）	介助（半自理）	介护（不能自理）		
全国	**10278**	**14030**	**390**	**14260**	**8035**	**2403**	**1384695**	**1246047**
中央级								
北京								
天津	56	131		140	47		33384	9677
河北	411	429	2	348	457	37	37055	87308
山西	521	876	17	822	534	58	68253	81193
内蒙古	72	388	10	387	81	2	44359	30424
辽宁	1222	891	2	1964	128	23		54798
吉林	882	251		151	852	130	4067	48828
黑龙江	109			109				2400
上海								
江苏	427	633	6	717	283	66		37741
浙江	56	144		164	30	6		21500
安徽	78	418	4		500		37969	13000
福建	412	240		318	27	307	13000	17092
江西	25			25				500
山东	1071	1123	51	1922	258	65	124462	126739
河南	67	533		600			25020	3000
湖北	1060	2618	82	2174	1139	447	494502	289677
湖南	663	1014	77	497	676	581	159611	144628
广东	562	1334	101	884	910	203	29079	49612
广西	375	861	14	476	597	177	129588	76297
海南								
重庆								
四川	1515	1504	12	2081	747	203	74838	39934
贵州								5620
云南	88	286		20	348	6	6070	56480
西藏								
陕西	363	177	12	353	157	42	20130	35076
甘肃	112	47		39	101	19	77273	6658
青海								
宁夏								
新疆	131	132		69	163	31	6035	7863

单位：人、人次、平方米、万元

增加值合计	执行行政事业单位会计制度财务指标					
	固定资产原价	上年结转和结余	本年收入合计	本年支出合计	收支结余	行政事业单位增加值
120836.1	**219734.9**	**24636.5**	**239031.6**	**226443.2**	**9649.6**	**120836.1**
1932.2	4239.5	346.2	2739.9	2570.4	515.6	1932.2
5731.5	19928.3	345.5	10302.3	9337.3	855.0	5731.5
7149.5	16050.1	2815.5	14850.7	15880.0	345.8	7149.5
2986.5	2547.0		4662.5	4662.5		2986.5
5294.6	9709.9	3891.7	9159.3	10618.5		5294.6
4184.7	9464.5	350.0	7554.5	6886.8	829.0	4184.7
35.5	887.0		497.0	497.0		35.5
8315.3	19672.7	794.4	10573.3	9722.4	3.4	8315.3
1414.0	1877.7	272.2	2164.5	1606.7	592.4	1414.0
1908.4	2178.5		4979.5	3072.7		1908.4
1394.0	437.8		5396.9	3265.5	652.0	1394.0
0.7	16.6		5.5	5.5		0.7
17054.9	28242.3		34827.3	34827.3		17054.9
8354.8	4684.1		6254.0	6694.0	794.1	8354.8
21551.5	39851.5	302.1	50162.1	48943.0	1478.8	21551.5
9285.6	8140.6		16441.5	14830.7		9285.6
7150.3	12340.0	1778.3	12964.9	10864.0	776.2	7150.3
5194.0	10519.6	3388.8	15627.5	13782.3		5194.0
8175.8	16814.5	2957.5	20441.8	17198.4	334.5	8175.8
992.8	2719.4	2486.7	2383.0	1854.6	1078.4	992.8
1948.5	5589.4	2353.1	2118.2	5938.6	1394.4	1948.5
605.2	3307.3	2554.5	4306.8	2766.4		605.2
175.7	516.6		618.6	618.6		175.7

C-2-10 为儿童提供住宿的

地区	单位数	单位数按登记类型分			单位数按床位数量分	
		编制登记	民政登记	一个机构多个牌子	0~99张	100~299张
全国	**890**	**443**	**35**	**412**	**524**	**264**
中央级						
北京	13	12	1		5	5
天津	2	2				1
河北	13	7		6	11	2
山西	10	5	2	3	8	2
内蒙古	8	7	1		2	4
辽宁	12	9	1	2	7	3
吉林	18	9		9	7	9
黑龙江	16	15	1		2	13
上海	4	3	1		2	1
江苏	45	14		31	31	9
浙江	16	11		5	5	8
安徽	52	30	1	21	26	20
福建	12	6	3	3	6	5
江西	17	9		8	13	2
山东	26	16		10	7	5
河南	22	18	2	2	11	7
湖北	117	35		82	93	15
湖南	72	27	2	43	52	15
广东	39	27	9	3	20	14
广西	37	7		30	24	12
海南	2	2			1	1
重庆	15	5	1	9	9	3
四川	117	36	1	80	90	19
贵州	25	16		9	10	12
云南	37	20	1	16	18	18
西藏	15	11	4		7	6
陕西	13	11		2	3	7
甘肃	27	16	2	9	12	12
青海	22	6	1	15	15	3
宁夏	10	6		4	6	2
新疆	56	45	1	10	21	29

社会服务机构总表

单位:个、人

		年末职工人数		年末职工人数按登记类型分		
300～499张	500张以上		女性	编制登记	民政登记	一个机构多个牌子
69	**33**	**14817**	**9540**	**11197**	**632**	**2988**
2	1	565	414	529	36	
	1	124	82	124		
		101	53	61		40
		131	58	71	11	49
1	1	331	175	329	2	
	2	568	348	482	9	77
1	1	369	173	323		46
1		458	292	444	14	
	1	471	407	418	53	
3	2	662	462	539		123
2	1	430	316	391		39
5	1	1024	639	769	20	235
1		152	105	111	21	20
2		177	92	128		49
10	4	628	434	456		172
2	2	886	743	857	18	11
7	2	1237	769	481		756
4	1	778	388	371	49	358
4	1	1076	702	765	287	24
1		636	456	474		162
		19	14	19		
1	2	360	254	278	16	66
7	1	956	572	647	4	305
2	1	332	183	183		149
1		347	218	231	4	112
1	1	221	139	166	55	
1	2	257	146	242		15
2	1	405	184	323	17	65
1	3	196	128	167	10	19
1	1	273	217	245		28
6		647	377	573	6	68

C-2-10续表1

地区	受教育程度		职业资格水平		按人员性质分	
	大学专科人数	大学本科及以上人数	助理社会工作师人数	社会工作师人数	管理人员	专业技术技能人员
全　国	**4703**	**3786**	**394**	**466**	**5973**	**8844**
中央级						
北　京	193	256	15	13	148	417
天　津	35	62	4	11	30	94
河　北	16	6		1	34	67
山　西	32	23	2	9	62	69
内蒙古	137	89	10	13	141	190
辽　宁	145	342	6	5	183	385
吉　林	62	68		2	95	274
黑龙江	165	130	2	20	280	178
上　海	116	129	20	42	59	412
江　苏	196	207	28	48	142	520
浙　江	114	165	16	21	152	278
安　徽	259	173	31	21	524	500
福　建	56	60	7	8	86	66
江　西	69	26	7	1	143	34
山　东	211	255	14	17	165	463
河　南	486	109	8	28	571	315
湖　北	372	229	22	21	381	856
湖　南	267	125	17	13	367	411
广　东	197	117	55	39	463	613
广　西	190	182	19	17	207	429
海　南	2			1	10	9
重　庆	126	162	17	20	127	233
四　川	327	234	40	25	624	332
贵　州	113	109	11	3	248	84
云　南	77	125	5	19	124	223
西　藏	31	14	2		75	146
陕　西	84	76	4	6	91	166
甘　肃	125	72	11	6	156	249
青　海	96	29	4	1	64	132
宁　夏	82	89	4	12	64	209
新　疆	322	123	13	23	157	490

单位:人、个、人次、时

年龄结构				志愿服务	
35岁及以下 人数	36岁至45岁 人数	46岁至55岁 人数	56岁及以上 人数	志愿者 服务人次数	志愿 服务时间
6061	**5368**	**2896**	**492**	**20250**	**58513.0**
207	223	108	27	137	187.0
59	34	25	6		
37	36	24	4		
30	65	33	3		
167	98	54	12		
265	145	144	14		
159	112	56	42		
212	158	85	3	30	120.0
233	100	113	25		
231	197	198	36	3448	10017.0
168	136	116	10	671	1536.0
331	366	294	33	1952	6320.0
54	63	32	3		
67	64	42	4	132	528.0
327	182	97	22	9598	26457.0
291	432	159	4		
441	534	230	32	1345	4038.0
267	350	139	22	676	2807.0
428	397	183	68		
315	197	108	16	5	6.0
1	12	4	2		
220	84	44	12	97	253.0
366	368	181	41	180	920.0
138	128	59	7	1001	1989.0
134	150	61	2	120	480.0
135	75	11		19	54.0
101	92	58	6	188	606.0
152	166	71	16		
94	81	19	2	516	1416.0
126	92	41	14	135	775.0
305	231	107	4		4.0

C-2-10续表2

地区	增加值合计	执行行政事业单位会计制度财务指标						为儿童提供服务机构床位数
		固定资产原价	上年结转和结余	本年收入合计	本年支出合计	收支结余	行政事业单位增加值	
全　国	**123665.5**	**381548.5**	**39615.8**	**266086.5**	**241069.8**	**21354.2**	**123665.5**	**107701**
中央级								
北　京	8148.9	18300.4	667.2	17022.3	16348.2	873.4	8148.9	1978
天　津	2692.7	1623.9	541.4	5233.2	4983.4	791.2	2692.7	823
河　北	526.7	1619.3	341.0	1524.6	1441.6	100.0	526.7	834
山　西	946.9	1680.7	819.6	2164.4	2335.0	6.0	946.9	974
内蒙古	3110.5	9790.5	543.4	6166.9	5176.3	1536.0	3110.5	1683
辽　宁	5902.0	10723.8	9002.7	14984.7	16745.6	361.5	5902.0	4024
吉　林	1738.1	11455.7	109.6	3794.7	3589.4	191.1	1738.1	3990
黑龙江	4162.0	20882.9	450.0	13351.8	6701.1	224.8	4162.0	2837
上　海	7471.1	18309.7	367.3	15680.7	15417.4	611.9	7471.1	2233
江　苏	10267.5	11280.3	4854.4	13635.3	13307.1	4742.5	10267.5	4674
浙　江	7396.2	14086.0	1832.3	11611.8	11653.7	876.5	7396.2	2867
安　徽	6197.6	22185.6	717.2	11907.3	10576.0	102.0	6197.6	6725
福　建	2233.7	3288.3	1174.9	5606.7	3254.4	464.6	2233.7	1554
江　西	929.9	7632.8		1668.3	1308.8		929.9	1460
山　东	7815.4	24336.6		16997.1	16997.1		7815.4	7406
河　南	2390.7	10946.8	601.1	7143.7	6634.3	1008.1	2390.7	3864
湖　北	6338.3	27562.2	90.1	13841.8	13736.1	223.0	6338.3	7863
湖　南	4260.6	10689.4	7.2	8748.5	8826.5		4260.6	5356
广　东	5890.0	25536.2	1303.6	12420.7	12033.3	834.7	5890.0	4889
广　西	3940.4	11619.6	1235.1	7158.7	7051.0	1336.7	3940.4	2973
海　南	51.1	660.0	17.0	80.3	81.0		51.1	163
重　庆	3944.4	7286.4	675.9	12824.5	11691.0	1809.3	3944.4	3390
四　川	7019.0	18730.4	5856.2	12653.8	13142.1	1418.3	7019.0	7987
贵　州	3035.4	6149.3	787.9	4743.1	5677.8	311.9	3035.4	3279
云　南	2402.7	16241.7	1225.1	6610.8	5445.3	585.9	2402.7	3853
西　藏	884.5	8450.3	56.0	3326.3	2110.4		884.5	2802
陕　西	4286.7	10370.8	1946.8	18982.5	9078.8	915.4	4286.7	3065
甘　肃	2592.4	16237.3	704.2	3924.9	3494.9	138.7	2592.4	3791
青　海	200.3	4172.0	72.0	368.7	372.2		200.3	1992
宁　夏	2283.0	12814.2	871.7	3357.5	3633.5	586.7	2283.0	1330
新　疆	4606.5	16885.4	2744.9	8550.9	8226.5	1304.0	4606.5	7042

单位：万元

按登记类型分			为儿童提供服务机构年末收养人数			按登记类型分		
编制登记	民政登记	一个机构多个牌子		女性	儿童	编制登记	民政登记	一个机构多个牌子
79358	**3037**	**25306**	**59142**	**21068**	**55510**	**48721**	**2041**	**8380**
1778	200		1477	342	1413	1386	91	
823			648	246	630	648		
499		335	246	21	246	173		73
566	140	268	698	219	678	398	86	214
1651	32		863	354	816	840	23	
3849	50	125	2779	1019	2558	2726	19	34
3000		990	1669	127	1596	1454		215
2737	100		1476	539	1284	1446	30	
2163	70		2111	868	2111	2041	70	
3095		1579	2384	1006	1853	1923		461
2466		401	1711	599	1622	1461		250
4635	130	1960	3306	1207	2494	2556	14	736
1130	155	269	921	343	896	661	148	112
1242		218	746	119	611	744		2
5216		2190	3433	1629	3433	2808		625
3649	200	15	3115	1267	3108	2928	187	
3211		4652	4048	1567	3439	2171		1877
3085	450	1821	2630	1564	2527	1966	289	375
3846	843	200	2500	838	2464	1816	609	75
1110		1863	1190	443	1014	770		420
163			72	27	72	72		
2380	50	960	1417	667	1417	947	42	428
5490	20	2477	3111	1147	2888	2626	2	483
2134		1145	1414	583	1375	964		450
2509	54	1290	1931	351	1911	1433	31	467
2490	312		2222	751	2162	1962	260	
2903		162	2093	775	2093	2092		1
2726	116	949	2515	645	2503	1945	45	525
1730	50	212	1279	499	1279	1245	30	4
1083		247	433	154	433	354		79
5999	65	978	4704	1152	4584	4165	65	474

C-2-11 儿童

地区	单位数	0～99张	100～299张	300～499张	500张以上	年末职工人数	女性
全国	**545**	**219**	**229**	**65**	**32**	**12768**	**8730**
中央级							
北京	11	5	4	1	1	514	393
天津	2		1		1	124	82
河北	12	10	2			88	52
山西	7	5	2			114	53
内蒙古	8	2	4	1	1	331	175
辽宁	10	5	3		2	547	342
吉林	18	7	9	1	1	369	173
黑龙江	15	2	12	1		450	286
上海	3	2			1	406	347
江苏	14	3	6	3	2	578	419
浙江	16	5	8	2	1	430	316
安徽	42	19	17	5	1	967	627
福建	12	6	5	1		152	105
江西	5	2	1	2		81	58
山东	18		4	10	4	575	420
河南	18	7	7	2	2	854	733
湖北	52	35	9	6	2	902	611
湖南	18	3	10	4	1	311	225
广东	37	19	14	3	1	958	664
广西	14	5	8	1		513	403
海南	2	1	1			19	14
重庆	9	3	3	1	2	334	243
四川	48	25	15	7	1	714	485
贵州	20	6	11	2	1	303	170
云南	27	10	16	1		315	202
西藏	15	7	6	1	1	221	139
陕西	12	2	7	1	2	243	141
甘肃	17	3	12	1	1	319	154
青海	7	2	2	1	2	177	122
宁夏	5	1	2	1	1	238	206
新疆	51	17	28	6		621	370

收养机构

单位:个、人

受教育程度		职业资格水平		按人员性质分		年龄结构	
大学专科人数	大学本科及以上人数	助理社会工作师人数	社会工作师人数	管理人员	专业技术技能人员	35岁及以下人数	36岁至45岁人数
3929	**3318**	**334**	**421**	**4765**	**8003**	**5311**	**4587**
183	218	10	11	97	417	187	208
35	62	4	11	30	94	59	34
16	3		1	24	64	36	35
27	20	2	9	45	69	25	62
137	89	10	13	141	190	167	98
132	334	6	5	165	382	259	140
62	68		2	95	274	159	112
165	122	2	20	277	173	209	153
92	123	19	39	41	365	190	86
161	195	26	47	113	465	196	161
114	165	16	21	152	278	168	136
235	168	31	21	490	477	320	332
56	60	7	8	86	66	54	63
12	12		1	75	6	24	28
197	236	13	16	144	431	306	164
468	102	7	28	554	300	275	418
259	160	16	16	219	683	311	417
94	47	10	7	107	204	119	126
171	104	48	28	370	588	397	377
140	138	14	12	133	380	276	157
2			1	10	9	1	12
113	154	15	17	103	231	210	73
232	165	32	19	449	265	273	265
97	100	10	3	224	79	126	119
66	120	3	19	106	209	119	138
31	14	2		75	146	135	75
81	67	4	6	82	161	92	89
92	58	6	5	107	212	128	133
82	28	4		46	131	86	71
70	66	4	12	54	184	117	77
307	120	13	23	151	470	287	228

C-2-11续表1

地 区	年龄结构		志愿服务		年末床位数		年在院总人天数
	46岁至55岁人数	56岁及以上人数	志愿者服务人次数	志愿服务时间		光荣间床位	
全 国	**2528**	**342**	**18857**	**53687.0**	**96117**	**797**	**16862725**
中央级							
北 京	97	22	137	187.0	1510		515662
天 津	25	6			823		221920
河 北	14	3			804	35	69520
山 西	24	3			859		217695
内蒙古	54	12			1683		316555
辽 宁	134	14			3954	75	1013045
吉 林	56	42			3990	4	166645
黑龙江	85	3	30	120.0	2737		327525
上 海	105	25			2133		768316
江 苏	188	33	3361	9681.0	3695	6	752976
浙 江	116	10	671	1536.0	2867		557780
安 徽	283	32	1662	5680.0	6066	25	1108623
福 建	32	3			1554		271635
江 西	29		132	528.0	965		88336
山 东	85	20	9187	25218.0	6976		1177379
河 南	158	3			3754		980791
湖 北	165	9	1218	3637.0	6146	195	1115499
湖 南	63	3	218	715.0	3786	388	675463
广 东	171	13			4559		791428
广 西	73	7			1965		243953
海 南	4	2			163		26308
重 庆	39	12	95	245.0	3180		350800
四 川	147	29	180	920.0	6342	29	831067
贵 州	53	5	1001	1989.0	3142	21	504926
云 南	56	2	120	480.0	3461		401364
西 藏	11		19	54.0	2802		614203
陕 西	57	5	188	606.0	3053		695000
甘 肃	50	8			3238	19	446634
青 海	18	2	503	1312.0	1780		211474
宁 夏	34	10	135	775.0	1183		110730
新 疆	102	4		4.0	6947		1289473

单位:人、人次、时、张、人天

年末在院人数		在院人员按性质分				在院人员按年龄分		
	女性	优抚对象	“三无”和五保对象	自费人员	其他社会救济对象	老人	青壮年	少年儿童
57441	**20576**	**2308**	**49123**	**2181**	**699**	**1706**	**1926**	**53809**
1423	339		1408	15		1	63	1359
648	246		40	18			18	630
246	21	17	222					246
697	219		677	20			20	677
863	354		785				47	816
2779	1019	1902	769	45	63		221	2558
1669	127	10	1588	58		73		1596
1456	534	140	1181	135		161	31	1264
2053	855		1929	124				2053
2367	1003	4	2161	141		178	353	1836
1711	599		1265	446		52	37	1622
3280	1202	34	2888	209	57	328	484	2468
921	343		878		43		25	896
744	119		744				135	609
3385	1621		3385					3385
3040	1231	30	2770	75	165		7	3033
3726	1439		3328	127	200	537	72	3117
2341	1501	18	2294	19		85	18	2238
2370	838		1992	309	2	2	34	2334
1079	412		820				176	903
72	27		72					72
1397	662		1314	1				1397
2984	1121	8	2533	47	132	188	35	2761
1412	583	4	1350	2	32	4	35	1373
1901	340		1773			20		1881
2222	751	8	945	53		60		2162
2092	775		2092					2092
2156	491	2	2017	127		12		2144
1275	499	29	954	200				1275
428	153		376					428
4704	1152	102	4573	10	5	5	115	4584

C-2-11续表2

地区	在院人员按类型分			康复和医疗门诊人次数	家庭寄养儿童数量	机构建筑面积
	自理（完全自理）	介助（半自理）	介护（不能自理）			
全　国	**24287**	**13467**	**19687**	**909956**	**23319**	**2258840**
中央级						
北　京	271	78	1074	1116	623	56259
天　津	151	92	405	270		20251
河　北	192	10	44		104	13883
山　西	331	152	214	730	70	19362
内蒙古	373	175	315	166714	17	48048
辽　宁	2038	661	80	23588	224	109011
吉　林	1278	316	75	12642	24	22984
黑龙江	996	271	189	185	126	57299
上　海	280	267	1506		1259	35074
江　苏	553	234	1580	15133	256	108259
浙　江	126	480	1105	22788	356	73704
安　徽	881	946	1453	13184	2255	226242
福　建	268	411	242	110	669	30179
江　西	359	147	238	30	200	21750
山　东	868	921	1596	61949	365	211901
河　南	1233	976	831	6633	545	102487
湖　北	1221	1283	1222	56029	5411	101517
湖　南	592	549	1200	3191	1628	59409
广　东	618	580	1172	179314	171	72688
广　西	89	427	563	14368	142	48918
海　南	30	15	27			2600
重　庆	405	285	707	163153	1049	86922
四　川	1459	956	569	33028	1614	141669
贵　州	816	483	113	672	295	49257
云　南	637	415	849	3595	1044	101822
西　藏	2186	34	2		28	140819
陕　西	621	440	1031		410	61894
甘　肃	1038	581	537	39851	114	63270
青　海	588	687		41		27517
宁　夏	144	95	189	263	119	22900
新　疆	3645	500	559	91379	4201	120946

单位：人、人次、平方米、万元

增加值合计	执行行政事业单位会计制度财务指标					
	固定资产原价	上年结转和结余	本年收入合计	本年支出合计	收支结余	行政事业单位增加值
111562.8	**340722.5**	**36785.8**	**241737.7**	**217399.6**	**19042.2**	**111562.8**
7182.4	17685.7	444.7	14884.6	14484.7	622.2	7182.4
2692.7	1623.9	541.4	5233.2	4983.4	791.2	2692.7
331.5	1274.3		643.6	613.6		331.5
936.8	1427.5	530.3	2034.7	2228.1	6.0	936.8
3110.5	9790.5	543.4	6166.9	5176.3	1536.0	3110.5
5524.0	10100.8	8950.4	14505.9	16220.7	361.5	5524.0
1738.1	11455.7	109.6	3794.7	3589.4	191.1	1738.1
3985.6	19667.9	450.0	13069.3	6443.6	199.8	3985.6
6669.3	17802.6	0.8	14507.7	14241.4	264.1	6669.3
9852.4	9118.2	4854.4	12777.1	12524.4	4742.5	9852.4
7396.2	14086.0	1832.3	11611.8	11653.7	876.5	7396.2
5965.0	21361.9	717.2	11050.9	9701.5	102.0	5965.0
2233.7	3288.3	1174.9	5606.7	3254.4	464.6	2233.7
714.7	4240.8		1445.2	1085.7		714.7
7129.0	22894.6		15945.3	15945.3		7129.0
2347.2	10463.8	601.1	6996.7	6489.3	1008.1	2347.2
5261.1	20450.4	90.1	11757.5	11623.6	223.0	5261.1
1877.4	6215.3		3574.1	3490.9		1877.4
4719.8	17762.3	1303.6	9358.4	9100.5	834.7	4719.8
3240.5	9418.7	857.0	5412.9	5763.5	507.1	3240.5
51.1	660.0	17.0	80.3	81.0		51.1
3796.7	6802.6	675.9	12637.6	11504.1	1809.3	3796.7
6223.7	17625.7	5300.1	11407.4	11836.3	938.2	6223.7
2445.2	5875.0	679.1	4146.9	5013.1	311.9	2445.2
2328.1	15908.5	1222.0	6425.2	5292.6	585.9	2328.1
884.5	8450.3	56.0	3326.3	2110.4		884.5
4263.3	9785.9	1946.8	18982.5	9078.8	915.4	4263.3
2219.3	14173.3	599.1	3223.3	2825.1	138.7	2219.3
177.3	3670.0		363.6	363.6		177.3
1905.6	11781.2	629.7	2655.9	2947.9	337.7	1905.6
4360.0	15860.8	2658.9	8111.5	7732.7	1274.7	4360.0

C-2-12 未成年人

地　区	单位数					年末职工人数	
		0～99张	100～299张	300～499张	500张以上		女性
全　国	**345**	**305**	**35**	**4**	**1**	**2049**	**810**
中央级							
北　京	2		1	1		51	21
天　津							
河　北	1	1				13	1
山　西	3	3				17	5
内蒙古							
辽　宁	2	2				21	6
吉　林							
黑龙江	1		1			8	6
上　海	1		1			65	60
江　苏	31	28	3			84	43
浙　江							
安　徽	10	7	3			57	12
福　建							
江　西	12	11	1			96	34
山　东	8	7	1			53	14
河　南	4	4				32	10
湖　北	65	58	6	1		335	158
湖　南	54	49	5			467	163
广　东	2	1		1		118	38
广　西	23	19	4			123	53
海　南							
重　庆	6	6				26	11
四　川	69	65	4			242	87
贵　州	5	4	1			29	13
云　南	10	8	2			32	16
西　藏							
陕　西	1	1				14	5
甘　肃	10	9		1		86	30
青　海	15	13	1		1	19	6
宁　夏	5	5				35	11
新　疆	5	4	1			26	7

救助保护中心

单位:个、人

受教育程度		职业资格水平		按人员性质分		年龄结构	
大学专科人数	大学本科及以上人数	助理社会工作师人数	社会工作师人数	管理人员	专业技术技能人员	35岁及以下人数	36岁至45岁人数
774	**468**	**60**	**45**	**1208**	**841**	**750**	**781**
10	38	5	2	51		20	15
	3			10	3	1	1
5	3			17		5	3
13	8			18	3	6	5
	8			3	5	3	5
24	6	1	3	18	47	43	14
35	12	2	1	29	55	35	36
24	5			34	23	11	34
57	14	7		68	28	43	36
14	19	1	1	21	32	21	18
18	7	1		17	15	16	14
113	69	6	5	162	173	130	117
173	78	7	6	260	207	148	224
26	13	7	11	93	25	31	20
50	44	5	5	74	49	39	40
13	8	2	3	24	2	10	11
95	69	8	6	175	67	93	103
16	9	1		24	5	12	9
11	5	2		18	14	15	12
3	9			9	5	9	3
33	14	5	1	49	37	24	33
14	1		1	18	1	8	10
12	23			10	25	9	15
15	3			6	20	18	3

C-2-12续表1

地区	年龄结构		志愿服务		本年在站救助人次数	从其他站转入的	女性
	46岁至55岁人数	56岁及以上人数	志愿者服务人次数	志愿服务时间			
全　国	**368**	**150**	**1393**	**4826.0**	**41979**	**4846**	**6954**
中央级							
北　京	11	5			483		20
天　津							
河　北	10	1			45		
山　西	9				17		
内蒙古							
辽　宁	10				80	5	20
吉　林							
黑龙江					18		
上　海	8				75		39
江　苏	10	3	87	336.0	2345	197	263
浙　江							
安　徽	11	1	290	640.0	1030	251	172
福　建					3		
江　西	13	4			1471	118	162
山　东	12	2	411	1239.0	432	21	78
河　南	1	1			547		55
湖　北	65	23	127	401.0	8132	454	495
湖　南	76	19	458	2092.0	8392	1454	2920
广　东	12	55			701	561	171
广　西	35	9	5	6.0	5668	63	1262
海　南							
重　庆	5		2	8.0	583	244	143
四　川	34	12			6572	863	835
贵　州	6	2			565	324	137
云　南	5				1222	24	59
西　藏							
陕　西	1	1			12		
甘　肃	21	8			1051	52	39
青　海	1		13	104.0	127		8
宁　夏	7	4			1992	215	28
新　疆	5				416		48

单位：人、人次

未成年人	老年人	肢体残疾人	智障及精神病人	救治的危重病人	自主返乡	跨省接送
41979		**1240**	**3290**	**122**	**4802**	**2803**
483						81
45						
17						1
80		13	31		1	
18						
75						
2345		39	18		107	494
1030		98	94			121
3						
1471		44	32		65	341
432		30	14	3	115	23
547		62	150		100	
8132		156	145	15	822	510
8392		531	1803	40	274	282
701		25	74			237
5668		58	665	31	1674	156
583		8	7		175	127
6572		11	149	23	291	181
565		68	15	2		106
1222		76	5	3	845	62
12						
1051		4	49		221	18
127						
1992		17	26	2	105	63
416			13	3	7	

C-2-12续表2

地区	床位数			年末在站人数			本年在站人天数	在站滞留三个月以上人数
		成年人床位数	儿童床位数		女性	儿童		
全　国	**11584**		**11584**	**1701**	**492**	**1701**	**465386**	**811**
中央级								
北　京	468		468	54	3	54	21618	3
天　津								
河　北	30		30					
山　西	115		115	1		1	1	
内蒙古								
辽　宁	70		70				956	
吉　林								
黑龙江	100		100	20	5	20	400	
上　海	100		100	58	13	58	19615	
江　苏	979		979	17	3	17	18579	44
浙　江								
安　徽	659		659	26	5	26	14496	11
福　建								
江　西	495		495	2		2	7451	
山　东	430		430	48	8	48	2975	3
河　南	110		110	75	36	75	11413	61
湖　北	1717		1717	322	128	322	125970	217
湖　南	1570		1570	289	63	289	48319	19
广　东	330		330	130		130	52786	139
广　西	1008		1008	111	31	111	63851	266
海　南								
重　庆	210		210	20	5	20	1883	13
四　川	1645		1645	127	26	127	40045	16
贵　州	137		137	2		2	1807	2
云　南	392		392	30	11	30	930	
西　藏								
陕　西	12		12	1		1	318	2
甘　肃	553		553	359	154	359	5650	
青　海	212		212	4		4	50	
宁　夏	147		147	5	1	5	4373	15
新　疆	95		95				21900	

单位:张、人、人天、万元

残疾人人数	未成年人人数	增加值合计	执行行政事业单位会计制度财务指标：固定资产原价	上年结转和结余	本年收入合计	本年支出合计	收支结余	行政事业单位增加值
149	**521**	**12102.7**	**40826.0**	**2830.0**	**24348.8**	**23670.2**	**2312.0**	**12102.7**
	3	966.5	614.7	222.5	2137.7	1863.5	251.2	966.5
		195.2	345.0	341.0	881.0	828.0	100.0	195.2
		10.1	253.2	289.3	129.7	106.9		10.1
		378.0	623.0	52.3	478.8	524.9		378.0
		176.4	1215.0		282.5	257.5	25.0	176.4
		801.8	507.1	366.5	1173.0	1176.0	347.8	801.8
4	44	415.1	2162.1		858.2	782.7		415.1
2	11	232.6	823.7		856.4	874.5		232.6
		215.2	3392.0		223.1	223.1		215.2
1	3	686.4	1442.0		1051.8	1051.8		686.4
	61	43.5	483.0		147.0	145.0		43.5
12	115	1077.2	7111.8		2084.3	2112.5		1077.2
14	17	2383.2	4474.1	7.2	5174.4	5335.6		2383.2
99	139	1170.2	7773.9		3062.3	2932.8		1170.2
1	100	699.9	2200.9	378.1	1745.8	1287.5	829.6	699.9
11		147.7	483.8		186.9	186.9		147.7
	16	795.3	1104.7	556.1	1246.4	1305.8	480.1	795.3
	2	590.2	274.3	108.8	596.2	664.7		590.2
		74.6	333.2	3.1	185.6	152.7		74.6
	2	23.4	584.9					23.4
		373.1	2064.0	105.1	701.6	669.8		373.1
		23.0	502.0	72.0	5.1	8.6		23.0
5	8	377.4	1033.0	242.0	701.6	685.6	249.0	377.4
		246.5	1024.6	86.0	439.4	493.8	29.3	246.5

C-2-13 其他提供住宿的

地区	单位数	单位数按登记类型分			单位数按	
		编制登记	民政登记	一个机构多个牌子	0～99张	100～299张
全国	**2623**	**1955**	**262**	**406**	**1906**	**651**
中央级	1	1				1
北京	24	23		1	13	7
天津	14	14			11	2
河北	169	65	61	43	107	57
山西	101	85	3	13	84	15
内蒙古	48	41	2	5	39	8
辽宁	117	81	28	8	83	32
吉林	63	61		2	45	18
黑龙江	117	83	31	3	98	18
上海	21	21			16	3
江苏	96	77	4	15	65	28
浙江	92	65	1	26	71	20
安徽	115	88	1	26	65	48
福建	85	65		20	65	20
江西	106	89		17	80	25
山东	76	70		6	44	31
河南	128	101	5	22	82	39
湖北	126	83	29	14	100	24
湖南	143	107	3	33	118	25
广东	97	85	10	2	53	35
广西	77	68	5	4	59	18
海南	10	9		1	5	5
重庆	42	42			36	6
四川	233	138	53	42	161	61
贵州	84	70		14	68	13
云南	127	93	6	28	89	34
西藏	8	6		2	5	3
陕西	101	98		3	83	15
甘肃	58	44	2	12	47	11
青海	23	7	2	14	16	7
宁夏	15	12	3		13	2
新疆	106	63	13	30	85	20

社会服务机构总表

单位:个、人

床位数量分		年末职工人数		年末职工人数按登记类型分		
300～499张	500张以上		女性	编制登记	民政登记	一个机构多个牌子
40	**26**	**28666**	**11390**	**23683**	**3250**	**1733**
		165	115	165		
1	3	788	360	786		2
	1	236	83	236		
2	3	1780	835	798	795	187
2		717	264	664	12	41
1		549	174	525	9	15
	2	1482	522	1237	163	82
		1012	319	1006		6
	1	966	376	843	116	7
	2	669	299	669		
3		1005	420	920	26	59
1		828	321	740	7	81
2		1125	457	1007	8	110
		587	213	532		55
1		884	310	833		51
1		755	260	729		26
4	3	1750	618	1588	51	111
1	1	1324	486	1087	180	57
		1335	466	1172	23	140
6	3	2273	880	1988	281	4
		742	267	690	45	7
		142	50	137		5
		385	131	385		
9	2	3009	1609	1283	1414	312
1	2	710	269	620		90
2	2	1020	424	848	57	115
		49	12	29		20
2	1	1055	387	1048		7
		536	182	492	9	35
		89	18	54	2	33
		102	34	87	15	
1		597	229	485	37	75

C-2-13续表1

地　区	受教育程度		职业资格水平		按人员性质分		年龄	
	大学专科人数	大学本科及以上人数	助理社会工作师人数	社会工作师人数	管理人员	专业技术技能人员	35岁及以下人数	36岁至45岁人数
全　国	**9126**	**6392**	**572**	**545**	**15546**	**13120**	**8624**	**10595**
中央级	66	99		1	16	149	122	27
北　京	164	281	20	3	381	407	299	239
天　津	49	62	2	8	82	154	75	54
河　北	294	232	8	16	596	1184	570	699
山　西	290	144	6	13	407	310	248	239
内蒙古	223	180	5	10	301	248	150	169
辽　宁	494	405	18	20	864	618	394	513
吉　林	258	223	5	3	534	478	254	476
黑龙江	377	212	7	10	705	261	242	361
上　海	203	176	22	26	337	332	213	201
江　苏	286	321	41	52	459	546	288	373
浙　江	253	245	22	17	493	335	249	310
安　徽	311	170	29	27	576	549	241	434
福　建	143	199	18	21	464	123	180	191
江　西	308	136	23	9	576	308	232	362
山　东	283	272	28	30	295	460	224	263
河　南	619	317	21	31	987	763	666	646
湖　北	429	213	14	9	562	762	399	547
湖　南	518	204	22	20	790	545	465	569
广　东	823	535	110	84	1565	708	717	835
广　西	211	216	34	18	402	340	180	248
海　南	34	37	3	3	42	100	44	49
重　庆	159	161	9	5	332	53	115	137
四　川	801	461	51	57	1437	1572	726	1037
贵　州	280	183	12	5	445	265	251	252
云　南	350	223	17	24	565	455	254	467
西　藏	9	11		1	17	32	13	27
陕　西	381	153	8	12	623	432	390	368
甘　肃	183	109	7	7	297	239	166	181
青　海	41	11	2	1	49	40	29	42
宁　夏	34	44	6		55	47	24	46
新　疆	252	157	2	2	292	305	204	233

单位：人、人次、时、张、人天

结构		志愿服务		年末床位数				年在院（站）总人天数
46岁至55岁人数	56岁及以上人数	志愿者服务人次数	志愿服务时间		编制登记	民政登记	一个机构多个牌子	
7047	**2400**	**20872**	**58060.6**	**170029**	**131623**	**23088**	**15318**	**16422761**
12	4			150	150			47998
179	71	318	1335.6	8042	7625		417	1523738
78	29	2000	4000.0	1489	1489			20575
426	85	1049	4299.0	14410	4684	7614	2112	1820694
193	37	140	474.0	3120	2798	130	192	278742
192	38	50	300.0	2582	2317	132	133	202204
434	141	95	156.0	8134	6834	663	637	680219
233	49	100	300.0	3047	3030		17	149171
273	90	116	436.0	4879	4680	132	67	152725
164	91	669	3111.0	2808	2808			715992
241	103	1800	8577.0	6407	5887	121	399	780620
199	70	4106	6455.0	5246	4596	36	614	386048
323	127	705	2248.0	6941	5851	103	987	731242
176	40	79	210.0	3695	3426		269	274619
224	66	272	1104.0	4933	4745		188	379903
222	46	4614	10820.0	5853	5513		340	365162
351	87	20	60.0	11333	7740	1260	2333	971874
274	104	554	1103.0	7130	5883	795	452	933138
236	65	1731	6886.5	6415	5463	246	706	719872
578	143			11666	10885	763	18	817996
214	100	215	456.0	3807	3499	260	48	337988
41	8			592	572		20	74468
99	34	1312	3150.0	1886	1886			125858
694	552	253	580.0	20891	9489	8226	3176	2087521
177	30	334	793.0	4082	3664		418	238671
246	53	16	39.0	6656	4783	1530	343	775866
9				953	613		340	505
229	68	310	1079.5	4526	4441		85	343722
152	37	10	80.0	2714	2409	55	250	144552
15	3			645	326	180	139	48094
25	7	4	8.0	586	436	150		53556
138	22			4411	3101	692	618	239428

C-2-13续表2

地区	增加值合计	执行行政事业单位会计制度财务指标				
		固定资产原价	上年结转和结余	本年收入合计	本年支出合计	收支结余
全　国	**236995.6**	**523725.4**	**48528.8**	**412614.7**	**421084.7**	**29405.6**
中央级	2549.9	1910.3	28.0	4921.2	4946.2	3.0
北　京	9489.3	7449.0	1851.8	18857.5	17149.6	1673.7
天　津	1722.2	2363.8	1429.2	2192.1	3267.0	27.1
河　北	8396.5	35249.0	3110.6	16035.3	13702.8	4542.3
山　西	4586.8	5718.8	1878.5	8196.6	8347.8	1019.6
内蒙古	4686.0	8693.6	1052.3	7993.1	8198.5	1023.1
辽　宁	8225.6	21021.9	1106.8	15250.0	14879.7	486.2
吉　林	5300.8	7462.2	207.7	7348.5	7690.1	253.3
黑龙江	4806.8	13188.4	688.4	6451.3	7017.0	86.3
上　海	10828.8	26081.3	5837.3	21494.2	20656.9	2768.5
江　苏	12972.4	35276.9	2347.2	23805.7	23197.5	1182.6
浙　江	13940.6	22718.9	872.4	24228.3	23428.1	-412.5
安　徽	6489.0	24596.9	1033.5	11964.5	12646.7	204.2
福　建	5486.3	8945.7	2845.4	12074.9	9740.2	3769.1
江　西	4142.4	11187.6	1273.3	7632.3	7892.9	373.7
山　东	8920.6	17039.6		14586.6	14586.6	
河　南	10396.2	20421.1	2758.1	17000.1	18072.5	2119.0
湖　北	9207.3	22056.9	201.7	18026.0	18094.6	971.9
湖　南	8304.7	16417.4	343.1	17656.8	18687.7	291.9
广　东	33123.5	62180.3	2925.6	52340.3	50722.0	1793.5
广　西	6245.4	12152.2	2836.6	13511.7	12766.0	1999.7
海　南	2439.7	2534.7	923.9	4630.7	3814.5	402.8
重　庆	5052.5	7629.5	155.4	9334.7	9372.2	117.9
四　川	13341.6	38646.8	3670.8	23654.4	24967.3	1348.8
贵　州	13067.5	9292.4	1103.8	13502.3	26685.7	686.0
云　南	7277.1	21608.2	1920.3	11770.0	12085.1	1400.6
西　藏	182.3	1321.0		135.0	470.1	
陕　西	7692.8	34827.6	1031.0	11266.7	11224.6	219.9
甘　肃	2561.6	7584.0	1541.8	4687.0	4521.0	520.3
青　海	300.2	788.8		1021.9	1024.9	
宁　夏	1404.3	2255.5	537.0	2338.6	1695.2	26.0
新　疆	3855.0	15105.1	3017.3	8706.4	9533.7	507.1

单位：万元

行政事业单位增加值	执行民间非营利组织单位会计制度财务指标				
	固定资产原价	上年结余	本年收入合计	本年费用合计	社会组织增加值
232227.9	**29850.9**	**3480.0**	**7862.6**	**11029.5**	**4767.7**
2549.9					
9489.1	1360.2			0.2	0.2
1722.2					
7669.1	9655.9	-126.5	1447.5	1546.1	727.4
4586.8	11.0				
4649.8	126.3		63.4	63.4	36.2
8141.7	495.0		97.7	171.9	83.9
5300.8					
4237.2	77.2	147.0	39.1	734.3	569.6
10828.8					
12965.4	2.0		0.7	7.0	7.0
13915.6	100.0		50.0	50.0	25.0
6429.0	100.0	100.0		70.0	60.0
5486.3					
4142.4					
8920.6					
10395.5	100.0		90.0	5.0	0.7
9059.2	253.0		375.8	375.8	148.1
8293.7	4.0	3.0	8.0	15.0	11.0
32563.7	266.4	169.8	1196.3	1108.0	559.8
6188.6	374.0	23.6	33.3	120.3	56.8
2439.7					
5052.5					
10883.8	16675.9	3163.1	4415.8	6714.3	2457.8
13067.5					
7277.1					
182.3					
7692.8					
2561.6					
297.0	190.0			3.2	3.2
1383.3	60.0		45.0	45.0	21.0
3855.0					

C-2-14 生活无着人员

地区	单位数	0~99张	100~299张	300~499张	500张以上	年末职工人数	女性
全　国	**1949**	**1680**	**226**	**26**	**17**	**17848**	**5977**
中央级							
北　京	20	13	4		3	588	251
天　津	13	11	1		1	212	68
河　北	83	74	9			532	134
山　西	90	80	8	2		591	209
内蒙古	40	36	3	1		422	132
辽　宁	66	51	14		1	855	268
吉　林	52	45	7			757	245
黑龙江	75	67	7		1	678	207
上　海	19	16	2		1	351	76
江　苏	74	61	10	3		717	279
浙　江	77	70	7			589	193
安　徽	75	62	11	2		521	164
福　建	69	62	7			405	133
江　西	93	80	12	1		597	204
山　东	57	44	12	1		480	157
河　南	97	79	13	3	2	1085	360
湖　北	87	73	12	1	1	886	306
湖　南	124	113	11			1003	326
广　东	74	46	19	6	3	1744	555
广　西	58	54	4			429	141
海　南	8	5	3			104	36
重　庆	38	36	2			319	110
四　川	147	127	17	2	1	1135	410
贵　州	70	63	5	1	1	402	155
云　南	94	86	7		1	522	165
西　藏	7	5	2			45	12
陕　西	90	82	5	2	1	901	327
甘　肃	46	44	2			400	152
青　海	15	14	1			58	11
宁　夏	10	9	1			74	21
新　疆	81	72	8	1		446	170

救助管理站

单位：个、人

受教育程度		职业资格水平		按人员性质分	
大学专科人数	大学本科及以上人数	助理社会工作师人数	社会工作师人数	管理人员	专业技术技能人员
6435	**4718**	**455**	**464**	**10840**	**7008**
134	248	17	2	327	261
49	52	2	8	74	138
119	109	3	11	222	310
243	119	5	12	344	247
170	150	5	9	223	199
368	271	11	17	517	338
171	182	2	1	393	364
286	165	5	5	523	155
131	142	17	24	281	70
229	265	39	45	366	351
213	216	20	16	381	208
176	146	16	24	335	186
106	164	15	21	316	89
213	105	23	8	400	197
179	198	21	27	184	296
414	191	13	24	598	487
303	147	14	9	390	496
424	161	20	19	584	419
641	418	98	70	1315	429
128	134	13	17	251	178
30	31	3	3	34	70
135	130	7	4	272	47
436	294	44	51	808	327
179	116	9	4	282	120
206	143	10	10	304	218
7	10		1	13	32
327	135	8	12	530	371
155	88	5	7	241	159
35	8	2	1	33	25
21	40	6		47	27
207	140	2	2	252	194

C-2-14续表1

地区	年龄结构				志愿服务	
	35岁及以下人数	36岁至45岁人数	46岁至55岁人数	56岁及以上人数	志愿者服务人次数	志愿服务时间
全国	**5959**	**6572**	**4152**	**1165**	**19071**	**51704.0**
中央级						
北京	264	166	126	32		
天津	75	53	63	21	2000	4000.0
河北	169	195	132	36	755	3258.0
山西	224	193	144	30	140	474.0
内蒙古	119	119	153	31	50	300.0
辽宁	259	276	244	76	20	40.0
吉林	215	340	169	33	100	300.0
黑龙江	182	266	200	30	116	436.0
上海	121	78	88	64	380	1600.0
江苏	250	257	154	56	1752	8522.0
浙江	185	232	121	51	3902	5779.0
安徽	165	183	136	37	461	1646.0
福建	162	137	80	26	39	90.0
江西	174	251	131	41	140	576.0
山东	172	168	114	26	4614	10820.0
河南	466	369	201	49	20	60.0
湖北	296	340	178	72	517	961.0
湖南	382	438	142	41	1731	6886.5
广东	487	678	467	112		
广西	114	143	114	58	215	456.0
海南	36	34	27	7		
重庆	86	119	85	29	1262	3050.0
四川	379	433	270	53	203	500.0
贵州	156	154	76	16	314	743.0
云南	142	232	122	26	16	39.0
西藏	11	25	9			
陕西	348	314	180	59	310	1079.5
甘肃	142	128	101	29	10	80.0
青海	17	24	14	3		
宁夏	16	35	16	7	4	8.0
新疆	145	192	95	14		

单位：人、人次、时

本年在站救助人次数	从其他站转入的	女性	未成年人	老年人	肢体残疾人
2953359	**161190**	**568551**	**115938**	**326355**	**157262**
584594	2689	190156	8475	15602	1949
11510	179	1007	222	663	227
61763	1011	10017	2253	8634	2775
82942	2801	7572	6763	10318	6902
38706	6680	5482	3755	8311	3911
49239	1562	7780	3184	7678	3154
46046	4299	11323	1289	9831	5640
30709	3903	4759	2102	5323	2946
27920	220	5696	1830	3529	813
92945	8452	14522	9110	11247	6079
59656	1794	9988	2234	6156	2382
127507	12751	15618	5227	15475	5163
101602	2554	6358	2463	7195	3999
103909	8162	11013	3741	16454	7380
83601	2941	13573	3833	7489	4618
149149	9374	27185	7450	17211	10462
264712	10574	53411	6881	36485	8645
277203	11732	54389	7963	44483	19928
153326	12287	15874	6873	12623	7801
53345	3417	11373	1830	5550	2593
29848	2055	6081	664	862	532
54583	3240	10462	844	7027	2649
174498	25571	30374	9959	23910	14228
80706	8577	9558	4966	11865	5558
55699	4331	7481	2825	6232	8643
7607		689	297	384	984
79216	4737	11992	4290	9973	5415
29473	3458	5673	1176	5867	2008
10747	123	1621	139	862	3486
6456	856	1128	923	623	224
24142	860	6396	2377	8493	6168

C-2-14续表2

地　区	智障及精神病人	救治的危重病人	自主返乡	跨省接送	床位数	成年人床位数	儿童床位数
全　国	**241537**	**29353**	**1010428**	**93650**	**99222**	**78630**	**20592**
中央级							
北　京	5971	622	11631	1654	6815	6607	208
天　津	2211	21	5692	131	1289	1081	208
河　北	4585	852	31496	2711	3542	2671	871
山　西	6332	537	39743	1214	2414	1588	826
内蒙古	5526	686	18677	1934	1887	1458	429
辽　宁	4827	564	18153	3133	4940	3288	1652
吉　林	4495	1026	23009	3230	2037	1337	700
黑龙江	2888	322	9090	2628	3488	1945	1543
上　海	1503	251	13505	691	1829	1595	234
江　苏	11951	2643	44726	5841	4278	3582	696
浙　江	7592	1124	32395	1998	3133	2558	575
安　徽	11128	3370	49359	3820	4523	3448	1075
福　建	2471	575	51665	1519	2233	1605	628
江　西	8197	137	29102	4582	3640	2904	736
山　东	6848	242	32191	4739	3628	2784	844
河　南	12682	1188	48553	4949	6822	5318	1504
湖　北	41000	1802	82169	9292	4515	3610	905
湖　南	38996	5148	100902	10687	4817	4448	369
广　东	6571	1777	79814	2969	7757	6060	1697
广　西	9642	339	27826	2957	1918	1509	409
海　南	2079	125	13657	339	453	347	106
重　庆	4084	336	40631	749	1446	1216	230
四　川	17822	2895	85959	9886	7234	6220	1014
贵　州	4838	481	30063	4099	2930	1853	1077
云　南	3098	253	22513	1539	1947	1751	196
西　藏	3	15	8		953	652	301
陕　西	4450	994	40195	2405	4032	3433	599
甘　肃	1957	104	16402	2072	1541	1263	278
青　海	5327	3	1180	24	269	255	14
宁　夏	756	184	2113	480	396	293	103
新　疆	1707	737	8009	1378	2516	1951	565

单位：人、张、人天、人次

年末在站人数			本年在站人天数	本年不在站救助人次数	
	女性	儿童			未成年人
24513	**5238**	**3175**	**8255041**	**521185**	**12095**
2397	90	549	1399293	3854	16
439	3	57	20575	204	6
906	253	62	299618	20812	304
490	188	44	166158	20539	1708
197	39	9	94156	23368	247
1379	101	135	168325	5078	224
			94786	15503	
209	34	57	65635	583	29
898	350	61	376649	983	29
1322	499	84	530786	7469	80
802	274	47	267557	1183	64
997	375	88	347079	38092	186
224	71	15	131977	11064	713
567	36	32	155353	9876	262
1047	344	19	357046	43842	1290
1807	583	562	465828	52256	1411
2056	486	123	689290	27766	560
1494	303	75	414533	38710	524
1634	235	253	657595	45506	419
388	147	13	145087	24362	722
461	117	17	74468	5614	7
197	39	11	100308	9664	48
2035	306	250	547076	51840	928
337	66	46	112116	16409	598
148	22	5	104995	9581	102
250		246	505	329	22
915	143	61	289272	17816	174
333	25	99	87372	7491	784
			6863	4688	91
81	8	6	17991	2189	73
503	101	149	66749	4514	474

C-2-14续表3

地 区	在站滞留三个月以上人数	残疾人人数	未成年人人数	增加值合计
全 国	**15058**	**7806**	**1187**	**162686.5**
中央级				
北 京	11	1	1	7551.7
天 津	16	8		1345.1
河 北	676	331	51	4010.4
山 西	552	383	35	3674.9
内蒙古	238	102	12	3491.7
辽 宁	215	150		6060.8
吉 林	469			4148.7
黑龙江	41	15	3	2847.5
上 海	788	743	56	6227.7
江 苏	1287	960	29	9634.9
浙 江	846	149	34	10486.1
安 徽	849	641	23	3695.7
福 建	260	202	12	3519.3
江 西	218	170	14	2858.5
山 东	635	465	18	5917.5
河 南	828	164	408	6290.0
湖 北	1747	1204	92	6222.8
湖 南	506	324	18	6314.3
广 东	1447	509	190	26596.7
广 西	500	99	24	3362.8
海 南	335	335		2402.7
重 庆	225	43	8	4174.2
四 川	1020	311	80	8724.2
贵 州	369	57	15	6579.2
云 南	30	21	4	3591.8
西 藏				182.3
陕 西	457	240	24	6498.9
甘 肃	53	50	2	1787.4
青 海	70	12	3	248.2
宁 夏	56	49	4	1201.0
新 疆	314	68	27	3039.5

单位：人、万元

执行行政事业单位会计制度财务指标					
固定资产原价	上年结转和结余	本年收入合计	本年支出合计	收支结余	行政事业单位增加值
336615.9	**39895.5**	**310191.0**	**320715.1**	**24602.3**	**162686.5**
4605.2	1776.1	15519.4	13958.1	1525.4	7551.7
1677.3	41.2	1637.8	1566.6	27.1	1345.1
16480.7	2139.4	11188.6	9076.9	3739.3	4010.4
4074.6	1817.0	7113.5	7248.0	1006.4	3674.9
6061.9	973.8	6222.3	6498.6	934.2	3491.7
11937.0	448.6	11869.4	11572.3	480.4	6060.8
4746.3	207.7	5775.1	6030.3	174.3	4148.7
5944.6	489.9	4540.9	5094.6	68.9	2847.5
16770.0	5666.9	14821.2	14318.9	2264.3	6227.7
24602.3	1419.9	19819.0	19197.9	1123.4	9634.9
9337.8	1800.2	18053.5	17457.6	249.4	10486.1
13033.7	891.3	8983.4	10118.2	83.2	3695.7
4437.9	2331.8	8166.0	6887.7	2189.8	3519.3
4871.9	831.8	5948.8	6076.3	373.7	2858.5
12867.8		10541.0	10541.0		5917.5
8488.2	2323.8	11231.9	12316.8	2147.9	6290.0
19158.8	44.0	14370.7	14300.7	943.7	6222.8
12684.9	314.5	15063.1	15531.9	152.5	6314.3
48378.1	2179.1	44229.5	43036.6	1792.0	26596.7
7248.9	1517.5	8815.7	8241.5	1601.0	3362.8
1734.4	814.5	4129.1	3328.5	402.8	2402.7
6387.8	155.4	7953.0	7990.5	117.9	4174.2
27088.8	3250.3	20434.8	21744.7	1104.9	8724.2
6185.4	1263.0	5045.7	18922.0	431.3	6579.2
9378.5	1198.9	6181.1	6590.1	644.0	3591.8
1321.0		15.0	350.1		182.3
31191.6	956.9	9808.5	9665.9	152.5	6498.9
4786.1	1487.7	3593.9	3474.2	484.0	1787.4
494.2		795.0	798.0		248.2
1528.8	537.0	1943.2	1432.2		1201.0
9111.4	3017.3	6380.9	7348.4	388.0	3039.5

C-2-15 军

地区	单位数	0～99张	100～299张	300～499张	500张以上
全　国	**327**	**200**	**98**	**20**	**9**
中央级					
北　京	1			1	
天　津	1		1		
河　北	9	7	2		
山　西	6	4	2		
内蒙古	5	3	2		
辽　宁	12	9	2		1
吉　林	11	7	4		
黑龙江	11	5	6		
上　海	1		1		
江　苏	17	11	5	1	
浙　江	11	6	4	1	
安　徽	35	28	6	1	
福　建	12	8	4		
江　西	13	8	3	2	
山　东	19	9	8	2	
河　南	25	13	10		2
湖　北	9	4	3	1	1
湖　南	12	8	3	1	
广　东	13	6	5	1	1
广　西	13	8	3	2	
海　南	2	2			
重　庆	4	3		1	
四　川	14	8	1	4	1
贵　州	9	5	3	1	
云　南	24	11	12	1	
西　藏	1	1			
陕　西	10	8	2		
甘　肃	9	6	2		1
青　海	5	4	1		
宁　夏	1				1
新　疆	12	8	3		1

供站

单位:个、人

年末职工人数	女性	受教育程度		职业资格水平	
		大学专科人数	大学本科及以上人数	助理社会工作师人数	社会工作师人数
5344	**2085**	**1684**	**1052**	**56**	**46**
44	12	5	25		
24	15		10		
88	31	18	35		
106	40	46	25	1	1
102	28	50	21		1
225	71	80	56	3	2
255	74	87	41	3	2
172	68	76	47	2	5
43	10	12	5	2	
249	112	57	56	2	7
146	63	39	29	2	1
527	270	118	19	10	2
132	65	30	27	2	
287	106	95	31		1
275	103	104	74	7	3
591	213	193	123	5	7
229	78	82	46		
259	117	77	40	1	1
248	113	92	83	2	9
241	87	71	70	4	1
38	14	4	6		
66	21	24	31	2	1
205	69	78	32	5	1
87	30	24	18		1
309	155	84	47	1	
4		2	1		
124	52	50	17		
121	26	28	15	2	
23	7	6	3		
10	2	8	2		
114	33	44	17		

C-2-15续表1

地 区	按人员性质分		年龄
	管理人员	专业技术技能人员	35岁及以下人数
全 国	**2845**	**2499**	**1120**
中央级			
北 京	44		6
天 津	8	16	
河 北	41	47	24
山 西	49	57	19
内蒙古	68	34	28
辽 宁	138	87	37
吉 林	141	114	39
黑龙江	111	61	44
上 海	38	5	7
江 苏	85	164	22
浙 江	94	52	14
安 徽	184	343	68
福 建	98	34	14
江 西	176	111	58
山 东	111	164	52
河 南	339	252	180
湖 北	86	143	51
湖 南	179	80	68
广 东	153	95	62
广 西	132	109	48
海 南	8	30	8
重 庆	60	6	29
四 川	109	96	40
贵 州	72	15	41
云 南	163	146	41
西 藏	4		2
陕 西	63	61	42
甘 肃	49	72	24
青 海	8	15	12
宁 夏	4	6	2
新 疆	30	84	38

单位：人、人次、时

结构			志愿服务	
36岁至45岁人数	46岁至55岁人数	56岁及以上人数	志愿者服务人次数	志愿服务时间
2079	**1668**	**477**	**577**	**1515.0**
21	6	11		
1	15	8		
13	36	15		
45	37	5		
41	28	5		
89	73	26		
136	64	16		
69	50	9		
5	19	12		
102	81	44	48	55.0
50	64	18	66	88.0
233	174	52	244	602.0
43	64	11		
111	93	25	132	528.0
95	108	20		
244	129	38		
98	56	24	37	142.0
91	80	20		
92	75	19		
90	77	26		
15	14	1		
18	14	5	50	100.0
75	68	22		
23	19	4		
148	96	24		
2				
43	36	3		
44	47	6		
10	1			
3	5			
29	39	8		

C-2-15续表2

地 区	增加值合计	执行行政事业单位			
		固定资产原价	上年结转和结余	本年收入合计	本年支出合计
全 国	**49266.3**	**138397.3**	**7102.0**	**74051.3**	**73399.9**
中央级					
北 京	1028.9	1921.0		1704.0	1629.0
天 津	377.1	686.5	1388.0	554.3	1700.4
河 北	1140.5	3779.4	622.3	2080.7	1499.7
山 西	875.9	744.2	61.5	1083.1	1099.8
内蒙古	965.4	2553.4	30.5	1539.5	1458.3
辽 宁	756.6	3381.3	572.4	1615.7	1616.6
吉 林	1152.1	2715.9		1573.4	1659.8
黑龙江	1389.7	7243.8	198.5	1910.4	1922.4
上 海	1034.8	2569.7	71.2	1465.8	1403.1
江 苏	3294.5	10374.6	927.3	3946.7	3959.6
浙 江	3223.1	13379.1	-927.8	5878.8	5673.5
安 徽	2510.4	11268.7	72.6	2632.2	2202.0
福 建	1290.5	3201.4	154.0	1923.6	1830.3
江 西	1283.9	6315.7	441.5	1683.5	1816.6
山 东	3003.1	4171.8		4045.6	4045.6
河 南	4029.7	11899.4	434.3	5689.1	5676.6
湖 北	2809.6	2228.1	157.7	3625.3	3763.9
湖 南	1925.6	3557.7	0.4	2390.0	2996.7
广 东	5233.9	12225.2	746.5	7195.7	6770.3
广 西	2619.3	4901.3	1209.1	4503.2	4193.5
海 南	37.0	800.3	109.4	501.6	486.0
重 庆	878.3	1241.7		1381.7	1381.7
四 川	1620.7	5051.0	198.9	2542.1	2833.7
贵 州	1304.3	696.0	-215.9	2800.9	2589.8
云 南	2857.9	9726.8	721.4	4250.5	4139.3
西 藏				120.0	120.0
陕 西	899.4	2844.0	74.1	1458.2	1283.1
甘 肃	701.0	2217.3	54.1	1013.9	986.8
青 海	48.8	294.6		226.9	226.9
宁 夏	180.3	676.7		395.4	263.0
新 疆	794.2	5730.7		2319.5	2171.9

单位：万元、张、人次、人天

会计制度财务指标		床位数	接待人次数		本年在站人天数
收支结余	行政事业单位增加值			接待军队人次数	
2895.3	**49266.3**	**37396**	**4561682**	**3438585**	**3322412**
	1028.9	349	14500	14500	
	377.1	200			
803.0	1140.5	552	90972	77242	60958
13.2	875.9	418	61458	49479	89334
88.9	965.4	483	63990	63990	73617
	756.6	1361	46212	36767	338980
79.0	1152.1	1010	78236	49373	54385
17.4	1389.7	1259	31965	25067	49294
132.9	1034.8	179	83096	42976	65335
59.2	3294.5	1832	226719	102072	167584
-661.9	3223.1	1401	356380	236195	89766
121.0	2510.4	2109	227608	163101	314177
256.9	1290.5	1227	124783	115262	115997
	1283.9	1293	180151	116916	224550
	3003.1	2225	243279	243260	8116
-28.9	4029.7	3171	425322	224657	178216
28.2	2809.6	1740	158620	146263	113493
139.4	1925.6	1128	315482	260910	250106
1.5	5233.9	3146	214957	203745	100525
398.7	2619.3	1609	93629	90787	122012
	37.0	139	44765	44765	
	878.3	440	141704	141704	25550
243.9	1620.7	3558	327480	320480	168528
197.5	1304.3	949	129041	100560	94389
756.6	2857.9	2777	469239	215339	399450
			52000	52000	
67.4	899.4	444	86919	86919	54450
36.3	701.0	1038	74005	74005	47000
	48.8	156	88200	88200	
26.0	180.3				
119.1	794.2	1203	110970	52051	116600

C-2-16 其他提供住宿的

地区	单位数	0～99张	100～299张	300～499张	500张以上	年末职工人数	女性
全国	**334**	**214**	**98**	**14**	**8**	**5104**	**3219**
中央级	1		1			165	115
北京	3		2	1		156	97
天津							
河北	77	33	39	2	3	1160	670
山西	5	4	1			20	15
内蒙古	3	3				25	14
辽宁	39	32	6		1	402	183
吉林							
黑龙江	31	31				116	101
上海	1				1	275	213
江苏	5	4	1			39	29
浙江	4	1	2	1		93	65
安徽	3	1	2			27	11
福建							
江西							
山东							
河南	6	3	1	1	1	74	45
湖北	30	27	3			209	102
湖南	4	2	2			25	13
广东	10	7	3			281	212
广西	6	5	1			72	39
海南							
重庆							
四川	71	33	30	7	1	1628	1119
贵州	3	3				70	31
云南	9	3	3	2	1	189	104
西藏							
陕西							
甘肃	3	3				15	4
青海	3	2	1			8	
宁夏	4	4				18	11
新疆	13	13				37	26

社会服务机构

单位：个、人

受教育程度		职业资格水平		按人员性质分	
大学专科人数	大学本科及以上人数	助理社会工作师人数	社会工作师人数	管理人员	专业技术技能人员
915	**588**	**55**	**35**	**1658**	**3446**
66	99		1	16	149
25	8	3	1	10	146
157	88	5	5	333	827
1				14	6
3	9			10	15
46	78	4	1	209	193
15				71	45
60	29	3	2	18	257
				8	31
1				18	75
14	1	2	1	11	16
12	3	3		50	24
44	20			86	123
4	2			17	8
90	34	10	5	97	184
12	12	17		19	53
282	133	1	5	518	1110
17	31	1		26	44
60	33	6	14	98	91
	6			7	8
				8	
5	2			4	14
1				10	27

C-2-16续表1

地　区	年龄结构 35岁及以下人数	36岁至45岁人数	46岁至55岁人数	56岁及以上人数	志愿服务 志愿者服务人次数
全　国	**1492**	**1822**	**1087**	**703**	**1184**
中央级	122	27	12	4	
北　京	29	52	47	28	318
天　津					
河　北	377	491	258	34	294
山　西	5	1	12	2	
内蒙古	3	9	11	2	
辽　宁	98	148	117	39	75
吉　林					
黑龙江	16	26	23	51	
上　海	85	118	57	15	289
江　苏	16	14	6	3	
浙　江	50	28	14	1	138
安　徽	4	11	6	6	
福　建					
江　西					
山　东					
河　南	20	33	21		
湖　北	52	109	40	8	
湖　南	6	13	5	1	
广　东	168	65	36	12	
广　西	18	15	23	16	
海　南					
重　庆					
四　川	304	511	341	472	50
贵　州	21	27	18	4	20
云　南	71	87	28	3	
西　藏					
陕　西					
甘　肃		9	4	2	
青　海		8			
宁　夏	6	8	4		
新　疆	21	12	4		

单位：人、人次、时、张、人天

志愿服务时间	年末床位数	光荣间床位	年在院总人天数	年末在院人数	女性
4721.6	**32862**	**478**	**4768223**	**16585**	**4467**
	150		47998	149	78
1335.6	878		124445	349	204
1041.0	10316	319	1460118	4531	614
	288	40	23250	157	15
	212		34431	95	
116.0	1833	6	172914	688	238
	132		37796	125	23
1511.0	800		274008	761	318
	297		82250	177	87
588.0	712		28725	213	11
	269		55386	155	15
	1340	20	327830	793	83
	875	80	130355	594	234
	356	2	30708	152	12
	763		59876	380	61
	280		70889	205	47
80.0	10069	4	1360967	5413	2087
50.0	123	7	31801	101	58
	1932		271421	815	107
	135		10180	83	
	220		41231	169	85
	190		35565	104	56
	692		56079	376	34

C-2-16续表2

地区	在院人员按性质分				在院人员按年龄分	
	优抚对象	“三无”和五保对象	自费人员	其他社会救济对象	老人	青壮年
全国	**354**	**3872**	**11750**	**1774**	**14290**	**1671**
中央级			149		57	28
北京		4	345	346	346	3
天津						
河北	47	566	3876	914	4473	51
山西		31	110	15	125	1
内蒙古		19	76		66	29
辽宁	54	154	388	109	600	54
吉林						
黑龙江	32	1	92	36	122	
上海		585	176		46	715
江苏		80	89	8	177	
浙江	8		205		201	12
安徽		62	93		155	
福建						
江西						
山东						
河南	22	552	219		773	
湖北		219	375		541	22
湖南	1	104	47		150	
广东		137	217		29	128
广西		185	20	64	64	10
海南						
重庆						
四川	134	449	4555	94	5141	205
贵州	50	8	59	41	75	17
云南	5	683	127	104	570	245
西藏						
陕西						
甘肃	1	27	55		83	
青海		6			17	151
宁夏			101	3	103	
新疆			376	40	376	

单位：人、人次、平方米

少年儿童	在院人员按类型分			康复和医疗门诊人次数	机构建筑面积
	自理（完全自理）	介助（半自理）	介护（不能自理）		
624	**8465**	**4930**	**3190**	**36933**	**712991**
64	32	106	11	4135	
	171	50	128	5014	35581
7	1941	1857	733	1467	185735
31	147	7	3		7438
	23	72		368	3320
34	289	283	116	2131	48269
3	64	53	8		29420
	37	226	498	761	24050
	105	72		3374	2840
	204	4	5	435	3200
	56	19	80		2000
20	710	42	41	250	39953
31	333	214	47	7090	15908
2	137	7	8	133	2310
223	97	25	258	3181	28442
131	176	28	1	23	8020
67	2908	1492	1013	7540	212590
9	85	10	6	990	8600
	535	85	195		37415
	51	14	18	26	4800
1	165	4		15	3500
1	35	69			2800
	164	191	21		6800

C-2-16续表3

地区	增加值合计	执行行政事业单位会计制度财务指标				
		固定资产原价	上年结转和结余	本年收入合计	本年支出合计	收支结余
全　国	**20855.5**	**45381.7**	**1017.2**	**22798.9**	**21996.4**	**533.6**
中央级	2549.9	1910.3	28.0	4921.2	4946.2	3.0
北　京	908.7	922.8	75.7	1634.1	1562.5	148.3
天　津						
河　北	3245.6	14988.9	348.9	2766.0	3126.2	
山　西	36.0	900.0				
内蒙古	228.9	78.3	48.0	231.3	241.6	
辽　宁	1408.2	5703.6	85.8	1764.9	1690.8	5.8
吉　林						
黑龙江	569.6					
上　海	3566.3	6741.6	99.2	5207.2	4934.9	371.3
江　苏	43.0	300.0		40.0	40.0	
浙　江	231.4	2.0		296.0	297.0	
安　徽	91.0	24.0		30.0	30.0	
福　建						
江　西						
山　东						
河　南	76.5	33.5		79.1	79.1	
湖　北	174.9	670.0		30.0	30.0	
湖　南	33.8	120.0		100.0	96.0	
广　东	1292.9	1577.0		915.1	915.1	
广　西	263.3	2.0	110.0	192.8	331.0	
海　南						
重　庆						
四　川	2860.0	6459.3	221.6	646.1	208.8	
贵　州	2327.3	1551.9		2521.5	2038.1	5.2
云　南	827.4	2502.9		1338.4	1355.7	
西　藏						
陕　西						
甘　肃	73.2	580.6		79.2	60.0	
青　海	3.2					
宁　夏	23.0	50.0				
新　疆	21.3	263.0		6.0	13.4	

单位：万元

行政事业单位增加值	执行民间非营利组织单位会计制度财务指标				
	固定资产原价	上年结余	本年收入合计	本年费用合计	社会组织增加值
16087.8	**29850.9**	**3480.0**	**7862.6**	**11029.5**	**4767.7**
2549.9					
908.5	1360.2			0.2	0.2
2518.2	9655.9	-126.5	1447.5	1546.1	727.4
36.0	11.0				
192.7	126.3		63.4	63.4	36.2
1324.3	495.0		97.7	171.9	83.9
	77.2	147.0	39.1	734.3	569.6
3566.3					
36.0	2.0		0.7	7.0	7.0
206.4	100.0		50.0	50.0	25.0
31.0	100.0	100.0		70.0	60.0
75.8	100.0		90.0	5.0	0.7
26.8	253.0		375.8	375.8	148.1
22.8	4.0	3.0	8.0	15.0	11.0
733.1	266.4	169.8	1196.3	1108.0	559.8
206.5	374.0	23.6	33.3	120.3	56.8
402.2	16675.9	3163.1	4415.8	6714.3	2457.8
2327.3					
827.4					
73.2					
	190.0			3.2	3.2
2.0	60.0		45.0	45.0	21.0
21.3					

C-2-17 不提供住宿的

地 区	机构和设施数			
		工商登记	编制登记	民政登记
全 国	**334083**	**16534**	**6962**	**25746**
中央级	1		1	
北 京	11830	574	302	424
天 津	2097	223	51	246
河 北	31842	615	253	253
山 西	3963	374	331	351
内蒙古	3034	145	126	22
辽 宁	8431	1749	189	330
吉 林	1218	318	201	71
黑龙江	2889	440	241	721
上 海	4842	928	147	709
江 苏	35933	2718	230	14267
浙 江	32047	1933	189	1178
安 徽	8226	341	267	145
福 建	5629	277	126	85
江 西	3761	296	266	1475
山 东	27907	1221	380	654
河 南	4895	813	291	589
湖 北	10064	533	355	472
湖 南	8645	491	297	75
广 东	55890	138	345	680
广 西	10332	123	192	56
海 南	1718	13	15	206
重 庆	5967	745	132	64
四 川	15294	692	629	860
贵 州	20048	38	268	94
云 南	2301	260	152	162
西 藏	103	3	27	32
陕 西	4248	197	227	682
甘 肃	6667	65	182	50
青 海	489	35	14	93
宁 夏	959	74	61	298
新 疆	2813	162	475	402

社会服务机构和设施总表

单位:个、人

年末职工人数	女性	工商登记	编制登记	民政登记
2369608	**817568**	**1250701**	**67611**	**130980**
135	53		135	
65390	28171	26086	3743	2178
25544	10710	15835	549	1201
96639	33417	34804	2953	1256
48477	12881	35764	2741	1355
21996	9065	8650	1668	84
130514	50147	89134	1803	1411
21702	7012	15440	2579	347
27817	10321	14417	1793	4163
100568	39171	74486	3558	8742
413220	139095	249796	2111	73318
274646	95246	204006	1659	3151
54917	21075	17312	2597	643
37881	13122	18090	931	339
37299	12744	24901	1673	6237
198799	67903	91981	4168	3800
75124	26231	54557	3261	2010
70450	26352	34357	3132	2134
61203	20254	30688	3304	396
158866	48063	13465	3402	2150
28982	8595	8126	1738	484
9803	2682	1221	156	1150
85068	31004	67826	1064	272
102105	36637	53854	3944	4388
93217	23110	1984	4578	591
42618	11604	32472	1216	843
560	244	201	91	155
29774	11378	12060	2204	2679
20929	6368	3663	1397	269
3310	1218	2048	139	181
9566	4457	4899	757	1498
22489	9238	8578	2567	3555

C-2-17续表1

地区	受教育程度		职业资格水平	
	大学专科人数	大学本科及以上人数	助理社会工作师人数	社会工作师人数
全国	**326285**	**146464**	**14225**	**6457**
中央级	10	125		1
北京	11892	9875	2367	885
天津	4117	2189	500	107
河北	6792	2232	83	145
山西	4199	1793	100	60
内蒙古	5324	3101	223	114
辽宁	16960	9796	466	299
吉林	3182	971	411	258
黑龙江	5629	2033	161	62
上海	5440	3033	413	270
江苏	51428	21767	1762	693
浙江	24310	10262	1124	735
安徽	10452	2998	467	192
福建	2677	1308	348	260
江西	2680	631	75	55
山东	43691	20158	380	244
河南	11114	4667	165	154
湖北	10014	3848	342	89
湖南	8576	3197	465	126
广东	24821	15169	3100	890
广西	3024	1689	164	88
海南	1119	399	51	12
重庆	10586	5252	266	186
四川	19108	5375	426	284
贵州	19111	6018	58	38
云南	2751	1222	60	42
西藏	142	67		2
陕西	6152	1880	110	45
甘肃	3520	1786	39	54
青海	366	168	22	10
宁夏	1140	571	8	7
新疆	5958	2884	69	50

单位：人、人次、时

年龄结构				志愿服务	
35岁及以下人数	36岁至45岁人数	46岁至55岁人数	56岁及以上人数	志愿者服务人次数	志愿服务时间
762739	**928981**	**521393**	**156495**	**7659574**	**18263552.7**
76	21	28	10		
18505	24744	17858	4283	5177669	12975703.4
9700	8943	5628	1273	62935	94873.0
31597	35761	22251	7030	9407	38116.0
13952	18339	13160	3026	1074	2284.4
7011	8846	5344	795	18121	36518.0
38201	54272	28337	9704	10612	18299.0
5315	10673	3517	2197	300	350.0
9777	11539	5042	1459	34154	71590.0
29482	34539	27093	9454	41448	124610.0
120145	163989	102403	26683	301826	643729.0
79599	95566	65304	34177	450918	768977.8
15525	24382	12594	2416	60874	100683.0
12288	15462	7542	2589	106131	325983.0
13996	15817	5700	1786	1019	2449.7
74849	75708	38090	10152	257483	587454.4
32083	30485	10496	2060	135	494.0
20848	32774	13999	2829	4782	9120.0
15135	29845	13726	2497	18760	59572.0
56857	60169	32300	9540	4750	10122.0
9125	8982	7364	3511	419	1366.0
2843	4161	2161	638	8560	15319.0
26602	34769	19141	4556	286099	669305.0
37616	42033	18598	3858	58860	138251.0
34660	35270	18460	4827	695749	1409787.0
17422	16890	7266	1040	7	13.0
292	197	57	14		
10500	10956	6891	1427	17489	44661.0
7416	7869	4204	1440	11643	60586.0
1298	1488	457	67	5	12.0
2772	4563	1812	419	31	8.0
7252	9929	4570	738	18314	53316.0

C-2-17续表2

地区	增加值合计	执行企业会计制度单位财务指标					执行行政	
		固定资产原价	营业收入	费用合计	营业利润	企业单位增加值	固定资产原价	上年结转和结余
全 国	**9598481.8**	**18063804.7**	**47441863.4**	**5790124.5**	**1271884.0**	**7571319.8**	**4179271.3**	**416077.1**
中央级	3788.8						32675.5	14718.3
北 京	353094.7	405663.8	586023.0	98909.7	4805.2	131413.3	183244.2	146132.8
天 津	78808.8	229039.3	349012.1	85796.5	5048.4	60450.9	120678.1	832.0
河 北	228778.2	475207.5	1231453.4	101384.2	8294.5	176917.9	132876.7	6369.7
山 西	56816.0	324806.5	442043.7	40859.6	-15471.6	43010.6	45332.0	3284.7
内蒙古	41174.0	67104.9	60340.3	11843.9	1939.2	15370.6	57875.1	8076.4
辽 宁	394218.6	1430175.8	1905689.6	205563.4	61656.0	352023.4	85488.5	16862.4
吉 林	29458.2	109584.8	240973.7	28409.7	417.5	20323.2	36989.6	2670.9
黑龙江	81850.1	104443.6	157916.0	35190.2	4946.7	34144.8	80894.9	4492.4
上 海	823328.3	1334572.2	3150759.7	319347.1	179063.7	758082.3	131486.3	5701.4
江 苏	1530553.3	3495563.8	11150010.4	1262609.2	233461.4	1312526.1	472931.5	23510.0
浙 江	2745367.2	5304150.4	15604251.3	2269745.9	493977.5	2528737.3	543844.5	45877.0
安 徽	143411.6	128278.1	930406.5	59297.8	17996.2	63888.7	263753.3	7046.7
福 建	72047.1	169980.9	315338.0	48052.1	1520.7	54335.8	56948.9	4624.2
江 西	30713.0	100414.0	2186710.8	19408.8	2946.9	16564.5	30070.3	3474.8
山 东	906916.6	1031038.7	1715529.3	320611.0	140573.7	597446.2	168598.0	3058.8
河 南	150343.5	388437.0	769064.4	90855.8	19358.2	115797.6	115234.7	4549.6
湖 北	139522.4	209498.8	370299.5	95405.6	10275.1	79730.9	158459.2	962.5
湖 南	121399.7	275084.6	578552.4	61963.6	9349.1	82242.4	117769.7	4013.6
广 东	175325.4	263188.1	297472.8	36914.0	5820.3	61369.2	290061.0	14000.1
广 西	61351.1	62014.8	297312.4	11543.7	-2029.5	22130.2	108077.9	1374.2
海 南	13856.8	21504.6	49843.3	7466.7	354.4	7444.8	17113.7	1950.2
重 庆	374130.7	705319.5	1943941.3	226364.6	43152.2	338322.7	101331.3	25475.3
四 川	404574.9	452387.5	1418186.2	98137.9	24656.4	322395.5	138069.1	13104.6
贵 州	83591.9	6908.5	18872.8	2915.1	917.5	2559.8	127591.6	13925.5
云 南	109686.6	501380.6	1059401.6	158278.6	-11500.5	49531.6	315121.8	7701.6
西 藏	1952.1	3414.8	398.0	222.5	26.0	67.9	15292.0	830.0
陕 西	315075.5	147931.1	340976.7	44261.7	19440.4	264048.5	99329.1	13315.3
甘 肃	17059.6	29769.5	9953.7	2432.3	84.8	3465.9	48336.0	710.7
青 海	6141.1	9282.5	16223.0	3682.6	426.2	5041.4	17763.1	0.1
宁 夏	20065.2	103286.5	48836.3	11731.4	3794.1	16053.1	11640.9	4193.7
新 疆	84079.2	174372.0	196071.2	30919.3	6583.3	35882.6	54392.8	13237.6

单位：万元

事业单位会计制度财务指标				执行民间非营利组织单位会计制度财务指标				
本年收入合计	本年支出合计	收支结余	行政事业单位增加值	固定资产原价	上年结余	本年收入合计	本年费用合计	社会组织增加值
3548540.6	**3340738.8**	**395186.6**	**1495482.5**	**1894514.3**	**31413.8**	**810128.0**	**843721.8**	**531679.5**
104266.2	66297.2	52687.2	3788.8					
362743.4	334886.6	178710.0	220604.5	2262.9	775.7	3343.1	3493.6	1076.9
64298.2	61678.2	1993.1	16030.9	2576.7	212.7	3299.2	3725.9	2327.0
125484.8	117636.6	7352.2	44504.0	47439.0	873.7	8306.0	10680.7	7356.3
44257.2	35112.9	4824.7	11638.7	5585.3	21.9	2157.4	4309.8	2166.7
67228.3	59260.9	15841.8	25050.9	4074.0		1319.9	1288.9	752.5
101089.5	108229.2	1479.3	38587.8	11689.4	438.3	6584.9	7531.4	3607.4
30207.8	31468.3	1411.7	8708.5	800.2		2510.8	1148.5	426.5
56347.9	57288.0	54.2	47102.9	3071.3	1000.0	1182.3	936.9	602.4
139630.8	125057.5	6449.4	47785.4	20213.1	12293.9	52027.6	31847.4	17460.6
216535.2	224405.4	31481.1	131649.6	348981.0	420.6	179112.6	175821.5	86377.6
618096.0	336588.6	8000.5	189369.8	156323.3	1561.7	67673.0	68124.2	27260.1
107588.4	103862.4	2473.9	58042.3	87746.1	180.0	15723.4	31014.0	21480.6
38271.6	35415.6	3363.0	14859.4	34570.4	52.7	5411.7	7339.6	2851.9
24697.1	20970.0	-61.0	8901.4	12127.1		5930.3	7311.4	5247.1
181526.8	184636.4		61674.2	422628.5		326223.7	326223.7	247796.2
190251.2	178254.0	2772.3	31392.6	13103.7	751.6	1988.6	5105.2	3153.3
99532.0	98534.3	506.0	50692.8	19099.9	66.0	16258.1	15776.0	9098.7
104400.4	88901.3	6139.8	35503.0	15456.1	52.6	8984.9	8434.3	3654.3
216527.9	448375.5	15099.3	94474.1	102854.6	1748.8	32800.1	35032.0	19482.1
80108.9	70128.9	3047.1	33002.1	31967.6	68.4	1819.5	7589.3	6218.8
27701.0	27572.2	2777.1	6020.2	1554.5		732.6	1074.7	391.8
68727.3	68070.7	25954.2	31807.5	37685.4	8.0	8059.8	7634.1	4000.5
104734.7	99958.2	3852.7	59301.3	95931.6	2399.5	28431.8	32575.0	22878.1
72860.0	64851.2	4284.3	50013.8	172950.7	8404.6	27499.6	42114.6	31018.3
80306.1	76651.0	4076.0	58751.5	218905.3	3.0	194.5	1955.0	1403.5
10476.1	10355.0		1884.2	28.0				
98374.9	101715.9	6114.6	50696.3	3711.1	1.7	129.7	669.7	330.7
20604.9	22368.2	786.3	10908.9	11813.8	78.4	1454.0	3637.8	2684.8
1304.0	1229.0		903.8	7404.0		157.9	362.1	195.9
11292.8	10841.7	-479.4	3818.4	672.0		688.2	737.5	193.7
79069.2	70137.9	4195.2	48011.4	1287.7		122.8	227.0	185.2

C-2-18 社区服务

地　区	机构和设施数	农村社区服务机构	可以为居民提供便民办事服务的机构	可以为居民提供活动场所的机构	可以为居民提供养老等服务的机构
全　国	**251368**	**102588**	**155890**	**64830**	**32391**
中央级					
北　京	10911	4955	8761	4013	631
天　津	1793	360	1258	379	41
河　北	10028	6549	2287	2404	5153
山　西	2910	1167	1773	738	287
内蒙古	2227	82	1528	451	210
辽　宁	6295	986	4520	395	1041
吉　林	633	157	560	28	28
黑龙江	2204	112	1462	439	103
上　海	3810	356	2240	1033	40
江　苏	29324	12279	15083	5623	8747
浙　江	23544	14079	15463	3809	2761
安　徽	6097	1832	4367	782	388
福　建	3183	908	2129	470	599
江　西	3137	249	1788	1035	62
山　东	22758	9642	20272	8898	4354
河　南	3226	636	1693	772	279
湖　北	8692	1953	5610	2092	366
湖　南	5421	997	3944	1757	583
广　东	55011	17883	25906	21624	1547
广　西	906	73	507	159	51
海　南	1658	1254	1218	284	47
重　庆	4107	1422	2231	1276	1089
四　川	12790	5399	9560	1831	947
贵　州	17589	14737	14539	1759	735
云　南	1547	408	1170	128	179
西　藏	39	10	33	11	6
陕　西	3153	786	2120	750	109
甘　肃	4999	2999	1780	1169	1874
青　海	271	41	156	81	
宁　夏	805	242	417	263	96
新　疆	2300	35	1515	377	38

机构和设施总表

单位:个、人

农村	可以为居民提供便民信息服务的机构	年末职工人数	女性	受教育程度	
				大学专科人数	大学本科及以上人数
19081	**45952**	**928607**	**348557**	**211547**	**93062**
60	3504	37036	18453	9459	8260
15	315	9174	5992	3015	1638
3995	511	24164	8850	3765	894
211	116	9249	3763	1966	724
23	198	11978	6125	3766	2459
313	733	38667	22257	12083	7180
	18	3909	2441	2057	200
24	331	12177	5288	4140	1547
8	502	25159	12947	3470	2055
5056	4017	140127	44029	27666	11782
2340	2282	60454	23997	12158	5043
215	775	27399	11534	7870	2055
91	285	14067	5761	1862	815
15	264	10831	4746	1459	207
1937	12709	87670	34086	29504	12914
189	506	13750	5627	3723	1045
115	1091	31561	12829	7291	2315
123	3231	19236	8362	4891	1527
599	6894	142225	42279	23337	13886
4	247	8218	4034	1575	837
15	129	8403	2298	972	311
827	575	14571	6893	4664	2154
535	3201	42396	14503	10554	3156
625	2500	82921	19908	17049	4890
120	95	8353	3026	1510	580
6	6	223	126	92	45
59	229	13889	6114	3779	877
1536	222	13528	4081	2766	1372
	34	941	342	278	109
4	56	3893	2411	531	140
21	376	12438	5455	4295	2045

C-2-18续表1

地区	职业资格水平		年龄结构			
	助理社会工作师人数	社会工作师人数	35岁及以下人数	36岁至45岁人数	46岁至55岁人数	56岁及以上人数
全　国	**11015**	**4618**	**302509**	**367641**	**201323**	**57134**
中央级						
北　京	2314	827	10720	13132	10465	2719
天　津	438	86	3332	3042	2380	420
河　北	37	95	8539	8878	5159	1588
山　西	50	23	2550	3875	2186	638
内蒙古	185	88	4798	4932	1805	443
辽　宁	364	247	13129	14844	6950	3744
吉　林	6	59	578	2813	459	59
黑龙江	130	45	3945	5570	1714	948
上　海	291	193	4835	9650	8335	2339
江　苏	1356	478	40068	56275	33936	9848
浙　江	948	520	19310	22763	13739	4642
安　徽	253	97	8327	12828	5512	732
福　建	308	199	4603	5454	2958	1052
江　西	32	33	3183	4313	2050	1285
山　东	186	140	33986	33761	15090	4833
河　南	89	56	4466	6517	2147	620
湖　北	107	66	10326	13590	6076	1569
湖　南	145	75	5499	7465	5671	601
广　东	2904	808	49463	54149	29831	8782
广　西	127	37	3878	2595	1423	322
海　南	29	8	1980	3792	2015	616
重　庆	194	100	4710	6045	3017	799
四　川	329	219	12348	18671	9564	1813
贵　州	34	18	30867	31627	16381	4046
云　南	23	19	2719	3650	1603	381
西　藏		2	170	53		
陕　西	53	22	3935	5336	3811	807
甘　肃	20	26	4866	4578	3090	994
青　海	7	7	401	340	200	
宁　夏	5	2	912	2054	885	42
新　疆	51	23	4066	5049	2871	452

单位：个、人次、张、人 、时

志愿服务		床位数合计	日间照料床位数		住宿收养床位数	
志愿者服务人次数	志愿服务时间			农村		农村
7170316	**17100578.4**	**662894**	**451046**	**207718**	**211848**	**109869**
5152994	12943228.4	5415	4116	1004	1299	84
59935	88873.0	5327	4323	1747	1004	389
3266	9356.0	62211	40294	28458	21917	16905
868	2266.0	9717	7942	3550	1775	397
17999	36396.0	9090	7465	329	1625	747
4928	10683.0	24674	14241	2013	10433	4805
		3844	3239	300	605	66
15985	47601.0	3104	2036	127	1068	218
39684	118586.0	4837	3950	237	887	209
251949	526125.0	126518	93895	38708	32623	11176
390917	686468.8	95000	76722	55469	18278	10200
29005	56796.0	41654	11670	2656	29984	19637
		12313	9469	2363	2844	298
656	1158.0	6151	4015	1906	2136	1874
192470	430392.2	52297	45037	13982	7260	1678
		14609	5096	958	9513	4752
3010	5054.0	10219	7143	1206	3076	1336
7999	18757.0	5792	3511	561	2281	809
3330	6622.0	37994	17841	7433	20153	7907
60	130.0	1472	957		515	49
8560	15319.0	2108	577	12	1531	560
269281	627095.0	23053	9141	3335	13912	10526
8497	25036.0	28686	20109	6910	8577	2246
690634	1393400.0	18382	14722	10926	3660	2795
		9644	4661	1649	4983	3311
		47			47	
10299	26513.0	6163	4109	1619	2054	830
1790	10050.0	37604	30897	20091	6707	5641
3		1278	1278			
		1250	1214	141	36	54
6197	14673.0	2441	1376	28	1065	370

C-2-18续表2

地区	年末收养人数合计	日间照料人数	农村	住宿收养人数	农村
全国	**105782**	**62501**	**24501**	**43281**	**22939**
中央级					
北京	1564	937	390	627	18
天津	366	269	81	97	97
河北	889	489	177	400	350
山西	1418	1378	1235	40	40
内蒙古	1780	1628	28	152	95
辽宁	4331	1072	179	3259	2226
吉林	53	53			
黑龙江	115	28	7	87	83
上海	1687	1686		1	
江苏	16132	12770	5521	3362	1756
浙江	7133	2136	1605	4997	24
安徽	16739	3350	1667	13389	7239
福建	2528	2307	130	221	16
江西	3861	2037	1794	1824	1794
山东	25271	22329	8040	2942	1279
河南	3389	231	80	3158	2155
湖北	1102	696	51	406	12
湖南	1976	775	55	1201	558
广东	1289	575	340	714	349
广西	296	136		160	14
海南					
重庆	4857	1448	302	3409	3281
四川	3469	3097	1922	372	119
贵州	1512	803	465	709	470
云南	1252	120	70	1132	669
西藏					
陕西	1016	572	16	444	68
甘肃	542	383	284	159	158
青海	514	514			
宁夏	313	313	56		54
新疆	388	369	6	19	15

单位：人、人次、人天、个、平方米

本年收养照料人天数	老年人活动人次数	社区服务志愿者组织数	注册社区志愿者人数	城镇便民、利民服务网点数	机构建筑面积
6383985	**7882590**	**101526**	**2536003**	**302039**	**49165154**
313729	1573719	10253	1444406	10372	2002650
		795		5683	433763
18345	1068	587	252	4338	1579355
291830	295225	613	10920	5400	464014
182341	287356	1136	11113	8816	596126
6076	100	1182	39571	8704	992885
8395	31189			273	95908
	44605	1823	44528	7307	506680
221753	83327	3509	123399	16243	881719
1161203	3334772	12186	160186	39851	7354795
27701	452404	2286	35973	63830	4895551
12000	73490	898	8820	7333	1358265
	1650	603	17	2687	564376
23449	39318	1013	2250	3060	558937
2487130	523795	5622	26419	31033	7341811
2535	42743	130	858	1400	1178425
31160	226795	590	3803	3177	1572080
5598	25623	1232	744	4416	890136
	2020	1228	266774	8514	6731744
26555	37727	34		1286	313602
		1	15	19	286202
1400828	623448	34063	218219	11478	1232197
43296	94419	5931	87582	24826	2046818
	185	14480	10242	15509	2725194
92606				23	446632
				6	12574
25042	35621	500	39335	2455	719153
	16923			8318	645529
					102305
35	3718	140		950	157470
2378	31350	691	577	4732	478258

C-2-18续表3

地区	增加值合计	执行企业会计制度单位财务指标					执行行政	
		固定资产原价	营业收入	费用合计	营业利润	企业单位增加值	固定资产原价	上年结转和结余
全国	**1091474.8**	**185091.9**	**17512.7**	**7497.6**	**6087.0**	**14734.4**	**2006764.0**	**64059.5**
中央级								
北京	45468.6	71660.6	8379.8	2951.0	6009.7	8514.6	52190.1	3575.8
天津	8382.9						66369.8	-26.1
河北	13848.0	659.0	41.2	59.9		2.2	18411.2	63.0
山西	4063.6						15203.9	203.0
内蒙古	9849.2	980.0	729.8	21.0		298.7	14259.1	226.0
辽宁	9792.9	728.5		126.0		27.2	18948.7	158.2
吉林	1159.1	3.0	10.3	9.3		13.3	2092.0	239.0
黑龙江	42607.0	14.0	4.0	2.1		284.7	59170.1	2.3
上海	34032.3	1.0		10.0		-20.0	13246.7	2335.1
江苏	176413.4	1488.7	424.7	163.7	46.7	114.0	288703.7	1037.3
浙江	164521.9	15158.8	1463.0	455.2	-1.6	50.8	474785.8	30998.9
安徽	41973.6	720.0	943.7	659.7		247.4	105906.0	3556.0
福建	5879.7	631.5	416.6	392.6	8.3	33.3	17970.4	22.8
江西	6659.9	3975.4	207.0	72.0		10.5	4052.5	6.1
山东	223484.8						16031.0	
河南	9888.4	1174.1	1083.4	463.3	9.5	693.6	19232.8	150.5
湖北	36353.7	2491.0	1598.0	1755.0	9.7	59.5	78490.9	262.0
湖南	17037.1	393.0	52.0	2.0		2383.3	17603.4	8.3
广东	73390.1	47240.6	1875.0	89.4		1308.8	199607.9	7192.3
广西	2565.5	317.0		1.1		3.0	4732.4	58.0
海南	2075.2	1527.3				0.2	11008.2	5.6
重庆	18555.5	28415.2	11.0	11.0			52794.1	30.6
四川	37688.3	2795.0	141.0	99.7	2.7	209.8	51802.2	5152.7
贵州	61707.4	400.4	63.0	11.7		21.9	44595.0	5754.0
云南	16172.2	1602.2	3.0		1.0	2.0	267693.3	2148.1
西藏	827.4						4882.0	680.0
陕西	10742.4	4.0					46395.1	48.0
甘肃	4669.8	520.7	5.0	11.1		52.7	12176.6	15.5
青海	382.5	326.0	3.0			2.0	2200.0	
宁夏	556.7	214.0				2.5	2796.5	32.0
新疆	10725.1	1650.9	58.2	130.8	1.0	418.4	23412.6	124.5

单位：万元

事业单位会计制度财务指标				执行民间非营利组织单位会计制度财务指标				
本年收入合计	本年支出合计	收支结余	行政事业单位增加值	固定资产原价	上年结余	本年收入合计	本年费用合计	社会组织增加值
1144078.1	**1122752.4**	**10409.0**	**618765.5**	**1477541.3**	**24246.9**	**709309.1**	**736195.2**	**457974.9**
49806.0	54154.4	556.9	36038.3	963.8	775.7	3201.0	3316.8	915.7
3365.5	3413.9		6060.6	2426.7	212.7	3295.1	3719.8	2322.3
13156.1	13114.7		11535.6	14524.1	136.7	2916.1	3572.3	2310.2
2354.0	2273.1		1981.6	5368.3	15.9	2109.4	4114.5	2082.0
12604.0	12891.8	191.5	9056.1	3237.0		1013.9	981.9	494.4
9176.4	10353.6	34.0	6216.7	10521.6	432.8	6559.9	7411.0	3549.0
1091.3	1220.9	1.0	719.3	800.2		2510.8	1148.5	426.5
45670.0	46535.3		41760.9	3071.3	1000.0	961.3	857.9	561.4
44816.7	37213.8	652.3	16632.6	20108.0	12293.9	51627.7	31770.3	17419.7
99755.8	113168.7	3115.7	96445.0	290336.1	417.6	163660.2	165556.0	79854.4
513583.2	236359.2	2249.7	144737.0	131716.3	1326.3	60121.0	56506.3	19734.1
36708.1	37426.7		25280.2	47024.5	180.0	9537.0	24383.3	16446.0
8488.7	8651.0	4.5	3854.5	12134.9	25.1	3442.9	5488.9	1991.9
2670.7	2229.9	10.5	1415.1	11247.1		5930.3	7298.6	5234.3
13605.5	13643.5		9793.3	277933.9		279338.8	279338.8	213691.5
9062.6	9612.0	99.7	6272.1	11315.2	748.6	1928.9	4828.8	2922.7
41535.9	40987.2		29692.1	12581.9	66.0	12123.7	11581.6	6602.1
23706.0	19869.4		13023.2	7260.3	49.6	5098.3	4160.9	1630.6
82080.1	334817.0	1450.9	53273.3	102170.1	1721.8	31945.1	33866.1	18808.0
1107.0	1084.7		1248.8	4411.3	58.4	235.7	1442.8	1313.7
2708.8	2831.3		1683.2	1554.5		732.6	1074.7	391.8
20733.1	20802.2	61.0	14935.1	33117.4	8.0	7589.4	7167.0	3620.4
25873.4	22935.9	824.2	15715.6	90357.3	2393.5	25996.9	30409.8	21762.9
38867.8	34238.9	642.3	32184.4	143922.7	2301.2	25037.5	39677.9	29501.1
6621.3	5949.6	466.5	14876.2	218389.3	3.0	94.5	1756.4	1294.0
880.0	844.4		827.4	28.0				
12662.2	12853.5	13.2	10531.3	2026.7	1.7	104.6	278.5	211.1
3197.0	2797.1	15.1	2264.8	9751.1	78.4	1227.6	3203.2	2352.3
82.4	106.6		184.6	7404.0		157.9	362.1	195.9
814.3	825.5		360.5	672.0		688.2	737.5	193.7
17294.2	19546.6	20.0	10165.5	1165.7		122.8	183.0	141.2

C-2-19 社区服务

地　区	单位数	农村社区服务机构	可以为居民提供便民办事服务的机构	可以为居民提供活动场所的机构	可以为居民提供养老等服务的机构
全　国	**918**	**32**	**631**	**163**	**94**
中央级					
北　京	17		12	4	2
天　津	13		10	3	
河　北	27		21	4	2
山　西	24	3	12	5	
内蒙古	4		2	2	
辽　宁	29	1	13	7	2
吉　林	27	3	18	1	
黑龙江	40		24	7	1
上　海	8		6		
江　苏	68	1	47	6	3
浙　江	29	1	16	3	1
安　徽	41	1	32	1	3
福　建	26		18	4	1
江　西	45		28	8	3
山　东	120		113	45	22
河　南	51	5	30	7	8
湖　北	32	1	28	2	2
湖　南	56	3	52	10	9
广　东	35	6	21	3	5
广　西	2		1		
海　南	2				2
重　庆	12		7	4	
四　川	80	1	40	13	13
贵　州	18	1	14	2	4
云　南	5		5		
西　藏	6		5	1	
陕　西	55		35	9	3
甘　肃	26	5	11	6	8
青　海					
宁　夏	6		4		
新　疆	14		6	6	

指导中心

单位:个、人

农村	可以为居民提供便民信息服务的机构	年末职工人数	女性	受教育程度：大学专科人数	受教育程度：大学本科及以上人数
6	**277**	**8735**	**3961**	**2303**	**1771**
	7	478	283	94	180
	1	71	29	18	31
	3	264	108	66	16
	8	101	51	20	9
		23	16	11	5
1	8	233	131	98	87
	8	576	414	67	63
	8	318	178	116	111
	2	100	54	34	54
	18	507	240	140	105
1	11	1126	174	97	94
1	7	427	153	64	37
	3	136	76	17	25
	6	250	142	60	29
	81	1555	757	673	503
1	7	442	200	99	37
	4	278	127	70	55
	44	395	180	110	46
1	8	203	103	48	83
	1	10	8	8	1
		4	1	3	
	2	39	17	12	16
1	22	425	179	132	75
	1	98	34	29	10
		19	8	5	9
		19	9	6	
	11	322	131	132	26
	1	86	41	22	2
	3	88	40	15	21
	2	142	77	37	41

C-2-19续表1

地　区	职业资格水平		年龄结构			
	助理社会工作师人数	社会工作师人数	35岁及以下人数	36岁至45岁人数	46岁至55岁人数	56岁及以上人数
全　国	**300**	**135**	**2897**	**4062**	**1508**	**268**
中央级						
北　京	66	17	130	195	135	18
天　津	1		27	22	17	5
河　北	1		115	112	31	6
山　西	2	2	35	36	25	5
内蒙古			5	14	4	
辽　宁	2	2	74	113	43	3
吉　林	2	3	81	344	144	7
黑龙江	7	12	131	138	47	2
上　海	3	6	46	29	19	6
江　苏	21	8	168	179	120	40
浙　江	18	5	198	862	59	7
安　徽	93	11	185	196	45	1
福　建	1	9	37	69	22	8
江　西	5	1	59	146	33	12
山　东	11	16	766	581	158	50
河　南	6	3	154	162	112	14
湖　北	2	5	74	142	52	10
湖　南	15	4	126	168	87	14
广　东	16	15	70	83	37	13
广　西			5	3	2	
海　南		1		3	1	
重　庆	3	3	9	23	7	
四　川	12	6	121	132	156	16
贵　州	1		45	34	18	1
云　南			5	11	2	1
西　藏			11	8		
陕　西	11	5	102	117	81	22
甘　肃	1		35	31	16	4
青　海						
宁　夏			29	43	14	2
新　疆		1	54	66	21	1

单位：人次、张、人 、时

志愿服务		床位数合计	日间照料床位数		住宿收养床位数	
志愿者服务人次数	志愿服务时间			农村		农村
146304	**390439.0**	**19045**	**12858**	**4070**	**6187**	**146**
98916	297960.0	1107	111		996	
13600	14500.0	110	110			
822	3545.0	662	142	20	520	10
6	6.0	85	79	32	6	6
		60	60			
30	60.0	432	418	10	14	
		1410	1355	195	55	10
		216	142		74	
30	240.0					
402	1888.0	458	456		2	
		3009	3008	2893	1	
2625	3348.0	261	198		63	20
		88	45		43	
		582	427		155	
28454	63841.0	1987	1683		304	
		2634	272	27	2362	28
		353	271		82	
87	532.0	328	210		118	
		307	175	50	132	
		20	20			
		249	130		119	
152	703.0	2428	2044	770	384	
121	380.0	292	86	50	206	50
		173	35		138	
1049	3386.0	1375	1020		355	
		387	345	23	42	22
		32	16		16	
10	50.0					

C-2-19续表2

地区	年末收养人数合计	日间照料人数	农村	住宿收养人数	农村
全　国	**2774**	**1659**	**40**	**1115**	**38**
中央级					
北　京	609			609	
天　津	40	40			
河　北					
山　西	24	24			
内蒙古	42	42			
辽　宁					
吉　林					
黑龙江					
上　海					
江　苏	109	109			
浙　江					
安　徽	42	37		5	2
福　建					
江　西	37	7		30	
山　东	1034	879		155	
河　南	82	26	26	56	26
湖　北					
湖　南	213	144		69	
广　东	26	19	4	7	
广　西					
海　南					
重　庆	11	7		4	
四　川	32	32			
贵　州	76			76	
云　南	56			56	
西　藏					
陕　西	341	293	10	48	10
甘　肃					
青　海					
宁　夏					
新　疆					

单位：人、人次、人天、个、平方米

本年收养照料人天数	老年人活动人次数	社区服务志愿者组织数	注册社区志愿者人数	城镇便民、利民服务网点数	机构建筑面积
264466	**164749**	**4640**	**704639**	**14031**	**936887**
222285	86200	2968	631379	46	131841
		20		20	9043
					19779
1825	226	3		21	5445
126	1755	1			6105
					6116
					5660
				1	19575
		1023	68450	220	6589
8339	3480	269	54	2129	144256
				1816	59017
	5350	3	410	50	20404
		66		1597	15426
600		5		41	14865
10539	44728	192	3647	4444	224059
	1325			177	36622
	2910	2		1308	41174
180	8912	17	21	192	41078
		2	4	567	16019
					200
					355
	5000	30	570	49	9350
	500	1	4	1289	28022
				1	3020
					4946
				2	1120
20572	4100	16	100	33	53076
	263			28	7855
					1588
		22			4282

C-2-19续表3

地区	增加值合计	执行企业会计制度单位财务指标					执行行政	
		固定资产原价	营业收入	费用合计	营业利润	企业单位增加值	固定资产原价	上年结转和结余
全　国	**36821.8**	**718.7**	**470.8**	**255.9**	**40.8**	**199.8**	**85781.4**	**3272.0**
中央级								
北　京	14049.9						29212.4	2033.9
天　津	687.3						1569.4	-26.1
河　北	162.6		41.2	59.9		2.2	568.2	
山　西	68.5						50.1	
内蒙古	96.6						517.0	
辽　宁	217.9						198.0	22.0
吉　林	226.1		9.0	9.0		12.0	1077.0	1.0
黑龙江	1045.5	4.0					318.0	
上　海	1550.9						5265.7	486.3
江　苏	3335.3	35.7	42.7	35.7	31.7	64.0	3303.7	273.3
浙　江	1182.4	80.0					2153.8	361.9
安　徽	642.0	320.0	234.7	74.7		58.5	3684.4	
福　建	190.7	26.0	31.6	7.6	8.3	33.3	70.0	
江　西	341.0			0.1			450.8	
山　东	5061.6						8447.4	
河　南	899.2			4.0		2.0	4359.0	10.0
湖　北	1018.7						7402.0	
湖　南	773.3	4.0					2894.2	
广　东	1573.0						4477.7	53.7
广　西	0.9						22.6	
海　南	9.0							
重　庆	210.8		11.0	11.0			1350.0	
四　川	406.5	50.0	63.6	45.3	0.8	16.7	718.7	42.0
贵　州	84.3	51.0	32.0	3.5		10.1	66.0	10.0
云　南	59.5	107.0					405.0	
西　藏	107.7						1714.2	
陕　西	2647.0						4962.6	1.0
甘　肃	41.0		5.0	5.1		1.0	34.4	
青　海								
宁　夏	15.0						125.0	2.0
新　疆	117.2	41.0					364.1	1.0

单位：万元

事业单位会计制度财务指标				执行民间非营利组织单位会计制度财务指标				
本年收入合计	本年支出合计	收支结余	行政事业单位增加值	固定资产原价	上年结余	本年收入合计	本年费用合计	社会组织增加值
51137.3	**50608.9**	**991.8**	**33007.6**	**21444.5**	**1142.1**	**5474.0**	**6250.9**	**3614.4**
23602.7	24330.2	-40.7	14049.9					
363.4	419.5		441.1	102.8	4.3	24.5	645.9	246.2
258.5	282.0		142.8	529.5		34.8	28.1	17.6
78.7	93.1		47.9	29.2		42.0	37.5	20.6
186.5	186.5		96.6					
313.9	308.9	17.0	177.6	116.4		68.8	69.0	40.3
288.4	281.4		212.2	6.0		3.5	3.7	1.9
1024.8	1023.8		1013.2	1030.0	1000.0	72.3	49.6	32.3
3635.5	3450.3	612.7	1512.5	1.4		79.5	48.8	38.4
3976.9	3725.6	276.9	2839.0	1360.4		763.7	984.2	432.3
1887.0	2026.0	14.1	1052.2	173.6	12.5	259.6	165.8	130.2
640.1	542.1		543.3	1049.0		92.0	68.2	40.2
255.2	162.2		132.8	44.0	11.0	42.5	41.0	24.6
289.4	295.9		229.4	871.0		180.0	220.8	111.6
3886.3	3906.3		2886.6	13865.1		3367.7	3367.7	2175.0
1571.8	926.1	99.7	845.0	418.0	1.0	55.0	105.0	52.2
2089.1	1899.1		992.7	25.0	10.0	26.0	36.0	26.0
951.4	834.3		751.3	91.0		89.7	39.0	22.0
2102.1	2139.3	12.1	1532.0	48.5		10.0	41.0	41.0
			0.9					
				5.0		23.0	21.0	9.0
356.6	356.4		203.8	156.0		7.0	7.0	7.0
368.8	350.1		300.7	503.5	102.6	195.9	198.5	89.1
32.8	33.5		35.0	164.0	0.7	28.4	52.0	39.2
45.3	45.3		59.5					
	42.0		107.7					
2723.6	2752.3		2644.6	46.0		3.0	3.8	2.4
92.9	63.4		25.7	47.1		5.1	15.3	14.3
12.0	12.0		15.0					
103.6	121.3		116.2	762.0			2.0	1.0

C-2-20 社区服务

地　区	单位数	农村社区服务机构	可以为居民提供便民办事服务的机构	可以为居民提供活动场所的机构	可以为居民提供养老等服务的机构
全　国	**23088**	**7657**	**16149**	**4724**	**2809**
中央级					
北　京	193	19	152	75	21
天　津	273	136	134	130	4
河　北	785	122	141	195	416
山　西	530	200	257	217	43
内蒙古	982	28	782	186	72
辽　宁	738	59	492	117	87
吉　林	349	104	304	19	19
黑龙江	466	51	360	64	16
上　海	249	12	215	14	4
江　苏	2550	979	1546	539	661
浙　江	2438	1665	1669	386	342
安　徽	1240	653	836	129	192
福　建	225	50	125	52	46
江　西	339	53	213	83	12
山　东	1221	350	1004	549	364
河　南	599	130	415	68	75
湖　北	558	70	418	100	44
湖　南	490	73	463	93	48
广　东	2741	928	1786	715	29
广　西	80	3	29	32	2
海　南	71		61	2	8
重　庆	282	22	212	141	9
四　川	1726	297	1522	172	59
贵　州	1564	775	1404	124	61
云　南	109	5	74	18	12
西　藏	15	3	14	6	6
陕　西	514	224	383	121	6
甘　肃	986	621	574	184	145
青　海	29	13	6	18	
宁　夏	74	9	53	19	3
新　疆	672	3	505	156	3

中心

单位:个、人

农村	可以为居民提供便民信息服务的机构	年末职工人数	女性	受教育程度	
				大学专科人数	大学本科及以上人数
1043	**3030**	**134915**	**51410**	**36898**	**18082**
	87	1800	1027	520	835
	25	1797	1094	549	328
117	74	2436	1242	519	141
	14	1922	743	470	154
2	61	7003	3503	2176	1458
15	80	5710	2918	1915	1478
	8	1726	815	764	113
	61	4756	1626	1693	646
	16	4903	2557	1577	1237
237	185	21282	4412	6927	1008
293	59	11541	4590	2615	1324
96	174	6859	2653	1752	784
5	13	1258	530	220	119
	35	1451	738	312	43
64	668	7640	2838	2704	1741
49	41	3353	1447	856	277
6	50	3369	1271	600	238
7	444	2672	1115	593	278
19	285	11033	4563	2127	2213
	17	304	131	76	31
		739	186	80	26
	84	1727	805	483	268
7	291	6979	2434	1696	587
37	102	11005	3598	2645	1633
3	13	774	327	178	102
6	6	83	49	13	7
1	4	2471	798	503	144
79	106	3099	1013	642	231
	5	141	35	37	28
	8	514	399	84	32
	14	4568	1953	1572	578

C-2-20续表1

地区	职业资格水平		年龄结构			
	助理社会工作师人数	社会工作师人数	35岁及以下人数	36岁至45岁人数	46岁至55岁人数	56岁及以上人数
全　国	**2196**	**884**	**48726**	**52882**	**26051**	**7256**
中央级						
北　京	37	29	524	670	495	111
天　津	121	22	547	735	434	81
河　北	8	10	897	913	519	107
山　西	4	5	687	864	295	76
内蒙古	153	78	2676	3106	1040	181
辽　宁	23	14	1912	2212	1219	367
吉　林	2	7	430	1032	228	36
黑龙江	57	13	1267	1642	1105	742
上　海	156	120	2129	1430	927	417
江　苏	196	101	8463	8798	3325	696
浙　江	410	95	3719	3603	3116	1103
安　徽	49	30	2036	3170	1401	252
福　建	32	10	335	614	269	40
江　西	12	16	457	610	339	45
山　东	14	6	3460	2788	1061	331
河　南	21	20	1414	1384	456	99
湖　北	20	22	1120	1271	811	167
湖　南	18	7	822	1289	471	90
广　东	748	166	4978	3541	2030	484
广　西	11		116	113	61	14
海　南	3	3	197	338	156	48
重　庆	20	17	466	817	385	59
四　川	41	53	2261	3422	989	307
贵　州	2	6	4078	4010	2241	676
云　南	5	7	214	284	218	58
西　藏		2	68	15		
陕　西	8		756	824	625	266
甘　肃	3	8	1169	1017	587	326
青　海	3		46	46	49	
宁　夏	1		135	271	102	6
新　疆	18	17	1347	2053	1097	71

单位：人、人次、时、张

志愿服务		床位数合计	日间照料床位数		住宿收养床位数	
志愿者服务人次数	志愿服务时间			农村		农村
2502183	**5684465.1**	**104705**	**72533**	**20012**	**32172**	**10720**
2046463	4776808.9	636	592	81	44	
45285	72273.0	2411	2074	670	337	
1588	4475.0	8482	6504	2225	1978	516
312	760.0	2584	1601	104	983	
5455	8004.0	4673	4201	58	472	
1012	2263.0	2879	1842	215	1037	136
		1812	1325		487	
		751	563	93	188	
11601	26813.0	2497	2178	5	319	35
6302	15360.0	14547	10234	2394	4313	2926
178410	313402.0	12990	12090	7225	900	239
3164	6923.0	19649	7896	2598	11753	5505
		588	302	94	286	46
20	60.0	697	697	11		
83175	181980.2	5361	4556	743	805	12
		2953	1449	202	1504	476
81	166.0	1059	693	64	366	10
3438	7500.0	554	439	33	115	
2370	3140.0	1916	1291	609	625	290
		153	68		85	7
		571	253		318	
33710	92556.0	1562	964		598	30
5851	9536.0	5749	2822	98	2927	31
67396	145652.0	2283	1894	823	389	178
		1231	664	10	567	5
		47			47	
723	1944.0	681	498	168	183	53
190	1120.0	3908	3431	1489	477	225
		959	959			
		85	75		10	
5637	13729.0	437	378		59	

C-2-20续表2

地区	年末收养人数合计	日间照料人数	农村	住宿收养人数	农村
全 国	**24131**	**10549**	**2501**	**13582**	**6294**
中央级					
北 京	153	153	38		
天 津	179	179	31		
河 北	15	15	5		
山 西	92	92	76		
内蒙古	969	959	28	10	
辽 宁	509	334		175	
吉 林	53	53			
黑龙江	6	6			
上 海	849	849			
江 苏	1714	688	76	1026	879
浙 江	241	197	5	44	10
安 徽	13464	2807	1667	10657	4985
福 建					
江 西	106	106			
山 东	2791	2293	479	498	
河 南	908	107	17	801	265
湖 北	6	6			
湖 南	225	168	17	57	
广 东	87	54	28	33	28
广 西	13	13			
海 南					
重 庆	215	215			
四 川	357	303	9	54	
贵 州	332	129	17	203	115
云 南					
西 藏					
陕 西	89	78	3	11	3
甘 肃	39	30	5	9	9
青 海	514	514			
宁 夏	12	12			
新 疆	193	189		4	

单位：人、人次、人天、个、平方米

本年收养照料人天数	老年人活动人次数	社区服务志愿者组织数	注册社区志愿者人数	城镇便民、利民服务网点数	机构建筑面积
808460	**1737474**	**45079**	**746194**	**170792**	**7606564**
11716	895069	3887	555591	4950	251461
		57		2749	115109
305	590	344	222	4228	157480
535	159	585	10920	4080	92398
100476	220199	970	9504	7108	370395
		244	340	3270	155979
8395	31189			273	62308
		28		6281	128635
218029	5532	2176	39428	15307	136695
73212	130504	612	13950	8078	1212181
726	98811	1285	29603	55638	873902
12000	11250	103	1300	2453	379470
		137		392	91683
12728	3067	513	1935	1627	71892
337340	176486	1423	11054	10816	738786
	10429	41	206	800	273760
	67087	204		498	119474
	4127	213	95	1029	148744
		429	75	905	657497
				20	34435
					12430
32830	25635	29342	46817	3422	157151
	20133	211	20596	14044	343157
	185	1670	3898	13456	449471
				1	45355
				4	3734
136	122	68	83	504	151513
	1900			5984	145980
					12333
	3650			634	13066
32	31350	537	577	2241	200090

C-2-20续表3

地区	增加值合计	执行企业会计制度单位财务指标						执行行政
		固定资产原价	营业收入	费用合计	营业利润	企业单位增加值	固定资产原价	上年结转和结余
全　国	**205763.7**	**6368.1**	**1248.3**	**751.0**	**23.4**	**377.2**	**336455.9**	**20780.3**
中央级								
北　京	12103.5	8.0	546.3	151.1	3.5	139.1	12276.6	1277.3
天　津	3990.8						61101.3	
河　北	1566.3	58.0					3714.2	
山　西	871.1						2952.1	8.0
内蒙古	4797.0	387.0	103.0	15.0		4.0	8791.9	8.0
辽　宁	1735.6	253.1				14.2	4174.6	55.0
吉　林	555.4	3.0	1.3	0.3		1.3	1003.0	228.0
黑龙江	2690.5	4.0	4.0	2.1		4.0	19539.0	2.0
上　海	8407.8	1.0				-20.0	6567.2	1623.7
江　苏	23441.9	6.0	22.0	22.0			42583.6	503.0
浙　江	30711.2	2032.0	257.1	252.4	0.7	19.4	23770.0	8674.9
安　徽	21575.7	11.5					38106.5	795.6
福　建	419.5	7.5	85.0	84.0			3816.4	5.0
江　西	1018.9	65.0		4.9		10.5	2285.1	6.0
山　东	21056.4						4088.8	
河　南	2857.4	54.3	167.6	104.6	9.5	85.5	6727.6	139.5
湖　北	3785.4	78.0	5.0	5.0	9.7	9.7	4583.4	
湖　南	3796.3	7.0	2.0	2.0		3.0	3806.5	
广　东	22767.7	736.3	0.2			0.2	7953.6	1476.8
广　西	102.9						677.9	8.0
海　南	122.1	5.8					1030.1	4.6
重　庆	2855.8	1645.0					10852.5	20.8
四　川	7982.1	560.0	24.2	17.7		17.1	13318.3	1281.2
贵　州	17700.8						11034.3	4473.5
云　南	687.1						2779.6	46.9
西　藏	118.9						1119.1	85.0
陕　西	2123.6						17024.4	
甘　肃	1034.2	103.6				10.5	4252.0	9.5
青　海	32.3	12.0	3.0			2.0	253.0	
宁　夏	67.7						287.5	
新　疆	4787.7	330.0	27.6	89.9		76.7	15985.8	48.0

单位：万元

事业单位会计制度财务指标				执行民间非营利组织单位会计制度财务指标				
本年收入合计	本年支出合计	收支结余	行政事业单位增加值	固定资产原价	上年结余	本年收入合计	本年费用合计	社会组织增加值
216469.8	**207056.2**	**2564.1**	**147336.2**	**165477.6**	**1079.3**	**70749.4**	**91405.3**	**58050.3**
16257.2	18216.0	597.6	11964.4					
911.3	903.6		3415.4	770.7	34.4	1012.8	1028.3	575.4
1515.3	1405.6		1382.9	2325.4	18.0	172.0	273.5	183.4
747.1	747.2		524.3	1151.0		702.0	855.2	346.8
7225.1	7221.3		4443.4	1699.0		706.9	636.6	349.6
1921.8	2169.4		1314.1	3191.3	14.0	1652.7	904.2	407.3
632.1	720.7	1.0	399.8	75.2		347.3	284.1	154.3
2560.9	2607.3		2556.3	385.1		230.0	240.4	130.2
28181.8	21922.4	30.7	8260.4	227.9	220.1	983.5	1090.8	167.4
16090.9	15297.3	271.0	14177.8	22134.5	11.0	15017.0	15377.1	9264.1
33935.1	32025.6	263.2	28191.0	11152.6	68.0	4950.5	4358.6	2500.8
12011.9	11079.0		8617.9	14031.0		2836.7	17338.6	12957.8
2001.4	2017.4	2.0	295.3	323.4	0.2	217.4	332.0	124.2
768.3	758.1		627.0	2786.2		768.6	1318.8	381.4
5415.3	5433.3		3937.6	43546.8		25631.7	25631.7	17118.8
2663.3	3945.5		1967.8	7046.4	15.8	655.7	1223.9	804.1
4067.0	4013.5		2915.2	935.4	28.0	1447.7	1630.2	860.5
7947.9	6864.1		3659.3	487.2		650.1	524.3	134.0
30213.2	28171.7	52.2	17181.8	7630.3	261.0	5764.6	9348.3	5585.7
73.3	72.4		102.0	0.1			1.1	0.9
260.0	310.0		41.2	100.0		40.0	150.5	80.9
3122.1	3129.9	61.0	2605.6	6847.5		737.8	559.8	250.2
8177.7	8691.1	613.8	5310.4	22894.9	208.9	3628.1	4425.3	2654.6
19455.5	16920.7	636.6	15259.0	12880.7	193.9	2296.6	3113.0	2441.8
850.2	722.5		637.1	600.0		10.0	68.0	50.0
110.0	100.3		118.9	28.0				
1925.9	2365.2		2112.4	30.0		1.0	12.2	11.2
1088.2	873.5	15.0	646.5	799.0	6.0	101.7	508.6	377.2
10.0	10.0		18.1	1181.0		10.0	13.0	12.2
70.0	76.2		67.0	12.0		55.2	3.0	0.7
6260.0	8265.4	20.0	4586.2	205.0		121.8	154.2	124.8

C-2-21 社区

地　区	单位数	农村社区服务机构	可以为居民提供便民办事服务的机构	可以为居民提供活动场所的机构	可以为居民提供养老等服务的机构
全　国	**120188**	**58228**	**86826**	**25637**	**14288**
中央级					
北　京	6350	3666	5217	3094	601
天　津	1263	182	987	163	21
河　北	1515	52	1113	196	376
山　西	1827	731	1340	366	37
内蒙古	709	33	410	165	62
辽　宁	3987	638	3053	219	479
吉　林	257	50	238	8	9
黑龙江	1340	52	796	339	34
上　海	2878	329	1458	989	31
江　苏	14704	7817	7352	1933	5901
浙　江	11648	8872	8805	1520	874
安　徽	2891	750	2349	348	28
福　建	2780	832	1930	383	498
江　西	1058	71	616	310	31
山　东	10558	5868	9644	4850	3024
河　南	905	147	734	86	9
湖　北	4529	893	3237	872	201
湖　南	2987	735	2368	849	265
广　东	12992	6080	8429	3772	185
广　西	524	31	383	30	32
海　南	1443	1143	1059	264	11
重　庆	2097	375	1485	770	197
四　川	7926	3649	6086	1007	462
贵　州	15608	13828	12956	1515	581
云　南	1240	271	1079	94	2
西　藏	18	7	14	4	
陕　西	2146	325	1516	442	35
甘　肃	1708	530	830	572	219
青　海	242	28	150	63	
宁　夏	641	233	325	225	81
新　疆	1417	10	867	189	2

服务站

单位：个、人

农村	可以为居民提供便民信息服务的机构	年末职工人数	女性	受教育程度	
				大学专科人数	大学本科及以上人数
7849	**24058**	**494254**	**193024**	**117562**	**46140**
59	3225	27923	14124	7148	5932
2	266	6537	4488	2306	1226
	39	7272	3957	2265	438
25	84	5857	2354	1171	492
2	111	2837	1531	852	518
98	467	25107	14822	8759	5076
	2	1607	1212	1226	24
15	227	5632	2706	1878	616
7	402	12167	6436	1424	489
3956	1865	64468	23259	12519	4979
674	908	29489	10765	5350	2088
1	278	13684	5896	3949	963
73	255	11409	4643	1564	647
	106	3738	1675	505	69
1650	5746	47149	19279	15498	6347
4	77	4177	1779	1052	321
77	526	18223	6935	4319	1288
75	2243	10618	4765	3163	1052
27	920	45881	13886	7014	3032
	134	5635	2833	1133	596
	129	7316	2001	838	284
41	322	9441	4806	3579	1473
367	2580	25244	8776	7114	1765
527	2362	69731	15680	13925	3157
	75	6863	2484	1285	422
		121	68	73	38
3	192	9858	4769	3053	703
162	102	5428	1780	1437	546
	29	800	307	241	81
4	27	2864	1825	349	83
	359	7178	3183	2573	1395

C-2-21续表1

地区	职业资格水平		年龄结构			
	助理社会工作师人数	社会工作师人数	35岁及以下人数	36岁至45岁人数	46岁至55岁人数	56岁及以上人数
全　国	**5743**	**2387**	**161729**	**194217**	**109216**	**29092**
中央级						
北　京	2052	748	8053	9890	7931	2049
天　津	311	56	2663	2009	1618	247
河　北	14	9	3221	2480	1282	289
山　西	17	4	1550	2395	1443	469
内蒙古			1241	1017	392	187
辽　宁	201	128	8613	9362	4119	3013
吉　林	2	49	67	1437	87	16
黑龙江	62	20	2152	2838	452	190
上　海	94	57	1205	5294	4370	1298
江　苏	798	262	15989	25860	17813	4806
浙　江	408	301	9402	10739	6808	2540
安　徽	80	50	4172	6505	2715	292
福　建	273	180	4135	4374	2314	586
江　西	10	15	1361	1753	590	34
山　东	113	88	17898	18092	8228	2931
河　南	17	5	1677	1472	731	297
湖　北	71	31	5500	7890	3716	1117
湖　南	94	46	2951	3938	3400	329
广　东	556	113	17350	16927	9812	1792
广　西	69	16	3004	1697	837	97
海　南	26	4	1742	3191	1816	567
重　庆	140	55	3527	3711	1828	375
四　川	223	116	7355	10738	6020	1131
贵　州	21	4	25795	26991	13801	3144
云　南	13	2	2399	3020	1225	219
西　藏			91	30		
陕　西	33	9	2869	3997	2546	446
甘　肃	10	6	2243	1990	922	273
青　海	4	7	355	294	151	
宁　夏	4	2	682	1548	603	31
新　疆	27	4	2467	2738	1646	327

单位：人次、张、人 、时

志愿服务		床位数合计	日间照料床位数		住宿收养床位数	
志愿者服务人次数	志愿服务时间			农村		农村
4380281	**10743835.3**	**238450**	**205585**	**95138**	**32865**	**13585**
2969920	7807795.5	2817	2688	838	129	84
1050	2100.0	2349	2025	1057	324	46
752	1137.0	6550	4314	170	2236	
550	1500.0	3527	3468	1587	59	40
11784	25889.0	2309	1826	247	483	159
3830	8304.0	7774	6164	307	1610	305
		622	559	105	63	56
13017	40845.0	1110	1042	34	68	4
22325	84084.0	2235	1672	227	563	174
204293	425803.0	63828	61058	29821	2770	1498
210876	369178.8	44446	39655	29349	4791	4451
22004	42942.0	4164	3094	20	1070	39
		6292	5711	1952	581	127
636	1098.0	899	857	21	42	
36992	83787.0	28195	25169	8996	3026	960
		1434	1131	77	303	22
2658	4192.0	4306	3145	853	1161	335
3666	8989.0	1730	1295	131	435	
960	3482.0	6582	3559	1192	3023	318
		537	405		132	
8560	15319.0	852	304	12	548	206
230587	525376.0	4312	3191	405	1121	29
2346	14399.0	11487	7712	2658	3775	1980
623110	1247345.0	13682	11321	8950	2361	2023
		2657	2309	571	348	158
8257	20530.0	2029	1245	283	784	150
1560	8870.0	9397	8732	5111	665	344
3		319	319			
		1047	1037	141	10	54
545	870.0	962	578	23	384	23

C-2-21续表2

地区	年末收养人数合计	日间照料人数	农村	住宿收养人数	农村
全国	**35084**	**32712**	**14487**	**2372**	**1347**
中央级					
北京	802	784	352	18	18
天津	50	50	50		
河北	157	107	2	50	
山西	569	529	529	40	40
内蒙古	415	390		25	
辽宁	451	451	21		
吉林					
黑龙江	26	22	7	4	
上海	833	833			
江苏	11160	10775	5013	385	272
浙江	1976	1899	1571	77	
安徽	488	350		138	
福建	275	235	130	40	16
江西	130	130			
山东	13411	12729	5723	682	584
河南	111	53	23	58	
湖北	282	232	35	50	10
湖南	426	318	12	108	
广东	69	61	58	8	8
广西	14	14			
海南					
重庆	813	813	128		
四川	904	865	433	39	18
贵州	847	472	271	375	322
云南	70	70	70		
西藏					
陕西	476	201	3	275	5
甘肃	10	10			
青海					
宁夏	301	301	56		54
新疆	18	18			

单位：人、人次、人天、个、平方米

本年收养照料人天数	老年人活动人次数	社区服务志愿者组织数	注册社区志愿者人数	城镇便民、利民服务网点数	机构建筑面积
2441020	**4828184**	**48820**	**921143**	**96303**	**23601741**
79728	582322	3232	245564	5376	1130374
		718		2914	246328
18040	160	243	30	69	240711
138338	238250			1253	290500
34161	60762	163	1559	1674	127777
1696	100	938	39231	4976	586379
					27940
	30066	1426	32919	730	301805
3724	77795	284	13327	618	646123
898389	2950062	10757	138871	24815	4010557
15880	277097	935	5820	6357	2343805
	48890	787	7060	3994	593008
	1000	300	17	698	414609
10121	36251	476	290	1342	171896
1048155	132352	3719	10131	14010	3248891
2535	4850	20		99	377906
15860	39972	373	3625	1177	951067
5418	10340	965	65	3095	392761
		402	144104	2050	1627957
		34		1249	98847
		1	15	19	258462
154066	222795	4139	166425	7891	706461
14100	70902	5443	66594	4836	1191363
		12810	6344	2032	2209303
				22	278745
					7720
774	29390	383	39152	1900	443144
	14760			1300	214257
					89972
35	68	140		316	132616
		132		1491	240457

C-2-21续表3

地区	增加值合计	执行企业会计制度单位财务指标					执行行政	
		固定资产原价	营业收入	费用合计	营业利润	企业单位增加值	固定资产原价	上年结转和结余
全　国	**542581.4**	**156408.2**	**9569.0**	**3919.1**	**6008.2**	**11650.1**	**722189.0**	**31095.6**
中央级								
北　京	17295.0	71637.6	7833.5	2726.9	6006.2	8302.5	7928.5	230.5
天　津	2908.4						2182.2	
河　北	8663.6	113.0					7331.5	45.0
山　西	2390.9						10179.3	194.0
内蒙古	3673.2	552.8	617.8	1.0		294.7	3077.9	218.0
辽　宁	5300.1	266.0				8.0	6168.7	79.2
吉　林	377.6						12.0	10.0
黑龙江	36083.8	6.0					9036.3	0.3
上　海	11795.4			10.0			1133.7	41.6
江　苏	98621.3	6.0					145879.5	223.0
浙　江	61353.1	12831.0	18.0	16.0			75299.5	14284.7
安　徽	15812.7	22.0				68.0	47938.5	2633.4
福　建	4980.2	558.0	300.0	300.0			13722.8	17.8
江　西	2294.5	3710.4	17.0	17.0			661.7	
山　东	111381.2						2602.8	
河　南	2390.5	165.4	162.9	129.1		141.8	1540.5	
湖　北	20791.6	1095.0	468.0	630.0		45.6	44304.6	255.0
湖　南	9744.8	262.0	50.0			2317.9	8358.8	1.8
广　东	24719.1	36741.7				256.6	134390.3	4966.6
广　西	2102.5	257.0					1628.6	
海　南	1813.0	1444.8				0.2	9978.1	1.0
重　庆	11956.0	23602.7					28047.2	2.8
四　川	22780.9	830.0	53.2	36.7		116.6	32439.5	3778.6
贵　州	42534.8	332.4	19.0	8.2		11.8	33102.3	1270.5
云　南	6650.1	59.2	3.0		1.0	2.0	57591.6	2099.3
西　藏	600.8						2048.7	595.0
陕　西	5272.8	4.0					22289.7	40.0
甘　肃	2083.0	403.1		5.3		30.2	2696.3	2.0
青　海	350.2	314.0					1947.0	
宁　夏	464.8	214.0				2.5	2384.0	30.0
新　疆	5395.5	980.1	26.6	38.9	1.0	51.7	6286.9	75.5

单位：万元

事业单位会计制度财务指标				执行民间非营利组织单位会计制度财务指标				
本年收入合计	本年支出合计	收支结余	行政事业单位增加值	固定资产原价	上年结余	本年收入合计	本年费用合计	社会组织增加值
495099.6	**442372.9**	**3344.6**	**307576.4**	**902455.2**	**7010.7**	**327914.4**	**356703.8**	**223354.9**
9547.1	10505.5		8992.5		4.0			
1707.4	1707.4		1774.4	922.5		1378.8	1532.6	1134.0
8819.6	9246.5		8531.9	3835.4		281.2	331.8	131.7
1049.2	959.8		926.2	3347.1	15.9	1133.9	2786.4	1464.7
4041.9	4064.7	191.5	3356.3	138.0		113.0	112.5	22.2
5476.8	6300.5	17.0	3470.4	5373.8	374.1	3610.9	4759.0	1821.7
170.8	218.8		107.3	719.0		2160.0	860.7	270.3
40750.7	41602.7		35797.6	1062.0		539.4	310.2	286.2
11187.8	10147.7	9.9	6576.2	12838.2	1930.5	12256.5	14298.4	5219.2
63842.8	77609.8	5.0	63892.4	158398.4	143.6	75199.3	76096.9	34728.9
171537.1	108675.0	1044.3	54142.0	55088.1	144.7	20734.6	16783.8	7211.1
21165.7	22786.4		13892.3	17573.0		4048.7	4276.7	1852.4
6073.5	6303.9	2.5	3273.2	9587.1	10.7	2763.3	4680.6	1707.0
729.1	676.4	10.5	381.1	3792.7		2433.9	2728.7	1913.4
3368.5	3368.5		2045.8	157722.8		143416.1	143416.1	109335.4
1876.2	2174.1		1519.1	441.8		293.8	1053.8	729.6
24850.9	24451.7		17072.6	6607.1	28.0	7457.2	6698.2	3673.4
11208.2	9156.7		6664.3	2891.1	48.6	2207.0	2114.4	762.6
29449.4	29880.2	1383.1	19667.7	40221.6	737.8	701.2	7921.6	4794.8
842.9	848.6		924.1	3316.3		56.6	1211.8	1178.4
2368.8	2368.8		1510.9	1449.5		669.6	903.2	301.9
14341.3	14335.8		9705.7	17714.0		5113.4	4844.3	2250.3
15449.7	12235.1	209.4	8372.4	48931.7	2048.2	17877.6	20180.1	14291.9
19093.9	17092.3	5.6	16696.8	126931.3	1488.6	21868.6	34861.7	25826.2
5427.8	4890.2	465.7	5633.5	213222.4	3.0		1371.8	1014.6
770.0	702.1		600.8					
7245.8	6978.1		5227.0	1275.0		52.6	45.8	45.8
1171.4	1245.2	0.1	1037.1	2120.3	33.0	766.3	1523.6	1015.7
72.4	96.6		166.5	6223.0		147.9	349.1	183.7
732.3	733.3		274.5	660.0		633.0	650.0	187.8
10730.6	11010.5		5343.8	52.0				

C-2-22 其他社区服务

地　区	单位数	农村社区服务机构	可以为居民提供便民办事服务的机构	可以为居民提供活动场所的机构	可以为居民提供养老等服务的机构
全　国	**107174**	**36671**	**52284**	**34306**	**15200**
中央级					
北　京	4351	1270	3380	840	7
天　津	244	42	127	83	16
河　北	7701	6375	1012	2009	4359
山　西	529	233	164	150	207
内蒙古	532	21	334	98	76
辽　宁	1541	288	962	52	473
吉　林					
黑龙江	358	9	282	29	52
上　海	675	15	561	30	5
江　苏	12002	3482	6138	3145	2182
浙　江	9429	3541	4973	1900	1544
安　徽	1925	428	1150	304	165
福　建	152	26	56	31	54
江　西	1695	125	931	634	16
山　东	10859	3424	9511	3454	944
河　南	1671	354	514	611	187
湖　北	3573	989	1927	1118	119
湖　南	1888	186	1061	805	261
广　东	39243	10869	15670	17134	1328
广　西	300	39	94	97	17
海　南	142	111	98	18	26
重　庆	1716	1025	527	361	883
四　川	3058	1452	1912	639	413
贵　州	399	133	165	118	89
云　南	193	132	12	16	165
西　藏					
陕　西	438	237	186	178	65
甘　肃	2279	1843	365	407	1502
青　海					
宁　夏	84		35	19	12
新　疆	197	22	137	26	33

机构和设施

单位:个、人

		年末职工人数	女性	受教育程度	
农村	可以为居民提供便民信息服务的机构			大学专科人数	大学本科及以上人数
10183	**18587**	**290703**	**100162**	**54784**	**27069**
1	185	6835	3019	1697	1313
13	23	769	381	142	53
3878	395	14192	3543	915	299
186	10	1369	615	305	69
19	26	2115	1075	727	478
199	178	7617	4386	1311	539
9	35	1471	778	453	174
1	82	7989	3900	435	275
863	1949	53870	16118	8080	5690
1372	1304	18298	8468	4096	1537
117	316	6429	2832	2105	271
13	14	1264	512	61	24
15	117	5392	2191	582	66
223	6214	31326	11212	10629	4323
135	381	5778	2201	1716	410
32	511	9691	4496	2302	734
41	500	5551	2302	1025	151
552	5681	85108	23727	14148	8558
4	95	2269	1062	358	209
15		344	110	51	1
786	167	3364	1265	590	397
160	308	9748	3114	1612	729
61	35	2087	596	450	90
117	7	697	207	42	47
55	22	1238	416	91	4
1295	13	4915	1247	665	593
	18	427	147	83	4
21	1	550	242	113	31

C-2-22续表1

地区	职业资格水平		年龄结构			
	助理社会工作师人数	社会工作师人数	35岁及以下人数	36岁至45岁人数	46岁至55岁人数	56岁及以上人数
全国	**2776**	**1212**	**89157**	**116480**	**64548**	**20518**
中央级						
北京	159	33	2013	2377	1904	541
天津	5	8	95	276	311	87
河北	14	76	4306	5373	3327	1186
山西	27	12	278	580	423	88
内蒙古	32	10	876	795	369	75
辽宁	138	103	2530	3157	1569	361
吉林						
黑龙江	4		395	952	110	14
上海	38	10	1455	2897	3019	618
江苏	341	107	15448	21438	12678	4306
浙江	112	119	5991	7559	3756	992
安徽	31	6	1934	2957	1351	187
福建	2		96	397	353	418
江西	5	1	1306	1804	1088	1194
山东	48	30	11862	12300	5643	1521
河南	45	28	1221	3499	848	210
湖北	14	8	3632	4287	1497	275
湖南	18	18	1600	2070	1713	168
广东	1584	514	27065	33598	17952	6493
广西	47	21	753	782	523	211
海南			41	260	42	1
重庆	31	25	708	1494	797	365
四川	53	44	2611	4379	2399	359
贵州	10	8	949	592	321	225
云南	5	10	101	335	158	103
西藏						
陕西	1	8	208	398	559	73
甘肃	6	12	1419	1540	1565	391
青海						
宁夏			66	192	166	3
新疆	6	1	198	192	107	53

单位：人次、张、人 、时

志愿服务		床位数合计	日间照料床位数		住宿收养床位数	
志愿者服务人次数	志愿服务时间			农村		农村
141548	**281839.0**	**300694**	**160070**	**88498**	**140624**	**85418**
37695	60664.0	855	725	85	130	
		457	114	20	343	343
104	199.0	46517	29334	26043	17183	16379
		3521	2794	1827	727	351
760	2503.0	2048	1378	24	670	588
56	56.0	13589	5817	1481	7772	4364
2968	6756.0	1027	289		738	214
5728	7449.0	105	100	5	5	
40952	83074.0	47685	22147	6493	25538	6752
1631	3888.0	34555	21969	16002	12586	5510
1212	3583.0	17580	482	38	17098	14073
		5345	3411	317	1934	125
		3973	2034	1874	1939	1874
43849	100784.0	16754	13629	4243	3125	706
		7588	2244	652	5344	4226
271	696.0	4501	3034	289	1467	991
808	1736.0	3180	1567	397	1613	809
		29189	12816	5582	16373	7299
60	130.0	782	484		298	42
		665			665	354
4984	9163.0	16930	4856	2930	12074	10467
148	398.0	9022	7531	3384	1491	235
7	23.0	2125	1421	1103	704	544
		5583	1653	1068	3930	3148
270	653.0	2078	1346	1168	732	627
40	60.0	23912	18389	13468	5523	5050
		86	86			
5	24.0	1042	420	5	622	347

C-2-22续表2

地区	年末收养人数合计	日间照料人数	农村	住宿收养人数	农村
全国	**43793**	**17581**	**7473**	**26212**	**15260**
中央级					
北京					
天津	97			97	97
河北	717	367	170	350	350
山西	733	733	630		
内蒙古	354	237		117	95
辽宁	3371	287	158	3084	2226
吉林					
黑龙江	83			83	83
上海	5	4		1	
江苏	3149	1198	432	1951	605
浙江	4916	40	29	4876	14
安徽	2745	156		2589	2252
福建	2253	2072		181	
江西	3588	1794	1794	1794	1794
山东	8035	6428	1838	1607	695
河南	2288	45	14	2243	1864
湖北	814	458	16	356	2
湖南	1112	145	26	967	558
广东	1107	441	250	666	313
广西	269	109		160	14
海南					
重庆	3818	413	174	3405	3281
四川	2176	1897	1480	279	101
贵州	257	202	177	55	33
云南	1126	50		1076	669
西藏					
陕西	110			110	50
甘肃	493	343	279	150	149
青海					
宁夏					
新疆	177	162	6	15	15

单位:人、人次、人天、个、平方米

本年收养照料人天数	老年人活动人次数	社区服务志愿者组织数	注册社区志愿者人数	城镇便民、利民服务网点数	机构建筑面积
2870039	**1152183**	**2987**	**164027**	**20913**	**17019962**
	10128	166	11872		488974
					63283
	318			41	1161385
151132	56590	25		46	75671
47578	4640	2	50	34	91849
4380				458	244411
	14539	369	11609	295	56665
		26	2194	98	92312
181263	250726	548	7311	4829	1987801
11095	76496	66	550	19	1618827
	8000	5	50	836	365383
	650	100			42658
		19	25	50	300284
1091096	170229	288	1587	1763	3130075
	26139	69	652	324	490137
15300	116826	11	178	194	460365
	2244	37	563	100	307553
	2020	395	122591	4992	4430271
26555	37727			17	180120
					14955
1213932	370018	552	4407	116	359235
29196	2884	276	388	4657	484276
				20	63400
92606					117586
3560	2009	33		18	71420
				1006	277437
					10200
2346				1000	33429

C−2−22续表3

地区	增加值合计	执行企业会计制度单位财务指标					执行行政	
		固定资产原价	营业收入	费用合计	营业利润	企业单位增加值	固定资产原价	上年结转和结余
全　国	**306307.9**	**21596.9**	**6224.6**	**2437.7**	**14.6**	**2507.3**	**862337.7**	**8911.6**
中央级								
北　京	2020.2	15.0		73.0		73.0	2772.6	34.1
天　津	796.4						1516.9	
河　北	3455.5	488.0					6797.3	18.0
山　西	733.1						2022.4	1.0
内蒙古	1282.4	40.2	9.0	5.0			1872.3	
辽　宁	2539.3	209.4				5.0	8407.4	2.0
吉　林								
黑龙江	2787.2					280.7	30276.8	
上　海	12278.2						280.1	183.5
江　苏	51014.9	1441.0	360.0	106.0	15.0	50.0	96936.9	38.0
浙　江	71275.2	215.8	1187.9	181.0	-2.3	31.4	373562.5	7677.4
安　徽	3943.2	366.5	709.0	585.0		120.9	16176.6	127.0
福　建	289.3	40.0					361.2	
江　西	3005.5	200.0	190.0	50.0			654.9	0.1
山　东	85985.6						892.0	
河　南	3741.3	954.4	752.9	225.6		464.3	6605.7	1.0
湖　北	10758.0	1318.0	1125.0	1120.0		4.2	22200.9	7.0
湖　南	2722.7	120.0				62.4	2543.9	6.5
广　东	24330.3	9762.6	1874.8	89.4		1052.0	52786.3	695.2
广　西	359.2	60.0				3.0	2403.3	50.0
海　南	131.1	76.7						
重　庆	3532.9	3167.5					12544.4	7.0
四　川	6518.8	1355.0			1.9	59.4	5325.7	50.9
贵　州	1387.5	17.0	12.0				392.4	
云　南	8775.5	1436.0					206917.1	1.9
西　藏								
陕　西	699.0						2118.4	7.0
甘　肃	1511.6	14.0		0.7		11.0	5193.9	4.0
青　海								
宁　夏	9.2							
新　疆	424.7	299.8	4.0	2.0		290.0	775.8	

单位：万元

事业单位会计制度财务指标				执行民间非营利组织单位会计制度财务指标				
本年收入合计	本年支出合计	收支结余	行政事业单位增加值	固定资产原价	上年结余	本年收入合计	本年费用合计	社会组织增加值
381371.4	**422714.4**	**3508.5**	**130845.3**	**388164.0**	**15014.8**	**305171.3**	**281835.2**	**172955.3**
399.0	1102.7		1031.5	963.8	771.7	3201.0	3316.8	915.7
383.4	383.4		429.7	630.7	174.0	879.0	513.0	366.7
2562.7	2180.6		1478.0	7833.8	118.7	2428.1	2938.9	1977.5
479.0	473.0		483.2	841.0		231.5	435.4	249.9
1150.5	1419.3		1159.8	1400.0		194.0	232.8	122.6
1463.9	1574.8		1254.6	1840.1	44.7	1227.5	1678.8	1279.7
1333.6	1301.5		2393.8	594.2		119.6	257.7	112.7
1811.6	1693.4	-1.0	283.5	7040.5	10143.3	38308.2	16332.3	11994.7
15845.2	16536.0	2562.8	15535.8	108442.8	263.0	72680.2	73097.8	35429.1
306224.0	93632.6	928.1	61351.8	65302.0	1101.1	34176.3	35198.1	9892.0
2890.4	3019.2		2226.7	14371.5	180.0	2559.6	2699.8	1595.6
158.6	167.5		153.2	2180.4	3.2	419.7	435.3	136.1
883.9	499.5		177.6	3797.2		2547.8	3030.3	2827.9
935.4	935.4		923.3	62799.2		106923.3	106923.3	85062.3
2951.3	2566.3		1940.2	3409.0	731.8	924.4	2446.1	1336.8
10528.9	10622.9		8711.6	5014.4		3192.8	3217.2	2042.2
3598.5	3014.3		1948.3	3791.0	1.0	2151.5	1483.2	712.0
20315.4	274625.8	3.5	14891.8	54269.7	723.0	25469.3	16555.2	8386.5
190.8	163.7		221.8	1094.9	58.4	179.1	229.9	134.4
80.0	152.5		131.1					
2913.1	2980.1		2420.0	8399.9	8.0	1731.2	1755.9	1112.9
1877.2	1659.6	1.0	1732.1	18027.2	33.8	4295.3	5605.9	4727.3
285.6	192.4	0.1	193.6	3946.7	618.0	843.9	1651.2	1193.9
298.0	291.6	0.8	8546.1	4566.9		84.5	316.6	229.4
766.9	757.9	13.2	547.3	675.7	1.7	48.0	216.7	151.7
844.5	615.0		555.5	6784.7	39.4	354.5	1155.7	945.1
	4.0		4.0				84.5	5.2
200.0	149.4		119.3	146.7		1.0	26.8	15.4

C-2-23 老龄事业

地区	单位数				年末职工人数	女性	受教育
		编制登记	民政登记	设施			大学专科人数
全国	**2558**	**1897**	**87**	**574**	**10044**	**4410**	**3747**
中央级							
北京	19	18	1		181	77	22
天津	14	11		3	59	28	18
河北	78	45	4	29	268	132	80
山西	111	104		7	500	210	232
内蒙古	38	27		11	131	70	47
辽宁	67	47	5	15	271	138	92
吉林	47	44		3	195	90	60
黑龙江	103	74	14	15	332	165	119
上海	20	18	2		160	94	40
江苏	68	51	2	15	265	124	78
浙江	94	55	1	38	337	160	114
安徽	104	78	1	25	258	88	84
福建	63	52		11	180	68	64
江西	108	94	1	13	398	156	196
山东	150	138		12	1042	322	397
河南	102	67	8	27	378	176	133
湖北	84	57	1	26	332	132	135
湖南	133	57		76	414	192	162
广东	111	68	1	42	348	148	129
广西	59	39	1	19	189	86	84
海南	8	5	2	1	24	15	10
重庆	31	21		10	115	53	47
四川	213	186	2	25	667	310	274
贵州	97	78	4	15	340	165	156
云南	127	75	10	42	537	215	228
西藏	4	1	3		5	1	1
陕西	102	99	1	2	663	299	224
甘肃	101	85	2	14	497	210	120
青海	42	3		39	76	40	14
宁夏	26	24	2		105	44	49
新疆	234	176	19	39	777	402	338

机构情况

单位：个、人、人次、时

程度	职业资格水平		年龄结构				志愿服务	
大学本科及以上人数	助理社会工作师人数	社会工作师人数	35岁及以下人数	36岁至45岁人数	46岁至55岁人数	56岁及以上人数	志愿者服务人次数	志愿服务时间
3481	**92**	**140**	**2574**	**3867**	**3024**	**579**	**301865**	**686486.0**
144	1	6	44	70	54	13	20962	27668.0
37		2	22	16	18	3	1000	2000.0
78	3	3	91	110	60	7	41	140.0
87	6	9	153	203	113	31	200	
77		4	27	49	46	9	122	122.0
118	3	1	87	89	79	16	5339	6964.0
53	3	1	48	90	50	7	300	350.0
101	10	3	68	127	111	26	18112	23827.0
97	2	16	47	57	49	7	1058	2614.0
108	4	7	72	81	89	23	928	3860.0
132	7	5	86	129	98	24	38808	48010.0
118	2	10	59	94	84	21	26963	31697.0
66	1		32	62	71	15	106122	325932.0
61		6	113	159	108	18		
456	2	13	254	383	324	81	1388	3952.0
84	10	5	168	154	51	5	12	75.0
105		1	61	127	110	34	1096	2305.0
86	2	5	109	157	134	14	3202	13958.0
135	9	11	108	131	90	19	1420	3500.0
61	2		33	71	72	13	182	1236.0
11		1	4	14	5	1		
51	2	3	19	31	51	14	4196	13004.0
263	4	5	155	255	220	37	49639	112159.0
136	2		61	121	141	17	2256	8971.0
184	2	4	116	195	192	34	5	13.0
3			1	1	3			
185	1	1	206	256	170	31	6335	15238.0
96	3		112	204	158	23	61	236.0
6			9	50	17		2	12.0
44		1	18	34	47	6	2	8.0
298	11	17	191	347	209	30	12114	38635.0

C-2-23续表

地 区	增加值合计	固定资产原价	执行 上年结转和结余
全 国	**74394.9**	**79310.6**	**7626.4**
中央级			
北 京	2081.2	1007.8	841.3
天 津	2779.8	279.1	630.2
河 北	913.9	330.4	176.0
山 西	1090.3	821.8	179.4
内蒙古	1333.2	366.3	199.1
辽 宁	1574.3	485.8	52.7
吉 林	838.0	733.3	20.0
黑龙江	1331.8	3022.8	40.2
上 海	3380.8	4985.3	561.3
江 苏	2949.3	13663.9	4.9
浙 江	3735.0	3313.1	202.8
安 徽	1259.7	654.1	18.1
福 建	1459.0	665.9	509.2
江 西	946.6	837.4	12.3
山 东	6234.8	4773.1	
河 南	2060.3	3140.4	16.0
湖 北	2020.1	2256.8	
湖 南	1219.2	1366.1	2.6
广 东	5192.3	8220.9	208.4
广 西	3336.2	807.5	28.9
海 南	114.5	30.5	245.3
重 庆	1424.7	1612.6	7.0
四 川	6309.2	5091.9	457.1
贵 州	2422.7	1348.7	704.2
云 南	2124.9	11045.8	1739.7
西 藏	14.7	213.5	
陕 西	11431.3	2485.5	471.8
甘 肃	1272.5	1714.2	100.1
青 海	50.3	326.3	0.1
宁 夏	539.0	1030.0	81.9
新 疆	2955.1	2679.8	115.8

单位：万元

行政事业单位会计制度财务指标

本年收入合计	本年支出合计	收支结余	行政事业单位增加值
278122.8	**270796.9**	**5114.6**	**74394.9**
18398.9	14016.4	945.3	2081.2
4991.9	4501.9	1115.7	2779.8
1417.3	1412.7	40.9	913.9
3191.8	3219.9	18.6	1090.3
2856.7	2886.4	96.8	1333.2
3154.4	3905.7	28.3	1574.3
1415.8	1451.9		838.0
2529.1	3375.6	0.6	1331.8
16313.5	15652.2	649.2	3380.8
5492.9	5432.3	24.3	2949.3
12156.9	12417.2	36.3	3735.0
2374.8	2369.0		1259.7
6446.7	6570.8	263.2	1459.0
1688.7	1636.3		946.6
12409.4	12409.4		6234.8
82643.8	82626.8		2060.3
4444.4	4444.4		2020.1
2683.6	2813.4	6.3	1219.2
16212.9	10728.8	32.8	5192.3
3996.1	4000.3	21.4	3336.2
45.1	545.1	361.2	114.5
3471.2	3465.8	12.4	1424.7
13192.3	13572.8	268.8	6309.2
5199.6	4525.0	67.7	2422.7
7988.4	8807.1	560.6	2124.9
15.9	7.0		14.7
33151.3	33132.9	535.6	11431.3
2579.4	2673.9		1272.5
279.3	180.1		50.3
2528.0	2724.0	24.2	539.0
4852.7	5291.8	4.4	2955.1

C-2-24 为老年人提供

地区	老龄人口情况					老龄系统接待来信来访次数	老年法律援助中心	老年维权
	60岁及以上老年人口数	65岁及以上老年人口数	80岁及以上老年人口数	100岁及以上老年人口数	纯老年人家庭人口数			涉老案件数
全 国	**204457512**	**132181739**	**27676545**	**65286**	**30821451**	**434284**	**20779**	**67500**
中央级								
北 京	2933046	2020650	498277	2016	485679	62733	378	769
天 津	2154229	1379649	306569	1239	358636	2771	97	3961
河 北	9857964	6325994	1129931	1962	850920	3925	315	570
山 西	4531021	2648961	566034	977	584389	11046	714	3098
内蒙古	3297836	2122339	409079	352	571863	2888	216	306
辽 宁	7473530	4639452	958894	1460	2081369	16302	1549	3355
吉 林	4251165	460492	90510	186	139159	948	34	163
黑龙江	4861140	3596293	687266	656	917071	3555	512	1032
上 海	4047859	2691794	734001	2107	945468	46373	133	8084
江 苏	15067145	10498515	2243525	5221	2978907	29861	1508	4019
浙 江	9751583	6018100	1397925	1950	2515059	36152	863	4762
安 徽	10719202	7094780	1476336	3541	1873009	9927	580	1166
福 建	4924740	3269889	781655	1732	984591	7771	1013	1916
江 西	6389800	3510772	765583	1230	329897	3690	579	577
山 东	16080700	10626637	2284514	5295	4163835	7419	2070	2124
河 南	11656693	7783575	1767007	4799	1073644	6381	1032	937
湖 北	8914311	5894205	1106582	2560	851532	12359	834	1331
湖 南	10392562	7021829	1588930	2487	1394267	25121	751	2115
广 东	11065406	7502811	1920194	6453	908673	17284	537	637
广 西	7812535	5164626	1100861	5143	429975	14762	268	1104
海 南	1232315	830561	227917	1847	70399	1767	12	154
重 庆	6561690	4395010	933766	1356	1634346	9545	383	10923
四 川	16490319	11142812	2092863	4835	2030515	39379	1514	3724
贵 州	5214964	3401736	567127	1156	463868	6894	1192	1054
云 南	5497775	3399295	699207	1331	569837	9549	1688	4804
西 藏	182835	86349	21207	32	1071	560		
陕 西	5330453	3491097	595540	800	605804	18146	662	2050
甘 肃	3712309	2482402	337980	380	334154	7961	765	715
青 海	653908	459934	70613	161	139463	11	3	20
宁 夏	612166	391313	55372	90	83575	8083	111	163
新 疆	2786311	1829867	261280	1932	450476	11121	466	1867

的居家养老服务情况

单位：人、人次、件、个、张

老龄事业发展情况								
	老年活动设施			老年福利			老年医疗护理机构	
维权协调组织数	老年活动站/中心/室数	老年人参与人数	年末活动人次数	享受高龄补贴的老年人数	享受护理补贴的老年人数	享受养老服务补贴的老年人数	老年医院数	床位数
79543	**349040**	**46547094**	**230885033**	**17196147**	**199797**	**1547289**	**3169**	**131378**
3608	6281	799772	5267444	320552	330	99081	17	3126
1847	2239	579074	726134	23278	1246	7412	32	1746
1997	9739	1300708	39014658	565949	5487	8784	158	2865
6042	17358	1164935	3160833	301906	170		98	2462
339	1383	262099	5665502	391413	56	2896	2	150
2642	7669	1123124	2924316	89707	136	1312	45	3390
616	1028	96442	149952	18302	2239	1538	86	1317
963	3288	526487	2546401	112520	5016	2172	261	3205
3447	6426	754241	7774980	154326	57181	179216	33	4092
6691	19579	4784388	79264241	2163510	26264	118699	393	20635
4105	32112	7495455	19068925	1168933	25496	127918	30	4628
2597	7435	1347810	3779887	1064425	20310	27807	227	13202
1642	17035	1556009	2942651	366736	852	24343	55	3407
1957	11083	1504900	2281551	330318	1115	548	56	2872
6149	53095	2697823	4311043	1193880	15021	161858	103	10615
3057	32925	1307140	1865176	316499	1390	12254	226	4811
2870	9615	1812850	8116183	719540	6129	9784	108	5426
4018	19125	2448393	3218792	256208	8000	114364	165	8378
1477	14066	2054257	5786260	1804285	232	101650	78	6202
1685	6299	1063091	2147690	463873	850	3650	38	4694
118	1049	158662	201044	162968		1274		
2440	5544	1868120	2486662	286159	395	14957		
9163	24445	4105924	14092499	951032	8920	292325	566	13756
1889	4224	944990	2082370	259445	1494	196134	99	1263
2687	12995	2511839	8397662	854808	386	8955	72	4202
	9	3389	3448	19659	292	2706		
2652	6568	944755	1347643	2134621	9152	12283	147	3251
1778	4017	584937	1015620	101234	1470	3986	60	445
	659	98033	133164	305119				
585	749	124841	330453	31500	8	314	4	76
482	11001	522606	781849	263442	160	9069	10	1162

C-2-24续表

地区	老年医疗护理机构			老龄事业				
	老年临终关怀医院数	床位数	年底在院人数	老年人协会个数	参加人数	村、居老年人协会	参加人数	乡、街道老年人协会
全　国	**802**	**37907**	**16725**	**438742**	**46775222**	**362197**	**34935832**	**39988**
中央级								
北　京	2	233	103	5563	374226	5298	330912	126
天　津	1	30	25	3459	379114	3183	312035	186
河　北	43	351	64	23355	688039	18016	518657	3137
山　西	75	5709	918	19198	915132	16860	756723	1046
内蒙古				1746	198787	1177	87347	322
辽　宁	8	930	211	10841	1188884	8801	728806	1170
吉　林	1	50	44	1109	141042	843	59594	142
黑龙江	44	1283	550	7294	867902	5063	539428	1753
上　海	9	238	173	1722	192845	1477	144607	198
江　苏	72	8409	4822	20502	4083189	18548	3492070	1336
浙　江	4	1387	669	30439	6884836	28931	6416977	743
安　徽	13	215	112	11637	1368924	10242	995502	988
福　建	41	1818	949	15667	2109225	14221	1821409	844
江　西	9	322	224	12200	1609274	9966	790850	1052
山　东	40	1771	888	67473	2180702	55706	1547421	7501
河　南	21	423	289	18566	1135273	14628	826358	1133
湖　北	88	613	338	13262	2149619	10824	1319911	1172
湖　南	89	2653	1002	35954	2968041	27045	2040152	2449
广　东	32	3845	2124	16207	2352235	12770	1804520	1201
广　西	3	200	133	10625	1924284	8915	1379520	884
海　南				772	133484	583	76930	129
重　庆	4	148	96	9558	2239655	6218	1498135	2864
四　川	129	3845	1213	33652	5291166	28784	3532428	3625
贵　州	20	133	43	17114	983971	13673	759138	1826
云　南	12	1270	800	16565	2315725	10152	1656506	1765
西　藏				8	1445			
陕　西	16	1091	373	15647	1171216	13772	803867	873
甘　肃	16	650	430	10977	565187	9979	496736	702
青　海				734	29988	685	12454	35
宁　夏	2	40		1419	57316	1280	43852	112
新　疆	8	250	132	5477	274496	4557	142987	674

单位：张、个、人、万元

发展情况

参加人数	县、市老年人协会	参加人数	老年基金会	事业投入经费	其他老年社团组织	参加人数	老年学校个数	老年学校在校人数
7587321	**6621**	**2988818**	**11646**	**28985**	**44359**	**4371699**	**54458**	**7331490**
57108	4	10301	6	74	5519	523606	2469	243878
49416	8	3361			1196	148624	484	184145
82573	857	132168	503	27	146	127196	290	42978
118159	747	63490	12	156	5482	207812	1319	239138
61381	198	49941			14	6889	58	9855
331752	148	33076			1294	54754	1202	156931
80561	5	4469	1	6	155	22646	319	25755
342838	55	14237	1894	20	866	218849	261	20687
48093	10	4065	15	4472	994	26648	1406	517203
427698	145	92893	9	6064	9934	616579	3813	1012370
421459	43	372051	266	1608	979	145135	9769	896760
200989	191	61284	6	13	918	89467	2611	228081
213168	99	35058	356	7801	833	251672	11731	924290
279856	348	172960	7163	101	1454	96234	1073	206004
326857	517	226988	7	295	2963	108816	3051	370379
130653	352	37345	15	59	312	34813	2300	158308
534033	272	319799	5	43	573	202841	1014	198162
526734	528	233911	35	327	866	184661	1137	179672
255266	242	68672	480	3603	3215	155609	507	102493
281663	111	86411	435	111	849	85320	792	84247
34933	36	18542	189		60	7715	9	2799
602901	253	271493	6	342	1000	321241	1554	300921
1427809	462	398590	5	213	1298	413973	2077	637428
170910	239	56927	14	383	1022	67373	1717	174068
248061	461	125243	49	1002	900	124321	2015	289253
	4	713						
117910	90	30640	30	416	539	90789	267	52463
123200	66	18923	40	15	568	27915	124	13272
13877	6	2237	94	1824	87	1558	103	4855
11105	17	4731			20	966	19	2324
66358	107	38299	11	11	303	7677	967	52771

C-2-25 为残疾人提供

地区	单位数	年末职工人数	#女性	#残疾职工	#女残疾职工	残疾职工工资总额	残疾职工养老保险总额
全国	**12890**	**998921**	**325360**	**374944**	**121595**	**4641426.7**	**206389.9**
中央级							
北京	543	24500	8122	9951	2932	25726.7	6002.5
天津	221	15828	4467	6401	1874	9624.1	3518.9
河北	384	26044	7592	10077	2651	3812155.4	4151.1
山西	220	25631	5824	9882	3187	33042.4	2548.3
内蒙古	61	3630	1482	1673	659	2703.6	621.5
辽宁	1407	69313	20566	31186	7707	44695.1	15559.0
吉林	318	15440	4035	6925	1738	1491.3	213.3
黑龙江	386	11872	3626	6365	2145	6592.0	1120.2
上海	913	73818	25544	24334	8170	100263.0	30899.2
江苏	2530	244943	85066	84818	29899	180700.6	41501.4
浙江	1713	186456	63291	60891	24387	164346.5	53611.7
安徽	237	13084	4591	5168	1577	10529.9	2268.7
福建	145	8255	3042	3790	521	4523.1	272.2
江西	253	20095	6018	8327	2527	10340.9	372.8
山东	1068	82407	23912	31367	8811	66754.1	22540.1
河南	640	39597	13506	18045	5378	20527.2	754.8
湖北	232	15355	4679	6947	2582	10447.9	1267.3
湖南	317	20610	5901	9591	2848	15691.6	3167.0
广东	110	10678	3792	4573	1664	9107.7	589.4
广西	48	2923	599	952	186	44044.6	1072.8
海南	4	204	34	99	29	236.4	14.2
重庆	398	31387	9616	11912	3241	26031.7	7193.4
四川	301	25761	10677	9687	3195	21877.4	3412.5
贵州	10	315	115	164	45	418.3	30.7
云南	89	10443	2407	3735	775	5394.5	1069.7
西藏							
陕西	166	9906	3002	3538	1137	5578.0	1372.3
甘肃	46	2854	996	1079	330	1961.6	310.1
青海	6	115	63	18	2	32.0	
宁夏	16	694	278	389	177	1866.0	11.7
新疆	108	6763	2517	3060	1221	4723.1	923.1

工作岗位的福利企业

单位:个、人、万元

残疾职工补贴	纳税总额	增值税总额	营业税总额	所得税总额	应减免税金总额	实际减免税金总额	盈利总额
25736.4	**1276258.6**	**946797.2**	**54098.7**	**171283.6**	**725496.2**	**669319.9**	**851560.7**
3037.7	22356.1	16663.4	644.1	1059.1	26466.3	23075.8	4087.2
27.7	5355.0	4189.9	191.6	1175.9	3718.0	3309.1	2341.2
331.5	29498.2	18068.8	1280.2	3609.6	13883.3	10365.4	11763.7
425.8	12863.0	10625.3	415.2	544.0	6546.5	5351.4	3636.2
65.1	5494.7	5823.7	177.7	154.6	4876.1	4488.1	1426.0
183.7	43221.4	43464.0	2907.9	4202.4	29027.3	33618.9	15008.3
20.7	858.0	800.3	19.0	38.7	779.0	752.7	10.4
260.0	3956.5	3498.1	3.7	339.2	3355.5	2908.0	12.1
8384.0	148687.0	93029.7	26173.9	52301.3	94451.5	88696.9	156658.2
3618.2	378176.5	307936.7	7481.0	37871.1	223360.5	184682.3	122135.5
649.3	354028.7	289495.8	3935.7	42034.5	144114.2	168059.3	407924.2
252.0	13048.3	11349.8	198.8	1157.0	7538.0	6941.4	11858.5
161.1	3757.3	2751.6	1.0	84.5	2703.8	2944.3	750.8
63.7	55943.2	3038.2	491.5	1746.3	18782.0	18805.5	6519.5
6258.7	110831.1	63385.9	7784.5	19442.6	69333.9	64392.0	71983.4
141.3	10809.4	6695.4	190.0	840.3	8340.7	7213.1	3566.4
184.8	8965.1	3441.8	23.8	1587.5	5401.1	2179.4	3186.6
632.1	5741.8	2982.0	800.0	167.3	4129.7	3297.0	1087.6
207.4	6926.2	1973.6	66.9	269.7	3674.8	3093.4	3516.0
2.5	421.2	2827.2	18.1	12.1	1817.2	1817.2	3357.6
			0.4	0.4			
396.7	44596.7	36018.4	96.6	2129.1	45880.5	26589.0	25266.2
185.5	1292.3	770.4	160.0	48.9	1225.2	539.0	4944.1
20.0	43.4	43.4					
70.9	4251.3	3029.5	31.8	30.3	1911.0	2890.7	-19099.1
95.6	1509.7	12038.9	344.0	344.7	772.3	431.8	7897.6
11.0	5.0						
6.7	605.0		605.0		1526.0	1526.0	355.0
42.7	3016.5	2855.4	56.3	92.5	1881.8	1352.2	1367.5

C-2-25续表1

地区	单位数	年末职工人数	受教育程度		职业资
			大学专科人数	大学本科及以上人数	助理社会工作师人数
全　国	**12890**	**998921**	**67320**	**26019**	**1309**
中央级					
北　京	543	24500	1804	743	21
天　津	221	15828	990	332	54
河　北	384	26044	1219	585	7
山　西	220	25631	1251	454	11
内蒙古	61	3630	326	76	23
辽　宁	1407	69313	3224	1193	74
吉　林	318	15440	661	378	383
黑龙江	386	11872	970	145	8
上　海	913	73818	1697	639	98
江　苏	2530	244943	20001	8312	237
浙　江	1713	186456	10064	4004	115
安　徽	237	13084	935	203	22
福　建	145	8255	178	52	4
江　西	253	20095	733	191	3
山　东	1068	82407	9467	4078	42
河　南	640	39597	3341	885	16
湖　北	232	15355	383	276	5
湖　南	317	20610	1154	252	7
广　东	110	10678	720	481	69
广　西	48	2923	166	32	2
海　南	4	204	1		
重　庆	398	31387	2334	1311	20
四　川	301	25761	3043	514	37
贵　州	10	315	39	11	
云　南	89	10443	420	55	4
西　藏					
陕　西	166	9906	1226	467	38
甘　肃	46	2854	81	30	1
青　海	6	115	6	9	5
宁　夏	16	694	10	5	2
新　疆	108	6763	876	306	1

单位:个、人、人次、时

格水平	年龄结构				志愿服务	
社会工作师人数	35岁及以下人数	36岁至45岁人数	46岁至55岁人数	56岁及以上人数	志愿者服务人次数	志愿服务时间
727	**321581**	**385862**	**220595**	**70883**	**31635**	**59968.0**
4	6415	10318	6388	1379	930	1080.0
16	6206	5762	3068	792	1000	2000.0
4	11076	9877	4313	778	1243	5321.0
3	6882	9687	7748	1314		
11	966	1626	919	119		
29	19301	29443	16678	3891	200	400.0
191	3835	6685	2812	2108		
4	4682	4126	2622	442		
45	24199	24399	18331	6889	270	850.0
93	72460	97131	60264	15088	8633	16403.0
171	52757	61069	44952	27678	16591	26326.0
6	3988	6160	2640	296	248	1345.0
6	2687	4004	1238	326		
2	8308	8545	2874	368	27	
14	32717	30812	15366	3512	924	3164.0
30	18922	14567	5357	751	7	21.0
2	5210	6571	2953	621	10	80.0
2	4208	12619	3092	691	455	1211.0
21	5006	4053	1274	345		
	1455	865	536	67	177	
	83	82	29	10		
35	9379	13105	7390	1513	189	853.0
21	10055	10943	3793	970	600	600.0
	85	145	79	6		
1	3167	4372	2736	168		
10	4467	3551	1653	235	71	174.0
1	774	1401	392	287	60	140.0
	12	52	28	23		
	225	431	30	8		
5	2054	3461	1040	208		

C-2-25续表2

地区	增加值合计	执行企业会计制度单位财务指标				
		固定资产原价	营业收入	费用合计	营业利润	企业单位增加值
全国	**6510182.8**	**15417610.6**	**40747380.0**	**5003339.9**	**1134655.1**	**6507498.1**
中央级						
北京	115353.6	298180.1	547729.0	83742.2	-777.4	115353.6
天津	60448.6	228953.2	348963.8	85777.2	5048.4	60448.6
河北	141280.3	367878.9	955873.6	68759.0	6858.3	141280.3
山西	33139.0	242935.6	348138.1	29778.4	-11993.9	33139.0
内蒙古	8653.1	38621.9	44379.3	7253.8	329.2	8653.1
辽宁	279141.8	1283292.4	1401752.8	162104.7	43589.8	279141.8
吉林	20309.9	109581.8	240963.4	28400.4	417.5	20309.9
黑龙江	27880.0	91894.3	125122.7	25208.3	4235.5	27880.0
上海	753525.1	1327350.3	3127025.5	314475.7	178117.2	753525.1
江苏	1297844.0	3451093.3	11045040.8	1251536.4	231773.2	1297844.0
浙江	2410432.7	5012310.1	14166092.5	2185572.1	487710.7	2410432.7
安徽	44439.6	83080.4	716002.1	42014.2	8164.0	44439.6
福建	41758.1	92382.1	204813.4	18338.8	980.0	41758.1
江西	15186.6	93148.6	2185969.8	19302.8	2946.9	15186.6
山东	545044.1	924189.3	1522147.6	289759.9	129646.8	545044.1
河南	90035.9	339021.7	613860.5	68045.9	11092.6	90030.4
湖北	37190.2	68863.8	180458.5	49161.1	10374.2	37190.2
湖南	35196.6	104341.1	402947.2	26981.2	1144.7	35123.9
广东	46340.8	198718.1	237640.5	26014.0	5542.6	46325.8
广西	6746.5	25763.7	111830.2	7147.1	-1690.9	6746.5
海南	1610.0	5006.0	18910.0	2222.0	323.0	1610.0
重庆	145200.9	326425.3	642695.5	72213.4	8100.7	145200.9
四川	258912.2	234038.4	841398.8	50889.3	11260.6	257372.7
贵州	1687.9	1426.1	5952.2	661.1	366.6	885.2
云南	11202.6	188882.1	313061.4	20598.8	-22295.8	10964.4
西藏						
陕西	40111.0	87367.5	193175.4	30349.1	16193.5	40109.3
甘肃	2376.6	8187.1	4783.2	420.1	-34.2	2376.6
青海	9.3	570.0				
宁夏	6594.9	19574.5	19047.0	10321.5	478.8	6594.9
新疆	32530.7	164532.9	181605.2	26291.4	6752.5	32530.7

单位：万元

执行行政事业单位会计制度财务指标					
固定资产原价	上年结转和结余	本年收入合计	本年支出合计	收支结余	行政事业单位增加值
4485.1	**91.0**	**4043.7**	**4112.0**	**28.9**	**2684.7**
14.9		42.6	42.6		5.5
154.0		56.5	56.5		72.7
		15.0	15.0		15.0
3199.9	15.9	2471.1	2460.4	28.9	1539.5
562.1	75.1	1163.9	1205.8		802.7
278.4		294.6	331.7		238.2
42.1					1.7
233.7					9.3

C-2-26 为残疾人提供服务的

地区	单位数	年末职工人数	#女性	#残疾职工	#女残疾职工	残疾职工工资总额	残疾职工养老保险总额
全国	**27**	**1560**	**497**	**179**	**68**	**69951.3**	**1172.9**
中央级							
北京	1	101	25	4		36.0	6.0
天津	1	5		1		3.0	1.0
河北	1	17	4	1	1	4.3	
山西	1	83	30	2		5.4	
内蒙古	1	41		25	16	61.2	12.6
辽宁	1	48	18	17	4	2.0	
吉林							
黑龙江	2	28	8	9	2	14.0	6.2
上海	1	83	30	2		17.5	
江苏	1	52	20	2		18.0	
浙江	1	64	23	3		69497.5	1117.3
安徽	1	10	10	2	1	5.0	
福建							
江西	1	68	9	14		16.8	0.3
山东	1	116	30	4		13.9	16.0
河南	2	128	34	12	2	7.0	
湖北	3	166	51	5	2	16.6	0.3
湖南	1	105	38	3	1	15.2	4.2
广东	2	86	20	10	3	25.0	
广西							
海南							
重庆							
四川	1	106	50	43	29	108.4	
贵州	1	58	22	2	1	9.8	
云南	1	74	33	5	1	30.1	
西藏							
陕西	1	88	24	12	4	39.0	9.0
甘肃							
青海							
宁夏							
新疆	1	33	18	1	1	5.6	

民政部门直属康复辅具机构

单位:个、人、万元

残疾职工补贴	纳税总额	增值税总额	营业税总额	所得税总额	应减免税金总额	实际减免税金总额	盈利总额
3282.6	**112.6**	**397.8**	**173.9**	**8.3**	**1293.0**	**1495.0**	**-50.0**
	23.0	1.0	22.0		372.0	372.0	-20.0
3.9	15.0	10.0	2.6	1.8	14.0	14.0	-25.0
3.3							
	66.9	52.7	4.9	0.5			2.1
3273.0							
0.2			11.4		7.6	7.6	
2.0					425.0	425.0	-10.0
0.2			5.6				
	7.7	3.2	4.5		355.4	355.4	
		128.9	122.9	6.0	119.0	119.0	2.9
		202.0				202.0	

C-2-26续表1

地 区	单位数	年末职工人数	受教育程度		职业资
			大学专科人数	大学本科及以上人数	助理社会工作师人数
全 国	**27**	**1560**	**398**	**340**	**25**
中央级					
北 京	1	101	26	29	
天 津	1	5			
河 北	1	17	4	5	
山 西	1	83	18	27	
内蒙古	1	41			
辽 宁	1	48			
吉 林					
黑龙江	2	28	10		
上 海	1	83	13	7	
江 苏	1	52	30	13	2
浙 江	1	64	14	24	
安 徽	1	10	2		
福 建					
江 西	1	68	9	4	1
山 东	1	116	27	22	
河 南	2	128	30	30	6
湖 北	3	166	43	25	
湖 南	1	105	30	25	
广 东	2	86	20	38	13
广 西					
海 南					
重 庆					
四 川	1	106	42	35	
贵 州	1	58	13	26	
云 南	1	74	33	9	1
西 藏					
陕 西	1	88	27	17	2
甘 肃					
青 海					
宁 夏					
新 疆	1	33	7	4	

单位:个、人、人次、时

格水平	年龄结构				志愿服务	
社会工作师人数	35岁及以下人数	36岁至45岁人数	46岁至55岁人数	56岁及以上人数	志愿者服务人次数	志愿服务时间
23	**411**	**438**	**484**	**227**		
1	46	21	21	13		
			5			
	5	4	4	4		
2	19	30	30	4		
		2	12	27		
	9	20	14	5		
	14	5	8	1		
	5	35	30	13		
1	10	14	19	9		
3	20	13	17	14		
1	2	4	4			
	8	8	16	36		
	10	31	65	10		
7	53	30	28	17		
1	45	39	58	24		
	35	34	23	13		
6	26	32	23	5		
	44	26	26	10		
	17	25	13	3		
1	29	9	34	2		
	8	38	29	13		
	6	18	5	4		

C-2-26续表2

地区	增加值合计	执行企业会计制度单位财务指标				
		固定资产原价	营业收入	费用合计	营业利润	企业单位增加值
全国	**16655.6**	**29461.2**	**20087.8**	**8804.5**	**-1405.5**	**5062.6**
中央级						
北京	540.2	2029.8	3223.7	841.8	-391.3	540.2
天津	2.3	86.0	48.3	19.3		2.3
河北	186.4					
山西	242.0	5340.0	737.0	233.0	-76.0	242.0
内蒙古	81.0	205.0	125.0	142.0	-24.0	81.0
辽宁	152.6	328.4	1056.2	42.1	10.3	152.6
吉林						
黑龙江	104.3	188.3	164.3	39.5	9.5	104.3
上海	722.5	2516.8	2201.4	1283.3	-255.7	722.5
江苏	2498.7					
浙江	429.6	6315.9	1813.3	903.2	-622.9	429.6
安徽	-3.7	474.0	979.0	394.0	-166.0	-3.7
福建						
江西	155.9					
山东	618.1	3261.0	2596.0	1383.0		618.1
河南	-19.7	4502.0	1983.0	775.0	-179.0	-19.7
湖北	2455.9	26.4	31.0	17.5	-0.9	10.0
湖南	980.9					
广东	1567.4	1579.6	3484.6	2350.8	242.5	1567.4
广西						
海南						
重庆						
四川	1521.3					
贵州	1597.0					
云南	1881.7					
西藏						
陕西	616.0	2608.0	1645.0	380.0	48.0	616.0
甘肃						
青海						
宁夏						
新疆	325.1					

单位：万元

执行行政事业单位会计制度财务指标					
固定资产原价	上年结转和结余	本年收入合计	本年支出合计	收支结余	行政事业单位增加值
15990.6	**2254.9**	**25068.3**	**22072.0**	**3530.0**	**11593.0**
84.0		199.0	199.0		186.4
5568.3		7021.4	7019.3	2.1	2498.7
539.0	-176.9	587.4	452.9	-42.4	155.9
3132.3		3953.1	4409.0	-455.9	2445.9
		5670.2	2268.4	3401.7	980.9
3199.9	15.9	2471.1	2442.2	28.9	1521.3
1445.1	2397.8	1016.7	1816.4	2.9	1597.0
1135.0	18.1	1853.7	1761.8		1881.7
887.0		2295.7	1703.0	592.7	325.1

C-2-27 其他为残疾人

地 区	单位数	年末职工人数	#女 性	#残疾职工	#女残疾职工	残疾职工工资总额	残疾职工养老保险总额
全 国	**3472**	**253570**	**77459**	**104336**	**28410**	**365453.1**	**44875.7**
中央级							
北 京	30	1578	629	488	154	953.1	295.8
天 津	1	2	1	10		10.0	2.0
河 北	156	8557	3354	3498	930	8847.6	1741.7
山 西	157	10264	2187	4912	1049	7636.9	752.1
内蒙古	82	4976	960	3109	939	3119.0	725.7
辽 宁	341	19773	6064	7856	2474	9306.2	2386.7
吉 林							
黑龙江	53	2520	863	1501	427	750.1	34.2
上 海	14	585	224	186	67	801.7	393.4
江 苏	77	4732	2003	1923	670	3254.3	683.6
浙 江	220	17550	4754	6577	1990	16874.9	5360.1
安 徽	105	4386	1521	1747	412	2869.9	929.3
福 建	132	9903	2640	4207	511	4437.8	506.4
江 西	44	4894	1409	1743	87	4816.8	6.8
山 东	153	9574	2608	3490	1122	7092.4	1896.2
河 南	173	14937	4341	6324	2209	9784.8	185.3
湖 北	299	19105	6569	6266	1792	14216.9	10210.5
湖 南	181	10749	2810	6194	1399	9545.4	1253.9
广 东	35	3053	652	1106	353	1592.2	140.4
广 西	76	5216	820	2226	478	111340.2	2127.8
海 南	9	1017	271	695	244	652.8	
重 庆	347	36439	13371	14156	4733	39732.0	10149.9
四 川	380	28522	9557	11780	3156	23367.8	3156.3
贵 州	30	1772	449	768	324	1646.6	224.9
云 南	177	22105	5553	8341	1671	74460.6	946.7
西 藏	3	201	75	99	30	143.6	22.4
陕 西	33	2110	758	938	417	1992.3	495.1
甘 肃	18	801	159	277	36	391.2	34.9
青 海	30	1946	706	933	302	1463.0	36.4
宁 夏	64	4500	1546	1945	165	3187.3	140.0
新 疆	52	1803	605	1041	269	1165.7	37.2

服务的福利机构

单位：个、人、万元

残疾职工补贴	纳税总额	增值税总额	营业税总额	所得税总额	应减免税金总额	实际减免税金总额	盈利总额
4720.4	**165980.4**	**109199.7**	**15301.0**	**14160.4**	**91898.1**	**81714.5**	**100395.5**
56.8	1171.5	148.3	643.5	126.3	1228.5	1145.6	304.3
101.0	6469.2	3446.9	25.1	722.0	5067.7	3180.0	1992.6
64.1	8539.9	7375.3	13.8	3.5	7230.9	4024.4	1836.5
69.0	3924.0	3683.4	138.0	56.0	1834.8	1803.8	1201.8
27.9	9294.5	7326.6	208.5	1097.8	6947.5	5104.6	5646.5
13.0							
281.8	359.2	312.4	38.8	8.0	281.2	242.9	1162.7
	2303.0	2964.2		62.8	2084.9	1068.7	939.4
	34510.8	24292.8	10749.0	102.0	9645.0	14541.4	13131.6
87.4	1732.6	1148.1	7.2	151.1	777.2	754.7	878.3
123.6	3567.0	566.0	17.0	16.7	365.2	260.8	3320.0
281.6	10050.9	5476.5	432.5	1318.7	7910.1	5314.1	4421.0
6.8	1620.2	1353.4	9.8	142.0	569.5	333.7	511.8
264.4	4822.3	5216.7	226.5	650.4	4640.1	3501.7	2244.8
873.8	2881.0	172.0	710.0	82.0	1494.0	1499.0	110.2
28.2	625.7	195.1	12.4	27.0	473.2	348.1	-101.4
11.4	450.9	4557.0	166.7		3407.7	3389.8	5621.9
	250.0	223.0	1.4	11.4	250.0	223.0	70.0
1099.9	64007.2	33261.9	1092.2	8809.9	31499.7	29101.1	52544.9
574.4	3583.9	3459.3	788.9	208.1	4575.8	4206.0	3005.4
30.3					15.0	15.0	
596.6	1343.8	256.5	8.0		545.1	545.1	-3203.6
70.9	4354.7	3720.6	1.5	560.4	795.2	840.3	4717.8
29.2	78.0	16.0	3.0	2.0			
20.8					251.4	251.4	
7.5	40.1	27.7	7.2	2.3	8.4	19.3	39.0

C-2-27续表1

地区	单位数	年末职工人数	受教育程度		职业资
			大学专科人数	大学本科及以上人数	助理社会工作师人数
全　国	**3472**	**253570**	**17013**	**6991**	**536**
中央级					
北　京	30	1578	84	46	2
天　津	1	2			
河　北	156	8557	225	82	9
山　西	157	10264	113	27	7
内蒙古	82	4976	862	218	
辽　宁	341	19773	982	498	12
吉　林					
黑龙江	53	2520	68	8	4
上　海	14	585	3	5	1
江　苏	77	4732	268	35	6
浙　江	220	17550	668	251	3
安　徽	105	4386	317	108	118
福　建	132	9903	81	100	
江　西	44	4894			1
山　东	153	9574	513	305	8
河　南	173	14937	2488	1860	
湖　北	299	19105	817	363	212
湖　南	181	10749	532	49	40
广　东	35	3053	113	30	
广　西	76	5216	384	135	2
海　南	9	1017	85	37	18
重　庆	347	36439	3032	1371	39
四　川	380	28522	3915	876	23
贵　州	30	1772	192		
云　南	177	22105	340	188	13
西　藏	3	201	1		
陕　西	33	2110	235	32	8
甘　肃	18	801	45	10	
青　海	30	1946	19	4	10
宁　夏	64	4500	421	276	
新　疆	52	1803	210	77	

单位:个、人、人次、时

格水平	年龄结构				志愿服务	
社会工作师人数	35岁及以下人数	36岁至45岁人数	46岁至55岁人数	56岁及以上人数	志愿者服务人次数	志愿服务时间
95	**89103**	**107209**	**47562**	**9696**	**16517**	**43989.0**
5	635	514	390	39	85	85.0
		1	1			
4	2807	3898	1515	337	23	168.0
3	3604	3369	2631	660		
	802	1763	2338	73		
9	4953	9068	4067	1685		
	790	1289	415	26		
	155	206	138	86	157	1256.0
7	1282	2236	904	310	55	125.0
	4128	8159	4492	771		
1	1496	1743	986	161	220	462.0
	3873	4020	1753	257		
	2045	2344	455	50		
3	2790	4022	2412	350	14	24.0
	6691	6535	1344	367		
	4117	10918	3777	293	57	171.0
4	2984	5300	2077	388	5354	18912.0
	1402	1012	590	49		
1	2475	1894	646	201		
2	718	213	77	9		
40	12047	14798	7741	1853	10377	22584.0
6	13387	10258	4149	728	2	12.0
	753	581	324	114	173	190.0
7	11116	8190	2431	368		
	46	97	45	13		
	800	747	484	79		
	350	374	70	7		
3	755	960	190	41		
	1442	1894	805	359		
	660	806	315	22		

C-2-27续表2

地区	增加值合计	执行企业	
		固定资产原价	营业收入
全　国	**1043476.6**	**2427376.7**	**6656679.9**
中央级			
北　京	7004.9	33793.3	26690.5
天　津		0.1	
河　北	35612.4	106439.6	275538.6
山　西	9629.6	76530.9	93168.6
内蒙古	6337.8	27296.0	15106.2
辽　宁	72726.8	145291.5	502880.6
吉　林			
黑龙江	5875.8	12347.0	32625.0
上　海	3854.7	4704.1	21532.8
江　苏	14439.1	42819.8	104393.9
浙　江	117813.3	270299.6	1434882.5
安　徽	19205.4	43981.2	212481.7
福　建	12100.2	74233.6	110056.0
江　西	1367.4	3290.0	534.0
山　东	51784.0	103588.4	190785.7
河　南	25067.3	43739.2	152137.5
湖　北	42471.2	138117.1	188212.0
湖　南	44795.2	170020.5	175553.2
广　东	12167.2	15643.8	54472.7
广　西	15380.7	35904.1	185482.2
海　南	5834.6	14971.3	30933.3
重　庆	193121.8	350431.0	1301234.8
四　川	64813.0	215544.1	576646.4
贵　州	1652.7	5082.0	12857.6
云　南	38565.2	310896.3	746337.2
西　藏	67.9	3414.8	398.0
陕　西	223323.2	57948.0	146156.3
甘　肃	1036.6	21059.7	5165.5
青　海	5039.4	8329.5	16220.0
宁　夏	9455.7	83472.0	29789.3
新　疆	2933.5	8188.2	14407.8

单位：万元

会计制度单位财务指标		
费用合计	营业利润	企业单位增加值
770482.5	**132547.4**	**1043476.6**
11374.7	-35.8	7004.9
32565.3	1436.2	35612.4
10848.2	-3401.7	9629.6
4427.1	1634.0	6337.8
43290.6	18055.9	72726.8
9940.3	701.7	5875.8
3578.1	1202.2	3854.7
10909.1	1641.5	14439.1
82815.4	6891.3	117813.3
16229.9	9998.2	19205.4
29320.7	532.4	12100.2
34.0		1367.4
29468.1	10926.9	51784.0
21571.6	8435.1	25067.3
44472.0	-107.9	42471.2
34980.4	8204.4	44795.2
8459.8	35.2	12167.2
4395.5	-338.6	15380.7
5244.7	31.4	5834.6
154140.2	35051.5	193121.8
47148.9	13393.1	64813.0
2242.3	550.9	1652.7
137679.8	10794.3	38565.2
222.5	26.0	67.9
13532.6	3198.9	223323.2
2001.1	119.0	1036.6
3682.6	426.2	5039.4
1409.9	3315.3	9455.7
4497.1	-170.2	2933.5

C-2-28 残疾人教育

地 区	职业培训基地数（个）	本年度城镇职业培训人数（人次）	残疾人就业服务机构（个）	残疾人就业人数（万人）
全 国	**6154**	**382490**	**2798**	**2159.6**
北 京	64	9260	17	13.7
天 津	30	2272	20	10.8
河 北	203	24912	189	107.6
山 西	588	7497	123	48.6
内蒙古	68	10881	78	37.8
辽 宁	163	16217	118	71.5
吉 林	199	12412	70	46.4
黑龙江	102	11835	127	36.9
上 海	30	16589	17	9.2
江 苏	234	21102	113	96.3
浙 江	333	14931	98	53.0
安 徽	82	11697	89	91.7
福 建	323	9421	92	40.9
江 西	229	4788	85	71.2
山 东	845	20627	132	162.7
河 南	251	41816	162	222.0
湖 北	277	11820	105	109.4
湖 南	243	6164	132	121.9
广 东	272	10919	134	81.2
广 西	70	10055	119	72.9
海 南	10	1969	21	8.1
重 庆	34	5092	35	60.3
四 川	424	34104	134	202.4
贵 州	40	5142	71	82.4
云 南	126	8843	130	106.3
西 藏	5	207	2	1.4
陕 西	372	12637	122	75.9
甘 肃	50	21659	95	64.0
青 海	31	1762	30	5.9
宁 夏	37	2232	19	13.6
新 疆	417	12714	94	30.3
兵团	2	914	24	1.8
黑龙江农垦			1	1.6

指标解释：

1.职业培训基地数：指承担着残疾人就业前培训，在职培训、下岗失业人员转岗转业培训、农村务工人员培训等项职能的实体的个数。

2.本年度城镇职业培训人数：指本年度城镇残疾人中在各类职业培训机构（基地）接受培训（含统计时正在接受培训）的实际人次数。

3.残疾人就业服务机构：指截止到本年度12月31日，省（自治区、直辖市）、地（州、盟）、市（地市级市、县级市）、县（旗）、市辖区各级残联所建的残疾人就业服务机构数。

4.残疾人就业人数：包括城镇就业残疾人和农村在业残疾人，其中城镇就业残疾人指截止到本年度12月31日城镇（非农业户口）残疾人集中就业、分散按比例就业（包括实施按比例就业前已在社会各单位就业的残疾人）、辅助性就业、公益性岗位就业、个体及其他形式就业的人数，农村在业残疾人指截止到本年度12月31日农村残疾人（农业户口）从事各种生产劳动，包括种植业、养殖业、家庭手工业及在各种类型企事业、服务业、商业及个体从业的实际人数。

就业情况

未入学残疾儿童、少年（人）	省市县乡残联实有人员（人）	高等院校录取残疾考生（人）	接收托养服务残疾人（人）	农村贫困残疾人危房改造（户）
80977	**114700**	**9542**	**931825**	**89566**
76	1214	240	107792	657
186	962	251	25329	1433
1028	5575	406	23017	2651
3683	4686	246	14801	9
1433	3174	239	19099	7033
2368	4232	336	35840	3074
2498	2865	367	16771	143
1039	2948	155	19516	1290
18	1194	64	28692	301
1300	4904	605	61312	682
394	4594	396	96574	3802
3794	3657	446	17945	6644
863	2654	307	27849	4269
6167	4361	242	15655	2413
5493	6180	393	45200	1986
7452	8180	759	20244	1636
1937	4220	369	23589	513
5011	5543	465	21935	6997
3693	7418	393	31206	1324
4910	3167	279	34304	5848
655	683	69	14963	318
1671	1960	186	21316	3607
4222	9116	415	44391	2889
3370	3237	417	14480	986
4688	3672	437	22709	2395
110	427	10	3168	28
4220	4608	302	27552	3168
3106	4020	243	20479	15020
749	1239	82	18034	2031
800	776	123	16249	75
3877	2885	273	32498	5140
39	130	26	7809	854
127	219	1	1507	350

5.未入学学龄残疾儿童少年总人数：指截止到本年度12月31日各级残联登记的，在省级人民政府依照《义务教育法》规定的入学年龄段内的，因各种原因未能入学的各类参加儿童少年人数。
6.高等院校录取残疾考生：指本年度高等特殊教育院校和普通高等院校录取的残疾考生数。
7.接收托养服务残疾人：指本年度接受机构托养和居家托养的智力、精神、无生活自理能力、长期需要专人照料或护理的残疾人数。
8.农村贫困残疾人危房改造：指本年度完成危房改造的农村贫困残疾人户数。

C-2-29 孤儿和

地 区	孤儿数	集中供养孤儿	社会散居孤儿	收养登记合计	中国公民收养登记
全 国	**525179**	**93522**	**431657**	**22772**	**19885**
中央级					
北 京	2287	1860	427	199	145
天 津	884	591	293	129	110
河 北	15663	2205	13458	400	346
山 西	15349	3091	12258	252	78
内蒙古	5883	1297	4586	225	132
辽 宁	7760	3149	4611	184	172
吉 林	5401	1549	3852	43	21
黑龙江	7884	1615	6269	47	29
上 海	2054	1955	99	255	182
江 苏	18445	3496	14949	2018	1828
浙 江	5088	2637	2451	4206	4126
安 徽	27073	3561	23512	1010	911
福 建	6437	2116	4321	1288	1233
江 西	24860	5746	19114	607	439
山 东	18023	3683	14340	2416	2312
河 南	45326	5911	39415	439	193
湖 北	26990	4637	22353	717	635
湖 南	45489	6338	39151	803	700
广 东	41711	10052	31659	1789	1308
广 西	23701	2491	21210	1624	1504
海 南	2152	318	1834	162	162
重 庆	12422	1430	10992	297	245
四 川	30174	4234	25940	1073	1022
贵 州	21646	2791	18855	426	260
云 南	22995	2294	20701	1239	1139
西 藏	5869	1563	4306	32	32
陕 西	13013	2794	10219	328	157
甘 肃	21999	3262	18737	130	64
青 海	15991	1453	14538	42	30
宁 夏	7077	442	6635	48	37
新 疆	25533	4961	20572	344	333

儿童收养

单位：人、件

香港居民	澳门居民	台湾居民	华　侨	外国人收养登记	协议解除收养关系登记	#中国公民
120	**12**	**39**	**20**	**2887**	**605**	**590**
		1		54	9	5
				19	3	3
				54	41	41
				174		
				93		
1		1	1	12	1	1
				22		
1				18	19	19
			1	73	2	2
1				190	15	15
			10	80	24	24
2				99	21	21
11	6	11	2	55	46	45
		1		168	61	59
		3	1	104	210	210
1		2		246	1	1
1		1		82	1	1
5		6		103	21	21
76	5	5	2	481	14	10
6	1	2		120	4	4
6		2				
4		2		52	36	36
5		2	2	51	52	52
			1	166	15	15
				100	1	1
				171	3	2
				66		
				12		
				11	1	
				11	4	2

C-2-30 被收养的

地区	被收				
	合计	#女性	残疾儿童	社会福利机构抚养的孤儿	#被外国人收养
全国	**22876**	**16158**	**2637**	**10336**	**2608**
中央级					
北京	199	107	43	52	52
天津	129	67	16	60	18
河北	400	239	70	167	54
山西	252	138	169	211	174
内蒙古	225	114	18	97	91
辽宁	185	94	5	98	12
吉林	43	17		26	22
黑龙江	47	31	13		
上海	255	182	72	165	73
江苏	2018	1469	172	857	190
浙江	4206	3327	58	2191	25
安徽	1013	758	100	371	99
福建	1292	991	56	466	54
江西	609	491	195	404	168
山东	2520	1590	181	986	104
河南	439	232	261	327	242
湖北	717	493	76	332	82
湖南	803	533	94	364	102
广东	1788	1296	416	1351	481
广西	1621	1379	91	537	
海南	162	124	11	59	
重庆	297	187	50	103	51
四川	1074	603	12	351	51
贵州	427	330	125	254	166
云南	1239	880	81	226	92
西藏	32	13		2	
陕西	328	191	157	197	171
甘肃	130	78	65	12	
青海	32	19	8	12	12
宁夏	48	31	15	19	11
新疆	346	154	7	39	11

儿童情况

单位：人

养人					
社会孤儿数	#被外国人收养	近亲属抚养人数	生父母有特殊困难无力抚养人数	#被外国人收养	其他
6802	**184**	**1375**	**527**	**29**	**3836**
111		11	2	2	23
5		47	4	1	13
99		42	8		84
15		9	2		15
44	1	13	26	1	45
54		29			4
		4	3		10
28	18	1	10		8
29		18	2		41
730		120	24		287
1530	37	73	25	18	387
401		56	17		168
518	1	32	1		275
109		36	5		55
588		244	12		690
30		33	15	4	34
136		66	46		137
190		99	24	1	126
216		92	9		120
582	120	41	31		430
62		24	7		10
103		27	14	1	50
334		81	78		230
51		4	36		82
616	7	58	34	1	305
15		3	12		
44		16	21		50
19		5	6		88
6		7	3		4
17		1	1		10
120		83	49		55

C-2-31 救助、低保

地 区	单位数	年末职工人数		受教育程度		职业资
			女性	大学专科人数	大学本科及以上人数	助理社会工作师人数
全 国	**992**	**7424**	**3283**	**2654**	**2784**	**112**
中央级						
北 京	17	121	65	29	86	4
天 津						
河 北	15	73	41	29	26	
山 西	99	766	363	281	277	17
内蒙古	21	239	133	73	148	9
辽 宁	12	80	24	13	31	
吉 林	65	819	205	177	179	10
黑龙江	34	295	135	122	122	1
上 海	7	76	48	7	57	14
江 苏	8	20	8	5	9	
浙 江	22	111	62	27	64	1
安 徽	32	125	44	49	56	4
福 建	23	82	46	28	34	4
江 西	68	434	198	161	89	13
山 东	11	53	23	19	29	2
河 南	38	246	122	70	54	2
湖 北	67	587	271	258	208	2
湖 南	83	723	299	288	205	6
广 东	4	31	15	1	24	3
广 西	96	470	256	176	234	1
海 南	3	18	11	5	12	
重 庆	35	260	143	85	166	6
四 川	57	274	133	108	96	6
贵 州	53	849	354	397	350	2
云 南	28	94	32	31	27	1
西 藏	8	14	6	6	2	
陕 西	28	259	130	103	71	2
甘 肃	23	160	66	45	74	
青 海	3	3	1		1	
宁 夏	13	85	41	31	40	1
新 疆	19	57	8	30	13	1

服务机构

单位:个、人、人次、时

格水平	年龄结构				志愿服务	
社会工作师人数	35岁及以下人数	36岁至45岁人数	46岁至55岁人数	56岁及以上人数	志愿者服务人次数	志愿服务时间
136	**3584**	**2973**	**761**	**106**	**2094**	**6733.0**
6	46	44	28	3	148	356.0
2	48	17	8		1	1.0
10	361	289	107	9	6	18.0
7	111	107	20	1		
2	38	18	8	16		
5	413	358	45	3		
3	108	144	39	4		
10	50	20	4	2		
1	8	7	5		13	35.0
10	54	44	11	2		
8	46	55	20	4	96	
7	34	44	4			
11	158	224	44	8	33	221.0
5	28	20	5			
1	125	96	24	1		
7	214	294	67	12	72	221.0
14	327	298	78	20	980	3520.0
	21	4	5	1		
2	208	204	55	3		
1	5	8	5			
2	131	95	30	4	313	926.0
10	134	111	25	4	100	400.0
5	581	218	48	2	292	815.0
	29	51	14			
	12	2				
2	150	75	30	4	20	160.0
2	101	47	10	2	20	60.0
		3				
3	13	56	16			
	30	20	6	1		

C-2-31续表

地区	增加值合计	固定资产原价	执行 上年结转和结余
全　国	**27902.0**	**14587.2**	**3467.0**
中央级			
北　京	1060.0	316.6	229.3
天　津			
河　北	37.2	39.1	
山　西	1623.2	1663.6	203.2
内蒙古	993.0	207.9	
辽　宁	276.7	86.7	30.6
吉　林	1529.7	635.3	250.9
黑龙江	869.3	918.4	
上　海	2058.7	304.9	146.8
江　苏	102.6	7.6	
浙　江	1323.4	199.8	57.1
安　徽	430.9	391.2	1.2
福　建	301.5	180.7	5.9
江　西	794.0	578.8	6.0
山　东	243.8	66.8	
河　南	604.3	937.4	
湖　北	3210.1	1492.6	21.1
湖　南	2771.8	1846.7	95.8
广　东	311.9	129.1	355.5
广　西	2329.9	1234.9	389.4
海　南	77.4	34.6	189.0
重　庆	1439.8	790.9	3.0
四　川	1174.1	397.7	
贵　州	2616.0	1193.5	64.9
云　南	290.8	26.0	1416.3
西　藏	18.5	64.0	
陕　西	1111.5	279.2	1.0
甘　肃	152.8	326.5	
青　海	1.0	25.0	
宁　夏	143.2	89.0	
新　疆	4.9	122.7	

单位：万元

行政事业单位会计制度财务指标			
本年收入合计	本年支出合计	收支结余	行政事业单位增加值
86804.4	**85269.3**	**2890.2**	**27902.0**
6897.5	6835.1	291.7	1060.0
99.6	99.6		37.2
5773.8	5893.0	2.0	1623.2
1397.7	1394.4	7.3	993.0
561.7	565.5	6.5	276.7
2533.6	2780.6	268.7	1529.7
1072.9	1084.6		869.3
9619.5	8884.0	530.9	2058.7
121.6	121.6		102.6
5268.5	4680.1	0.5	1323.4
830.1	871.0	5.4	430.9
423.2	416.6	4.3	301.5
1553.1	1573.9		794.0
294.4	294.4		243.8
954.2	926.0		604.3
5486.7	5507.8		3210.1
7454.2	6734.1	335.4	2771.8
1014.5	1145.8		311.9
12640.4	12456.9	18.1	2329.9
2855.3	2846.7	180.8	77.4
7536.0	7516.9	22.1	1439.8
2313.2	2509.0		1174.1
3323.2	3075.1	0.2	2616.0
4613.4	4890.9	1216.3	290.8
331.0	331.0		18.5
1417.4	1411.5		1111.5
209.5	218.0		152.8
4.1	4.1		1.0
177.1	174.1		143.2
27.0	27.0		4.9

C-2-32 城市居民最低生活

地 区	城市居民最低生活保障人数	按人员性质分类			老年人	成	
		#女 性	#残疾人	#三无人员		在职人员	灵活就业
全 国	**18770467**	**7924026**	**1611080**	**499649**	**3157500**	**375109**	**4258094**
中央级							
北 京	89135	39302	18526	1790	13292	5155	11861
天 津	135760	67607	20500	1049	15346	4109	12597
河 北	625264	262259	42961	12866	103389	11527	158305
山 西	726305	322227	49348	12681	79805	18580	218405
内蒙古	705833	347640	61028	160	97373	2245	210652
辽 宁	802412	342971	118118	11610	111170	7904	113958
吉 林	758758	378126	79580	7830	122850	15	547966
黑龙江	1273447	520225	142511	25197	132243	9355	251681
上 海	187290	69279	28603	591	4965	14398	2158
江 苏	306793	133792	39449	4844	81916	5704	34614
浙 江	64280	24669	15524	3188	14272	1634	9514
安 徽	724051	302240	79923	37593	211181	8766	142318
福 建	146613	53919	21615	5320	32556	2219	31008
江 西	983274	396530	136171	53010	196832	25739	220932
山 东	446119	181640	33235	8222	77482	18151	84874
河 南	1189092	484880	80049	37438	238595	12533	208088
湖 北	1070921	512467	67737	23373	197035	85007	353319
湖 南	1340135	544170	78894	49062	298993	16879	158827
广 东	315969	128012	39943	13299	66726	9169	68221
广 西	448016	157565	32806	27756	114967	9873	110544
海 南	110853	46388	8474	2684	25516	3477	23825
重 庆	409839	186404	63260	52	75984	860	82315
四 川	1734415	680265	107695	51909	325042	19440	370164
贵 州	476165	181363	28879	15027	74487	5818	102009
云 南	1008747	379120	54523	29709	158777	24263	212991
西 藏	47033	20768	3306	8519	10742	4845	10737
陕 西	577607	276207	26089	4771	42535	5575	122753
甘 肃	813897	298668	38175	14937	80540	14913	165403
青 海	203014	101861	8311	3383	20133	6151	36466
宁 夏	168317	69884	11998	4502	21507	2856	39147
新 疆	881113	413578	73849	27277	111249	17949	142442

保障及其他社会救济

单位：人、户

年人		未成年人		城市居民最低生活保障户数	城市“三无”救助人数
登记失业	未登记失业	在校生	其 他		
3125169	**3986851**	**2660398**	**1207346**	**10260755**	**75682**
23072	15459	13087	7209	52109	311
38674	28508	22448	14078	78539	
107474	117377	94633	32559	348487	148
82676	126810	154153	45876	367559	155
111629	204937	46170	32827	415696	13356
201567	181906	144363	41544	446049	1330
3659	7303	76896	69	484146	4586
278909	398471	158352	44436	713011	1567
61220	62764	39588	2197	127529	
39553	90749	39328	14929	166305	2452
9472	16013	8518	4857	42879	858
93435	146348	83656	38347	434611	1206
26007	34219	14297	6307	82466	820
184197	139081	123362	93131	456855	10796
119933	73903	52695	19081	232192	2051
226837	252570	145553	104916	671713	178
142602	182892	75234	34832	596401	8015
289010	311003	165955	99468	756731	2421
34609	65279	52310	19655	156836	4974
58158	73027	53981	27466	228360	1536
17212	19603	15733	5487	48738	240
58588	100600	70060	21432	241213	9997
255514	431134	216000	117121	989346	25
56492	127310	82282	27767	256103	1331
187454	198201	153027	74034	622637	50
4708	6402	6717	2882	27072	878
99417	65571	150345	91411	282378	2546
167895	182964	149040	53142	340894	1446
21159	48532	41950	28623	96891	59
23833	37320	33304	10350	87523	113
100204	240595	177361	91313	409486	2237

C-2-33 农村最低

地区	农村最低生活保障人数	女性	老年人	未成年人	残疾人	农村最低生活保障户数
全国	**52072404**	**18263506**	**20647701**	**5782892**	**4514417**	**29436178**
中央级						
北京	51324	20910	21072	6328	16366	31066
天津	101447	41676	27665	17389	17816	46881
河北	2098940	656342	1236467	116365	170323	1550568
山西	1407031	502789	803429	66857	149359	1120381
内蒙古	1221501	564736	679427	31400	92151	958970
辽宁	806706	289108	364439	62959	105059	504610
吉林	790473	373800	439837	27228	60442	597525
黑龙江	1172767	445743	537117	65607	79778	661127
上海	29763	14912	10046	1631	10124	23566
江苏	1190956	448973	474586	129096	133977	646637
浙江	507780	177802	187213	65489	108624	323949
安徽	2089224	761036	852138	180884	278501	1194527
福建	739188	252564	221104	78101	107910	378008
江西	1701223	643588	507524	295404	348789	768151
山东	2582089	911749	1503919	160532	212454	1820719
河南	3979447	1182854	2035005	317367	363953	3041457
湖北	2216478	1008160	911531	119196	251456	1479604
湖南	3160287	947772	1291029	304943	210151	1804369
广东	1587610	507617	459608	324111	143891	717464
广西	3289710	945611	1176031	551882	191522	1294495
海南	214757	72685	51406	33005	14248	85391
重庆	502387	225937	139063	88644	80773	277794
四川	4253319	1291536	1861781	455977	361682	2513702
贵州	4168251	1445023	1451350	636968	254651	2000526
云南	4589414	1722140	1358589	538793	263887	2488861
西藏	323440	122680	146240	66892	19765	116564
陕西	1816478	764357	607855	172431	144454	812001
甘肃	3389900	1139859	712453	540199	168986	1123096
青海	372005	98471	61385	66819	22205	147386
宁夏	391607	126232	130545	26339	39001	299657
新疆	1326902	556844	387847	234056	92119	607126

生活保障

单位：人、户

农村五保集中供养人数	女　性	老年人	未成年人	残疾人
1742580	**306114**	**1545681**	**51361**	**280033**
1964	202	1499	18	1050
1241	135	1112	6	283
66791	6567	59703	1022	12239
25313	1792	20610	449	5995
24910	1786	20897	167	5542
33672	3796	29221	582	6897
23942	2586	16584	145	7636
50949	9975	40315	1590	12785
1144	220	1039	4	217
102125	17450	96376	1185	13933
34841	5607	32785	326	5137
160969	22490	150612	2281	19080
9245	1212	8103	260	1586
120629	42797	101745	11685	15929
167909	31440	161679	1455	14930
186919	36187	170003	5754	26709
70094	13967	62931	565	12189
103482	22041	91372	4339	16342
27417	5513	25823	457	2653
22100	4070	20465	566	3500
2372	699	2308	39	121
64148	6716	55796	622	12255
269563	30816	234588	7328	45116
39250	7859	31167	4400	6255
39287	9388	32971	2013	8954
8220	3566	6973	710	904
48694	7620	39941	760	13700
12876	2139	10827	785	2655
4743	1860	4110	469	608
4032	769	3197	166	1293
13739	4849	10929	1213	3540

C-2-34 农村五保

地区	农村五保分散供养人数	女性
全国	**3548131**	**634960**
中央级		
北京	2230	161
天津	11043	1046
河北	164153	14960
山西	135007	13914
内蒙古	64049	5357
辽宁	104777	12213
吉林	91679	16644
黑龙江	85927	17227
上海	1570	218
江苏	96185	14156
浙江	843	140
安徽	269618	43956
福建	75325	11341
江西	108605	37835
山东	58105	11292
河南	300354	54720
湖北	186504	34717
湖南	400191	78290
广东	211498	35086
广西	267390	44898
海南	29043	8336
重庆	99446	9283
四川	235208	34085
贵州	78369	16973
云南	172068	42854
西藏	7591	3929
陕西	84179	13530
甘肃	109852	21916
青海	18676	6184
宁夏	10334	2545
新疆	68312	27154

供养情况

单位：人、户

老年人	未成年人	残疾人
2988892	**159456**	**647259**
1792	7	1161
9535	62	2520
145657	3318	29260
97703	6558	41054
51292	650	15447
89261	2703	21689
58237	1956	33767
61579	2529	28623
1274	11	463
90535	1498	10795
755	16	169
246637	4682	34332
61587	2956	19184
89626	11411	17059
55716	625	5157
271597	9731	37032
164696	2836	28781
337137	21920	66076
193695	7464	22242
238558	14089	35905
27288	748	2596
82797	2088	18746
202157	7789	41792
55532	14178	13205
119098	18230	48902
6442	722	1003
63997	3458	23703
91303	5248	23228
14644	3120	3427
6896	955	3448
51869	7898	16493

C-2-35 医疗救助及

地区	传统救济	临时救助户次	临时救助按户籍性质分类		临时救助按属地分类	
			城市家庭户次	农村家庭户次	当地常住人口户次	非当地常住人口户次
全国	**745110**	**6507059**	**3334639**	**3172420**	**6315296**	**191763**
中央级						
北京		69078	22442	46636	69078	
天津	161	88935	78790	10145	88929	6
河北	5181	113704	32654	81050	108883	4821
山西	6490	113721	28605	85116	108426	5295
内蒙古	24474	168017	55783	112234	154506	13511
辽宁	7172	313335	153071	160264	288801	24534
吉林	1783	208768	92840	115928	203221	5547
黑龙江	4364	246795	113042	133753	245529	1266
上海	13	1581290	1519217	62073	1555777	25513
江苏	73824	349379	120692	228687	345222	4157
浙江	59884	139545	27469	112076	138828	717
安徽	45585	93207	35987	57220	89677	3530
福建	4297	62609	20147	42462	61384	1225
江西	48005	129688	72955	56733	125910	3778
山东	783	354975	175284	179691	351789	3186
河南	23628	122315	31952	90363	113730	8585
湖北	21705	361484	160125	201359	355939	5545
湖南	110533	273925	89585	184340	248205	25720
广东	1661	162394	69390	93004	148417	13977
广西	117691	81696	5088	76608	80928	768
海南	48	29901	7155	22746	28457	1444
重庆	13439	199599	99157	100442	196299	3300
四川	61316	285846	80067	205779	279576	6270
贵州	21513	91978	15415	76563	85116	6862
云南	42915	305859	41623	264236	299286	6573
西藏		5892	3279	2613	5808	84
陕西	2615	206618	43078	163540	197515	9103
甘肃	33991	106341	27807	78534	103447	2894
青海	3	31736	5927	25809	31168	568
宁夏	67	45323	6653	38670	45009	314
新疆	11969	163106	99360	63746	160436	2670

其他农村救济

单位：人、户、人次

临时救助按救助类型分类		民政部门资助参保人数	民政部门资助参合人数	民政部门直接医疗救助人次数		
支出型临时救助户次	应急型临时救助户次				住院救助	门诊救助
5339203	**1167856**	**17019896**	**50217322**	**23953340**	**11066452**	**12886888**
68613	465	52689	60193	88873	22293	66580
87483	1452	299699		206819	74492	132327
83751	29953	164214	1966463	259394	191580	67814
91562	22159	591221	1374637	219675	174039	45636
132595	35422	609338	1090658	301882	218188	83694
220871	92464	755026	989984	742943	273233	469710
173555	35213	893377	962498	785516	333611	451905
226490	20305	1321037	1305028	629286	286004	343282
1418664	162626	83078	9946	100182	44516	55666
289815	59564	234149	1183613	3105574	632192	2473382
118499	21046	47714	679082	1536340	439548	1096792
76242	16965	537435	2373063	947237	797481	149756
54590	8019	34111	818470	799262	253531	545731
111162	18526	1012542	2512733	1549447	459783	1089664
249179	105796	327748	2221243	269221	237782	31439
72876	49439	638930	3251200	856734	687044	169690
312929	48555	1368879	2636370	1017299	735112	282187
194388	79537	1167786	2619463	979548	573842	405706
121575	40819	857794	1455188	987009	306054	680955
72900	8796	215286	2538267	423063	383660	39403
27436	2465	112962	274431	85001	45585	39416
174606	24993	619569	1136501	2599734	637702	1962032
192177	93669	1553654	4752619	1762508	1175895	586613
59473	32505	336152	3195982	302232	273305	28927
259663	46196	1063220	4537519	822477	623131	199346
3753	2139	30636	18376	39382	37320	2062
163365	43253	103254	811373	389375	275362	114013
82839	23502	772431	3409308	409042	292700	116342
24605	7131	208529	457380	285590	147989	137601
40858	4465	154872	263147	330888	126829	204059
132689	30417	852564	1312587	1121807	306649	815158

C-2-36 救灾储

地区	单位数	年末职工人数		受教育程度		职业资
			女性	大学专科人数	大学本科及以上人数	助理社会工作师人数
全国	**868**	**2321**	**713**	**784**	**643**	**29**
中央级						
北京	20	55	14	12	20	
天津	2	27	10	7	17	3
河北	11	50	11	14	16	
山西	75	187	58	79	34	5
内蒙古	12	35	7	16	8	
辽宁	27	140	53	67	53	
吉林	16	59	17	19	8	
黑龙江	10	32	8	13	11	
上海	1	1				
江苏	7	17	5	7	8	
浙江	63	119	35	23	17	2
安徽	13	33	12	16	5	1
福建	25	52	21	7	20	3
江西	16	41	17	7	3	
山东	6	29	8	9	12	2
河南	13	82	16	25	25	1
湖北	48	127	54	57	36	1
湖南	14	39	10	20	10	
广东	68	201	81	63	62	3
广西	20	53	24	15	24	2
海南	3	12	5	3	9	
重庆	38	63	20	15	22	1
四川	98	262	80	106	78	1
贵州	14	35	8	17	14	
云南	40	133	45	53	53	4
西藏	40	65	13	18	7	
陕西	20	78	21	20	18	
甘肃	41	106	28	25	18	
青海	77	94	15	15	10	
宁夏	11	37	7	14	5	
新疆	19	57	10	22	20	

备机构

单位：个、人、人次、时

格水平	年龄结构				志愿服务	
社会工作师人数	35岁及以下人数	36岁至45岁人数	46岁至55岁人数	56岁及以上人数	志愿者服务人次数	志愿服务时间
38	**821**	**903**	**482**	**115**	**845**	**2175.0**
	14	25	12	4		
	18	5	2	2		
4	16	15	15	4		
1	58	87	33	9		
	13	11	10	1		
1	51	47	31	11		
1	26	22	9	2		
	11	13	8		7	56.0
				1		
2	8	3	5	1		
1	36	46	29	8		
2	8	11	11	3		
3	20	19	11	2		
	17	11	12	1		
	5	13	9	2		
2	25	19	31	7		
2	41	59	21	6	125	140.0
	20	14	5		27	70.0
3	83	85	31	2		
	10	23	17	3		
	9	2	1			
	17	28	11	7	577	1607.0
7	101	114	44	3	4	14.0
	22	10	2	1	81	128.0
4	50	51	30	2	2	
	41	20	4			
1	19	23	26	10	9	72.0
	26	40	25	15	10	80.0
	23	55	14	2		
	17	12	6	2		
4	16	20	17	4	3	8.0

C-2-36续表

地　区	增加值合计	执行行政事业单位会计制度财务指标				
		固定资产原价	上年结转和结余	本年收入合计	本年支出合计	收支结余
全　国	**15166.2**	**120282.3**	**11025.1**	**47899.3**	**57408.9**	**75530.3**
中央级						
北　京	529.2	2194.3		5440.1	17952.1	11104.0
天　津	530.8	2156.5		665.5	653.0	
河　北	243.0	577.3	68.0	387.8	358.2	748.0
山　西	554.9	1183.7	381.6	3205.2	1810.3	12605.0
内蒙古	308.1	2103.4	373.4	1023.5	543.9	
辽　宁	997.7	3941.0	755.8	2482.0	2175.6	420.0
吉　林	243.3	1231.8	40.0	356.9	1027.2	180.0
黑龙江	273.5	650.4	59.4	697.9	429.9	
上　海						
江　苏	117.2	1069.6	1584.3	5191.5	4359.0	750.0
浙　江	539.2	3157.8	512.0	1507.9	1614.8	1000.0
安　徽	271.6	2785.7	108.7	173.2	283.5	1000.0
福　建	260.6	842.6	270.7	468.4	375.8	800.0
江　西	88.6	908.0		119.4	126.2	
山　东	462.5	4005.1	19.2	936.8	968.8	
河　南	929.9	1981.4	4.6	1192.1	1930.1	
湖　北	469.1	3339.3	2.0	1227.1	1148.4	3730.0
湖　南	57.1	421.6		72.6	70.1	11000.0
广　东	1495.0	8322.9	1979.8	7572.9	6426.9	12800.0
广　西	448.2	4017.6	219.8	2181.6	2148.5	700.0
海　南	123.7	953.2	33.5	278.2	296.9	1823.3
重　庆	228.1	2770.2		1325.7	1325.7	3405.0
四　川	2078.4	20761.8	404.3	4777.6	2920.5	8581.0
贵　州	165.7	1478.2	17.6	152.5	130.2	400.0
云　南	947.1	6956.9	1248.8	1723.9	2517.7	314.0
西　藏	363.7	8442.5	150.0		46.0	1060.0
陕　西	601.9	4391.8	75.5	930.7	779.6	1580.0
甘　肃	546.6	8134.3	402.0	1029.5	641.0	
青　海	638.7	14481.1		364.2	364.2	650.0
宁　夏	230.6	3189.8	2314.0	1454.5	194.7	
新　疆	422.3	3832.5	0.1	960.1	3790.1	880.0

单位：万元、平方米、顶

行政事业单位增加值	库房建筑面积	仓储面积	#租用仓储面积	#空余仓储面积	仓储物资种类			
					单帐篷	#中央储备	棉帐篷	#中央储备
15166.2	**951152.6**	**806263.6**	**75530**	**61721**	**513342**	**127315**	**159163**	**60008**
529.2	71079.0	65794.0	11104	2080	37472	1126	13447	
530.8	10466.0	9420.0		60	8010	8010	3916	3916
243.0	15391.8	10379.0	748	720	1347	20	1660	
554.9	24501.5	28953.0	12605	1364	14205		9156	
308.1	35133.2	31610.8		650	902	85	1682	15
997.7	47675.0	41855.0	420	1237	16885	9739	12810	12302
243.3	4945.0	4525.0	180	20	1124		345	300
273.5	4300.0	3280.0		485	300			
	2000.0	2000.0			120			
117.2	9797.0	8237.0	750		2321		500	
539.2	15631.3	12500.0	1000	1000	360	55	50	
271.6	15570.0	13838.0	1000	4958	13123	6599	1090	
260.6	25159.0	22659.0	800	290	14114	1271	200	
88.6	9899.0	7941.0		420	2850	50	690	200
462.5	11095.0	10300.0			8310	3680	2040	
929.9	21220.0	16543.0		1350	36412	13078	2037	1900
469.1	46891.0	32507.0	3730	2340	24252	17295	8851	8485
57.1	17008.0	25453.0	11000	815	10211	8141	2636	1036
1495.0	60194.9	54059.0	12800	4820	22562		290	
448.2	17359.0	14589.0	700	1360	3902	70	1037	
123.7	4155.0	4113.3	1823	300	9088	63		
228.1	17278.0	16040.0	3405	541	14028		2632	
2078.4	191915.4	138996.5	8581	24495	154425	23615	29435	4268
165.7	12703.0	10279.0	400	315	837	40	6918	
947.1	58293.7	43794.6	314	4018	37504	9611	2026	20
363.7	34331.3	29403.3	1060	1450	6501	4017	7396	636
601.9	54281.0	54230.0	1580	460	38790	9409	18659	16400
546.6	43973.0	35914.0		4862	7261	150	3673	
638.7	46211.4	38785.0	650	211	560		5502	200
230.6	2170.1	1985.1		200	13055		7781	
422.3	20525.0	16280.0	880	900	12511	11191	12704	10330

C-2-37 民政部门

地区	直接接收捐赠情况			间接接收
	捐赠款数额	捐赠衣被合计	捐赠其他物资价值	捐赠款数额
全 国	**795542.9**	**5244.5**	**80053.2**	**21519.1**
中央级	3059.9			
北 京	81436.6	176.6	20610.1	
天 津	5629.3		299.3	141.4
河 北	1140.8	1.2	1.0	30.0
山 西	1147.5	20.5	108.7	23.2
内蒙古	668.4	0.9	8086.1	22.3
辽 宁	42595.6	2.9	659.0	187.2
吉 林	21107.8			
黑龙江	1074.5		20.0	5.0
上 海	18124.6	37.3	150.0	
江 苏	145768.3	63.1	2135.6	1864.8
浙 江	93149.8	31.0	649.2	861.2
安 徽	286.5			62.5
福 建	8476.9	5.6	5044.8	163.7
江 西	9074.1	148.4	31948.4	446.5
山 东	19348.2			
河 南	3313.5	905.1	34.0	250.6
湖 北	7876.9	3.3	3263.0	146.3
湖 南	24777.7	7.8	2155.2	1732.9
广 东	116588.6	3194.4	1265.8	5476.4
广 西	677.6	22.0	29.9	330.0
海 南	1541.4	0.2		903.4
重 庆	49418.0	2.7	2534.6	3645.7
四 川	26216.1	409.6	322.0	4002.7
贵 州	7890.6	1.6	147.2	8.4
云 南	98716.9	195.8	540.9	803.3
西 藏	1916.1		7.0	
陕 西	364.1	0.5	28.3	154.1
甘 肃	855.6	7.6	6.0	
青 海	508.0			60.0
宁 夏	412.9	1.5		197.5
新 疆	2380.1	4.9	7.1	

接收的社会捐赠

单位：万元、万件、人次、个

捐赠情况		受益人次数	社会捐赠接收工作站、点数		
捐赠衣被合计	捐赠其他物资价值			社会捐赠接收工作站数	慈善超市数
105.6	**39011.6**	**16949213**	**32061**	**14126**	**10174**
		2836465	1788	36	218
		98840	1255	446	38
		8354	720	532	117
		44076	1037	531	251
0.1		1454	441	12	166
0.8	6.0	734530	1325	961	296
		192954	500	417	84
		14796	1199	337	853
		312426	2809	200	132
	36783.3	1425155	3695	1008	2438
		649361	919	454	341
		32831	365	266	99
	20.0	192626	791	310	460
0.6		388534	552	221	61
		182607	2149	1136	704
7.6		171249	737	463	43
0.6	1360.0	203716	719	499	262
2.7	538.3	394974	1544	670	767
6.2	17.0	1789168	819	511	133
5.0		164077	1160	733	220
		7310	39	13	8
0.1	279.2	5683339	1767	957	551
0.1	1.9	547085	2742	1337	1418
0.1	0.6	439068	1175	764	195
		348962	181	166	12
1.7	5.3	52	37	34	2
		15379	403	178	38
		23693	296	223	75
			60	51	2
		15850	236	161	83
80.0		30282	601	499	107

C-2-38 福利彩票发

地 区	单位数				年末职工人数		受教育
		编制登记	民政登记	设施		女性	大学专科人数
全 国	**893**	**707**	**56**	**130**	**11206**	**4610**	**3725**
中央级	1	1			135	53	10
北 京	17	17			141	59	43
天 津	11	10	1		111	48	15
河 北	16	15		1	287	120	80
山 西	12	12			257	129	111
内蒙古	16	16			292	131	134
辽 宁	20	20			459	184	185
吉 林	53	45		8	619	131	93
黑龙江	21	20		1	175	72	68
上 海	18	4	11	3	196	84	39
江 苏	79	74	2	3	787	338	250
浙 江	72	38	6	28	579	275	200
安 徽	37	24	5	8	583	294	229
福 建	13	10	1	2	333	135	102
江 西	48	33	4	11	164	56	46
山 东	18	18			700	265	202
河 南	73	47	13	13	590	246	205
湖 北	54	40	1	13	380	170	158
湖 南	75	75			583	240	186
广 东	65	55	1	9	731	323	221
广 西	32	26	1	5	669	267	310
海 南	3	3			47	19	22
重 庆	1	1			152	37	46
四 川	12	11		1	631	322	280
贵 州	13	13			236	97	73
云 南	17	11	3	3	116	53	42
西 藏	2	1	1		33	14	14
陕 西	41	28	1	12	548	129	127
甘 肃	20	12	3	5	234	113	57
青 海	2	2			27	13	1
宁 夏	8	5	2	1	197	105	71
新 疆	23	20		3	214	88	105

行机构情况

单位：个、人、人次、时

程度	职业资格水平		年龄结构				志愿服务	
大学本科及以上人数	助理社会工作师人数	社会工作师人数	35岁及以下人数	36岁至45岁人数	46岁至55岁人数	56岁及以上人数	志愿者服务人次数	志愿服务时间
3466	**152**	**104**	**5736**	**3681**	**1488**	**301**	**2299**	**6284.7**
125		1	76	21	28	10		
80	3	4	57	46	29	9	4	8.0
70		1	57	32	21	1		
64	4		171	82	26	8	5	
97	1		131	88	30	8		
61		1	156	83	40	13		
207			246	125	74	14	16	32.0
98	5	1	304	254	49	12		
44	2	7	68	79	25	3	20	20.0
53		1	94	52	37	13	50	120.0
274	31	19	377	272	119	19	945	2691.0
149	4	5	283	215	66	15	516	1170.0
187	6	5	375	139	60	9	233	593.0
82			125	122	77	9		
16	5	1	58	74	26	6	111	422.7
314	12	21	343	230	108	19		
161	20	2	303	205	77	5		
96	2	1	165	150	62	3	100	307.0
176	5	11	326	190	59	8	65	225.0
253	26	11	370	238	102	21		
120	9	4	351	237	72	9		
12	4		18	14	15			
91	1		81	47	21	3		
170	2		422	154	46	9		
102		3	147	74	12	3	121	350.0
30	5		55	37	20	4		
7			17	12	4			
105	1	4	217	176	93	62	74	316.0
91	3	1	113	90	29	2	10	30.0
11			14	11	2			
55			134	48	13	2	29	
65	1		82	84	46	2		

C-2-38续表

地区	增加值合计	执行	
		固定资产原价	上年结转和结余
全国	**176968.1**	**697224.5**	**126879.3**
中央级	3788.8	32675.5	14718.3
北京	2862.0	15432.6	85.8
天津	2636.9	15945.1	226.5
河北	3310.0	32356.0	252.6
山西	1912.2	11172.7	711.0
内蒙古	5719.9	28946.7	5497.5
辽宁	-1615.6	34100.4	15116.8
吉林	4033.3	25248.5	1605.7
黑龙江	1746.7	11258.6	3969.5
上海	2288.1	34701.6	343.3
江苏	13199.3	72158.6	20485.3
浙江	10168.0	41012.2	12237.4
安徽	5095.7	23354.3	2639.4
福建	3036.9	5635.0	1628.6
江西	3774.6	13371.1	3563.5
山东	11926.8	68556.8	3039.6
河南	7806.2	32459.5	1879.1
湖北	3649.1	28832.7	181.9
湖南	5687.7	30356.3	2012.1
广东	15543.0	38624.5	2430.2
广西	6971.6	12814.4	166.9
海南	1252.9	430.9	401.3
重庆	7776.8	11961.9	25399.4
四川	1235.4	716.6	797.5
贵州	2893.8	14299.0	4585.5
云南	34681.3	8523.6	172.7
西藏	587.2	433.4	
陕西	3691.3	24070.3	101.9
甘肃	2189.5	12978.8	120.3
青海	2.4	60.0	
宁夏	2453.1	3730.1	1749.0
新疆	6662.8	11006.8	760.7

单位：万元

行政事业单位会计制度财务指标

本年收入合计	本年支出合计	收支结余	行政事业单位增加值
1144068.9	**996442.7**	**157713.2**	**176968.1**
104266.2	66297.2	52687.2	3788.8
28493.0	22894.9	5538.2	2862.0
49668.5	48144.8	299.0	2636.9
57660.3	52789.5	805.0	3310.0
19600.2	11445.7	2828.4	1912.2
39943.4	33058.3	12355.9	5719.9
52306.0	54441.4	89.9	-1615.6
22357.0	21883.3	529.0	4033.3
4686.6	4095.7	53.0	1746.7
27026.5	23980.6	2201.2	2288.1
68321.2	65330.2	25422.2	13199.3
50158.8	44946.8	4916.5	10168.0
37664.3	33693.5	2413.2	5095.7
13784.8	11338.1	1860.5	3036.9
15604.9	12165.6		3774.6
96555.1	99594.7		11926.8
75808.4	64254.1	2367.9	7806.2
27586.0	26832.4		3649.1
49940.0	43359.8	2309.0	5687.7
79773.4	68532.5	8863.6	15543.0
40643.0	29880.2	1455.8	6971.6
18747.0	18025.6	974.3	1252.9
27494.8	27079.9	25814.3	7776.8
2163.3	1945.6	43.7	1235.4
17476.9	14156.9	3429.2	2893.8
52925.4	48490.2	863.3	34681.3
9229.2	9101.6		587.2
18025.9	13812.9	154.0	3691.3
6761.8	9290.3		2189.5
301.0	301.0		2.4
6125.6	6789.4	-590.1	2453.1
22970.4	8490.0	29.0	6662.8

C-2-39 优抚对象享受

地 区	抚恤、补助优抚对象总人数	在院集中供养人数	定期抚恤人数合计	烈 属	城 市
全 国	**9173281**	**95487**	**311210**	**197955**	**41714**
中央级					
北 京	44537	264	1708	512	240
天 津	46188	125	809	320	125
河 北	566354	3565	14181	7877	1348
山 西	181493	2936	8234	5670	414
内蒙古	47950	1531	1875	977	451
辽 宁	235280	3456	7241	2997	736
吉 林	127717	3061	5053	3011	1423
黑龙江	123871	3832	5625	3731	1686
上 海	40403	391	5763	4463	3902
江 苏	495485	5246	16477	8574	1147
浙 江	276256	1591	4897	2523	501
安 徽	475231	2707	11091	6128	1480
福 建	187777	1008	9757	7564	662
江 西	322352	6784	27800	25038	3700
山 东	959504	11773	34443	21528	3780
河 南	753265	13362	17930	9325	1566
湖 北	479130	8767	31670	23612	3371
湖 南	877665	8274	26893	17700	3898
广 东	432929	2137	7838	5209	2155
广 西	294547	496	4412	2838	356
海 南	26913	41	3682	3362	383
重 庆	280078	616	5621	3024	812
四 川	860036	8492	28595	16302	4082
贵 州	232737	287	3652	1967	382
云 南	351828	416	6837	3940	810
西 藏	4643	542	2164	1438	400
陕 西	268055	2350	11265	5877	834
甘 肃	120836	664	2653	913	257
青 海	14705	96	745	325	112
宁 夏	11532	173	496	257	133
新 疆	33984	504	1803	953	568

定期抚恤、补助情况

单位：人

农　村	因公牺牲军人遗属	城　市	农　村	病故军人遗属	城　市	农　村
156241	**48179**	**12524**	**35655**	**65076**	**19177**	**45899**
272	150	71	79	1046	674	372
195	133	50	83	356	235	121
6529	2664	551	2113	3640	872	2768
5256	921	209	712	1643	353	1290
526	420	178	242	478	234	244
2261	1428	461	967	2816	799	2017
1588	807	431	376	1235	660	575
2045	860	465	395	1034	562	472
561	150	121	29	1150	971	179
7427	2074	501	1573	5829	882	4947
2022	892	226	666	1482	455	1027
4648	2187	559	1628	2776	858	1918
6902	1187	182	1005	1006	272	734
21338	1270	391	879	1492	484	1008
17748	5945	1391	4554	6970	1996	4974
7759	4070	882	3188	4535	1173	3362
20241	4779	771	4008	3279	692	2587
13802	3879	1275	2604	5314	1700	3614
3054	929	494	435	1700	813	887
2482	572	117	455	1002	231	771
2979	152	75	77	168	58	110
2212	1057	310	747	1540	482	1058
12220	5905	1340	4565	6388	1703	4685
1585	645	156	489	1040	237	803
3130	1040	226	814	1857	512	1345
1038	199	57	142	527	37	490
5043	2442	506	1936	2946	622	2324
656	697	160	537	1043	277	766
213	139	53	86	281	53	228
124	131	38	93	108	50	58
385	455	277	178	395	230	165

C-2-39续表

地区	定期补助人数合计	在乡退伍红军老战士	在乡西路红军老战士	红军失散人员	在乡复员军人
全　国	**8095950**	**341**	**87**	**11269**	**993204**
中央级					
北　京	31392	1			3727
天　津	38366				2219
河　北	505823				40353
山　西	149179	7		1	23776
内蒙古	34221	5		2	9392
辽　宁	198246	4	4		28328
吉　林	103961			1	21732
黑龙江	100195	11	1	15	30910
上　海	27551				2345
江　苏	430258			1	49168
浙　江	249113			62	20736
安　徽	430565	3	1	2004	40096
福　建	166263			245	16815
江　西	270969	10		4938	34889
山　东	816732				105629
河　南	671793	8		396	59599
湖　北	416252	2	1	360	44743
湖　南	799994	3		1675	123882
广　东	401041			49	22847
广　西	279486	15		262	30757
海　南	21384			40	5010
重　庆	253389				29879
四　川	771798	9	57	600	115791
贵　州	214284	1		6	29089
云　南	326574			3	32196
西　藏	711	90			69
陕　西	234343	165		601	44757
甘　肃	107718	5	17	6	11878
青　海	10555				1747
宁　夏	8946		2	1	1866
新　疆	24848	2	4	1	8979

单位：人

抗 日	带病回乡退伍军人	60岁以上农村籍退伍军人	参战退役人员	参试退役人员	部分60周岁以上烈士子女(含错杀被平反人员子女)	其 他
40462	**1242020**	**3748039**	**1448018**	**188072**	**229308**	**235592**
286	1579	19944	3147	814	1990	190
139	11383	14307	7620	180	1229	1428
5831	49245	315221	50302	19442	30038	1222
2490	25868	67926	8755	6644	12495	3707
218	9212	12636	1843	111	790	230
373	16448	110119	6980	3500	2266	30597
486	11679	63135	3676	1579	1846	313
737	11384	50827	4944	219	1335	549
29	558	21559	2459	526		104
5049	52751	234077	33045	4602	15032	41582
165	20193	176109	24563	2341	1343	3766
1555	138475	189410	35213	11145	6527	7691
36	10443	96602	31205	340	7521	3092
263	49799	87793	44082	3278	44453	1727
11637	96609	479621	76144	15944	42785	
3199	92221	383318	94236	24073	15284	2658
2722	109302	166341	66939	8985	12471	7108
792	161957	311048	179184	7807	11630	2808
350	31424	150372	151108	8839	2678	33724
83	4058	86340	86853	3221	3236	64744
623	1494	7286	6591	214	231	518
47	68544	84007	62839	6096	1232	792
363	184454	298724	132284	20619	7323	11937
222	16649	81284	86598	263	283	111
87	24194	89415	174938	110	1787	3931
	290	143	12			107
1177	28239	77276	50660	25406	2470	4769
425	5461	63585	17888	5915	731	2232
2	1304	3403	1032	1589	147	1333
31	821	3211	1100	289	40	1616
1045	5982	3000	1778	3981	115	1006

C-2-40 伤残人员

地区	伤残人员合计	按伤残				
		一级				二级
			因战	因公	因病	
全国	**766121**	**3452**	**905**	**2283**	**264**	**2118**
中央级						
北京	11437	46	1	41	4	37
天津	7013	32		30	2	19
河北	46350	230	24	186	20	99
山西	24080	91	36	52	3	53
内蒙古	11854	57	14	41	2	18
辽宁	29793	106	31	72	3	73
吉林	18703	140	26	105	9	74
黑龙江	18051	70	12	43	15	34
上海	7089	24	2	21	1	17
江苏	48750	183	50	121	12	141
浙江	22246	58	9	45	4	94
安徽	33575	149	33	106	10	39
福建	11757	44	4	37	3	24
江西	23583	179	45	65	69	155
山东	108329	300	81	211	8	284
河南	63542	285	59	196	30	207
湖北	31208	159	51	95	13	67
湖南	50778	293	134	151	8	204
广东	24050	97	18	66	13	45
广西	10649	42	20	20	2	24
海南	1847	7		7		2
重庆	21068	135	50	75	10	35
四川	59643	205	69	130	6	154
贵州	14801	104	34	70		37
云南	18417	133	37	86	10	73
西藏	1768	7		7		13
陕西	22447	118	39	77	2	37
甘肃	10465	72	19	51	2	17
青海	3405	19	3	15	1	3
宁夏	2090	25		25		9
新疆	7333	42	4	36	2	30

享受抚恤情况

单位：人

等级分类						
因战	因公	因病	三级	因战	因公	因病
292	**1335**	**491**	**17870**	**4919**	**10450**	**2501**
3	26	8	201	36	131	34
1	15	3	122	28	75	19
10	65	24	827	207	461	159
11	35	7	479	178	228	73
2	11	5	176	33	121	22
17	44	12	662	199	403	60
22	36	16	672	213	341	118
	24	10	382	81	179	122
1	16		117	22	77	18
32	92	17	1402	572	712	118
	53	41	468	46	278	144
11	18	10	744	229	441	74
2	16	6	162	16	126	20
12	20	123	597	114	277	206
12	242	30	3589	1051	2276	262
24	148	35	1236	376	602	258
9	40	18	659	119	412	128
52	133	19	1314	386	760	168
5	18	22	435	111	262	62
7	12	5	201	66	110	25
	2		55	13	36	6
3	21	11	459	106	293	60
18	118	18	1266	285	841	140
12	19	6	273	94	159	20
10	30	33	421	147	171	103
	9	4	63	1	61	1
12	23	2	417	113	268	36
1	14	2	208	39	135	34
	3		61	14	45	2
	7	2	43	6	33	4
3	25	2	159	18	136	5

C-2-40续表1

地区	按伤残					
	四级				五级	
		因战	因公	因病		因战
全国	**11592**	**1404**	**6381**	**3807**	**55448**	**17543**
中央级						
北京	141	24	81	36	508	106
天津	80	13	51	16	520	72
河北	603	90	259	254	3451	940
山西	232	35	107	90	1675	702
内蒙古	109	14	54	41	639	125
辽宁	239	81	101	57	2021	743
吉林	585	144	265	176	2339	694
黑龙江	299	7	63	229	1375	651
上海	99	12	55	32	377	104
江苏	974	140	569	265	3624	1225
浙江	389	20	142	227	1269	218
安徽	220	44	122	54	2173	709
福建	132	11	65	56	1172	130
江西	667	27	146	494	1765	423
山东	2199	139	1860	200	8542	3897
河南	1686	190	659	837	4994	1284
湖北	441	38	274	129	1871	402
湖南	538	104	325	109	4137	1337
广东	234	46	115	73	1474	383
广西	66	16	39	11	722	271
海南	14	1	8	5	110	28
重庆	291	46	178	67	1275	430
四川	693	88	477	128	4050	1159
贵州	93	13	68	12	810	334
云南	192	25	55	112	1120	460
西藏	40		37	3	93	2
陕西	110	8	47	55	1693	425
甘肃	92	9	57	26	681	134
青海	15	3	12		233	41
宁夏	26	5	19	2	135	20
新疆	93	11	71	11	600	94

单位：人

等级分类					
因公	因病	六级	因战	因公	因病
25930	**11975**	**174777**	**44986**	**92095**	**37696**
338	64	1892	357	1291	244
231	217	1449	242	898	309
1336	1175	11248	2534	5319	3395
716	257	5063	1914	2268	881
437	77	3183	432	2351	400
1054	224	6506	2161	3628	717
1452	193	5724	1513	3698	513
550	174	3797	1713	1501	583
199	74	1191	260	679	252
1368	1031	12537	3578	6282	2677
515	536	4385	520	2041	1824
1050	414	8077	1961	4067	2049
402	640	3452	327	1362	1763
807	535	4740	1302	2256	1182
3862	783	28661	9101	15527	4033
1955	1755	15519	3899	7861	3759
991	478	6643	1159	3503	1981
2095	705	11278	3043	5884	2351
584	507	4712	1098	2444	1170
376	75	1963	631	938	394
61	21	370	134	162	74
646	199	3936	989	2153	794
2001	890	12627	2624	6960	3043
380	96	2536	703	1368	465
489	171	3192	966	1595	631
88	3	231	4	224	3
769	499	5154	1080	2623	1451
456	91	2026	299	1226	501
174	18	584	117	420	47
90	25	474	81	333	60
458	48	1627	244	1233	150

C-2-40续表2

地区	按伤残							
	七级	因战	因公	八级	因战	因公	九级	因战
全国	**230108**	**60417**	**169691**	**223406**	**65760**	**157646**	**29318**	**1263**
中央级								
北京	3610	681	2929	3951	719	3232	774	15
天津	2031	303	1728	2234	361	1873	336	3
河北	13816	3702	10114	13543	3444	10099	1725	33
山西	7722	2792	4930	6848	2377	4471	742	19
内蒙古	3747	685	3062	3231	665	2566	486	12
辽宁	9088	3158	5930	9660	3701	5959	963	32
吉林	4010	865	3145	3297	782	2515	1024	15
黑龙江	5917	3130	2787	5850	3460	2390	247	5
上海	2062	421	1641	2661	557	2104	361	15
江苏	13403	3878	9525	13794	4356	9438	1702	140
浙江	5685	792	4893	8695	1065	7630	888	18
安徽	10054	2361	7693	9874	2729	7145	1459	29
福建	2788	469	2319	3178	627	2551	597	12
江西	6082	1493	4589	7425	2292	5133	471	20
山东	33733	10810	22923	25986	9409	16577	3329	61
河南	18342	4580	13762	16107	4256	11851	2743	197
湖北	9770	1586	8184	9310	1849	7461	1529	40
湖南	14832	3947	10885	15237	4713	10524	1999	220
广东	6892	1569	5323	8436	2554	5882	1255	65
广西	3261	1052	2209	3590	1401	2189	561	27
海南	552	204	348	581	217	364	128	9
重庆	7251	1703	5548	6486	1980	4506	800	58
四川	18922	4058	14864	18000	4721	13279	2124	77
贵州	4886	1323	3563	5161	1853	3308	554	26
云南	5971	1911	4060	6435	2511	3924	601	43
西藏	565	8	557	424	5	419	259	3
陕西	7395	1651	5744	6796	1705	5091	498	22
甘肃	3580	434	3146	3275	553	2722	351	12
青海	1384	267	1117	912	262	650	128	2
宁夏	615	138	477	598	134	464	105	13
新疆	2142	446	1696	1831	502	1329	579	20

单位：人

等级分类				按人员种类分类				优抚对象享受医疗保障人数
	十　级			残疾军人	伤残国家机关工作人员	伤残人民警察	伤残民兵民工	
因　公		因　战	因　公					
28055	**18032**	**1882**	**16150**	**711299**	**31140**	**18655**	**5027**	**4746407**
759	277	6	271	10325	417	653	42	16393
333	190	4	186	6345	134	500	34	23913
1692	808	19	789	44227	1279	620	224	214759
723	1175	59	1116	22613	1020	266	181	95065
474	208	3	205	8988	1920	806	140	33777
931	475	8	467	26646	1203	1497	447	66045
1009	838	13	825	14091	2406	2056	150	50395
242	80	6	74	17161	440	372	78	57998
346	180	10	170	6584	128	364	13	14382
1562	990	77	913	47085	883	639	143	265802
870	315	19	296	21466	454	173	153	91807
1430	786	30	756	30756	1972	638	209	233062
585	208	3	205	11191	293	197	76	80545
451	1502	1028	474	21596	1249	562	176	102744
3268	1706	32	1674	105071	1723	1052	483	553563
2546	2423	135	2288	60312	1946	1097	187	347766
1489	759	29	730	29476	995	651	86	344214
1779	946	98	848	46120	3064	1517	77	739944
1190	470	54	416	23441	201	354	54	218222
534	219	25	194	9642	302	174	531	122559
119	28	3	25	1779	28	27	13	18590
742	400	50	350	19895	656	421	96	240444
2047	1602	65	1537	55663	2321	1303	356	340213
528	347	40	307	13377	897	468	59	145909
558	279	31	248	16492	832	618	475	168371
256	73	2	71	760	736	174	98	2632
476	229	14	215	21286	829	213	119	94241
339	163	7	156	9606	534	235	90	38546
126	66		66	2450	564	280	111	4518
92	60	3	57	1752	185	102	51	5626
559	230	9	221	5103	1529	626	75	14362

C-2-41 优待、烈士褒扬和

地区	优待				烈士
	优待优抚对象户数	优待军属户数	优待总金额	固定优待军属总额	本年批准烈士人数
全　国	**3354536**	**883066**	**1510251.5**	**693200.5**	**267**
中央级					
北　京	31462	6381	34863.0	16454.5	2
天　津	9108	5325	10208.2	7293.5	8
河　北	183757	50655	82725.5	49183.3	2
山　西	59246	23690	48446.3	30089.8	7
内蒙古	25211	10193	26277.7	6230.2	5
辽　宁	75273	16311	29418.5	8805.8	
吉　林	23521	4227	11114.1	4729.4	5
黑龙江	42603	10579	14825.7	3341.7	1
上　海	24432	8052	37619.5	16331.5	8
江　苏	276477	46956	132729.1	50688.3	4
浙　江	131389	39840	87177.4	45004.3	24
安　徽	145057	44695	63712.1	30237.4	15
福　建	126484	15724	34754.1	14552.5	5
江　西	72545	33431	29454.8	11472.9	1
山　东	600062	94016	191089.3	120701.6	40
河　南	258896	92849	102986.6	72391.5	15
湖　北	196629	40595	90200.9	34371.6	7
湖　南	214819	61347	50828.6	25311.9	15
广　东	88665	33564	55810.0	21993.3	
广　西	144026	32657	29808.8	9695.8	10
海　南	10658	3937	4154.1	1243.3	4
重　庆	175846	25985	32836.6	15616.5	4
四　川	218367	79904	98678.7	38691.5	20
贵　州	45746	26697	22525.0	16897.6	8
云　南	60962	23279	14858.7	5885.5	14
西　藏	1218	324	923.9	692.6	5
陕　西	46532	24831	152128.1	25372.8	14
甘　肃	25547	13655	7007.4	3557.8	5
青　海	2220	1451	1414.2	970.2	1
宁　夏	3040	1551	1404.3	627.9	
新　疆	34738	10365	10270.3	4764.0	18

义务兵、士官安置

单位：户、万元、人、处

褒扬	安置退役士兵、复员干部				
零散烈士纪念建筑物数		自主就业退役士兵	安排工作退役士兵	供养退役士兵	复员干部
11365	**443824**	**402639**	**37490**	**1157**	**2538**
186	4284	3626	619		39
5	3198	2869	321		8
1120	22403	19437	2846	85	35
1547	8951	5808	3097	1	45
132	4859	3630	1188	4	37
133	7537	6712	544	79	202
527	12456	10777	1642	13	24
88	4715	4418	197	49	51
5	4564	4198	353		13
855	26967	25831	698	1	437
270	18907	18160	671		76
382	26008	24471	1329		208
257	13927	13483	366	50	28
531	17061	15307	1728	7	19
504	43647	39219	4317	39	72
453	47561	42419	4567	325	250
618	28506	27067	1382	16	41
246	23879	21170	2659	16	34
745	18659	18063	407		189
536	13737	13082	634	5	16
79	3018	2462	310	186	60
378	11784	11365	402	1	16
508	37258	35053	1981	6	218
520	9172	8495	667		10
181	11515	9894	1487	12	122
1	286	165	119		2
178	4515	3538	946	1	30
296	6759	5770	897		92
38	1428	1169	172		87
	2446	2114	196	134	2
46	3817	2867	748	127	75

C-2-42 离退休、

地　区	本年接收人员合计	军队离退休干部	离　休	地方离退休干部	离　休	军队退休士官	军队无军籍职工
全　国	**27699**	**10067**	**246**	**221**	**9**	**503**	**16908**
中央级							
北　京	5008	2780	9	3		6	2219
天　津	243	234				2	7
河　北	1244	798	79	58	2	93	295
山　西	337	48	5	2		3	284
内蒙古	150	87	1			7	56
辽　宁	2617	554	24	1	1	12	2050
吉　林	621	136				17	468
黑龙江	343	163	1	14	1	1	165
上　海	1024	378	1			4	642
江　苏	1568	658	11	5	2	28	877
浙　江	593	243	3	4	1	9	337
安　徽	287	132	15	2		24	129
福　建	474	104		3		21	346
江　西	256	53	2	2		2	199
山　东	1786	583				81	1122
河　南	1139	302	4	5		44	788
湖　北	1309	394	15	37		27	851
湖　南	663	107	1	18		11	527
广　东	671	177				5	489
广　西	314	72				2	240
海　南	602	204	10				398
重　庆	326	160		1		11	154
四　川	1756	430	26	17	1	45	1264
贵　州	119	32		4			83
云　南	625	217	2			5	403
西　藏	74	60		10			4
陕　西	1544	511	2			9	1024
甘　肃	1008	172	2	17	1	26	793
青　海	192	50	29				142
宁　夏	145	2	1	7		2	134
新　疆	661	226	3	11		6	418

退职人员

单位：人

本年实有人数合计	军队离退休干部	离　休	地方离退休干部	离　休	军队退休士官	军队无军籍职工	军队离退休干部服务站
356049	**212273**	**21026**	**29395**	**1360**	**6739**	**107642**	**199**
70258	43777	1911	6545	7	566	19370	
7761	5155	519	919	17	82	1605	13
19527	11838	1254	1685	87	1098	4906	16
6693	3617	472	393	27	246	2437	8
4098	2658	314	389	22	58	993	7
30685	21787	1933	1358	191	357	7183	26
2414	305	48	258	13	41	1810	2
5536	3484	367	43	4	75	1934	12
11429	7291	597	113	5	27	3998	7
20612	12539	1334	2314	192	248	5511	3
7755	4253	664	1384	51	46	2072	9
5242	3161	650	553	109	207	1321	9
8264	3618	494	3477	10	86	1083	4
4111	1174	435	1419	49	59	1459	2
25511	17917	2994	751	34	1190	5653	10
12321	7140	968	1156	146	529	3496	8
13916	7454	1030	1460	89	186	4816	1
12205	5369	683	2243	94	182	4411	7
12756	7869	791	414	21	62	4411	4
3458	1933	164	63		53	1409	9
1727	628	49	21	1	10	1068	2
5818	3712	168	132	1	140	1834	9
16453	9452	787	997	27	484	5520	17
2291	1320	187	266	15	11	694	
11734	6694	787	287	10	79	4674	2
1197	499				11	687	
15634	9805	916	262	35	223	5344	6
6788	2850	295	313	27	253	3372	2
2178	762	2	15	3	31	1370	
870	618	47	7		9	236	
6807	3594	166	158	73	90	2965	4

C-2-43 军队离退休

地区	单位数	年末职工人数		受教育程度		职业资
			女性	大学专科人数	大学本科及以上人数	助理社会工作师人数
全　国	**185**	**2426**	**1128**	**728**	**1276**	**45**
中央级						
北　京	32	392	198	105	247	15
天　津	1	41	26	10	31	1
河　北	24	307	158	99	99	4
山　西	2	21	9		15	
内蒙古	1	14	7	5	8	
辽　宁	11	422	153	70	288	1
吉　林						
黑龙江	2	9	3	9		
上　海	7	106	54	49	37	2
江　苏	1	2	1	1	1	
浙　江	13	147	79	30	106	
安　徽	8	51	20	21	19	2
福　建	5	12	7	1		
江　西	1	3	1	2		
山　东	7	151	54	39	86	1
河　南	7	96	47	57	27	3
湖　北	4	54	14	19	33	
湖　南	6	33	20	9	16	
广　东	6	88	38	23	57	8
广　西	4	55	27	11	36	2
海　南	1	5	2	2		
重　庆	5	46	17	26	13	1
四　川	14	132	84	63	38	1
贵　州	2	5	2	2	1	
云　南	10	103	52	31	49	1
西　藏	2	5	3	3	2	
陕　西	4	54	23	11	33	
甘　肃	1	2	1		2	
青　海						
宁　夏	1	1				
新　疆	3	69	28	30	32	3

人员管理中心

单位：个、人、人次、时

格水平	年龄结构				志愿服务	
社会工作师人数	35岁及以下人数	36岁至45岁人数	46岁至55岁人数	56岁及以上人数	志愿者服务人次数	志愿服务时间
72	**957**	**747**	**589**	**133**	**955**	**3792.0**
22	119	134	129	10		
1	25	10	4	2		
4	171	88	41	7	796	3405.0
3	9	9	2	1		
	7	2	5			
1	142	116	117	47	86	86.0
	6	3				
	40	25	29	12	21	168.0
		1	1			
3	61	35	42	9	6	48.0
1	17	16	15	3		
	3	5	3	1		
	1	2				
11	65	47	34	5		
5	27	44	19	6		
	7	13	28	6		
3	12	19	2			
14	36	38	13	1		
2	29	19	6	1		
	1	2	2			
	18	7	20	1		
	42	41	37	12		
	3	2				
	41	39	20	3		
		5				
1	44	5	5		46	85.0
	1	1				
1		1				
	30	18	15	6		

C-2-43续表

地区	增加值合计	执行行政事业单位会计制度财务指标		
		固定资产原价	上年结余	收入合计
全　国	**398317.3**	**142280.8**	**175241.1**	**542238.8**
中央级				
北　京	172886.5	70206.9	138732.7	247850.5
天　津	398.0	500.0		426.0
河　北	17289.3	7693.0	3219.6	26708.5
山　西	1523.9	680.0	428.3	1757.0
内蒙古	5882.3	116.9	1198.8	7203.9
辽　宁	27650.6	8327.3		26379.8
吉　林				
黑龙江	12.0			12.0
上　海	15562.8	4388.8	860.1	28578.5
江　苏	30.0	500.0		15.0
浙　江	22981.8	3674.0	955.1	25477.3
安　徽	6978.2	878.9	21.8	8225.8
福　建	218.2	108.3	44.7	457.3
江　西	3.1	3.0		
山　东	19384.5	5396.1		21800.8
河　南	2103.9	2069.9	1657.5	4512.0
湖　北	4880.0	13450.3	805.0	8397.5
湖　南	798.0	191.0		956.0
广　东	13758.7	5391.2	448.8	14432.7
广　西	10406.3	3611.3	40.2	11006.8
海　南	0.8	21.0		
重　庆	1805.5	779.5		3062.6
四　川	24726.5	2332.7	3735.7	46599.1
贵　州	25.7	1.8	6.2	21.8
云　南	2523.1	1730.2	792.0	3557.4
西　藏	22.5	44.1		20.0
陕　西	19618.6	355.5	12315.7	26605.4
甘　肃	4.5			
青　海				
宁　夏	9.0			10.0
新　疆	26832.9	9829.1	9978.9	28165.1

单位：人、万元

支出合计	收支结余	行政事业单位增加值	年末机构管理军休干部人数	分散安置人数	本年发放离退休金
508246.1	**186364.9**	**398317.3**	**25507**	**14657**	**231828**
212291.2	169711.0	172886.5	855	46	32197
426.0		398.0	412	412	4413
23787.4	5501.6	17289.3	2683	1344	16952
1593.4	161.9	1523.9	133	133	1265
6193.6	2209.1	5882.3	571	571	5129
31063.1	550.7	27650.6	3351	1355	20243
12.0		12.0	16		
27185.3	835.5	15562.8	1904	1033	16466
15.0		30.0			
25135.7	146.7	22981.8	2525	1640	23016
7327.4	55.8	6978.2	669	43	3236
458.6	43.4	218.2	60	51	428
3.0		3.1	2		
21800.8		19384.5	1728	1306	19989
2938.5	248.7	2103.9	287	109	1931
8430.5	805.0	4880.0			
975.9	17.5	798.0	84	75	356
14408.1	20.0	13758.7	914	646	10552
10727.5	319.4	10406.3	743	743	8892
		0.8			
2785.2		1805.5	144	41	1269
45189.6	599.6	24726.5	4435	1423	25136
28.0		25.7			
3167.1		2523.1	105	13	1058
23.0		22.5	173		222
34082.6	5155.9	19618.6	1813	1773	16459
5.5		4.5			
10.0		9.0			
28182.1	-16.9	26832.9	1900	1900	22621

C-2-44 军队离退休

地区	单位数	年末职工人数		受教育程度		职业资
			女性	大学专科人数	大学本科及以上人数	助理社会工作师人数
全国	**30**	**661**	**258**	**178**	**187**	**6**
中央级						
北京	12	498	188	116	119	4
天津	1	11	3		11	
河北	1	3		3		
山西						
内蒙古						
辽宁	2	13	5	3	10	
吉林						
黑龙江	1	4		3	1	
上海	2	49	23	16	25	2
江苏	3	15	6	4	8	
浙江						
安徽						
福建						
江西	1	23	14	10	3	
山东						
河南						
湖北	1	6	4	3	3	
湖南						
广东						
广西						
海南	1	17	6	14	1	
重庆	1	2			2	
四川	3	14	5	5	4	
贵州						
云南						
西藏						
陕西	1	6	4	1		
甘肃						
青海						
宁夏						
新疆						

人员活动中心

单位:个、人、人次、时

格水平	年龄结构				志愿服务	
社会工作师人数	35岁及以下人数	36岁至45岁人数	46岁至55岁人数	56岁及以上人数	志愿者服务人次数	志愿服务时间
4	**257**	**198**	**153**	**53**	**5**	**5.0**
3	212	153	99	34		
	4	1	4	2		
	2		1			
	5	2	6		5	5.0
	2	2				
1	18	12	15	4		
	2	4	8	1		
	1	3	11	8		
	1	3	2			
	5	8	2	2		
		2				
	1	6	5	2		
	4	2				

C-2-44续表

地区	增加值合计	固定资产原价	执行 上年结转和结余
全国	**10033.7**	**69511.7**	**2930.8**
中央级			
北京	3953.3	29902.1	1880.5
天津	920.1	18853.0	
河北	71.0	654.0	
山西			
内蒙古			
辽宁	690.1	6614.2	
吉林			
黑龙江	98.0		
上海	872.5	5418.2	175.7
江苏	431.6	2173.6	42.8
浙江			
安徽			
福建			
江西	136.6	258.1	-43.7
山东			
河南			
湖北	280.6	3180.8	
湖南			
广东			
广西			
海南	2491.4	2141.3	875.5
重庆	5.0		
四川	69.0	248.4	
贵州			
云南			
西藏			
陕西	14.5	68.0	
甘肃			
青海			
宁夏			
新疆			

单位：万元

行政事业单位会计制度财务指标

本年收入合计	本年支出合计	收支结余	行政事业单位增加值
16309.3	**14432.3**	**2769.1**	**10033.7**
3931.4	4402.8	1411.6	3953.3
1935.0	1871.0		920.1
201.0	199.0		71.0
1527.5	776.2		690.1
398.0	398.0		98.0
3926.5	2769.8	322.5	872.5
424.9	439.4	18.3	431.6
281.4	281.8	-44.1	136.6
549.3	549.3		280.6
3054.6	2654.4	1060.8	2491.4
11.0	11.0		5.0
68.7	67.6		69.0
	12.0		14.5

C-2-45 烈士纪念

地区	单位数	年末职工人数		受教育程度		职业资
			女性	大学专科人数	大学本科及以上人数	助理社会工作师人数
全国	**1516**	**10201**	**4031**	**3137**	**1973**	**117**
中央级						
北京	5	61	26	10	22	2
天津	9	140	56	31	36	
河北	106	885	326	195	200	19
山西	59	388	165	123	51	2
内蒙古	13	116	39	39	38	3
辽宁	46	329	134	101	113	2
吉林	30	376	93	115	55	4
黑龙江	25	201	75	91	52	1
上海	11	236	89	97	55	
江苏	88	685	267	183	196	17
浙江	40	185	83	37	75	5
安徽	51	396	164	123	50	7
福建	54	182	68	38	32	1
江西	67	293	120	56	35	
山东	116	938	360	372	301	10
河南	99	1359	637	470	173	13
湖北	56	690	298	273	85	1
湖南	42	390	160	101	35	4
广东	115	318	131	68	70	5
广西	23	307	126	72	63	9
海南	8	38	12	5	6	
重庆	20	72	25	31	27	
四川	165	444	169	162	49	7
贵州	55	137	34	49	24	
云南	64	162	27	54	18	1
西藏	5	14	6	7	1	
陕西	41	352	186	112	40	1
甘肃	79	385	109	84	41	2
青海	1	9	3	7	2	
宁夏	9	29	11	8	6	
新疆	14	84	32	23	22	1

建筑物管理机构

单位：个、人、人次、时

格水平	年龄结构				志愿服务	
社会工作师人数	35岁及以下人数	36岁至45岁人数	46岁至55岁人数	56岁及以上人数	志愿者服务人次数	志愿服务时间
172	**3110**	**3941**	**2553**	**597**	**23446**	**59627.4**
2	29	17	10	5	226	238.0
	36	46	46	12	1000	2000.0
20	269	341	216	59	943	3395.0
6	93	137	131	27		0.4
3	27	42	37	10		
4	102	105	89	33	38	129.0
	111	166	93	6		
	47	80	65	9	30	86.0
3	39	60	91	46	208	1016.0
32	149	257	233	46	1821	6718.0
9	53	68	53	11	686	2273.0
14	88	180	117	11	1021	2121.0
1	30	74	57	21		
	72	115	100	6	192	648.0
21	348	348	198	44	14942	35306.0
33	593	496	245	25	6	18.0
2	200	279	143	68	312	842.0
	126	166	90	8	224	565.0
2	75	121	106	16		
3	85	98	65	59		
	17	11	10			
	18	41	11	2	79	265.0
7	104	217	89	34	18	30.0
	29	54	44	10	1530	3437.0
1	37	84	36	5		
	5	7	1	1		
4	153	148	45	6	150	430.0
4	140	137	94	14	20	110.0
	1	1	6	1		
	8	14	7			
1	26	31	25	2		

C-2-45续表

地　区	增加值合计	执行行政事业单位会计制度财务指标				
		固定资产原价	上年结转和结余	本年收入合计	本年支出合计	收支结余
全　国	**84413.4**	**511874.9**	**15528.0**	**164144.0**	**162170.6**	**12738.0**
中央级						
北　京	968.4	11915.4	742.6	1684.0	2132.2	299.6
天　津	2299.6	12146.4	1.4	2904.6	2323.0	578.4
河　北	6239.1	26117.7	1895.9	17997.0	17794.8	904.6
山　西	2930.6	14414.3	1178.2	8319.9	8822.2	479.3
内蒙古	1510.4	8970.1	581.6	1887.1	1980.5	189.2
辽　宁	1953.5	7300.6	656.5	4083.0	3739.9	459.9
吉　林	1344.9	7048.7	515.3	2453.2	3104.4	613.0
黑龙江	1010.7	5874.6	421.0	1277.4	1352.9	0.6
上　海	6963.8	68440.8	1275.6	9017.0	9040.1	1256.9
江　苏	8356.9	36419.0	334.4	13956.2	13450.1	514.2
浙　江	2457.1	10649.0	798.7	5113.1	4804.0	629.8
安　徽	3583.8	24934.2	48.4	4438.1	4050.2	4.3
福　建	1317.0	4548.5	406.6	3449.4	2806.4	847.6
江　西	1577.8	9520.4	107.5	2191.5	2310.4	
山　东	10974.3	58204.1		31956.2	31956.2	
河　南	4604.6	26291.2	62.9	8215.3	8169.6	54.7
湖　北	4029.8	24082.9	-309.5	6207.8	6081.1	-45.0
湖　南	2440.9	21577.6	46.3	2842.0	2775.4	-5.1
广　东	4044.7	18873.0	1384.1	14780.8	11655.6	4364.4
广　西	3123.5	16613.0	0.4	5014.6	6071.1	994.6
海　南	272.7	2404.0	200.0	12.0	372.2	200.0
重　庆	533.3	4455.8	35.3	1311.1	1302.0	44.4
四　川	3326.1	47650.7	2420.5	3282.5	3784.4	198.1
贵　州	905.6	9776.9	32.4	583.5	609.0	19.3
云　南	644.1	8332.9	148.0	405.9	439.3	
西　藏	50.2	1212.5			2.0	
陕　西	2364.1	15208.7	264.4	3397.0	3415.4	53.4
甘　肃	3847.2	5043.1	6.8	4423.5	4325.9	4.7
青　海	17.5	437.0		273.0	273.0	
宁　夏	83.0	805.5	16.8	183.3	124.0	77.1
新　疆	638.1	2606.3	2255.9	2484.0	3103.3	

单位：万元、平方米、个、人次

行政事业单位增加值	管理单位占地面积	烈士纪念建筑物面积	烈士纪念建筑物数	纪念馆（陈列馆）个数	藏品数	参观人次数	本机构管理的其他烈士纪念园地数
84413.4	**45641179.7**	**5695009.9**	**9289**	**1299**	**226061**	**75613996**	**505**
968.4	83326.0	22895.0	41	6	1093	295500	7
2299.6	339913.3	43191.3	35	14	1563	711890	
6239.1	3114255.3	241711.4	472	95	38963	4116593	86
2930.6	1580862.0	340349.0	152	54	3927	1563121	
1510.4	583223.0	51162.0	33	17	335	371665	2
1953.5	1701772.4	268155.0	630	26	14350	1034158	2
1344.9	634570.0	26304.0	395	27	5437	765279	7
1010.7	426538.7	101164.7	403	16	7595	2683669	1
6963.8	374550.0	42204.7	65	16	2607	1781302	5
8356.9	3040645.5	518669.0	366	108	19980	7461252	4
2457.1	1105412.1	89190.3	136	39	6664	1760568	21
3583.8	4864859.8	282425.0	926	199	5840	4170081	5
1317.0	754954.6	70611.7	175	23	1578	3224037	22
1577.8	657444.8	180221.0	218	19	7928	962026	46
10974.3	5430657.0	520130.1	711	164	31357	16294761	10
4604.6	2528256.9	233071.2	895	100	10441	3569641	85
4029.8	2343902.7	189096.5	493	71	18167	3555224	60
2440.9	1245392.1	337262.9	102	19	3461	1472334	1
4044.7	1476463.0	156093.7	251	13	1072	5002884	7
3123.5	2267419.4	173777.1	64	10	2199	1163536	2
272.7	547571.0	159801.0	485	21	1181	935485	25
533.3	217590.0	70665.8	124	18	2931	2327448	35
3326.1	5556599.9	768796.6	931	95	9642	3355578	25
905.6	879679.0	272384.0	239	13	424	1195908	11
644.1	984989.1	239150.8	212	20	2311	700007	12
50.2	63920.0	15454.0	12	4	5702	16433	1
2364.1	496923.0	91464.0	413	38	4589	1666747	2
3847.2	650048.0	85905.0	260	37	7846	2526722	20
17.5	59236.8	9990.0	12	2	5400	45000	
83.0	293044.0	41579.6	9	5	859	127959	
638.1	1337160.3	52133.5	29	10	619	757188	1

C-2-46 自然灾害损失

地区	人口受灾情况				
	受灾人口	死亡人口	失踪人口	紧急转移安置人口	需紧急生活救助人口
合计	**24353.7**	**1583**	**235**	**601.7**	**298.3**
北京	32.1	1			
天津	3.7	1			
河北	1716.1	13			2.5
山西	476	9		0.5	0.8
内蒙古	644.5	17		0.8	0.6
辽宁	746.7	8		0.1	
吉林	545.5	1		1.1	0.2
黑龙江	257.4	11		2.4	6.3
上海					
江苏	548.4	1		0.1	
浙江	471.4	19	1	50.3	6.6
安徽	1201.6	6		5.6	0.8
福建	155.8	22	1	28.3	1.3
江西	634.2	50		47	21.4
山东	959.8	1		1.6	3
河南	2491	10		0.6	
湖北	986.9	22	2	5.8	6
湖南	1704.9	65	6	79.5	47.8
广东	742.8	66	5	54	19.6
广西	1100.5	59	1	54.1	28.8
海南	621.4	27	7	29	9
重庆	649.7	111	18	44.4	12.9
四川	1611.9	57	6	33.9	22.7
贵州	1493.8	126	20	73.6	44.4
云南	1414.8	777	165	58.6	39.2
西藏	17.6	18		0.2	
陕西	1208.5	37		21.3	1.8
甘肃	1052.7	7	2	0.3	0.2
青海	129.8	9	1	0.1	0.5
宁夏	220.6	4			1.4
新疆	433.4	24		8.1	7.3
兵团	80.2	4		0.4	13.2

情况总表

单位：万人次、人、千公顷、万间、亿元

农作物受灾情况		房屋倒损情况			直接经济损失
受灾面积	绝收面积	倒塌房屋	严重损坏房屋	一般损坏房屋	
24890.7	**3090.3**	**45**	**98.5**	**255.7**	**3373.8**
53.3	11.3			0.5	10.5
10.3	4.3				1.3
1435.7	176.7			0.6	135.1
1173.5	113.7	0.2	0.4	0.9	50.8
1878.3	258.9	0.1	0.3	0.8	113.1
1931.4	550.6			0.1	169.6
689.3	117.8	0.3	0.8	0.8	117.4
810	114.3	0.3	1.2	2.1	55.8
554.1	39.8			0.2	14
204	13.8	0.3	0.9	10.8	64.4
641.3	22	0.2	0.2	0.4	29.4
102.6	11.1	0.2	0.3	3.1	45.4
487.1	46.6	1.8	1.6	5.7	72.8
886.1	76.7	0.1	0.1	0.8	82.4
1905.2	210.4	0.3	0.2	0.7	118.7
1058.8	72.8	1.5	1.7	3.6	68.4
1136.1	192	4	6.6	18.2	206.5
842.4	159.5	3.3	6.8	9	337.1
1212.7	61.1	2.1	3.2	24.8	191.7
309.4	110.8	2.5	14.2	4.6	177.4
280.9	34.4	6.1	6.6	10.4	98.5
919.3	80.9	3.9	8.9	24.5	205.4
626.7	97.4	3.2	7.3	23.7	198
882	87.4	11.1	28.8	90	444.2
12.9	4.6	0.1	0.2	0.5	1.9
772.2	102.6	1.8	2.9	8	93.4
1618.4	66.8	0.1	0.5	1.3	74.6
169.8	18.1		0.1	0.3	9.3
438.3	38.8		0.3	0.3	16.6
1137.7	140.6	1.5	4	8.2	115.6
710.9	54.5		0.4	0.8	54.5

C−2−47 旱灾

地 区	人口受灾情况		
	受灾人口	因旱需生活救助人口	因旱饮水困难需救助人口
合 计	**10194.7**	**1473.1**	**1012.5**
北 京	18.4	1.2	0.8
天 津			
河 北	1275.4	98.7	35.3
山 西	155	10.8	3.8
内蒙古	482.1	200.8	125.5
辽 宁	659.7	126.6	37.3
吉 林	506.3	170.7	15.7
黑龙江	12.3		
上 海			
江 苏	475.1		
浙 江			
安 徽	593.6	5.8	5.8
福 建			
江 西			
山 东	751.9	55.2	26.1
河 南	2365.3	153.9	147.4
湖 北	522.5	121.3	97.5
湖 南			
广 东			
广 西	28.1	6.1	2.8
海 南			
重 庆	31.1	3.7	2.6
四 川	593.8	177.2	128.7
贵 州	18	1.1	1.1
云 南	420.3	121.9	253
西 藏	4.4	2.7	
陕 西	870.2	81.9	59.9
甘 肃	142.5	19.2	10.6
青 海	10.2	0.7	0.1
宁 夏	120.1	78.1	51.3
新 疆	125.7	27.2	6.5
兵 团	12.7	8.3	0.7

损失情况

单位:万人次、千公顷、万头、亿元

农作物受灾情况		损失情况	
受灾面积	绝收面积	饮水困难大牲畜	直接经济损失
12271.7	**1484.7**	**1157.2**	**835.6**
26.1	6.8		3.7
1027.9	107.8	15.6	102.1
721.6	41.4	1.6	11
1313.6	183.5	420.1	85.9
1811.4	543.7	7.8	162.8
568.3	97.3	1.9	104.8
61.8	10.8		3
473.9	34.5		10.2
283.3	16.5		10
688.5	60		51
1809.3	203.8	21.9	110.6
633.5	21.8	24	23.1
15.6	0.2		0.5
7.6	1.1	3.1	0.3
576.8	21.3	89.7	17.4
9.5		0.5	0.3
332	19.1	150	14.5
4.1	1.5		0.3
434.7	42.7	9	44.3
644.2	13.9		9.4
23.9	0.1	10.5	0.1
227.8	12.9	55.1	5.8
435.8	32.5	346.4	50.6
140.5	11.5		13.9

C-2-48 风雹灾害

地区	人口受灾情况				
	受灾人口（万人次）	死亡人口（人）	失踪人口（人）	紧急转移安置人口	需紧急生活救助人口
合 计	**2226.7**	**161**	**6**	**9.7**	**17.9**
北 京	13.7	1			
天 津	3.7	1			
河 北	296.7	3			1.7
山 西	106.2	1		0.1	0.7
内蒙古	117.8	12		0.7	0.6
辽 宁	19.4	4			
吉 林	24.9	1			0.1
黑龙江	49.8	4		0.1	
上 海					
江 苏	52.3	1		0.1	
浙 江	22.4	1			
安 徽	6.1	4			
福 建	6.7			0.1	0.1
江 西	34.2	22		0.7	0.4
山 东	64.4	1			
河 南	51.4	5			
湖 北	35.8	5	1	0.3	0.2
湖 南	37.2	7		0.6	0.4
广 东	7.7	21	1	0.5	0.3
广 西	39.5	13		1.1	0.7
海 南					
重 庆	63.4	5		0.4	0.4
四 川	62.6	1		0.2	0.6
贵 州	343	6	2	2.7	1.3
云 南	176.6	16	1	0.3	2.2
西 藏	3.6	15			
陕 西	148.6	1		0.1	
甘 肃	139.1		1	0.1	
青 海	47.9	2			
宁 夏	47.2	4			0.4
新 疆	181	4		1.6	5.1
兵 团	23.8				2.7

损失情况

单位：万人次、人、千公顷、万间、亿元

农作物受灾情况		房屋倒损情况			直接经济损失
受灾面积	绝收面积	倒塌房屋	严重损坏房屋	一般损坏房屋	
3225.4	**457.7**	**1.3**	**4**	**25.7**	**276.7**
27.2	4.5			0.5	6.8
10.3	4.3				1.3
254.2	26.3			0.3	20.5
153.9	19.9		0.1	0.4	12.7
439.4	50.9	0.1	0.2	0.6	22.5
24.1	5.5			0.1	4.1
89.2	14.4			0.3	6.3
234.9	34.7		0.2	0.4	8.5
56.3	5			0.2	2.8
5.3	0.2			0.2	1.5
9.8					0.4
2.7	0.2			1.5	0.8
42.4	4.4	0.2	0.1	1	4.6
57.7	13.8		0.1	0.2	22.5
37.7	2.9	0.1	0.1	0.2	3.8
48.8	4.2	0.1	0.1	0.2	2.8
21.4	4.2	0.1	0.3	0.7	2.4
15.3	0.6		0.6	0.9	4.1
14.8	1.1	0.1	0.2	1.7	1.8
20.7	2	0.1	0.2	1.5	2.1
29.8	5	0.1	0.2	1.2	4
160.9	30.4	0.2	0.8	5.2	14.9
157.1	19.3		0.3	6	16.9
4.7	2	0.1	0.1		0.5
189.8	31.8		0.1	0.8	21.1
143.1	22.1		0.1	0.3	13.9
67.5	9.7				3.9
94.2	23.1			0.2	6.9
586	89	0.1	0.2	0.9	44
226.2	26.2			0.2	18.3

C-2-49 台风灾害

地区	人口受灾情况				
	受灾人口	死亡人口	失踪人口	紧急转移安置人口	需紧急生活救助人口
合计	**2659.5**	**94**	**17**	**177.3**	**45**
北京					
天津					
河北					
山西					
内蒙古					
辽宁	9.4			0.1	
吉林					
黑龙江					
上海					
江苏	16.2				
浙江	158.5			32.9	0.2
安徽	68.9			2.5	0.1
福建	70.9			21.2	0.8
江西	52	10		4.1	2.8
山东	54.2			0.8	0.1
河南					
湖北					
湖南					
广东	554.5	2		35	7.5
广西	766	15		47.1	22.9
海南	612.4	27	7	28.6	9
重庆					
四川					
贵州	15.8			0.4	0.1
云南	280.7	40	10	4.6	1.5
西藏					
陕西					
甘肃					
青海					
宁夏					
新疆					
兵团					

注：台风灾害损失包含台风风暴潮。

损失情况

单位:万人次、人、千公顷、万间、亿元

农作物受灾情况		房屋倒损情况			直接经济损失
受灾面积	绝收面积	倒塌房屋	严重损坏房屋	一般损坏房屋	
2483.1	**348.7**	**5.2**	**24.4**	**38.2**	**693.4**
8.9	0.7				0.9
21.1	0.3				0.7
57.3	3.1			0.1	10.8
38.1	0.7	0.1	0.1	0.1	2.8
48.5	4.8		0.1	0.3	16.5
35.2	6.8	0.1	0.2	0.5	12.2
73.8	2.4	0.1		0.4	6.1
699.6	147.6	0.7	5.8	6.6	255.3
1050.8	47.9	1.3	2.4	21.4	170.1
307.8	110.7	2.5	14.2	4.6	176.9
7	1.4		0.1	0.1	1.4
135	22.3	0.4	1.5	4.1	39.7

C-2-50 地震灾害

地区	人口受灾情况				
	受灾人口	死亡人口	失踪人口	紧急转移安置人口	需紧急生活救助人口
合计	**310.6**	**624**	**112**	**65.9**	**35.7**
北京					
天津					
河北	0.1				
山西					
内蒙古					
辽宁					
吉林	0.3			0.3	
黑龙江					
上海					
江苏					
浙江	13.8			4.7	
安徽	0.1				
福建					
江西					
山东	1.3				
河南					
湖北	4.1				0.1
湖南					
广东					
广西					
海南					
重庆					
四川	20.3	5		2	0.8
贵州	1.6			0.8	
云南	220.5	619	112	52.2	34.8
西藏	0.3				
陕西					
甘肃	0.4				
青海					
宁夏					
新疆	45.9			5.5	
兵团	1.9			0.4	

损失情况

单位：万人次、人、千公顷、万间、亿元

农作物受灾情况		房屋倒损情况			直接经济损失
受灾面积	绝收面积	倒塌房屋	严重损坏房屋	一般损坏房屋	
36.4	**2.8**	**11.5**	**33.3**	**104**	**408**
				0.1	
			0.1	0.1	0.2
			0.7	9.2	6.4
				0.1	0.3
			0.1	0.6	0.5
			2.7	9.7	38.7
0.7			0.2	0.7	2.8
35.7	2.8	10.3	26.2	78	346.4
				0.2	
				0.3	0.1
		1.2	2.9	4.3	11
			0.4	0.5	1.6

C–2–51 低温冷冻和

地区	人口受灾情况				
	受灾人口	死亡人口	失踪人口	紧急转移安置人口	需紧急生活救助人口
合　计	**1761.4**	**17**		**1.8**	**21.4**
北　京					
天　津					
河　北	82.8				
山　西	149.7				0.1
内蒙古	31.5				
辽　宁	53				
吉　林	4.6				0.1
黑龙江	55.4				
上　海					
江　苏					
浙　江	4.9	10		0.2	
安　徽	62.5				
福　建	0.4				
江　西	36.9				
山　东	2.4			0.1	0.1
河　南	10.5				
湖　北	86.2				0.3
湖　南	124.7			0.8	2.1
广　东	6.8				
广　西	21.9			0.2	1.2
海　南					
重　庆	10.1				1
四　川	32.3				0.5
贵　州	101.5			0.3	2.6
云　南	82.3				0.2
西　藏	2.2	2			
陕　西	3.1				
甘　肃	602.8				
青　海	56.8				0.1
宁　夏	50.8				1
新　疆	43.8	1		0.2	1.6
兵　团	41.5	4			10.5

雪灾损失情况

单位:万人次、人、千公顷、万间、亿元

农作物受灾情况		房屋倒损情况			直接经济损失
受灾面积	绝收面积	倒塌房屋	严重损坏房屋	一般损坏房屋	
2132.5	**168.2**	**0.1**	**0.5**	**1.2**	**129.2**
105.2	38.1				9
207.7	38.7				20.9
47.5	0.2				1.6
72.9					0.8
7.5					0.6
					5.4
0.5					0.1
6.5					0.7
41	0.1				1.6
2.1					
28.4	0.1				1.1
0.2					0.1
9.9					0.3
82.9	10.7			0.1	3.5
73.2	4.9		0.1	0.4	3.9
5.3	0.1				0.6
15.1	0.9				1.1
1.7	0.3				0.4
17.5	2.5				2.6
43.9	1.9			0.1	1.6
74.5	5			0.1	3.1
0.2					0.2
4.5	1.1				0.4
675.8	22.8				36.4
64.3	5.5				3.6
114.7	2.8			0.1	3.8
85.6	15.7	0.1	0.4	0.3	5.2
343.9	16.8			0.1	20.6

C－2－52 洪涝、滑坡和

地区	人口受灾情况				
	受灾人口	死亡人口	失踪人口	紧急转移安置人口	需紧急生活救助人口
合计	**7200.1**	**631**	**97**	**347**	**178.3**
北京					
天津					
河北	61.1	9			0.8
山西	65.1	8		0.4	
内蒙古	13.1	5		0.1	
辽宁	5.2	4			
吉林	9.4			0.8	
黑龙江	139.9	7		2.3	6.3
上海					
江苏	4.8				
浙江	271.8	5		12.5	6.4
安徽	470.4	1		3.1	0.7
福建	77.8	15	1	7	0.4
江西	511.1	18		42.2	18.2
山东	85.6			0.7	2.8
河南	63.8	2		0.6	
湖北	338.3	16	1	5.5	5.4
湖南	1543	54	6	78.1	45.3
广东	173.8	31	2	18.5	11.8
广西	245	28	1	5.7	4
海南	9			0.4	
重庆	545.1	106	18	44	11.5
四川	902.2	49	6	31.7	20.8
贵州	1013.9	114	18	69.4	40.4
云南	234.4	95	42	1.5	0.5
西藏	7.1	1		0.2	
陕西	186.6	30		21.2	1.8
甘肃	167.9	7	1	0.2	0.2
青海	14.9	7	1	0.1	0.4
宁夏	2.5				
新疆	37	19		0.8	0.6
兵团	0.3				

泥石流灾害损失情况

单位:万人次、人、千公顷、万间、亿元

农作物受灾情况		房屋倒损情况			直接经济损失
受灾面积	绝收面积	倒塌房屋	严重损坏房屋	一般损坏房屋	
4738.9	**628.2**	**26.9**	**36.3**	**86.8**	**1029.8**
48.4	4.5			0.2	3.5
90.3	13.7	0.2	0.3	0.5	6.2
77.8	24.3		0.1	0.2	3.1
14.1	0.7				0.8
24.3	6.1	0.3	0.7	0.4	5.5
513.3	68.8	0.3	1	1.7	38.9
2.3					0.2
134.9	10.5	0.3	0.2	1.3	45
269.1	4.7	0.1	0.1	0.3	14.6
49.3	6.1	0.2	0.2	1.3	27.4
381.1	35.3	1.5	1.3	4.2	54.9
65.9	0.5			0.1	2.4
48.3	3.7	0.2	0.1	0.5	4
293.6	36.1	1.4	1.5	2.7	38.5
1041.5	182.9	3.9	6.2	17.1	200.2
122.2	11.2	2.6	0.4	1.5	77.1
116.4	11	0.7	0.6	1.7	18.2
1.6	0.1				0.5
250.9	31	6	6.4	8.9	95.7
292.5	52.1	3.8	6	13.6	142.6
404.7	63.7	3	6.2	17.6	177
147.7	18.9	0.4	0.8	1.8	23.6
3.9	1.1		0.1	0.3	0.9
143.2	27	1.8	2.8	7.2	27.5
155.3	8	0.1	0.4	0.7	14.8
14.1	2.8		0.1	0.3	1.7
1.6			0.3		0.1
30.3	3.4	0.1	0.5	2.7	4.8
0.3					0.1

C-3-1 成员组

地 区	单位数	民政登记	依法成立	年末职工人数	女性	受教育程度 大学专科人数	大学本科及以上人数
全 国	**1288192**	**606048**	**682144**	**9624685**	**2770933**	**1651158**	**1002070**
中央级	2252	2252		33101	14510	368	23872
北 京	15952	9083	6869	138430	55260	32939	44520
天 津	10002	4729	5273	63474	27657	16991	20694
河 北	70113	17642	52471	445436	103796	57568	35111
山 西	42684	12330	30354	259464	69104	48000	24057
内蒙古	25217	11790	13427	140129	43817	30751	11882
辽 宁	35800	20137	15663	276118	92214	59169	39421
吉 林	21829	10521	11308	90318	23601	11477	4092
黑龙江	24220	12479	11741	191756	68057	30207	9968
上 海	18092	12365	5727	184712	48996	65503	22036
江 苏	92971	71571	21400	644141	180718	142830	88677
浙 江	72162	39844	32318	482528	143611	109857	58842
安 徽	40592	22549	18043	308726	83705	64425	35928
福 建	38105	21357	16748	329505	71627	31289	23568
江 西	34555	14236	20319	257293	73362	28267	9246
山 东	121180	41165	80015	662816	173985	152908	92296
河 南	78914	27572	51342	433007	119368	75762	37669
湖 北	56195	26560	29635	468260	136693	84843	29233
湖 南	70634	24011	46623	407790	128456	77328	41820
广 东	73613	47680	25933	697549	280274	151974	102511
广 西	36504	20321	16183	402166	88969	49035	30280
海 南	7883	4847	3036	61013	20828	9167	3988
重 庆	25417	14387	11030	200061	81445	43412	38259
四 川	90923	37800	53123	727622	198747	105280	65784
贵 州	28187	9424	18763	262882	63447	32412	38297
云 南	33445	19207	14238	520084	176248	45240	24583
西 藏	6064	600	5464	37091	9847	1047	576
陕 西	46811	18050	28761	360353	79288	33157	13987
甘 肃	31697	14400	17297	237484	44808	19973	8683
青 海	7970	3362	4608	35087	7952	2855	792
宁 夏	7065	4324	2741	71827	15691	7852	4558
新 疆	21144	9453	11691	194462	44852	29272	16840

织总表

单位：个、人、人次、时

职业资格水平		年龄结构			志愿服务		
助理社会工作师人数	社会工作师人数	35岁及以下人数	36岁至45岁人数	46岁至55岁人数	56岁及以上人数	志愿者服务人次数	志愿服务时间
31381	**14442**	**2857661**	**3709919**	**2178135**	**878970**	**2801900**	**7589678.5**
749	1471	10074	11516	6620	4891		
3766	1838	35882	46347	36820	19381	162568	521477.0
859	226	16135	19101	17950	10288	21492	61376.0
1379	710	132922	181548	102791	28175	50563	236936.0
162	161	76747	91448	64160	27109	4472	6842.0
118	32	42872	53359	31824	12074	10590	30744.0
1226	424	70196	100712	63240	41970	41006	54830.0
575	238	18458	60361	8944	2555	21	30.0
356	177	69196	73063	39141	10356	20538	54217.0
1185	523	52368	61775	46339	24230	470060	997516.0
5216	1412	180395	237938	162419	63389	281822	688578.5
1951	979	144835	184717	99861	53115	162790	365092.0
2450	580	87053	119242	77052	25379	98530	229993.0
778	376	76048	110890	87052	55515	20087	40252.0
665	157	77989	117796	47856	13652	1546	4118.0
867	370	188576	277655	151611	44974	245855	629502.0
340	172	141667	171875	90190	29275	59	33.0
422	271	143059	161359	140904	22938	22845	73380.0
531	198	131233	166200	83233	27124	151666	514586.0
3370	2914	299894	216417	134615	46623	36773	98155.0
742	171	98329	153755	105840	44242	7362	17724.0
27	3	20735	27964	9294	3020		
1097	335	71978	67191	40872	20020	365119	1063468.0
1390	388	241501	269095	135327	81699	88575	291693.0
123	28	68686	114800	58927	20469	494602	1507125.0
535	105	145785	176875	108925	88499	1311	2705.0
		7947	13577	10324	5243		
118	45	87574	130129	113761	28889	3741	12307.0
131	49	49426	122344	53600	12114	58	40.0
52	10	8506	14622	9665	2294	23619	44511.0
30	4	9240	47215	11608	3764	265	350.0
171	75	52355	109033	27370	5704	13965	42098.0

C-3-1续表

地区	增加值合计	执行企业会计制度单位财务指标						执行行政
		固定资产原价	营业收入	费用合计	营业利润	企业单位增加值	固定资产原价	上年结转和结余
全　国	**10816988.3**	**2863527.7**	**1362536.0**	**39664.3**	**24846.5**	**212970.2**	**15388113.1**	**1257310.1**
中央级	200422.1							
北　京	631024.7	2461730.3	1300932.8	37799.2	23912.1	183221.3	526232.8	188033.2
天　津	77768.8						186878.4	19854.4
河　北	324399.5	355.0					601962.3	17628.9
山　西	212668.2						461064.7	3348.5
内蒙古	79720.2	30.0	2.0	2.0			87149.5	3528.6
辽　宁	299859.8	1771.9				11.0	197433.3	15739.4
吉　林	28339.8						72034.2	1968.3
黑龙江	137109.3	4318.5	14.0	14.8		100.2	350133.9	295822.7
上　海	763504.2	329337.5	59220.0	1538.3	928.4	21045.6	1021996.8	135631.4
江　苏	1287837.3		140.0	105.0			2169608.8	85330.3
浙　江	939315.0	1626.0					3420466.4	91541.4
安　徽	294216.1						347930.0	10185.2
福　建	162652.5	100.3	385.0				116211.8	3579.9
江　西	251287.7	12593.0	1568.0	201.0	6.0	421.1	118702.1	1370.2
山　东	1271440.1						1399096.4	
河　南	164088.2	6748.0	36.0				245667.9	3462.2
湖　北	331884.0	1898.4					446958.8	3818.2
湖　南	300495.2	12.0					267321.3	7993.0
广　东	1602515.3	26058.5	215.2			8152.6	1715670.5	87720.0
广　西	106111.7	211.0				15.4	170845.5	1388.4
海　南	57012.6	2.5					25637.7	1255.9
重　庆	191073.2	14.0					165063.4	10580.0
四　川	364096.9	3041.4					257128.1	161985.1
贵　州	116748.1	75.0					39455.6	4077.6
云　南	226589.3	1162.6		2.0		19.0	393352.5	87707.3
西　藏	2266.3	7491.0					21357.5	8.2
陕　西	210246.7						173632.6	1723.4
甘　肃	62411.3	30.5					145180.0	3509.2
青　海	10330.2						4907.1	28.0
宁　夏	30739.0	1558.0				26.0	140004.9	4675.0
新　疆	78814.5	3362.3	23.0	2.0		-42.0	99028.3	3816.2

单位：万元

事业单位会计制度财务指标				执行民间非营利组织单位会计制度财务指标				
本年收入合计	本年支出合计	收支结余	行政事业单位增加值	固定资产原价	上年结余	本年收入合计	本年费用合计	社会组织增加值
8388876.7	**11462858.9**	**32143.6**	**3839288.6**	**17841106.8**	**8014435.3**	**22305318.3**	**19956262.4**	**6764729.5**
				760245.7		4300338.0	3583248.7	200422.1
253518.0	329772.5	3177.6	237521.0	673642.1	938559.3	1292623.9	1000789.5	210282.4
151053.3	152332.2		35522.1	96222.5	20909.7	190319.9	170381.1	42246.7
330059.2	328596.0		88098.7	1041865.4	446993.5	351099.6	384330.0	236300.8
151956.7	169252.4	5.3	101896.5	253192.3	12454.9	175187.2	169521.0	110771.7
56885.9	61162.5	2.2	37546.9	88759.3	268.4	76029.5	77430.3	42173.3
105928.0	171486.1	3717.7	101226.7	475135.9	384510.9	362688.6	514493.7	198622.1
31814.9	29262.6	26.2	15282.3	11061.8	375.3	14866.6	22402.4	13057.5
52693.2	57580.9		42875.8	133787.1	802.6	32100.6	190070.2	94133.3
461963.8	393031.8	7428.1	214920.6	295334.2	2138298.5	2529959.4	2058285.0	527538.0
797255.2	964406.2	1493.9	529773.9	2303505.5	1636584.5	2771276.5	2219139.8	758063.4
1204645.3	1021754.4	8854.5	558106.4	2057434.8	591325.8	1373243.3	1234707.8	381208.6
131662.8	128445.9	355.6	88150.3	813553.0	11991.2	426543.7	415641.0	206065.8
133368.2	135485.1	44.0	37001.0	362080.7	149916.8	234803.9	250528.8	125651.5
60363.6	62246.9	538.0	36249.7	267797.5	7031.6	241145.9	915254.4	214616.9
1175714.0	1175714.0		678407.5	653346.7	72.0	845096.9	846158.7	593032.6
124443.6	128655.9	248.8	54863.4	456525.5	38803.2	253560.9	197615.6	109224.8
199064.1	203138.1		119587.2	537128.0	18276.5	499384.3	464920.3	212296.8
254774.0	254786.1	834.3	150114.1	411780.6	66844.6	308298.8	314233.0	150381.1
817800.0	604854.4	725.6	341925.3	2668583.0	229479.3	2494792.6	2104318.8	1252437.4
88116.3	53877.7	149.0	46523.2	155627.6	72387.5	91943.7	88602.2	59573.1
20247.7	19268.1	247.7	10107.1	150097.0	211.2	60498.6	57880.8	46905.5
65741.6	72179.7	3287.9	44649.9	648516.9	190333.7	674214.0	606688.0	146423.3
1354184.3	1354184.1	584.6	92867.8	799416.0	650387.5	698563.6	845752.6	271229.1
25619.6	25518.6	2.7	24448.5	337351.6	41685.4	161215.0	142435.0	92299.6
82732.6	76451.6	384.9	42810.2	546217.8	243089.7	260004.7	322790.5	183760.1
741.9	759.1		858.4	5866.8	13056.5	3076.8	2688.6	1407.9
67114.3	63771.3		48206.6	520659.8	5443.7	56582.9	220503.9	162040.1
66427.7	26796.6	10.0	22927.9	106599.1	2888.6	1383510.4	56513.4	39483.4
778.9	685.4		279.9	54186.3	632.7	33150.1	28258.9	10050.3
80195.0	4185.5		8906.8	54365.9	22952.0	38254.8	376342.3	21806.2
42013.0	3393217.2	25.0	27632.4	101220.4	77868.2	70943.6	74336.1	51224.1

C-3-2 社会组

地区	单位数	年末职工人数	女性	受教育程度		职业资格水平	
				大学专科人数	大学本科及以上人数	助理社会工作师人数	社会工作师人数
全国	**606048**	**6822623**	**2003785**	**1304048**	**887693**	**16651**	**9324**
中央级	2252	33101	14510	368	23872	749	1471
北京	9083	104147	37214	22174	36845	1086	888
天津	4729	38270	15926	10850	17917	119	71
河北	17642	260419	71292	46143	33187	1252	619
山西	12330	148571	42896	36427	19196	46	70
内蒙古	11790	87880	26901	24263	9918	12	7
辽宁	20137	204806	62657	38676	32876	362	91
吉林	10521	55888	11843	11034	3744	556	223
黑龙江	12479	138980	50623	18749	7760	107	135
上海	12365	157443	33570	58955	18957	511	273
江苏	71571	533822	146460	117621	79030	2115	554
浙江	39844	356994	107451	89500	51753	345	279
安徽	22549	231774	60682	53932	33808	1632	310
福建	21357	259139	55110	28253	22914	562	257
江西	14236	179910	53139	24479	8843	551	147
山东	41165	342065	80613	96969	67676	551	284
河南	27572	221127	71200	46154	29940	285	88
湖北	26560	355090	100503	74020	27299	253	203
湖南	24011	241550	80367	60624	38274	313	128
广东	47680	574091	244758	136335	96772	2076	2412
广西	20321	321481	69324	42705	29034	631	120
海南	4847	45476	17317	7436	3659	4	3
重庆	14387	146041	63672	33160	35384	688	220
四川	37800	514534	146467	82904	58972	955	255
贵州	9424	173845	43795	26939	37485	105	17
云南	19207	448907	161589	40273	23443	476	89
西藏	600	12452	4398	656	469		
陕西	18050	252343	52503	30241	13141	85	24
甘肃	14400	169563	32146	15700	7035	87	40
青海	3362	16880	3982	2100	603	39	9
宁夏	4324	60510	11989	6659	4382	4	3
新疆	9453	135524	28888	19749	13505	94	34

织总表

单位：个、人、人次、时

年龄结构				建立党组织的社会组织	社会组织中中共党员人数	志愿服务	
35岁及以下人数	36岁至45岁人数	46岁至55岁人数	56岁及以上人数			志愿者服务人次数	志愿服务时间
2274867	**2483570**	**1390303**	**673883**	**82995**	**864630**	**459162**	**1275281.0**
10074	11516	6620	4891	1143	19446		
28394	35147	24741	15865	1215	25516	15	
9172	11492	10325	7281	2795	13474	700	1400.0
98236	98881	46127	17175	4781	41133	5812	23095.0
53424	49064	30102	15981	1032	15161	1678	1975.0
29975	30561	18773	8571	1649	11077	1347	3730.0
52908	72965	42915	36018	1401	18229	5674	12352.0
17968	26584	8812	2524	299	4350	20	30.0
59046	43183	27976	8775	789	4958	10500	27800.0
47055	54163	36243	19982	4141	35366	2994	23682.0
154181	193782	129617	56242	4307	73333	70466	166323.0
118583	130809	63268	44334	5367	51876	48708	98257.0
72982	82478	55602	20712	2810	33605	34965	73674.0
62199	75955	68465	52520	2205	21263		
61253	75495	32531	10631	2015	21637	10	50.0
119736	137017	64158	21154	12586	86471	100444	266581.0
98480	79924	30152	12571	3696	29847	52	33.0
118447	112048	107278	17317	3718	37346	2929	6174.0
96675	85586	41666	17623	3077	40621	109038	366370.0
276741	173054	91046	33250	1513	21409	36705	98032.0
85835	125665	75358	34623	985	42994		
18023	21062	4785	1606	260	6505		
59103	44185	25833	16920	867	19391	22535	86176.0
195966	178584	77049	62935	5603	65903	2	14.0
48433	78680	33550	13182	2963	21078	2611	12900.0
126837	146009	91318	84743	2259	27471	205	636.0
4503	5351	1997	601	153	1714		
70113	84310	78558	19362	1393	17856	1233	4449.0
34699	88330	38072	8462	4208	24701	50	40.0
4774	6464	4395	1247	1089	4023	141	468.0
6707	42434	8023	3346	1127	7535	77	200.0
34345	82792	14948	3439	1549	19341	251	840.0

C-3-2续表1

地 区	行政执法	行政处罚数	并处没收违法经营额/违法所得	并处罚款
全 国	**4246**	**4200**	**1**	
中央级	12	12		
北 京	110	109		
天 津				
河 北	408	408		
山 西	83	83		
内蒙古				
辽 宁	9	8		
吉 林				
黑龙江	1	1	1	
上 海	25	20		
江 苏	437	433		
浙 江	14	14		
安 徽	61	61		
福 建	4	4		
江 西				
山 东	2377	2345		
河 南	7	7		
湖 北	32	32		
湖 南	4	4		
广 东	245	242		
广 西				
海 南				
重 庆	121	121		
四 川	169	169		
贵 州	12	12		
云 南				
西 藏				
陕 西				
甘 肃				
青 海				
宁 夏	3	3		
新 疆	112	112		

单位：起、万元

(1) 警告	(2) 限期（责令）停止活动	(3) 撤销登记	取缔非法社会组织	#并处没收非法财产
811	**255**	**3134**	**46**	
6	4	2		
7		102	1	
		408		
3	1	79		
1	1	6	1	
	1			
		20	5	
30	21	382	4	
14				
2		59		
		4		
663	105	1577	32	
		7		
3	12	17		
		4		
38	93	111	3	
44	7	70		
		169		
		12		
	3			
	7	105		

C-3-2续表2

地区	增加值合计	执行行政事业单位会计制度财务指标				
		固定资产原价	上年结转和结余	本年收入合计	本年支出合计	收支结余
全 国	**6503187.8**	**259575.3**	**21959.1**	**378379.6**	**89551.3**	**1492.5**
中央级	200422.1					
北 京	210282.4					
天 津	42228.7					
河 北	235418.1	3111.1	15.0	537.3	275.1	
山 西	109389.7	3754.2	66.7	1570.5	1358.8	1.3
内蒙古	41081.7	5550.6	4.4	3523.6	4314.4	2.2
辽 宁	189355.5	793.1	270.7	4167.0	4046.2	
吉 林	13394.7	394.0	15.0	1029.1	752.1	
黑龙江	90320.2	845.5	4.0	262437.3	418.4	
上 海	527112.4					
江 苏	746656.6	156843.9	18541.4	57485.5	46641.8	60.0
浙 江	335686.5	10.0				
安 徽	187342.0	204.5		602.1	578.1	
福 建	108755.7	5573.0		2321.3	2140.0	44.0
江 西	206042.9	9360.2		1760.0	1674.7	538.0
山 东	593032.6					
河 南	92232.0	3716.3	186.5	2095.6	1494.1	
湖 北	189924.9	1198.0		3645.5	3640.5	
湖 南	153599.9	8456.5	1495.4	7277.0	7463.5	834.3
广 东	1229360.2	7625.5	235.4	7254.4	876.5	
广 西	58812.7	2067.2	17.0	974.9	851.9	
海 南	46945.5	501.0		524.0	524.0	
重 庆	135189.8	3233.6	9.0	5767.7	5767.7	
四 川	250438.4	10617.1		1887.4	947.0	
贵 州	54071.6	2600.2	32.0	1444.9	1160.6	2.7
云 南	173881.2	7006.7	451.5	1665.2	1116.1	
西 藏	1523.1	3080.7	12.0	8.2	9.2	
陕 西	162062.9	569.3	7.2	768.9	590.6	
甘 肃	40338.1	12628.2	161.8	3259.6	1959.2	10.0
青 海	6997.0	198.0		28.0	3.0	
宁 夏	21208.4	5264.8		4636.0		
新 疆	50080.0	4372.1	434.1	1708.6	947.8	

单位：万元

行政事业单位增加值	执行民间非营利组织单位会计制度财务指标				
	固定资产原价	上年结余	本年收入合计	本年费用合计	社会组织增加值
82604.7	**15346719.3**	**7923623.1**	**20059288.4**	**19122330.6**	**6420583.1**
	760245.7		4300338.0	3583248.7	200422.1
	673642.1	938559.3	1292623.9	1000789.5	210282.4
	96199.6	20909.7	190319.9	170345.1	42228.7
436.2	1020414.1	446752.5	346613.1	379087.1	234981.9
1210.1	232635.0	12418.9	170608.0	162008.2	108179.6
3188.6	72329.2	238.4	67709.8	70495.6	37893.1
4271.0	404943.6	382020.9	336953.0	488666.6	185084.5
337.2	11061.8	375.3	14866.6	22402.4	13057.5
640.6	125625.4	755.6	25244.3	184557.8	89679.6
	295334.2	2138298.5	2529958.4	2057786.8	527112.4
47255.4	1738514.4	1635656.1	2562226.8	2034691.9	699401.2
0.4	1294418.1	588019.6	1115571.7	1044170.3	335686.1
225.9	684340.7	9309.0	396349.8	383173.2	187116.1
955.9	244166.3	127091.0	172089.8	199007.5	107799.8
1598.1	250605.3	5958.6	228575.4	900652.6	204444.8
	653346.7	72.0	845096.9	846158.7	593032.6
575.5	357713.8	38779.2	210351.4	151007.3	91656.5
3017.4	490504.3	17554.5	429280.1	408768.9	186907.5
5921.7	387598.8	66844.6	303531.3	309999.1	147678.2
1292.7	2511529.0	219169.2	2466117.1	2063881.8	1228067.5
437.3	153247.8	72353.5	91002.3	87235.5	58375.4
40.0	150097.0	211.2	60498.6	57880.8	46905.5
4747.1	574355.0	189700.7	640586.6	574035.0	130442.7
1303.6	739249.5	649008.8	679759.3	812373.0	249134.8
1027.5	193305.5	12196.2	99413.2	81876.2	53044.1
672.2	444157.6	228559.6	242091.5	301598.9	173209.0
115.2	5530.8	13056.5	3076.8	2688.6	1407.9
22.8	520659.8	5443.7	56582.9	220503.9	162040.1
2243.5	93542.9	2888.6	46872.8	55117.8	38094.6
7.9	24235.2	601.2	27558.5	21986.5	6989.1
210.6	50789.2	22952.0	37538.0	374928.0	20997.8
850.0	92380.9	77868.2	69882.6	71207.3	49230.0

C-3-3 社会

地区	单位数	年末职工人数	女性	受教育程度		职业资
				大学专科人数	大学本科及以上人数	助理社会工作师人数
全国	**309736**	**3736265**	**815873**	**520520**	**362026**	**7360**
中央级	1941	29608	12940		23646	749
北京	3730	37242	10882	7167	19644	295
天津	2215	11483	4024	1535	7287	10
河北	9810	131274	18113	14702	11606	1035
山西	6855	80241	17131	17698	10517	23
内蒙古	7044	55876	14224	15710	6239	4
辽宁	8966	107695	17504	14642	12672	27
吉林	5671	34920	4264	4634	1540	379
黑龙江	5471	96425	37014	8030	4043	57
上海	3909	31355	5383	13307	3949	276
江苏	32706	216457	53350	54752	22071	765
浙江	19430	132073	31271	36803	18410	123
安徽	11977	103447	14910	16477	9020	1256
福建	13892	187430	26293	16479	8035	185
江西	8030	94098	18719	13982	4430	25
山东	17738	139121	26659	35333	27739	172
河南	11183	74266	17924	10453	5646	105
湖北	11878	220021	48239	27669	8754	18
湖南	12194	123396	31401	23655	15714	95
广东	22132	184832	49820	34955	22860	194
广西	12311	241198	34433	24121	18316	454
海南	2334	21475	5486	3658	669	
重庆	7049	46082	8571	7274	6806	259
四川	20030	319728	69043	33732	32833	565
贵州	5624	131701	25676	15545	29490	9
云南	12987	386579	130751	29214	12785	96
西藏	570	12224	4311	600	408	
陕西	9907	168539	25546	12977	4176	31
甘肃	10742	146582	25440	9341	4120	63
青海	2209	11725	2412	1265	345	19
宁夏	3129	53168	7993	3977	1662	2
新疆	6072	106004	16146	10833	6594	69

团体

单位:个、人、人次、时

格水平	年龄结构				志愿服务	
社会工作师人数	35岁及以下人数	36岁至45岁人数	46岁至55岁人数	56岁及以上人数	志愿者服务人次数	志愿服务时间
3537	**933883**	**1403517**	**908719**	**490146**	**199462**	**516493.0**
1471	8882	10363	5922	4441		
98	5818	9758	11668	9998		
6	2695	3524	2682	2582	500	1000.0
300	47948	49682	23904	9740	1319	5022.0
19	17807	29416	20929	12089	1604	1906.0
3	16010	20107	13256	6503	712	2484.0
17	17824	36123	23545	30203	266	568.0
86	11374	16076	6307	1163		
62	45962	26971	18017	5475	5000	5000.0
134	7079	9535	7976	6765	516	3858.0
156	44723	77281	60003	34450	38957	99978.0
154	30447	53055	35385	13186	40818	82099.0
174	23132	40424	27019	12872	8810	18428.0
28	29605	54316	55616	47893		
25	26443	37204	22726	7725	10	50.0
92	41855	53496	30619	13151	40257	108798.0
24	27078	29198	12354	5636		
31	66254	61416	82974	9377	578	1236.0
55	37596	44485	28227	13088	51026	152641.0
217	39778	68474	53719	22861		
66	49246	95858	63316	32778		
	8240	9747	2688	800		
99	9292	14436	12142	10212	7615	28743.0
117	102362	106687	54986	55693	2	14.0
2	27174	66161	27410	10956	589	1939.0
48	96038	123126	84537	82878	143	435.0
	4427	5265	1947	585		
13	35023	53059	66375	14082	561	1874.0
15	27182	81082	31136	7182	40	
3	2878	3991	3797	1059	52	150.0
	4122	39330	7145	2571	77	200.0
22	19589	73871	10392	2152	10	70.0

C-3-3续表1

地　区	社会组织负责人	女性	中央级社团	省级社团	按活动区域分 地级社团
全　国	**638943**	**107343**	**1941**	**27973**	**76211**
中央级	25334		1941		
北　京	25636	4862		1488	
天　津	5816	465		955	
河　北	15001	1883		818	2691
山　西	8699	823		926	2161
内蒙古	11706	2661		727	2260
辽　宁	12718	1993		802	3727
吉　林	6501	702		763	1889
黑龙江	9208	1210		999	2214
上　海	12795	4155		1189	
江　苏	50740	7259		995	5807
浙　江	43134	7787		1076	4571
安　徽	16978	1791		989	3570
福　建	18061	2971		1005	3113
江　西	11980	2118		779	2399
山　东	55172	11114		868	5536
河　南	15942	3193		1098	4008
湖　北	27810	4884		956	3348
湖　南	28542	5002		877	3846
广　东	51220	16834		1570	7833
广　西	18759	2290		824	2451
海　南	3714	611		818	371
重　庆	22769	3680		985	
四　川	36637	5932		1187	4208
贵　州	36584	4894		722	1232
云　南	17836	2313		884	2663
西　藏	867	57		216	139
陕　西	17157	2553		858	1916
甘　肃	13897	1614		608	1625
青　海	2280	191		537	448
宁　夏	3634	88		645	541
新　疆	11816	1413		809	1644

单位：人、个

县级社团	建立党组织的社会组织	社会组织职工中中共党员人数	当年新增单位数	当年年检单位数	行业性社团
203611	**52188**	**526172**	**31477**	**94565**	**40028**
	1017	17355	32	1782	401
2242	709	18392	256	1229	149
1260	1451	7765	99	345	248
6301	3145	25455	705	2760	1607
3768	504	9326	444	3286	906
4057	1067	6987	822	2543	1804
4437	897	11024	288	1638	2302
3019	252	2918	1262	222	279
2258	558	3472	284	179	438
2720	1289	11973	164	2530	120
25904	2644	36784	6635	10001	3445
13783	3144	24887	1736	8594	1643
7418	1939	16705	1081	4752	1497
9774	1637	18260	1128	2473	2386
4852	1411	8068	337	1015	442
11334	7400	45613	1586	13319	6716
6077	2631	13716	749	1230	975
7574	1439	16444	1111	7473	1169
7471	2510	25839	1008	3479	1980
12729	876	10801	3200	4562	1700
9036	830	38183	1565	1308	592
1145	82	5226	175	598	293
6064	455	7718	549	4043	1010
14635	3901	48754	1732	4905	2486
3670	2031	14107	664	1912	892
9440	1160	22302	1467	1834	982
215	135	1621	14	169	79
7133	944	12068	664	3078	884
8509	3354	20099	858	373	598
1224	660	2543	135	928	500
1943	900	6114	404	670	166
3619	1216	15653	323	1335	1339

C-3-3续表2

地区	社会组织					
	科技与研究	生态环境	教育	卫生	社会服务	文化
全　国	**16923**	**6964**	**11412**	**10060**	**44630**	**30101**
中央级	58	4	36	19	20	45
北　京	324	68	154	158	460	346
天　津	39	19	54	46	196	106
河　北	568	155	265	473	1397	961
山　西	448	118	340	188	1074	907
内蒙古	475	129	318	165	910	638
辽　宁	282	148	1041	412	1105	715
吉　林	183	71	248	173	1406	522
黑龙江	270	88	216	250	1061	705
上　海	653	50	163	193	531	312
江　苏	1421	530	920	913	7310	3436
浙　江	1289	498	845	586	2052	1853
安　徽	677	242	331	389	1964	1223
福　建	513	386	659	404	2198	1641
江　西	265	210	384	444	1204	779
山　东	1345	349	541	515	2439	1940
河　南	843	345	506	387	1314	1317
湖　北	862	236	279	409	1548	1176
湖　南	794	402	530	458	1638	1158
广　东	1233	299	780	541	3618	2411
广　西	567	124	243	227	1853	673
海　南	278	19	74	51	129	294
重　庆	483	99	263	174	624	583
四　川	758	637	826	837	3042	1784
贵　州	229	101	150	146	704	586
云　南	403	217	299	469	1406	1273
西　藏	29	22	21	26	119	44
陕　西	530	134	201	218	953	1209
甘　肃	260	900	178	256	1151	801
青　海	139	130	82	207	223	159
宁　夏	182	87	302	102	247	160
新　疆	523	147	163	224	734	344

单位：个

按行业分类

体育	法律	工商业服务	宗教	农业及农村发展	职业及从业组织	国际及涉外组织	其他
20848	**3270**	**34099**	**4898**	**60202**	**19867**	**516**	**45946**
17	4	1533	4	9	2	27	163
240	56	520	43	601	164		596
63	20	83	15	144	81	7	1342
589	115	1088	191	1785	657	17	1549
619	91	710	94	733	430	8	1095
403	41	790	71	1496	268	8	1332
538	113	721	138	1326	727	23	1677
297	105	233	64	674	226	10	1459
402	75	446	80	836	543	11	488
361	39	737	70	64	248	14	474
4360	316	3113	389	3590	1663	4	4741
1589	203	3387	364	1551	2020	97	3096
847	144	1136	183	2775	918	14	1134
847	150	1349	353	2009	1072	53	2258
623	120	741	158	1289	597	13	1203
1020	168	2003	225	4614	1335	35	1209
690	164	1421	288	1880	703	13	1312
766	145	1505	185	1942	647	15	2163
626	163	1348	236	2000	1196	41	1604
1655	120	3518	249	1573	1075	31	5029
381	49	730	98	4847	528	15	1976
163	3	366	12	466	140	5	334
382	42	830	93	2341	419	3	713
1238	220	1380	354	4511	1487		2956
344	54	689	115	1195	541	1	769
633	221	1103	301	3789	662	22	2189
11	9	32	9	121	8		119
380	54	885	180	4050	430	10	673
225	63	434	163	4635	692	5	979
208	62	122	37	441	36		363
60	50	152	36	1223	95		433
271	91	994	100	1692	257	14	518

C-3-3续表3

地 区	行政执法	行政处罚数	并处没收违法经营额/违法所得	并处罚款
全 国	**2312**	**2308**	**1**	
中央级	12	12		
北 京	55	54		
天 津				
河 北	81	81		
山 西	39	39		
内蒙古				
辽 宁	9	8		
吉 林				
黑龙江	1	1	1	
上 海				
江 苏	398	398		
浙 江	6	6		
安 徽	58	58		
福 建	2	2		
江 西				
山 东	1258	1258		
河 南	6	6		
湖 北	26	26		
湖 南	4	4		
广 东	136	134		
广 西				
海 南				
重 庆	40	40		
四 川	63	63		
贵 州	12	12		
云 南				
西 藏				
陕 西				
甘 肃				
青 海				
宁 夏	3	3		
新 疆	103	103		

单位：起

(1) 警告	(2) 限期（责令）停止活动	(3) 撤销登记	取缔非法社会组织	并处没收非法财产
361	**156**	**1791**	**4**	
6	4	2		
7		47	1	
		81		
3	1	35		
1	1	6	1	
	1			
14	8	376		
6				
2		56		
		2		
293	63	902		
		6		
3	7	16		
		4		
18	56	60	2	
8	5	27		
		63		
		12		
	3			
	7	96		

C-3-3续表4

地区	增加值合计	执行行政事业单位会计制度财务指标				
		固定资产原价	上年结转和结余	本年收入合计	本年支出合计	收支结余
全国	**1793300.7**	**259575.3**	**378379.6**	**21959.1**	**89551.3**	**1492.5**
中央级	144700.6					
北京	43489.8					
天津	9374.5					
河北	21781.5	3111.1	537.3	15.0	275.1	
山西	38114.7	3754.2	1570.5	66.7	1358.8	1.3
内蒙古	13151.6	5550.6	3523.6	4.4	4314.4	2.2
辽宁	43023.8	793.1	4167.0	270.7	4046.2	
吉林	5881.6	394.0	1029.1	15.0	752.1	
黑龙江	25037.2	845.5	262437.3	4.0	418.4	
上海	41267.8					
江苏	165726.2	156843.9	57485.5	18541.4	46641.8	60.0
浙江	102406.1	10.0				
安徽	50624.5	204.5	602.1		578.1	
福建	29478.1	5573.0	2321.3		2140.0	44.0
江西	52920.8	9360.2	1760.0		1674.7	538.0
山东	159483.0					
河南	15666.1	3716.3	2095.6	186.5	1494.1	
湖北	49902.9	1198.0	3645.5		3640.5	
湖南	36655.6	8456.5	7277.0	1495.4	7463.5	834.3
广东	458023.0	7625.5	7254.4	235.4	876.5	
广西	19060.2	2067.2	974.9	17.0	851.9	
海南	10391.7	501.0	524.0		524.0	
重庆	29801.2	3233.6	5767.7	9.0	5767.7	
四川	55348.2	10617.1	1887.4		947.0	
贵州	17317.1	2600.2	1444.9	32.0	1160.6	2.7
云南	32181.5	7006.7	1665.2	451.5	1116.1	
西藏	476.8	3080.7	8.2	12.0	9.2	
陕西	84081.7	569.3	768.9	7.2	590.6	
甘肃	22121.1	12628.2	3259.6	161.8	1959.2	10.0
青海	3664.6	198.0	28.0		3.0	
宁夏	4236.9	5264.8	4636.0			
新疆	7910.0	4372.1	1708.6	434.1	947.8	

单位：万元

	执行民间非营利组织单位会计制度财务指标				
行政事业单位增加值	固定资产原价	上年结余	本年收入合计	本年费用合计	社会组织增加值
82604.7	**3117213.4**	**2824873.5**	**4916826.3**	**5333017.6**	**1710696.0**
	660106.0		1569386.3	1234633.5	144700.6
	215901.2	477654.3	401949.4	270756.9	43489.8
	24633.7	571.1	53665.8	82137.9	9374.5
436.2	58488.7	383387.6	69706.9	53694.3	21345.3
1210.1	73800.6	5611.8	58388.2	56483.5	36904.6
3188.6	19358.4	80.0	22932.7	22568.4	9963.0
4271.0	288434.4	257518.2	51450.7	89373.9	38752.8
337.2	5319.4	15.0	6131.7	10981.1	5544.4
640.6	18560.1	160.1	6464.2	38448.0	24396.6
	22509.2	557996.7	403398.0	343688.1	41267.8
47255.4	484041.1	9692.7	382056.3	385461.5	118470.8
0.4	122424.3	80339.5	261058.7	251432.3	102405.7
225.9	124948.0	3076.9	95298.2	80521.2	50398.6
955.9	25987.7	104879.7	72624.6	77508.2	28522.2
1598.1	70414.1	1195.1	31997.8	685057.6	51322.7
	122231.2	3.0	233881.7	235083.3	159483.0
575.5	39250.0	4932.6	33126.1	29589.9	15090.6
3017.4	62328.0	16160.7	147108.6	130114.6	46885.5
5921.7	53211.5	393.6	72639.8	65751.9	30733.9
1292.7	133161.5	80786.2	531095.4	649915.6	456730.3
437.3	35920.9	71677.0	17747.2	24205.9	18622.9
40.0	44358.5	100.6	14126.1	14950.0	10351.7
4747.1	49151.8	12490.7	112598.2	120074.7	25054.1
1303.6	99988.7	635816.8	100908.8	120987.1	54044.6
1027.5	86801.3	9542.9	48907.5	30116.8	16289.6
672.2	58673.0	31759.7	35828.0	56249.4	31509.3
115.2	4294.8	265.2	306.0	463.0	361.6
22.8	46139.1	2316.2	14681.0	107718.6	84058.9
2243.5	31192.1	47.0	25266.7	29575.6	19877.6
7.9	10207.2	390.0	23593.2	16179.3	3656.7
210.6	10481.2		7998.4	7608.1	4026.3
850.0	14895.7	76012.6	10504.1	11687.4	7060.0

C-3-4 基金

地区	单位数	年末职工人数	女性	受教育程度		职业资
				大学专科人数	大学本科及以上人数	助理社会工作师人数
全　国	**4117**	**20394**	**5420**	**4210**	**4930**	**90**
中央级	227	1992	728			
北　京	318	2304	1088	340	1155	
天　津	64	111				
河　北	49	271	103	85	164	1
山　西	59	143	59	98	45	
内蒙古	91	373	125	306	56	
辽　宁	69	536	142	245	126	25
吉　林	79	103	23			
黑龙江	76	132				
上　海	199	1095	192	728	233	
江　苏	483	1664	434	54	73	3
浙　江	381	1013	374	415	494	2
安　徽	80	202	27	26	41	
福　建	179	1079	151	8	50	12
江　西	50	233	51	134	74	
山　东	92	322	81	170	116	7
河　南	104	382	44	228	152	
湖　北	95	847	155	296	370	
湖　南	189	1047	118	252	604	
广　东	558	3090	899	154	286	
广　西	49	378	143	64	19	1
海　南	56	280	84	84	112	
重　庆	54	401	134	140	227	10
四　川	128	900				
贵　州	40	203	5	94	34	17
云　南	75	209	75	58	135	12
西　藏	13	71	22	19	24	
陕　西	88	480	21	16	33	
甘　肃	53	9	1	5		
青　海	27	45	10	12	8	
宁　夏	55	275	125	90	184	
新　疆	37	204	6	89	115	

会

单位：个、人、人次、时

格水平	年龄结构				志愿服务	
社会工作师人数	35岁及以下人数	36岁至45岁人数	46岁至55岁人数	56岁及以上人数	志愿者服务人次数	志愿服务时间
76	**5771**	**5958**	**5261**	**3404**	**1268**	**4720.0**
	598	697	398	299		
10	708	538	507	551		
				111		
4	98	73	53	47		
2	23	20	31	69	53	
	135	92	59	87		
6	135	102	238	61		
	89	14				
5			132			
30	381	344	201	169		
4	587	342	537	198		
2	407	390	156	60		
	15	39	62	86		
	146	264	341	328		
	48	169	16			
2	162	145	10	5	1000	3000.0
	29	16	151	186		
	190	314	245	98		
	213	260	322	252		
	990	771	852	477		
1	70	130	149	29		
	84	112	56	28		
7	91	191	45	74	215	1720.0
	200	364	336			
	61	62	72	8		
3	43	67	55	44		
	23	28	14	6		
	106	134	130	110		
	3	6				
	15	24	6			
	69	141	44	21		
	52	109	43			

C-3-4续表1

地区	社会组织负责人数		按性质分		
		女性	公募基金会	非公募基金会	涉外基金会
全　国	**8952**	**1687**	**1470**	**2610**	**9**
中央级	1564	7	93	97	9
北　京	700	190	41	277	
天　津	64	25	20	44	
河　北	72	25	9	40	
山　西	59	3	24	35	
内蒙古	96	24	91		
辽　宁	69		69		
吉　林	61	12	24	55	
黑龙江	47	17	37	39	
上　海	667	192	56	143	
江　苏	531	111	161	322	
浙　江	429	74	138	243	
安　徽	89		23	57	
福　建	184	22	36	143	
江　西	124	22	18	32	
山　东	79	15	38	54	
河　南	206	52	39	65	
湖　北	680	128	22	73	
湖　南	913	122	111	78	
广　东	1278	514	114	444	
广　西	71	14	20	29	
海　南	56	17	17	39	
重　庆	190	24	28	26	
四　川	128	5	52	76	
贵　州	63	13	30	10	
云　南	69		41	34	
西　藏	23	8	8	5	
陕　西	312	34	30	58	
甘　肃	2		22	31	
青　海	22	5	13	14	
宁　夏	55	11	25	30	
新　疆	49	1	20	17	

单位:人、个

境外基金代表机构	建立党组织的社会组织	社会组织职工中中共党员人数	当年登记单位数	当年年检单位数
28	**615**	**7336**	**522**	**782**
28	90	1725	11	
	21	908	37	
	64	200	9	
	43	150		
	1	16	4	51
	10	60	1	
	7	21	13	
			10	
	24	551	49	148
	4	1060	42	3
	21	421	54	292
	35	132	9	8
	146	476	18	2
	4	15	6	
	32	149	6	85
	2	228	6	
	7	214	18	76
	45	500	19	
		63	123	6
	24	79	9	1
		123	5	
	1	8	6	46
			19	
	2	6	8	
		1	11	
	7	36	2	11
	20	68	6	
			13	
		2	4	50
	5	124	4	3

C-3-4续表2

地 区	社会组织					
	科技与研究	生态环境	教育	卫生	社会服务	文化
全 国	**89**	**57**	**1183**	**147**	**1323**	**243**
中央级	1		2		8	1
北 京	21	10	59	20	139	48
天 津	3		24	3	21	8
河 北	1		7	1	1	
山 西			23		27	9
内蒙古		2	25	46	1	3
辽 宁						
吉 林		2	20	1	46	1
黑龙江	2	5	17	4	38	2
上 海	10	6	54	16	74	19
江 苏	3	3	142	6	158	15
浙 江	7		156	5	123	16
安 徽	3	3	23	1	25	5
福 建		3	92	6	63	5
江 西	2	1	20	1	20	1
山 东	4	2	30	3	14	7
河 南			16			6
湖 北		3	44	1	26	6
湖 南	2		124		9	10
广 东	17	5	127	18	326	42
广 西			12	2	29	
海 南	1	2	20	2	8	7
重 庆	2		18	2	24	3
四 川	4		50	2	14	4
贵 州			5		30	
云 南		6	20	4	28	5
西 藏		1	4	1	1	4
陕 西	1		19	2	4	13
甘 肃	4	3	15		24	3
青 海			3			
宁 夏	1		10		39	
新 疆			2		3	

单位：个

按行业分类

体育	法律	工商业服务	宗教	农业及农村发展	职业及从业组织	国际及涉外组织	其他
34	**36**	**227**	**25**	**46**	**18**	**3**	**686**
		209				2	4
5	3			2			11
2							3
			3				36
							14
							69
	8	1					
2	1	1	1	1	1		1
3		8	1	1	2		5
3	3	2	3	22	4		119
4	1		2	9			58
1	1	1			7		10
		3	1				6
1	2		2				
1	1			1			29
2							80
2	4		1	2			6
2	1		4	1	2		34
4				1			18
				1			5
	4	1	4	2			5
	1	1	2				1
1	2			1	1		49
1							4
	1					1	10
	2						
	1		1	1			46
				1	1		2
							24
							5
							32

C-3-4续表3

地　区	行政执法	行政处罚数	(1) 警告	(2) 限期（责令）停止活动	(3) 撤销登记	取缔非法社会组织
全　国	14	13	8	2	3	1
中央级						
北　京	1	1			1	
天　津						
河　北						
山　西						
内蒙古						
辽　宁						
吉　林						
黑龙江						
上　海						
江　苏						
浙　江	8	8	8			
安　徽						
福　建						
江　西						
山　东						
河　南						
湖　北						
湖　南						
广　东	4	3		2	1	1
广　西						
海　南						
重　庆	1	1			1	
四　川						
贵　州						
云　南						
西　藏						
陕　西						
甘　肃						
青　海						
宁　夏						
新　疆						

单位：起、万元

执行民间非营利组织单位会计制度财务指标				
固定资产原价	上年结余	本年收入合计	本年费用合计	社会组织增加值
245010.7	**2749297.4**	**4604338.2**	**3051775.6**	**231673.6**
72053.3		2633316.3	2249936.6	42730.3
8976.1	241958.8	177433.7	35878.6	30457.1
3000.0	10000.0	1750.0	950.0	426.3
1427.9	14836.5	14654.3	708.6	339.0
1300.0		10773.0	9973.0	406.0
381.0		10521.0	8018.0	5390.1
1110.0		30053.9	36973.5	802.4
328.7			1007.9	62.0
225.0		210.0	473.0	322.5
	933698.2	353497.7	180428.6	65379.3
802.9	1449865.0	640881.8	40775.6	26291.0
8064.1	70357.0	117335.2	90608.5	1396.9
1462.0		1574.0	449.3	207.7
27891.0	500.0	30751.0	27762.5	21831.2
715.0		10988.0	8930.4	8024.8
792.7		3017.3	2701.5	416.0
126.0	35.0	132.0	150.0	124.3
1178.7		53034.9	29587.7	5856.6
		5.0	5.0	10124.0
18735.6	10.0	424253.8	249410.3	4243.8
381.2	4.9	52.0	72.5	70.5
		2800.0	560.0	560.0
66011.2	44.8	53887.8	43275.6	401.5
				1001.7
361.2			365.9	200.7
40.0	24.8	15925.0	13284.1	1113.9
733.5	12301.4	2237.5	1823.7	778.3
1310.0		1237.0	928.0	48.5
				409.4
4250.0		1152.0	865.0	13.3
13313.6	15661.0	12824.0	13882.2	814.5
10040.0		40.0	1990.0	1430.0

C-3-5 民办

地区	单位数	年末职工人数		受教育程度		职业资
			女性	大学专科人数	大学本科及以上人数	助理社会工作师人数
全 国	**292195**	**3065964**	**1182492**	**779318**	**520737**	**9201**
中央级	84	1501	842	368	226	
北 京	5035	64601	25244	14667	16046	791
天 津	2450	26676	11902	9315	10630	109
河 北	7783	128874	53076	31356	21417	216
山 西	5416	68187	25706	18631	8634	23
内蒙古	4655	31631	12552	8247	3623	8
辽 宁	11102	96575	45011	23789	20078	310
吉 林	4771	20865	7556	6400	2204	177
黑龙江	6932	42423	13609	10719	3717	50
上 海	8257	124993	27995	44920	14775	235
江 苏	38382	315701	92676	62815	56886	1347
浙 江	20033	223908	75806	52282	32849	220
安 徽	10492	128125	45745	37429	24747	376
福 建	7286	70630	28666	11766	14829	365
江 西	6156	85579	34369	10363	4339	526
山 东	23335	202622	53873	61466	39821	372
河 南	16285	146479	53232	35473	24142	180
湖 北	14587	134222	52109	46055	18175	235
湖 南	11628	117107	48848	36717	21956	218
广 东	24990	386169	194039	101226	73626	1882
广 西	7961	79905	34748	18520	10699	176
海 南	2457	23721	11747	3694	2878	4
重 庆	7284	99558	54967	25746	28351	419
四 川	17642	193906	77424	49172	26139	390
贵 州	3760	41941	18114	11300	7961	79
云 南	6145	62119	30763	11001	10523	368
西 藏	17	157	65	37	37	
陕 西	8055	83324	26936	17248	8932	54
甘 肃	3605	22972	6705	6354	2915	24
青 海	1126	5110	1560	823	250	20
宁 夏	1140	7067	3871	2592	2536	2
新 疆	3344	29316	12736	8827	6796	25

非企业

单位:个、人、人次、时

格水平	年龄结构				志愿服务	
社会工作师人数	35岁及以下人数	36岁至45岁人数	46岁至55岁人数	56岁及以上人数	志愿者服务人次数	志愿服务时间
5711	**1335213**	**1074095**	**476323**	**180333**	**258432**	**754068.0**
	594	456	300	151		
780	21868	24851	12566	5316	15	
65	6477	7968	7643	4588	200	400.0
315	50190	49126	22170	7388	4493	18073.0
49	35594	19628	9142	3823	21	69.0
4	13830	10362	5458	1981	635	1246.0
68	34949	36740	19132	5754	5408	11784.0
137	6505	10494	2505	1361	20	30.0
68	13084	16212	9827	3300	5500	22800.0
109	39595	44284	28066	13048	2478	19824.0
394	108871	116159	69077	21594	31509	66345.0
123	87729	77364	27727	31088	7890	16158.0
136	49835	42015	28521	7754	26155	55246.0
229	32448	21375	12508	4299		
122	34762	38122	9789	2906		
190	77719	83376	33529	7998	59187	154783.0
64	71373	50710	17647	6749	52	33.0
172	52003	50318	24059	7842	2351	4938.0
73	58866	40841	13117	4283	58012	213729.0
2195	235973	103809	36475	9912	36705	98032.0
53	36519	29677	11893	1816		
3	9699	11203	2041	778		
114	49720	29558	13646	6634	14705	55713.0
138	93404	71533	21727	7242		
15	21198	12457	6068	2218	2022	10961.0
38	30756	22816	6726	1821	62	201.0
	53	58	36	10		
11	34984	31117	12053	5170	672	2575.0
25	7514	7242	6936	1280	10	40.0
6	1881	2449	592	188	89	318.0
3	2516	2963	834	754		
12	14704	8812	4513	1287	241	770.0

C-3-5续表1

地区	民间组织负责人	女性	法人	按性质分 合伙
全国	**412609**	**139488**	**228366**	**7033**
中央级	206		82	1
北京	13168	6342	4150	13
天津	3232	1348	2370	10
河北	9981	3034	4802	367
山西	6553	1610	4931	136
内蒙古	6042	1753	2953	181
辽宁	11912	4127	8440	175
吉林	5741	1672	2762	45
黑龙江	7854	2905	3743	189
上海	20341	8947	7675	37
江苏	44732	11535	33607	818
浙江	26035	9315	16400	451
安徽	13374	4040	7425	545
福建	8431	2880	6007	348
江西	10446	3361	3978	244
山东	53375	15722	17813	443
河南	20882	7087	11800	457
湖北	18703	5634	12002	387
湖南	18673	6162	7625	371
广东	29816	11275	22637	103
广西	8418	3269	5339	205
海南	2523	1218	2244	6
重庆	16246	7361	6387	108
四川	24169	8670	13724	504
贵州	4669	1423	1993	245
云南	6446	2197	4212	196
西藏	12	3	14	2
陕西	10285	3493	5522	215
甘肃	4531	1165	2615	118
青海	1100	251	1045	24
宁夏	1250	232	917	39
新疆	3463	1457	3152	50

单位：人、个

个体	建立党组织的社会组织	社会组织职工中中共党员人数	当年登记单位数	当年年检单位数
56796	**30192**	**331122**	**42056**	**94589**
1	36	366	18	53
872	485	6216	431	2498
70	1280	5509	179	462
2614	1593	15528	1162	2035
349	527	5819	754	1772
1521	572	4030	842	1550
2487	504	7205	726	1890
1964	40	1411	900	369
3000	231	1486	467	910
545	2828	22842	744	4833
3957	1659	35489	9093	9897
3182	2202	26568	2781	7495
2522	836	16768	1740	3808
931	422	2527	629	1708
1934	600	13554	419	341
5079	5154	40709	3600	16544
4028	1063	15903	3194	2657
2198	2272	20688	1057	8422
3632	522	14282	1641	5460
2250	637	10545	3578	4623
2417	131	4732	1677	1074
207	178	1156	318	443
789	411	11665	950	4211
3414	1702	17149	2049	6184
1522	930	6965	594	1182
1737	1099	5168	885	719
1	11	57		16
2318	429	5720	678	2005
872	854	4602	493	153
57	429	1480	50	100
184	227	1419	156	143
142	328	3564	251	1032

C-3-5续表2

地　区	社会组织					
	科技与研究	生态环境	教育	卫生	社会服务	文化
全　国	**15110**	**398**	**163681**	**23404**	**42244**	**14148**
中央级	21		6	3	16	17
北　京	314	8	3007	339	707	233
天　津	41	3	1001	173	377	105
河　北	548		4214	1457	719	253
山　西	508	7	3305	324	515	283
内蒙古	336	4	2981	238	559	166
辽　宁	331	8	6279	1720	1521	273
吉　林	185		3118	225	900	102
黑龙江	592	3	4518	179	1016	138
上　海	364	18	3221	153	2623	450
江　苏	848	48	8599	2543	17609	2246
浙　江	1284	20	11921	813	1993	1132
安　徽	490	9	5897	1691	1340	337
福　建	422	9	5215	365	254	394
江　西	243	2	4517	501	368	194
山　东	3331	11	9684	2725	2356	2018
河　南	921	77	9614	2551	1058	725
湖　北	678	96	6527	1104	1442	1149
湖　南	309	16	9186	711	354	494
广　东	947	19	17208	616	2393	1213
广　西	196	4	6751	189	299	153
海　南	158	1	1596	302	103	140
重　庆	129		5219	90	1062	97
四　川	457	9	12440	1752	843	509
贵　州	177	2	2594	369	275	77
云　南	175	4	4710	392	243	178
西　藏	2		8			2
陕　西	507	6	5022	1044	522	464
甘　肃	364	6	1876	416	211	302
青　海	49		719	64	52	99
宁　夏	54	8	613	46	135	82
新　疆	129		2115	309	379	123

单位：个

按行业分类							
体育	法律	工商业服务	宗教	农业及农村发展	职业及从业组织	国际及涉外组织	其他
11901	**490**	**3120**	**82**	**1415**	**890**	**4**	**15308**
1	1	12					7
319	22	14		6	5		61
249	2	17		1	388		93
289	6	51	1	38	5		202
225	17	64	1	11	14		142
141	5	28	3	13	8		173
394	9	62	18	11	14		462
167	3	11	1	6	1		52
318	6	15	2	2	6		137
524	31	219		49	33	4	568
1901	37	630	16	206	71		3628
935	17	225		39	16		1638
329	1	89	7	92	8		202
370	2	80	3	5	12		155
189	3	14		15	2		108
1458	144	388	5	52	49		1114
821	12	75	3	3	8		417
298	68	211	5	642	108		2259
187	3	106	4	34	5		219
792	11	210	4	8	36		1533
256	1	18		1	2		91
62		24		1	22		48
302	2	54		55	14		260
363	34	322	3	57	12		841
129	4	22		11	5		95
268	4	27	3	5	6		130
	1	2					2
189	30	52		11	3		205
110	11	40	3	39	27		200
28	2	1			1		111
88		30		2	9		73
199	1	7					82

C-3-5续表3

地　区	行政执法	行政处罚数	(1) 警告	(2) 限期(责令)停止活动	(3) 撤销登记	取缔非法社会组织
全　国	**1920**	**1879**	**442**	**97**	**1340**	**41**
中央级						
北　京	54	54			54	
天　津						
河　北	327	327			327	
山　西	44	44			44	
内蒙古						
辽　宁						
吉　林						
黑龙江						
上　海	25	20			20	5
江　苏	39	35	16	13	6	4
浙　江						
安　徽	3	3			3	
福　建	2	2			2	
江　西						
山　东	1119	1087	370	42	675	32
河　南	1	1			1	
湖　北	6	6		5	1	
湖　南						
广　东	105	105	20	35	50	
广　西						
海　南						
重　庆	80	80	36	2	42	
四　川	106	106			106	
贵　州						
云　南						
西　藏						
陕　西						
甘　肃						
青　海						
宁　夏						
新　疆	9	9			9	

单位：起、万元

增加值合计	执行民间非营利组织单位会计制度财务指标				
	固定资产原价	上年结余	本年收入合计	本年费用合计	社会组织增加值
4478213.5	**11984495.2**	**2349452.2**	**10538123.9**	**10737537.4**	**4478213.5**
12991.2	28086.4		97635.4	98678.6	12991.2
136335.5	448764.8	218946.2	713240.8	694154.0	136335.5
32427.9	68565.9	10338.6	134904.1	87257.2	32427.9
213297.6	960497.5	48528.4	262251.9	324684.2	213297.6
70869.0	157534.4	6807.1	101446.8	95551.7	70869.0
22540.0	52589.8	158.4	34256.1	39909.2	22540.0
145529.3	115399.2	124502.7	255448.4	362319.2	145529.3
7451.1	5413.7	360.3	8734.9	10413.4	7451.1
64960.5	106840.3	595.5	18570.1	145636.8	64960.5
420465.3	272825.0	646603.6	1773062.7	1533670.1	420465.3
554639.4	1253670.4	176098.4	1539288.7	1608454.8	554639.4
231883.5	1163929.7	437323.1	737177.8	702129.5	231883.5
136509.8	557930.7	6232.1	299477.6	302202.7	136509.8
57446.4	190287.6	21711.3	68714.2	93736.8	57446.4
145097.3	179476.2	4763.5	185589.6	206664.6	145097.3
433133.6	530322.8	69.0	608197.9	608373.9	433133.6
76441.6	318337.8	33811.6	177093.3	121267.4	76441.6
134165.4	426997.6	1393.8	229136.6	249066.6	134165.4
106820.3	334387.3	66451.0	230886.5	244242.2	106820.3
767093.4	2359631.9	138373.0	1510767.9	1164555.9	767093.4
39682.0	116945.7	671.6	73203.1	62957.1	39682.0
35993.8	105738.5	110.6	43572.5	42370.8	35993.8
104987.1	459192.0	177165.2	474100.6	410684.7	104987.1
194088.5	639260.8	13192.0	578850.5	691385.9	194088.5
36553.8	106143.0	2653.3	50505.7	51393.5	36553.8
140585.8	385444.6	196775.1	190338.5	232065.4	140585.8
268.0	502.5	489.9	533.3	401.9	268.0
77932.7	473210.7	3127.5	40664.9	111857.3	77932.7
17807.6	62350.8	2841.6	21606.1	25542.2	17807.6
3319.1	9778.0	211.2	2813.3	4942.2	3319.1
16157.0	26994.4	7291.0	16715.6	353437.7	16157.0
40740.0	67445.2	1855.6	59338.5	57529.9	40740.0

C-3-6 自治组

地　区	单位数	居民1000户以下	居民1000户－3000户	居民3000户以上	社区居委会（村委会）成员	#中共党员
全　国	**682144**	**488185**	**157850**	**36109**	**2802062**	**1580888**
中央级						
北　京	6869	4203	2144	522	34283	19502
天　津	5273	3836	1178	259	25204	9251
河　北	52471	42140	8921	1410	185017	90790
山　西	30354	25023	4462	869	110893	51690
内蒙古	13427	9097	3715	615	52249	25220
辽　宁	15663	7641	5893	2129	71312	37196
吉　林	11308	6731	3464	1113	34430	482
黑龙江	11741	5869	4768	1104	52776	23731
上　海	5727	2149	3306	272	27269	13863
江　苏	21400	8808	9712	2880	110319	72203
浙　江	32318	24312	7041	965	125534	57346
安　徽	18043	8004	7447	2592	76952	50317
福　建	16748	12227	4029	492	70366	25625
江　西	20319	12613	6880	826	77383	32166
山　东	80015	65847	11619	2549	320751	245758
河　南	51342	34116	14682	2544	211880	113515
湖　北	29635	20675	6880	2080	113170	76143
湖　南	46623	35683	8630	2310	166240	108504
广　东	25933	16392	7242	2299	123458	85570
广　西	16183	10928	4465	790	80685	54165
海　南	3036	2593	311	132	15537	11958
重　庆	11030	6069	3905	1056	54020	32758
四　川	53123	40015	10387	2721	213088	114366
贵　州	18763	15726	2460	577	89037	41690
云　南	14238	9278	4294	666	71177	48394
西　藏	5464	5381	78	5	24639	17801
陕　西	28761	24210	3631	920	108010	51135
甘　肃	17297	13663	3042	592	67921	28618
青　海	4608	3994	343	271	18207	7096
宁　夏	2741	1971	576	194	11317	7067
新　疆	11691	8991	2345	355	58938	26968

织总表

单位:个、人

#女性	社区居委会（村委会）主任	#主任、书记“一肩挑”	#中共党员	#女性	受教育程度 大学专科人数
767148	**680089**	**245295**	**503248**	**111109**	**347110**
18046	6692	3828	5469	2087	10765
11731	5201	1983	3600	1311	6141
32504	52382	10795	30174	5446	11425
26208	30217	12840	21038	3279	11573
16916	13395	2892	7710	2900	6488
29557	15628	7043	11287	4001	20493
11758	11308	6609	7541	2699	443
17434	11603	2402	6489	3218	11458
15426	5621	1300	3841	2589	6548
34258	21297	5621	17208	4710	25209
36160	32075	2837	17618	4097	20357
23023	18028	3721	15510	2605	10493
16517	16692	898	7544	2016	3036
20223	20231	2955	10806	3546	3788
93372	80015	58724	77793	12397	55939
48168	51186	21545	38151	11633	29608
36190	29562	24106	27541	2604	10823
48089	46588	22191	40987	7771	16704
35516	25871	18806	21847	3355	15639
19645	16174	4184	12493	1968	6330
3511	3034	2143	2693	184	1731
17773	11010	774	9238	1865	10252
52280	52995	4276	36433	9193	22376
19652	18700	1667	12274	2831	5473
14659	14172	6199	10906	1632	4967
5449	5463	2664	3868	1128	391
26785	28717	1966	19278	3939	2916
12662	17263	1647	10046	2471	4273
3970	4604	1329	2961	654	755
3702	2722	1350	1935	307	1193
15964	11643	6000	8969	2673	9523

C-3-6续表1

地区	受教育程度	职业资格水平		年龄结构			
	大学本科及以上人数	助理社会工作师人数	社会工作师人数	35岁及以下人数	36岁至45岁人数	46岁至55岁人数	56岁及以上人数
全　国	**114377**	**14730**	**5118**	**582794**	**1226349**	**787832**	**205087**
中央级							
北　京	7675	2680	950	7488	11200	12079	3516
天　津	2777	740	155	6963	7609	7625	3007
河　北	1924	127	91	34686	82667	56664	11000
山　西	4861	116	91	23323	42384	34058	11128
内蒙古	1964	106	25	12897	22798	13051	3503
辽　宁	6545	864	333	17288	27747	20325	5952
吉　林	348	19	15	490	33777	132	31
黑龙江	2208	249	42	10150	29880	11165	1581
上　海	3079	674	250	5313	7612	10096	4248
江　苏	9647	3101	858	26214	44156	32802	7147
浙　江	7089	1606	700	26252	53908	36593	8781
安　徽	2120	818	270	14071	36764	21450	4667
福　建	654	216	119	13849	34935	18587	2995
江　西	403	114	10	16736	42301	15325	3021
山　东	24620	316	86	68840	140638	87453	23820
河　南	7729	55	84	43187	91951	60038	16704
湖　北	1934	169	68	24612	49311	33626	5621
湖　南	3546	218	70	34558	80614	41567	9501
广　东	5739	1294	502	23153	43363	43569	13373
广　西	1246	111	51	12494	28090	30482	9619
海　南	329	23		2712	6902	4509	1414
重　庆	2875	409	115	12875	23006	15039	3100
四　川	6812	435	133	45535	90511	58278	18764
贵　州	812	18	11	20253	36120	25377	7287
云　南	1140	59	16	18948	30866	17607	3756
西　藏	107			3444	8226	8327	4642
陕　西	846	33	21	17461	45819	35203	9527
甘　肃	1648	44	9	14727	34014	15528	3652
青　海	189	13	1	3732	8158	5270	1047
宁　夏	176	26	1	2533	4781	3585	418
新　疆	3335	77	41	18010	26241	12422	2265

单位：个、人、人次、时

志愿服务		居民(村民)小组	当年完成选举的居(村)委会数	当年完成选举的居(村)选民登记总数			
志愿者服务人次数	志愿服务时间				本届登记选民数	参加投票人数	委托投票人数
2342738	**6314397.5**	**6062180**	**330169**	**429867123**	**398331991**	**343615676**	**28635936**
162553	521477.0	83028	834	401962	382463	207921	22576
20792	59976.0	99266	2200	2130195	2007174	1822972	34952
44751	213841.0	323541	3921	2833440	2779069	2103401	45637
2794	4867.0	120157	23316	16034888	15386807	13094900	787660
9243	27014.0	70630	1				
35332	42478.0	190511	1623	3859892	2837653	2175964	68529
1		74350	5425	2803305	2345550	1938205	39595
10038	26417.0	137956	4582	10851422	7701740	6607064	99177
467066	973834.0	208627					
211356	522255.5	345779	2536	6609494	6491047	5436929	403133
114082	266835.0	330908	3498	6749629	6370110	6317590	421999
63565	156319.0	295584	10916	32214846	27837043	25247772	1655931
20087	40252.0	156607	1170	1026300	1003720	901468	8448
1536	4068.0	174199	1435	2130361	1592020	1688092	109095
145411	362921.0	550047	66315	55500876	52296416	43100024	5452308
7		401242	40273	55785394	51801063	44708095	2478183
19916	67206.0	242197	24451	26820086	25165734	19280131	4679333
42628	148216.0	487064	40713	40335803	37682512	35165649	2334927
68	123.0	254204	25783	56212770	54436543	48638977	3040379
7362	17724.0	275694	11571	25810424	25056691	21632393	2240196
		28449	1411	2034888	1874831	1345799	60583
342584	977292.0	94045	1503	4455714	4165728	2905844	316001
88573	291679.0	425898	30736	38043599	35080410	30297269	2850865
491991	1494225.0	182809	10256	16611249	15773175	13045404	675580
1106	2069.0	171312	3310	8074086	7299999	6553074	200895
		16383	3085	1044307	996532	944587	20509
2508	7858.0	146071	173	517925	336614	247657	8603
8		92572	4722	6836702	5947636	5410567	242218
23478	44043.0	14959	2884	2728470	2578471	2039489	333108
188	150.0	15696	540	468925	381238	317021	1212
13714	41258.0	52395	986	940171	724002	441418	4304

C-3-6续表2

地区	增加值合计	执行企业会计制度单位财务指标					执行行政	
		固定资产原价	营业收入	费用合计	营业利润	企业单位增加值	固定资产原价	上年结转和结余
全国	**4313800.5**	**2863527.7**	**1362536.0**	**294416.3**	**24846.5**	**212970.2**	**15128537.8**	**878930.5**
中央级								
北京	420742.3	2461730.3	1300932.8	259860.4	23912.1	183221.3	526232.8	188033.2
天津	35540.1						186878.4	19854.4
河北	88981.4	355.0					598851.2	17091.6
山西	103278.5						457310.5	1778.0
内蒙古	38638.5	30.0	2.0	2.5			81598.9	5.0
辽宁	110504.3	1771.9		8.1		11.0	196640.2	11572.4
吉林	14945.1						71640.2	939.2
黑龙江	46789.1	4318.5	14.0	186.4		100.2	349288.4	33385.4
上海	236391.8	329337.5	59220.0	32772.2	928.4	21045.6	1021996.8	135631.4
江苏	541180.7		140.0	140.0			2012764.9	27844.8
浙江	603628.5	1626.0					3420456.4	91541.4
安徽	106874.1						347725.5	9583.1
福建	53896.8	100.3	385.0	385.0			110638.8	1258.6
江西	45244.8	12593.0	1568.0	843.6	6.0	421.1	109341.9	-389.8
山东	678407.5						1399096.4	
河南	71856.2	6748.0	36.0	36.0			241951.6	1366.6
湖北	141959.1	1898.4					445760.8	172.7
湖南	146895.3	12.0					258864.8	716.0
广东	373155.1	26058.5	215.2	106.0		8152.6	1708045.0	80465.6
广西	47299.0	211.0				15.4	168778.3	413.5
海南	10067.1	2.5					25136.7	731.9
重庆	55883.4	14.0					161829.8	4812.3
四川	113658.5	3041.4		9.1			246511.0	160097.7
贵州	62676.5	75.0					36855.4	2632.7
云南	52708.1	1162.6		64.0		19.0	386345.8	86042.1
西藏	743.2	7491.0					18276.8	
陕西	48183.8						173063.3	954.5
甘肃	22073.2	30.5					132551.8	249.6
青海	3333.2						4709.1	
宁夏	9530.6	1558.0				26.0	134740.1	39.0
新疆	28734.5	3362.3	23.0	3.0		-42.0	94656.2	2107.6

单位：万元

事业单位会计制度财务指标				执行民间非营利组织单位会计制度财务指标				
本年收入合计	本年支出合计	收支结余	行政事业单位增加值	固定资产原价	上年结余	本年收入合计	本年费用合计	社会组织增加值
8366917.6	**11373307.6**	**30651.1**	**3756683.9**	**2494387.5**	**90812.2**	**2246029.9**	**833931.8**	**344146.4**
253518.0	329772.5	3177.6	237521.0					
151053.3	152332.2		35522.1	22.9			36.0	18.0
330044.2	328320.9		87662.5	21451.3	241.0	4486.5	5242.9	1318.9
151890.0	167893.6	4.0	100686.4	20557.3	36.0	4579.2	7512.8	2592.1
56881.5	56848.1		34358.3	16430.1	30.0	8319.7	6934.7	4280.2
105657.3	167439.9	3717.7	96955.7	70192.3	2490.0	25735.6	25827.1	13537.6
31799.9	28510.5	26.2	14945.1					
52689.2	57162.5		42235.2	8161.7	47.0	6856.3	5512.4	4453.7
461963.8	393031.8	7428.1	214920.6			1.0	498.2	425.6
778713.8	917764.4	1433.9	482518.5	564991.1	928.4	209049.7	184447.9	58662.2
1204645.3	1021754.4	8854.5	558106.0	763016.7	3306.2	257671.6	190537.5	45522.5
131662.8	127867.8	355.6	87924.4	129212.3	2682.2	30193.9	32467.8	18949.7
133368.2	133345.1		36045.1	117914.4	22825.8	62714.1	51521.3	17851.7
60363.6	60572.2		34651.6	17192.2	1073.0	12570.5	14601.8	10172.1
1175714.0	1175714.0		678407.5					
124257.1	127161.8	248.8	54287.9	98811.7	24.0	43209.5	46608.3	17568.3
199064.1	199497.6		116569.8	46623.7	722.0	70104.2	56151.4	25389.3
253278.6	247322.6		144192.4	24181.8		4767.5	4233.9	2702.9
817564.6	603977.9	725.6	340632.6	157054.0	10310.1	28675.5	40437.0	24369.9
88099.3	53025.8	149.0	46085.9	2379.8	34.0	941.4	1366.7	1197.7
20247.7	18744.1	247.7	10067.1					
65732.6	66412.0	3287.9	39902.8	74161.9	633.0	33627.4	32653.0	15980.6
1354184.3	1353237.1	584.6	91564.2	60166.5	1378.7	18804.3	33379.6	22094.3
25587.6	24358.0		23421.0	144046.1	29489.2	61801.8	60558.8	39255.5
82281.1	75335.5	384.9	42138.0	102060.2	14530.1	17913.2	21191.6	10551.1
729.9	749.9		743.2	336.0				
67107.1	63180.7		48183.8					
66265.9	24837.4		20684.4	13056.2		1336637.6	1395.6	1388.8
778.9	682.4		272.0	29951.1	31.5	5591.6	6272.4	3061.2
80195.0	4185.5		8696.2	3576.7		716.8	1414.3	808.4
41578.9	3392269.4	25.0	26782.4	8839.5		1061.0	3128.8	1994.1

C-3-7 村民

地区	单位数	居民1000户以下	居民1000户-3000户	居民3000户以上	社区居委会（村委会）成员
全　国	**585451**	**450122**	**114850**	**20479**	**2305024**
中央级					
北　京	3937	3599	321	17	14294
天　津	3698	3472	214	12	15197
河　北	48636	40535	7137	964	166067
山　西	28072	24273	3198	601	100090
内蒙古	11192	8474	2445	273	41011
辽　宁	11558	6922	3883	753	45492
吉　林	9313	6102	2426	785	27933
黑龙江	8902	5089	3326	487	39128
上　海	1605	1000	557	48	6157
江　苏	14428	6727	6146	1555	72219
浙　江	27997	22351	5236	410	105530
安　徽	14786	6983	5879	1924	60130
福　建	14440	11088	3071	281	58491
江　西	17011	10902	5495	614	64711
山　东	73388	61944	9583	1861	289019
河　南	46938	32053	12922	1963	190481
湖　北	25448	19058	5249	1141	92955
湖　南	41523	33096	6754	1673	143895
广　东	19347	14254	4341	752	85577
广　西	14291	10260	3608	423	68939
海　南	2561	2347	171	43	12791
重　庆	8255	5240	2711	304	37732
四　川	46318	36641	8148	1529	182594
贵　州	16747	14555	1788	404	77406
云　南	12035	8456	3318	261	58280
西　藏	5255	5211	40	4	23273
陕　西	26608	23202	2819	587	97283
甘　肃	15957	13103	2422	432	61345
青　海	4157	3740	172	245	16186
宁　夏	2274	1860	374	40	8973
新　疆	8774	7585	1096	93	41845

委员会

单位:个、人

#中共党员	#女性	社区居委会（村委会）主任	#主任、书记“一肩挑”	#中共党员	#女性
1315790	**526409**	**583980**	**205981**	**428203**	**71666**
10302	4235	3841	2237	3072	294
5223	3739	3646	871	2332	226
82142	22949	48583	9524	27560	3856
46856	20565	27964	11777	19433	2284
20006	9997	11164	1980	6155	1527
24793	11315	11535	4123	7738	1264
35	9306	9313	5698	6107	1746
19121	8256	8773	1355	4629	1330
4531	2000	1581	507	1248	353
48602	17155	14393	3346	11723	2144
45840	26183	27800	1726	14601	2479
40612	15534	14774	2819	12782	1493
20866	11502	14395	633	6290	1142
27199	14883	16937	2204	8925	2439
223247	83180	73388	54247	71283	10026
104370	39188	46798	20065	35145	10006
63286	26598	25382	21117	23823	924
94030	38941	41496	19626	36437	6035
61106	18419	19304	13895	16051	1219
47390	14123	14283	3644	10985	1323
9995	2574	2561	1767	2247	105
22840	9542	8246	271	6800	798
97230	41418	46230	3290	31328	7197
36355	14384	16692	1316	10843	1973
39986	10621	11985	5366	9137	1138
16714	5153	5255	2620	3722	1095
45906	21653	26573	1461	17651	3178
25958	9860	15927	1289	9194	1941
6057	2879	4156	1078	2579	458
5882	2056	2258	1111	1614	92
19310	8201	8747	5018	6769	1581

C-3-7续表1

地区	受教育程度		职业资格水平	
	大学专科人数	大学本科及以上人数	助理社会工作师人数	社会工作师人数
全　国	**212881**	**55939**	**1579**	**516**
中央级				
北　京	3306	1146	90	18
天　津	2125	490	2	3
河　北	7072	541	19	15
山　西	8535	3760	2	6
内蒙古	3127	703	8	3
辽　宁	9119	1472	44	26
吉　林	11	6		
黑龙江	6823	972	160	10
上　海	1864	655	69	26
江　苏	13676	4429	579	132
浙　江	13997	3387	124	39
安　徽	6256	1055	111	26
福　建	1615	233	6	10
江　西	2058	186	1	1
山　东	46286	18189	51	7
河　南	24744	6588	19	46
湖　北	5590	674	5	5
湖　南	11375	2097	44	27
广　东	4685	774	123	49
广　西	3538	253	9	12
海　南	1125	112		
重　庆	4854	729	23	8
四　川	15985	4982	50	18
贵　州	3477	477	1	7
云　南	2585	395	6	1
西　藏	320	68		
陕　西	836	123	5	15
甘　肃	2957	870	5	4
青　海	255	46	5	
宁　夏	350	43	1	
新　疆	4335	484	17	2

单位：人、人次、时

年龄结构				志愿服务	
35岁及以下人数	36岁至45岁人数	46岁至55岁人数	56岁及以上人数	志愿者服务人次数	志愿服务时间
440983	**1017619**	**670031**	**176391**	**984024**	**2941713.5**
1224	4696	6442	1932		
2983	4984	5189	2041	13792	38476.0
28315	74937	52592	10223	37585	180246.0
20103	37778	31656	10553	807	1803.0
9020	17732	11049	3210	121	152.0
7632	17799	15093	4968	1521	2750.0
5	27898	17	13	1	
6350	22507	8957	1314	514	1727.0
1375	1905	2340	537	14735	51670.0
15977	28882	22409	4951	74259	170337.5
20001	45792	31917	7820	35516	97150.0
9516	29189	17414	4011	32201	83198.0
11141	29463	15428	2459	20084	40252.0
13398	35495	13127	2691	2	6.0
60850	126623	79659	21887	121677	306157.0
36697	82261	55803	15720		
19173	40663	28187	4932	262	886.0
28273	70256	36850	8516	28299	107632.0
12953	28536	33279	10809	68	123.0
9161	23712	27385	8681	193	324.0
2063	5670	3867	1191		
7244	16507	11559	2422	110248	331712.0
37302	77548	50964	16780	56802	218384.0
17326	31506	22312	6262	426648	1287621.0
15856	25339	14297	2788	724	1364.0
3154	7766	7954	4399		
14911	41433	32118	8821	1405	4426.0
12726	30784	14390	3445	8	
3114	7049	5063	960	6432	15317.0
1676	3647	3253	397	120	
11464	19262	9461	1658		

C-3-7续表2

地区	当年完成选举的村委会数	当年完成选举的村选民登记数	本届登记选民数	参加投票人数	委托投票人数
全国	**302832**	**368872058**	**343801097**	**301390325**	**26221084**
中央级					
北京	729	215435	195936	172554	22353
天津	1976	1856152	1825677	1678748	24283
河北	3738	2629190	2581926	1947252	43985
山西	22866	15555318	14919910	12791419	772285
内蒙古	1				
辽宁	1207	2456917	2291502	1977945	63499
吉林	4829	1902152	1815113	1581613	35720
黑龙江	4318	10060678	7063743	6095868	94516
上海					
江苏	1404	3605690	3573978	3189946	269366
浙江	2840	4704220	4352875	4466826	356197
安徽	10065	29490252	25661786	23527730	1515289
福建	883	619071	616015	570922	7159
江西	1247	1764589	1388583	1421722	24129
山东	61109	48183478	45940381	38062933	5018401
河南	39232	54255204	50389612	43522805	2454178
湖北	24009	25303292	23686204	18224469	4656187
湖南	40625	40019879	37366875	34850204	2334927
广东	19312	40550291	39491427	37458379	2547557
广西	10256	21029091	20372329	17832695	1987069
海南	1186	1687902	1685512	1181214	54789
重庆	1047	2469482	2246492	1618050	209743
四川	27235	31291205	29046643	25068022	2504393
贵州	8975	13669045	12967017	10999711	493940
云南	2766	5888216	5670307	5312133	182742
西藏	3007	988379	948288	893824	19648
陕西	77	254494	236149	221900	7650
甘肃	4153	5145004	4403344	4234776	216965
青海	2574	2400016	2264077	1782051	299477
宁夏	450	360101	356955	314790	1207
新疆	716	517315	442441	389824	3430

单位：个、人、次

经推举产生的村民代表数	女性	当年召开村民会议次数	当年召开村民代表会议的次数	自然村	村委会小组数
14697883	**3149748**	**506434**	**867222**	**1922379**	**4704267**
31057	9835	596	2059	3591	28641
30142	8772	177	2048	3009	37001
77979	13134	2766	9574	68622	281605
454237	49493	20705	43896	45267	104180
1226	195	22	33	34382	50453
237318	6060	432	1250	32680	76911
35003	3365	352	523	10682	48325
670814	17776	15386	1973	16578	72465
		101	136	1278	26769
127283	34013	7330	27160	72830	208179
166077	55593	23127	19014	89577	259621
542402	147105	6995	17845	135904	244814
53929	11555	480	720	64676	131043
30099	7979	58	89	113533	159967
1837798	456662	181732	369039	91828	465817
1939575	553054	44859	50562	155355	366972
827035	184654	27812	73169	98104	195904
2640464	638649	28087	50462	124885	431411
1326648	294527	21869	40394	141674	204295
1506080	203622	27634	36514	156989	241286
38094	6824	1037	2342	16671	25053
32305	3730	1391	3792	6127	68520
732608	107108	26863	39315	81625	369754
745275	219961	41349	44794	78141	158934
254385	78601	5136	2478	117391	148030
51154	5238	559	509	14248	15390
3924	79	15122	21575	64632	133054
181129	19087	1904	2908	60710	86207
83224	8511	2147	1863	5591	13782
13475	2014	308	599	4800	13796
27144	2552	98	587	10999	36088

C-3-7续表3

地　区	增加值合计	执行企业会计制度单位财务指标					执行行政	
		固定资产原价	营业收入	费用合计	营业利润	企业单位增加值	固定资产原价	上年结转和结余
全　国	**3215299.5**	**2844361.1**	**1361651.8**	**293554.5**	**24840.5**	**211296.2**	**11872976.6**	**718386.8**
中央级								
北　京	317866.2	2461730.3	1300932.8	259860.4	23912.1	183221.3	392152.2	170965.2
天　津	26871.5						169421.6	19658.9
河　北	78645.1						551639.6	8964.4
山　西	54328.7						438462.5	1665.0
内蒙古	27587.4	8.0	2.0	2.5			63531.9	5.0
辽　宁	52343.7	1360.9		7.8		11.0	168853.7	9058.5
吉　林	12454.9						66656.2	788.6
黑龙江	30848.1	15.5	2.0	30.5		0.9	122827.4	33191.4
上　海	187063.5	329334.5	59220.0	32772.2	928.4	21045.6	861669.1	94855.3
江　苏	338337.8		140.0	140.0			1366617.4	24847.2
浙　江	471552.3	1626.0					2951387.1	59009.9
安　徽	83087.4						267613.2	1814.6
福　建	43968.1	0.3					78852.2	1616.8
江　西	34370.0	10668.0	1168.0	584.0		298.8	90211.2	-445.3
山　东	581848.0						1118724.5	
河　南	62706.8	5943.0	30.0	30.0			209041.3	1199.9
湖　北	109412.5	1176.4					307821.0	1.7
湖　南	107469.9	12.0					192495.9	697.6
广　东	256384.4	21296.6	157.0	68.0		6673.2	1305305.8	52888.7
广　西	39108.3	28.0				15.4	140951.4	298.3
海　南	6677.1						21128.9	317.5
重　庆	33237.0	14.0					95863.2	3758.8
四　川	88525.2	2891.4		9.1			186394.2	152721.5
贵　州	52875.4	75.0					33004.9	2191.7
云　南	34891.4	425.0		50.0		13.0	265955.3	77109.7
西　藏	276.7	6001.0					6916.8	
陕　西	43666.2						154969.3	927.3
甘　肃	17314.0	29.5					63575.7	229.0
青　海	2712.2						4461.9	
宁　夏	8523.2	1143.7				12.0	128780.0	39.0
新　疆	10346.5	582.0				5.0	47691.2	10.6

单位：万元

事业单位会计制度财务指标				执行民间非营利组织单位会计制度财务指标				
本年收入合计	本年支出合计	收支结余	行政事业单位增加值	固定资产原价	上年结余	本年收入合计	本年费用合计	社会组织增加值
6513868.4	**6235315.0**	**22160.4**	**8464.0**	**2046643.1**	**61850.9**	**2087395.3**	**669026.0**	**266737.9**
131794.7	194702.7	184.3	3.4					
139603.3	140436.5							
312726.1	312117.2		3.0	20063.3	229.0	3964.8	4727.0	1141.5
90634.1	90602.3	4.0	252.5	18183.3	36.0	4275.2	6914.9	2301.4
42984.9	42959.6			14925.6		6958.7	5504.0	3350.5
55281.6	99771.2	3717.2	3491.0	63630.4	1237.0	20573.2	19170.6	8389.6
26593.7	24071.9	26.2						
39197.7	42802.4			7503.0	47.0	6361.2	4994.3	4142.5
321225.4	261605.0	9232.5	680.6					
489893.4	652894.0	1484.8	1061.3	399059.4	218.4	145376.0	133938.8	39615.7
959547.4	815831.6	3774.2	592.0	730565.3	3306.2	237990.2	167238.2	37696.0
103189.6	97744.7	312.6	1.6	98559.6	2638.4	23093.5	25527.7	14884.1
99817.0	99548.6		10.0	85954.6	11336.0	48973.0	39560.5	13959.8
47473.8	47842.6			15322.3	993.0	9921.0	10654.5	7139.1
986096.3	986096.3							
106962.9	109822.7	242.2		92284.8	4.0	40798.5	43703.7	16292.3
151016.0	151247.8			40848.4	694.0	62008.4	51150.0	23238.1
184301.1	181194.8			20011.7		3721.9	3487.1	2303.4
512905.7	322482.0	1.3	1960.4	119365.0	10019.1	27889.2	25528.1	16091.6
78196.5	43093.3	149.0		648.3	34.0	900.2	1227.8	1115.3
13576.2	12064.6	247.7						
36708.2	37900.4	2596.8		55498.2	393.0	24724.9	23730.9	11547.8
1323778.8	1305548.3	151.6	211.6	49221.1	1042.9	14544.8	27901.0	18526.4
21075.7	20229.7		15.8	126230.9	27619.0	54348.7	51628.8	34015.3
50808.8	46459.1	36.0	19.0	39935.0	1973.9	8536.5	11989.4	4677.3
725.9	725.9			105.0				
60845.3	56963.8		57.0					
32766.8	21511.9			12370.2		1336625.1	1332.5	1326.7
767.0	672.5			24212.2	30.0	4357.9	5077.3	2460.0
79535.8	3506.3			3428.5		673.4	1233.9	710.8
13838.7	12865.3		104.8	8717.0		779.0	2805.0	1812.7

C-3-8 社区

地区	单位数	居民1000户以下	居民1000户–3000户	居民3000户以上	社区居委会（村委会）成员
全国	**96693**	**38063**	**43000**	**15630**	**497038**
中央级					
北京	2932	604	1823	505	19989
天津	1575	364	964	247	10007
河北	3835	1605	1784	446	18950
山西	2282	750	1264	268	10803
内蒙古	2235	623	1270	342	11238
辽宁	4105	719	2010	1376	25820
吉林	1995	629	1038	328	6497
黑龙江	2839	780	1442	617	13648
上海	4122	1149	2749	224	21112
江苏	6972	2081	3566	1325	38100
浙江	4321	1961	1805	555	20004
安徽	3257	1021	1568	668	16822
福建	2308	1139	958	211	11875
江西	3308	1711	1385	212	12672
山东	6627	3903	2036	688	31732
河南	4404	2063	1760	581	21399
湖北	4187	1617	1631	939	20215
湖南	5100	2587	1876	637	22345
广东	6586	2138	2901	1547	37881
广西	1892	668	857	367	11746
海南	475	246	140	89	2746
重庆	2775	829	1194	752	16288
四川	6805	3374	2239	1192	30494
贵州	2016	1171	672	173	11631
云南	2203	822	976	405	12897
西藏	209	170	38	1	1366
陕西	2153	1008	812	333	10727
甘肃	1340	560	620	160	6576
青海	451	254	171	26	2021
宁夏	467	111	202	154	2344
新疆	2917	1406	1249	262	17093

居委会

单位:个、人

#中共党员	#女性	社区居委会（村委会）主任	#主任、书记“一肩挑”	#中共党员	#女性
265098	**240739**	**96109**	**39314**	**75045**	**39443**
9200	13811	2851	1591	2397	1793
4028	7992	1555	1112	1268	1085
8648	9555	3799	1271	2614	1590
4834	5643	2253	1063	1605	995
5214	6919	2231	912	1555	1373
12403	18242	4093	2920	3549	2737
447	2452	1995	911	1434	953
4610	9178	2830	1047	1860	1888
9332	13426	4040	793	2593	2236
23601	17103	6904	2275	5485	2566
11506	9977	4275	1111	3017	1618
9705	7489	3254	902	2728	1112
4759	5015	2297	265	1254	874
4967	5340	3294	751	1881	1107
22511	10192	6627	4477	6510	2371
9145	8980	4388	1480	3006	1627
12857	9592	4180	2989	3718	1680
14474	9148	5092	2565	4550	1736
24464	17097	6567	4911	5796	2136
6775	5522	1891	540	1508	645
1963	937	473	376	446	79
9918	8231	2764	503	2438	1067
17136	10862	6765	986	5105	1996
5335	5268	2008	351	1431	858
8408	4038	2187	833	1769	494
1087	296	208	44	146	33
5229	5132	2144	505	1627	761
2660	2802	1336	358	852	530
1039	1091	448	251	382	196
1185	1646	464	239	321	215
7658	7763	2896	982	2200	1092

C-3-8续表1

地区	受教育程度		职业资格水平	
	大学专科人数	大学本科及以上人数	助理社会工作师人数	社会工作师人数
全国	**134229**	**58438**	**13151**	**4602**
中央级				
北京	7459	6529	2590	932
天津	4016	2287	738	152
河北	4353	1383	108	76
山西	3038	1101	114	85
内蒙古	3361	1261	98	22
辽宁	11374	5073	820	307
吉林	432	342	19	15
黑龙江	4635	1236	89	32
上海	4684	2424	605	224
江苏	11533	5218	2522	726
浙江	6360	3702	1482	661
安徽	4237	1065	707	244
福建	1421	421	210	109
江西	1730	217	113	9
山东	9653	6431	265	79
河南	4864	1141	36	38
湖北	5233	1260	164	63
湖南	5329	1449	174	43
广东	10954	4965	1171	453
广西	2792	993	102	39
海南	606	217	23	
重庆	5398	2146	386	107
四川	6391	1830	385	115
贵州	1996	335	17	4
云南	2382	745	53	15
西藏	71	39		
陕西	2080	723	28	6
甘肃	1316	778	39	5
青海	500	143	8	1
宁夏	843	133	25	1
新疆	5188	2851	60	39

单位：人、人次、时

年龄结构				志愿服务	
35岁及以下人数	36岁至45岁人数	46岁至55岁人数	56岁及以上人数	志愿者服务人次数	志愿服务时间
141811	**208730**	**117801**	**28696**	**1358714**	**3372684.0**
6264	6504	5637	1584	162553	521477.0
3980	2625	2436	966	7000	21500.0
6371	7730	4072	777	7166	33595.0
3220	4606	2402	575	1987	3064.0
3877	5066	2002	293	9122	26862.0
9656	9948	5232	984	33811	39728.0
485	5879	115	18		
3800	7373	2208	267	9524	24690.0
3938	5707	7756	3711	452331	922164.0
10237	15274	10393	2196	137097	351918.0
6251	8116	4676	961	78566	169685.0
4555	7575	4036	656	31364	73121.0
2708	5472	3159	536	3	
3338	6806	2198	330	1534	4062.0
7990	14015	7794	1933	23734	56764.0
6490	9690	4235	984	7	
5439	8648	5439	689	19654	66320.0
6285	10358	4717	985	14329	40584.0
10200	14827	10290	2564		
3333	4378	3097	938	7169	17400.0
649	1232	642	223		
5631	6499	3480	678	232336	645580.0
8233	12963	7314	1984	31771	73295.0
2927	4614	3065	1025	65343	206604.0
3092	5527	3310	968	382	705.0
290	460	373	243		
2550	4386	3085	706	1103	3432.0
2001	3230	1138	207		
618	1109	207	87	17046	28726.0
857	1134	332	21	68	150.0
6546	6979	2961	607	13714	41258.0

C-3-8续表2

地 区	当年完成选举的居委会数	当年完成选举的居选民登记数	本届登记选民数
全 国	**27337**	**60995065**	**54530894**
中央级			
北 京	105	186527	186527
天 津	224	274043	181497
河 北	183	204250	197143
山 西	450	479570	466897
内蒙古			
辽 宁	416	1402975	546151
吉 林	596	901153	530437
黑龙江	264	790744	637997
上 海			
江 苏	1132	3003804	2917069
浙 江	658	2045409	2017235
安 徽	851	2724594	2175257
福 建	287	407229	387705
江 西	188	365772	203437
山 东	5206	7317398	6356035
河 南	1041	1530190	1411451
湖 北	442	1516794	1479530
湖 南	88	315924	315637
广 东	6471	15662479	14945116
广 西	1315	4781333	4684362
海 南	225	346986	189319
重 庆	456	1986232	1919236
四 川	3501	6752394	6033767
贵 州	1281	2942204	2806158
云 南	544	2185870	1629692
西 藏	78	55928	48244
陕 西	96	263431	100465
甘 肃	569	1691698	1544292
青 海	310	328454	314394
宁 夏	90	108824	24283
新 疆	270	422856	281561

单位：个、人

参加投票人数	委托投票人数	居委会小组数
42225351	**2414852**	**1357913**
35367	223	54387
144224	10669	62265
156149	1652	41936
303481	15375	15977
		20177
198019	5030	113600
356592	3875	26025
511196	4661	65491
		181858
2246983	133767	137600
1850764	65802	71287
1720042	140642	50770
330546	1289	25564
266370	84966	14232
5037091	433907	84230
1185290	24005	34270
1055662	23146	46293
315445		55653
11180598	492822	49909
3799698	253127	34408
164585	5794	3396
1287794	106258	25525
5229247	346472	56144
2045693	181640	23875
1240941	18153	23282
50763	861	993
25757	953	13017
1175791	25253	6365
257438	33631	1177
2231	5	1900
51594	874	16307

C-3-8续表3

地区	增加值合计	执行企业会计制度单位财务指标					执行行政	
		固定资产原价	营业收入	费用合计	营业利润	企业单位增加值	固定资产原价	上年结转和结余
全　国	**1098501.0**	**19166.6**	**884.2**	**861.8**	**6.0**	**1674.0**	**3255561.2**	**160543.7**
中央级								
北　京	102876.1						134080.6	17068.0
天　津	8668.6						17456.8	195.5
河　北	10336.3	355.0					47211.6	8127.2
山　西	48949.8						18848.0	113.0
内蒙古	11051.1	22.0					18067.0	
辽　宁	58160.6	411.0		0.3			27786.5	2513.9
吉　林	2490.2						4984.0	150.6
黑龙江	15941.0	4303.0	12.0	155.9		99.3	226461.0	194.0
上　海	49328.3	3.0					160327.7	40776.1
江　苏	202842.9						646147.5	2997.6
浙　江	132076.2						469069.3	32531.5
安　徽	23786.7						80112.3	7768.5
福　建	9928.7	100.0	385.0	385.0			31786.6	-358.2
江　西	10874.8	1925.0	400.0	259.6	6.0	122.3	19130.7	55.5
山　东	96559.5						280371.9	
河　南	9149.4	805.0	6.0	6.0			32910.3	166.7
湖　北	32546.6	722.0					137939.8	171.0
湖　南	39425.4						66368.9	18.4
广　东	116770.7	4761.9	58.2	38.0		1479.4	402739.2	27576.9
广　西	8190.7	183.0					27826.9	115.2
海　南	3390.0	2.5					4007.8	414.4
重　庆	22646.4						65966.6	1053.5
四　川	25133.3	150.0					60116.8	7376.2
贵　州	9801.1						3850.5	441.0
云　南	17816.7	737.6		14.0		6.0	120390.5	8932.4
西　藏	466.5	1490.0					11360.0	
陕　西	4517.6						18094.0	27.2
甘　肃	4759.2	1.0					68976.1	20.6
青　海	621.0						247.2	
宁　夏	1007.4	414.3				14.0	5960.1	
新　疆	18388.0	2780.3	23.0	3.0		-47.0	46965.0	2097.0

单位：万元

事业单位会计制度财务指标				执行民间非营利组织单位会计制度财务指标				
本年收入合计	本年支出合计	收支结余	行政事业单位增加值	固定资产原价	上年结余	本年收入合计	本年费用合计	社会组织增加值
1853049.2	**5137992.6**	**8490.7**	**1019418.5**	**447744.4**	**28961.3**	**158634.6**	**164905.8**	**77408.5**
121723.3	135069.8	2993.3	102876.1					
11450.0	11895.7		8650.6	22.9			36.0	18.0
17318.1	16203.7		10158.9	1388.0	12.0	521.7	515.9	177.4
61255.9	77291.3		48659.1	2374.0		304.0	597.9	290.7
13896.6	13888.5		10121.4	1504.5	30.0	1361.0	1430.7	929.7
50375.7	67668.7	0.5	53012.6	6561.9	1253.0	5162.4	6656.5	5148.0
5206.2	4438.6		2490.2					
13491.5	14360.1		15530.5	658.7		495.1	518.1	311.2
140738.4	131426.8	-1804.4	48902.7			1.0	498.2	425.6
288820.4	264870.4	-50.9	183796.4	165931.7	710.0	63673.7	50509.1	19046.5
245097.9	205922.8	5080.3	124249.7	32451.4		19681.4	23299.3	7826.5
28473.2	30123.1	43.0	19721.1	30652.7	43.8	7100.4	6940.1	4065.6
33551.2	33796.5		6036.8	31959.8	11489.8	13741.1	11960.8	3891.9
12889.8	12729.6		7719.5	1869.9	80.0	2649.5	3947.3	3033.0
189617.7	189617.7		96559.5					
17294.2	17339.1	6.6	7873.4	6526.9	20.0	2411.0	2904.6	1276.0
48048.1	48249.8		30395.4	5775.3	28.0	8095.8	5001.4	2151.2
68977.5	66127.8		39025.9	4170.1		1045.6	746.8	399.5
304658.9	281495.9	724.3	107013.0	37689.0	291.0	786.3	14908.9	8278.3
9902.8	9932.5		8108.3	1731.5		41.2	138.9	82.4
6671.5	6679.5		3390.0					
29024.4	28511.6	691.1	18213.6	18663.7	240.0	8902.5	8922.1	4432.8
30405.5	47688.8	433.0	21565.4	10945.4	335.8	4259.5	5478.6	3567.9
4511.9	4128.3		4560.9	17815.2	1870.2	7453.1	8930.0	5240.2
31472.3	28876.4	348.9	11936.9	62125.2	12556.2	9376.7	9202.2	5873.8
4.0	24.0		466.5	231.0				
6261.8	6216.9		4517.6					
33499.1	3325.5		4697.1	686.0		12.5	63.1	62.1
11.9	9.9		19.8	5738.9	1.5	1233.7	1195.1	601.2
659.2	679.2		895.8	148.2		43.4	180.4	97.6
27740.2	3379404.1	25.0	18253.6	122.5		282.0	323.8	181.4

C-3-9 其他社会服务

地区	单位数	工商登记	编制登记	民政登记	设施	年末职工人数	女性	受教育大学专科人数
全国	**6795**	**737**	**4148**	**627**	**1283**	**93412**	**30044**	**26177**
中央级								
北京	68	4	64			1849	612	373
天津	43	2	34	6	1	942	275	213
河北	254	4	212	9	29	3965	1216	804
山西	146	11	87	11	37	1304	443	453
内蒙古	169	15	126	4	24	2208	657	707
辽宁	398	34	240	103	21	5755	1874	1733
吉林	215	32	156	3	24	4972	619	1652
黑龙江	229	14	163	34	18	3440	1142	1142
上海	93	56	36		1	3229	1322	570
江苏	345	56	232	43	14	4975	1634	1382
浙江	299	56	197	12	34	3915	1076	1080
安徽	269	23	167	21	58	3406	1167	885
福建	209	30	138	2	39	3051	859	519
江西	236	6	152	42	36	2264	716	388
山东	288	19	248	6	15	4429	1436	1554
河南	305	30	235	17	23	6251	1983	1782
湖北	275	18	202	14	41	4286	1611	1512
湖南	348	31	190	6	121	3769	1315	1309
广东	448	52	243	30	123	8335	2317	1735
广西	171	24	109		38	2200	809	713
海南	31	6	22	2	1	309	77	66
重庆	167	26	95	26	20	2403	990	763
四川	426	45	257	22	102	4860	1804	1441
贵州	316	56	94	16	150	3784	1456	1098
云南	299	21	160	37	81	1670	500	561
西藏	27		3	24		77	35	29
陕西	177	31	117	12	17	2822	1024	741
甘肃	221	17	60	21	123	1181	440	329
青海	49	9	11	6	23	185	46	43
宁夏	81	3	20	54	4	217	64	77
新疆	193	6	78	44	65	1359	525	523

机构总表

单位：个、人、人次、时

程度	职业资格水平		年龄结构				志愿服务	
大学本科及以上人数	助理社会工作师人数	社会工作师人数	35岁及以下人数	36岁至45岁人数	46岁至55岁人数	56岁及以上人数	志愿者服务人次数	志愿服务时间
11249	**803**	**681**	**31720**	**35618**	**20088**	**5986**	**20539**	**62397.0**
456	59	36	616	567	480	186	148	568.0
244	2	5	269	260	269	144	300	700.0
306	15	22	1467	1532	767	199	351	1588.0
234	2	8	514	511	231	48		
258	9	11	630	846	588	144		
951	41	44	1969	1976	1355	455	150	278.0
453	6	13	1381	1736	1318	537		
457	17	16	871	1463	874	232		
356	12	23	780	1012	963	474	1815	9292.0
736	77	51	1493	1942	1196	344	1308	5003.0
613	41	37	1166	1380	1005	364	5482	9000.0
258	100	37	1084	1396	742	184	1776	4870.0
261	33	41	925	1279	670	177	6	16.0
102	29	24	798	995	390	81	359	1090.0
806	45	62	1599	1690	897	243	3770	10065.0
500	52	46	3076	2146	819	210	100	150.0
391	32	16	1419	1717	964	186	410	1260.0
516	22	15	1522	1501	619	127	1231	5234.0
763	95	47	2708	3341	1828	458	20	43.0
307	26	14	781	888	393	138		
28	2		100	137	60	12		
361	9	15	786	930	520	167	2126	6958.0
536	43	42	1571	1985	1029	275	2	4.0
384	5	12	1397	1569	690	128	941	5175.0
238	13	19	599	644	242	185	14	39.0
19			51	17	9			
293	8	16	1035	1051	577	159	114	624.0
187	3	2	456	413	275	37		
14			51	93	39	2		
79	1	6	42	105	60	10		
142	4	1	564	496	219	80	116	440.0

C-3-9续表

地区	增加值合计	执行企业会计制度单位财务指标					执行行政	
		固定资产原价	营业收入	费用合计	营业利润	企业单位增加值	固定资产原价	上年结转和结余
全国	**994065.3**	**922067.8**	**909193.5**	**239462.2**	**171638.9**	**334903.6**	**1858650.8**	**109889.2**
中央级								
北京	47596.9	23994.2	57498.0	20150.4	16225.6	24392.4	104351.3	3490.7
天津	17446.6	5981.2	3416.0	1944.4	124.3	1226.8	31934.8	12049.0
河北	21018.5	3700.7	3499.0	3380.0	-603.6	206.9	70918.0	2437.8
山西	8621.8	8777.0	2763.0	971.0	-40.0	1463.5	31476.2	1009.5
内蒙古	13782.6	14559.1	5630.9	3123.0	80.0	1183.3	31055.2	646.1
辽宁	53417.5	38442.0	27964.5	15554.0	1391.4	13636.9	84132.6	3437.2
吉林	11407.7	19147.3	821.2	45.7	27.7	420.7	71800.6	395.0
黑龙江	26986.0	18478.2	7898.4	4784.5	1536.0	4022.9	71097.3	2357.7
上海	150178.7	246924.6	375773.9	70388.8	90349.1	147402.2	2087.0	1909.8
江苏	101704.8	38734.1	57870.4	9464.4	30209.9	35835.4	181217.4	13904.4
浙江	64260.5	34434.8	54490.1	10823.2	7284.5	12479.3	98033.7	9040.8
安徽	28148.2	16912.1	10234.9	4415.6	1069.6	4814.6	51519.0	1684.2
福建	29279.4	56454.9	25963.0	10182.8	3001.2	12171.8	42623.1	5067.8
江西	12291.8	7376.4	3238.0	913.9	148.0	783.8	26608.9	229.4
山东	43074.1	7293.9	4626.4	2006.9	377.1	1722.9	96033.2	
河南	20160.5	18621.0	9099.4	3486.1	794.5	3388.8	51975.3	318.9
湖北	36796.7	12268.4	9643.7	4108.3	1086.6	3158.8	90257.0	172.6
湖南	24455.4	33565.2	11435.2	5238.1	527.8	3173.4	138685.1	445.6
广东	110073.6	50201.0	38320.1	12250.4	5721.0	13871.9	249538.6	8261.8
广西	25145.7	28275.1	67440.8	7131.1	1163.8	8401.3	34986.7	9479.7
海南	3496.5	7084.0	3893.1	1961.7	1112.6	2318.6	8339.6	1717.8
重庆	22741.0	27784.8	22421.2	6000.1	789.1	2952.9	44116.2	1739.9
四川	47106.6	38728.8	33549.9	11581.6	1592.1	7560.7	93893.3	21599.9
贵州	22845.8	89790.9	38248.5	16350.3	3839.7	17423.7	21990.1	495.1
云南	12812.8	42062.2	4601.1	1853.8	581.5	3371.9	35274.7	1039.1
西藏	333.1	388.8				0.4	1801.2	140.0
陕西	17256.5	18121.6	20408.3	9184.5	1866.8	4422.1	21685.1	4834.3
甘肃	8415.4	3909.8	6095.9	917.4	1274.1	2668.6	20282.7	94.1
青海	602.4	1441.0	213.0	213.0		65.0	1536.5	
宁夏	1647.5	433.0	402.0	324.0	7.0	45.3	8492.5	930.8
新疆	10959.9	8181.7	1733.6	713.2	101.5	316.9	40907.9	960.2

单位：万元

事业单位会计制度财务指标				执行民间非营利组织单位会计制度财务指标				
本年收入合计	本年支出合计	收支结余	行政事业单位增加值	固定资产原价	上年结余	本年收入合计	本年费用合计	社会组织增加值
1462109.8	**1367846.6**	**63252.4**	**654281.5**	**57747.2**	**2992.7**	**13247.5**	**10394.6**	**4880.2**
120708.4	119268.5	2119.2	23204.5					
36425.4	44351.7	12413.3	16209.4	39.0		100.0	59.3	10.4
41566.7	39490.5	3308.6	20810.1	150.0		95.7	10.0	1.5
24849.2	23091.1	-14.7	7155.3	1.0		7.0	7.0	3.0
21442.1	20479.9	983.7	12547.3			203.0	203.0	52.0
81576.7	78121.9	4035.8	38970.2	3656.9	503.5	1206.8	1130.1	810.4
14740.1	14525.8	1011.6	10987.0					
42774.8	40041.8	83.5	22893.3	462.0		218.0	103.8	69.8
8430.7	8162.6	1796.3	2776.5					
129547.2	118721.6	11159.9	65082.0	5500.3		3397.5	2627.2	787.4
101231.3	91112.6	4340.2	51431.0	733.0	1209.5	1494.5	849.2	350.2
43087.5	41115.5	1468.4	23063.1	2527.1	260.0	1121.6	957.7	270.5
37190.2	38709.3	2186.0	17085.6	5.0		137.3	127.6	22.0
20378.0	17827.1	-4.7	11500.8	15.0		18.0	13.3	7.2
75548.3	75548.3		40874.3	2598.4		786.5	786.5	476.9
32766.2	30356.1	1031.8	16765.6	383.0		152.0	8.7	6.1
80197.5	80085.6	274.0	33628.0	62.0		18.0	18.0	9.9
124995.9	123235.0	285.7	21256.0	1670.0		186.5	69.0	26.0
198236.2	148783.5	6509.9	96147.4	1812.3	99.2	102.5	82.9	54.3
29043.6	28108.3	1738.4	16744.4			63.0		
5387.5	3187.5	2570.5	1177.9					
40596.9	38473.6	3171.1	19510.9	13243.0		429.5	416.1	277.2
65563.5	55846.7	443.7	38393.8	13077.5	698.5	2795.8	1899.1	1152.1
6593.8	8268.8	-32.5	5198.8	4171.5		441.7	590.6	223.3
14031.1	11671.5	711.2	9421.9	38.0		19.7	28.5	19.0
557.0	586.9		332.7					
24263.1	27729.9	1176.2	12831.4	1091.0		12.0	9.0	3.0
11569.8	11583.7		5734.5	83.2		15.6	22.7	12.3
795.4	744.0		508.9	4167.0		59.3	45.1	28.5
4005.8	4259.6	483.5	1541.2	652.0	222.0	38.0	81.0	61.0
24009.9	24357.7	1.8	10496.8	1609.0		128.0	249.2	146.2

C-3-10 婚姻登记

地区	单位数				年末职工人数		受教育程度	
		编制登记	民政登记	设施		女性	大学专科人数	大学本科及以上人数
全　国	**2236**	**1258**	**279**	**699**	**10761**	**7064**	**4403**	**2916**
中央级								
北　京	14	14			146	107	32	107
天　津	15	8	6	1	124	82	45	46
河　北	71	44	5	22	523	405	161	71
山　西	81	45	6	30	330	214	166	74
内蒙古	40	32	2	6	179	118	94	57
辽　宁	105	89	9	7	701	487	274	281
吉　林	69	63	2	4	481	302	110	92
黑龙江	80	41	25	14	341	233	146	80
上　海	18	17		1	149	108	45	80
江　苏	87	61	18	8	611	443	249	177
浙　江	74	49	3	22	355	266	125	171
安　徽	81	47	8	26	428	268	180	89
福　建	51	32	1	18	167	117	69	53
江　西	97	43	26	28	338	226	97	26
山　东	115	101		14	920	602	396	334
河　南	46	29	4	13	336	202	116	63
湖　北	97	84	4	9	591	427	276	117
湖　南	116	82	2	32	651	405	313	130
广　东	133	65	11	57	669	403	294	158
广　西	64	48		16	258	177	136	71
海　南	14	13	1		40	21	13	7
重　庆	51	38	13		309	173	107	122
四　川	121	60	11	50	573	364	297	143
贵　州	168	30	5	133	301	169	154	98
云　南	89	25	18	46	233	143	90	59
西　藏	25	1	24		46	30	22	11
陕　西	66	47	6	13	384	254	148	69
甘　肃	146	25	14	107	363	213	161	63
青　海	14	4	1	9	16	5		4
宁　夏	54	2	49	3	74	29	31	38
新　疆	34	19	5	10	124	71	56	25

服务机构总表

单位:个、人、人次、时、处

职业资格水平		年龄结构				志愿服务		办理婚姻登记事务的处数
助理社会工作师人数	社会工作师人数	35岁及以下人数	36岁至45岁人数	46岁至55岁人数	56岁及以上人数	志愿者服务人次数	志愿服务时间	
173	**200**	**5263**	**4094**	**1287**	**117**	**12257**	**30325.0**	**6797**
7	4	88	40	17	1	7	7.0	19
		59	39	22	4	200	500.0	18
3	9	282	211	29	1	121	563.0	345
1	4	169	121	37	3			137
		59	91	28	1			122
10	10	343	252	94	12	48	94.0	210
6	5	211	171	90	9			69
6	1	169	142	28	2			180
3	13	64	60	17	8			20
20	15	334	200	60	17	362	1113.0	114
14	11	185	124	42	4	4927	7806.0	115
15	10	194	178	53	3	483	1126.0	114
7	13	69	87	9	2			136
5	6	162	128	47	1	78	234.0	524
14	29	433	358	120	9	3770	10065.0	170
6	9	225	93	16	2	100	150.0	196
15	6	270	244	74	3	40	130.0	126
3	5	362	213	73	3	561	2554.0	154
11	11	322	250	91	6			342
4	1	94	124	37	3			127
		25	14	1				180
4	12	117	138	51	3	1384	5176.0	86
13	15	255	236	69	13			843
1	3	166	100	35		136	637.0	681
5	5	80	130	23		9	24.0	592
		36	7	3				109
	2	207	138	39		31	146.0	141
		211	100	46	6			425
		4	5	7				225
	1	15	46	12	1			102
		53	54	17				175

C-3-10续表

地 区	增加值合计	执行企业会计制度单位财务指标					执行行政	
		固定资产原价	营业收入	费用合计	营业利润	企业单位增加值	固定资产原价	上年结转和结余
全 国	**36572.7**	**497.3**	**623.6**	**486.3**	**58.1**	**469.6**	**92189.3**	**1107.1**
中央级								
北 京	1308.5						627.2	11.5
天 津	712.4	66.0	187.2	254.9	27.5	170.2	565.5	56.8
河 北	665.5	22.5					433.5	3.5
山 西	408.1						182.0	6.9
内蒙古	645.2		5.0				324.2	
辽 宁	2485.4	0.8	41.5	2.5		14.0	2261.3	31.1
吉 林	1122.9	6.4				24.0	565.5	4.0
黑龙江	447.9	30.0	1.1	2.0	1.0	32.0	2478.6	1.6
上 海	1703.5						1357.2	95.2
江 苏	3112.7	20.0	114.8	104.2	10.6	20.6	1374.8	10.1
浙 江	2283.5						1600.8	63.4
安 徽	1032.7						1174.8	48.3
福 建	489.1	1.0					477.6	52.4
江 西	297.6	48.0	31.0	2.8		22.8	585.6	
山 东	5119.8						4225.6	
河 南	433.8						189.4	
湖 北	2142.8						1430.6	
湖 南	3883.1						61467.5	17.0
广 东	1751.2	26.5	8.0				2639.8	400.5
广 西	584.6	62.0	130.0	102.1	11.0	103.0	590.7	34.3
海 南	85.4	1.5					28.3	5.6
重 庆	1418.1		50.0			15.0	1626.2	41.3
四 川	1496.3	3.0					3147.1	9.0
贵 州	727.4	12.0				24.0	391.9	2.0
云 南	423.0	62.0	55.0	17.8	8.0	40.6	440.2	14.0
西 藏	89.5	21.6				0.4	458.2	140.0
陕 西	1244.0						484.1	45.7
甘 肃	142.1						608.9	0.1
青 海	14.9	30.0					42.4	
宁 夏	106.5	25.0				3.0	208.1	10.0
新 疆	195.3	59.0					201.7	2.8

单位：万元

事业单位会计制度财务指标				执行民间非营利组织单位会计制度财务指标				
本年收入合计	本年支出合计	收支结余	行政事业单位增加值	固定资产原价	上年结余	本年收入合计	本年费用合计	社会组织增加值
129024.7	**130343.2**	**310.9**	**35405.0**	**1243.1**		**1549.0**	**1115.8**	**698.1**
2051.1	2046.7	21.1	1308.5					
82.4	606.3	11.5	531.8	39.0		100.0	59.3	10.4
1090.6	1075.8	5.2	665.5			3.5		
477.1	590.2	1.2	405.1	1.0		7.0	7.0	3.0
884.0	872.5	6.5	645.2					
3226.2	3420.5	1.9	2466.2	6.0		10.8	13.8	5.2
1284.5	1327.3	0.8	1098.9					
3183.9	3215.4		390.5	213.0		218.0	39.4	25.4
4460.9	4299.6	17.8	1703.5					
4403.2	4359.0	54.3	2970.1	68.8		324.2	212.8	122.0
3035.5	3166.2	8.8	2187.9	168.0		256.0	164.0	95.6
1418.5	1445.2	-4.3	1010.6	23.1		34.1	32.7	22.1
769.1	764.8	21.5	484.6	5.0		6.6	4.5	4.5
556.1	547.4	2.8	267.6	15.0		18.0	13.3	7.2
5972.3	5972.3		4990.3	120.0		169.5	169.5	129.5
565.3	578.4		431.6	3.0			3.2	2.2
2719.5	2743.5		2142.3	20.0		3.0	3.0	0.5
82128.4	82166.0	9.0	3883.1			6.5		
2684.4	2851.7	8.4	1740.9	15.0		12.0	14.8	10.3
498.8	521.6	6.3	481.6			63.0		
91.7	125.4	2.0	85.4					
2851.9	2763.4	134.3	1340.6	383.0		78.6	75.6	62.5
1517.4	1650.7		1377.8	42.5		170.3	195.1	118.5
477.9	627.1		646.2	77.5		35.2	68.3	57.2
429.5	413.3		363.4	38.0		19.7	28.5	19.0
109.0	85.2		89.1					
1520.9	1556.7		1244.0					
184.3	202.6		139.1	5.2		10.0	11.0	3.0
19.0	19.6		14.9					
104.2	103.2		103.5			3.0		
227.1	225.6	1.8	195.3					

C-3-11 结婚登

地　区	登记结婚件数	登记结婚人数	按居住 内地居民登记结婚件数	内地居民登记结婚人数	涉外及华侨、港澳台居民登记结婚件数
全　国	**13067426**	**26134852**	**13020405**	**26035446**	**47021**
中央级					
北　京	170027	340054	168878	337756	1149
天　津	99394	198788	99031	198062	363
河　北	661326	1322652	660732	1321464	594
山　西	350711	701422	350557	700034	154
内蒙古	216787	433574	216596	433192	191
辽　宁	345097	690194	343228	686456	1869
吉　林	235243	470486	234285	468570	958
黑龙江	352253	704506	350401	700802	1852
上　海	141939	283878	139977	279954	1962
江　苏	834497	1668994	832902	1665804	1595
浙　江	436802	873604	433144	866288	3658
安　徽	798907	1597814	798017	1596034	890
福　建	375330	750660	368993	737986	6337
江　西	371233	742466	369985	739970	1248
山　东	831823	1663646	830458	1660916	1365
河　南	1175822	2351644	1174641	2349282	1181
湖　北	621946	1243892	620489	1241012	1457
湖　南	621995	1243990	620198	1240396	1797
广　东	891457	1782914	883056	1764438	8401
广　西	472298	944596	470645	941290	1653
海　南	90036	180072	89234	177342	802
重　庆	304493	608986	303713	607426	780
四　川	774240	1548480	772685	1545228	1555
贵　州	437203	874406	436794	873588	409
云　南	464805	929610	460983	921966	3822
西　藏	19561	39122	19548	37728	13
陕　西	381221	762442	380760	761520	461
甘　肃	201813	403626	201676	403352	137
青　海	54021	108042	53995	107984	26
宁　夏	55958	111916	55912	111824	46
新　疆	279188	558376	278892	557782	296

记服务

单位:对、人

地分类

内地居民	#女 性	香港居民	澳门居民	台湾居民	华 侨	外国人
45618	**29116**	**5033**	**1457**	**9092**	**6750**	**26092**
1052	733	45	4	158	40	999
359	251	16	2	42	15	292
593	304	20	3	65	14	493
154	92	7	2	22	2	121
177	105	4	3	20	5	173
1857	1436	30	19	206	112	1514
955	644	24	6	131	41	759
1846	1171	37	14	178	346	1283
1817	1380	131	19	316	53	1588
1572	1261	57	15	483	35	1028
2764	1535	59	9	234	2801	1449
888	432	19	5	190	11	667
6316	3765	785	101	1884	1111	2477
1248	544	59	18	266	28	877
1339	837	35	11	203	39	1103
1142	679	85	12	373	31	719
1453	1178	155	56	513	33	704
1794	1506	160	51	842	45	702
8329	5977	2630	948	887	1825	2183
1653	1150	144	52	504	64	889
802	663	219	20	420	24	119
777	633	75	24	251	16	417
1555	1241	124	35	477	27	892
409	333	51	15	156	12	175
3807	515	21	3	83	7	3723
13	61					13
460	350	18	4	127	7	306
137	108	9	3	38	4	83
25	18	1		3	1	22
29	21	10	2	10		41
296	193	3	1	10	1	281

C-3-11续表

地区	按婚姻状况分类			
	初婚人数	再婚人数	#女性	#恢复结婚件数
全国	**22868064**	**3266788**	**1686629**	**348285**
中央级				
北京	253774	86280	41213	9765
天津	173945	24843	12158	10147
河北	1099881	222771	118880	2199
山西	637477	63945	34811	5216
内蒙古	336032	97542	53459	10391
辽宁	627524	62670	30279	22652
吉林	429146	41340	20759	18263
黑龙江	617682	86824	43843	25766
上海	201404	82474	40601	14506
江苏	1418389	250605	128632	38065
浙江	732704	140900	73208	10305
安徽	1368811	229003	119072	24929
福建	680224	70436	35823	538
江西	658658	83808	43452	8727
山东	1358269	305377	159228	3566
河南	2285917	65727	33024	28127
湖北	1182271	61621	29736	7447
湖南	1060729	183261	97096	11721
广东	1620113	162801	76146	19607
广西	845449	99147	54326	6069
海南	166292	13780	6493	1164
重庆	432617	176369	92155	15794
四川	1209165	339315	179730	27843
贵州	852237	22169	11267	6471
云南	814658	114952	57003	3137
西藏	35364	3758	1602	33
陕西	655587	106855	57991	1910
甘肃	391891	11735	6125	2134
青海	99514	8528	4251	194
宁夏	97313	14603	7408	1339
新疆	525027	33349	16858	10260

单位:对、人

按年龄分类				
20～24岁	25～29岁	30～34岁	35～39岁	40岁及以上
7782331	**9930636**	**2964981**	**1635040**	**3821864**
30087	168414	70745	25910	44898
38794	89201	34052	14027	22714
546937	472074	117979	55289	130373
232665	249093	70440	41348	107876
106523	173965	59816	29212	64058
127219	287960	102290	52471	120254
102057	166064	60953	40111	101301
121426	203013	87229	64667	228171
25349	114527	57358	26327	60317
487823	586152	137615	87541	369863
170884	388053	111763	54096	148808
566904	513986	129364	95513	292047
212433	316724	85453	41307	94743
266724	265226	76094	51763	82659
491946	770751	164536	79123	157290
857516	860633	221841	136186	275468
355872	486422	130631	74065	196902
371729	525812	150871	67761	127817
550911	758750	241158	91820	140275
258514	379232	147702	65097	94051
47879	60190	29108	12992	29903
179831	208495	64878	40676	115106
466900	534962	164932	117068	264618
247696	269937	111742	78977	166054
278045	294044	117956	81229	158336
19910	13659	3116	1674	763
228374	341048	77742	37044	78234
138970	167491	41307	17665	38193
26390	41940	15014	9663	15035
39113	38304	11409	6934	16156
186910	184514	69887	37484	79581

C-3-12 离婚办

地区	总计	民政部门合计	内地居民登记离婚	涉外及华侨、港澳台居民登记离婚	#外国人
全国	**3636754**	**2957295**	**2950581**	**6714**	**2702**
北京	65623	56192	55989	203	146
天津	44500	38954	38874	80	53
河北	185721	146877	146817	60	39
山西	65583	47894	47877	17	14
内蒙古	88421	66587	66369	218	16
辽宁	152715	126197	125952	245	177
吉林	122133	107357	107248	109	74
黑龙江	187285	157983	157780	203	120
上海	61480	52981	52608	373	234
江苏	218310	178180	177951	229	122
浙江	135823	111040	110637	403	161
安徽	171015	139468	139384	84	44
福建	87289	70341	69168	1173	360
江西	89415	72909	72785	124	75
山东	234143	181336	181185	151	114
河南	230850	193499	193380	119	50
湖北	157395	133723	133549	174	69
湖南	175983	146449	146197	252	69
广东	177945	151645	150151	1494	264
广西	100919	80818	80614	204	97
海南	14111	10846	10734	112	25
重庆	132589	115359	115232	127	56
四川	274972	229572	229353	219	94
贵州	95714	70848	70785	63	19
云南	100464	79190	79029	161	135
西藏	2640	2067	2067		
陕西	85072	68268	68221	47	22
甘肃	42231	25221	25206	15	5
青海	12549	7480	7477	3	2
宁夏	15820	11281	11274	7	2
新疆	108044	76733	76688	45	44

理服务

单位：件(对)、人

法院部门合计	判决离婚	调解离婚	离婚案件收案	判决不离	调解不离
679459	**186220**	**493239**	**1318744**	**225274**	**72618**
9431	2971	6460	20168	3697	337
5546	1527	4019	13216	2861	588
38844	10467	28377	77950	12443	3165
17689	4284	13405	38319	4718	5186
21834	5599	16235	38819	2022	3303
26518	7934	18584	49957	8096	1398
14776	4709	10067	28083	2804	707
29302	5348	23954	44439	1228	1708
8499	2588	5911	18061	4283	442
40130	9748	30382	91710	22155	6070
24783	7103	17680	50063	12122	1635
31547	8231	23316	64575	14600	1732
16948	7128	9820	34689	7609	803
16506	5168	11338	33667	6442	2176
52807	16500	36307	115323	24102	7617
37351	11536	25815	78128	16485	2692
23672	6155	17517	46406	9315	1878
29534	9508	20026	58532	12776	4130
26300	10117	16183	49213	9336	2199
20101	7137	12964	34970	6959	1302
3265	1076	2189	5498	782	732
17230	5287	11943	34206	7381	1094
45400	10601	34799	84691	13695	4671
24866	5564	19302	41126	4186	1672
21274	5571	15703	37228	3934	3050
573	91	482	832	14	118
16804	3148	13656	31328	2632	3874
17010	3998	13012	33626	4642	2852
5069	1022	4047	9134	622	911
4539	1314	3225	9992	1655	693
31311	4790	26521	44795	1678	3883

C-3-13 殡葬服务

地区	单位数	工商登记	编制登记	民政登记	年末职工人数	女性	受教育程度 大学专科人数	大学本科及以上人数
全国	**4559**	**737**	**2890**	**348**	**82651**	**22980**	**21774**	**8333**
中央级								
北京	54	4	50		1703	505	341	349
天津	28	2	26		818	193	168	198
河北	183	4	168	4	3442	811	643	235
山西	65	11	42	5	974	229	287	160
内蒙古	129	15	94	2	2029	539	613	201
辽宁	293	34	151	94	5054	1387	1459	670
吉林	146	32	93	1	4491	317	1542	361
黑龙江	149	14	122	9	3099	909	996	377
上海	75	56	19		3080	1214	525	276
江苏	258	56	171	25	4364	1191	1133	559
浙江	225	56	148	9	3560	810	955	442
安徽	188	23	120	13	2978	899	705	169
福建	158	30	106	1	2884	742	450	208
江西	139	6	109	16	1926	490	291	76
山东	173	19	147	6	3509	834	1158	472
河南	259	30	206	13	5915	1781	1666	437
湖北	178	18	118	10	3695	1184	1236	274
湖南	232	31	108	4	3118	910	996	386
广东	315	52	178	19	7666	1914	1441	605
广西	107	24	61		1942	632	577	236
海南	17	6	9	1	269	56	53	21
重庆	116	26	57	13	2094	817	656	239
四川	305	45	197	11	4287	1440	1144	393
贵州	148	56	64	11	3483	1287	944	286
云南	210	21	135	19	1437	357	471	179
西藏	2		2		31	5	7	8
陕西	111	31	70	6	2438	770	593	224
甘肃	75	17	35	7	818	227	168	124
青海	35	9	7	5	169	41	43	10
宁夏	27	3	18	5	143	35	46	41
新疆	159	6	59	39	1235	454	467	117

机构总表

单位:个、人、人次、时

职业资格水平		年龄结构				志愿服务	
助理社会工作师人数	社会工作师人数	35岁及以下人数	36岁至45岁人数	46岁至55岁人数	56岁及以上人数	志愿者服务人次数	志愿服务时间
630	**481**	**26457**	**31524**	**18801**	**5869**	**8282**	**32072.0**
52	32	528	527	463	185	141	561.0
2	5	210	221	247	140	100	200.0
12	13	1185	1321	738	198	230	1025.0
1	4	345	390	194	45		
9	11	571	755	560	143		
31	34	1626	1724	1261	443	102	184.0
	8	1170	1565	1228	528		
11	15	702	1321	846	230		
9	10	716	952	946	466	1815	9292.0
57	36	1159	1742	1136	327	946	3890.0
27	26	981	1256	963	360	555	1194.0
85	27	890	1218	689	181	1293	3744.0
26	28	856	1192	661	175	6	16.0
24	18	636	867	343	80	281	856.0
31	33	1166	1332	777	234		
46	37	2851	2053	803	208		
17	10	1149	1473	890	183	370	1130.0
19	10	1160	1288	546	124	670	2680.0
84	36	2386	3091	1737	452	20	43.0
22	13	687	764	356	135		
2		75	123	59	12		
5	3	669	792	469	164	742	1782.0
30	27	1316	1749	960	262	2	4.0
4	9	1231	1469	655	128	805	4538.0
8	14	519	514	219	185	5	15.0
		15	10	6			
8	14	828	913	538	159	83	478.0
3	2	245	313	229	31		
		47	88	32	2		
1	5	27	59	48	9		
4	1	511	442	202	80	116	440.0

C-3-13续表1

地　区	火化炉数	全年处理遗体数	国际运尸数	外国人	港澳台	侨民
全　国	**5908**	**4593037**	**820**	**215**	**260**	
中央级						
北　京	90	90584	58	56	2	
天　津	66	66628				
河　北	374	206290				
山　西	65	22250				
内蒙古	158	65801				
辽　宁	364	278253				
吉　林	167	75583				
黑龙江	251	165362				
上　海	94	123203	36	35	1	
江　苏	533	475387				
浙　江	346	307311				
安　徽	258	259527				
福　建	218	197564				
江　西	201	89767				
山　东	494	581500				
河　南	315	222705	345			
湖　北	318	208065				
湖　南	151	82367				
广　东	409	474196	374	119	255	
广　西	91	77139				
海　南	7	2990	4	3	1	
重　庆	116	79011	3	2	1	
四　川	281	206120				
贵　州	124	72147				
云　南	174	61581				
西　藏	6	829				
陕　西	89	53377				
甘　肃	54	17954				
青　海	43	7483				
宁　夏	8	3669				
新　疆	43	18394				

单位:具、个、台

穴位数	#本年销售穴位数	安葬数	#本年安葬数	格位数	#格位存放数	#本年格位存放数
14318347	**641659**	**8963554**	**604033**	**817348**	**389078**	**71359**
674637	18286	527153	21231	24784	12427	438
182012	5667	204713	6875	38883	33985	2995
252100	8659	91499	8963	8582	6753	1079
101615	4118	51318	3783	14406	5954	581
339128	24165	266304	25395	21355	7922	2433
715776	64986	421326	28190	6612	3869	1442
31211	1638	17576	3070	30075	27008	11883
223027	18755	188537	24214			
1862568	66604	1308034	55286	131675	110889	7341
1434539	90089	1141412	55028	50708	37245	5041
1034916	32189	760379	39300	33844	9871	581
325129	22821	280630	34632	18954	2811	1780
215806	14218	154383	15242	22899	6046	426
189187	16073	62937	17792			
253284	7832	154480	8808	3660	757	189
255698	8616	131107	10643	10246	5374	1671
897021	25931	579579	45487	11418	2057	183
430598	24049	202092	22931	2720	1370	296
1099501	29325	627058	29036	217156	73391	10860
255235	9372	122806	7482	17481	8035	3644
31228	2115	15989	1968			
493019	18251	286988	17883	37245	7485	1000
1151568	56286	669948	53188	16567	4509	302
362301	25292	146823	18478	11845	2066	408
475604	9508	124559	14573			
308648	16292	276607	13935	84231	17453	15218
106612	6704	82120	6313			
5357	1121	2200	464			
27918	3305	19140	3007			
583104	9392	45857	10836	2002	1801	1568

C-3-13续表2

地区	增加值合计	执行企业会计制度单位财务指标					执行行政	
		固定资产原价	营业收入	费用合计	营业利润	企业单位增加值	固定资产原价	上年结转和结余
全　国	**957492.6**	**921570.5**	**908569.9**	**238975.9**	**171580.8**	**334434.0**	**1766461.5**	**108782.1**
中央级								
北　京	46288.4	23994.2	57498.0	20150.4	16225.6	24392.4	103724.1	3479.2
天　津	16734.2	5915.2	3228.8	1689.5	96.8	1056.6	31369.3	11992.2
河　北	20353.0	3678.2	3499.0	3380.0	-603.6	206.9	70484.5	2434.3
山　西	8213.7	8777.0	2763.0	971.0	-40.0	1463.5	31294.2	1002.6
内蒙古	13137.4	14559.1	5625.9	3123.0	80.0	1183.3	30731.0	646.1
辽　宁	50932.1	38441.2	27923.0	15551.5	1391.4	13622.9	81871.3	3406.1
吉　林	10284.8	19140.9	821.2	45.7	27.7	396.7	71235.1	391.0
黑龙江	26538.1	18448.2	7897.3	4782.5	1535.0	3990.9	68618.7	2356.1
上　海	148475.2	246924.6	375773.9	70388.8	90349.1	147402.2	729.8	1814.6
江　苏	98592.1	38714.1	57755.6	9360.2	30199.3	35814.8	179842.6	13894.3
浙　江	61977.0	34434.8	54490.1	10823.2	7284.5	12479.3	96432.9	8977.4
安　徽	27115.5	16912.1	10234.9	4415.6	1069.6	4814.6	50344.2	1635.9
福　建	28790.3	56453.9	25963.0	10182.8	3001.2	12171.8	42145.5	5015.4
江　西	11994.2	7328.4	3207.0	911.1	148.0	761.0	26023.3	229.4
山　东	37954.3	7293.9	4626.4	2006.9	377.1	1722.9	91807.6	
河　南	19726.7	18621.0	9099.4	3486.1	794.5	3388.8	51785.9	318.9
湖　北	34653.9	12268.4	9643.7	4108.3	1086.6	3158.8	88826.4	172.6
湖　南	20572.3	33565.2	11435.2	5238.1	527.8	3173.4	77217.6	428.6
广　东	108322.4	50174.5	38312.1	12250.4	5721.0	13871.9	246898.8	7861.3
广　西	24561.1	28213.1	67310.8	7029.0	1152.8	8298.3	34396.0	9445.4
海　南	3411.1	7082.5	3893.1	1961.7	1112.6	2318.6	8311.3	1712.2
重　庆	21322.9	27784.8	22371.2	6000.1	789.1	2937.9	42490.0	1698.6
四　川	45610.3	38725.8	33549.9	11581.6	1592.1	7560.7	90746.2	21590.9
贵　州	22118.4	89778.9	38248.5	16350.3	3839.7	17399.7	21598.2	493.1
云　南	12389.8	42000.2	4546.1	1836.0	573.5	3331.3	34834.5	1025.1
西　藏	243.6	367.2					1343.0	
陕　西	16012.5	18121.6	20408.3	9184.5	1866.8	4422.1	21201.0	4788.6
甘　肃	8273.3	3909.8	6095.9	917.4	1274.1	2668.6	19673.8	94.0
青　海	587.5	1411.0	213.0	213.0		65.0	1494.1	
宁　夏	1541.0	408.0	402.0	324.0	7.0	42.3	8284.4	920.8
新　疆	10764.6	8122.7	1733.6	713.2	101.5	316.9	40706.2	957.4

单位：万元

事业单位会计制度财务指标				执行民间非营利组织单位会计制度财务指标				
本年收入合计	本年支出合计	收支结余	行政事业单位增加值	固定资产原价	上年结余	本年收入合计	本年费用合计	社会组织增加值
1333085.1	**1237503.4**	**62941.5**	**618876.5**	**56504.1**	**2992.7**	**11698.5**	**9278.8**	**4182.1**
118657.3	117221.8	2098.1	21896.0					
36343.0	43745.4	12401.8	15677.6					
40476.1	38414.7	3303.4	20144.6	150.0		92.2	10.0	1.5
24372.1	22500.9	-15.9	6750.2					
20558.1	19607.4	977.2	11902.1			203.0	203.0	52.0
78350.5	74701.4	4033.9	36504.0	3650.9	503.5	1196.0	1116.3	805.2
13455.6	13198.5	1010.8	9888.1					
39590.9	36826.4	83.5	22502.8	249.0			64.4	44.4
3969.8	3863.0	1778.5	1073.0					
125144.0	114362.6	11105.6	62111.9	5431.5		3073.3	2414.4	665.4
98195.8	87946.4	4331.4	49243.1	565.0	1209.5	1238.5	685.2	254.6
41669.0	39670.3	1472.7	22052.5	2504.0	260.0	1087.5	925.0	248.4
36421.1	37944.5	2164.5	16601.0			130.7	123.1	17.5
19821.9	17279.7	-7.5	11233.2					
69576.0	69576.0		35884.0	2478.4		617.0	617.0	347.4
32200.9	29777.7	1031.8	16334.0	380.0		152.0	5.5	3.9
77478.0	77342.1	274.0	31485.7	42.0		15.0	15.0	9.4
42867.5	41069.0	276.7	17372.9	1670.0		180.0	69.0	26.0
195551.8	145931.8	6501.5	94406.5	1797.3	99.2	90.5	68.1	44.0
28544.8	27586.7	1732.1	16262.8					
5295.8	3062.1	2568.5	1092.5					
37745.0	35710.2	3036.8	18170.3	12860.0		350.9	340.5	214.7
64046.1	54196.0	443.7	37016.0	13035.0	698.5	2625.5	1704.0	1033.6
6115.9	7641.7	-32.5	4552.6	4094.0		406.5	522.3	166.1
13601.6	11258.2	711.2	9058.5					
448.0	501.7		243.6					
22742.2	26173.2	1176.2	11587.4	1091.0		12.0	9.0	3.0
11385.5	11381.1		5595.4	78.0		5.6	11.7	9.3
776.4	724.4		494.0	4167.0		59.3	45.1	28.5
3901.6	4156.4	483.5	1437.7	652.0	222.0	35.0	81.0	61.0
23782.8	24132.1		10301.5	1609.0		128.0	249.2	146.2

C-3-14 殡仪

地区	单位数	年末职工人数		受教育程度		职业资
			女性	大学专科人数	大学本科及以上人数	助理社会工作师人数
全国	**1801**	**45767**	**11637**	**12896**	**4408**	**367**
中央级						
北京	12	581	125	140	102	23
天津	11	454	92	97	95	2
河北	154	2812	583	518	166	12
山西	26	398	110	93	75	1
内蒙古	60	1190	310	435	110	3
辽宁	78	2693	726	772	280	10
吉林	47	1966	107	1210	228	
黑龙江	98	2424	715	788	276	10
上海	15	714	163	175	118	3
江苏	95	2806	670	737	342	45
浙江	77	2193	449	659	236	20
安徽	70	2009	595	461	100	59
福建	63	1826	453	226	77	16
江西	85	1371	345	165	38	5
山东	123	2825	574	960	387	27
河南	114	3558	1003	1032	214	23
湖北	85	2449	841	864	200	16
湖南	70	1489	424	460	233	8
广东	90	4126	943	805	297	57
广西	32	723	231	232	54	6
海南	2	65	21	10	9	
重庆	37	915	307	321	119	3
四川	87	1834	521	499	160	12
贵州	48	1643	586	324	118	
云南	79	734	168	264	97	1
西藏	2	31	5	7	8	
陕西	41	1049	291	393	145	2
甘肃	25	314	90	76	84	1
青海	20	94	21	35	10	
宁夏	6	58	19	13	14	
新疆	49	423	149	125	16	2

馆

单位：个、人、人次、时

格水平	年龄结构				志愿服务	
社会工作师人数	35岁及以下人数	36岁至45岁人数	46岁至55岁人数	56岁及以上人数	志愿者服务人次数	志愿服务时间
239	**14798**	**17525**	**10323**	**3121**	**5260**	**21082.0**
13	148	172	176	85	52	52.0
	119	90	146	99	50	100.0
10	914	1130	624	144	205	870.0
4	101	146	118	33		
4	332	471	297	90		
15	873	990	613	217	46	87.0
3	394	649	533	390		
14	550	1012	684	178		
3	191	204	203	116	1515	8992.0
20	767	1035	788	216	469	1252.0
13	589	842	581	181	166	353.0
20	613	828	457	111	635	1600.0
15	551	716	441	118		
2	440	617	260	54	281	856.0
23	915	1080	631	199		
14	1812	1178	471	97		
8	796	979	530	144	225	680.0
1	551	599	284	55	635	2550.0
16	1294	1689	914	229		
6	312	237	121	53		
	20	26	16	3		
3	310	347	211	47	557	1421.0
14	578	777	373	106	2	4.0
4	578	749	282	34	381	1950.0
5	325	281	106	22		
	15	10	6			
6	383	345	260	61	30	240.0
1	106	109	84	15		
	34	44	16			
1	10	23	19	6		
1	177	150	78	18	11	75.0

C-3-14续表1

地区	火化炉数	全年处理遗体数	国际运尸数	外国人
全国	**5908**	**4593037**	**820**	**215**
中央级				
北京	90	90584	58	56
天津	66	66628		
河北	374	206290		
山西	65	22250		
内蒙古	158	65801		
辽宁	364	278253		
吉林	167	75583		
黑龙江	251	165362		
上海	94	123203	36	35
江苏	533	475387		
浙江	346	307311		
安徽	258	259527		
福建	218	197564		
江西	201	89767		
山东	494	581500		
河南	315	222705	345	
湖北	318	208065		
湖南	151	82367		
广东	409	474196	374	119
广西	91	77139		
海南	7	2990	4	3
重庆	116	79011	3	2
四川	281	206120		
贵州	124	72147		
云南	174	61581		
西藏	6	829		
陕西	89	53377		
甘肃	54	17954		
青海	43	7483		
宁夏	8	3669		
新疆	43	18394		

单位:具、个、台

港澳台	侨民	穴位数	#本年销售穴位数	安葬数	#本年安葬数
260		**2290894**	**84990**	**1048271**	**159190**
2		8203	143	7932	149
		7345	796	3550	710
		55171	3889	24436	3741
		103713	11901	88601	13042
		29619	1772	32651	4751
		2900	175	5808	1646
		112780	2208	110394	13176
1		62	62	62	62
		96598	2862	77561	2819
		110337	2940	62419	12232
		31256	828	38630	16153
		108522	7531	80631	7814
		170631	15042	50620	16279
		28032	616	8245	939
		30213	1209	14637	3550
		95229	6550	106018	27721
		146771	5127	93888	7002
255		82236	1609	31135	1989
		4612	1350	1094	68
1					
1		102147	2806	64505	3828
		23507	910	14992	1793
		35349	2249	3419	2299
		286894	4227	46409	8741
		55395	990	47031	919
		20456	1633	16255	1500
		4664	740	1533	743
		538252	4825	15815	5524

C-3-14续表2

地区	增加值合计	执行企业会计制度单位财务指标					执行行政	
		固定资产原价	营业收入	费用合计	营业利润	企业单位增加值	固定资产原价	上年结转和结余
全　国	**482706.7**	**332494.8**	**146086.5**	**51344.3**	**17694.7**	**64242.7**	**1304394.0**	**57601.4**
中央级								
北　京	8925.7						54573.1	803.0
天　津	8957.5						21664.7	222.0
河　北	16153.9	464.6	393.0	359.0	-94.0	106.0	59735.3	1785.5
山　西	5430.2	629.0	54.0	42.0	18.0	70.0	23192.6	756.6
内蒙古	9138.4	3801.0	1306.9	1769.0		394.7	27555.1	211.7
辽　宁	29471.5	10153.1	5371.5	3505.3	131.6	2294.2	67002.6	3381.4
吉　林	6626.8	17177.0	92.0	4.0		27.1	63654.5	
黑龙江	19215.9	10678.4	1912.4	1527.0	130.0	987.2	55613.4	1410.7
上　海	32049.9	94627.6	75717.3	16056.9	13521.0	32049.9		
江　苏	42953.1	8605.7	2816.3	498.5	659.2	1152.6	157245.3	7910.3
浙　江	40173.6	5313.4	3904.6	1451.0	445.7	1859.6	86036.1	4297.7
安　徽	16326.2	5163.3	2114.2	1062.0	128.0	1530.2	34616.6	523.5
福　建	17387.3	48063.6	15768.0	7233.5	1420.1	8685.8	32326.3	1343.1
江　西	9414.9	5890.0	894.0	229.1	39.0	88.6	20437.7	202.2
山　东	32686.1	634.0	69.0	143.0		76.8	81068.9	
河　南	12184.6	4788.1	1097.5	390.2	112.0	410.0	46576.6	216.2
湖　北	23983.9	823.1	397.0	378.5	-4.7	27.4	61609.7	172.6
湖　南	12007.8	9381.2	3577.0	1810.4	-51.6	1273.6	39380.4	302.3
广　东	62721.6	5879.5	2525.9	1692.3	35.7	437.2	161122.9	4389.4
广　西	6414.4	10520.6	1777.8	1154.3	-514.6	-143.0	17324.3	1240.9
海　南	1003.0	5080.0	1426.0	1436.0	6.0	734.5	527.8	38.8
重　庆	9132.2	10211.3	3121.6	1311.5	87.0	682.7	29323.9	1570.2
四　川	23493.9	11671.7	6375.2	2068.3	152.8	1907.0	59680.8	20544.4
贵　州	12346.9	49520.4	14000.9	6751.7	1473.5	9314.7	17663.2	469.2
云　南	7830.5	4831.0	100.0	10.0			30143.6	882.4
西　藏	243.6	367.2					1343.0	
陕　西	9243.5	1430.0	122.2	52.0		118.0	18077.5	4681.0
甘　肃	3747.6	200.0	15.0	6.0		10.1	18719.6	42.0
青　海	517.0	1101.0	183.0	183.0		35.0	1187.0	
宁　夏	843.1	10.0		5.0			6600.6	204.3
新　疆	2082.2	5479.0	954.2	214.8		113.1	10390.9	

单位：万元

事业单位会计制度财务指标				执行民间非营利组织单位会计制度财务指标				
本年收入合计	本年支出合计	收支结余	行政事业单位增加值	固定资产原价	上年结余	本年收入合计	本年费用合计	社会组织增加值
887219.3	**819899.1**	**29437.6**	**417680.4**	**23875.0**	**222.0**	**1969.2**	**1625.1**	**783.6**
36926.3	37061.8	-908.4	8925.7					
17189.2	19788.2	1248.7	8957.5					
31466.3	30071.0	1795.0	16046.4	150.0		92.2	10.0	1.5
16278.4	17203.0	-16.5	5360.2					
14997.0	14106.9	885.8	8743.7					
55999.0	53607.3	3374.4	27177.1	55.0			1.0	0.2
8121.6	8392.3	-44.2	6599.7					
30108.2	27003.8	83.5	18228.0	3.0			0.8	0.7
91738.5	83448.0	7735.7	41477.5	2389.0		448.0	448.0	323.0
78698.4	71362.3	2350.7	38314.0					
28167.0	27034.6	731.1	14605.8	1209.0		772.0	741.0	190.2
21150.7	19754.4	1630.0	8701.5					
15136.0	13617.9	-11.6	9326.3					
60114.7	60114.7		32609.3					
24797.1	22473.3	1001.2	11774.5	370.0		150.0	0.2	0.1
53882.9	53762.5	274.0	23954.3	5.0		3.0	3.0	2.2
31113.5	29733.3	266.3	10734.2					
144775.8	106829.7	3346.7	62284.4					
11628.9	11542.0	847.3	6557.4					
558.6	595.9	282.2	268.5					
28155.8	27044.4	2691.6	8286.5	12735.0		306.7	268.0	163.0
34701.4	31728.5	365.3	21586.9					
4411.2	5139.7	-134.5	3023.2	1280.0		70.0	17.0	9.0
11930.7	9597.3	677.7	7830.5					
448.0	501.7		243.6					
19200.6	22832.0	943.9	9124.5	150.0		10.0	7.0	1.0
8653.8	8603.3		3737.5					
702.0	650.0		454.3	4144.0		56.3	42.1	27.7
1071.4	1267.4	21.7	782.1	652.0	222.0	35.0	81.0	61.0
5096.3	5031.9		1965.1	733.0		26.0	6.0	4.0

C-3-15 公

地　区	单位数	年末职工人数		受教育程度		职业资
			女性	大学专科人数	大学本科及以上人数	助理社会工作师人数
全　国	**1598**	**26895**	**8813**	**5681**	**2195**	**161**
中央级						
北　京	34	1022	339	191	173	28
天　津	7	247	75	35	49	
河　北	16	462	194	91	52	
山　西	27	490	91	157	68	
内蒙古	28	554	166	82	44	4
辽　宁	163	1967	562	529	278	12
吉　林	52	2167	175	272	105	
黑龙江	37	496	138	138	52	1
上　海	50	2316	1032	333	134	5
江　苏	109	1166	390	272	104	5
浙　江	75	912	261	116	78	2
安　徽	80	746	239	172	36	22
福　建	29	390	140	58	37	1
江　西	13	173	50	41	22	10
山　东	41	623	243	182	70	4
河　南	52	1124	399	283	83	6
湖　北	68	936	256	246	45	1
湖　南	103	1113	384	325	87	8
广　东	113	2204	690	323	126	18
广　西	27	580	241	158	77	5
海　南	7	147	23	33	4	2
重　庆	54	1033	458	263	73	2
四　川	141	1964	758	436	182	15
贵　州	54	1483	636	448	88	
云　南	73	441	122	95	19	4
西　藏						
陕　西	38	1125	396	122	27	5
甘　肃	35	418	112	66	23	1
青　海	12	64	15	3		
宁　夏	5	25	4	11	5	
新　疆	55	507	224	200	54	

墓

单位：个、人、人次、时

格水平	年龄结构				志愿服务	
社会工作师人数	35岁及以下人数	36岁至45岁人数	46岁至55岁人数	56岁及以上人数	志愿者服务人次数	志愿服务时间
107	**8169**	**9940**	**6537**	**2249**	**2392**	**8939.0**
15	342	324	264	92	81	501.0
	64	93	60	30		
3	209	141	82	30	25	155.0
	215	213	52	10		
	155	165	193	41		
6	647	578	542	200	46	77.0
2	722	688	638	119		
1	104	245	106	41		
	516	729	726	345	300	300.0
10	275	541	257	93	449	2575.0
1	200	256	296	160	351	687.0
4	229	290	171	56	576	1836.0
	100	188	79	23		
15	58	88	19	8		
7	236	220	133	34		
14	370	467	195	92		
	265	359	284	28	145	450.0
8	400	457	203	53	30	120.0
1	645	835	548	176		
3	184	281	91	24		
	38	75	31	3		
	321	364	237	111	33	56.0
12	590	757	477	140		
2	483	590	333	77	285	1883.0
3	113	123	65	140		
	329	472	237	87	26	114.0
	101	177	130	10		
	7	40	16	1		
	5	13	7			
	246	171	65	25	45	185.0

C-3-15续表1

地区	增加值合计	执行企业会计制度单位财务指标				
		固定资产原价	营业收入	费用合计	营业利润	企业单位增加值
全国	**393596.8**	**571676.3**	**758951.1**	**185643.5**	**153388.6**	**268976.5**
中央级						
北京	32860.5	23994.2	57498.0	20150.4	16225.6	24392.4
天津	5077.4	5915.2	3228.8	1689.5	96.8	1056.6
河北	2313.0	3213.6	3106.0	3021.0	-509.6	100.9
山西	2143.0	8148.0	2709.0	929.0	-58.0	1393.5
内蒙古	2524.4	10758.1	4319.0	1354.0	80.0	788.6
辽宁	19748.5	28288.1	22551.5	12046.2	1259.8	11328.7
吉林	1998.3	1840.7	729.2	41.7	27.7	369.6
黑龙江	6215.2	7191.8	5234.9	2494.7	1215.0	2792.4
上海	115352.3	152297.0	300056.6	54331.9	76828.1	115352.3
江苏	50685.9	26576.8	54939.3	8861.7	29540.1	34662.2
浙江	15405.2	29029.7	49901.3	9317.9	6720.0	10404.7
安徽	8955.4	11748.8	8120.7	3353.6	941.6	3284.4
福建	6684.8	7767.3	9204.0	2556.3	1410.1	3027.0
江西	1161.4	1433.4	2313.0	682.0	109.0	672.4
山东	4637.0	6659.9	4557.4	1863.9	377.1	1646.1
河南	5087.1	13832.9	8001.9	3095.9	682.5	2978.8
湖北	9099.9	11422.3	9246.7	3729.8	1091.3	3131.4
湖南	6431.7	17580.0	7491.2	2911.7	579.4	1821.8
广东	30082.3	44262.0	35683.2	10440.1	5693.3	13360.7
广西	10001.5	17692.5	65533.0	5874.7	1667.4	8441.3
海南	1589.0	2002.5	2467.1	525.7	1106.6	1584.1
重庆	10906.7	14073.5	19084.6	4677.6	703.1	2236.2
四川	17959.9	26638.5	26970.9	9475.3	1419.1	5570.4
贵州	8471.4	39961.7	24189.6	9590.1	2366.2	8056.4
云南	3747.8	37169.2	4446.1	1826.0	573.5	3331.3
西藏						
陕西	4728.6	16327.6	20286.1	9132.5	1866.8	4304.1
甘肃	4117.2	3346.8	6060.9	859.4	1264.1	2648.5
青海	41.6	310.0	30.0	30.0		30.0
宁夏	375.5	358.0	387.0	305.0	7.0	42.3
新疆	5193.9	1836.2	604.1	475.9	105.0	167.2

单位：万元

执行行政事业单位会计制度财务指标					
固定资产原价	上年结转和结余	本年收入合计	本年支出合计	收支结余	行政事业单位增加值
251554.8	**21675.7**	**291489.3**	**258832.8**	**22643.2**	**122314.5**
29638.7	2673.5	64669.1	60167.1	5917.0	8468.1
8554.2	4159.8	16904.0	19502.4	7476.5	4020.8
3004.1	17.3	4614.6	3980.8	645.0	2212.1
7798.8	246.0	7269.8	4470.8		749.5
1206.8	339.8	3025.6	2943.5	5.0	1683.8
13207.8	17.6	18604.5	17349.0	635.6	7615.2
1648.3		3103.2	2465.5	605.0	1628.7
8091.4	945.4	7461.5	7351.2		3379.1
19052.5	1858.7	28642.7	24042.8	1294.7	15724.4
6855.5	4323.1	10184.3	7079.7	1947.7	4902.4
8846.6	1112.4	10270.1	9677.7	741.1	5612.8
680.5	2.0	6436.2	5929.2	283.0	3640.3
1191.7		718.0	719.0		489.0
9936.8		8723.7	8723.7		2822.1
3662.6	40.1	4268.3	4143.4	11.5	2106.1
21479.6		18462.6	18447.1		5961.3
27645.5	126.3	8943.6	8697.7	-5.1	4583.9
22328.6	2648.9	22375.3	14166.0	1893.8	16679.1
2464.0	573.6	3540.4	3380.7	512.9	1560.2
120.0	996.0	644.0	157.0		4.9
11307.0	8.0	7437.1	6610.0	128.4	8618.8
23713.6	433.5	24771.4	18020.2	52.4	12055.9
2171.0	0.5	210.0	1082.1	0.5	257.9
4058.7	101.0	328.3	309.5	1.0	416.5
829.0		1216.8	1165.6	59.5	424.5
614.9	8.0	2182.2	2225.3		1459.4
20.0		30.0	30.0		10.8
997.8	520.2	2255.9	2335.9	437.7	333.2
10428.8	524.0	4196.1	3659.9		4893.5

C-3-15续表2

地区	执行民间非营利组织单位会计制度财务指标					穴位数
	固定资产原价	上年结余	本年收入合计	本年费用合计	社会组织增加值	
全　国	**21160.3**	**2698.2**	**8180.9**	**5250.1**	**2305.8**	**12027453**
中央级						
北　京						666434
天　津						174667
河　北						196929
山　西						101615
内蒙古			203.0	203.0	52.0	235415
辽　宁	3593.9	503.5	1195.4	1114.7	804.6	686157
吉　林						28311
黑龙江	246.0			63.6	43.7	110247
上　海						1862506
江　苏	2831.1		1712.5	1110.4	299.3	1337941
浙　江	395.0	1140.0	1110.5	487.7	98.1	924579
安　徽	1295.0	260.0	315.5	184.0	58.2	293873
福　建			130.7	123.1	17.5	107284
江　西						18556
山　东	2380.0		224.0	224.0	168.8	225252
河　南				3.3	2.2	225485
湖　北	37.0		12.0	12.0	7.2	801792
湖　南	1670.0		180.0	69.0	26.0	283827
广　东	1782.3	96.2	88.5	65.6	42.5	1017265
广　西						250623
海　南						31228
重　庆	125.0		44.2	72.5	51.7	390872
四　川	3035.0	698.5	2517.5	804.0	333.6	1128061
贵　州	2814.0		336.5	505.3	157.1	326952
云　南						188710
西　藏						
陕　西						253253
甘　肃	77.0		5.6	11.7	9.3	86156
青　海	23.0		3.0	3.0	0.8	5357
宁　夏						23254
新　疆	856.0		102.0	193.2	133.2	44852

单位:万元、个、具

#本年销售穴位数	安葬数	#本年安葬数	格位数	格位存放数	本年格位存放数
556669	**7915283**	**444843**	**766725**	**351168**	**66334**
18143	519221	21082	24784	12427	438
4871	201163	6165	38883	33985	2995
4770	67063	5222	8582	6753	1079
4118	51318	3783	14406	5954	581
12264	177703	12353	21355	7922	2433
63214	388675	23439	6612	3869	1442
1463	11768	1424	30075	27008	11883
16547	78143	11038			
66542	1307972	55224	131675	110889	7341
87227	1063851	52209	8047	1995	336
29249	697960	27068	27366	7998	347
21993	242000	18479	18954	2811	1780
6687	73752	7428	22899	6046	426
1031	12317	1513			
7216	146235	7869	3660	757	189
7407	116470	7093	10246	5374	1671
19381	473561	17766	11418	2057	183
18922	108204	15929	2720	1370	296
27716	595923	27047	217156	73391	10860
8022	121712	7414	17481	8035	3644
2115	15989	1968			
15445	222483	14055	36245	6981	964
55376	654956	51395	16567	4509	302
23043	143404	16179	11845	2066	408
5281	78150	5832			
15302	229576	13016	84231	17453	15218
5071	65865	4813			
1121	2200	464			
2565	17607	2264			
4567	30042	5312	1518	1518	1518

C-3-16 其他殡葬

地区	单位数	年末职工人数		受教育程度		职业资
			女性	大学专科人数	大学本科及以上人数	助理社会工作师人数
全国	**1160**	**9989**	**2530**	**3197**	**1730**	**102**
北京	8	100	41	10	74	1
天津	10	117	26	36	54	
河北	13	168	34	34	17	
山西	12	86	28	37	17	
内蒙古	41	285	63	96	47	2
辽宁	52	394	99	158	112	9
吉林	47	358	35	60	28	
黑龙江	14	179	56	70	49	
上海	10	50	19	17	24	1
江苏	54	392	131	124	113	7
浙江	73	455	100	180	128	5
安徽	38	223	65	72	33	4
福建	66	668	149	166	94	9
江西	41	382	95	85	16	9
山东	9	61	17	16	15	
河南	93	1233	379	351	140	17
湖北	25	310	87	126	29	
湖南	59	516	102	211	66	3
广东	112	1336	281	313	182	9
广西	48	639	160	187	105	11
海南	8	57	12	10	8	
重庆	25	146	52	72	47	
四川	77	489	161	209	51	3
贵州	46	357	65	172	80	4
云南	58	262	67	112	63	3
西藏						
陕西	32	264	83	78	52	1
甘肃	15	86	25	26	17	1
青海	3	11	5	5		
宁夏	16	60	12	22	22	1
新疆	55	305	81	142	47	2

服务机构

单位：个、人、人次、时

格水平	年龄结构				志愿服务	
社会工作师人数	35岁及以下人数	36岁至45岁人数	46岁至55岁人数	56岁及以上人数	志愿者服务人次数	志愿服务时间
135	**3490**	**4059**	**1941**	**499**	**630**	**2051.0**
4	38	31	23	8	8	8.0
5	27	38	41	11	50	100.0
	62	50	32	24		
	29	31	24	2		
7	84	119	70	12		
13	106	156	106	26	10	20.0
3	54	228	57	19		
	48	64	56	11		
7	9	19	17	5		
6	117	166	91	18	28	63.0
12	192	158	86	19	38	154.0
3	48	100	61	14	82	308.0
13	205	288	141	34	6	16.0
1	138	162	64	18		
3	15	32	13	1		
9	669	408	137	19		
2	88	135	76	11		
1	209	232	59	16	5	10.0
19	447	567	275	47	20	43.0
4	191	246	144	58		
	17	22	12	6		
	38	81	21	6	152	305.0
1	148	215	110	16		
3	170	130	40	17	139	705.0
6	81	110	48	23	5	15.0
8	116	96	41	11	27	124.0
1	38	27	15	6		
	6	4		1		
4	12	23	22	3		
	88	121	59	37	60	180.0

C-3-16续表

地区	增加值合计	执行企业会计制度单位财务指标					执行行政	
		固定资产原价	营业收入	费用合计	营业利润	企业单位增加值	固定资产原价	上年结转和结余
全　国	**81189.1**	**17399.4**	**3532.3**	**1988.1**	**497.5**	**1214.8**	**210512.7**	**29505.0**
北　京	4502.2						19512.3	2.7
天　津	2699.3						1150.4	7610.4
河　北	1886.1						7745.1	631.5
山　西	640.5						302.8	
内蒙古	1474.6						1969.1	94.6
辽　宁	1712.1						1660.9	7.1
吉　林	1659.7	123.2					5932.3	391.0
黑龙江	1107.0	578.0	750.0	760.8	190.0	211.3	4913.9	
上　海	1073.0						729.8	1814.6
江　苏	4953.1	3531.6					3544.8	4125.3
浙　江	6398.2	91.7	684.2	54.3	118.8	215.0	3541.3	356.6
安　徽	1833.9						6881.0	
福　建	4718.2	623.0	991.0	393.0	171.0	459.0	9138.7	3670.3
江　西	1417.9	5.0					4393.9	27.2
山　东	631.2						801.9	
河　南	2455.0						1546.7	62.6
湖　北	1570.1	23.0					5737.1	
湖　南	2132.8	6604.0	367.0	516.0		78.0	10191.7	
广　东	15518.5	33.0	103.0	118.0	-8.0	74.0	63447.3	823.0
广　西	8145.2						14607.7	7630.9
海　南	819.1						7663.5	677.4
重　庆	1284.0	3500.0	165.0	11.0	-1.0	19.0	1859.1	120.4
四　川	4156.5	415.6	203.8	38.0	20.2	83.3	7351.8	613.0
贵　州	1300.1	296.8	58.0	8.5		28.6	1764.0	23.4
云　南	811.5						632.2	41.7
西　藏								
陕　西	2040.4	364.0					2294.5	107.6
甘　肃	408.5	363.0	20.0	52.0	10.0	10.0	339.3	44.0
青　海	28.9						287.1	
宁　夏	322.4	40.0	15.0	14.0			686.0	196.3
新　疆	3488.5	807.5	175.3	22.5	-3.5	36.6	19886.5	433.4

单位：万元、个

事业单位会计制度财务指标				执行民间非营利组织单位会计制度财务指标					殡仪服务站
本年收入合计	本年支出合计	收支结余	行政事业单位增加值	固定资产原价	上年结余	本年收入合计	本年费用合计	社会组织增加值	
154376.5	**158771.5**	**10860.7**	**78881.6**	**11468.8**	**72.5**	**1548.4**	**2403.6**	**1092.7**	**26**
17061.9	19992.9	-2910.5	4502.2						2
2249.8	4454.8	3676.6	2699.3						
4395.2	4362.9	863.4	1886.1						2
823.9	827.1	0.6	640.5						
2535.5	2557.0	86.4	1474.6						1
3747.0	3745.1	23.9	1711.7	2.0		0.6	0.6	0.4	
2230.8	2340.7	450.0	1659.7						
2021.2	2471.4		895.7						
3969.8	3863.0	1778.5	1073.0						
4762.8	6871.8	2075.2	4910.0	211.4		912.8	856.0	43.1	
9313.1	9504.4	33.0	6026.7	170.0	69.5	128.0	197.5	156.5	
3231.9	2958.0	0.5	1833.9						
8834.2	12260.9	251.5	4259.2						4
3967.9	2942.8	4.1	1417.9						4
737.6	737.6		452.6	98.4		393.0	393.0	178.6	
3135.5	3161.0	19.1	2453.4	10.0		2.0	2.0	1.6	
5132.5	5132.5		1570.1						
2810.4	2638.0	15.5	2054.8						
28400.7	24936.1	1261.0	15443.0	15.0	3.0	2.0	2.5	1.5	
13375.5	12664.0	371.9	8145.2						
4093.2	2309.2	2286.3	819.1						
2152.1	2055.8	216.8	1265.0						2
4573.3	4447.3	26.0	3373.2	10000.0		108.0	900.0	700.0	5
1494.7	1419.9	101.5	1271.5						
1342.6	1351.4	32.5	811.5						
2324.8	2175.6	172.8	2038.4	941.0		2.0	2.0	2.0	
549.5	552.5		398.5	1.0					
44.4	44.4		28.9						
574.3	553.1	24.1	322.4						1
14490.4	15440.3		3442.9	20.0			50.0	9.0	5

C-4-1 其他

地区	单位数			年末职工人数		受教育程度	
		编制登记	民政登记		女性	大学专科人数	大学本科及以上人数
全国	**2263**	**2149**	**114**	**19204**	**8519**	**4874**	**6391**
中央级	29	29		1416	696	157	1155
北京	75	75		774	368	140	473
天津	21	21		189	100	57	102
河北	53	51	2	647	403	121	95
山西	74	74		512	252	137	145
内蒙古	25	25		342	132	83	93
辽宁	107	103	4	847	297	204	278
吉林	34	31	3	277	77	44	34
黑龙江	43	43		542	285	117	133
上海	111	39	72	978	379	368	334
江苏	68	68		674	326	272	241
浙江	169	168	1	752	365	164	347
安徽	28	28		156	61	49	41
福建	66	65	1	287	146	70	141
江西	441	439	2	1936	701	310	242
山东	55	55		473	209	148	155
河南	145	144	1	2125	956	593	617
湖北	75	67	8	677	303	207	230
湖南	113	112	1	992	470	322	291
广东	42	40	2	461	225	131	215
广西	76	76		1205	466	225	148
海南	18	18		103	42	50	36
重庆	21	21		147	57	49	61
四川	140	140		893	394	295	308
贵州	81	65	16	575	233	173	143
云南	28	28		179	93	81	61
西藏							
陕西	43	43		513	256	144	105
甘肃	33	32	1	246	72	54	76
青海	14	14		43	23	8	11
宁夏	8	8		53	19	12	11
新疆	27	27		190	113	89	69

事业单位

单位：个、人、人次、时

职业资格水平		年龄结构				志愿服务	
助理社会工作师人数	社会工作师人数	35岁及以下人数	36岁至45岁人数	46岁至55岁人数	56岁及以上人数	志愿者服务人次数	志愿服务时间
291	**407**	**6856**	**6675**	**4080**	**1593**	**8209**	**21311.0**
13	37	663	366	317	70		
30	32	257	241	206	70		
1	7	45	73	49	22	500	1000.0
5	5	358	216	60	13		
	18	115	217	145	35		
4	5	117	125	87	13	3	9.0
	5	263	317	168	99	2	6.0
5	2	133	89	36	19		
6	5	176	151	186	29		
12	36	330	329	195	124	71	308.0
17	26	294	204	148	28	560	1760.0
20	50	278	254	186	34	3508	6524.0
6	4	25	63	61	7	74	160.0
6	19	109	105	65	8	8	64.0
31	13	690	936	286	24	728	2844.0
6	9	191	137	114	31	2223	6754.0
39	23	857	669	452	147		
10	14	210	272	152	43	55	130.0
3	15	365	367	175	85	391	1629.0
3	13	175	156	91	39		
23	25	233	319	179	474		
6	4	37	35	28	3		
1	1	41	63	37	6		
27	29	308	315	199	71		
5	1	190	195	151	39	6	18.0
1		76	47	47	9		
1		191	201	102	19	50	65.0
3	2	63	91	78	14	30	40.0
2	2	15	22	6			
		5	13	27	8		
5	5	46	87	47	10		

C-4-1续表

地区	增加值合计	执行企业会计制度单位财务指标				
		固定资产原价	营业收入	费用合计	营业利润	企业单位增加值
全　国	**197303.5**	**48889.8**	**27874.4**	**19548.4**	**-2684.5**	**5997.4**
中央级	21221.1	38641.5	21386.9	13778.6	-2236.5	4571.1
北　京	39985.9	58.3	1243.1	132.0	14.8	25.2
天　津	1756.5	625.4				
河　北	1783.1					
山　西	4115.3					
内蒙古	2190.7					
辽　宁	5155.9					
吉　林	667.3					
黑龙江	3046.7					
上　海	9670.8					
江　苏	10148.2	49.6	1108.3	539.4	18.4	211.3
浙　江	18263.9	1258.2	68.4	500.9	-450.0	-634.7
安　徽	513.1	210.0	103.0	38.0	-33.0	-19.8
福　建	2596.0					
江　西	4028.0	187.8	106.7	88.6		78.3
山　东	4133.6					
河　南	10687.5					
湖　北	7497.9					
湖　南	6032.1					
广　东	10304.1					
广　西	7780.2	5885.1	3518.0	1601.2	1.8	1516.6
海　南	4180.5					
重　庆	1120.3					
四　川	5353.1					2.0
贵　州	4876.3	1952.9	340.0	2869.7		247.4
云　南	1184.7					
西　藏						
陕　西	3322.8					
甘　肃	1428.7					
青　海	303.1					
宁　夏	414.7					
新　疆	3541.5	21.0				

单位：万元

执行行政事业单位会计制度财务指标					
固定资产原价	上年结转和结余	本年收入合计	本年支出合计	收支结余	行政事业单位增加值
419440.1	**67201.6**	**401709.4**	**380163.6**	**75846.7**	**191306.1**
98564.5	9329.2	66926.0	50484.2	24742.5	16650.0
49869.1	33391.4	62943.4	67285.3	21952.5	39960.7
1309.2	-396.5	2619.6	2848.0	15.8	1756.5
5148.8	7.6	3576.6	3437.4	3.4	1783.1
2771.3	90.4	7229.6	4729.8	6.0	4115.3
1516.2	645.5	4361.6	4629.7	2984.1	2190.7
9366.6	575.5	13828.3	15695.3	184.1	5155.9
128.6	28.7	871.2	878.7	6.9	667.3
8502.1	54.8	4420.1	4416.2		3046.7
30743.7	2914.1	25165.9	22222.5	-1153.2	9670.8
17939.5	1997.2	30004.9	29810.4	2454.8	9936.9
12845.7	4093.5	29983.6	29596.1	1724.5	18898.6
624.8	0.3	882.9	918.3	15.4	532.9
5697.5	564.2	4678.3	11084.6	887.2	2596.0
7847.1	477.3	7368.1	6192.6	2734.4	3949.7
2390.9	46.7	5785.0	5879.3		4133.6
11662.5	3839.7	14599.3	18533.2	7020.2	10687.5
15822.0	45.3	12265.0	12064.3	245.4	7497.9
13318.8	-538.8	16127.2	15700.3	222.7	6032.1
39361.5	2297.3	15838.4	15929.3	449.7	10304.1
24931.4	856.2	10633.5	8529.0	155.8	6263.6
1313.6	494.7	7384.3	6779.2	1041.7	4180.5
2609.7	42.6	1972.6	2056.8	79.8	1120.3
20154.4	871.5	25973.6	19533.1	6208.6	5351.1
4302.2	1813.1	7733.7	6144.2	189.2	4628.9
3126.0	154.8	1406.4	1297.9		1184.7
14064.5	2019.3	6483.7	5043.8	137.2	3322.8
1533.1	1.4	2360.9	2320.6	13.0	1428.7
1240.7		310.3	310.3		303.1
481.0	83.0	460.3	451.3	6.0	414.7
10253.1	1401.6	7515.1	5361.9	3519.0	3541.5

附 录

06

《中国民政统计年鉴-2014》勘误

一、151页 表B-1-18 中央彩票公益金使用情况，单位应为“亿元”。

二、157页 表B-1-22 中央彩票公益金用于基本建设投资情况，缺少单位，应为单位：亿元。

三、581页 表C-3-4 基金会，中央级社会组织增加值应为34243.6万元。